COGNITIVE
STUDIES

COGNITIVE
STUDIES

Volume 1

Jerome Hellmuth, Editor

BRUNNER / MAZEL Publishers

TABLE OF CONTENTS

PREFACE

One greets the publication of a new annual at this point in psychological history with a certain ambivalence—particularly if it is a topical volume. For in many respects psychology and the behavioral sciences generally are undergoing a fragmentation that is surely serious in its consequences—though it is debatable whether the consequences tend toward the good side or the bad. In any case the behavioral sciences are dividing into many subspecialties, and plainly this division represents itself in many new journals that are read by specialists in the particular field and rather rarely by "outsiders."

Were there a broader enterprise that could properly be called "general psychology," with agreed upon axioms, beliefs, or deep hypotheses, the occurrence of such specialism in general and in the pattern of publishing would all be to the good. But in fact it is unclear what constitutes the "core" or axiomatic agreement of psychology, and in consequence it is hard to discern the relation between one specialty and another. One is put in mind of C. K. Ogden's joke about the scholar who, thwarted in his efforts to find any material on Chinese metaphysics, decided to consult two articles in the BRITANNICA, "China" and Metaphysics." If you should wish to delve into, say the development of perception, you would do about as well looking up "Perception" and "Development."

But that is all on the negative side of the ambivalence that greets a new topical journal or, more properly, a new series of volumes, of which this is the first. There is a positive side as well, and that is why I am pleased to see this series come into being. The positive side derives, for me, from a view of the history of science that is inherent in the writing of three friends, all of whom, at one time or another, have been colleagues and all of whom, by their conversation and writing, have made a case for the noncumulative or discontinuous nature of scientific development. All of them—Edwin Boring, James Conant, and Thomas Kuhn—have made a strong case for the importance of the paradigm or model or theoretical framework as critical in the growth of science. Each in his way has argued that, in the absence of, say, a Copernican model or of the conservation theorems or of a cell theory, there is little point in pursuing pseudo-consensus by acting as if there were an axiomatic unity in a field of study.

Rather, one does better to pursue the quest for unity in the spirit of high adventure, which in science means the construction of bold hypotheses that can come as close as possible to accounting for as much as possible, yet that manage to generate new observations and new technique. Plainly we do not know where the great breakthroughs will occur to provide the paradigms, but it is always worth cultivating the parts of the field where the action seems lively in the interest of placing one's bets wisely. And surely the area chosen for this set of volumes seems lively indeed—*cognitive development.* It is an approach to problems (rather than a set of topics) that has generated much work of a varied yet surprisingly coherent nature.

Developmental biology, computer sciences, linguistics, developmental behavioral studies of striking variety, inquiries into pathology, neurochemistry and cross-cultural studies seem to converge in studying the ontogenesis of information processing in man and his forebears. Though the enterprise has the vigor of diversity, it also has the sins of diversity.

Yet as one reads through the papers in this volume, it becomes apparent that diversity has its perils. One such is in the sheer magnitude of the task of keeping up with the relevant literature. There are papers in this volume—excellent ones, too—that are without any references at all to major architects of the topics they are considering. It is plain from the high quality of the discussion in these papers that coteries are still a feature of modern science and that is is a way of life based on selective feeding. So there is an American Learning Coterie, a Piaget Coterie, and others less exclusive, each with its way of focusing attention, solemnizing conclusions, celebrating heroes, plotting data, leaving out antiheroes, etc. One hopes that a journal such as this might provide a new occasion for hospitality to the Out Group. For surely, House and Zeaman can live with Vygotsky, Piaget and Hess and Shipman can occupy the same house, the Kendlers and Bruner are on the same intellectual continent, the contents of *ENFANCE* are not antithetical to what appears in the JOURNAL OF EXPERIMENTAL CHILD PSYCHOLOGY.

Yet it can probably be demonstrated by learned historians that the synoptic intelligence and the eclectic temperament do not move the mountains of the mind. So perhaps, too, one had better celebrate our parochialism, hoping only that we will quarrel with each other about the virtues of contending viewpoints rather than ignoring our rivals. The reader of these pages may come away with the conviction that we are not contending enough, that we have set up our stalls and are showing our wares for sale to whomsoever may be tempted. We are insufficiently bad tempered, perhaps, and ought to have it out more often. Time will tell.

Let me turn now to some trends and antinomies that are apparent in this collection of papers. The first, typically Anglo-American, is an enormous involvement (however theoretical its expression) in the problem of early education—aid to the socially disadvantaged child, assistance to the handicapped, curriculum for the early school years. An exquisitely observant, theoretically subtle article dealing (as did Bishop Berkeley) with the integration of the supposedly separate modalities by which space is represented, leads in the end to a discussion of intellectual enrichment and its nature. Another that explores the cultural patterning of cognitive activity and reviews the converging literature in that field nonetheless manages to stay within critical hailing distance of the issues of educational theory.

Yet as one author remarks, though there is great interest in such pragmatic issues, there is at the same time a fascination with, indeed a virtual run on Piaget, though Piaget has very little to say directly about education or the optimum patterning of experience for learning or problem solving. What he has to say is mostly about leaving the child to próceed on his own—which surely is not the most interesting or the most pertinent advice possible. Why, then, the adulation of Piaget after the long years of neglect of this gifted and fecund man?

The answer, I believe, reveals some important trends and, indeed, even leads to some predictions. For one thing, Piaget represents a comprehensive and powerful point of view about the nature of the growth of intelligence. It is in sharp contrast to what several authors lament as the atomism and lazy empiricism of the sort of experimental research on children leading to the important though banal conclusion that as we grow older we know more, are more skillful, are more aware of the world. All is to be explained by accretion through the unexamined operation of learning. What is pertinent about Piaget is that even if he is *very* wrong, his formulations lead to alternative conjectures of some substance. The scale is right.

But Piaget has meant more than comprehensive theory. He has been the model observer, the ethologist of the human infant, the man who could take a single norm in a Gesell volume of norms and, by theoretically informed microscopy, reveal in it the essence of growth (as seen in Geneva). Such, for example, is the work on conservation, on object identity, on decentration.

But this systematist and exquisite observer leaves little for education. This is not to say that experience and action do not play a central role in Piaget's theory of assimilation and accommodation. They do. Rather, it is that by this theory it matters little in what order or in what way action and experience occur—so long as they are appropriate to the stage of development. And while there must be deep truth in this point, it is surely far from the whole truth.

So, as I read these papers, I am led to predict that the Piaget vogue in its collision with the desire to aid the struggling young learner will produce before long a new and productive turmoil within the community of developmentalists.

While noting the extraordinary rise of Piaget, one is equally struck by the decline of Freud and orthodox psychoanalytic doctrine. Extravagant reconstructions of the infantile mind from the data of pathology in the adult are of the past. The effort is to examine the establishment of coping strategies and modes of control. But psychoanalysis is without a new program of research.

One cannot help but be struck by the progress that has been made in reformulating some of the deep issues of development, issues that are as ancient as concern with psychology itself. The distinction between heredity and environment, once treated so woodenly as if one were drawing the ultimate distinction, has now become eased by several new formulations. There is alive a new sense of the role of environment in changing not only the organic substrate of behavior, its morphology and neurochemistry, but also the way in which the hereditary code gets spelled out. Early handling, we now know, can alter enzyme reactions in a manner to change the expression of genetic information. So the opportunity for experience and chance encounters with stress not only negate the simple distinctions dear to the hearts of the combatting nativist and empiricist, but also make somewhat dubious a sharp distinction between "mind" and "body."

It is this new work in developmental biology, neurochemistry, and neurophysiology that has made the field of cognitive development become concerned with organic substrata of a most important and interesting kind. This shift is reflected in this volume and, hopefully, will be the more so in later volumes. The volumes edited by Newton and Levine (EARLY EXPERIENCE AND BEHAVIOR, 1968) and by Ambrose (EARLY STIMULATION, to appear in 1969) have much to tell us about the biological bases of cognitive development.

Another trend in the volume is a willingness to accept as alternative modes of functioning what a decade ago were taken as canonically exclusive points of view about behavior. In several papers, for example, there is a ready acceptance of the existence of *both* incremental learning *and* step-wise hypothesis testing and an effort to find the conditions producing each. This formerly bitter issue used to be argued as hypothesis *versus* chance in discrimination learning.

Finally, what comes through forcefully is the vitality of the field of cognitive development—if a field it really is. The work one encounters in these pages seems to be, in the main, general psychology put into a fresh context—the context of development. After all, there is a very limited number of ways of achieving useful data in psychology, and it usually by comparing: the immature with the mature, the sick with the well, one species with another, organism with automaton, the familiar and the culturally exotic. The first of these has been the ordinary domain of developmental work. But it is plain that workers in this burgeoning field are using all of these comparisons to achieve some workable idea about growth and about cognitive functioning generally. It is a good sign.

Jerome S. Bruner
Cambridge, Massachusetts

AUTHOR AFFILIATIONS

Silvano Arieti, M.D.
Clinical Professor of Psychology
New York Medical College

Thomas J. Banta, Ph.D.
Department of Psychology
University of Cincinnati

Jerome S. Bruner, Director
Center for Cognitive Studies
Harvard University

Joseph Church, Ph.D.
Department of Psychology
Brooklyn College

Martin V. Covington, Ph.D.
University of California
Berkeley, California

David Elkind, Ph.D.
Department of Psychology
The University of Rochester

Hans. G. Furth, Ph.D.
Center for Research in Thinking
 and Language
The Catholic University of America

Eugene S. Gollin, Ph.D.
Professor, Department of Psychology
University of Colorado

Jacqueline Goodnow, Ph.D.
Department of Psychology
George Washington University

Jane W. Kessler, Ph.D.
Director, Mental Development Center
Case Western Reserve University

G. A. Kohnstamm
University of Utrecht
Institute of Child Development
 and Education
Utrecht, Holland

Melvin Manis, Ph.D.
Professor of Psychology
University of Michigan

Sonia F. Osler, Ph.D.
Professor of Psychology
Institute of Advanced Psychological Studies
Adelphi University

Walter R. Reitman, Ph.D.
Department of Psychology and
 Mental Health Research Institute
University of Michigan

Anne Saravo, Ph.D.
Research Associate
The Fels Research Institute
Yellow Springs, Ohio

Arthur Staats, Ph.D
Professor of Psychology and
 of Educational Psychology
University of Hawaii

Burton White, Ph.D.
Department of Psychology
The University of Rochester

Martin Whiteman, Ph.D.
The Columbia University School
 of Social Work

Leon J. Yarrow, Ph.D.
Chief, Social and Behavioral Sciences Branch
National Institute of Child Health and
 Human Development
National Institutes of Health
Bethesda, Maryland

Herbert Zimiles, Ph.D.
Chariman, Research Division
Bank Street College of Education
New York City, New York

COGNITIVE
STUDIES

TECHNIQUES FOR THE DIFFERENTIAL STUDY
OF COGNITION IN EARLY CHILDHOOD

Joseph Church, Ph.D.

It is hardly news any longer that the past ten years have seen a tremendous revival of interest in cognitive processes and, more particularly, cognitive development. Most conspicuous has been the renewal of attention to the work of Piaget and, to a lesser extent, Werner. On the theoretical and empirical side, there has been an upsurge of experimental research, testing, modifying, and elaborating Piaget's formulations. On the educational and psychometric side, there have been numerous attempts to apply Piaget's ideas to problems of early education and its evaluation, as in programs for the disadvantaged.

And yet, for all the ferment, one has the feeling of a certain sterility. Much of the experimental literature seems obsessed with subtle, arcane points of doctrine. Many of the workers in the Piaget tradition seem to have accepted without question Piaget's early and since-abandoned view of cognitive development as the product of autonomous maturation of neural structures. Those who have bothered to take note of individual differences in cognitive development are all too ready to ascribe them to biological differences, and those who take note of group differences seem ready to attribute them to racial differences. But the research designed to show either the relevance or the irrelevance of experience for cognitive development is so consistently unimaginative (with a few happy exceptions) that one can conclude very little from it. Many of those who are applying Piaget's ideas to problems of measurement seem prepared to repeat the logical and psychological errors that have haunted the mental measurements movement from its birth. Those who study "cognitive development" in the Piaget tradition seem to treat language as merely a superficial garment for the true structures of perception and thought, and those who study language development in the fast-growing tradition of Chomsky seem unconcerned with the psychological functions of language. All in all, the field of cognitive development seems to be blighted with a barren formalism seriously divorced from human realities. As one observer put it, people are so busy studying Piaget or Chomsky that they have forgotten to study children.

Before I go on to talk about techniques and their relevance, let me say that, in my opinion, tradition developmental psychology is a thing of the past. Cognitive psychology has effectively killed, cooked, consumed, and digested personality psychology. But we have become aware that our knowledge of human cognition is inescapably relativistic, that is, we know that there are radical individual and group

Parts of the chapter have been taken, with some modifications, from a paper presented at a study group on "Mechanisms of Language Development," sponsored by The Centre for Advanced Study in the Developmental Sciences and The Ciba Foundation, May 20-24, 1968.

differences in the way self and world are perceived, thought about, talked about, valued, categorized, and acted with and towards. Thus, the quest for universals has proven largely futile. This is not to say that there are no cognitive universals. Certain basics of perception, for instance, are so categorically imperative that without them we are likely to be dead. There must be a kind of universal figure-ground organization so that we do not constantly walk into obstacles on the assumption that they are the spaces in between objects. Without a visual cliff response, real precipices would be a danger. Even with respect to the visual cliff, however, there are some ambiguities. Some babies and some puppies, as I have recorded elsewhere, far from retreating from the drop-off, try to fling themselves into space, as though they see the cliff as inviting rather than menacing. We have called this form of behavior the "Geronimo response." Also, some older children act as though the visual cliff response has dropped out with the passage of time—and there are enough fatal falls to make this a serious practical consideration. Schiff's (1965) looming effect seems to be another universal, but again I am moved to wonder why it does not get young children out of the path of approaching cars.

But such basics aside, many aspects of cognition seem neither innate nor the simple products of maturation. Even the much-touted wisdom of the body is liable to betray us, and at a relatively early age it is as likely to be our cultural learning as our spontaneous reactions that dictates which foods look appetizing and which nauseous. Burghardt and Hess (1966) have demonstrated that even in the lowly snapping turtle early experience can be a potent determiner of food preferences. Even when we assume that a given cognitive skill will appear sooner or later in just about everybody, there may still be marked cultural differences in the age of emergence. Here too, however, I have gone too fast, acting as though we were in basic agreement on what we mean by cognition. This is almost certainly not the case. I have before me the outline of a first graduate course in developmental psychology. It has segments devoted to learning, perception, language, and, almost as though it were a residual term, cognition. I suspect that it was only through an oversight that the framers of this course omitted yet another unit devoted to intelligence. This kind of fragmentation permits the writing of learned treatises on the effects of cognition on perception or of intelligence on cognition. In our pursuit of abstractions, we sometimes lose sight of our basic subject matter, human organisms making their way through space, society, and life. And in doing so, we bear out the general semanticist's thesis that we end up by reifying our own abstractions. In keeping with the Zeitgeist, I have been interested for several years in ways to study early cognitive development and the origins of cognitive differences. To this end, I have been combing the literature and finding, to my surprise, what a wealth of techniques has been available to us for some time. It is not always easy to recognize useful techniques. For instance, the Cattell scale (Cattell, 1940) has an item called "glass frustration," which seems to make it primarily a matter of affect, and I had to have pointed out to me that this task was identical to one that I referred to as "ability to detour around a transparent barrier," which is a matter of perceiving spatial relations. Other tasks—for want of a better word—came from observations of babies and young children coping with their everyday surroundings. We tend to forget that the world is an intelligence test, and that babies in normal environments spend much of their waking time exploring those environments and solving the puzzles that they present. By watching babies encounter and cope with objects, one can find a great many situations that are easily adaptable to formal testing.

I have now amassed something like 200 tasks applicable to the study of cognitive development between birth and age four. Some of these tasks ask the child to interact with stimulus objects, while others are questions designed to elicit information from the child's caretaker. For instance, I am interested in early manifestations of guilt feelings as an aspect of self-awareness. I have not yet found a way of eliciting guilt in the laboratory, but every mother I have asked has given me a sensible answer to the question, "How does he act when you catch him doing something he isn't supposed to do?" Apparently, every baby old enough to move around under his own power engages in forbidden behavior, apparently they all get caught—at least sometimes—and apparently all mothers note how their babies react. How verbal the tasks are depends, obviously, on the age of the child. At the earliest ages, it is the demand qualities of the stimulus objects that, quite reliably, tell the child what to do.

The set of tasks overlaps somewhat with those assembled by Bettye Caldwell (1964), by Uzgiris and Hunt (1966) and, most especially, by Audrey Little (n.d.) at Western Australia. At older ages, my tasks have much in common with the Early Childhood Inventories developed by Coller and Victor (1967). There are, however, some important differences. One, of course, is that the overlap among sets is far from complete. I have been to some pains to exclude tasks whose cognitive relevance is not clear, even though they are clearly developmental in character. In line with some recent comments by Charlesworth (1968), I place more reliance than the others on affective indicators of what is cognized, and how. The model for this approach is Tinkelpaugh's (1928) study in which monkeys manifested great distress at finding a less favored foodstuff, such as lettuce, in a place where they had been led to expect to find bananas or peanuts. By the same token, the baby's differential emotional reactions to strangers and familiar people can be taken as evidence that schemata of the known are being established. Another difference is that my colleagues seem to be working within an essentially psychometric framework, whereas I have been groping towards a comparative phenomenology of infancy and early childhood, an attempt to depict, analyze, and characterize the life space as it is given at different ages and in different cultures. I find Uzgiris and Hunt's structuralism, derived from

Piaget, somewhat alien to my own orientation, which seeks to find the key to mental organization in the structure of the real world and symbolic and schematic representations thereof. I am willing to grant only semi-autonomy to mental mechanisms and operations. And I would make them contingent on the organism's interactions with objects, human and otherwise. If we assume that there is some kind of structure, neural or whatever, corresponding to every sort of operation, we end up packing the child as full of structures as MacDougall and his followers did with propensities. While the baby may indeed have pre-wired, as the current jargon phrases it, sensitivities to certain aspects of the world, the model breaks down when we consider all the artifacts, real and symbolic, with all their multifarious morphologies and workings, to which the child learns to adapt. The matter becomes even more complicated when we consider cultural and subcultural differences, unless, of course, we are willing to ascribe such differences to genetic, organic—in the end, racial—factors. I prefer to think that semi-autonomous structures arise out of the child's direct and socially mediated congress with the world around him and with himself.

Thus, a chief concern in using these tasks was to establish the early origins of cultural differences in cognition and, eventually, to relate these to cultural differences in child-rearing practices. This is in line with the conviction that simple normative studies, unrelated to antecedent variables, whether introduced experimentally or occurring naturally, are a thing of the past. We already have some evidence of early cultural differences in the sphere of motor and postural development, as in Mead and MacGregor's (1951) observations on the early acquisition of styles of movement and in Marcelle Geber's (1958) observations on the remarkable precocity of African babies reared in the tribal fashion. Caudill (1966) has demonstrated sharp divergences in temperament between Japanese and American middle-class babies from a few months of age. It seems reasonable, then, to assume that early differences in cognition can likewise be demonstrated. One might also find some diagnostic uses for these tasks, singly or in combination. They may suggest some techniques in early education and provide a means of evaluating the effectiveness of such efforts. Finally, they may be useful in studying the way non-linguistic aspects of cognitive development relate to the acquisition of language, the way language influences and fails to influence perception and thought at early ages. I might say, in passing, that I am also working on a scheme for the analysis of early language. This approach seeks to categorize communicative acts and operations, with the study of vocabulary and grammatical, syntactic, and compositional means subordinated to an understanding of what the child is trying to say, his attempts to represent real or imaginary states of affairs. Some categories, for example, are drawing contrasts, question types, and making contingency statements. I am collecting longitudinal date, and progress is very slow.

I have grouped my cognitive tasks into six sets, dealing respectively with 1) self-awareness, 2) social and personal awareness, and affect, including observations designed to study the baby's developing reactions to medical personnel and preventive medical procedures—in short, learning to anticipate pain from his monthly check-ups, 3) imitation, 4) perception of space, spatial relations, and physical causation, 5) perception of objects and object attributes, and 6) perception of pictures and other two-dimensional arrays.

I hope I need not explain the mechanics and ethics of working with babies and young children. The problem of stranger anxiety is a constant one and becomes especially serious when working with babies of a different race or subculture, for whom everything about the experimenter may be wrong and terrifying, from his skin color, to his accent, to his smell. Particularly in medical settings, the examiner may take on the dreaded connotations of doctor. These problems can be solved—usually—with a bit of patience; it may be just as important to allay the mother's or caretaker's stranger anxiety, too. Very young babies are tested propped up in a baby carrier and older ones in a feeding table with an extended top provided with sockets into which various screen and panels can be fitted.

SELF-AWARENESS

The earliest test of self-awareness with which I am familiar is to interrupt the baby's visual contact with the world by draping a cleaning tissue over the upper part of his face. There seems to be a fairly stable developmental sequence of reactions, from no response, to vocal fussing, to whole-body activity, to head-wagging, to diffuse reaching in which the baby seems to want to use his hands but doesn't know where to apply them, to more localized but still ineffectual reaching in the vicinity of the head, to removal of the tissue by wiping it away, to, typically by age five months, reaching up, grasping the tissue, and pulling it off. This last, most mature response itself comes in three stages. The first consists of the baby's remaining still, and even tense, for as long as thirty seconds, as though trying to figure out what to do before reaching up to grasp the tissue. The second is immediate grasping and removal. The third is to remove the tissue and then put it back, as though initiating a game of peek-a-boo.

Another indicator of self-awareness is the baby's reaction to being tickled. A cleaning tissue is twisted to form a point which is then moved lightly back and forth across, in random order, the outer surface of each calf, the skin of each forearm, and the top of the baby's head. The developmental sequence in this case is from no response to a change of facial expression (typically a smile or a puzzled or quizzical frown), to generalized movement, to moving the tickled member, to looking towards the tickling, to touching the spot being tickled.

Although these reactions have been set forth in sequence, the range of ages at which each appears is wide. It is not too surprising that one-month-old babies should fail to react to this minimal stimulation; but babies as old as three or four months may also show no response. Responding in terms of a change of expression has been observed between ages one month and four months. Generalized movement occurs over the entire one-to-six month range. Movement just of the member tickled has been observed as young as one month and as late as five months. Visual orientation to the site of tickling seems not to begin until age four months. Manual localization—touching or rubbing or scratching the tickled spot is so far only an adultomorphic projection—no subject under six months of age has reacted this way in my presence (although I have seen much younger babies scratching their eczema), and most babies older than six months are too active for this test. One can detect the baby's beginning shift from almost total dependency to partial autonomy by asking the mother, "How do you know when he wakes up?" Characteristically, at about age four months, the baby no longer howls for attention as soon as he awakes, but instead spends some time amusing himself, crowing or cooing, playing with his fingers, exploring his surroundings, and in general being self-sufficient. It is worth emphasizing that virtually all parents notice this change in behavior upon awakening, if only because it means that they now wake up of their own accord rather than in response to the baby's crying. At least some babies reach a point where this solitary interlude becomes an essential transition between sleeping and waking, so that they actively resent adult interruption. It would be interesting to find out whether this first autonomy is made possible by the attainment of visually guided reaching and grasping. It seems connected, as implied above, with the child's discovery of his hands.

The baby's knowledge of his own body seems to develop through a fairly stable series of discoveries. One can see the baby's discovery of his hands, and later of his feet, as things to be inspected, played with, and mouthed, and most parents can describe their children's status in this respect. I have not thought it worthwhile to ask about the baby's discovery of his navel, a standard but often unnoticed event, or prudent to ask about the discovery of the genitalia, which many parents regard as wicked or shameful.

The baby's ability to feed himself tells us something about the coordination of his body schema. The progression seems to go from soft foods, which can be licked from the fingers or crammed directly into the mouth with the palm, to biting off mouthfuls from something held in the hand, such as a cracker or an apple slice, to picking up pellet-like bits, whether a pea or a piece of meat, and popping it into the mouth. Biting-off behavior is interesting because one can often observe the baby learning that it is necessary to align a cracker, say, just so for it to fit into the mouth. However, these remarks are based on casual observations, and I have not undertaken any systematic studies, which should ideally be longitudinal over the 6-18 month age period.

Stages in the baby's recognition of his own reflection in the looking glass have been studied by Dixon (1957). In middle-class babies, recognition occurs at about age 10 months. A report on the early education project in the Baltimore City Public Schools (1964), however, indicates that lower-class four-year-olds may not recognize their own reflections. I have tried to verify this observation with a sample of lower-class four-year-olds in Poughkeepsie but found that they all recognized themselves. I abandoned this approach, only to find that my wife, working with a group of disadvantaged Hawaiian and part-Hawaiian three- and four-year-olds, had observed in them a failure of self-recognition. The question is still moot.

Negativism is an indicator of autonomy and hence self-awareness, but I have so far found no way to study it in the laboratory. One can get at early manifestations of conscience, as I have said, by asking the mother, "How does he act when you catch him doing something he's not supposed to do?" This is, admittedly, a beating-your-wife kind of question, but so far it has always worked. I find the variety of behaviors described quite fascinating: no reaction; hurries to finish before he can be interrupted; tries to hide activity; flees or hides; stops activity and feigns innocence; cries woefully, cries angrily; acts fearful; proffers the forbidden object to the adult; and makes a lavish display of affection.

At younger ages starting at about 12 months, one can ask the baby to indicate facial features and body parts that the examiner names, and at later ages one can ask the child to name anatomy that the examiner indicates. Striking social class differences exist in performance on these tasks. Sphincter control is an index of self-awareness, and the attainment thereof can be gauged roughly by whether the baby wears diapers or pants. Play-acting, pretending to be somebody or something else, would be a useful indicator if we knew how to elicit it.

What I have called the Cyclops effect (Church, 1966) is an interesting if transitory phenomenon that waxes and wanes between ages one and two. One peers at the baby through a tube (I use the cardboard rollers from paper towels), saying "Boo!" or "Hi!" to make sure the baby is attending, and then when he has responded (typically with a smile), hands him the tube with a reasonable expectation that he will try to reciprocate. At its full flower, the Cyclops effect consists in the baby's planting the tube squarely between his eyes and being baffled as to why he cannot see through it. At ages younger than a year, babies seem not to try to look through the tube. When they first begin to try, they may place the tube in the midline of the head, but below eye level—most often over the nose, but in one case over the mouth (I discarded one 20-month-old who apparently was using the tube as a wind instrument). Whatever the baby's knowledge of his own binocularity, vision seems to be phenomenologically centered in a unitary field. By age two, most babies fit the tube over one eye.

One can ask babies from a year and a half on to perform arbitrary, abstract actions of the kind that seemed to baffle Goldstein and Scheerer's (1941) brain-injured patients: "Open your mouth"; "Close your eyes"; "Touch your hair"; etc. One can ask children age two and over how many they have of various body parts: "How many ears have you got?"; "How many noses?" etc.—children seem to be neither amused nor disturbed by the plural designation of singular traits. The baby's knowledge of his own age is yet another useful index, even though he may have no idea of what the numbers and time designations stand for.

Somewhere between ages two and three, children begin to apply trait adjectives (*big, strong, good, pretty, fat*) to themselves and to be able to specify some of their competences and incompetences ("I don't know how to read yet"), but I have so far not found any way to incorporate these self-verbalizations into a set of formal measures.

A more advanced self-awareness item asks the child to talk about sensory functions. Notice that there are two sorts of questions. One kind goes from function to organ ("What do you smell [taste, touch] with?") and the other from organ to function ("What are your eyes [ears] for?"). Here we recognize that of the five commonly known senses, only two operate through highly specialized receptors—one may taste with one's tongue, but one also talks with it, licks stamps with it, and so forth.

Most middle-class three-year-olds can cope with this task, and they seem to do equally well on all five subtasks with the exceptions noted below. Lower-class four-year-olds do somewhat less well (no statistical comparisons involving three-year-olds were possible, since the three-year-old data were collected by two students who graduated before the analysis was begun). The lower-class four-year-olds had difficulty with all the senses except vision. Several of our middle-class four-year-olds had difficulty with taste (5/16 Ss) and touch (6/16 Ss).

The problem of recognizing a photograph of oneself is akin to recognizing one's reflection in a mirror, but is made more difficult by several important differences: A photograph is considerably less than life size, it may be black and white rather than living color, and it is static (videotape recording may make it possible to study the child's recognition of pictures of himself in action). Sharp social class differences have been reported in recognition of one's own picture. The Polaroid camera is a very useful instrument in this area of study, and many teachers of disadvantaged children make the Polaroid camera a teaching instrument as well. Similarly, the tape recorder should enable us to test for recognition by the child of his own voice.

SOCIAL AND PERSONAL AWARENESS

The chief stimulus material for the study of early social awareness is the experimenter. If, however, the experimenter is too exclusively an aversive stimulus (a matter that is seldom discussed in reports of research), he can for some tasks make the mother his surrogate. (While mothers can be helpful, they sometimes have to be restrained—verbally—either from empathizing with the baby to the point of distraction or even from actively intervening to help the baby solve an experimental problem).

One notes first of all whether the baby attends to the experimenter's face at close range. A surprising number of babies do not, and I suspect—without real evidence—that such inattention may be pathognomic. One then begins speaking to see if the experimenter's voice elicits a change of state. One finds out by asking the mother whether the baby smiles at people (I have had little luck making very young babies to whom I was a stranger smile), and, at a somewhat later age, whether the baby laughs. From age two months, one speaks in short bursts to the baby to see whether he shows any signs of trying to answer back—several mothers have told me that the exchange of conversational babbles is something the baby does only with his father.

From age three months on, one looks for signs of tension or reserve in the baby's reaction to the test situation, the examiner himself, or to the test materials. From age five months one tries to play social games with the child: saying "Boo!", pretending to be angry, playing peek-a-boo, this little piggy, give and take, pat-a-cake, and waving bye-bye. One leaves a plaything on the table top to see if the baby will drop it overboard and then look to an adult to retrieve it. If the baby is able to creep, one asks the mother if he likes to be chased and if he himself initiates the chasing game. One also asks if he likes to hide and be found. One tries giving the child a plaything and then abruptly taking it away from him—this is a test of conservation, but it is also a test of how conservation is manifested emotionally and behaviorally, by puzzlement, woe, anger, or active searching or reaching.

One asks the mother to reach out her arms to the baby to see if he responds in kind, and, once he has been picked up, what manifestations of affection— hugging, snuggling, kissing—appear. The question about early manifestations of guilt can logically be considered to belong here as well as in the category of self-awareness.

REACTIONS TO MEDICAL PERSONNEL AND PROCEDURES

On the basis of observations of my own children, I hypothesized a developmental increase in the gradient of anticipatory fear that babies will show towards visits to the pediatrician. I later learned that this had been the topic of a somewhat abortive study by David Levy (1960). Here I must specify that in the United States most babies are taken for monthly medical examinations during the first year of life, and receive an immunizing injection at almost every visit. On the first visit or two, the baby has no reason to expect pain, and he does not begin to scream until the needle actually goes in—it may even take him until several seconds after the injection to realize that something unpleasant has happened. Once the baby has begun to learn his lesson, he shows signs of fear at increasingly earlier stages in the process: the doctor's approach, being undressed for the examination, entering the examining room, entering the waiting room, approaching the doctor's office—by age one, leaving home to go to the doctor's. As one mother told me, "We always take a taxi to come to the doctor's. Now, whenever he sees the taxi pull up to the house, he starts to howl."

Alas, my study aborted as thoroughly as Levy's. The reasons might be psychologically interesting if I could be sure what they were. I worked in the office of a pediatrician with a largely Japanese-American practice, and what I think I observed was the precocious development of a massive imperturbability, the babies stoically enduring without protest whatever was done to them. This observation is wholly consonant with Caudill's findings. The matter is mooted, however, by the pediatrician's enlightened technique—injections were given quickly and skillfully from behind, in a buttock, and were, moreover, accompanied by a lollipop which seemed to distract the baby from any pain or discomfort.

IMITATION

I had hoped to demonstrate, via a stable sequence of emergence of imitative behavior, the origins of imitation in a general emphathic capacity rather than in the reinforcement paradigm of various learning theories. Let me say immediately that I failed, but not without, I hope, learning something along the way. Following Zazzo (1957) the stimulus-action that I emitted for the youngest babies was sticking out my tongue. Zazzo reports that babies 10-20 days old imitate tongue-protrusion, and I myself have observed it in a number of babies in this age range. However, with one part-Hawaiian sample (27 babies, ages 1-9 months), I could not elicit tongue-protrusion before age two months, and three of the five two-month-olds who responded did so only inconsistently. Nevertheless, tongue-protrusion was the form of imitation that appeared earliest in this sample. As mentioned under the rubric of social and personal awareness, a kind of quasi-imitation that appears at about age two months in American middle-class babies is the infant's trying to speak back when spoken to—his reaction takes the form of twisting and squirming, miscellaneous mouth movements including smiling, and sometimes the production of a strangled sound or two. I succeeded in eliciting such behavior from only three of 150-odd Hawaiian subjects; one was three months old and the others were five months old.

Some of the other stimuli used with varying degrees of success and failure are: lip-smacking, arm-waving, head-wagging, sniffing, blowing and whistling (which are on Little's scale; obviously, one does not expect an infant to whistle, but I have observed a number of them trying to), vocalizations like ah-ah-ah and dah-dah-dah (which are on the Cattell scale at the nine-month level), slapping the table top (which Cattell places in the twelfth month but which my Hawaiian babies responded to quite reliably from age seven months on—obviously, one can test for this only with babies mature enough to sit up in a high chair or feeding table), making a great show of effort about picking something up, knocking over a plaything set in front of the baby, inverting a cup, hand-clapping, playing peek-a-boo, and waving bye-bye.

Other acts of imitation that I have observed adventitiously are copying the ding! of a kitchen timer, the sound of an internal combustion engine, the squeak made by a squeeze toy, and dropping a block through a cardboard tube. A number of babies have been reported to croon to music from as young as age three months, but I have yet to settle on the right stimulus. (Two tasks in the area of spatial relations—pouring from cup to cup and using a stick to reach a lure—involve learning by imitation, and both work with children in the 14-24 - month range.)

PERCEPTION OF SPACE, SPATIAL RELATIONS, AND CAUSATION

Several people have questioned why I consider the tasks that follow to be tests of space perception. I in turn have difficulty understanding the question, but these tasks all have to do with the location, orientation, or direction of movement of objects with respect to other objects, to the concrete settings in which the objects are situated, or to abstract spatial coordinates such as up and down—and eventually, of course, even more abstract ones such as north and south. Here let it be noted that we are dealing with everyday three-dimensional space, which I take to be the primary sphere of orientation. Some references to two-dimensional space come later.

Some aspects of spatial perception have been demonstrated so often that we need mention them only in passing. Everybody is confident now that newborn babies track moving objects with their eyes, and a few neonates by moving their heads. From the age of a few weeks babies can track a moving person as far as they can swivel their heads, although this observation was treated as a major heresy just a few years ago. White and collaborators (White, Castle, and Held, 1964) have studied visually guided reaching and grasping to the point where little seems to remain to be said.

More in doubt is the age at which babies first orient visually to a source of sound. Wertheimer (1961) thought that he observed such orienting in freshly newborn babies, but later began to have his own doubts. My own observations of 32 Hawaiian babies between the ages of one and seven months led me to conclude that age four months was the turning point. One day, though, the mother of a two-month-old spoke from behind him and he immediately twisted his head around in her direction. At that point I had almost finished running subjects, but I used a few more mothers as stimuli and decided that, although the baby probably does not orient to inanimate sounds of moderate intensity until age four months, he turns to a familiar voice at age two months. There, as far as I know, the matter rests. There is also a related observation which I have found no way to study formally. This is searching not for the source of a sound, but for the sound itself, as though at least some sounds (a chord struck on the piano, a handclap) have for the baby an autonomous, visible existence.

I have already mentioned the next task, having to do with the development of the baby's ability to cope with a transparent barrier between him and some desired object, included in the Cattell Scale under the name of "glass frustration." It is one of Little's tasks as well. I have tried several forms of glass frustration, such as interposing a glass or a coarse wire mesh screen between the baby and the lure, but the one that I like best is to drop a colored plastic clothespin into a wide-mouth, shallow, clear plastic container and set it down in front of the baby. Up to the age of eight or ten months (Cattell gives the 13th or 14th month as the norm), the baby, if he responds to the clothespin at all, tries persistently to grasp it through the side of the container. Notice that the container is visible to him—he may even grasp its edge in one hand while trying with the other to penetrate its side. He may also, in the course of his struggles, accidently spill out the clothespin, but he does not benefit from this experience: as soon as the clothespin is returned to the container, he resumes his attempted penetration. Observe also that the idea of taking something out of a container is by no means beyond him: if one uses an opaque container he immediately removes the lure.

A related but somewhat more advanced task is to give the baby a lure in a transparent bottle with an opening too narrow to accommodate his hand. Here, of course, the solution is to invert the bottle and let gravity do the work. According to Cattell, babies can solve this problem imitatively in the 13th or 14th month, and spontaneously in the 15th or 16th month. In my sample, only three children older than a year failed to solve the problem spontaneously, and two one-year-olds and one 14-month-old solved it.

Observing babies exploring space in their free play, I have gotten the impression that babies at first are insensitive to the different dynamics of horizontal surfaces and vertical or tilted ones as these relate to objects other than the baby himself. As regards his own migrations through space, the baby is highly sensitive not only to vertical drop-offs but also to the threat of surfaces that slope away from him. However, he does not seem to grasp spontaneously that the same laws apply to his playthings. I think I have been babies try to set things down on a wall, like the comedian who hangs his coat on a nonexistent coathook. It comes as a great surprise even to one-and-a-half-year-olds that a toy car placed at the top of an incline should roll down it.

To try to test for this effect in the laboratory, I built two benches, one with a horizontal top and the other with a top pitched at 30° from the horizontal. These were placed so as to form a right angle, a plaything was placed on the floor near their junction, and then the S was placed by the toy, in the expectation that he would try to set it on one of the benches. The notion was that younger babies would choose at random between the benches, whereas older ones would show a consistent preference for the level top. I never found out, since this seemingly innocuous partial enclosure proved to be so disturbing to babies that they either simply cried or fled.

A task, included also in Little's set, which is placed here for want of a better location, is to confront the baby with three playthings in a row. These must be objects small enough to pick up in one hand but not small enough to be picked up two to a hand. Reliably, the baby will want to pick up all three playthings. The discontinuity comes when he realizes that he hasn't got enough hands to go around, and that he will have to put down (or tuck under an arm) one of the two playthings he has already picked up before he can pick up the remaining one. In one small sample, about age eight months seem to be the turning point, although eight-month-olds may go through a period of bafflement, looking back and forth among hands and objects, before the light dawns.

Piaget, by way of Kohlberg, has given us the interesting task of asking the baby to extrapolate the path of a moving object which disappears behind an opaque screen and then reappears on the far side. The least mature response is simply to lose interest as soon as the object disappears. A more mature response is to continue watching the point of disappearance as though in expectation that the object will reappear (it should be made explicit that the baby's response is scored only after several repetitions in the course of which it is ensured that he sees where the object actually emerges from behind the screen). The most mature response, which seems to appear after about eight months of age, is to swivel the gaze to the far edge of the screen in anticipation of the object's reappearance.

From the primate literature has come the task of securing a visible but out-of-reach lure by pulling on a string tied to it. This task has been used by Little and Cattell, the latter of whom places it in the eighth month. There seem to be several developmental steps in the mastery of this problem: paying no attention to either the lure or the string; trying to reach the lure but giving up; playing with the string but failing to notice that the lure moves when the string moves; discovering the correlated movement of string and lure and then capitalizing on the discovery to obtain the lure; and, finally, simply grabbing the string and pulling in the lure. Like Cattell, I find solutions to the problem appearing between ages seven and eight months. One can also distinguish between a less mature way of pulling in the lure with a single, whole-arm sweep and a more mature one of reeling it in hand over hand. A variant of this task is the crossed string problem, which adds noise to the system in the form of one or more extra lengths of string that lead nowhere. In my experience, every baby who solved the simple string problem also solved crossed string problems, which suggests that this complication tells us nothing further.

The next group of spatial tasks represents a failure in human engineering. I made the mistake of constructing a single panel—analogous to an "activity board"—containing a great many stimuli. As a result, my Ss were very easily distracted, and the research needs to be repeated with only one task to a panel.

One group of tasks was designed to test the baby's ability to manipulate various kinds of latches to open doors in the panel: a simple pull-knob (the door being held closed by a magnet), a spring-return latch of the kind found on ordinary doors, a rotary level latch, a lift latch, a hook and eye, and a sliding bolt. Provisionally, this arrangement of tasks corresponds to a developmental sequence between ages nine months and two years. Opening doors and peering through them at the world beyond the panel seems to be intrinsically rewarding, but one can place a mirror or picture behind the door.

The same panel also contained a narrow slot and a small (about 1 cm) circular hole, to see if I could elicit the exploratory probing with the forefinger that one so often sees in the everyday behavior of older infants. A few babies obliged, but for most Ss these stimuli semed not to be very compelling in their complicated surroundings.

Also mounted on this panel was a socket containing a 15-watt light bulb turned on and off by a pull-chain switch with a length of string attached. To attract the baby's attention, I would turn the light on and off a few times and then wait to see what happened. Babies between the ages of nine and fifteen months characteristically touched, pushed, pulled, or twisted the bulb itself, as though direct action would make it work. A few babies in this range tried to use the string, but without success. When the subject could not work the switch, I proceeded to two levels of training. First, I demonstrated again the correct procedure, moving my hand slowly and exaggeratedly. This procedure worked with a number of babies in the one-to-two year range. If it did not work, I folded the baby's hand around the string, clasped his hand in mine, and worked the switch in this way. This technique was successful with all babies past a year in age, although some continued to have trouble controlling the direction of their pull, and some needed further instruction to teach them that they had to release the tension at the end of each pull to reset the switch.

As most parents know, a spatial skill that comes in late infancy is removing the screw caps from bottles and tubes, often with messy results. At a somewhat later age, the baby becomes able to screw caps back on. I provided my Ss with a small green plastic bottle (of the kind in which one buys liquid for blowing bubbles) with a full-diameter white metal screw-on cap. The successive stages, between nine months and two years, in removing the cap were: no response to the cap as such, trying simply to pull the cap off, twisting the cap back and forth (which sometimes worked), and finally, unscrewing the cap with a series of rotary motions. This last response was observed in one nine-month-old, but appears more characteristically at age one and a half. Putting the cap back on appeared in a similar sequence between ages one and somewhere after two years: no attempt to replace, trying to force the cap back on, back-and-forth twisting, and screwing the cap on.

In late infancy, babies seem to become sensitive to the "correct" up-down orientation of those objects that have a standard up and down. This is shown in everyday life by the baby's almost compulsive setting upright of whatever capsized objects he encounters in his migrations. In the laboratory, one simply places an object on its side on the tabletop in front of the baby. The test objects used were a rubber effigy of a rabbit sitting up on its haunches and a white-painted wooden cone some 15 cm in height. Three kinds of response occurred: The baby simply picked up the object and started to play with it (typically, he stuck it in his mouth—since the cone had a fairly sharp point, I had to be alert to keep it away from the baby's face); the baby picked up the object, aligned it with his own up-down body axis, and then set about playing with it; or the baby first set the object upright on the table and then was free to manipulate it. This last form of response seems to appear at 9-10 months in middle-class babies, but not until 14 months or later in my Hawaiian sample. It made no difference whether the stimulus object was a real-life representation or an abstract geometric form. Strictly speaking, since this response is one that appears and then disappears, one cannot know for sure whether the baby who fails to show it has not yet reached this phase or has already left it behind. Thus, a longitudinal approach to the matter would be desirable.

As we have seen, babies from age one year on can pour things out of containers (although they may not yet know how to *stop* pouring). A more difficult task is to pour something out of one container and into another. I set two large plastic cups in front of the baby, placed a pingpong ball in one cup, slowly poured the ball back and forth from cup to cup several times, and then set the cups, one of them containing the ball, back in front of the baby. Most babies younger than age one fail to get the message. Most typically, they try to drink the ball from the cup, as though they perceived it as milk. In babies past age one, there are three steps in responding: undirected pouring, where the baby makes no apparent attempt to aim the ball into the second cup; aimed but inaccurate pouring; and accurate pouring from one cup to another.

From the primate literature comes the task of using a stick to rake in a lure too distant to be grasped with the hand. Ideally, this task can be scaled from very easy (a rake-like instrument in place with its cross-piece ready to draw in the lure) to very hard (a simple stick placed out of the baby's field of view while he is oriented to the lure, so that he is obliged to search for it). In the hurly-burly of practice, these complications proved unworkable, and I lost a good many Ss finding out as much. What I arrived at, with seven Ss between the ages of one and two, was to place the lure, an animal figurine, at the far edge of the feeding table, and the stick along its side edge. If the baby failed to see the connection between the stick and the lure, I, from a position behind the baby, picked up the stick, raked in the lure, allowed the baby to play with it briefly, and then restored the status quo ante. Only one baby, a 12½-month old girl whose parents had more education than was typical of my sample, spontaneously used the stick to get the lure. Three babies, 15-19 months of age, failed to benefit from my example. Three others, 13, 22, and 26 months of age, learned to use the stick as an extension of the arm.

Another task from the primate literature that should be usable, but which I have not tried, requires the subject to move a stool to where he can stand on it and procure a lure placed too high for him to reach. It seems intuitively that this is a variant on the stick task, and we should expect performance on the two to be highly correlated.

Two tests of the perception of relative size come to us from the manufacturers of commercial playthings: pierced disks, graduated in size, that fit on a spindle, and nesting boxes. As some critics have pointed out, in the commercial versions elements that differ in size also differ in color, and the disks or boxes should be homogenized as to color before being used. The disks that I worked with were actually shallow plastic cups, which permitted, logically, errors of inversion. In fact, only one baby ever put a disk on upside down, and he corrected himself. The varieties of response observed were: removes only a few disks from the spindle, replaces none (two 15-month-olds); removes all the disks, replaces none (a one-year-old, a 15-month-old, and an 18-month-old); replaces some disks but in mixed order (nine babies, 14-26 months); replaces some disks in sequence, but with gaps (one 18-month-old); and correct sequence, no gaps (one 14-month-old, who reversed the expected pattern by putting the smallest disk on the bottom and built up to the largest). While no clear-cut developmental pattern emerges from these findings, I believe that the addition of older subjects would reveal an age trend. One would also expect analogous responses to the nesting boxes, but in fact none of my Ss showed enough interest in the boxes to justify categorizing their responses.

I tried, with my four-year-old samples, a test of passive spatial vocabulary (*near, far, in between, on, under,* etc.) but it turned out to be too easy for both middle-class and disadvantaged children. By contrast, to my surprise, a test of simple time words turned out to be much too hard.

PERCEPTION OF OBJECTS AND OBJECT ATTRIBUTES

An index of early learning is the baby's visual recognition of the nursing bottle, shown by his opening his mouth and straining towards the bottle. Cattell places this behavior in the third month, but I find it—in bottle-fed babies, I need not add—by age one month. A complication, however, is that the one-month-old does not discriminate between a nursing bottle and a host of other objects, and it remains to be seen how wide a range of equivalent stimuli he will react to, and at what age he reacts only to the bottle.

Visually guided reaching and grasping can also be understood as an aspect of object perception in that it implies that the object exists for the baby as a graspable solid. Both Little and I have been interested in the baby's systematic visual inspection of novel objects, although I am still in search of the ideal stimulus. Piaget, Cattell, Little, and Kohlberg have studied object conservation, most successfully, I believe, by the technique of slowly lowering an object behind an opaque screen, the index of conservation being whether the baby tries to rise upward to follow the downward vanishing object.

A learned dynamic of wheeled vehicles is that they roll, and one can see the contrast between younger babies, who move a toy car without regard to the wheels, and older ones who consistently move the car only forward or backwards. I have long intended to study the baby's tactual exploration of textured surfaces (*e.g.*, window screening, fur, sandpaper, *etc.*) but have not yet done so, although one can observe such exploration in everyday life.

A standard plaything of middle-class babies is the kitchen pots and pans, which he learns to disassemble and, eventually, to reassemble. There seem to be marked social-class differences in the sophistication with which babies deal, specifically, with a double-boiler, related, apparently, to the restricted access poor children have to such playthings. A middle-class family is not much concerned about the fate of its to them inexpensive utensils, but a poor family has to be.

We move here into the linguistic sphere, testing the baby's passive and active knowledge of object names, color names, and size terms. It still comes as a surprise to many people to learn that disadvantaged four-year-olds are likely not to know color names, which many middle-class two-year-olds have mastered.

With three- and four-year-olds we have used various tests of sameness and difference (a key concept in the Coller and Victor tasks), with middle-class three-year-olds surpassing disadvantaged four-year-olds in their ability both to say correctly whether two objects are the same or different and, when the objects are different, to put into words the nature of the difference. We have also used a five-object oddity task, using five blocks of five colors, five sizes, and two shapes (four of the blocks are triangular and the fifth is a cube; the triangular—strictly speaking, prisms—blocks are taken from the Hanfmann-Kasanin test, and the cube from the Merrill-Palmer test.). The same social-class differences are observable in ability to point out the odd block and to verbalize the difference (it is enough for our purposes that the child be able to say something to the effect that these blocks look like tents and this one doesn't; or even "they're sort of different here," pointing to the corners).

PERCEPTION OF PICTURES AND OTHER TWO-DIMENSIONAL ARRAYS

Although I find the study of the perception of two-dimensional patterns a fascinating pursuit, I have found and developed only a few tasks in this area. Western adults take picture perception—and educated adults the perception of maps, diagrams, charts, graphs, and all the rest—so much for granted that they may fail to notice that skills in this area have to develop, and may have to be cultivated. Studies of neonatal and infantile perception, usually by the preference method but also by tracing eye movements, indicate that babies can find some kind of meaning in two-dimensional patterns right from the beginning. The problem is to know what kind. A controversy, reminiscent of that between the atomists and Gestaltists during the 1930's and '40's, seems to be boiling up between elementalists, inspired by Hebb's cell-assembly view of development, and globalists, marching under the banner of Werner's differentiation-integration view. For the moment I see no ready empirical answer to the problem. I will say only that one cannot safely infer that the baby sees only the point he is fixating at a given moment. That is, there is no reason to assume that the baby's visual experience is punctiform, but there is every reason to assume that there is some kind of temporal integration involved in coming to terms with any new perceptual object, whether it be a picture, a piece of music, or a roomful of people. I keep trying to ally myself with the Gibsons to say that three-dimensional perception is the basic kind, with perception of two-dimensional patterns a more difficult and intricate a process, and the Gibsons consistently keep repudiating me. I think part of the difficulty lies in their adherence to stimulus properties, as in their study of which kinds of deformations of letter-like forms can be accepted as equivalent to a standard, whereas I am somewhat more concerned with subject variables that, for instance, will permit equivalence between forms having little in common morphologically: consider the difference among printed and cursive, capital and small forms of many actual letters of the alphabet, which are nonetheless treated by the child as equivalent.

One can sometimes get evidence of picture recognition even from preverbal babies—indeed, the Hayeses (Hayes, 1951) observed picture recognition in their chimpanzee, Viki. The baby usually demonstrates his recognition by some appropriate action: rocking to a picture of a rocking horse, making the sound of a motor to a picture of a car, petting a pictured animal, smelling the picture of a flower, or, like Viki, trying to hear the ticking of a pictured watch. My attempts to duplicate such responding in test situations have been a failure, partly, perhaps, because I could not find culturally relevant pictures for my Hawaiian sample. My pictures included an apple and a banana, both of which are common in Hawaii, but neither of which can be considered a really gripping stimulus. For what it is worth, none of my Hawaiian one-to-two-year-olds reacted to a picture card as picture. They chewed, bent, pounded, and threw the cards, but they seemed impervious to the fact that the cards bore meaningful representations of objects.

There are several tasks which test perceptual organization in three-, four-, and five-year-olds. For instance, asking the child simply to trace a looping line indicates that younger children do not see the good continuation of the line, as shown by the way they detour around the loops. A similar effect is seen in asking the child to color two crossed oblongs, the "nearer" of which masks the center section of the "more distant" one. The youngest children ignore the lines separating the two oblongs and simply color the cross as a whole. Somewhat older subjects are likely to color the two exposed ends of the partly masked oblong different colors, suggesting that they appear disconnected. It is only at about age four or even five that children consistently begin to assign the same color to the exposed ends of the rearward oblong.

A number of people have studied the development of ability to copy geometric forms. I have data indicating reliably superior performance of middle-class four-year-olds over disadvantaged four-year-olds on the task of copying the block capital letters **A, E, M,** and **P**. The examiner first prints the letter on a blank sheet of paper and then hands the pencil to the child with an invitation to make the letter, which is named. Here an important procedural note is in order. When making the standard for the child to copy, one must sit behind him or beside him. If one sits acorss a table from the child and forms the letter upside down so that it is properly oriented for the child, he may try to reciprocate. A number of children have transcended their egocentrism to the extent of making the letter upside down, for the examiner's benefit, but none has transcended egocentrism so far as to do it correctly. Performance on each letter is scored zero for no response (although every effort is made to teach the child the operation, to the point of moving his hand through the necessary strokes), one point for any effort resulting in a mark or scribble, two points for a form obviously derived from the model (such as a zigzag in response to **M**) but not recognizable as the particular letter, and three points for a recognizable copy, no matter how poor (*e.g.*, any perceptible bit of stem below and to the left of the loop in the **P** differentiating it from an **O** or a **D** or a **Q**). With the maximum individual score being 12, middle-class four-year-olds had a mean of 10.56 and deprived four-year-olds a mean of 7.46.

Drawing a person is a task ambiguously both two-dimensional and three-dimensional, but in any case, middle-class four-year-olds do significantly better at it than their disadvantaged age-mates. In fact, the performance of deprived four-year-olds is at about the same level as that of middle-class three-year-olds.

Paper-and-pencil mazes, as Porteus has always proclaimed, are a sensitive measure of age differences, although the age norms embodied in the different mazes are probably too low. In our comparison of middle-class and disadvantaged four-year-olds, we used the age four mazes to demonstrate the task, and the age five mazes as a test. We ignored Porteus' scoring, which penalizes the child for bumping into the walls, on the ground that our interest in fine motor control was minimal. Let me say simply that the middle-class group did significantly better than the disadvantaged group, who in this case again performed at about the same level as middle-class three-year-olds. Two interesting kinds of response showed up in deprived children. One I call "short-cut": after following the maze for a while, the child travels in a straight line to the exit, disregarding the barriers. Six out of twenty-eight disadvantaged children responded thus. The other, which appeared in two other deprived children, I call "roundabout": instead of tracing a line through the maze, the children detoured around the outside of the maze from entrance to exit.

We attempted to use the jigsaw puzzles from the Merrill-Palmer scale with our groups, but they proved too easy for all our subjects.

Anne Berens and I (Berens and Church, in preparation) have done a study comparing deprived (in this case part-Hawaiian) and middle-class (miscellaneous hypenated-Americans, largely Japanese) three-to-five-year-olds on a task of completing various geometric forms (and some real-life equivalents) with a corner left off. The demands of Pragnanz, or good form, became apparent to our middle-class subjects at age four or five, whereas younger middle-class *S*s and all our disadvangated *S*s completed the break simply by drawing a line directly between the two ends. It made no detectable difference whether abstract or concrete forms were used.

Let me end on a note of even more unfinished business. I have worked out an *a priori* scheme for the analysis of picture descriptions. This scheme has something in common with the Hemmendinger-Siegel-Philips (Hemmendinger, 1951) developmental scoring system for Rorschach responses. Picture descriptions can be scored in terms of a) whether they begin with an integral statement of what the picture is about, and whether this statement is further elaborated, or whether the response consists of the enumeration of isolated objects or features; b) the specification of object attributes; c) specification of concrete relations between people or objects (*e.g.* "she's washing the dishes" or "the wagon is bumping into the tree"); d) specification of social roles (*e.g.*, "daddy", "policemen") or of formal relationships; e) reference to psychological states such as motives or feelings; f) mention of antecedent or subsequent events that put the picture in temporal, historical, or evolutionary perspective; and g) gross misperceptions of content. Notice that the emphasis here is on cognitive powers of analysis and integration, and not on projective themes.

The reason that this technique remains untested is that I have never managed to find the right pictures. For my purposes, if I am going to keep my stimuli constant, I need interracial pictures, and good, interesting, interracial pictures suitable for the preschool years are far from abundant. However, a graduate student at the City University has found some materials for use with school-age children, and is now making a comparison of the responses of normal and disturbed middle-years children, which may provide a test of the method.

Even though I was not successful with my tests of spatial and temporal words, other approaches can undoubtedly be devised. The child's ability to count objects, although it belongs with verbal tests, is a useful index of cognitive development. It should be possible to adapt Guilford's Unusual Uses technique for preschool children.

In closing, then, let me stress the wealth of techniques available to us. Furthermore, these techniques are not merely techniques: they reveal important facts of cognitive development. These facts do not yet exist in any organized pattern, but even in their present incoherent state they carry some implications. It seems to me, for instance, that there can no longer be any serious question about discontinuities in cognitive development. We are now in a position to move on to the more interesting problems of differential cognitive development and its occasions. And we are in a favorable position to reintegrate the study of linguistic and cognitive development, which have tended recently to go their separate ways. Instead of debating the Whorfian hypothesis, we can begin in earnest to investigate it.

References

Baltimore City Public Schools. AN EARLY SCHOOL ADMISSION PROJECT: PROGRESS REPORT 1963-64. Baltimore: Baltimore City Public School, 1964.

Berens, A. E., and Church, J. SUBCULTURAL AND AGE DIFFERENCES IN PERFORMANCE ON FIGURE-COMPLETION TASKS. In preparation.

Burghardt, G. M., and Hess, E. H. "Food imprinting in the snapping turtle, Chelydra serpentina." SCIENCE, 151: 108-109, 1966.

Caldwell, B. M. DIRECTIONS FOR SETTING UP CHILD-ENVIRONMENT INTERACTIONS AND A CHECK-LIST FOR OBSERVED REACTIONS, and EARLY LANGUAGE ASSESSMENT SCALE. Mimeographed, 1964.

Cattell, P. INFANT INTELLIGENCE SCALE, record form. New York: Psychological Corporation, 1940.

Caudill, W., and Weinstein, H. "Maternal care and infant behavior in Japanese and American urban middle class families." In Konig, R., and Hill, R. (Eds.). YEARBOOK OF THE INTERNATIONAL SOCIOLOGICAL ASSOCIATION, 1966.

Charlesworth, W. R. "Cognition in infancy: Where do we stand in the mid-sixties?" MERRILL-PALMER QUARTERLY, 14: 25-46, 1968.

Church, J. LANGUAGE AND THE DISCOVERY OF REALITY. New York: Vintage, 1966.

Coller, A. R., and Victor, J. EARLY CHILDHOOD INVENTORIES PROJECT. New York: New York University School of Education, Institute for Developmental Studies, 1967.

Dixon, J. D., "Development of self recognition." JOURNAL OF GENETIC PSYCHOLOGY, 91:251-256, 1957.

Geber, M. "The psycho-motor development of African children in the first year and the influence of maternal behavior." JOURNAL OF SOCIAL PSYCHOLOGY, 47: 185-195, 1958.

Goldstein, K., and Scheerer, M. "Abstract and concrete behavior." PSYCHOLOGICAL MONOGRAPHS, 53 (no. 2), 1941.

Hayes, C. THE APE IN OUR HOUSE. New York: Harper, 1951.

Hemmendinger, L. A GENETIC STUDY OF STRUCTURAL ASPECTS OF PERCEPTION AS REFLECTED IN RORSCHACH TEST PERFORMANCE. Ph.D. Dissertation, Clark University, 1951.

Levy, D. M. "The infant's earliest memory of inoculation: A contribution to public health procedures." JOURNAL OF GENETIC PSYCHOLOGY, 96: 3-46, 1960.

Little, A. OBJECT RELATIONSHIPS, DIFFERENTIATION OF SPACE, CAUSALITY SEQUENCE, TEMPORAL (MEMORY) SEQUENCE , AND IMITATION SEQUENCE. University of Western Australia, Department of Psychology, mimeographed, no date.

Mead, M., and Macgregor, F. C. GROWTH AND CULTURE: A PHOTOGRAPHIC STUDY OF BALINESE CHILDHOOD. New York: Putnam, 1951.

Schiff, W. "Perception of impending collision." PSYCHOLOGICAL MONOGRAPHS, 79 (no. 11), 1965.

Tinklepaugh, O. L. "An experimental study of representative factors in monkeys." JOURNAL OF COMPARATIVE PSYCHOLOGY, 8: 197-236, 1928.

Uzgiris, I. C., and Hunt, J. McV. AN INSTRUMENT FOR ASSESSING INFANT PSYCHOLOGICAL DEVELOPMENT. University of Illinois, Psychological Development Laboratory, mimeographed, 1966.

Wertheimer, M. "Psychomotor coordination of auditory and visual space at birth." SCIENCE, 134: 1692, 1961.

White, B. L., Castle, P., and Held, R. "Observations on the development of visually directed reaching." CHILD DEVELOPMENT, 35: 349-364, 1964.

Zazzo, R. "Le probleme de l'imitation chez le nouveau-ne." ENFANCE, 2:135-142, 1957.

THE INITIAL COORDINATION OF SENSORIMOTOR SCHEMAS
IN HUMAN INFANTS: PIAGET'S IDEAS AND
THE ROLE OF EXPERIENCES*

Burton White, Ph.D.

During the last ten years, increasing numbers of American psychologists have turned to the study of human infancy. Characteristically, recent research in this country has been carefully designed and executed. Another feature shared by most modern studies is the modesty of their scope. Visual orientation, auditory sensitivity, heart-rate patterns, conditioned reflexes, etc., typify the target phenomena under study. Valuable as these studies are, they seem to leave the student of human development in a state of deprivation. Some sense of how the entire human infant functions during his first encounters with the world is indispensable and yet not easily available. It would be fair to say that few American developmental psychologists have much first-hand knowledge about infant behavior beyond the scope of their admittedly narrowly defined studies. I think part of the enormous respect many of us have for Jean Piaget is due to his contribution to our understanding of the nature of the normally functioning human infant.

THE ORIGINS OF INTELLIGENCE IN CHILDREN (Piaget, 1952), is in my opinion, far and away the most outstanding body of work we have on human infancy. It represents the work of a truly remarkable observer, theoretician, and experimenter. It is one of the few examples of behavioral research on a grand scale. Actually, the approach Piaget used is more familiar to biologists and ethologists than to psychologists. Defining intelligence as the prime human adaptive tool, Piaget traced the etiology of this vital asset from its first manifestations in the sensorimotor behavior of the newborn to the emergence of ideational forms at the end of the second year. He did this using a combination of fundamental scientific tools. The combination was a simple one: 1) selection of the general topic—the ontogenesis of intelligence; 2) general theorizing—e.g. continuous efforts towards adaptation involving assimilation, accommodation, and schemas; 3) observations—thousands of hours spent identifying the multiplicity of manifestations of the processes under study; 4) experimentation—e.g. on object permanence, means-ends behavior, and so on; 5) refinement and integration of theory.

Along the way, Piaget identified behavioral signs of the emergence of several related fundamental processes such as: intentionality, curiosity, symbolic behavior, the transition from trial and error to insightful behavior, and so on. It is truly amazing that virtually no one (Charlesworth, 1964, excepted) has pursued subsequently the

*From STUDIES IN COGNITIVE DEVELOPMENT: ESSAYS IN HONOR OF JEAN PIAGET, edited by David Elkind and John H. Flavell. Copyright 1968 by Oxford University Press, Inc. Reprinted by permission.

study of these processes in infants although it has been thirty years since Piaget's observations were published.

When one describes this work in 1967, one gets a feeling of remoteness from modern American studies. There is no mention of independent variables, operational definitions, elaborate experimental design, nonparametric statistics, and so forth, nor their counterparts of the 1930's. Yet, neither is there a feeling of artificiality, arbitrariness, and atomism characteristic of modern studies. Perhaps the most unique contribution Piaget has made to the study of infancy is to suggest a viable alternative to the conventional approach used in our field.

Bear with me for a moment while I compare the tasks of understanding early human development and manufacturing a suit of clothes. Most modern studies are primarily empirical, restricted in scope, and scientifically respectable. Such studies produce dependable findings. In the preparation of our suit of clothes, these well-shaped findings are comparable to finely cut lapels, or pockets, or buttonholes, or cuffs, or what have you. They are unquestionably excellently made but it is not as if we have all of the pieces that only remain to be put together. Rather, we have perhaps less than 5 percent of the total, and in fact, there are those producing such pieces, lapels perhaps, who would have us believe that the entire suit is simply a very large lapel. I find less to quarrel with with them, however, than with others in our field who claim to have fine suits available when we know they have not taken the time and trouble to procure any fabric let alone lapels or pockets. Their suits are splendidly advertised but seem to lack substance. Piaget, on the other hand although admittedly having studied only one of several major developmental processes, and only in his own three children, has manufactured a complete suit. It is undoubtedly improperly cut. It would be miraculous if it were a perfect fit. Nonetheless, it has a general shape that probably bears a strong generic relationship to the product we seek. He has very few genuine competitors.

Let me make explicit what I have implied. There seem to be in current use three ways of studying infant development: 1) empirical studies of high dependability and molecular scope; 2) theoretical work, broad in scope but supported by negligible amounts of data (as for example, modern explanatory systems of language acquisition); and 3) bold frontal assaults on the **total** course of the developmental process via intensive first-hand longitudinal observations combined with cumulative experimentation, and an irreligious attitude towards laboratory methods, experimental design, and statistics. It is my contention that Piaget's infancy work is an example of style 3 and constitutes the single most important contribution to our understanding of early human intellectual development. It is the only system based on empirical evidence that addresses the question, "What does the human child know of the world during his first two years of life?" Perhaps it is time we asked whether the traditional approaches in which we have been investing virtually all of our resources (styles 1 and 2) have been sufficiently productive.

Personally, I find my professional bearings with Piaget's studies. Right or wrong, he offers a powerful framework for guidance in investigating human behavior; a framework that is sufficiently complicated for the obviously complex creature involved, and one that pulls together the bewildering pieces of infant behavior into a believable system. I never cease to be amazed at how often my own observations on several hundred infants confirm Piaget's observations on only three.

Perhaps the feature of Piaget's theory that attracted me most was its focus on the intimate interaction between infant and environment. Here, after all, is where the processes that concern psychologists take place. Even though he did not concern himself with possible optimal arrangements of environmental circumstances of "aliments," he did not open the door for anyone who would care to sponsor schema development, complication, and proliferation. The studies I have been involved with over the last several years (White, et al., 1964; Haynes, et al, 1965; White & Castle, 1964; White & Held, 1966; White, 1967) have been oriented toward the determination of optimal rearing conditions for human infants. I have consciously tried to utilize both styles 2 and 3 in my approach to the problem. As a result, I feel my colleagues and I have gained some dependable knowledge about fundamental sensorimotor acquisitions as visually-directed reaching, accommodation, and exploration. In addition, we believe we have gained some preliminary but dependable knowledge about the complicated interrelations between early experience and development.

In this report, I should like to present some hitherto unpublished data on one phase of sensorimotor theory. These data concern the integration of schemas or in Piaget's terms the "reciprocal coordinations" of the second stage. During a series of studies on the effects of differential rearing conditions, we routinely included an "object-in-hand" test. According to Piaget, the behavior seen when an object is grasped by an infant of one to five months of age reveals the degree of interrelationship among the grasping, sucking and looking schemas. The one-month-old infant is capable of grasping a rattle, looking at it, or sucking it. Further, each of these behaviors can be elicited if the rattle is used as directed "aliment," that is, if it is brought to the infant's mouth, he will suck it; if it is pressed in the infant's palm, he will grasp it, and so on. However, at one month of age, according to Piaget, these schemas exist in isolation. This means that, unlike an adult, a one-month-old infant will not look at something he is grasping, nor grasp what he is sucking, and so forth. During the months that follow, these schemas become coordinated. The steps as spelled out by Piaget (1952, pp. 88-122) are as follows:

1–2 MONTHS*—The hand does not grasp an object that is being sucked, even though the hand itself is occasionally brought to the mouth and sucked. Further, the eyes do not regard the object grasped (or the hand). Vision is therefore not so advanced as sucking when compared with control of the hands.

2–3 MONTHS—The eyes follow the motion of the hands but the hands are not under the control of the visual system; they move in and out of the visual field apparently independently. The hand does not try to grasp what the eye sees. Continuing the primacy of sucking as a controlling function, the hand brings grasped objects to the mouth where they are sucked rather than to the visual field for viewing.

3–4 MONTHS—The hand grasps the object that is being sucked and reciprocally the object grasped is brought to the mouth to be sucked. However, if the object is in view before it is grasped, there is a delay before the object is brought to the mouth. In addition, vision seems to influence hand movements, maintaining their presence in the visual field and "augmenting" their activity (Piaget, 1952, p. 102).

4–5 MONTHS—The hand grasps the seen object for the first time. Prehension results when hand and object are simultaneously in view.

5-6 MONTHS—True visually directed reaching emerges. After the object is grasped the infant routinely glances at it before bringing it to the mouth for sucking. Occasionally, viewing is prolonged and the object is not brought to the mouth at all. It should be noted that in sensorimotor theory the intersection of several schemas provides the basis for the emergence of object permanence. An object that is simultaneously looked at, reached for, and felt, as in the prehensory act, is more than a part of a single activity schema. It serves a truly unique function when it participates in three schemas at once, and from this special role true object permanence normally develops. (Hunt, 1961).

The data to be presented in this paper address two questions: 1) Does the sequence described by Piaget fit the facts gathered on a larger group of subjects? 2) Do modifications in rearing conditions that accelerate the acquisition of visually directed reaching affect other important steps in the sequence?

*Ages cited are approximations.

Unfortunately, placing an object in the hand of an infant (our method) is an inadequate test of the entire developmental sequence in question. For example, a test situation where an object (perhaps a pacifier) was placed in the infant's mouth would be necessary as well as a situation where the infant could view the object before he grasped it. Nonetheless, we may be able to learn something from this admittedly partial view of the situation when the results are combined with those of tests of prehension in the same subjects.

THE TEST PROCEDURE

Once each week, beginning at 36 days, each infant was brought to the testing room. After a five- to ten-minute acclimatization period, the infant was given three opportunities to respond to the presentation of the test object (for details see White, et al., 1965). This procedure took about five minutes. The last phase of the session consisted of the object-in-hand test. The test object was a paper party toy. It was approximately five inches in length and one half inch in diameter along the handle or stem. At one end there was a wooden mouthpiece through which air could be blown to extend a red coiled section. To this coiled section were attached two feathers. When coiled, this section is surrounded by orange and yellow fringes. The overall diameter of this display was about one and a half inches: The object is a common five-and-ten-cent store item and was used because it is easily grasped and retained by young infants and features a complex contour field with highly contrasting orange, red, and yellow lines previously found attractive to most infants (White, et al., 1964).

Subjects were physically normal infants born and reared in an institution. As part of a larger study, some of these infants had been reared in a variety of systematically varied rearing conditions designed to accelerate sensorimotor development. (For details see White & Held, 1966; White, 1967.) The data presented in this paper are from two groups: Forty-three controls including eleven babies who had received extra handling during the first 36 days of life, and sixteen modified enrichment infants. In brief, the experimental group was reared under conditions designed to increase the occurrence of certain forms of motility in sensorily enriched surroundings. Such experiences produced markedly precocious visually directed reaching and heightened visual attentiveness.

HYPOTHESES

1. Control babies would exhibit behaviors consistent with Piaget's observations on the development of reciprocal coordinations among looking, sucking, and grasping schemas.

2. Increased looking at and palpating of nearby objects (induced via enrichment procedures) would result in acceleration of the coordination process.

RESULTS

1. The normal developmental sequence:

On the basis of Piaget's discussion of the development of prehension schemas (1952, pp. 88-122) one would expect a developmental pattern somewhat like that described in Table 1.

TABLE 1

The Normal Developmental Sequence According to Piaget

Test		Object-in-Hand	Prehension
AGE (months)	N	RESPONSE	RESPONSE
1-2	3	1 Retains only	-
2-3	"	I Brought to mouth for sucking	-
3-4	"	1 Brought to mouth for sucking	-
4-5	"	1 Brought to mouth for sucking	Fourth-stage reaching (if hand and object simultaneously in view)
5-6	"	1 Brief regard then brought to mouth for sucking	
			True reaching
		2 Prolonged regard	

Responses to the object-in-hand test in our control group are shown in Table 2.

Description of responses:

Retains only—The infant holds the test object for more than three seconds.

Views—The infant holds the test object and either glances at it one or more times or regards it steadily for up to two minutes.

Brought to mouth—The infant holds the object and without viewing,

TABLE 2

The Sequence Exhibited by Control Subjects

Test				Object-In-Hand		Prehension	
	AGE (Months)	No.*	RESPONSE	SUBJECTS EXHIBITING N	RESPONSE † PER CENT	N	RESPONSE
	1.5-2	23	1 Retains only	22	95.8		
			2 Brought to mouth	5	21.7		
			3 Views	3	13.0		
	2-2.5	27	1 Retains only	23	85.2		
			2 Views other hand	3	11.1		
			3 Views other hand raised	2	7.4		
	2.5-3	25	1 Retains only	21	84.1		
			2 Views	18	72.1		
			3 Brought to mouth	6	24.0		
			4 Views other hand	5	20.0		
			5 Monitored mutual play	0	0.0		
	3-3.5	27	1 Views	24	89.0		
			2 Retains only	16	59.3		
			3 Monitored mutual play	7	25.9		
			4 Brought to mouth	6	22.2		

Age	N	Response		%		
3.5-4	25	1 Views	20	80.0		
		2 Monitored mutual play	13	52.0		
		3 Views then to mouth	7	28.0		
		4 Retains only	6	24.0		
		5 Brought to mouth	6	24.0		
		6 Views other hand raised	6	24.0		
		7 Monitored mutual play then to mouth	3	12.0		
4-4.5	21	1 Views	17	81.0	12	Fourth-stage reaching (median-130 days)
		2 Monitored mutual play	15	71.5		
		3 Views other hand raised	7	33.3		
4.5-5	16	1 Views	12	75.0	14	True reaching (median-147 days)
		2 Monitored mutual play	9	56.3		
		3 Brought to mouth	6	37.5		
		4 Views then to mouth	6	37.5		
		5 Monitored mutual play then to mouth	1	6.3		

Total N = 164   Total trials = 560

*Each test consisted to two trials. Average number of tests/subjects was 1.71. Average number of responses per trial was 1.21; increasing steadily with age.
†Only the responses occurring in 20 percent or more of the subjects of either the control or experimental group are recorded.

TABLE 3

The Sequence Exhibited by Experimental Subjects

Test			Object-In-Hand			Prehension	
	AGE (Months)	N*	RESPONSE	SUBJECTS EXHIBITING N	RESPONSE PER CENT	N	RESPONSE
	1.5-2	16	Retains only	16	100.0		
			Views	10	62.6		
			Brought to mouth	6	37.5		
	2-2.5	16	Retains only	15	93.9		
			Views	10	62.6		
			Views other hand raised	5	31.3		
			Views other hand	4	25.0		
			Brought to mouth	4	25.0		
	2.5-3	14	Views	13	93.0	13	True reaching (median-89 days)
			Retains only	7	50.0		
			Views other hand	6	42.8		
			Monitored mutual play	5	35.7		
			Views other hand	4	28.6		

Age	N		Count	%	4th stage reaching (median-95 days)
3-3.5	12	Views	10	83.6	8
		Retains only	7	58.3	
		Views other hand	6	50.0	
		Monitored mutual play	4	33.3	
		Views other hand	3	25.0	
3.5-4	12	Views	10	83.6	
		Monitored mutual play	7	58.3	
		Views other hand	4	33.3	
		Monitored mutual play then to mouth	3	25.0	
		Views then to mouth	1	8.3	
		Retains only	1	8.3	
4-4.5	11	Views	9	82.8	
		Monitored mutual play	9	82.8	
		Views other hand	4	36.4	
4.5-5	9	Monitored mutual play	8	88.9	
		Views	7	77.8	
		Views then to mouth	3	33.3	
		Views other hand	3	33.3	
		Monitored mutual play then to mouth	2	22.2	
		Brought to mouth	0	00.0	

Total N = 90   Total trials = 380

*Average number of tests/subject was 1.90. Average numbers of responses/trial was 1.13, increasing steadily with age.

TABLE 4

Significance Levels for Differences Between Control and Experimental Subjects—Object-In-Hand-Test

Response	Percent Exhibiting Response*		t	df	Significance Level (1-tailed tests)
	CONTROLS	EXPERI-MENTALS			
Retains only	24.0	8.3	1.34	35	N. S.
Views	13.0	62.6	3.56	37	.001
Views with other hand raised	7.4	31.3	1.90	41	N. S.
Brought to mouth	37.5	0.0	3.10	23	.005
Views other hand	20.0	42.8	1.47	27	N. S.
Monitored mutual play	35.7	64.3	2.79	27	.005
Monitored mutual play then to mouth	12.0	25.0	0.93	35	N. S.
Views then to mouth	28.0	8.3	1.64	35	N. S.

*In this analysis the following procedure was followed:

(a) Identify responses that occurred in at least 20 percent of either group

(b) Determine the number of age periods when each response occurred in at least 20 percent of either group

34

(c) Calculate the probability of any single comparison between groups for any two-week interval for an overall significance level of .05 according to the following formula:

$$p = (1 - \alpha)^n$$ where n = number of 2-week periods where response occurred in at least 20 percent of either group

(d) Test most extreme group differences against adjusted significance levels

N	1	2	3	4	5	6	7
	.050	.025	.017	.012	.010	.008	.007

TABLE 5

Distribution of Schemas as a Function of Age for Control and Experimental Groups—Object-in-Hand Test

AGE (Months)	Control				Experimental			
	RESPONSE*	SCHEMAS INVOLVED †	PERCENT SHOWING	WEIGHTED SCORE	RESPONSE	SCHEMAS INVOLVED	PERCENT SHOWING	WEIGHTED SCORE
1.5-2	Retains only	1	95.8	95.8	Retains only	1	100.0	100.0
	Brought to mouth	2	21.7	43.4	Views	2	62.6	125.2
					Brought to mouth	2	37.5	75.0
Group score				139.2				300.2
2-2.5	Retains only	1	85.2	85.2	Retains only	1	93.9	93.9
					Views	2	62.6	125.2
					Views other hand raised	3	31.3	93.9
					Views other hand	2	25.0	50.0
					Brought to mouth	2	25.0	50.0
Group score				85.2				413.0
2.5-3	Retains only	1	84.1	84.1	Views	2	93.0	186.0
	Views	2	72.1	144.2	Retains only	1	50.0	50.0
					Views other hand	2	42.8	85.6
					Monitored mutual play	3	35.7	107.1
					Views other hand raised	3	28.6	85.8
Group score				228.3				514.5

Age group	Behavior	n			Behavior	n		
3-3.5	Views	2	89.0	178.0	Views	2	83.6	167.3
	Retains only	1	59.3	59.3	Retains only	1	58.3	58.3
	Monitored mutual play	3	25.9	77.7	Views other hand raised	3	50.0	150.0
	Brought to mouth	2	22.2	44.4	Monitored mutual play	3	33.3	99.9
					Views other hand	2	25.0	50.0
Group score				359.4				535.4
3.5-4	Views	2	80.0	160.0	Views	2	83.6	167.2
	Monitored mutual play	3	52.0	156.0	Monitored mutual play	3	58.3	174.9
	Views then to mouth	3	28.0	84.0	Views other hand raised	3	33.3	99.9
	Retains only	1	24.0	24.0	Monitored mutual play	4	25.0	100.0
	Views other hand raised	3	24.0	72.0				
Group score				544.0				542.0
4-4.5	Views	2	81.0	162.0	Views	2	82.8	165.6
	Monitored mutual play	3	71.5	214.5	Monitored mutual play	3	82.8	248.4
	Views other hand raised	3	33.3	100.0	Views other hand raised	3	36.4	109.2
Group score				476.5				523.2
4.5-5	Views	2	75.0	150.0	Monitored mutua play	3	88.9	266.7
	Monitored mutual play	3	56.3	168.9	Views	2	77.8	155.6
	Brought to mouth	2	37.5	75.0	Views then to mouth	3	33.3	99.9
	Views then to mouth	3	37.5	112.5	Views other hand raised	3	33.3	99.9

Monitored mutual play then to mouth

Group score	506.4	22.2	88.8
			710.9

4

Group differences are significant beyond .02 level-Randomization test (Siegel, 1956).
*Only responses occurring in at least 20 percent of the subjects are included.
†Schemas were assigned as follows:

RESPONSE	SCHEMAS INVOLVED	TOTAL SCHEMAS
Retains only	Grasp	1
Brought to mouth	Grasp	2
	Sucking	
Views	Grasp	2
	Vision	
Views—other hand	Grasp	2
	Vision	
Views—other hand raised	Grasp	3
	Vision	
	"Other Arm"	
	Movement	
Views then to mouth	Grasp	3
	Vision	
	Sucking	
Monitored mutual play	Grasp	
	Vision	
	Tactual	
Monitored mutual play then to mouth	Grasp	4
	Vision	
	Tactual	
	Sucking	

brings it to the mouth one or more times briefly or manages to keep it at the mouth and gum or suck it.

Monitored mutual play—The object is brought to the midline where it is simultaneously viewed and tactually explored by the other hand.

Views then to mouth—Responses 2 and 3 combined.

Views—other hand raised—The infant retains the object and extends and raises both arms while viewing the object.

Views—other hand—The infant retains the object and views the free hand.

Monitored mutual play—then to mouth—Responses 4 and 3 combined.

Although fourth- and fifth-stage reaching occurred about as predicted by Piaget's work, this was not the case for the object-in-hand data. The number of response patterns seen was considerably greater than expected, the influence of the sucking schemas was much less than expected, and that of vision was strikingly greater than expected.

2a. Is the developmental sequence influenced by rearing conditions? Table 3 contains responses to the object-in-hand test shown by the experimental group. Table 4 indicates that the groups differ significantly.

b. Is the rate of coordination of schemas influenced by rearing conditions?

Table 5 shows comparative data for the experimental and control groups. The schemata listed are not necessarily the only ones involved in the behaviors seen.*

It is clear that the coordination of schemas as described in this analysis has been accelerated for the experimental group. With respect to prehension, the median

---

*Piaget does not give precise guidelines for assigning schemas to behavior. I have tried to be conservative in assigning schemas to the behavior patterns in question. There seem to be at least five schemas involved: (1) the grasp schema—retention of the object; (2) the visual schema—glances or prolonged viewing of the object; (3) the sucking schema—the object is brought to the mouth for attempts at sucking; (4) the tactual schema—the other hand joins with the hand holding the object to either feel it or take it away; and (5) the "other" arm movement schema—the other hand is raised. This last schema reflects the ambiguities in assigning schemas to complicated behavior patterns. Since all behaviors require a schema in Piaget's system, and since hand-raising occurs rather often, I have postulated a schema for it. Actually, hand-raising is a part of another schema, bilateral hand-raising, which is a behavior pattern often seen between 7 and 11 weeks of age in our control group.

dates of onset for stages four and five were 95 to 89 days respectively compared to 130 and 147 days for the control group. These shifts are highly significant (p < .001—Mann-Whitney U Test, Siegel, 1956).

DISCUSSION

The first hypothesis, that the sequences described by Piaget would be repeated in a larger subject group, was only partly confirmed. We did not find the sucking schema to be dominant in our groups. Further, the influence of vision was markedly greater than expected. In addition, the complexity of the sequence in terms of number of responses shown was greater than expected. Finally, the influence of postural factors such as the tonic neck reflex and the favored hand was both marked and unexpected. During the third month of life, a child would often view the object placed in his favored hand, and again view that hand when the object was placed in the other hand. Another manifestation of this asymmetry was seen a few weeks later when the infant would merely stare at the object in the favored hand (views object) but would bring the favored hand over to join or tactually explore the object when it was held by the other hand (monitored mutual play). Responses during the second month involved only one hand. During the third and fourth months there was a steady increase in bilateral hand and arm involvement that paralleled the oft-noted reduction in the influence of the tonic neck reflex (Gesell and Amatruda, 1941). This paves the way for the coordination of the visual and tactual schemas of each hand with the other. It is of course possible that the fact that Piaget's children were breast fed, whereas the subjects in this study were not, would account for some or even all of the differences.

The second hypothesis predicting plasticity of development was amply confirmed. The results of both the object-in-hand and the prehension tests indicate important functional relationships between rearing conditions and the developmental processes in question. Further, it is to be noted that the degree of acceleration involved in the experimental group is more than nominal even though the experimental modification of rearing conditions were little more than first attempts. Of course, at this time no claim can be made for precise understanding of the role of experience; however, some discussion of the design of the experimental rearing conditions is in order at this point.

It is customary to select independent variables primarily on the basis of the theory underlying one's study. In experiments where the subjects are human adults, for example, whether or not the subject is inclined to act as required during the experimental treatment is rarely a problem. If a subject should prove reluctant, he may be replaced. In our studies of infant development as in Piaget's, the situation is different for two reasons. First, we are unable, and in fact, unwilling to demand actions of our subjects that are very different from what they tend to do normally. Second, we depend much more on induction in designing experiments than on existing theories. This latter fact means that we take pains to discover via extensive naturalistic observations what infants actually do in the hope that an analysis of actual experiences when meshed with general theoretical notions will yield experiments of definite relevance to human development. This process has a parallel in studies of the acquisition of language. For many years now, psychologists and educators have marvelled at how quickly all children acquire the complicated rules involved in understanding and producing their native language. It has frequently been noted that little or no active tuition is necessary. But, few, if any, investigators have attempted to learn how this remarkable natural achievement occurs. It seems most likely that we would learn a great deal about the learning processes involved were we to study the details of the experiences involved. Is it not likely that the differential experiences undergone by extreme groups (very fast versus very slow progress in language acquisition) would provide a wealth of information about the processes involved?

During the first six months of life children are not usually able to locomote; in fact, they have limited abilities in most all developmental areas. In addition, their experiential histories are very brief. These factors combined suggest that an analysis of the opportunities for learning is more feasible for this period than for subsequent ones. Piaget has provided some clues by describing the developing sensorimotor structures. Only lengthy longitudinal observations can complete the picture, however. These we have done for one population. We have observed several hundred physically normal, hospital-reared infants for three continuous hours each week from birth to six months (White et al., 1964; White & Castle, 1965). The favorite activities of these children when awake and not distressed or drowsy are visual exploration, especially of their own hands, tactual exploration, and combined visual and tactual exploration, again usually of their own hands. From about the fourteenth week on if given the opportunity, they will usually view areas several yards away. When placed in the prone position prior to that time, however, their visual interest and tactual interest seem to be restricted primarily to the 24 inches or so around them. On the basis of unsystematic observations, it would appear that home-reared babies do not differ radically in these respects. The major visual-motor activities of this time of life primarily consists of the internal ocular adjustments of accommodation and position, including convergence and pursuit; rotations of the head; movements of the arm, hand, and fingers within the visual field; head rearing (in the prone position); and from about the fifth month on, turning the torso from side to side and occasionally completely over.

Our modified enrichment group was given extra handling during the first 36 days of life when visual motor activities do not occupy much of the infant's day (White &

Held, 1966; White, 1967). During the second month an attempt was made to optimize learning conditions for the acquisition of visual control over the hand that seems to be a major if not *the* major sensorimotor acquisition of the first half year of life. Visual -monitored batting and tactual exploration of nearby objects were induced (White & Held, 1966; White, 1967). During the third month, similar activities plus heightened visual scanning was induced by the presence of new viewable and palpable objects as well as routine prone placement of the subjects (White & Held, 1966; White, 1967).

Obviously, we have dealt with molar experiences rather than isolated independent variables. The scientific task that awaits is the sorting of what is and what is not relevant within the gross experimental treatment. It is here that refined theory is sooner or later necessary; I, however, do not believe that one should proceed hastily towards extended theoretical analyses. Rather, I would advocate modest theoretical distinctions followed by empirical test leading to new theoretical deviations slightly more specific, followed by test, and so on.

CONCLUSION

Piaget's general position which holds that infant behavior consists at first of sequential activation of isolated schemas and, from the third month on, their reciprocal coordination, is amply supported by this study. On the other hand, two major amplifications are also revealed. First, that the number of schemas involved in prehensory development is, for the subject groups of this study at least, many times what Piaget saw in his own children. In addition, and of obvious importance for developmental psychology, is the demonstration of the functional relevance of experience to the developments in question. Although this study requires replication, and is only an early attempt in a complicated area of investigation, it appears that major effects on the rate of development may be induced with ease using innocuous alterations in rearing conditions. Let me point out, however, that the design of enrichment conditions in this study or "the match" as Hunt would put it, presupposes dependable knowledge about infant capacities and preferences. This information is expensive to obtain coming as it does from hundreds of hours of naturalistic observations and the results of standardized test sessions.

At various stages, extending over the last six years, this research has received support from Grant M-3657 from the National Institute of Mental Health; Grant 61-234 from the Foundation's Fund for Research in Psychiatry; Grants HD-00761 and HD-K 02054 from the National Institutes of Health, the Optometric Extension Program; Grant NSG-496 from the National Aeronautics and Space Administration; Grant AF-AFOSR354-63 from Office of Scientific Research, United States Air Force; and the Rockefeller Foundation. The research was conducted at the Tewksbury Hospital, Tewksbury, Massachusetts. I am very grateful for the assistance of Dr. Richard Held, Mr. Peter Castle, and Miss Kitty Riley and for the consideration and aid given by Drs. John Lu, Solomon J. Fleischman, Peter Wolff, and Lois Crowell and head nurses Helen Efstathiou, Frances Craig, and Virginia Donovan.

References

Charlesworth, W. R. "Instigation and maintenance of curiosity behavior as a function of surprise versus novel and familiar stimuli." CHILD DEVELPM., 35:1169—1186, 1964.

Gesell, A. & Amatruda, C. DEVELOPMENTAL DIAGNOSIS. New York: Hoeber, 1941.

Haynes, H., White, B. L., & Held, R. Visual accommodation in human infants. SCIENCE, 148:528-530, 1965

Hunt, J. McV. INTELLIGENCE AND EXPERIENCE. New York: Ronald, 1961.

Piaget, J. THE ORIGINS OF INTELLIGENCE IN CHILDREN. (2nd ed.) New York: Internat. Univer. Press, 1952.

Siegel, S. NONPARAMETRIC STATISTICS FOR THE BEHAVIORAL SCIENCES. New York: McGraw-Hill, 1956. Pp. 116-117.

White, B. L., & Castle, P. W. Visual exploration behavior following postnatal handling of human infants. PERCEPT. MOT. SKILLS, 18:497-502, 1964.

White, B. L., Castle, P. W., & Held, R. M. Observations on the development of visually-directed reaching. CHILD DEVELPM., 35:349-364, 1964.

White, B. L., & Held, R. Plasticity of sensorimotor development in the human infant. In J. F. Rosenblith, & W. Allinsmith (Eds.), CAUSES OF BEHAVIOR: READINGS IN CHILD DEVELOPMENT AND EDUCATIONAL PSYCHOLOGY. (2nd ed.) Boston, Mass.: Allyn & Bacon, 1966. Pp. 60-71.

White, B. L. An experimental approach to the effects of experience on early human behavior. In J. P. Hill (Ed.), MINN. SYMPOS. CHILD PSYCHOL. Minneapolis: Univer. of Minn. Press, I, 1967. Pp. 497-502.

DEVELOPMENTAL AND EXPERIMENTAL
APPROACHES TO CHILD STUDY

David Elkind, Ph.D.

Two of the many new trends that have marked the course taken by American psychology over the past decade are the rapid rise of developmental psychology as a discipline and the equally rapid growth of experimental child psychology. The reasons for these trends are multiple but most certainly include the pressures toward curricular reform which arose from the attacks upon American education in the nineteen fifties and the pressures towards social reform which arose from the civil rights movement and the "War on Poverty". Both of these pressures created demands for people trained in child development and in research with children. These demands, coupled with government support, made training in child development and research with children possible on a scale that would have seemed meglomanical if someone had suggested it a decade earlier.

While developmental and experimental child psychology are both concerned with young people, however, their approaches to child study stem from quite different traditions. The developmental psychologist, whose tradition is European in its nativistic, biological holism, tends to view the child as a *growing* organism. For the developmentalist, the child's growth is a matter of epigenesis, increasing differentiation and hierarchical integration of progressively elaborated structures which makes the child a different organism in kind from the adult. The experimental child psychologist, whose tradition is English in its empiricist, physicalistic associationism, sees the child as a naive organism. For the child experimentalist, growth is a matter of gaining increasing sophistication as a consequence of accumulated experience—a circumstance which makes the child different only in *degree* from the adult.

The purpose of present paper is neither to attack, nor to defend either of these orientations. Rather, what I wish to do is to outline what seem to be three basic differences in their approaches to child behavior. Only when we truly appreciate the differences between these two orientations can we hope to integrate them in meaningful and productive way. In the following pages these two orientations will be compared with regard to their conceptions of: a) the unit of psychological analysis; b) the relative activity or passivity of the subject; and c) the importance of content and process. A final section will suggest a possible underlying cause for the orientational differences in these domains.

Before proceeding, however, it is perhaps well to say that I am aware of the fact that there is no single generally accepted theory of learning which unites all child experimentalists and that the same holds true for developmental psychologists. It may well be the case that differences within learning and developmental theories can in some cases be greater than the differences between such theories. Likewise, the experimentalist may well employ age differences in his investigations just as the developmentalist often uses experimental control and manipulation of variables. There is, nonetheless, a very real difference in orientation (Kaplan, 1967; Russell, 1957) between the child experimentalist and developmentalist which justifies treating them as distinct and worthy of comparison. In short, I am using the terms child experimentalist and developmentalist in the broad sense of a set of attitudes or assumptions about the nature of child study and not in the more narrow senses either of a particular theory or research methodology.

The Unit of Analysis

Every science begins with one or more fundamental units of analysis and investigation. In physics one such element is the atom while in biology the comparable element is the cell. Progress within a particular science often comes about because new data or theoretical constructions challenge the previous interpretations of these basic concepts. The conception of the atom, for example, has undergone a series of metamorphoses and the modern view bears little resemblance to the notions of the Greek "atomists." Likewise, within biology, the concept of the cell has been radically transformed, particularly within the last few decades. Today with the "breaking" of the DNA code and the knowledge of the relation between genes and enzymes, even the concept of "protoplasm," is regarded as quaint.

The choice of a unit of analyses within a science is, therefore, of very great significance for it is the unit which often determines the direction and hence the fruitfulness of the research enterprise. Although in most sciences the choice of the unit is relatively straightforward, it poses very real problems in the social sciences and especially in psychology which stands somewhere between the social and biological domains. The problem is of course that at the level of the individual or of the group there are so many possible units of analysis that it is difficult to find common genotypes such as the atom which can account for the variety of phenotypic phenomena encompassed by the discipline. Within psychology, for example, we study intellectual abilities, personality traits, social attitudes, learning sets and so on without having any generally accepted unit which could be said to underly all of these elements and integrate their various manifestations. One of the major divergences between the experimental and developmental orientations rests in their choice of a unit of analysis.

Within the field of learning the basic unit is regarded as more or less complex association between behavioral and environmental events. The behavioral event can be a simple response such as lever pressing or a more complex pattern of mediating internal responses which are said to account for directed thinking (Berlyne, 1965). Likewise the environmental event can be a simple signal, a complex visual array or even a drug injection. Whether the behavioral and environmental events are conceived in a broad or narrow sense is less significant than the fact that they are said to form a unit which in principle should be able to account for a considerable variety of human behaviors. Looked at in this broad sense, that is in the sense wherein response and stimulus can be defined in simple or complex terms, it is reasonable to say that for the experimentalist, the basic unit of behavioral analysis is the S-R, or S-O-R, bond.

Within developmental psychology, however, the unit of behavioral analysis is regarded differently as becomes readily apparent when one reads developmentalists such as Freud (1953), Piaget (1950) or Werner (1957). The unit is not an S-R bond (in the broad sense described above) but rather a system or organization that possesses certain properties. Since the unit of developmental psychology is perhaps less well known or at least not as well highlighted as the unit of the learning theory orientation, it might be well to describe it with illustrative examples.

In Freud's (1938) book on the interpretation of dreams there is some admittedly associationistic psychology but there is also a good description of the "dream work," i.e., the rules and principles which govern primary process thought such as condensation and displacement. Primary process thought is described in terms of its own structures and its interrelated rules of organization. It is, then, a *system* of thinking which can be used to interpret a wide variety of behaviors from dreams to slips of the tongue. In the work of Piaget (1950) the same holds true. Piaget has been progressively elaborating the *systems* of thinking which exist at different age levels and has tried to specify these terms of their group or logical properties. The system of concrete operations, for example, which emerges at about the age of six or seven, is characterized by the following set of operations:

$$\text{Associativity} \qquad A + (B + C) = (A + B) + C$$

$$\text{Combinatively} \qquad A \, Y \, B = AB$$

$$\text{Identity} \qquad A + A = 0$$

As in the case of Freud, Piaget believes that these systems are the basic units of analyses and should be the starting point for interpreting many different forms of behavior at the age levels where they are present.

The foregoing difference between the experimental and developmental approaches with respect to their basic units of analysis is not absolute but relative. Within the developmental framework, it is more usual to think of systems as primary and of particular structures, such as Piaget's operations and schemas, as secondary and derivative parts of these larger organizations. Within the experimental orientation, in contrast, it is more usual to think in terms of S-R bonds as primary and their associated systems, such as habit family hierarchies, as derivative. The difference between the developmental and experimental orientations does not lie, then, in the fact that one advocates organizations and the other atomistic elements. In both the experimentalist and developmentalist orientations there are both wholes and parts and the difference lies in that the developmentalist derives the parts from the whole while the reverse holds true for the experimentalist.

It must also be said that the difference in choice of a unit for the two orientations does not necessarily imply anything with respect to their origin in nature or nurture. While it is usual to suppose that S-R bonds are derived from nurture whereas mental systems derive from nature, such presuppositions cannot hold up under close scrutiny. If the system is held to be native or innate as, for example, some modern linguists (e.g. Chomsky, 1957) assert with respect to language structures, this innateness can only be relative. The emergence of structures common to different individuals is not independent of the environment but rather presupposes what Hartmann (1951) has called a "normal expectable environment". When the environment deviates markedly from the norm, the expected system may not appear or may appear in a distorted form. The language of the autistic child, to the extent that such autism is environmentally induced, demonstrates the relativity even of supposed innate structures to environmental influence.

The role of the environment in altering structures and systems is illustrated in some experiments reported by Waddington (1962). When the fly grub (Drosophilia) is placed on a high salt diet sufficient to kill a large number of them, those that survive become somwhat modified in their body structure. Under the high salt diet, some of these Drosophilia develop enlarged anal papillae. After twenty generations, a large proportion of the population was able to survive the high salt diet. Two results were found. The overall size of the papillae were increased and the readiness to become enlarged under high salt condition was also increased. When the new population was put back on the old, low salt, diet, the change in papillae size did not entirely reverse itself. Waddington calls this "genetic assimilation" and points out that it resembles the inheritance of acquired characteristics inasmuch as it demonstrates that a structure acquired under changed environmental conditions does not revert to its original state when the environment is restored to its previous condition. There is, of course, selection operating and that is why these findings are not evidence in support of Lamarck.

Piaget (1929) has reported similar results with molluscs moved from quiet ponds to lakeside and back again. The swirls common to the lake molluscs were gradually acquired by the pond molluscs which Piaget transported to the lake shores. When this new generation of molluscs was returned to the banks of quiet ponds, the swirls common to the lake molluscs were retained after many generations. In short these studies give evidence that the environment can force selection in certain directions and that in some cases at least the results are partially irreversible. Hence we have a kind of inheritance of acquired characteristics which is mediated by selection.

These data are of importance because they suggest that the structures that are sometimes said to be innate and independent of the environment may, at an earlier point in time, have been a product of genetic assimilation. It is because of this incessant feedback between genetically determined structures and the environment that the term "innateness" loses its fixed connotation. Every structure has a history both within the organism and within the species and may have been at one time or another determined, at least in part, by environmental intrusions. It is for this reason that Piaget (1968) says that "every structure has a genesis and every genesis gives rise to structure."

It would be hard then, to make a case for the innateness of the structures or systems advocated by the developmentalist as the basic units of behavior. In a like manner, S-R bonds cannot be attributed solely to experience. The phenomena of generalization, for example, seems to presuppose structural systems which are themselves not learned. An animal which acquires a size discrimination will generalize this response to sets of stimuli other than those upon which it was originally practiced. Generalization is a system principle which cannot be explained entirely by reference to experience or training. In a more general way, White (1965) has recently brought together a large group of investigations which seem to show that in many different areas of learning there are significant changes between the ages of four and six. One interpretation of these findings is that the maturation of new mental systems alters the mode of learning. In short, learning and S-R bonds cannot be acquired without the intervention of organismic systems just as organismic systems cannot appear without the nutriments and directions provided by the environment.

Accordingly, the distinction between systems on the one hand and S-R bonds on the other does not reside in their relative innateness or acquiredness since both can be shown to depend, at some point in the history either of the individual or of the species, upon genetic as well as upon environmental factors. The real difference between these two units lies in their mode of definition. The S-R bond or habit must always be defined with reference to some form of environmental input whereas a system can be defined entirely in terms of its principles of organization. The mode of definition, however, says nothing with respect to the origins of these units. The fact, say, that Piaget's concrete operations can be defined without reference to environmental input does not imply that they are innate anymore than the fact that the S-R bond can be defined without reference to organismic systems implies that it is entirely acquired.

Passivity and Activity

Another major difference between the experimental and developmental orientations lies in the dimension of activity and passivity. In the sense in which these terms are used here, activity refers to self directed and self initiated behavior whereas passivity refers to behavior which has been or can be directed and initiated from without. By and large, the experimentalist prefers to study passive behaviors whereas the developmentalist seems to prefer the study of active behaviors. This is not surprising inasmuch as the experimentalist wants to test the effects of his experimental manipulations whereas the developmentalist wants to observe the effects of endogenous growth processes.

The distinction between active and passive behaviors must not be confused, as it often is, with certain assumptions about the nature of the organism. Because the experimentalist concerns himself with those behaviors which he can control and direct, this does not mean that he attributes passivity to the organism as a whole. He has merely selected from the individual's passive behavior repertoire and does not deny that the individual also has a repertoire of self initiated and directed behaviors. In the same manner, the fact that the developmentalist studies spontaneous behavior manifestations in no way connotes that he denies the existence of a repertoire of behaviors that can be controlled by environmental manipulation. In short, it is unfair and incorrect to say of the experimentalist that he views the organism as passive and that the developmentalist views him as active. For both the experimental and developmental psychologist the organism is both active *and* passive and their difference lies in which of these behavior reservoirs they choose to tap and not in their vision of the organism as a whole.

This difference in selection from active or passive behavior repertoires on the part of developmentalists and experimentalists, while quite relative, has nonetheless both methodological and practical consequences. Although the experimentalist does not gainsay the endogenous factors such as maturation and exploratory and curiosity drives which can initiate and direct behavior, he is unwilling to accept any change in behavior as being due to such factors until it has been shown that comparable changes cannot be produced by environmental manipulation. Without such a demonstration, says the experimentalist, the attribution of behavior changes to intrinsic factors, smacks of mysticism rather than science. One might just as well attribute the changes to some mythical cherubs who go about their merry work of instilling behaviors in the wee hours of the morning when no one is about. So, while the experimentalist can accept active, self initiated behaviors in principle he demands proof that there are no immediate environmental determinants of such behaviors.

The developmentalist, on the contrary, is much more willing to accept changes in behavior as being due to endogenous factors without testing whether or not the changes can be brought about by environmental manipulation. What is more important, from his point of view, is to determine whether or not the changes are indeed developmental. Piaget (1951) long ago laid down the criteria for such a determination on the cognitive plane. The criteria are as follows: a) In a true developmental sequence one finds both **anticipations** (types of behavior usually observed at a later age suggested in the behavior of young children) and adherences (remnants of behaviors from an earlier age suggested in the actions of older children); b) A true developmental sequence will be evidenced by a certain uniformity of responses within age groups which is greater than any uniformities between age groups; c) Finally, the direction of change from early to late childhood should be towards the adult norm. When these criteria have been established in a given area of behavior, one can be reasonably sure that a true developmental sequence has been observed. A somewhat different criterion has been suggested by Werner (1957) who speaks of it as the orthogenetic principle which holds that behavior is developmental to the extent that it manifests progressive differentiation and hierarchical integration with increasing age.

The preference for observing passive or active behaviors on the part of experimentalist and developmental psychologists is also reflected in their respective conceptions of control. Within the experimental orientation, the concept of control is one of manipulation. Everything in the situation except the environmental change or changes under investigation are kept constant in accord with Mill's maxim that a constant cannot be a source of change. The developmentalist, in contrast, has a somewhat different conception of control. He argues that if nothing is controlled, if everything is left to vary at random, other than the task itself, and if one still finds that the behaviors manifest the criteria described by Piaget and Werner, then such regularities must be regarded as genuine characteristics of the organism. The maxim here is that uncontrolled variation cannot be regarded as a cause of observed regularities.

Finally, the preference of the experimentalist for passive behaviors and of the developmentalist for active ones is also reflected in their approach to applied problems. There is, however, a paradox here. For, while the experimentalist prefers to study the passive behaviors of his subjects, he tends to be activist in his own behavior with respect to applied problems. He wants to teach young children to read, to program learning and to modify disturbed behavior. And, it must be added, he has had some notable successes in these areas. The developmentalist, who prefers the active behaviors of his subjects, tends to be passive in his approach to applied problems. He places emphasis on enriching the environment and providing the child with the opportunity to be active and self directive (as say, in the discovery method). In a phrase, the experimentalist wants to modify behavior to make it fit the environment whereas the developmentalist wants to modify the environment to fit behavior.

Content and Process

Psychology, like every other science, has both its inductive and its deductive moments. Developmental psychology has, until fairly recently, been primarily concerned with the inductive or "what" aspect of behavior. This has sometimes been called the "developmental descriptive" approach in that it concerns itself with the nature or content of children's minds at different age levels and with describing these contents as completely as possible. Comparative analysis of contents at successive age levels often leads to inductive generalizations regarding the principles which govern the growth of mental contents. Piaget, for example, on comparing the ideas of children at different age levels about the physical world suggested that as young people grow older their ideas become more relative, realistic and objective than they were in preceding epochs of their lives (Piaget, 1951).

The experimental orientation has, on the other hand, been primarily deductive in its approach. (Skinner is of course a quite notable exception but the premises which govern his methodology if not his conceptualizations are deductive in their orientation.) Starting from a set of principles regarding the nature of learning, consequences are deduced which are then put to test. Within this hypothetic-deductive context, the processes involved in learning, the "how" of S-R bonding is the prime focus of concern as are the variables and parameters that affect this bonding. Content is, from this point of view, a confounding factor which must be eliminated insofar as this is possible. Hence the use of nonsense syllables in memory experiments, geometric forms in concept attainment studies and so on.

This distinction, between the content orientation of the developmentalist and the process orientation of the experimentalist, is necessarily relative. The developmental psychologist is interested in processes, but of a somewhat different sort than those that concern the experimentalist. To appreciate this difference it is necessary to recall that psychology must of necessity deal with several different time scales. There is the scale of milliseconds, seconds and minutes with which neurophysiologists and psychophysicists are frequently involved when studying rate of response, thresholds and so on. Next there is the scale of hours and days which forms the background for most psychological investigations of learning, memory and problem solving. Finally, there is the scale of months and years which is the province of the developmental psychologist. I do not want to enter the continuity versus discontinuity argument here, but only to point out there there is no a priori reason why, if some processes take seconds and others hours and days, why still other processes could not take months and years.

Although it is difficult to do experimental work on these developmental processes in humans, some experimental work of this kind has been done with animals. The visual deprivation studies of Riesen (1961) demonstrate the effects of certain kinds of stimuli upon the development of sensory capacities. In a recent study by Young (1963) it was also shown that apes raised in a hemmed-in environment developed myopia as a result. But this process took months and not just hours or days and is, therefore, more difficult to manipulate and study experimentally. A good many of the studies aimed at teaching children conservation (*e.g.* Greco, 1959; Smedslund, 1959; Wohlwill, 1959, 1960) over a short period of time seem to have confused the products of developmental processes with those of short term learning processes. This probably explains why so many of these training studies have been failures.

While the developmentalist is concerned with both processes *and* content, the same does not seem to hold true for the experimentalist whose prime concern is with process. The experimentalist's reluctance to deal with content probably stems from the inherent difficulty in quantifying meaningful material. That this is not an insurmountable obstacle has been shown by Osgood, Suci and Tannenbaum (1957) in their work on the semantic differential—a notable step forward in the experimental study of content. The work of Attneave and Arnoult (1956) in the quantification of perceptual forms is another example of a successful attempt to measure what seems to be unmeasurable.

In closing this section, on content and process, it is perhaps appropriate to point out that while the neglect of content in animal investigations can be defended, the same may not be true in studies with children. Content clearly has attentional and motivational properties that are relevant to the learning process. The banality and boredom of the "Look Spot Run" type primer in contrast with the attractiveness of comic books for young readers is but one example of the importance of content in human learning. It is to be hoped that the efforts of workers such as Osgood and Suci and Attneave and Arnoult will, in the future, encourage other experimentalists to systematically explore the role which content plays in learning.

DISCUSSION

In the foregoing pages it has been pointed out that the experimental and developmental approaches differ in their choice of psychological units and in their preferences for studying active as opposed to passive behaviors and contents as opposed to processes. While, as I have tried to indicate, these differences are only relative, they nonetheless exist and need to be accounted for. In part these differences can be explained in terms of the different traditions out of which the orientations originate. But what is the central difference between the biological, holistic and nativistic tradition on the one hand and the physicalistic, associationistic and environmental tradition, on the other hand? It is with this question that the present concluding section is concerned.

One essential difference, or so it seems to the writer, lies in the perspectives which are regarded as permissible under these two traditions. More particularly, the difference may revolve around the investigator's willingness to take his subject's point of view and to construct concepts and study relations from this perspective. By and large, the experimentalist tradition sees such an approach as inherently invalid and unscientific—more art than science. The developmentalist, in contrast, regards taking the subject's point of view as a legitimate procedure and at least some of his concepts (such as Piaget's "conservation" concept) only make sense when the subject's point of view is taken into account. In the following paragraphs, I want to show how the willingness or unwillingness to take the subject's point of view can account for the differences in orientation that have been noted in the preceding sections. Let us take up the experimental orientation first.

The Experimental Orientation

One of the basic premises of the experimental orientation is that of an absolute separation between: a) the stimulus and the response on the one hand and b) the observer and what is being observed on the other. From this standpoint, the subject of investigation always appears separate from the stimuli which impinge upon him. In a Skinner box, for example, the animal is a separate entity from the lever which he presses and animal and lever must be defined independently of one another. Likewise, the investigator regards himself as entirely separate from the objects of his investigation.

This separation between subject and object and experimenter and data is an inevitable consequence of an investigator who stands outside the objects of his investigations and refuses to project himself into his subjects or to anthropomorphize. It follows, from such a position, that the major problem is to determine how the separate stimuli and behaviors get linked together in adaptive ways. The choice of an S-R bond as a basic unit of inquiry is a logical consequence of this standpoint. Likewise, the preference for observing passive behaviors can be derived from the same perspective. When subjects are looked at only from the outside, it is much easier to deal with those behaviors which can be initiated or controlled from without than to try and surmise what goes on inside the "black box" to account for spontaneous behaviors. Finally, when subjects are viewed from without, content becomes unimportant because to deal with meaning and understanding on the part of the subject presupposes that one can take the subject's point of view.

In short, the experimentalists' insistence on standing outside the subject-object, stimulus response interaction leads inevitably to the choice of an S-R bond as a unit, and to the preference for passive over active behaviors and for process over content.

The Developmental Orientation

The developmentalist, while he recognizes the value of the observer's perspective, also sees value in attempting to put himself in the subject's position and in attempting to see things from the subject's point of view. The greatest difficulty is always of objectifying this perspective and of integrating it with the perspective of the outside observer. Piaget's (1952, 1954) work on the "Origins of Intelligence in Children" and "The Construction of Reality in the Child" is a remarkable example of how such observations can be made and integrated. The "Origins" book presents an interpretation of intellectual development from without while the "Construction" book presents the same development from the standpoint of the child. Both types of interpretation are tied at every point to concrete observations.

It is the developmentalists' willingness to take the point of view of his subject which helps account for his choice of system as a unit of psychological analysis. As soon as one takes the subject's point of view, it becomes clear that many events are happening simultaneously and that they do not come in a hodge-podge but are rather patterned and organized. Consequently systems have to be postulated to account for this patterning and organization. Likewise, the preference for the study of active as opposed to passive behaviors derives, it would seem, directly from putting one's self in the subject's position and seeing things from his point of view. Once in the subject's perspective it becomes clear that stimuli are always interpreted and that there are compulsions to activity from within, such as curiosity, need for practice and exercise, needs for exploration which lead to self initiated and directed behaviors. Finally, from the standpoint of the subject, content is important because it determines his interest, motivation and comprehension.

In summary, then, it is suggested here that one of the central differences between the experimental and developmental orientations lies in their respective unwillingness or willingness to take the observer's point of view and to formulate concepts and rules of behavior from this perspective. While the problem of the experimenter's projection of himself into his subject's position is full of dangers from a scientific standpoint, it may nonetheless be necessary for a full accounting of human behavior. The task is to make such an approach scientifically acceptable. When that is done, the major differences between the developmental and experimental orientation will, in all probability, disappear and we will have a unified discipline of child psychology that is at once experimental and developmental.

References

Attneave, F., & Arnoult, M.D. "The quantitative study of shape and pattern perception." PSYCHOLOGICAL BULLETIN, 53: 452-471, 1956.

Chomsky, N. SYNTACTIC STRUCTURES. The Hague: Mouton, 1957.

Freud, S. "The interpretation of dreams." In A. A. Brill (Ed.) THE BASIC WRITINGS OF SIGMUND FREUD. New York: Modern Library, 1938.

Freud, S. "Formulations regarding the two principles of mental functioning." In COLLECTED PAPERS, V. IV. London: Hogarth, pp. 13-21, 1953.

Greco, P. "L'apprentissage dans une situation a structure operatoire concrete: les inversions successives de l'ordre lineaire par des rotations de 180°." In J. Piaget (Ed.) ETUDES D' EPISTEMOLOGIE GENETIQUE, Vol. 8. Paris: Universitaires de France, pp. 68-182, 1959.

Hartman, H. "Ego psychology and the problem of adaptation." In D. Rapaport (Ed.) THE ORGANIZATION AND PATHOLOGY OF THOUGHT. New York: Columbia University Press, 1951.

Kaplan, B. "Meditations on genesis." HUMAN DEVELOPMENT, 10: 65-87, 1967.

Osgood, C. E., Suci, G. J., and Tannenbaum, P. H. THE MEASUREMENT OF MEANING. Urbana: University of Illinois Press, 1957.

Piaget, J. "L'adaptation limnaea stagnalis au milieu lacoustres de la Suisse comande." REVUE SUISSE DE ZOOLOGIE, 36: 263-531, 1929.

Piaget, J. THE PSYCHOLOGY OF INTELLIGENCE. London: Routledge & Kegan Paul, 1950.

Piaget, J. THE CHILD'S CONCEPTION OF THE WORLD. London: Routledge & Kegan Paul, 1951.

Piaget, J. THE ORIGINS OF INTELLIGENCE IN CHILDREN. New York: International Universities Press, 1952.

Piaget, J. THE CONSTRUCTION OF REALITY IN THE CHILD. New York: Basic Books, 1954.

Piaget, J. SIX PSYCHOLOGICAL STUDIES. New York: Random House, 1968.

Riesen, A. H. "Stimulation as a requirement for growth and function in behavioral development." In D. W. Fiske and S. R. Maddi (Eds.) FUNCTIONS OF VARIED EXPERIENCE. Homewood, Ill.: Dorsey Press, 57-80, 1961.

Russell, W. A. "An experimental psychology of development: Pipe dream or possibility." In D. B. Harris (Ed.) THE CONCEPT OF DEVELOPMENT. Minneapolis: University of Minnesota Press, 162-174, 1957.

Smedslund, J. "Apprentissage des notions de la conservation et de la transitivite du poids." In J. Piaget (Ed.) ETUDES D' EPISTEMOLOGIE GENETIQUE, Vol. 9. Paris. Presses Universitaires de France, pp. 85-124, 1959.

Waddington, C. H. THE NATURE OF LIFE. New York: Atheneum, 1962.

Werner, H. "The concept of development from a comparative and organismic point of view." In D. B. Harris (Ed.) THE CONCEPT OF DEVELOPMENT. Minneapolis: University of Minnesota Press, 125-148, 1957.

White, S. A. "Evidence for a hierarchical arrangement of learning processes." In L. P. Lipsitt and C. C. Spiker (Eds.) ADVANCES IN CHILD DEVELOPMENT AND BEHAVIOR. New York: Academic Press, 187-220, 1965.

Wohlwill, J. F. "A study of the development of the number concept by scalogram analysis." JOURNAL OF GENETIC PSYCHOLOGY, 97: 345-377, 1960.

Wohlwill, J. F. "Un essai l'apprentissage dans le domaine de la conservation du nombre." In J. Piaget (Ed.) ETUDES D' EPISTEMOLOGIE GENETIQUE, Vol. 9. Paris: Presses Universitaires de France, pp. 125-35, 1959.

Young, F. A. "The effect of restricted visual space on the refractive error of the young monkey eye," INVESTIGATIVE OPHTHALMOLOGY. 2: 571-577, 1963.

A DEVELOPMENT ANALYSIS OF LEARNING

Eugene S. Gollin, Ph.D.

Anne Saravo, Ph.D.

"Developmental psychology differs from other branches of the science of behavior more in its viewpoint than in its precise method of investigation (Munn, 1965)." A developmental viewpoint shares much in common with a comparative approach, which tests the universality of sets of functional relations between response and stimulus events across species. Cross species comparisons are necessary because it is assumed that organisms with different biological capacities and qualities may respond differently to the same environmental conditions. Differences in sensory capacity and in preferred mode of environmental sampling, differences in temperament, differences in motivation, differences in storage capacity, and differences in life history also will contribute to differences in behavior. The purpose of comparative analysis is not only the establishment of universal principles but also the establishment of non-universal or specific characteristics and qualities of behavior.

Developmental analysis is concerned with intra-specific rather than with inter-specific questions. A cross-sectional analysis of ontogenesis assumes differences in experiential history, and possibly differences in the quality and functional maturity of the biological substrate. A longitudinal analysis explores the amount of variance imparted by individual differences along many dimensions over time. These differences may derive from genetic sources, from differences in pathological history, from differences in non-specific experiences, as well as from differences in more formalized instruction.

Developmental and comparative analyses come together when ontogenetic analysis is conducted inter-specifically. For example, in sensory deprivation studies one question dealt with is the degree to which organisms of different species require particular kinds and amounts of stimulus input in order for them to develop "normally" (Riesen, 1960, 1961).

Although concerned with the same general problems confronting other areas of psychology, developmental analysis also presents a special set of methodological, procedural, and design problems that are complicating factors. For example, a corollary of the assumption that subjects in different cross sections differ along a number of dimensions is that even when input variables are held constant from the experimenter's vantage point they are not constant from the vantage point of the subjects in the several cross-sectional slices. Therefore, developmental analysis is required to use what Bitterman (1960) has described as control by systematic variation, in contrast to control by equation. To offer an extreme case as illustration, if one wished to determine the response qualities, properties, or characteristics of a paramecium and an elephant under various conditions of deprivation, one would obviously use neither the same stimulus conditions nor would one use the same deprivation conditions. What one would try to do would be to vary the array of stimulus inputs and vary the array of deprivation conditions in both organisms in ways appropriate to those organisms. Out of such an analysis there should emerge a description of the functional relations between the various sets of stimulus and response events. If the systematic variation procedures have been sufficiently extensive it will be possible to make some comparative statements.

When looked at in this context developmental and comparative psychology become ways of approaching problems rather than subject matters *per se*. A developmental approach has certain advantageous characteristics. 1) It puts emphasis upon the history of behavioral phenomena. 2) It recognizes that organisms are ever changing and that the consequences of stimulation may be understood only if the nature of change is understood. 3) It directs attention to structures which may differ along neurophysiological or biochemical dimensions. 4) It is concerned with pre-existing capacities of organisms, that is, the quality and functional maturity of the biological substrate. 5) It recognizes that the psychological properties of an incoming stimulus are to some extent determined by the experiential history of the organism, that is, it is concerned with experience derived cognitive-affective dispositional systems. 6) It directs a search for rules which describe sequentiality, recognizing that all behavior is an interaction between organism and environment and that organism is constantly changing (Lehrman, 1953).

In sum, developmental analysis consists of a research strategy which is directed toward two interdependent goals; first, the obtaining of data which test the generality of existing theoretical formulations, and second, the specification of rules which describe behavioral change in ontogenetic and phylogenetic contexts.

In keeping with that definition, the present chapter will provide examples of current studies which illustrate developmental research strategy. In addition, we shall attempt to evaluate this research, and current theoretical interpretations, from a developmental vantage point and within the framework of a general hypothesis, that is, that there is a shift in cognitive behavior in the course of human ontogenesis from operations dominated by perceptual-motor tendencies to operations dominated by conceptual-verbal tendencies (Wohlwill, 1962; Gollin, 1968). Some theorists (Reese, 1962; White, 1965; Kendler & Kendler, 1962) have maintained that this change is largely due and confined to a transition in the use of mediational language which allegedly occurs between the ages 5-7. In other words, during this ontogenetic period, children begin to utilize verbal mediators and thus achieve a means for the control and direction of their own behavior.

In contrast to the viewpoint of Kendler & Kendler is that of Zeaman & House (1963), Mackintosh (1965), and Sutherland (1959). These adherents of attentional or observing response theories assert that organism-environment interactions are governed by invariant processes throughout ontogenesis and possibly throughout phylogenesis. This invariance of process is extended to include varieties of defective organisms as well (Zeaman & House, 1963).

Proponents of both the attentional and the verbal mediation viewpoint have demonstrated empirical support for their respective positions, but at present, no one theory is sufficiently comprehensive to deal with all the relevant findings. Demonstrations of invariance and/or the effects of language do not, however, preclude the eventual synthesis of the two theories. The futility of attempting to establish the null hypothesis is obvious, and both the Kendlers (Kendler & Kendler, 1966) and Zeaman & House (1963) have suggested that attention and verbal mediation are not mutually exclusive. Whether or not such a synthesis occurs, the questions raised by these two theories are of particular developmental importance: to what extent are functional differences in performance related to developmental parameters? And to what extent are these changes a function of underlying qualitative and/or quantitative differences in cognitive structure ?

Studies which provide information relevant to these issues will be used in the following sections to illustrate three major tactics of research which developmental analysis employs: a) the definition of the behavioral domain; b) specification of variables which alter that domain; and c) assessment of the degree to which those alterations transfer to other behavior areas (Gollin, 1965, 1968).

Definition of the Behavioral Domain

An organism-levels x task-levels design is used in developmental analysis to define the behavioral domain. Performance outcomes on tasks ordered along some dimension and by subjects ordered along some developmentally relevant dimension may be regarded as the objective at this stage of research. The specific levels of task complexity and the particular organism dimension employed will be dictated by theoretical issues or gaps in empirical information.

Experimenters often depend on standardization of research techniques to facilitate task-task comparisons, so that many relevant studies use only one level of either subjects or tasks, which may be called a subjects x task(s) design. Using either the subjects x task(s) or levels x levels type of design, singly or in combinations, there are several descriptions of behavioral domain which have been forthcoming in addition to the simple linear function: a) that illustrated by the Lashley three-dimentional representation; b) that represented by a relatively U-shaped curve; and c) that represented by an interrupted linear performance which is suggestive of a developmental inversion. Other curves are also possible; the ones illustrated in Figures 1-3 were selected for discussion because they are relevant to the developmental questions posed by current theories.

When Lashley (1929) compared the learning of groups of rats with different amounts of surgically induced brain damage on mazes of differing degrees of difficulty, he presented his results on a graph similar to that shown in Figure 1.

Rats, regardless of the degree of damage, showed little or no differences in performance on simple mazes, but marked performance differences, correlated with degree of brain damage, were observed on the complex mazes. This study is a prototype of the organism-levels x task-levels design.

Similarly, Kay (1954) presented problem-solving tasks representing different degrees of difficulty to subjects ranging in age from 20 through 69 years. He found that performances of younger and older subjects did not differ on easy problems but that

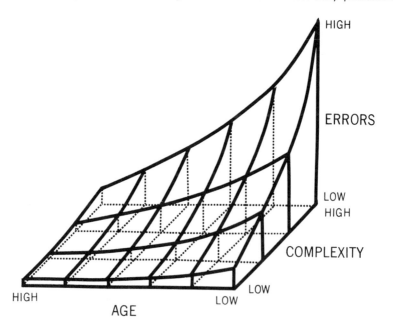

FIGURE 1

A three-dimensional graph showing the relationship between age, task complexity, and perform-ance scores. The age dimension is laid out to reflect comparisions utilizing very young Ss in comparison with older children and adults. If geriatric samples (see Kay, 1954) were employed and compared with younger adults, the values along the horizontal axis would be reversed. In the Lashley graph (1929) percent of cortical destruction was laid out along the horizontal axis.

as problem difficulty increased, the error scores of older subjects rose at a much greater rate than those of younger subjects. He was able to graph his data in a manner similar to that of Lashley.

Gollin (1965a) tested recognition performance of preschool children, first grade children, and adults on incomplete pictures after training on complete and intermediately complete representation of the test pictures. It was found that when training was conducted on the intermediate representations recognition scores of the three age groups were not significantly different; however, when the training materials consisted of the complete pictures there was a sharp increase in errors of first-graders over adults and of pre-schoolers over first-grade children. These data fell into the pattern illustrated by the Lashley graph.

Another example of the levels x levels design is a study by Hill (1965). She studied the performance of children at 1, 4, 6, and 12 years of age on three discrimination learning tasks: object discrimination, oddity and conditional oddity problems. She found that the majority of one and four year old children could solve an object discrimination problem, the oddity problem was solved by six year old children, and the conditional oddity problem was solved by children 12 years of age.

Hill also showed that position preference, which is a nonreward contingent response strategy, dominated the behavior of the one year old children, while older children exhibited both contingent (*e.g.* win-stay, lose-shift) and non-contingent (position preference) response patterns.

The increasing complexity of response strategies with age poses a problem for theories of problem—solving, such as that of Zeaman and House, which do not make allowances for integrated response chains that function as a unit. The performance of the one year olds, as Hill suggested, would be consistent with attention theory. For these children, only one response pattern seemed to be available, that of a preference response. Once this pattern was applied to the relevant dimension, object instead of position, the one year olds arrived at a solution of the object discrimination problem. To apply this formulation to the explanation of such a complex problem as conditional oddity (odd is correct when background is blue, non-odd is correct when background is yellow) seems to somehow beg the question. Form was the relevant dimension in all three problems. To be sure, once attention is directed to the relevant dimension, to the oddity relation among the cues of the vehicle dimension, to the background dimension, to the reversal principle conditional on the background cue, etc...the problem is solved. Certainly, attention is involved, but more important, what allows these Ss to entertain and dismiss such a possible variety of incorrect solutions? And, alternatively, what allows older children to chain such a long series of attentional and instrumental responses?

The answers to these questions would seem to necessitate the inclusion of some developmentally variant parameters in attention theory. At present, developmental factors have been linked to the distribution of probabilities of distracting dimensions and to the number of irrelevant dimensions. The theory can be developmentally predictive only if these links are made more explicit. At present, it remains to be seen whether or not these attention-theory formulations may be adequately extended to describe developmental findings.

In addition to the data which may be represented by Lashley's three-dimensional graph, a second type of performance curve may be forthcoming from explorations of the behavioral domain. In problem solving, for example, a succession of age-related strategies may be employed which produce similar outcomes at some points in the developmental continuum. The performance curves, in this case, may not rise dependably with age. The relationship between age and performance may be "U" shaped (Weir, 1964). Thus, very young children may, under certain experimental conditions or task demands, achieve higher performance scores than older children or even adults. However, it is possible that the very behavioral dispositions which produce success in one context may preclude it in other contexts. An example of this is shown in Figure 2 which is a facsimile of one of Weir's graphs (1964).

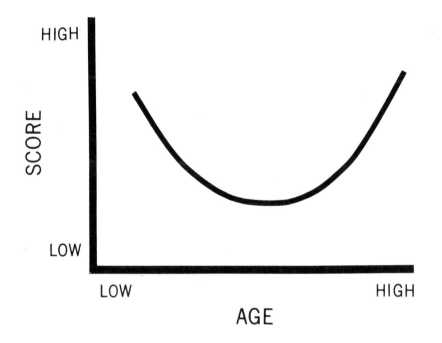

FIGURE 2

An illustration of the relations between performance and age comparable to that reproted by Weir (1964).

In Weir's experiment, subjects from the third through the eighteenth year were observed in a probability-learning task. The tendency to maximize response, that is, to push the higher pay-off button was greatest for the youngest (3 and 5 years) and the oldest subjects (18 years). Weir wrote, "There is no question that different processes must have led to this final level for groups so discrepant in age (1964, pp. 476)." His analysis of Ss learning curves supports his contention that similar terminal response rates arise from different cognitive strategies and also that the low level of maximizing shown by intermediate age groups (7-10) reflects their attempts to employ a strategy which was not suitable to a high pay-off rate.

A similar analysis was made of the performance of children, 3 to 9 years, on a simple discrimination task (Weir & Stevenson, 1969). In this study, an inverted "U" shape was obtained: the 3 and 9 year olds performed more poorly than the children of intermediate ages. The authors suggested that the older Ss developed complex hypotheses concerning the solution of the problem and that these hypotheses hindered their employment of the more simple, correct solution. A comparison of these two studies nicely illustrates the point that the sampling of organisms along a developmental continuum is in terms of a particular experimental context and does not necessarily imply functional invariance across tasks. Not only are the performance curves in the two studies different, which is not surprising in view of the different age range sample, but their points of inflection also do not correspond.

A study by Schusterman (1964) also found developmental differences in the repertoire of response strategies. He studied the choice behavior of mentally retarded children (MA approximately 5 years, CA approximately 10 years), and two groups of normal children, 5 and 10 years old, on a 2-choice problem with uncertain outcome, i.e. a 50:50 probability series. Performance on an initial position discrimination training problem was inversely related to MA; the 10 year olds began the task with complex pattern seeking behavior which interfered with learning in the simple continuous reinforcement problem. Analysis of strategies in the probability learning phase of the experiment indicated that while the low MA Ss tended to alternate or show a strong position preference, high MA Ss used strategies which were based on reward outcomes and choice patterns extending back over several trials.

These results suggest that at different periods during ontogenesis different cognitive strategies are available. Hill's one year old children were able to solve only simple problems because their repertoire of strategies is limited. With increasing age more strategies are available permitting solution of wider arrays of problems. But the increase in additional cognitive strategies with age is not to be regarded as simply leading to an increase in kinds of problems that may be solved. There are studies which suggest that one or another cognitive strategy may achieve dominance at particular periods in the course of development. Schusterman's study (1964) illustrates that a dominant strategy may or may not lead to problem solution depending upon the nature of the task. A dominant strategy may increase the number of errors committed even though it represents a developmental advance (Weir, 1964). When a new cognitive strategy is becoming established there may be a decline in performance since the child has not yet abandoned the old nor mastered the new (Friedman, 1965; Beilin, 1964). The specific cognitive strategy employed will be a function not only of its availability to the respondent but also of the nature of the task demand. Particular task arrangements may preclude the activation of problem solving strategies or approaches which might otherwise become manifest. The repertoire of response strategies available to a respondent, therefore, is only determinable if a wide array of task arrangements are employed. (Another problem, to be discussed, is the capacity of organisms to acquire strategies not yet available to them.)

A third empirical model contains properties found in each of the other two types of performance curves. While group performance curves generally rise with age there are points of inversion or depression. These reverses in performance efficiency may be regarded as symptomatic of shifts in cognitive operations. Figure 3 illustrates a

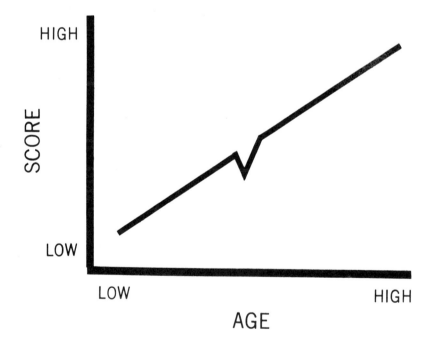

FIGURE 3

An illustration of a performance inversion comparable to that reported by Friedman (1965) and by Beilin (1964).

developmental inversion, such as reported by Freidman (1965) in a study of concept formation, and by Beilin (1964) whose subjects were presented with a conservation problem. Freidman found a general rise in performance from the first to the fifth grade which was interrupted at the fourth grade where a depression in performance was observed. He attributed the inversion to an attempt on the part of fourth grade children to introduce new cognitive techiniques, such as hypothesis testing rather than trial-and-error procedures. A similar inversion was reported by Beilin (1964): third graders showed less performance efficiency in a quasi-conservation task than either second or fourth grade children.

Such inversions suggest a transition period in cognitive functioning. Both authors, in somewhat different terms, attributed the inversion to the onset of a transition from perceptual to conceptual processes (Beilin) or trial-and-error learning to mediational hypothesis testing (Friedman). Thus, the performance efficiency of the child who is just beginning to be able to master a more efficient method of solution on a particular task, declines because the older cognitive mode is not fully abandoned and the newer one is not fully mastered. This latter statement would apply to any two response strategies, and is certainly not restricted to a developmental context with its implication of sequentiality. For example, anyone who first typed by the "hunt and peck" method and then attempts to type by the "touch system" is apt to be discouraged by the initial lowering of efficiency which occurs as the new system is being mastered. The significance of these periods of inversion (they may be instances of negative transfer or response competition) is that they provide an opportunity for the investigator to study the factors which influence transition from one cognitive strategy to another.

The major point which should be extracted from these studies is that the behavioral outcomes depicted on the curves can not be considered as characteristic of a particular age, or developmental level, alone. An implication of Werner's (1948) approach to development is that the curves depicted in Figures 2 and 3, the U shaped curve and the inversion, might be made to traverse the developmental continuum by appropriate manipulations of task complexity. For example, the developmental inversion might appear at age 7 for one task, but at age 9 for a more complex variation of that same task. That is, the points of inflection or inversion should depend not only on developmental level, but also on the task involved.

Wohlwill (1962) and Gollin (1968) have suggested several dimensions which may be used to more specifically define task complexity. Although they were originally introduced as dimensions along which perception and conception might be specified, they may also serve as indicators of the degree a particular task demands a shift towards an inferential or conceptual mode of problem solving. Task complexity would be said to increase if 1) input redundancy decreases, 2) irrelevant information increases, 3) temporal and spatial separation increases between relevant aspects of the stimulus complex (elements which must be integrated if task solution is to occur), 4) spatial and temporal crowding between relevant aspects of the stimulus complex increases, and 5) the number of diverse stimulus elements which must be integrated increases. These dimensions are similar to the developmental differences which, as Neal Miller (1967) suggests, are the consequences of increased numbers of traces which can be stored and increased capacities for performance resulting from superiorities in the complex neural networks for processing information after it is stored, or after it has been retrieved from storage and is involved in the initiation of behavior.

Variables Altering the Domain

The definition of the behavioral domain has suggested the second, not independent kind of developmental research: what are the variables which alter the domain? And what are the relationships between these variables and developmental status? The foregoing dimensions of complexity specify some of the more important task variables which may be manipulated to study the resulting change, or equally important, the lack of change, in cognitive behavior. Obviously they do not exhaust the range of effective task manipulations. In addition, certain other variables *e.g.*, practice, motivation, set, etc., need to be included; they have already been shown to be effective in changing the behavioral domain (Wolff, 1967; Harter, 1967; Maccoby, 1967).

There are a number of learning problems which appear to be particularly sensitive to both developmental differences and to attempts to alter these differences; reversal, oddity, and transposition problems are examples of those tasks. At present, there is some controversy as to whether or not developmental differences do indeed exist in these tasks, especially in both reversal learning and the relative ease of reversals and other concept-shift paradigms. There seem to be several reasons for this confusion. It must be realized that two very different questions are being asked. The first, "Are there developmental differences in learning?" has been confused with the second "What are the conditions under which performance differences associated with age are alterable?" Thus because large amounts of overtraining can produce similar reversal performance in two age groups, it does not follow that there are no age-related differences in reversal learning. Second, a box score approach, that is, comparisons between studies which confound both age and method, tend to be misleading or inconclusive on this point since the relevant variables which must be matched for these kinds of comparisons are, at best, incompletely specified. Third, despite a plethora of studies in the area, only a few have explored the relation of concept shifts and reversal learning in the appropriate developmental context. For example, Wolff (1966) could find only five studies which compared intra-dimensionnal and extra-dimensional shifting in which Ss were blocked by age, excluding studies performed by the Kendlers. Of these, only three included the reversal paradigm. They compared the performance of children 3 vs. 4 years (Cobb & Price, 1967); 6-7 vs. 8-10 yrs. (Milgram & Furth, 1964) and 10 vs. 11 years (Willer, 1963). Since the point of inflection for performance on this task has appeared to be at approximately 5-6 years, these age range comparisons are not those which would be expected to produce an age x shift interaction. However, several studies have shown age differences in the relative ease of reversal learning (Jeffrey, 1965, Saravo, 1967; Kendler, Kendler & Learnard, 1962, Gollin, 1964).

The alteration of performance differences has been obtained with novel stimuli (Blank, 1967), overtraining (see Wolff, 1967), delay between training and test (Gollin, 1964; Youniss & Furth, 1964; Stevenson & Weir, 1959), change of stimuli on an irrelevant dimension between training and test (Jeffrey, 1965); learning set (Saravo & Kolodny, 1968), and sophistication (Saravo & Gollin, 1968). Reversal performance is facilitated and age differences attenuate.

A comparable diminution of age differences on the oddity problem was achieved by increasing the number of non-odd cues, thus increasing the perceptual distinctiveness of the odd cue (Gollin, Saravo & Salten, 1967). Kindergarten children under this condition performed like second grade children, while their performance on the standard three—stimulus problem was inferior to that of the older children. Nursery school children were not affected by the introduction of additional non-odd cues. Neither practice nor increased perceptual distinctiveness could move their performance closer to that of the older children. Their tendency to respond to position, in part, apparently prevented response to the relevant stimuli or attention to the stimulus-reward contingencies of the task. While these results suggest developmental variations in the effects of certain training manipulations they are not so dramatic as the following studies.

Both Tempone (1965) using MA 6-10, and Mednick & Lehtinen, (1957) using CA 7-12, had reported an inverse relation between age and stimulus—generalization responsivity. The younger children showed higher, broader, curves, while the older children's generalization curves were steeper, more peaked. Using two age groups, 6-7 year olds and 10-11 year olds, Tempone (1966) investigated the effect of number of training trials on the responsivity of the two age groups. Instead of a diminution of age differences, as would be expected if the direction of the effect of practice were invariant with respect to age, the effects of training were divergent. Increased training resulted in increased generalization for the younger children, but decreased generalization for older Ss.

A similar developmentally variant effect of practice was found in a study on reversal learning (Gollin, 1964), albeit at younger age. Varying amounts of overtraining on a visual discrimination task were given to 3½-4 and 4½-5 year old children, who were then reversed on that task. In the younger group, negative transfer on the reversal task increased with overtraining, while in the older group, this effect was not obtained. The trend of the results indicated that overtraining tended to improve reversal learning apparently by facilitating the ability to inhibit or "turn off" the previously correct response once an informing error was made. This was reflected in the greater number of older children who gave an errorless performance after the first reversal trial (the informing trial). Both of these studies raise more questions than they answer, particularly with respect to the functions which would be obtained if an extended range of either practice or age were tested. Does the effect of practice describe a relatively stable, gradual "U" function on these tasks or are the apparent discontinuities in the developmental function also representative of that function described by training? What effect does practice have on the underlying mechanisms of problem solving which produce such disparate outcomes?

As noted previously, one mechanism which has been suggested is a mediating or attention response to the relevant dimension. The Kendlers have related this complex—problem—solving prerequisite to the acquisition of labels which delineate the relevant dimension (Kendler & Kendler, 1962; Kendler, Kendler & Learnard, 1962). Zeaman and House (1963) have argued that some sort of mediating response to a dimension does occur in even young children and that slow learning is caused by attention to the wrong dimension, or, at least, failure to attend to the relevant dimension. In support of this latter viewpoint, several studies have demonstrated that young children do dimensionalize stimuli, since they show strong dimensional preferences which affect both ease of discrimination and discrimination-reversal learning (Heal, Bransky & Mankinen, 1966; Smiley & Weir, 1966). The strongest test of mediational transfer would be a comparison of the intradimensional shift (a shift to new values along the previously relevant dimension) with an extradimensional shift (a shift to a previously irrelevant dimension). Delineation of the Task 1 relevant dimension should facilitate intradimensional shifting and retard extradimensional shifting. This result can only be attributed to mediation, however, if the novelty of the relevant dimension in the transfer task is appropriately controlled. Under these conditions intradimensional shift superiority has been found for both rats (Shepp & Eimas, 1964) and preschool children (Dickerson, 1966); although in the latter study, pretraining procedures and the possible sophistication of Ss (see Saravo & Gollin, 1968) may have nullified the expected developmental implications.

To summarize, evidence has been presented to show that age related differences do exist in problem solving behavior which cannot be attributed to simple linear increments in learning speed, or to ceiling floor artifacts in experimental design, or to the development of dimensional responding, alone. In addition, the effects of variables which change these differences have been shown to depend on the developmental status of the organism.

Transfer of Behavioral Alterations

The third phase of developmental analysis will be illustrated by a series of experiments in the area of discrimination learning. Each experiment was designed to determine the relations between various subject—task arrangements and transfer to a conditional discrimination problem.

The conditional discrimination problem is a useful method for developmental research because the problem contains within itself several levels of difficulty and because it is essentially a transfer task which permits an analysis of the effects of previous learning upon later performance. Figure 4 shows the stimulus patterns which were used throughout this experimental series.

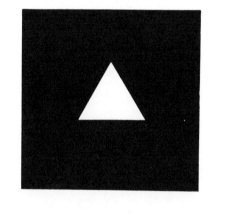
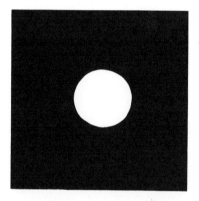

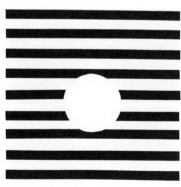

FIGURE 4
Stimulus patterns used in the conditional discrimination experiments.

A pair of cues, circle (*c*) and triangle (*t*) were presented upon one of the backgrounds, black (*b*) or striped (*s*). The subject responded to one or the other cue; a correct response produced a reward. This condition is referred to as original learning (OL). When criterion was reached on OL, usually 10 correct responses in succession, the cues were presented upon the other background. The previously unrewarded cue now was associated with reward. This condition is called reversal learning (RL). When criterion was reached on RL, the backgrounds were presented in alternation or in random order. In order to receive the reward the subject had to respond to the cue *c* or *t* when it appeared in that background condition which was associated with reward during OL and RL. This phase of the procedure was the random test (RT) of conditional discrimination (CD).

The subjects used in the first experiment fell in the age ranges 3½-4 years, 4½-5 years, and 5½-6 years. The outcomes of the initial experiment (Gollin & Liss, 1962) are represented in a three dimensional graph, which defined the domain to be explored in the experiments which follow. There were no differences between the age groups on OL. The youngest age group, however, showed a significant increase in

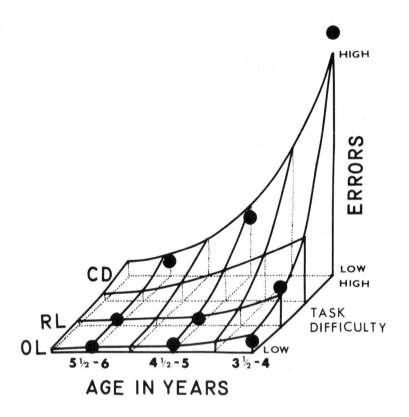

FIGURE 5
The base experiment: OL, RL and CD errors made by the three age groups.

trials to criterion on RL, i.e., negative transfer, but there was no comparable increase in errors among the older groups. The CD test extended the age related differences. The oldest children made fewest errors, and a majority of the youngest did not reach the CD criterion within 50 trials despite a procedure designed to help them to understand the problem. Although there were no differences in performance among groups on OL, the first transfer task (RL) produced differences between the youngest children and the two older groups, and the second transfer task (CD) accentuated the age-related differences. (See Figure 5.)

The experiments that follow may be thought of as constituting a series of experimental probes designed to clarify the relationships found in the first experiment. The first probe was designed to investigate the age-related differences in transfer effects from OL to RL (Gollin, 1964). Groups of children aged 3½-4 years and 4½-5 years served as subjects. Groups at each age level were assigned to one of three OL training conditions: zero, 10 or 20 postcriterion training trials. They were then given reversal learning (RL), followed by an alternation test in which OL and RL settings were presented on successive trials in single alternation order.

The overtraining variable was chosen because in a number of studies of visual discrimination it has been found to facilitate reversal learning (see Wolff, 1967). The expectation was that overtraining would facilitate the performance of both groups, perhaps to the extent of obliterating the previous age related differences in transfer between OL and RL. Contrary to this hypothesis, overtraining impeded learning on both the reversal and alternation reversal test for the younger children.

All children continued to respond to the previously rewarded cue on the first RL trial. Twenty-four of the 36 older children showed an "errorless" reversal performance; that is, after receiving no reward on the first RL trial they switched to the other cue and reached criterion without further error. This is in marked contrast to the behavior of the younger children; only one child out of the 36 in the younger groups produced an "errorless" reversal performance. In addition, although the trend was facilitative, the effects of overtraining did not reliably affect the performance of the older children until the alternation test. In this case, the overtrained groups reached criterion with fewer trials than the nonovertrained group.

The two age groups in this experiment appeared to differ qualitatively in their behavior, and the difference was apparently magnified by the overtraining variable. It has recently been suggested that reversal learning may be conceptualized as consisting of two phases. In the first there is extinction of the approach response to the previously positive stimulus and in the second phase there is acquisition of an approach response to the new positive stimulus (Paul, 1965). Using this explanation, it would seem all but impossible to account for the data of both the younger and older age groups without some further assumptions. Are the results, then, accountable in terms of verbal mediation? Possibly, but it should be pointed out that when an inquiry is conducted both age groups appear to be able to supply verbal labels for the cues and backgrounds, and some of the younger ones even appear able to state the "reversal" principle.

The possibility remained that the poor reversal performance of the younger children, as well as their inability to solve the CD problem was primarily due to insufficient experience with reversal tasks *per se*. A suggestion along these lines has been offered by Warren (1964) who successfully trained sophisticated monkeys in CD by using trial-to-trial variations of the several stimulus components in a modified learning set procedure. Furthermore, Warren noted that the performance of the monkeys in his study was actually superior to the 5½-6 year old children in the Gollin and Liss (1962) study. Warren attributed this only partly to the monkey's experimental sophistication. He also suggested that training on isolated parts of the CD task (*e.g.*, OL, RL, OL, etc.) before introducing trial-to-trial variation retarded the solution of the CD problem.

In the next experiment (Gollin, 1965b) therefore, trial-to-trial variation was introduced, that is, backgrounds were changed from trial-to-trial, and in order to make a rewarded response the subject had to shift from cue to cue on succcessive presentations. Three other conditions were added: background *Runs* of 2, 3, and 5. The subjects were 5½-6 year old children, 15 assigned to each condition. Fifty massed training trials were presented followed by the CD test.

The results showed that as the length of background runs in training increased, there was a corresponding increase in the number of *S*s who achieved a perfect score in the CD test. Furthermore, only the *Runs-of-5* group achieved a mean score reliably different from chance on this problem. Perhaps the sophistication of Warren's monkeys (they had previously been run on a variety of experimental problems) contributed to their superior performance.

Since the 5½-6 year old group was successful under the *Runs-of-5* condition in both the RL trials and on the CD problem, it was decided to try that variation with younger groups. Accordingly groups aged 3½-4 years and 4½-5 years were trained and tested in the same fashion as the older children. The outcome is shown in Figure 6 where age related trends in reversal errors and in the random test of CD are discernible.

Thus, although the *Runs-of-5* condition facilitated solution of the CD problem in the oldest group (5½-6 years) it did not have a comparable effect upon the CD performance of the two younger groups.

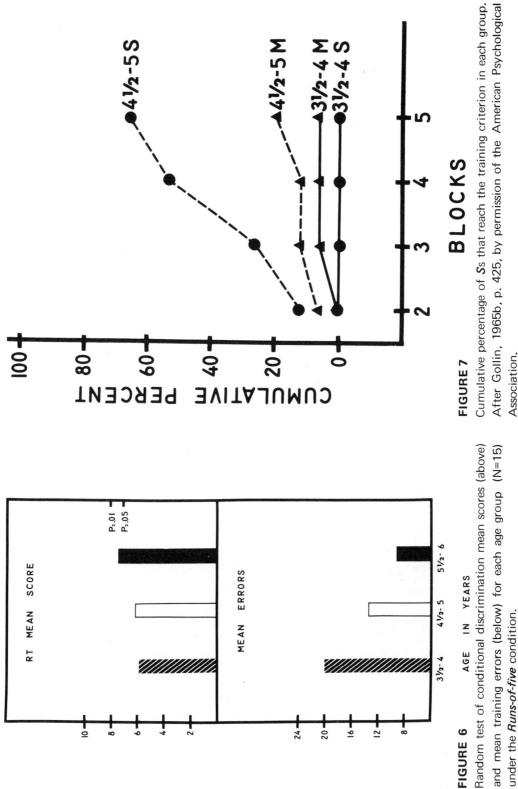

FIGURE 7

Cumulative percentage of *S*s that reach the training criterion in each group. After Gollin, 1965b, p. 425, by permission of the American Psychological Association.

FIGURE 6

Random test of conditional discrimination mean scores (above) and mean training errors (below) for each age group (N=15) under the *Runs-of-five* condition.

Did the crowding of trials under the massed condition interfere with learning in the younger groups? Would distributing the 50 training trials make a difference? In order to answer these questions additional groups of 3½-4 year olds, and 4½-5 year old children were recruited. They were given 10 training trials per day for five days and then given the CD problem. On each training day they were presented with the pair of cues five times in succession on each background.

Figure 7 shows the cumulative per cent of subjects under both the massed and distributed training conditions who reached criterion during the training blocks. Distribution of practice had a marked effect on the older groups' performance but no apparent effect upon the performance on the younger group. A similar result is apparent when the CD test data are examined. The only group that achieved a score significantly greater than chance is the 4½-5 year distributed practice group.

A further analysis of performance was undertaken by analyzing the Trial 2 outcomes in each block of training trials from the second block on. There were two reversals per block. This analysis is shown on Figure 8. The older children appear to grasp the "reversal principle", that is, the failure to receive a reward should be followed by a shift of response to the other cue. Note that the younger subjects, trained by distributed practice, seem to be approaching an understanding of the "reversal principle" by the last training block.

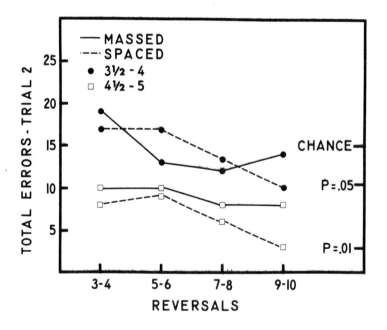

FIGURE 8

Total number of Trial 2 errors made by each group from the third reversal in blocks of 10 trials (two Trial 2 presentations per block). After Gollin, 1965b, p. 425, by permission of the American Psychological Association.

If a training procedure could be established which produced "errorless" reversal in 3½-4 year old children, would they then be able to master the CD problem? In an attempt to answer this question the training procedure was modified to include aspects of precious training procedures which had seemed to produce beneficial performance outcomes in older children. Subjects were trained to criterion on one background condition on Day 1 and then reversed on successive days for 5 days, thereby increasing background-run length and distributing practice. Then the test of conditional discrimination was administered. The results are shown in Figure 9. The first reversal block on Day 2 shows the usual negative transfer effect. On Day 5, the last training day, 8 out of the 16 children reversed without error, six made an error on the first reversal trial only, and two subjects made more than one error.

Despite the evidence of Day 5, suggesting that the "reversal principle" had been learned by most children, the performance on RT (the conditional discrimination problem) remained at chance level. The 3½-4 year old children were unable to transfer the training experience to the test situation (Gollin, 1965b.).

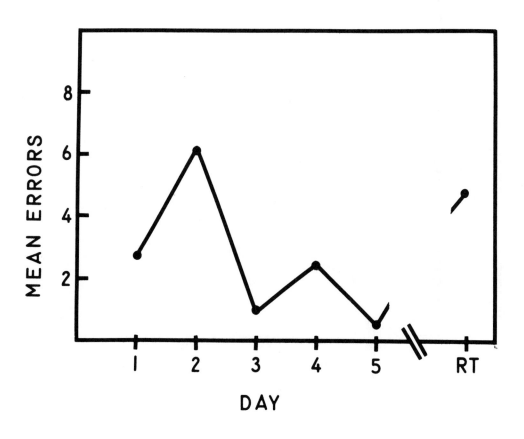

FIGURE 9
Mean errors on each training day and on the random test of CD.

A further test of the conditional principle is obtained by observing the Trial 1 performance of *S*s from the second reversal block. Figure 10 shows the Trial 1 outcomes for the three age groups under the condition of massed practice. Figure 11 shows the Trial 1 outcomes of the two younger groups under massed and distributed practice conditions. It will be noted that only 4½-5 year old children trained under the *Runs—of—5* distributed condition reached levels of performance significantly different from chance.

After having tried and, so far, failed to produce solution of the conditional discrimination in young children (3½-4), the last experiment in this series (Gollin, 1966) utilized the information from the previous studies and combined instruction, correction, and successive reversals in small blocks in an attempt to produce mastery of the CD problem among age groups younger than those that had been successful in earlier experiments. Children 3-5 years old were trained on a successive discrimination reversal using a correction procedure and verbalization techniques which required *S* to name the cues, and directed his attention to the background-stimulus-reward contingencies. These procedures were not used in the

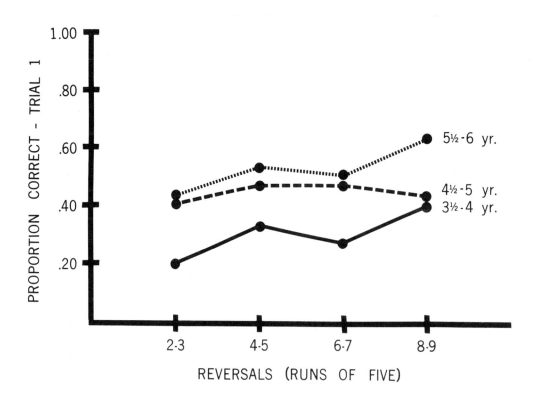

FIGURE 10

The proportion of *S*s in each age group that made a correct response on Trial 1 from the second reversal under the massed training condition.

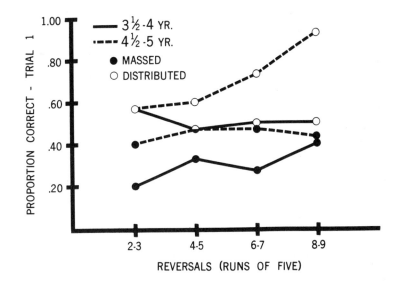

FIGURE 11

The proportion of *S*s in each age group that made a correct response on Trial 1 from the second reversal under the massed and distributed training condition.

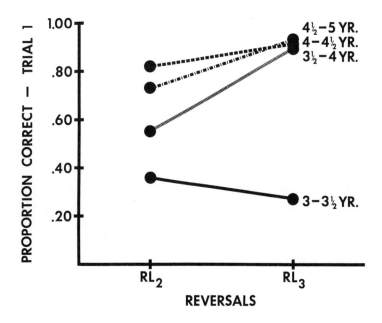

FIGURE 12

The proportion of *S*s in each age group that made a correct response on Trial 1 from the second and third reversals.

CD test. In addition, a more lenient criterion was used in the last two reversals (RL2 and RL3) in order to reduce the tendency of young S to perseverate to the cue of the preceding phase of training.

The result of these procedures was that the target group, 3½-4 year olds, was able to learn the reversal task and solve the conditional problem; only the youngest children, 3-3½, were unable to solve the CD problem and were also unsuccessful on the reversal task. The Trial 1 response on RL 3 (see Figure 12) suggested that all Ss but this group had learned the conditional principle, since approximately 90 per cent of the older Ss (including 89 per cent of the 3½-4 year olds) were correct on the first trial. On Trial 1 of RL2, however, only about half of the 3½-4 year old children were responding on the basis of the conditional principle.

In the context of the procedures used in this experiment, the 3½-4 year old Ss appeared to be in a transition group, while in the context of previous experiments, 4½-5 year olds showed transition characteristics with respect to solution of the CD problem. The defining characteristics of a "transition group" are, therefore, dependent not only on the developmental status of respondents but also on the training-test arrangements.

The conditional discrimination problem in the previous studies entailed successive reversals contingent on background change. Thus, it might be conceptualized as a within subject comparison of two problems, whose relationship to each other, or to the previous training, is a reversal. The two problems were not analyzed separately because there was no interest in the relative ease of those two problems, *per se*.

The next experiment to be discussed (Saravo & Kolodny, 1968) utilized the double-problem characteristics of the conditional discrimination to test the extent of transfer of learning set training on two different types of problems, a reversal and a nonreversal shift. Over a period of 2-3 weeks, 25 preschool children learned a series of 8 two-task transfer problems; half of these were reversal (RS) shifts, half were nonreversal shifts (NRS). This series of 8 problems was followed by a CD problem in which the transfer task constituted a mixed list, within subject comparison of both RS and NRS paradigms. The CD task required a reversal on half the trials and a nonreversal on the others. Figure 13 illustrates a specimen of the settings on problems 1, 2, and 9 (CD) for one S; for purposes of illustration, the left stimulus of each pair is positive.

Performance on OL, the first task in each problem, revealed that early in learning repeated shifts hindered Ss overall performance. For 3 year olds, this negative transfer was sufficiently disruptive to prevent most of them from finishing the series. Even the children who did finish the series showed a decrement in OL performance

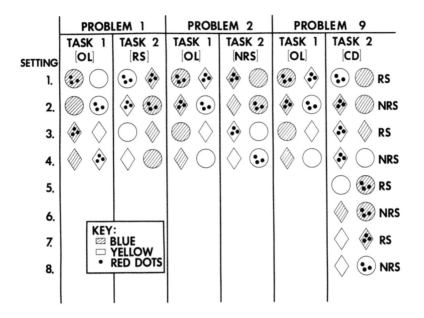

FIGURE 13

Stimulus settings for one subject of problems 1, 2, and 9, illustrating orignial learning tasks (OL), reversal and nonreversal shifts (RS and NRS, respectively) and conditional discrimination (CD). After Saravo and Kolodny, 1968 by permission of JOURNAL OF EXPERIMENTAL CHILD PSYCHOLOGY, (Academic Press).

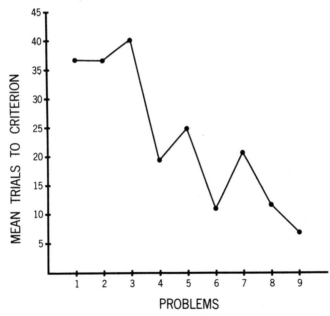

FIGURE 14

Mean trials to criterion on the first tasks (OL) of problems 1-9. After Saravo and Kolodny, 1968 by permission of the JOURNAL OF EXPERIMENTAL CHILD PSYCHOLOGY, (Academic Press).

in one or more problems when compared with the first problem. In general, however, the negative transfer produced early in learning was superseded by the formation of a learning set at the end of the series (see Figure 14).

Task two performance in problems 1-8 indicated that RS was the more difficult shift on the first two problems, but thereafter the children performed with equal facility on the two shifts. Performance improved reliably overall on RS, while NRS facilitation was dependent on an overall improvement in shifting to color.

When the children were given the CD comparison of RS and NRS, they returned to their initial superiority on NRS. Facilitation of reversal shifting, then, did not transfer to the CD problem although all but three Ss who were able to finish the series reached criterion on CD.

The early negative transfer found in OL and the inability of the youngest children to overcome this negative transfer is analogous to the previous finding (Gollin, 1964) that 3½-4 year old children were hindered in reversal performance by overtraining. In addition, the failure of RS-facilitation transfer suggests that preschool children are easily disrupted by problem changes, and that this disruption was in the form of a recovery of their previously extinguished modes of responding. These modes of responding would include attention responses to never-relevant dimensions, and a tendency towards cue perseveration.

DISCUSSION

These experiments, conducted as a comparative—developmental program of inquiry, indicate that there is a complicated interplay between the amount and kind of training, the temporal succession of stimulus events, the character or content of stimulus events, and ontogenetic status. There are marked differences between the age groups in the degree to which they are able to transfer their training experiences. The cognitive behavior of the youngest children is characterized by trial—and—error procedures, and a marked inability to extrapolate what has been learned.

In contrast, the "middle—aged" and older children appear to be able to learn a strategy or principle and to carry it over successfully to related tasks. In most of the experimental situations that have been used there is not much overlap between the performance scores of the 3 year and 4½ year old children. The data suggest that the cognitive behavior of these children, in these tasks, is mediated differently. The differences in mediation are specifiable in terms of the experimental operations carried out in the context of developmental—comparative analysis.

It should also be noted that experiments conducted within the comparative-developmental context raise questions for general psychological theories which must encompass the matrix of relationships that have been generated by this approach. The research approach to cognitive development illustrated by this series of experiments delineates a number of issues in discrimination learning and in developmental analysis:

1) Similar performance outcomes (*e.g.*, OL) by children of different ages may lead to quite different outcomes in transfer tasks (see Figure 5).

2) Identical experimental treatments, *e.g.*, practice, may affect transfer by apparently increasing response probability in one group, and decreasing that response probability in another group (Tempone, 1957; Saravo & Kolodny, 1968; Gollin, 1964).

3) An experimental treatment which produces a successful performance in an age group which has previously failed will not necessarily eliminate failure in a younger group (see Figure 7, 11, & 12).

4) Success during extended training which is dependent upon one solution strategy does not necessarily transfer to a test situation wherein a rearrangement of stimulus orders requires another strategy for solution (see Figure 9 and Saravo & Kolodny, 1968).

5) Transition rules are likely to vary as a function of the developmental status of the respondent. For example, although massed training under the *Runs—of—five* training condition did not lead to CD solutions for 4½-5 year old children, distributed training did produce success; for the 3½-4 year old children the distribution of training blocks was an ineffective training procedure. The oldest group of children (5½-6 years) were able to solve the problem under the massed training condition. However, the massed training procedure did not lead to CD success for the oldest children until the stimulus-compounds are grouped in background *Runs—of—five*.

6) Behavior theories in general, and learning theories in particular, must take into account not only divergencies in transition rules, and the "timeliness" of experimental treatments, but also those instances where the same treatment produces divergent performances, *e.g.*, the overlearning reversal effect function for 3½-4 year as contrasted to 4½-5 year old children.

Many of these findings represent an impasse for current theories of discrimination learning. For example, according to the Kendlers, a mediating response to a dimension, primarily verbal in nature, does not functionally control discriminative behavior until the ages of 5-7. As previously noted, there is much evidence to show that dimensional responding does occur in preverbal organisms. Moreover, recent work by Munsinger & Kessen (1966) suggests that young children may be more likely to dimensionalize stimuli than older children under certain experimental arrangements. In support of the Kendlers' thesis, many studies on the effect of verbalization training do show the expected facilitation (Silverman, 1966; Kendler, 1964; Jeffrey, 1953; Spiker, 1956; Katz, 1965), although these effects may just as easily support the position that relevant verbal mediators function through the acquisition of observing responses to the relevant dimension. As previously noted, proponents of both the attentional and verbal mediational formulations have stated that the two positions are not incompatible. Parenthetically, with the assumption that training equalizes approach and avoidance tendencies on values of the irrelevant dimensions (*e.g.*, Spence, 1936), "dimensional" responding may be also included within a one—stage discrimination model.

What the two—stage theories have in common is a postulation of some mediating response (attentional or verbal) to the relevant dimension, which is of central importance in discrimination learning. A corollary of this assumption would be that the more complex the discrimination, the greater the effect of dimension selection (Saravo, 1967).

Only the Kendlers, however, have attempted to account for age associated differences in reversal learning by this mechanism. House and Zeaman (1963, p. 190) recognized that the relative ease of reversal and nonreversal paradigms was indeterminate without some additional assumptions as to the course of learning of the instrumental habit in the reversal problem. Since dimensional responding does occur in preverbal organisms, however, neither the Kendlers nor Zeaman & House can explain age differences in reversal learning solely as a function of verbal mediators in the form of dimensionalization. It is clear, then, that neither of these theories can adequately handle developmental—reversal phenomena without modification.

What kinds of processes would account for these developmental differences in learning? Voronin (1962) has summarized Russian research which suggests that the rate of formation of simple associations in vertebrates is approximately the same, and consequently cannot reflect the level of phylogenesis. This agrees with House and Zeaman, whose analysis of data by backward learning curves shows an initial flat chance—level stage of performance followed by a final sharply rising portion of the curve. The length of the first part of the curve, they believe, is controlled primarily by attentional processes, while the last portion of the curve is largely indicative of instrumental learning. The slope of this portion, the learning rate, they, like Voronin, believe does not reflect species or developmental factors.

Voronin suggested two factors which appeared to reflect developmental differences in learning: 1) The length of the chain of reflexes (associations) which may be established appears to vary phylogenetically. This is most probably a direct function of the storage capabilities of the organism and would seem to be particularly relevant to Hill's (1965) data, in which only the older children were able to solve the problem requiring a long chain of attentional and instrumental responses. 2) The ability to inhibit a previous response also appears to be related to phyletic status.

It is this latter factor, the ability to "turn off", overcome, or inhibit a previous response which we feel is the basis for much of the unaccounted for developmental variation in discrimination learning. Most simple discrimination problems do not require lengthy chaining, and so are not directly sensitive to variations in this ability, although the storage capacity of the organism should be directly related to response inhibition. It is hypothesized that the basic underlying mechanism of response "turn off" is the discrimination of change. This of course is related to storage capacity since a requirement for the detection of change is the prior perception of sameness—a schema, representation, or strong habit must be activated.

An important distinction to be made is the one between not making a response because the subject decides that response is inappropriate and does not make it even though he remains capable of making it, and failure to make the response because some inhibitory process has been generated, or extinction has taken place. Reversals, therefore, may be facilitated by any operation which is likely to weaken the habit previously acquired, and also by any operation which permits the subject to say "not that one anymore".

Thus, there are two kinds of processes which may control the response inhibition mechanism, one continuous and available to all organisms and one discontinuous and characteristic of developmentally advanced human problem solving. The necessary conditions for each set of processes may be arranged in a variety of ways. The continuous process reflects stimulus generalization decrements such as produced by a discriminable change in the stimulus complex, including removal of reinforcement, change of pace of the experiment, change of stimuli, etc. or by conditioned inhibition, such as possible in learning set where S learns to inhibit a previous response when a change in the experimental situation occurs. The discontinuous process reflects the development of a representation of the situation so that in effect he says to himself "that response is no longer the one which is correct. I must try another response."

In lower organisms, the usual reversal technique does not afford a large enough change from training to reversal unless the salience of this change is heightened, for example, by overtraining, magnitude of reward, a longer delay between training and test than the usual intertrial interval, etc. With increased storage capacity for all components of the stimulus complex in more advanced organisms, the likelihood that a change is detected should also increase without inflection of salience by experimental manipulations.

In addition, the change in reward contingencies is likely to generate heightened attention to the properties of the stimulus array and facilitate alteration of Ss response pattern. It should also be noted that attentional factors function to decrease the storage necessary in order to include all relevant components of the stimulus complex, since to be selectively attentive also implies being selectively exclusive. Again, inclusiveness or exclusiveness may reflect either a very simple kind of associative incremental process which is possible for lower organisms, or a much more complex one which involves categorizing or the generation of classes.

For humans, the incremental mechanism may be supplemented and eventually by—passed by verbal processes—supplemental because language facilitates storage capacity via chunking (Miller, 1956) and therefore enhances the discrimination of change from training to reversal task. While language aids may be the preferred mode for humans they obviously are not for higher primates. Higher primates are able to learn reversal problems in one trial and therefore it must be assumed that some sort of schematic or structural systems exist without language. It is also likely that nonverbal mediators also operate at the human level.

In our view, verbal mediation as well as other forms of mediation essentially modify the environment to which children respond. There is a shift in saliencies, in causal attributions, in the ability to integrate events over time, in the ability to be selectively attentive, and in the ability to shift behavior in the face of changing environmental demand. In part, redefinition or reordering of the significance of environmental events is attributable to the emergence of verbal mediational systems, and, in part, to the refinement of other mediational systems which may not be exclusively verbal (*e.g.*, perceptual groupings akin to those dealt with by Gestalt laws).

The effect of overtraining is particularly difficult to predict since it both increases the probability of discriminating the discrepancy between training and transfer task, thereby facilitating reversal, and also increases the strength of the response, thereby retarding reversal. In lower organisms and young children overtraining is likely to be an impactful manipulation. It may at least, establish a very strong habit, schema, or structure, as Mandler (1962) suggests. When the reward contingency aspect of this relationship is violated the additional stimulation adds to the change in the stimulus complex and facilitates the weakening of the previously learned habit. Up to this point, however, overtraining also serves to strengthen associative bonds, and so would interfere with a subsequent reversal. This hypothesis predicts, tentatively, a curvilinear relationship between overtraining and reversal performance with the point of inflection a function of the difficulty of the discrimination (remembering, as previously discussed, that difficulty is a joint function of task complexity and developmental level). When a correct hypothesis or schema is already available, as with the older child or adult, the effects of overtraining are likely to be very slight. A single disconfirmation is likely to lead to a shift in response, regardless of the number of previously rewarded original learning responses.

Therefore, the development of hypothesis testing behavior allows for the apparent circumvention of this incremental and decremental system. Once a hypothesis or schema is available to the subject, only one or at the most a few disconfirmations are necessary for termination of that response. In this case, the response that is turned-off is no longer simply that of approaching or avoiding; the most important response is that of the cognitive strategy or the hypothesis which mediates the observed behavior. When and only when a correct hypothesis is unavailable or of low probability, is the S then forced to rely on incremental and decremental modes of problem solving. In other words, any organism, adult or otherwise, may under certain circumstances utilize in his behavior rote-kinds of processes. If task complexity or stimulus—response—reward relationships are complex, novel, or unreliable, the adult is likely to show in his initial behavior a pattern of response which is not discernibly different from that of a lower organism or young child. However, it should be noted that even in this latter case the adult is likely to come to the situation with a set to solve the problem to attempt to generate a variety of solutions which will yield dependable outcomes. With respect to the younger child, it is part of our thesis that depending upon the task complexity, his prior experience, and his capacity level he will under certain circumstances be an incremental and decremental organism and under other circumstances be an hypothesizing organism.

Preparation of this paper was aided by Grant No. HD-01570 and by Contract No. PH 43 65-1011 from NICHHD to the Fels Research Institute, E. S. Gollin, Principal Investigator.

References

Beilin, H. "Perceptual—cognitive conflict in the development of an invariant area concept." J. OF EXP. CHILD PSYCH., 1: 208-226, 1964.

Blank, Marion. "Effect of stimulus characteristics on dimensional shifting in kindergarten children." J. OF COMP. PHYS. PSYCH., 64: 522-525, 1967.

Bitterman, M. E. "Toward a comparative psychology of learning." AM. PSYCH., 15: 704-712, 1960.

Cobb, N. J. & Price, L. E. "Reversal and nonreversal shift learning in children as a function of two types of pretraining." PSYCH. REP., 19: 1003-1010, 1966.

Dickerson, D. J. "Performance of preschool children on three discrimination shifts." PSYCHONOMIC SC., 4: 417-418, 1966.

Friedman, S. R. "Developmental level and concept learning: confirmation of an inverse relationship." PSYCHONOMIC SC., 2: 3-4, 1965.

Gollin, E. S. "Reversal learning and conditional discrimination in children." J. OF COMP. PHYS. PSYCH., 58: 441-445, 1964.

Gollin, E. S. "A developmental approach to learning and cognition." In L. P. Lipsitt and C. C. Spiker (Eds.), ADVANCES IN CHILD DEVELOPMENT AND BEHAVIOR, Vol. 2, New York: Academic Press, Inc., pp. 159-186, 1965a.

Gollin, E. S. "Factors affecting conditional discrimination in children." J. OF COMP. PHYS. PSYCH. 58: 422-427, 1965b.

Gollin, E. S. "Solution of conditional discrimination problems by young children." J. OF COMP. PHYS. PSYCH. 62: 454-456, 1966.

Gollin, E. S. "Research trends in infant learning." In J. Hellmuth (Ed.), THE EXCEPTIONAL INFANT, VOLUME I: THE NORMAL INFANT. Seattle: Special Child Publications, pp. 243-266, 1967.

Gollin, E. S. "Conditions that facilitate or impede cognitive functioning: Implications for Developmental Theory and for Education." In R. D. Hess & R. M. Bear (Eds.), EARLY EDUCATION: CURRENT THEORY, RESEARCH, AND PRACTICE. Chicago, Illinois: Aldine Press, Chp. 4, pp. 53-62, 1968.

Gollin, E. S. & Liss, P. "Conditional discrimination in children." J. OF COMP. PHYS. PSYCH. 55: 850-855, 1962.

Gollin, E. S., Saravo, Anne & Salten, Cynthia. "Perceptual distinctiveness and oddity-problem solving in children." J. OF EXP. CHILD PSYCH., 5: 586-596, 1967.

Harter, Susan, "Mental age, IQ, and motivational factors in the discrimination learning set performance of normal and retarded children." J. OF EXP. CHILD PSYCH., 5: 123-141, 1967.

Heal, L. W., Bransky, M. L. & Mankinen, R. L. "The role of dimension preference in reversal and nonreversal shifts of retardates." PSYCHONOMIC SC. 6: 509-510, 1966.

Hill, S. D. "The performance of young children on three discrimination learning tasks." CHILD DEVELOP., 36: 425-435, 1965.

Jeffrey, W. E. "The effects of verbal and nonverbal responses in mediating an instrumental act." J. OF EXP. PSYCH. 45: 327-333, 1953.

Jeffrey, W. E. "Variables affecting reversal shifts in young children." AM. J. OF PSYCH., 78: 589-595, 1965.

Katz, P. A. "Effects of labels on children's perception and discrimination learning." J. OF EXP. PSYCH., 66: 423-428, 1963.

Kay, H. "The effects of position in a display upon problem solving." QUART. J. OF EXP. PSYCH., 6: 155-169, 1954.

Kendler, T. S. "Verbalization and optional reversal shifts amomong kindergarten children." J. OF VERBAL LEARN. AND VERBAL BEHAV., 3: 428-436, 1964.

Kendler, H. H. & Kendler, T. S. "Vertical and horizontal processes in problem solving." PSYCH. REV., 69: 1-16, 1962.

Kendler, T. S. & Kendler, H. H. "Optional shifts of children as a function of number of training trials on the initial discrimination." J. OF EXP. CHILD PSYCH., 3: 216-224, 1966.

Kendler, T. S., Kendler, H. H., & Learnard, B. "Mediated responses to size and brightness as a function of age." AM. J. OF PSYCH., 75: 571-586, 1962.

Lashley, K. S. BRAIN MECHANISM AND INTELLIGENCE: A QUANTITATIVE STUDY OF INJURIES TO THE BRAIN. Chicago: University of Chicago Press, 1929.

Lehrman, D. S. "A critique of Konrad Lorenz's theory of instinctive behavior." QUART. REV. OF BIO. 28: 337-363, 1953.

Maccoby, E. "Selective auditory attention in children," In Lipsitt, L. P. and Spiker, C. C. (Eds.) ADVANCES IN CHILD DEVELOPMENT AND BEHAVIOR, Vol. 3, New York: Academic Press, pp. 99-124, 1967.

Mackintosh, N. J. "Selective attention in animal discrimination." PSYCH. BULL., 64: 124-150, 1965.

Mandler, G. "From association to structure." PSYCH. REV. 69: 415-427, 1962.

Mednick, S. A. & Lehtinen, L. E. "Stimulus generalization as a function of age." J. OF EXP. PSYCH., 53: 180-183, 1957.

Milgram, N. A., & Furth, H. G. "Position reversal versus dimension reversal in normal and retarded children." CHILD DEVELOP., 35: 701-708, 1964.

Miller, G. A. "The magical number seven, plus or minus two: some limits on our capacity for processing information." PSYCH. REV., 63: 81-97, 1956.

Miller, N. E. "Laws of learning relevant to its biological basis." PROCEEDINGS OF THE AMERICAN PHILOSOPHICAL SOCIETY, Vol. III, No. 6, 315-325, December 1967.

Munn, N. L. THE EVOLUTION AND GROWTH OF HUMAN BEHAVIOR. Second edition. Boston: Houghton Mifflin, 1965.

Munsinger, H. & Kessen, W., "Stimulus variability and cognitive change." PSYCH. REV., 73: 164-178, 1966.

Paul, C. "Effects of overlearning upon single habit reversal in rats." PSYCH. BULL. 63: 65-72, 1965.

Reese, H. W. "Verbal mediation as a function of age level." PSYCH. BULL. 59: 502-509, 1962.

Riesen, A. H. "Receptor functions." In P. H. Mussen (Ed.), HANDBOOK OF RESEARCH METHODS IN CHILD DEVELOPMENT. New York: John Wiley & Sons, Chapter 7, pp. 284-307, 1960.

Riesen, A. H. "Stimulation as a requirement for growth and function in behavioral development." In D. W. Fiske & S. R. Maddi (Eds.), FUNCTIONS OF VARIED EXPERIENCE. Homewood, Illinois: Dorsey Press, Chapter 3, pp. 57-80, 1961.

Saravo, Anne. "Effect of number of variable dimensions on reversal and nonreversal shifts." J. OF COMP. PHYS. PSYCH., 64: 93-97, 1967.

Saravo, Anne & Kolodny, May. "Learning set and shift behavior in children."

JOURNAL OF EXPERIMENTAL CHILD PSYCHOLOGY. (In press).

Saravo, Anne, & Gollin, E. S. "Shift behavior in naive and sophisticated children." PSYCHONOMIC SC. (In press).

Schusterman, R. J. "Strategies of normal and mentally retarded children under conditions of uncertain outcome." AM. J. OF MENT. DEF., 69: 66-75, 1964.

Shepp, B. E. & Eimas, P. D. "Intradimensional and extradimensional shifts in the rat." J. OF COMP. PHYS. PSYCH., 57: 357-361, 1964.

Silverman, I. W. "Effect of verbalization on reversal shifts in children: Additional data." J. OF EXP. CHILD PSYCH., 4: 1-8, 1966.

Smiley, S. S., & Weir, M. W. "The role of dimensional dominance in reversal and nonreversal shift behavior." J. OF EXP. CHILD PSYCH., 4: 211-216, 1966.

Spence, K. W. "The nature of discrimination learning in animals." PSYCH. REV., 43: 427-449, 1936.

Spiker, C. C. "Stimulus pretraining and subsequent performance in the delayed reaction experiment." J. OF EXP. PSYCH., 52: 107-11, 1956.

Stevenson, H. W. & Weir, M. W. "Response shift as a function of overtraining and delay." J. OF COMP. PHYS. PSYCH., 52: 327-329, 1959.

Sutherland, N. S. "Stimulus analyzing mechanisms." In PROCEEDINGS OF A SYMPOSIUM ON THE MECHANIZATION OF THOUGHT PROCESSES. Vol. 2, London: Her Majesty's Stationery Office, 1959.

Tempone, V. J. "Stimulus generalization as a function of mental age." CHILD DEVELOPMENT, 36: 229-235, 1965.

Tempone, V. J. "Mediational processes in primary stimulus generalization." CHILD DEVELOPMENT, 37: 687-696, 1966.

Voronin, L. G. "Some results of comparative-physiological investigations of higher nervous activity." PSYCHOLOGICAL BULLETIN, 59: 161-195, 1962.

Warren, J. M. "Additivity of cues in conditional discrimination learning by rhesus monkeys." J. OF COMP. PHYS. PSYCH., 58: 124-126, 1964.

Weir, M. W. "Devlopmental changes in problem-solving strategies." PSYCHOLOGICAL REVIEW, 71: 473-490, 1964.

Weir, M. W. & Stevenson, H. W. "The effect of verbalization in children's learning as a function of chronological age." CHILD DEVELOPMENT, 30: 143-149, 1959.

Werner, H. COMPARATIVE PSYCHOLOGY OF MENTAL DEVELOPMENT. New York: Follett, 1948.

White, S. H. "Evidence for hierarchical arrangement of learning processes." In Lipsitt, L. P. & Spiker, C. C. (Eds.), ADVANCES IN CHILD DEVELOPMENT AND BEHAVIOR, Vol. 2, New York: Academic Press, pp. 187-220, 1965.

Willer, H. I. THE EFFECT OF INTERPOLATED TRAINING ON REVERSAL AND NONREVERSAL SHIFTS IN GRADE SCHOOL CHILDREN. (Doctoral dissertation, State University of Iowa) Ann Arbor: University Microfilms, No. 64-3439, 1963.

Wohlwill, J. F. "From perception to inference: a dimension of cognitive development." MONOGRAPHS OF THE SOCIETY FOR RESEARCH IN CHILD DEVELOPMENT, 27 (No. 2): 87-107, 1962.

Wolff, J. L. "Concept-shift and discrimination-reversal learning in humans." PSYCH. BULL. 68: 369-408, 1967.

Youniss, J., & Furth, H. G. "Reversal learning in children as a function of overtraining and delayed transfer." J. OF COMP. PHYS. PSYCH., 57: 155-157, 1964.

Zeaman, D., & House, B. J. "The role of attention in retardate discrimination learning." In N. R. Ellis (Ed.), HANDBOOK OF MENTAL DEFICIENCY, New York: McGraw-Hill, pp. 159-223, 1963.

THE ROLE OF COGNITION IN THE DEVELOPMENT OF INNER REALITY

Silvano Arieti, M.D.

Introduction

In a recent publication I wrote that "cognition is or has been, up to now, the Cinderella of psychoanalysis and psychiatry. No other field of the psyche has been so consistently neglected by clinicians and theoreticians alike. Isolated studies and manifestations of interest have not so far developed into a definite trend." (Arieti, 1965a) This situation is particularly unacceptable to people, like the present writer, who believe that cognition should receive the place of honor in psychiatric studies.

Perhaps historians of science will find deeply rooted cultural reasons for this neglect. They may interpret it as part of an overall anti-intellectual cultural climate which started toward the end of the 19th century and continued into the 20th. More specifically, psychologists and psychiatrists may believe that the behavioral school, with its emphasis on overt behavior, and the classic psychoanalytic school, with its emphasis on the study of psychic energy or libido, have been rather ill-disposed, and perhaps, even intolerant of studies on cognition.

An additional reason for this lack of concern is to be found in the fact that the authors who have studied cognition have done so in ways which could not be well integrated with the rest of psychiatric or psychoanalytic studies. If we take the example of Piaget, (1929, 1930, 1952, 1957) who perhaps is today the most prominent author in the field of cognition, we recognize that until recently, he was known only to an elite of psychologists, psychiatrists and psychoanalysts. This situation prevailed not only in the United States but also abroad. Odier (1956) made perhaps the most serious attempt to absorb the contributions of his countryman Piaget into the field of classic psychoanalysis, but he too failed to make a profound impact on psychoanalytic practice or theory. Perhaps it is possible to understand why for a long time even Piaget's most important contributions encountered so much resistance. Although they reveal very well the process of cognitive maturation and adaptation to environmental reality and disclose the various steps by which the child increases his understanding and mastery of the world, they do not represent *intrapsychic life* in its structural and psychodynamic

*This article contains some excerpts from the author's following writings: 1) SOME ELEMENTS OF COGNITIVE PSYCHIATRY, American Journal of Psychotherapy, Vol. 21, 723, 1967, 2) forthcoming new edition of INTERPRETATION OF SCHIZOPHRENIA (in preparation). 3) The Development of Inner Reality, in THE WORLD BIENNIAL OF PSYCHIATRY AND PSYCHOTHERAPY. N. Y.: Basic Books (in press).

aspects. And it is intrapsychic life, called also inner life, inner reality, intrapsychic self, etc., that constitutes the core of psychiatric and psychoanalytic studies.

Isolated perceptions, concepts, skills, problem solving, mathematical thinking, etc., are not in themselves psychiatrically important. A great part of psychic reality consists of more complex internal or internalized constructs. It is true that these constructs are made of elementary cognitive and affective elements, but they are much more than the sum of their parts and are governed by laws or principles different from those which apply to the parts. Piaget has dealt with internalization and inner representation but not to the extent of studying psychodynamically inner reality. The cognitive functions, as described by Piaget, seem really conflict-free, as the ego psychologists, following Hartmann (1950), have classified them. It will be one of the aims of this paper to show that they are not at all—either in their form or their content—alien to man's conflicts but originators of most of them.

Psychiatry and psychoanalysis have intensely studied inner life, but have failed to realize or at least to illustrate to what extent this inner life is made up of cognitive constructs. Many schools of psychiatry and psychoanalysis have stressed the biological aspect of the human being; how he is motivated by instinctual drives, or by basic physiological needs or functions. If the functioning of the human psyche could be reduced to these relatively simple biological mechanisms it would not be too dissimilar from that of subhuman animals. And yet we know how insufficient animal studies are for an understanding of human psychology and psychopathology. In addition to the biological root human psychology has at its disposal a potentially infinite universe of symbols—the vast cognitive field which exists only in a rudimentary form in the non-human. Although even this universe of symbols needs a biological substratum, it transcends its origin.

The human infant lives in poverty of symbols only in the first year of life or approximately during that period which Piaget described as characterized by sensorimotor intelligence. Although a great deal of psychopathology can occur during the first year of life, as Spitz (1945, 1965), Bowlby (1951, 1960) and many others have described, the first year of life from a cognitive point of view is mostly a preparation for what is to develop later. The baby probably experiences very early in life some kind of primitive identity, which includes items of motor behavior, awareness of one's body and of its contacts with the external world. From the end of the first year of life the baby internalizes; that is, he more and more retains as enduring inner objects mental representations of external objects, events and relations. These inner objects acquire a relative independence or autonomy from the external correspondent stimuli which elicited them. They will constitute the inner reality which from a psychological standpoint eventually becomes at least as important as external reality. A gradual building, accruing, and modification of inner reality will occur throughout the life of the individual. This inner reality will always consist of constructs, which do not lend themselves easily to objective, quantifiable or experimental procedures.

Cognition can be divided into three main categories: primary, secondary and tertiary. The designations primary and secondary derive, respectively, from Freud's original formulation of the primary and secondary processes, made in Chapter VII of THE INTERPRETATION OF DREAMS (1901). To quote Jones (1953)"...Freud's revolutionary contribution to psychology was not so much his demonstrating the existence of an unconscious, and perhaps not even his exploration of its content, as his proposition that there are two fundamentally different kinds of mental processes, which he termed primary and secondary...."

Freud gave the first description of the two processes and tried to differentiate the particular laws or principles which rule the primary process only. He called the primary process primary because, according to him, it occurs earlier in the ontogenetic development, and not because it is more important than the secondary. Freud elucidated very well two mechanisms by which the primary process operates: namely the mechanisms of displacement and condensation. However, after this original breakthrough, he did not make other significant discoveries in the field of cognition. This arrest of progress is to be attributed to several factors. First of all, Freud became particularly interested in the primary process as a carrier of unconscious motivation. Secondly, inasmuch as he interpreted motivation more and more in the function of the libido theory, the primary process came to be studied predominantly as a consumer of energy.

The Freudian school, as a rule, has continued to study the primary process almost exclusively from an "economic" point of view. Its main characteristic would be the fact that it does not bind the libido firmly, but allows it to shift from one investment to another (see, for instance, Arlow, 1958). Some Freudians, however, for instance, Schur (1966), reassert the preponderantly cognitive role of the primary process.

The present author is also particularly concerned with the cognitive functions of the primary process; namely what he calls primary cognition. He has described primary cognition in numerous publications, but to maintain the continuity of the exposition, he will repeat here briefly some of the main concepts.

Primary cognition prevails: 1) in those mental mechanisms that are classified in Freudian psychoanalysis as belonging to the id. The dream-work to a large extent follows primary cognition; 2) in the early stages of what Werner (1956) called the microgenetic process; 3) in psychopathological conditions. Its most typical forms occur in advanced stages of schizophrenia (Arieti, 1948, 1955, 1959, 1962). What is particularly important in the present context is that primary cognition appears 4) for a very short period of time early in life as a normal aspect of development. In most cases it is almost immediately overlapped by secondary cognition, so that it is difficult to retrieve it in pure forms, even in the young child.

Secondary cognition consists predominantly of conceptual thinking; it follows most of the time the laws of logic, and inductive and deductive processes. Tertiary cognition occurs in the process of creativity, and most of the time consists of specific combinations of primary and secondary forms of cognition. The important topic of tertiary cognition cannot be dealt with in this paper, and the reader is referred to other writings of the author (Arieti, 1966, 1967a).

In what follows the author will describe some developmental aspects of inner reality, with particular reference to early childhood and adolescence. The reader is reminded once again that by early childhood we refer to the period which starts approximately at a one and a half and includes the whole preschool age. We shall give particular consideration during this period to the formation of various forms of primary cognition, namely to imagery, endocept and prelogical thinking. Although for didactical purposes we may divide early childhood in stages, or in a hierarchy of levels, generally these levels occur in combination, with one or the other predominating at a certain time.

THE PHANTASMIC STAGE OF INNER REALITY

At first psychological internalization occurs through images (Arieti, 1967, chapter 5). An image is a memory trace which assumes the form of a representation. It is an internal quasi reproduction of a perception which does not require the corresponding external stimulus in order to be evoked. The image is indeed one of the earliest and most important foundations of human symbolism, if by symbol we mean something which stands for something else which is not present. For instance, the child closes his eyes and visualizes his mother. She may not be present, but her image is with him; it stands for her. The image is obviously based on the memory traces of previous perceptions of the mother. The mother then acquires a *psychic reality* which is not tied to her physical presence.

Image formation is actually the basis for all higher mental processes. It introduces the child into that inner world which I have called phantasmic (Arieti, 1967). It enables the child not only to re-evoke what is not present, but to retain an affective disposition for the absent object. For instance, the image of the mother may evoke the feelings that the child experiences toward her.

The image thus becomes a substitute for the external object. It is actually an *inner object*, although it is not well organized. It is the most primitive of the inner objects, if, because of their sensorimotor character, we exclude motor engrams from the category of inner objects. When the image's affective associations are pleasant, the evoking of the image reinforces the child's longing or appetite for the corresponding external object. The image thus has a motivational influence in leading the child to search out the actual object, which in its external reality is still more gratifying than the image. The opposite is true when the image's affective associations are unpleasant: the child is motivated not to exchange the unpleasant inner object for the corresponding external one, which is even more unpleasant.

Imagery soon constitutes the foundation of inner psychic reality. It helps the individual not only to understand the world better, but also to create a surrogate for it. Moreover, whatever is known or experienced tends to become a part of the individual who knows and experiences. *Thus cognition can no longer be considered a hierarchy of mechanisms, but also an enduring pyschological content which retains the power to affect its possessor, now and in the future.* *

The child who has reached the level of imagery is now capable of experiencing not only such simple emotions as tension, fear, rage and satisfaction, as he did in the first year of life. but also anxiety, anger, wish, perhaps in a rudimentary form even love and depression, and, finally, security. *Anxiety* is the emotional reaction to the expectation of danger, which is mediated through cognitive media. The danger is not immediate, nor is it always well defined. Its expectation is not the result of a simple perception or signal. At subsequent ages the danger is represented by complicated sets of cognitive constructs. At the age level that we are discussing now it is sustained by images. It generally refers to a danger connected with the important people in the child's life, mother and father, who may punish or withdraw tenderness and affection. *Anger*, at this age, is also rage sustained by images. *Wish* is also an emotional disposition, which is evoked by the image of a pleasant object. The image motivates the individual to replace the image with the real object satisfaction. *Depression* can be felt only at a rudimentary level at this stage, if by depression we mean an experience similar to the one the depressed adult undergoes. At this level depression is an unpleasant feeling evoked by the image of the loss of the wished object and by the experience of displeasure caused by the absence of the wished object. Love, at this stage, remains rudimentary. For the important emotion, or emotional tonality, called after Sullivan's security, the author must again refer the reader to another publication (Arieti, 1967).

*For a study of the phenomenology of images and the formations of their derivatives - paleosymbols - see Arieti (1967, chapter 5).

The child does not remain for a long time at a level of integration, characterized exclusively by sensorimotor behavior, images, simple interpersonal relations, and the simple emotions that we have mentioned. Higher levels impinge almost immediately, so that it is impossible to observe the phantasmic level in pure culture. Nevertheless we can recognize and abstract some of its general characteristics.

Images, of course, remain as a psychological phenomenon for the rest of the life of the individual. At a stage, however, during which language does not exist or is very rudimentary, they play a very important role. Unless initiated, checked or corrected by subsequent levels of integration (secondary process), they follow the rules of the primary process. They are fleeting, hazy, vague, shadowy, cannot be seen in their totality and tend to equate the part with the whole. For instance, if the subject tries to visualize his kitchen, now he reproduces the breakfast table, now a wall of the room, now the stove. An individual arrested at the phantasmic level of development would have great difficulty in distinguishing images and dreams from external reality. He would have no language and could not tell himself of others, "This is an image, a dream, a fantasy; it does not correspond to external reality." He would tend to confuse psychic with external reality, almost as a normal person does when he dreams. Whatever was experienced would become true for him by virtue of its being experienced. Not only is consensual validation from other people impossible at this level, but even intrapsychic or reflexive validation cannot be achieved. The phantasmic level of young children is characterized by what Baldwin (1929) called *adualism*, or at least by difficult dualism: lack of the ability to distinguish between the two realities, that of the mind and that of the external world. This condition may correspond to what orthodox analysts, following Federn (1952), call lack of ego boundary.

Another important aspect that the phantasmic level shares with the sensorimotor level of organization, is the lack of appreciation of causality. The individual cannot ask himself why certain things occur. He either naively accepts them as just happenings, or he expects things to take place in a certain succession, as a sort of habit rather than as a result of causality or of an order of nature. The only phenomenon remotely connected with causation is a subjective or experiential feeling of expectancy, derived from the observation of repeated temporal associations.

THE ENDOCEPT

The endocept is a mental construct representative of a level intermediary between the phantasmic and the verbal. At this level there is a primitive oranization of memory traces, images and motor engrams (or exocepts). This organization results in a construct which does not tend to reproduce reality, as it appears in perceptions or images: it remains nonrepresentational. The endocept, in a certain way, transcends the image, but inasmuch as it is not representational, it is not easily recognizable. On the other hand, it is not an engram (or exocept) which leads to prompt action. Nor can it be transformed into a verbal expression; it remains at a preverbal level. Although it has an emotional component, most of the time it does not expand into a clearly felt emotion.

The endocept is not, of course, a concept. It cannot be shared. We may consider it a disposition to feel, to act, to think, which occurs after simpler mental activity has been inhibited. The awareness of this construct is vague, uncertain and partial. Relative to the image, the endocept involves considerable cognitive expansion; but this expansion occurs at the expense of the subjective awareness, which is decreased in intensity. The endocept is at times experienced as an "atmosphere", an intention, a holistic experience which cannot be divided into parts or words—something similar to what Freud called oceanic feeling. At other times there is no sharp demarcation between endoceptual, subliminal experiences and some vague protoexperiences. On still other occasions, strong but not verbalizable emotions accompany endocepts.

For the evidence of the existence of endocepts and for their importance in adult life, dreams and creativity, the reader is referred elsewhere (Arieti, 1967, especially chapter 6). In children endocepts remain in the forms of vague memories which will affect subsequent periods of life. In adult life they often evoke memories expressed with mature language which was not available to the child when the experiences originally took place.

Endoceptual experiences exist even when the child has already learned some linguistic expressions; expressions, however, which are too simple to represent the complexities of these experiences. To avoid misinterpretations I wish to repeat at this point that the acquisition of language (that is, the verbal level) overlaps the endoceptual, phantasmic, and to a small degree, even the sensorimotor (or exoceptual) levels.

PRECONCEPTUAL LEVELS OF THINKING

It is beyond the purpose of this essay to study the child's acquisition of language and the experience of high level emotions, which presuppose verbal symbols. I am referring to the mature experience of depression, hate, love, joy and derivative emotions (see Arieti, 1967, chapter 7). From the acquisition of language (naming things) to a logical organization of concepts various substages follow each other so rapidly and overlap in so many multiple ways that it is very difficult to retrace and individualize them. These intermediary stages are more pronounced and more easily recognizable in pathological conditions.

Some of these stages, called by some authors prelogical and by Arieti (1948, 1955) paleological (or ancient logic) follow a type of cognition which is irrational according to our usual logical standards. However, paleologic thinking is not haphazard, but susceptible of being interpreted as following an organization or "logic" of its own. Paleologic thinking can be understood in accordance with Von Domarus' principle (1944), which (in a formulation slightly modified by me), states: Whereas in mature cognition or secondary cognition identity is accepted only upon the basis of identical subjects, in paleologic thinking identity is based upon the basis of identical predicates. In other publications (1965, 1967) I have illustrated the cognitive relations between part perception, paleologic thinking and some psychological mechanisms reported by ethologists, for instance Tinbergen (1951).

Paleologic cognition occurs for a short period of time early in childhood, from the age of one to three. It is difficut to recognize because it is, in most instances, overlapped by secondary cognition. Here are a few examples: an 18 month old child is shown pictures of different men. In each instance he says: "daddy, daddy". It is not enough to interpret this verbal behavior of the child by stating that he is making a mistake or that his mistake is due to lack of knowledge, inadequate experience of the world or inadequate vocabulary. Obviously he makes what we consider a mistake; however, even in the making of the mistake, he follows a mental process. From perceptual stimuli he proceeds to an act of individualization and recognition. Because the pictures show similarities with the perception of his daddy he puts all these male representations into one category: they are all daddy or daddies. In other words, the child tends to make generalizations and classifications, which are wrong according to a more mature type of thinking. Obviously there is in this instance what to the adult mind appears a confusion between similarity and identity. Children tend to give the role of an identifying or essential predicate to what is instead a secondary detail, attribute, part, or predicate. This part is the essential one to them either because of its conspicuous perceptual qualities or because of its association with previous very significant experiences. Levin reported that a child, twenty-five months old, was calling "wheel" anything which was made of white rubber, as for example, the white rubber guard which was supplied with little boys' toilet seats to deflect urine. The child knew the meaning of the word wheel as applied, for example, to the wheel of a toy car. This child had many toy cars whose wheels, when made of rubber, were always of white rubber. It is obvious that an identification had occurred because of the same characteristic, "white rubber".*

A girl, three years and nine months old, saw two nuns walking together, and told her mother, "Mommy, look at the twins". She thought that the nuns were twins because they were dressed alike. The characteristic of being dressed alike, which twins often

*This confusion between identity and similarity reacquires prominence in some psychopathological conditions. It has been studied intensely in schizophrenia by Von Domarus (1944) and later Arieti (1948, 1955).

have, led to the identification with the nuns.

Again it is not enough to say that the child made   an error, or that her error was due to the fact that she did not know the meaning of the word "twin". What we want to stress is that she had the propensity to put into the category "twin" people who are dressed alike.

At this age children have become aware of causality and repeatedly ask why. At first causality is teleological: events are believed to occur "because" they are willed or wanted by people or by anthropomorphized forces.

We should not concluded that young children *must* think paleologically: they only have a propensity to do so. Unless abnormal conditions (either environmental or biological) make difficult either the process of maturation or the process of becoming part of the adult world, this propensity is almost entirely and very rapidly overpowered by the adoption of secondary process cognition. In secondary process cognition the individual learns to distinguish essential from nonessential predicates, and develops more and more the tendency to identify subjects which are indissolubly tied to essential predicates.

THE IMAGE OF MOTHER AND THE SELF-IMAGE

The randomness of experience is more and more superseded by the gradual organization of inner constructs. These constructs continuously exchange some of their components, and increase in differentiation, rank and order. A large number of them, however, retain the enduring mark of their individuality. Although in early childhood they consist of the cognitive forms that we have described (images, endocepts, paleologic thoughts) and of their accompanying feelings (from sensations to emotions) they become more and more complicated and difficult to analyze. Some of them have powerful effects and have an intense life of their own, even if at the stage of our knowledge we cannot give them an anatomical location or a neurophysiological interpretation. They may be considered the very inhabitants of inner reality. The two most important ones in the preschool age, and the only two which we shall describe in this paper, are the image of mother and the self-image.

Before proceeding we must warn the reader about a confusion which may result from the two different meanings given to the word "image" in psychological and psychiatric literature. The word image is often used, as we did in a previous section of this paper, in reference to the simple sensorial images which tend to reproduce perceptions. With this term we shall now refer also to those much higher psychological constructs or inner objects which represent whatever is connected with a person: for instance, in this more elaborate sense, *the image of the mother* would mean a synthesis of what the child feels and knows about her. From the context the reader will easily realize which of the two connotations we refer to.

In normal circumstances the mother as an inner object will consist of a group of agreeable images: as the giver, the helper, the assuager of hunger, thirst, cold, loneliness, immobility and any other discomfort. She becomes the prototype of the good inner object.

The negative characteristics of mother play a secondary role which loses significance in the context of the good inner object. In pathological conditions the mother becomes a malevolent object and an attempt is made to repress this object from consciousness. (Arieti, 1967, 1968)

Much more difficult to describe in early childhood is the self-image. This construct will be easier to understand in later developmental stages. At the sensorimotor level the primordial self probably consisted of a bundle of relatively simple relations between feelings, kinesthetic sensations, perceptions, motor activity and a partial integration of these elements. At the phantasmic level the child who is raised in normal circumstances learns to experience himself not exclusively as a cluster of feelings and of self-initiated movements, but also as a body image and as an entity having many kinds of relations with other images, especially those of the parents. Inasmuch as the child cannot see his own face, his own visual image will be faceless— as, indeed, he will tend to see himself in dreams throughout his life. He wishes however, to be in appearance, gestures and actions like people toward who he has a pleasant emotional attitude or by whom he feels protected and gratified. The wish tends to be experienced as reality and he believes that he is or is about to become like the others or as powerful as the others. Because of the reality value of wishes and images, a feeling results which in psychoanalytic literature has been called feeling of omnipotence.

In the subsequent endoceptual and paleologic stages the self-image will acquire many more elements. However, these elements will continue to be integrated so that the self-image will continue to be experienced as a unity, as an entity separate from the rest of the world. The psychological life of the child will no longer be limited to acting and experiencing but will include also observing oneself and having an image of oneself.

In a large part of psychological and psychiatric literature a confusion exists between the concepts of self and of self-image. In this paper we cannot go into this complicated subject which we shall discuss in another publication. Also in a large part of the psychiatric literature the self and the consequent self-image are conceived predominantly in a passive role. For instance, Sullivan has indicated that the preconceptual and first conceptual appraisals of the self are determined by the relationships of the child with the significant adults. Sullivan (1953) considers the self (and self-image) as consisting of reflected appraisals from the significant adults: the child would see himself and feel about himself as his parents, especially the mother, see him and feel about him. What is not taken into account in this conception is the fact that the self is not merely a passive reflection. The mechanism of the formation of the self cannot be compared to the function of a mirror. If we want to use the metaphor of the mirror, we must specify that we mean an activated mirror which adds to the reflected images its own distortions, especially those distortions which at an early age are caused by primary cognition. The child does not merely respond to the environment. He integrates experiences and transforms them into inner reality, into increasingly complicated structures. He is indeed in a position to make a contribution to the formation of his own self.

The self-image consists of three parts: body-image, self-identity and self-esteem. The body-image consists of the internalized visual, kinesthetic, tactile, and other sensations and perceptions connected with one's body. The body is discovered by degrees. The body-image eventually will be connected with belonging to one of the two genders. Self-identity, called also personal identity or ego-identity, depends on the discovery of oneself not only as continuous and as same, but also as having certain characteristics, a role in the group to which the person belongs.

Self-esteem depends on the child's ability to do what he wants to do; but is also connected wih his capacity to avoid doing what the parents do not want him to do. Later it is connected also with his capacity to do what his parents want him to do. His behavior is explicitly or by implication classified by the adults as bad or good. Self-identity and self-esteem seem thus to be related, as Sullivan has emphasized, to the evaluation that the child receives from the significant adults. However, again, this self-evaluation is not an exact reproduction of the one made by the adults. The child is impressed more by the appraisals which hurt him the most or please him the most. These partial salient appraisals and the ways they are intergrated with other elements will make up the self-image.

Other authors have referred to other cognitive elements which enter in the develpment of the self-image, although they have not stressed their cognitive nature. For instance, Adler (1927) wrote extensively about the inferiority feeling or inferiority complex which he attributed to organic inferiority, or to the fact that the child feels little, helpless and insecure in an adult world. It seems to me that although the child is aware of his littleness he accepts it, because very early in life he discovers that he will grow up, that everybody expects him to grow up and become another adult. However, in the process of growing up and developing more and more his ability to imagine, to think and to infer, the child during the later part of childhood becomes more aware of a discrepancy between what he is and what he and the others wish him to be. Although he is not able to verbalize these ideas in definite formulations, he becomes aware that there is a gap between an ideal state which the others or he himself conceive and the reality of his personal situation. This gap becomes an inner construct, part of his inner reality. Elsewhere I have described how unconditional love from the parents early in childhood and feelings of basic trust later, will tend to neutralize the effect of this ideality gap, as I call it. (Arieti, 1967a, chapter 14)

In such conditions as psychoneurosis, but especially in psychopathic personality and schizophrenia, specific factors contribute to the development of abnormal self-image (Arieti, 1967a,b; 1968).

SECONDARY COGNITION: THE CONCEPT

It is beyond the scope of this paper to describe the stages intermediary between early childhood and mature adulthood. We shall consider only the role of concepts. As Vygotsky (1962) has illustrated, conceptual thinking starts early in life, but it is in adolescence that it acquires prominence. Conceptual life is a necessary and very important part of mature life. Many authors (Piaget, 1952; Bruner et al, 1956; Werner and Kaplan, 1963) have made important studies of the mechanisms involved in the formation of concepts and of concepts as psychological forms. We shall instead stress their content. This position is a departure from what this author has done in reference to less mature forms of cognition (Arieti, 1948, 1955). In fact in psychiatric studies, especially in conditions like schizophrenia where severe pathology is found, it is important to study not only content but also form; it is crucial to understand not only *what* the individual experiences but *how* he experiences. Is he perceiving in terms of parts of wholes? Is he using images, endocepts, paleologic cognition? How are these cognitive modalities varying during the course of the illness or even of the single therapeutic session? What is the meaning of such variety of forms? On the other hand, the psychiatrist's and analyst's main interest in concepts resides in determining how their content affects psychodynamically human life.

In a large part of psychiatric, psychoanalytic, and psychologic literature concepts are considered static, purely intellectual entities, separate from human emotions and unimportant in psychodynamic studies. The present author cannot adhere to this point of view. Concepts and organized clusters of concepts become depositories of emotions and also originators of new emotions. They have a great deal to do with the conflicts of man, his achievements and his frustrations, his states of happiness or despair, of anxiety or of security (Arieti, 1965). They become the repositories of intangible feelings and values. Not only every concept has an emotional counterpart, but concepts are necessary for high emotions. In the course of reaching adulthood, emotional and conceptual processes become more and more intimately interconnected. It is impossible to separate the two. They form a circular process. The emotional accompaniment of a cognitive process becomes the propelling drive not only toward action but also toward further cognitive processes. Only emotions can stimulate man to overcome the hardship of some cognitive processes and lead to complicated symbolic, interpersonal and abstract processes. On the other hand, only cognitive processes can extend indefinitely the realm of emotions. As I have illustrated elsewhere, some very important human emotions could not exist without a conceptual foundation (Arieti, 1967). For instance, depression should not be confused with the state of deprivation, discomfort or anaclitic frustration of lower animal forms or human babies. Depression requires an understanding of the meaning of loss (actual or symbolic) and a state of despair (which follows a belief that what is lost cannot be retrieved). The importance of this understanding is not recognized, because it is based on cognitive processes which often become almost immediately unconscious (see below). The conceptual presuppositions to mature love, to symbolic anxiety, to hate (as distinguished from rage or anger) have been described elsewhere (Arieti, 1967).

Reification of concepts (that is assumption that concepts faithfully correspond to external reality) is considered by science an invalid procedure. It is obvious that concepts may not correspond to external reality, but they nevertheless do have an enduring psychological reality. They remain as parts of inner reality; they do not fade with the termination of the neuronal mechanisms which were necessary for their occurrence.

Even what I said about the relative lack of importance of concepts as *forms* needs clarification. Concepts too undergo organization of increasing order, rank and level, and become components or organized conceptual constructs, whose grammar and syntax we do not know yet. Undoubtedly future studies will reveal the structure of these so-far obscure organizations.

From a psychiatric and psychoanalytic point of view the greatest importance of concepts resides in the fact that to a large extent they come to constitute the self-image (Arieti, 1965b). When this development occurs, the previous self-images that we have described are not completely obliterated. They remain throughout the life of the individual in the forms of minor components of the adult self-image or as repressed or suppressed forms. In adolescence, however, concepts emerge as the major part of the self-image. Concepts like inner worth, personal significance, mental outlook, more mature evaluations of appraisals reflected from others, attitudes toward ideals, aspirations, capacity to receive and give acceptance, affection, and love, are integral parts of the self and of the self-image, together with the emotions which accompany these concepts. These concepts and emotions which constitute the self are generally not consistent with one another, in spite of a prolonged attempt made by the individual to organize them logically.

The motivation of the human being varies according to the various levels of development. When higher levels emerge, motivations originated at lower levels do not cease to exist. At a very elementary sensorimotor level the motivation consists of obtaining immediate pleasure and avoidance of immediate displeasure. Gratification of bodily needs or states like hunger, thirst, and sexual urges are important motivational factors at this level. When imagery emerges, either phylogenetically or ontogenetically, the individual becomes capable of wishing for something which is not present and is motivated toward the fulfillment of his wishes. He will continue to be wish-motivated in more advanced stages of primary cognition, such as the paleological stage. Although the motivation can always be understood as a search for or as an attempt to retain pleasure and avoid unpleasure, gratification of the self becomes the main motivational factor at a conceptual level of development. Certainly, the individual is throughout his life concerned with danger: immediate danger, which elicits fear, and a more distant or symbolic danger which elicits anxiety. However, whereas at earlier levels of development this danger is experienced as a threat to the physical self, at higher levels it is many times experienced as a threat to an acceptable image of the self.

Many psychologic defenses are devices to protect the self or the self-image. Here are a few examples. The detached or schizoid person decreases his emotional or actual participation in life in order not to feel inadequate and injure his self-image. The hypochondriac protects his self by blaming only his body for his difficulties. These examples could be multiplied endlessly. In typical psychoneuroses, such as phobic conditions and obsessive-compulsive syndromes, the self is protected by a partial return to primary cognition. In the schizophrenic psychosis the self is defended by a much more extensive return to primary cognition.

The defenses we have referred to have most of the time an unconscious organization. Contrary to what is generally believed, repression and suppression from awareness do not apply only to primitive strivings and to the contents of primary cognition, but also to the content of high conceptual ideation. Important ideational constructs are in some cases completely repressed, because ungratifying or inconsistent with one's cherished self-image.

As described elsewhere, no anticipation and understanding of the future is possible without cognitive processes (Arieti, 1967b). In order to feed his present self-esteem and maintain an adequate self-image, the young individual has, so to say, to borrow from his expectations and hopes for the future. If he is disappointed about the present, he may secretly say to himself "one day it will happen." It is when he loses faith in the future, and a present vacillating self-esteem cannot be supported by hope for the future, that severe psychopathological conditions may develop (Arieti, 1967b).

Most concepts which affect the individual are learned from others, either private persons or social and cultural institutions. This point has been stressed in the Whorf-Sapir theory of cognition (Whorf, 1956). Culture, with its systems of knowledge, languages, beliefs, and values bestows upon each person a patrimony of concepts which becomes a part of the individual. This does not mean that a cognitive approach to psychiatry and psychoanalysis should be equated to an interpersonal-cultural one. Certainly a cognitive approach is closer to the cultural than to one based on instinctual theories. However, it does not conceive the individual as molded entirely by culture or by interpersonal relations. First of all, primary cognition affects the individual deeply and in various ways. Secondly, the person's various uses of the different modalities of cognition confers on him a certain individuality which is not a derivative of cultural factors.

Nevertheless, it is accurate to say that a given culture predisposes the individual to build some self-images rather than others and special patterns of defenses. This topic is too vast to be discussed here. However, it is relevant to mention that even the need to build and retain a self-image which is gratifying, is to a large extent culturally determined. In some medieval cultures, for instance, the prevailing philosophy was that of mortifying the self and of depicting the individual as an insignificant entity, a sinner, an individual who is not " his own". This self-effacing cultural attitude should not be confused with individualistic masochistic traits.

GENERAL ASPECTS OF INNER REALITY

We have attempted to describe in this paper several levels of inner reality, or organizational ranks, from the simplest to the most complex. Although inner constructs consist of cognitive and affective components, in this paper we have focused on the cognitive. Whereas some of these structures are relatively well known, the knowledge of others is still rudimentary. The methodology that we have followed is similar to that of Werner's (1957) comparative developmental approach.

The description of different levels of organization is occasionally criticized by some authors as something reducing the psyche to static layers, reminiscent of geological strata, not dealing with something vital and evolving. It would be something similar to "still pictures, not to a cinema." On the contrary, a developmental process must be conceived as something moving, emerging, a denouement in time. Undoubtedly we do not know all the laws which apply to inner structures or to their temporal unfolding. Probably, insights obtained through new approaches, like the one introduced by Von Bertalanffy's General Systems Theory (1956, 1966), will do much to clarify the mysteries of inner reality. Inner reality is indeed an "open system"; and is always related to external reality.

From a general point of view inner reality can be examined from three different aspects: 1) representational function, 2) subjectivity, 3) potentiality. These three aspects are so interrelated that we cannot understand any of them without taking into consideration the other two. For didactical reasons only we shall discuss them separately.

The representational function is the function which permits inner constructs to represent objects or events of the external world. The individual himself as an organism and as a person can be represented by the self-image. These representations are not exact or even analogic reproductions of what they intend to stand for. They are mediated by intrapsychic mechanisms and are under the influence of previous experience. Psychologically they may become more important than external reality.

The second aspect of inner reality refers to the fact that what is objective or objectivizable becomes subjective, is appropriated by the individual as a subjective experience, acquires a subjective reality and becomes part of the individual himself. This subjectivization is not adequately accounted for by psychological or psychiatric authors who give exclusive or almost exclusive importance to the environment. This subjectivization is a phenomenon as difficult to understand as the whole mind-body problem. The intensity of a subjective construct does not correspond to the external event or stimulus to which it refers. It depends, as we have already mentioned, on the selections of other constructs with which it is integrated, and on the mechanisms used in such integration. The subjective aspect of inner life is particularly evident when we study sensations and emotions, but it is obvious that emotions accompany and transform cognitive constructs and in their turn are transformed by them.

The potentiality of inner reality can be seen in the way 1) it affects the behavior of the individual, in relation to other people, himself, the world in general, 2) it affects itself. In other words, inner reality feeds on the external world as well as on itself.

How inner reality leads the individual to the states of mental health or mental disease is a topic too vast to be considered here. There is another subject, however, which we must consider before concluding this paper. In subhuman animals and during the first 1½-2 years of human life inner reality exists only a rudimentary form. In the growing and grown human being, however, it becomes so intense that sometime in the evolution of homo sapiens mechanisms become organized which had the purpose of decreasing its intensity and prominence. These various mechanisms have been described, under various terminologies, in psychological, psychiatric and psychoanalytic literatures. The following ones should be considered: 1) Displacement or transformation of a construct into another (like in regression, fixation, paleologic thinking, etc.) 2) Decrease of affective or sensuous content, for instance by the mechanisms called denial, reaction-formation, undoing, blunting of affect, depersonalization, alienation, hysterical anesthesia, etc. 3) Suppression, or more or less voluntary removal of some psychological content from the focus of attention or of consciousness. This content goes into a state of quiesence, like a language or skill that is not used. 4) Repression or removal of psychological content from consciousness. The study of this mechanism is the main topic of psychoanalysis.

These mechanisms alter and complicate but do not eliminate inner life.

References

Adler, A., UNDERSTANDING HUMAN NATURE. Garden City, N. Y. Garden City Publishing Co., 1927.

Arieti, S., "Special Logic of Schizophrenic and Other Types of Autistic Thought." PSYCHIATRY 11: 325, 1948.

Arieti, S., INTERPRETATION OF SCHIZOPHRENIA. Brunner, N. Y., 1955.

Arieti, S., "Schizophrenia. The Manifest Symptomatology, the Psychodynamic and Formal Mechanisms." In AMERICAN HANDBOOK OF PSYCHIATRY, Vol. 1. Arieti, S. (Ed.) Basic Books, N.Y., pp. 455-484, 1959.

Arieti, S. "The Microgeny of Thought and Perception." Arch. Gen. Psychiat., 6: 454, 1962.

Arieti, S., "Contributions to Cognition from Psychoanalytic Theory." In SCIENCE AND PSYCHOANALYSIS, Vol. 8. Masserman, J. (Ed.) Grune & Stratton, N. Y., pp. 16-37, 1965a.

Arieti, S., "Conceptual and Cognitive Psychiatry." AM. J. PSYCHIAT., 122, 361, 1965b.

Arieti, S., "Creativity and Its Cultivation: Relation to Psychopathology and Mental Health." In AMERICAN HANDBOOK OF PSYCHIATRY, Vol. 3. Arieti, S. (Ed.) Basic Books, N.Y., 1966.

Arieti, S., THE INTRAPSYCHIC SELF: FEELING, COGNITION AND CREATIVITY IN HEALTH AND MENTAL ILLNESS. Basic Books, N. Y., 1967a.

Arieti, S., "New Views on the Psychodynamics of Schizophrenia." AMER. J. PSYCHIAT. 124: 4, 1967b.

Arieti, S., "The Psychodynamics of Schizophrenia: A Reconsideration." AMER. J. PSYCHOTHERAPY, Vol. 22, July 1968.

Arlow, J. A., Report on Panel: "The Psychoanalytic Theory of Thinking." J. AM. PSYCHOANAL. ASS. 6: 143, 1958.

Baldwin, J. M., Quoted by Piaget (1929).

Bowlby, J., "Maternal Care and Mental Health." WHO MONOGRAPH SERIES, No. 2, 1951.

Bowlby, J., "Grief and Mourning in Infancy." THE PSYCHOANALYTIC STUDY OF THE CHILD, Vol. 15. Intern. Univ. Press, N.Y., 1960.

Bruner, J. S., Goodnow, J. J. and Austin, G. A. A STUDY OF THINKING. Wiley, N. Y., 1956.

Federn, P. EGO PSYCHOLOGY AND THE PSYCHOSES. Basic Books, N. Y., 1952.

Freud, S. THE INTERPRETATION OF DREAMS. Basic Books, N.Y., 1960.

Hartmann, H., "Psychoanalysis and Development Psychology." In PSYCHOANALYTIC STUDY OF THE CHILD, Vol. 5. Intern. Univ. Press, N.Y., 1950.

Jones, E., THE LIFE AND WORK OF SIGMUND FREUD, Vol. 1. Basic Books, N. Y., 1953.

Levin, M., "Misunderstanding of the Pathogenesis of Schizophrenia, Arising from the Concept of 'Splitting'." AMER. J. PSYCHIAT.94: 877, 1938.

Odier, C., ANXIETY AND MAGIC THINKING. Intern. Univ. Press, N. Y., 1956.

Piaget, J., THE CHILD'S CONCEPTION OF THE WORLD. Harcourt, Brace, N.Y., 1929.

Piaget, J., THE CHILD'S CONCEPTION OF PHYSICAL CAUSALITY. Harcourt, Brace, N.Y., 1930.

Piaget, J., THE ORIGINS OF INTELLIGENCE IN CHILDREN. Intern. Univ. Press, N.Y., 1952.

Piaget, J., LOGIC AND PSYCHOLOGY. Basic Books, N.Y., 1957.

Schur, M., THE ID AND THE REGULATORY PRINCIPLES OF MENTAL FUNCTIONING. Intern. Univ. Press, N.Y., 1966.

Spitz, R., "Diacritic and Coenesthetic Organization." PSYCHOANAL. REV., 32: 146, 1945.

Spitz, R., THE FIRST YEAR OF LIFE. A PSYCHOANALYTIC STUDY OF NORMAL AND DEVIANT DEVELOPMENT OF OBJECT RELATIONS. Intern. Univ. Press N. Y., 1965.

Sullivan, H.S., CONCEPTIONS OF MODERN PSYCHIATRY. Norton, N.Y., 1953.

Tinbergen, N., THE STUDY OF INSTINCT. Clarendon, Oxford., 1951.

Von Bertalanffy, L., "General Systems Theory." In Von Bertalanffy, L. and Rapaport, A. (Eds.) SOCIETY FOR THE ADVANCEMENT OF GENERAL SYSTEMS THEORY. Ann Arbor, Univ. of Michigan Press., 1956.

Von Bertalanffy, L., "General Systems Theory and Psychiatry." In AMERICAN HANDBOOK OF PSYCHIATRY, Vol. 3. Arieti, S. (Ed.) Basic Books, N. Y., 1966.

Von Domarus, E., "The Specific Laws of Logic in Schizophrenia." LANGUAGE AND THOUGHT IN SCHIZOPHRENIA: COLLECTED PAPERS. Kasamin, J. S., (Ed.) Univ. of California Press, 1944.

Vygotsky, L. S., THOUGHT AND LANGUAGE. M.I.T. Press, Cambridge, Mass., 1962.

Werner, H., "Microgenesis and Aphasia." J. ABNORM. SOC. PSYCHOL., 52: 347, 1956.

Werner, H., COMPARATIVE PSYCHOLOGY OF MENTAL DEVELOPMENT. Intern. Univ. Press, N.Y., 1957.

Werner, H. and Kaplan, B., SYMBOL FORMATION. AN ORGANISMIC-DEVELOPMENTAL APPROACH TO LANGUAGE AND THE EXPRESSION OF THOUGHT. Wiley, N.Y., 1963.

Whorf, B. L., LANGUAGE, THOUGHT AND REALITY. Wiley and Technology Press, N.Y., 1956.

CONTRIBUTIONS OF THE MENTALLY RETARDED
TOWARD A THEORY OF COGNITIVE DEVELOPMENT

Jane W. Kessler, Ph.D.

The psychological literature appearing since 1960 bears impressive witness to two major trends, both of which represent a revival of old interests. One of these is the attention given to the development of cognition, the processes by which the organism acquires, stores, and utilizes information. The second is the dramatic increase of research interest in the mentally retarded which coincided with the increased lay and professional interest in better services for the retarded. Although the change in attitude was accelerated by the Kennedy-sponsored task forces and ensuing federal legislation, it was preceded by a growing feeling in many quarters that the mentally retarded were being short-changed by the nihilism implicit in the Doll definition for mental retardation (1941) and by the assumptions that were made regarding the nature of the IQ and its supposedly inevitable effects on learning, personality, and social adjustment. Numerous reviews of behavioral and learning studies of the mentally retarded have appeared (Johnson and Blake, 1960; Ellis, 1963; Zigler, 1966a; Robinson and Robinson, 1965). These reviews have taken the mentally retarded as a special population and centered their attention around the similarities and differences of this group compared to normal populations, usually normal children. There has often been the implication that such research should be useful; *i.e.* commutable into therapeutic action to improve the functioning of the retarded. Indeed, McPherson complained when research was dictated more by theoretical considerations than by a true interest in mental retardation: "This impression of increased interest in the experimental approach to learning and mental deficiency is negated somewhat by the realization that four of these papers (14 studies in all) have utilized mental defectives because of their usefulness for learning data and theory *per se*, rather than because of an interest in this type of learner," (1958, p. 876). Robinson and Robinson also commented that "many learning theorists have been much more interested in learning processes *per se* than in the nature of the organism that is learning....When research is conceived in this fashion, it may well yield results which are very important to the scientist who is interested in general laws of behavior but it is of relatively little use to workers whose primary interest lies in the understanding of individual differences, particularly differences among retarded children and between them and children who are brighter than they"(1965, p. 327).

Contrary to these sentiments, in this review we will look at the recent research output to see what contributions have been made toward a theory of normal cognitive development rather than to the welfare of the mentally retarded. We should have reached the point where ideas can be exported out of the area of retardation as well as imported into it, thus bringing closer together these two major thrusts of interest which have tended to be parallel rather than interlocking. It is interesting to note that with the exception of Maccoby (1964), all the annual reviews of developmental psychology have specifically omitted the topic of mental retardation from their discussion. Our goal raises the question as to what the necessary ingredients would be for a complete theory of cognitive development which in turn depends on the definition of "cognition." There are as many definitions as there are writers on the subject, but we are thinking of it in the broadest sense possible, namely to refer to all those processes above the reflex level which produce some change in behavior. Key issues to which a theory should address itself include: 1) the neurophysiological correlates of learning; 2) the nature of changes which occur with development; 3) the relationship of perceptual and motor development to later cognitive functioning; 4) the relationship of language to cognitive development; 5) the sources of individual differences; and 6) the interdependence of affect and cognition. As the research material is presented, the reader will soon note that there is considerable overlapping in these areas, particularly between 2) and 5).

The author freely admits many arbitrary decisions in the categorization process. Also, the vast amount of material dealing with cultural factors and intellectual development is slighted because this topic is considered in several other chapters of this volume, whereas the neurophysiological correlates of learning are given relatively complete coverage. Finally, the reader will observe several detours from the path of true research reporting into the rough area of clinical practice. There are many issues regarding the diagnosis and treatment of mental retardation, and its first cousin, "cerebral minimal dysfunction," which are of timely concern and should be considered in the light of relevant research evidence, even when this is scanty or virtually nonexistent.

NEUROPHYSIOLOGICAL CORRELATES OF LEARNING

Neuroanatomical Approach

The general theoretical issue is clearly stated in Hebb's dictum: "Modern psychology takes completely for granted that behavior and neural function are perfectly correlated, that one is completely caused by the other" (1949, p. xiii). the first problem is the extent to which neural connections determine behavior which introduces the concepts regarding cortical localization. Historically, the relationship between brain structure and mental activity was first approached by matching the pathologic findings of structural brain lesions with the resultant psychological disorder. Broca (1861) was the first of the clinical neurologists who attempted to localize the cerebral areas responsible for such complex functions as speech, writing, calculation, reading, and so on. Lashley, an experimental psychologist, was one of the first to cast doubt on the specific action ascribed to the various circumscribed cortical areas which had been mapped out in this way. He found that rats which had been trained to run a maze could be retrained to criterion after extensive cortical ablations, regardless of the area which was removed. He countered the localization theory with a theory of "equipotentiality" to explain his thesis that the degree of functional impairment is proportional to the amount of tissue removed rather than dependent on the locus of lesion (1929).

In retrospect, it is clear that the original localization and equipotentiality theories equally over-simplified the brain-behavior relationship and modern concepts of brain function have combined features of both. There is no argument with the clinical facts that lesions in different parts of the brain give rise to different symptoms but the connection between the structural pathology and the psychological disorder is nowhere near as "clear" as it seemed initially. Isolated pathological foci affect behavioral functions multiply rather than singly; and conversely, the same psychological function can be disordered by lesions in varied parts of the cortex. Also, restoration of function after brain damage cannot be explained by the simple transfer of the disturbed function to the "vicarious" part of the symmetrically opposite hemisphere but, rather, in terms of a functional reorganization. Competencies like reading and speech are no longer regarded as unitary functions but rather as activities which must be further analyzed in terms of underlying mental processes. For instance, reading, which usually takes place by visual analysis and synthesis of letter signs, can be produced along different pathways of tactile and motor tracing of letters after damage to the occipital region (Luria, 1948). In his critique of the localization theory, Luria states: "These facts demonstrate conclusively that the complex forms of behavior activity cannot in any sense of the term be regarded as simple properties, incapable of further subdivision, and firmly associated with particular groups of nerve cells in the cortex...both the concept of functions and the simplified ideas of their direct localization in circumscribed areas of the brain require serious revision" (1966, p. 16).

In her impressive review of the literature, Rapin summarizes the current status regarding localization. The greatest specificity occurs in the sensory receiving and motor output zones of the cortex. It is virtually impossible to destroy complex behavior by a lesion at a single site. "Lesions of the dominant hemisphere interfere with verbal functions, those in the anterior half of the brain impair executive behavior, and those situated in the posterior half of the brain lead to perceptual deficits....Lesions in the mammillary bodies or bilateral removal of hippocampus and hippocampal gyrus destroy recent memory and the ability to learn. The limbic system and hypothalamus are concerned with motivation and the reticular formation with vigilance." (Rapin, 1965, p. 7). Luria makes an interesting suggestion that a lesion of the posterior (occipito-parietal) divisions of the dominant hemisphere leads to the disturbance of synthesis of individual elements into simultaneous groups but it does not affect the synthesis of elements organized serially in time. The opposite is true for lesions of the fronto-temporal divisions of the dominant hemisphere as shown by the patients' difficulties with auditory memory (which requires serial organization of the input) compared to their competence with visual memory (which requires simultaneous organization of the input in some kind of figure ground or spatial configuration) (1966). Although this idea has not received general support from other investigators, it has considerable heuristic value. It is certainly important to distinguish between the processes of organizing sensory input received at a single moment and those processes involved in organizing sensory input received over a period of time, although this often resolves into the traditional distinction of visual (simultaneous) versus auditory (serial) stimulation.

Developmental Considerations

Further complications are introduced when we look at the localization question from a developmental point of view. A lesion sustained early in life has different consequences compared to those resulting from a lesion occurring at maturity. Young children are much more likely than adults to recover normal function following a *focal* neurologic deficit (Rapin, 1965). Studies of Kennard (1938, 1942) and Benjamin and Thompson (1959) demonstrated that experimental lesions in young animals produced less motor and less sensory deficit than comparable lesions in older animals. Teuber and Rudel (1962) suggested that, particularly with simple functions, there may be comparatively larger areas of representation in the young brain, a greater plasticity and flexibility as to which neuronal circuits are potentially capable of establishing behavior functions. This can be seen in the fact that there is no difference in language development in children with right and left infantile hemiplegias (Basser, 1962). Apparently the cerebral hemispheres are equipotential in relation to language at birth, but once the specialization of definite cortical areas responsible for the development of speech takes place, the flexibility is lost. In children older than approximately 6 years and in adults, speech cannot shift to the opposite hemisphere so that a massive lesion in the speech area will almost always result in a permanent language deficit.

On the other hand, early injury seems to have a more pervasive effect on higher mental functions. Although the right and left infantile hemiplegics are equally good (or equally poor) in language development, they are likely to have generalized mental retardation which rarely accompanies acquired hemiplegia. Graham and her co-workers at the University of Wisconsin have reported a number of studies regarding the psychological effects of brain injury in the preschool child (Graham, *et al.*, 1963; Ernhart, *et al.*, 1963). To start with, they found that selecting a sample of preschool children with unequivocal evidence of brain damage was complicated by the frequency of mental retardation. In the final experimental group of 70 children, 15 had IQ's between 50 and 70, even though they had tried to eliminate mental retardation as a confounding variable. The pattern of psychological functioning in this group not only differed from that of uninjured children; it also differed from that found after injury to the adult brain (and also from that commonly assumed to typify the brain-injured child). Whereas the adult pattern is one of relatively greater impairment of conceptual and perceptual-motor functions with relatively unimpaired vocabulary performance, in the brain-injured preschool children, there were no significant differences in degree of impairment in these areas. Hebb also reported that damage to the infant brain affected later performance on vocabulary tests, information, and the like at least as much as performance on other tests (1942).

There may also be differences in effects of injuries occurring at different stages of early development. Graham *et al.* (1962) also studies a group of children who suffered perinatal anoxia and might therefore be "possibly injured." The anoxic group was less impaired on all functions than the known brain injured group, but even more important, the anoxic children were significantly impaired in vocabulary ability but were *not* impaired in perceptual-motor ability. Thus, vocabulary impairment (which correlates well with general intelligence measures) seems to be inversely related and perceptual-motor impairment directly related to the age at which injury occurs. In general, this supports the earlier conclusion reported by Hebb: "It appears, therefore, that an early injury may prevent the development of some intellectual capacities that an equally extensive injury at maturity would not have destroyed. To complete the picture, it should be said again that this relationship does not hold—at least not to the same degree—for all intellectual capacities; and sensory and motor capacities after damage to the infant brain tend to reach a higher level than that attained after destruction of the same regions at maturity" (1949, p. 292). He explained this physiologically by suggesting that some types of behavior that require a large amount of brain tissue for their first establishment can then persist when the amount of available tissue is decreased.

One of the real difficulties which arises in comparing research summaries is disagreement as to what is properly called a "simple function" or what measures are used to assess "perception" for instance. Birch and Lefford studied perception in a wide variety of congenitally, neurologically impaired children (including several groups of mentally retarded) in terms of simple form discrimination, perceptual analysis (identifying component parts of geometric forms), and perceptual synthesis (choosing the parts to make a whole form). They found that the neurologically impaired children differed from the normal only slightly in simple perceptual recognition but were significantly defective in both perceptual analytic and synthetic abilities. Particularly in perceptual synthesis, there was *no* curve of improvement in function related to chronological age (1964). Thus, this study could be used in part to support the hypothesis that perceptual impairment is inversely related to the age of the organism at the time of injury, but when the perceptual task is made more complex, impairment from early injury becomes apparent. Unfortunately, Birch and Lefford did not include an analysis of their data in terms of mental age so we cannot determine how the more complex aspects of perception related to other kinds of thought processes.

Another problem is introduced when we consider the age at which the particular function is evaluated. Children injured early tend to show relatively greater perceptual-motor deficits if examined *after* age 5, rather than before 5 years as in the Graham studies (Fraser and Wilks, 1959; Schachter and Apgar, 1959; Thurston, Middelkamp and Mason, 1955). The study by Teuber and Rudel (1962) is particularly illustrative of the complex relationship between development and the effects of brain injury. Comparing a group of children injured in the perinatal period with normal children between ages 5 and 18, they found that the performance of both groups changed systematically with age but differently for different functions. Thus the degree of impairment was not static but varied according to what was being tested and when.

Reviewing the research leaves one with a strong impression of the complexities involved in defining and evaluating psychological processes which seem simple at first. It also seems clear that we need more investigations which seek to replicate the findings of psychological colleagues, a research approach which is taken for granted in the physical sciences but not at all popular in the behavioral sciences. Finally, the need for longitudinal studies, or, in the least, follow-up studies, of the same children is obvious from theoretical considerations and the fact of the virtual non-existence of such studies to date.

Clinical Diagnosis of Brain Damage in Children

Most of the research cited in the preceding section was designed to study the psychological effects of *known* brain injury on psychological development. There is a large body of clinical research which has proceeded in the opposite direction, that is, the starting point is a study in psychological differences and the end point is the establishment of original cause. The experiments of Werner and Thuma are classic examples of this approach and the repercussions of their original work are still strong in clinical practice. In some 13 articles appearing between 1939 and 1947, these workers demonstrated significant differences between retardates matched for mental age and IQ and, further, found that these differences tended to cluster into two syndromes, one of which they labelled "endogenous mental deficiency" and the other "exogenous mental deficiency." Because of his background in Gestalt psychology and the influence of Goldstein's earlier work with brain-injured adults (1927, 1942), Werner stressed the problems of figure-ground perception and considered the other psychological characteristics (hyperactivity, perseveration, concrete thinking, etc.) to be secondary. The term "brain-injured" was soon substituted for "exogenous" and the concept was later enlarged to include "the clinical syndrome of the brain-injured child who is not mentally defective, but who in spite of 'normalcy of IQ' as tested is still 'defective'." (Strauss & Lehtinen, 1947). By defective, Strauss meant that the child has a school learning problem and/or behavioral difficulties, similar in kind to those described in the original "exogenous mental deficiency" group. Strauss, relying on a mass action view of brain function, stated that "all brain lesions, wherever localized, are followed by a similar kind of disordered behavior" (Strauss and Lehtinen, 1947). They proposed four criteria for the diagnosis of minimal brain injury: 1) a history of trauma or inflammatory processes before, during, or shortly after birth; 2) slight neurological signs; 3) the existence of immediate family of normal intelligence; and 4) the presence of psychological disturbances in perception and conceptual thinking of the order described in the research. According to Strauss, it would be legitimate to make a diagnosis on the evidence of psychological behavior alone.

Strauss' work has been criticized on three main grounds. First, his assumptions of a single syndrome as the unitary result of any and all brain damage has been amply disproved; in his review, Birch concluded that "in point of fact, there is not *a* minimally brain-damaged child but rather many varieties of brain-damaged children" (1964, p.6). The second line of criticism is perhaps the logical result of the first point; namely, attempts to replicate the original experiments of Strauss and Werner did not confirm their findings with respect to differences in perception of apparent motion and critical flicker frequency (Keller, 1962), distractibility (Cruse, 1962), and deficiency in abstract thinking (Weatherwax and Benoit, 1962). Schulman, Kaspar, and Throne (1965) undertook a clinical-experimental study to investigate all aspects of the diagnostic status of 35 boys between the ages of 11 and 15 years with IQ's ranging between 50 and 80. In this sample, no evidence was found of a brain damage syndrome as such; on the contrary, the neurological, psychological, and behavioral measures for "brain damage" did *not* co-vary significantly. Of particular interest, these workers found that hyperactivity was *not* a correlate of brain damage (as detected by other means). This might be attributed to maturational factors because these subjects were preadolescent, but the finding is in general accord with Graham's work with much younger children. The authors found the outside situation in which the child is placed to be one of the significant variables affecting level of activity. This suggests a functional element; the troublesome hyperactive child may not be consistently overactive because of inner "organic-drivenness," but he may react with characteristic overactivity in specific situations which are in some ways disturbing or frustrating to him.

Despite the contradictions in the research, the clinical diagnosis of organic brain damage is enjoying a current peak in popularity. The literature is replete with articles bearing witness to the importance of organic factors in the production of all kinds of behavioral and learning disorders and commenting on the unsatisfactory nature of "purely psychogenic and interpersonal explanations for any disorganized or poorly understood behavior" (Clements, 1966, p. 1). In practice, the diagnostic signs accepted as evidence of "minimal cerebral dysfunction" vary greatly from one clinician to another, both within and across professional fields such as psychology, pediatrics, or neurology. Quoting Birch (1964, p. 5), "In large part, our difficulties arise from the fact that a considerable proportion of the children who now come to our attention have rather subtle disturbances of the nervous system. Many of them do not exhibit the gross motor disturbances and alterations of normal reflex patterns that have classically been correlated with damage to the central nervous system. Instead, they present varied pictures of developmental lag, of behavioral disturbance, of transient or persistent motor awkwardness, of minor perceptual disturbance, of distractibility, of limitation of attention span, of thought disturbance, and of educational and emotional difficulties."

By and large, there is consensus about the varying effects of brain damage according to site, age at time of lesion, kind of lesion, time elapsed since injury, and probably, according to the inborn constitution of the individual. However, there is a second point which is much more controversial. Is it true, as stated by Birch, that the "behaviors described under the concept (of brain damage) almost never occur in the absence of cerebral damage?" Clinical observation has indicated that the sequelae of early deprivation look suspiciously like the brain damage syndrome (Provence and Lipton, 1962) and the GAP report on classification of psychopathological disorders in childhood says that "young children with significant psychological disturbance may also exhibit difficulties in impulse control, distractibility, and hyperactivity together with delayed perceptual-motor development and dysrhythmic electroencephalographic patterns, in the absence of any history or specific signs of brain damage....Signs of such cerebral dysfunction may not arise from somatic sources alone; therefore, diagnoses of organicity or minimal brain damage, based principally on behavioral manifestations, seem open to much question," (1966, p.266). There are many ways of interfering with development and it is probable that the mode of interference is not so important as the timing. Perhaps this could be experimentally verified with animals by interrupting development as specified ages with 1) sensory deprivation, 2) chemical inhibitors, and 3) severe trauma and comparing the results.

Turning to the experimental evidence with animals, environmental deprivation in critical periods has clear-cut organic effects on the nervous system of the growing organism (Riesen, 1958). Conversely, environmental enrichment has measurable effects on the central nervous system in the form of greater amount of cortical tissue (Krech, Rosenzweig, and Bennett, 1960), higher levels of acetylcholinesterase (Bennett, Diamond, Krech, and Rosenzweig, 1964), and increased number of glial cells (Altman and Das, 1964). When we examine the biochemistry of neuronal activity more closely in the next section, it becomes obvious that any dichotomy between genetically or organically determined structure and environmentally determined function is untenable. What is needed now is a bringing together of all kinds of facts to understand how external events change the nervous system and how the structure of the nervous system affects the acquisition, storage, and utilization of external data—the general subject of this review.

However, despite some lip service to the idea that there is no real distinction between the so-called organic and so-called functional disorders of childhood, it seems to be extraordinarily difficult to put it into practice and one is tempted to editorialize on the possible reasons. The need to specify "a cause" may be a hold-over from the medical disease model where one attempts to identify and treat the etiologic agent; it may represent an intellectual characteristic of man to find certainty where none exists; it may represent an emotional need to identify with one position or camp in opposition to another; it may represent a form of pragmatism where diagnosis depends on available treatments and what the traffic can bear; it may represent a genuine ignorance as to the options of explanations which are possible since so often the opposite to an organic explanation is "blame the parents"; or it may represent a failure in our teaching. It seems often that each generation must discover what the previous generation discarded. Whatever the reasons may be for dichotomizing, it should be borne in mind that "cerebral dysfunction" is a non-specific term which takes in the entire array of psychopathology of childhood regardless of the initial starting event.

Neurochemistry and Learning

Recently there has been a growing concern with the biochemical events in the brain and many excellent reviews have appeared (Rosenzweig and Leiman, 1968; Gaito and Zavala, 1964). The studies have followed two major lines of interest: one, the nature of chemical events which support transmission of neural impulses across the synaptic junctions, and two, possible molecular changes occurring in nervous tissue. The question posed by investigators in both areas is the neural basis of memory. There is agreement that there must be at least two stages involved in memory and that these stages extend over a period of time. Although he had relatively few biochemical facts at his disposal, Hebb's early theories are still very useful for conceptualizing the processes which may take place. He contrasts immediate memory which is also evanescent (so-called "short-term memory" in current research) with memories which are both instantaneously established and permanent. He suggests that input to the brain activates loops of neurons which may continue to fire one another in the fashion of a reverberatory circuit even after the stimulus is removed. If this continues long enough, some sort of structural change must take place to account for long-term memory. Glickman (1961) and Deutsch (1962) have reviewed research relevant to this "dual-trace" theory. Evidence that something continues to go on in the nervous system *after* the stimulus is removed is shown by the fact that if electroconvulsive shock or certain drugs are administered soon after a trial, learning is impaired, but learning is not affected if the interference is introduced an hour or more later. Along the same line, the fact that performance may improve over a period of time during which no overt practice occurs also shows that there must be continuing nervous activity. Similarly, the disturbing effect of presenting too many different learning activities spaced in close temporal sequence ("retroactive inhibition") bears out the notion that the person needs time to "digest" facts, that is, to consolidate the immediate memories into permanent structures. With some over-simplification of the theoretical distinctions involved, one may consider the neurochemistry of synaptic transmission as relevant to short-term memory and molecular approach as concerned with long-term memory.

What happens at the synapse to facilitate transmission? Structurally, one might speculate that it has something to do with proliferation or growth of the dendrites and/or axons, but this only leads to the further question as to how this comes about. Reeves (1966) reviewed neuropharmacological evidence which strongly suggests that acetylcholine is the most important single transmitter substance at many brain synapses. Reeves also reviewed the behavioral studies in which acetylcholine or its inhibitor, cholinesterase, were manipulated genetically or with drugs. Animals which are high in acetylcholine learn more rapidly when trials are massed but not when they are distributed, suggesting that the main functional difference is in rate of consolidation (McGaugh, Jennings, and Thompson, 1962). Animals raised in rich environments differ significantly in brain cholinesterase activity from animals raised in isolation (Krech, Rosenzweig, and Bennett, 1960). Acetylcholine is not viewed as the only transmitter in the central nervous system, but the investigators who are concentrating on the nature of the synapse believe that the change which underlies memory is an increase in the availability of some chemical transmitter substance (or substances) at the cell endfeet which were active in the particular neuronal circuit involved in the original learning experience.

In contrast to this, another group takes the position that intracellular changes are the basis of memory, and the favorite candidate seems to be ribonucleic acid (RNA). This hypothesis is derived from the discovery that the giant deoxyribonucleic acid

(DNA) molecule residing in the nucleus of each body cell contains the "genetic memory" of the organism. DNA directs the cell's activity by manufacturing different forms of RNA which acts as a messenger to "order" various forms of protein metabolism. Some investigators have offered the suggestion that RNA serves a similar function for experiential learning (Gaito, 1961, 1963; Gaito and Zavala, 1964; Booth, 1967). Briefly, they believe that the electrical impulses set off by the learning process modify the RNA in brain cells and other nerve cells that have taken part in a learning activity. The modification produces new forms of RNA molecules that specifically encode the fresh information.

Again, most of the supporting evidence has been obtained from animal experimentation. McConnell reported experiments in which he had trained flatworms to respond to a bright light and had fed the trained flatworms to untrained ones which could then be conditioned in half the time, presumably because the untrained worms had ingested "educated" RNA (McConnell, 1966). Hyden taught white rats to walk a tightwire and found that the trained rats had more RNA in brain cells and other nerve cells involved in learning this task than did untrained rats (Hyden & Egyhazi 1962). Hyden also found that in rats who had been deprived of stimulation in certain senses such as sight or hearing, the nerve cells involved contained a much lower than normal amount of RNA and proteins. Other investigators have studied the effects of interfering with the synthesis of normal RNA. Dingman and Sporn injected such a substance into the brains of rats and found they made twice as many errors as rats who had been injected with a placebo solution (1961). Working with another RNA-inhibiting drug, Flexner and Flexner found that mice conditioned to avoid shock forget their training after an injection 24 hours or even several days after training. They found that the longer after training the drug is given, the more of it must be given and into more places in the cortex (1966). Agranoff used the same drug with goldfish and concluded that short-term memory involves electrical states or other readily reversible phenomena, while long-term memory formation requires metabolic changes of which protein synthesis is a part (1966). In spirit, this agrees with Gaito's suggestion that short-term and long-term memory depend on different neurological sites. He proposes that synaptic changes may be preliminary in nature, facilitating or setting off reactions which allow changes to occur elsewhere in the nerve cell (1961). There is no question that the neurochemical approaches are incomplete and in a state of flux. Booth warns us that the relation of RNA or any biochemical substance to memory is not likely to be an experimental question with a single answer but a wide research field. Further, he adds that the biochemical search must be allied with the elucidation of functional neuroanatomy and all genetically or developmentally programmed organization of the central nervous system. He makes a plea for unified teams or individuals who are capable of professional competence in experimentation, critical evaluation, and inventiveness over the biochemical, physiological, and psychological levels simultaneously (1967). Although the biochemistry involved is awesome, some time ago Krech indicated that "It is the psychological data, in the last analysis, which must provide the tests of the adequacy of any theory of brain action" (1950, p. 346).

Memory Studies in Retardates

Various theories have been advanced by psychologists to explain the essential difference of mentally retarded individuals in terms of one or another psychological deficit (Zigler, 1966). The one most closely linked to the preceding neurophysiological discussion is the "stimulus-trace" theory proposed by Ellis (1963). He suggests that a defect in short-term memory characterizes the behavior of retarded individuals and that this can be explained on the basis that both the amplitude and duration of the stimulus trace for a perceptual event is diminished in the subnormal organism. He cites a series of experiments by Thompson and his students (*e.g.*, 1958) as evidence for a trace theory. In summary, these studies show that 1) memory in brain-injured animals is more susceptible to electroconvulsive shock than is memory in normal animals; 2) memory in young animals is more susceptible to electric shock than is memory in adult animals; 3) the deleterious effects of shock on memory of the young animal seem to be dependent on the stage of myelinization, and 4) shock-produced memory loss does not seem to depend upon the animals' previous visual experience or cerebral metabolism. Support for the stimulus trace theory was also given by Baumeister and Bartlett who factor analyzed the WISC performance of normals and retardates and found for both groups a General factor, a Verbal factor, and a Performance factor. In addition, a Trace factor was reported for the retarded group but not for the normal group. Coding, Arithmetic, and Digit Span were the subtests most closely identified with the Trace factor (1962).

There seems to be general agreement that retardates even when matched for mental age with individuals of normal IQ are deficient in short-term memory (Hermelin and O'Connor, 1964; Neufeldt, 1966; Fagan, 1967) but there is some argument as to why. Neufeldt puts the question in terms of information theory and suggests that organisms may differ in inherent short-term storage capacity or they may differ in strategy of encoding the available information. With a somewhat different slant based more on neurophysiological theories, Fagan similarly distinguishes between the acquisition phase (encoding) and retention phase (storage). In this connection, he contrasts the stimulus trace theory of Ellis with the "input organization" hypothesis of Spitz (1966). Spitz enunciated his theory in terms of Gestalt principles. When a figure is projected onto the brain, "the frequency of the impulses of the cortical cells representing the figure is at a different level from those representing the ground...the two chemically different regions of the tissue fluid plus the adjacent cells set up a current system. This current is greatest at the boundary line of figure and ground" (1963, p. 21). He goes on to state that the continued presence of this direct current polarizes all cell surfaces and establishes the condition of satiation. The original experiments which were used to apply the theory of differences in cortical satiation to mental retardates had to do with visual aftereffects, visual reversals with such familiar figures as the Necker cube, and perceptual illusions (Spitz, 1967). He hypothesized that cortical cells in mental retardates would be more "sluggish," slower in initial excitability and slower to return to original state after excitation. There is some electroencephalographic evidence which seems to bear out this notion. Baumeister and Hawkins reviewed other studies and offered their own data to show that EEG differences between persons differing in intelligence are more likely to be evident under conditions of stimulation and activity than under conditions of rest. Comparing individuals with IQ's ranging from 28 to 80, they found a significant correlation in responsiveness to a simple light stimulation and increasing IQ (1967). Spitz added a corollary to his hypothesis of cortical satiation (1966) namely, that the retardates' slower learning ability is further hampered by a deficit in the organization or grouping of the material to be learned because the ability to organize and isolate material presumably requires a level of neural flexibility which is generally beyond their threshold.

In his study of short-term memory, Fagan compared normal children with educable retarded children, matched for mental age, in terms of digit recall after a 2-second versus 10-second interval. He hypothesized that the Ellis notion of weakened amplitudes and durations of stimulus traces in mental retardates would lead to the prediction of both acquisition and retention slope differences whereas Spitz's assumption of retardate impairment in encoding material would yield a difference only in the 2-second recall. As expected, he found a deficit for the retardates in acquisition (2-second recall) but the rate of forgetting over the 10-second retention interval was no greater than that for the normals which he interpreted as supporting the Spitz hypothesis. If the retarded child can take in the information, he can retain it as well as the normal child. (In some ways this is similar to the conclusions reached by Zeaman and House from studies of discrimination learning. In discrimination learning they identified two stages, the first involving an intentional response and the second involving the specific instrumental response and the difference for the retardates is found only in the first stage. Once the retarded subject has identified the relevant stimulus dimension, he has no more difficulty learning the subsequent discrimination than the normal subject.)

There is no question that retardates have an acquisition deficit. The major point is that all these investigators are working on a neurophysiological base and trying to derive behavioral consequences therefrom. It is also interesting that they tend to take the view that all mental retardates are brain-damaged in one way or another, meaning by brain damage that there is a deficit or defect in the structure and/or functioning of the organism's brain mechanisms which has resulted in a lowered IQ

(Spitz, 1963). What light does this psychologically-oriented research focussing on the nature of the deficit in mental retardation shed on the broader issues of brain-behavior relationship? Not much as yet because the exciting developments in the neurochemistry of learning have had to extrapolate from animal research and there is no satisfactory method of obtaining similar data from the human brain. One can only speculate as to how the pieces might be fitted together. The psychological findings with mentally retarded indicate that the crucial difference is in the process of acquisition as measured by immediate recall rather than either short or long term memory. The data on long-term memory in mental retardation is relatively scant; Belmont located only 12 studies bearing directly on this subject. Most of them were subject to methodological criticism, but relying mainly on the findings of one complicated study by Klausmeier *et al.* (1959), Belmont concluded that normal and retardates seem to be equal in long term memory (1966). It appears that mentally retarded suffer mainly in the very first stage of information processing. This would seem to suggest some differences in synaptic transmitter mechanisms rather than a primary defect in protein synthesis necessary for RNA. However, it must be kept in mind that the neurophysiological aspects of learning are correlates, not causes, so that the ultimate "cure" may be either environmental or neurochemical manipulations, or both. A second important point is the unanswered question as to whether the differences between retarded and normal individuals of the same mental age are dichotomous or continuous. The finding of significant group differences does not tell us whether such differences are distributed in the normal, bell-shaped curve, in a linear relationship with intellectual differences, or whether these differences are sharp, qualitative rather than quantitative distinctions. Finally, it is probably unrealistic to expect hypotheses of short-term memory or consolidation deficits to explain all the varieties of ineffectual learning and maladaptive behavior which are gathered together under the heading of mental retardation. It would appear useful to select those particular mentally retarded individuals who show marked and specific deficits in short-term memory for further elucidation of the mechanisms involved by systematic manipulation of variables, which in turn might lead to some remedial teaching procedures, useful for at least *some* retarded individuals.

NATURE OF DEVELOPMENTAL CHANGES

Maturation Versus Learning

In this context, development refers to change in the individual which occurs over a period of time measured in months rather than hours or days. The critical issues have to do with the reason, or reasons, for the characteristic differences which appear as the child gets older. Twenty years ago, the controversy centered around maturation versus learning; that is, the importance of intrinsic, predetermined factors as opposed to extrinsic, experiential factors in the regulation of development. This question was in essence a variation of the earlier question regarding the relative roles of heredity and environment in determining intelligence, but maturational concepts included a broader range of functions than those usually subsumed under the term of "intelligence."

In recent years, the balance of power has swung over to the experiential side. The previously-cited evidence of changes in neural structure in animals *following* sensory deprivation or enrichment indicated the dependence of neurological growth on environmental factors. The long-lasting adverse effects of early maternal deprivation (usually associated with sensory deprivation) for infants in institutions gave further proof of the importance of environmental factors in the first two or three years of life (Dennis, 1960; Provence and Lipton, 1962). Researchers found that early infant development was susceptible to positive modification as well. Rheingold *et al.* (1959) demonstrated an increase in infant vocalizations by social conditioning, and White and Held (1966) reported that the median age for top level reaching was advanced to 98 days, about 60% of the time required by the control group, by providing heightened motility in an enriched visual surrounding. (It should be noted that these investigations were done with infants in institutions so that the comparison groups were in situations of comparative deprivation.)

Findings of this kind seem to invalidate earlier reports indicating that infant training, before the point of "maturational readiness" was inefficient and yielded no long-term benefit. Hunt has attempted to effect a reconciliation between the "old" and the "new" on the basis of two facts. First, the importance of experience or learning in development appears to increase up the phylogenetic scale, making the earlier work with lowly amphibia of doubtful relevance. Second, the emphasis in the "old" experiments was on restriction or practice of *motor* responses without interference of sensory input and it may well be that infants learn to "do" things by watching as well as by "doing" (Hunt, 1966). Hunt is concerned with the problem of timing of educational experiences, or "the problem of the match, " which he defines almost like "cognitive dissonance," as supplying the infant or the individual, at every stage of his development, with circumstances with an appropriate degree of incongruity to be interesting and/or somewhat surprising with not so much incongruity as to be frightening" (1966, p. 131).

The new look at early development has introduced what has been called a "revolution in learning" (Pines, 1967). Research findings have been translated into action programs emphasizing the importance of intellectual stimulation in the first two years of life. For instance, the conclusion stated by Bloom (1964) that, in terms of intelligence measured at age 17 years, 50% of the variance can be accounted for by age 4 years* and the reports of declining IQ's from infant scores to school-age

*It is interesting to compare this with an earlier statement made by Goodenough that one-half of an individual's ultimate mental stature is attained by the age of three years, but at that time (1946), it was explained on the basis of innate factors and it had no effect on educational thinking.

tests in culturally deprived populations (Gray and Klaus, 1965) has prompted Head Start workers to start nurseries for infants (Caldwell and Richmond, 1964; Caldwell, 1967). With reference to mental retardation, another approach towards prevention was hinted at in a little-noted article by Goshen who discussed severe maternal depression during the first year of child's life as a possible cause of mental retardation. He was particularly concerned about the mother's role in stimulating language. "Neurotic maternal attitudes which are characterized by a failure to stimulate and evoke meaningful signals during critical periods of life can result in failure on the child's part in grasping the significance of language, thus proceeding to a state recognizable as mental retardation" (1963, p. 174). Maternal depression is not restricted to any socioeconomic group and recognition of this condition in the mother might lead to early intervention for the child.

In the current zeal for acceleration through environmental enrichment, the possibility of over-stimulation should be kept in mind. Miller has elaborated on the consequences of "information input overload" (1960, 1964) and Thompson noted the curvilinear relationship between early experience and adult behavior with regard to the handling of animals (1962). Only careful, objective observations over a long period of time will provide the answers to the problem of match between external circumstances and internally developing structures.

Sequential Aspects of Development

In modern development theory, concern about the sequential aspects of development is kept very much alive by the contribution of Piaget and his co-workers. Piaget delineated four major epochs in the mental evolution of the child (sensorimotor, pre-operational, concrete operations, and formal operations) with substages in each (Flavell, 1963). He has stood firm in the central thesis that the sequence is inevitable although he is more than willing to concede that the age at which stages appear and their duration will vary as a function of hereditary potential and experience (Tanner and Inhelder, 1960). Considerable research has been done with mentally retarded individuals to see if they follow the same order of cognitive stages at a slowed down rate, and in general, this particular line of research has supported Piaget's position. Woodward, for example, took 147 subjects, seven to sixteen years of age, who were either profoundly or severely retarded, and presented them with a variety of problems relevant to each of the six stages of sensorimotor intelligence. By and large, they could solve all the problems of stages lower than that at which they were classified and there was consistency in their success or failure with different kinds of problems representing the same sensorimotor level (1959). A number of other English studies using retarded children have supported Piaget's notion of stages in the development of number concepts (Hood, 1962; Mannix, 1960 and Woodward, 1961). Although the mental age at which children entered the stage of concrete operations varied, no child with a mental age of less than six years performed at the level of concrete operations in all the tests, and no child with a mental age of more than six and a half years was at the pre-operational stage in all the tests. Following the pattern of normal children, the retarded child's ability to conserve quantity and number is arrived at gradually, and a period of nonconservation, or perceptual domination, is followed by a transitional stage before conservation becomes consistent. In the pre-conservation, or pre-operational period (particularly in the substage of "intuitive thinking" roughly spanning the ages from 4 to 7 years), the child centers his attention on one or another perceptual aspect of a stimulus situation; for instance, the amount of liquid in a tall, thin container will be judged as "more" than the same amount in a short, wide container because of the single dimension of "tallness." Similarly, in judging the equivalence of area or number, the young child will be distracted by the scattered or close grouping of the objects. Amongst other things, conceptual development requires an increasing ability to withstand the influence of perceptually prominent but irrelevant features, a factor of selective attention which appears as a recurrent theme in the research with mentally retarded.

One of the first longitudinal studies to appear indicated that the order of difficulty of conservation tasks was consistent for several samples of kindergarten, first and second grade children (Almy *et al.,* 1966). However, it was noted that children in a "lower-class" school did less well than those from a "middle-class" school and furthermore, that the second graders in the longitudinal study (with repeated interviewing) did better than the second graders in the cross-sectional study (76% conserved in all tasks as compared to 48%). Although this bears out the notion of a consistent progression, it also indicates the importance of general environmental factors and specific learning experience. The "educability" of Piaget concepts in children has been subjected to research investigation with conflicting results. Wohlwill and Lowe (1962) and Beilin and Franklin (1962) suggested that training in conservation was generally a failure, but this may be attributable to the particular method of training. Roeper and Sigel (1967) described these investigators as trying to teach conservation directly rather than building up to it by taking the child through the prerequisite steps. Using young, five-year-old gifted children, Roeper found that conservation could be achieved at an earlier age by demonstration and verbal discussion of the preliminary concepts of multiple classification, reversibility, and seriation. Wallach and Sprott found that opportunity for the children to manipulate the materials and thus "see" the reversibility was effective in the achievement of number conservation (1964). With respect to strategy of teaching in this area, Smedslund concluded that procedures which made the child stop and think and try out various possibilities were more effective than procedures which relied on the experimenter correcting or reinforcing specific responses (1961).

The educational message from Piaget-oriented investigations seems reasonably clear; the child learns best from his own experimentation. Almy *et al.* comments "While the vicarious is certainly not to be ruled out, it is direct experience that is the avenue to knowledge and logical ability. Language is important, but for Piaget, the ability to use language to express logic is an outcome of activity. Attempts to improve the child's logic solely through instructing him in the use of language are not likely to be very successful" (1966, p. 137). This view runs counter to the emphasis on drill in vocabulary and linguistic structure for preschool, culturally deprived children recommended by Bereiter and Engelman (1966). The answer obviously rests with follow-up studies. Unfortunately, however, many of the contemporary preschool programs have a true missionary purpose and the experimental group is being compared with a control group who receive "nothing" so that some of the important theoretical issues will not be answered. None of the special teaching procedures has been systematically tried out with mentally retarded individuals and it would be valuable to know if their attainment of concepts can be facilitated with the same strategies as those demonstrated for young, gifted children, for instance, in the Roeper and Sigel study. Conceivably, differences in cognitive styles and motivational characteristics do not allow the retarded child to profit as effectively from his own experimentation as from demonstration.

Continuity and Discontinuity

In Ausubel's opinion, "second only to the nature-nurture controversy in historical importance has been the great debate over whether development is a process of gradual, quantitative and continuous change or whether it is characterized by abrupt, uneven and discontinuous changes which are qualitatively different from one another" (1957, p. 93). With reference to cognitive development specifically, Robinson and Robinson laud Piaget because he "has given us a picture of a central nervous system which, as a result of its intercourse with the environment during the formative years, constantly forms levels of integration which are both quantitatively and qualitatively different from the syntheses out of which they are evolved. He thus sees the human mind as a computer which changes its data-processing characteristics as well as the amount of data it retains in its storage units" (1965, p. 356). Since "stages" always have their precursors and their remnants, the same data can be subjected to various interpretations depending on one's theoretical preference for continuity versus discontinuity; by and large, stimulus-response learning theorists emphasize the former and specialists in child development emphasize the latter. Ausubel, representing the child development point of view, states that "to demonstrate the existence of developmental stages it is only necessary to show that certain qualitative differences in process arise consistently at definite points in a developmental cycle which differentiate the greater mass of children at a given age level from adjacent age groups" (1957, p. 96). He allows that such stages need not be abrupt, or represent a complete departure from previous stages, or be totally consistent for every child in a given age bracket.

In his review of cognitive research stimulated by Piaget, Wallach identified two periods of major transition, or cognitive reorganization, one at approximately 18 months of age and a second between five and eight years (1963). He pointed out that prediction of later IQ from infant tests is notoriously poor (Stott and Ball, 1965; Bayley, 1955) whereas correlations between tests in middle childhood and retests in later childhood are considerably higher and statistically significant. This suggests that infant tests are, of necessity, measuring something different than the later tests of intelligence. Hofstaetter did a factor analysis of intelligence test scores obtained from the same individuals at a number of ages from 2 months to 17½ years (1954) and found that individuals maintained a consistent ranking, one to another, in three age periods, from 2 to 18 months; from 21 months to 4 years; and for tests given at 6 years and later. He identified three factors which he felt played successively important roles in determining IQ test scores: 1) sensorimotor alertness; 2) persistence; and 3) manipulation of symbols. These findings support the generalization that whatever is being assessed by IQ tests is structurally or qualitatively different in infancy, early childhood and middle childhood.

Corroboration of the notion of "stages" also comes from reseachers who are *not* following Piaget's lines of inquiry. White suggests the hypothesis that "cognitive development proceeds by hierarchical overlays of higher processes upon lower processes, the lower processes being inhibited in favor of the higher" (1963, p. 222), which suggests a "stepping up" on separate cognitive levels as opposed to progression on a sort of continuous moving stairway. However, this is a little different idea of stages than that advanced by Piaget because the hierarchical overlay is based on *active inhibition* of a more primitive response. White gives an example from the field of discrimination learning. Given the task of selecting the "correct" one of a pair of stimuli, young children, as well as animals, will start by using position (right or left) as the basis of selection. At some point, the position-guided behavior is superseded (inhibited) and the child starts to examine other attributes of the stimuli for the right cue. The primitive nature of the position response is corroborated by the fact that House and Zeaman were unable to establish cue-guided discrimination learning in severely retarded individuals but were able to establish position reversal set (House and Zeaman, 1959).

From a great variety of starting-points, many observers of child development, if not all, make the discovery of a turning point around the age of five years. White describes it as a developmental shift from associational to cognitive-verbal function and cites results from transposition experiments across different age levels.

In a typical experiment, stimuli varying in two dimensions, such as brightness and size, are used. Children first learn that black stimuli are correct and white stimuli are incorrect. Transfer to a condition where white stimuli are correct would constitute a reversal shift; transfer to a condition where large stimuli are correct would constitute a nonreversal shift.

If learning is proceeding by associative, S-R processes, the non-reversal shift should be easier than the reversal shift; this is true for animals (Kelleher, 1956) and for young children between three and four (Kendler, Kendler, and Wells, 1960). If verbal mediating processes are used, the reversal shift should be easier, and this is true for college students (Kendler, and D'Amato, 1955). Kendler and Kendler (1959) found that fast learners among a group five to seven years old were superior on a reversal shift, while slow learners did better on a nonreversal shift. Clearly a transition point is suggested at this age range. (White, 1963, p. 209).

Some of these ideas are further elaborated in the later section on the role of language and verbal mediation in cognitive development; the point to be made here is that there is agreement that something very important happens to the human being between five and seven years of age. The shift is probably related to developing language skills, but there is a circular effect involved. The child's ability to appreciate relationships and to "de-center" from the single perceptual aspect stimulates him to look for and to comprehend appropriate verbal explanations.

With reference to mental retardation, Inhelder felt that adult retardates might be classified according to the stage of mental development which they had attained. In her system, the severely mentally retarded adult is fixated at the level of sensorimotor intelligence; the moderately retarded adult is seen as fixated at the pre-operational intuitive subperiod; the mildly retarded adult operates at the level of concrete operations (1944). No one has taken up the challenge of trying to alter these "fixation points" by special training. It would seem that efforts of this kind would be invaluable in teasing out the steps involved in transition from one phase to another as it would provide the chance to watch the "cognitive movie" in very slow motion.

Mental Age Concept

In any discussion of stages in cognitive development, the mental age figures prominently as the substitute for chronological age in retarded individuals. The standard paradigm for comparative studies is to match "normal" subjects with "retarded" subjects on the basis of MA. The roughness of any such "match" should be kept in mind. The pioneer work of Werner and Strauss showing significant differences between retarded individuals of like MA and IQ is of lasting importance even if the etiologic distinctions are doubtful. The mental age is nothing but a composite test score, arrived at by averaging a number of subtest scores which in turn tap a number of intellective factors. The same score may result from an even, across-the-board performance, or from combinations of high and low points which can be the mirror opposite of one another. Not only may there be basic differences in the structures of abilities in retarded individuals, but other factors confound intelligence test scores as well as performance in research tasks. Baumeister lists such factors as institutionalization, school experience, socio-economic status, reinforcement history, reinforcement contingencies, comprehension of instructions, motor impairment, and so on, as deserving as much attention as MA (1967). In theory, one can only agree but in practice it is impossible to obtain groups who are so exhaustively studied that they can be matched in all respects and inevitably, the fact of being retarded has occasioned some difference in life experiences. However, it is imperative for the researcher to appreciate that matching for mental age does not guarantee homogeneity and to examine individual differences within the retarded and normal groups.

RELATIONSHIP OF PERCEPTUAL-MOTOR DEVELOPMENT TO COGNITIVE FUNCTIONING

Interest in this topic sharply increased in recent years for a number of reasons. First, Piaget's formulations established a functional continuity between the emergence of sensorimotor skills and the development of concept formation. Particularly with respect to children, the traditional boundaries between perception, judgment, memory thought, and imagination are arbitrary. "There are boundaries; but they are fluid, cloudlike, evanescent. Perceptual responses involve memories and judgments, lead on into thought and imagination; and the latter influence subsequent perception." (Solley and Murphy, 1960, p. 327). A second reason has emerged from the research with mentally retarded individuals suggestive of a primary deficit in the information encoding process (input organization in Spitz's terms), or initial perceptual process. A third reason for contemporary interest is the wave of special therapies which are directed at perceptual-motor dysfunction remediation as a means to the end of improved cognitive functioning. The following discussion is limited to those specific areas in this vast field where work with the retarded has made, or could make, a significant contribution.

Developmental Aspects of Perception

Theories about perception are as numerous as those about intelligence and revolve around the same issues: nativism versus empiricism; the mind-body problem; dependence or independence of affects, needs, values, etc. (Pronko, Ebert, and Greenberg, 1966). With regard to the origin of perception, the recent studies of Fantz have shown that the newborn's capacity for pattern discrimination is greater than formerly thought, thereby contradicting the view that form perception is acquired through an associational process. Using a visual preference technique, Fantz concluded that "visual patterning is intrinsically stimulating or interesting; it elicits much more visual attention from birth than do color and brightness alone...at some point in development, at least by the third month, the unlearned visual selectiveness begins to be modified by past visual experiences. One of the changes is decreased attention to familiar patterns and consequent increased attention to novel ones.... These findings give evidence that in development visual perception precedes action rather than the reverse as is often assumed" (1966, p. 171). Fantz also cited supporting neurological evidence showing that the vertebrate visual system is inherently receptive and responsive to patterned input, rather than simple brightness stimulation (Hubel and Wiesel, 1963; Sackett, 1963).

In a provocative, but as yet inconclusive study, Fantz and Nevis compared ten infants of university faculty, reared in private homes, with ten foundlings, reared in an institution. These two samples were selected as representing the upper and lower reaches of the intellectual continuum, to the degree that this is possible on the basis of parentage and environmental beginnings. With weekly testing from 2 to 24 weeks, they found that the two groups were similar in the nature of shifts in visual preferences but differed in rate. They also used an adaptation of the Griffiths Mental Development Scale, given weekly, which showed a significant difference from about 15 weeks of age and thereafter. Fantz and Nevis were cautious in the interpretation of their data: "We cannot differentiate among the various possible sources of difference, including genetic make-up, prenatal and postnatal care and nutrition, and early environment. . . . The rough correlation between the pattern preference scores and the scores on a 'mental development scale' both supports the group difference and suggests that it involves basic aspects of psychological development, which are revealed earlier by pattern preference changes than by the appearance of various active, coordinated behaviors. . . . There is some basis for a tentative conclusion that development of selective visual attention to configurational variables represents an early stage of basic perceptual-cognitive development—a stage which may be not only predictive of later stages in this development, but also may facilitate further development by making visual exploration of the environment a more effective learning process" (Fantz and Nevis, 1967, p. 105).

These findings should serve as a stimulus for much more research, and infants with Down's syndrome would seem to be particularly appropriate subjects. There have been reports of visual depth perception in infancy which also deserve replication with different groups and which might be linked developmentally with the visual preference findings cited above. Walk and Gibson found that normal infants at 6 or 7 months discriminated between a checkered surface immediately below a sheet of glass and a similar surface 4 feet below; they would crawl across the former but not the latter (1961). In this kind of study, it would also be interesting to determine the relationship between motor experience (*i.e.* reaching, rolling, crawling, etc.) and perception of distance or depth—does the infant recoil from the visual cliff as soon as he can crawl or does he need a prerequisite amount of crawling experience? Walk and Gibson's work with pairs of kittens showed different reactions to the visual cliff on the basis of different motor and identical visual experiences and this would suggest an affirmative answer (1961). If indeed motor experience is required for depth and distance perception, does it take the retarded child a longer time?

Figure-ground Perception

Figure-ground organization is a fundamental problem in perception, and like the field as a whole, it has been subjected to scrutiny with regard to its innate or learned character (Solley and Murphy, 1960). One interpretation of figure-ground perception in neurophysiological terms has already been discussed (see Spitz), but this does not answer the question of origin. There is no question that what is perceived as "figure" changes with age. One of the characteristics of the global perception of young children is the failure to isolate the parts within the whole, or to isolate objects from their surrounding context, "field," or "background." Using the Embedded Figures Test, Witkin *et al.* found that children between 8 and 10 years had great difficulty in identifying hidden figures; between 10 and 13 years there was a sudden, marked improvement (1954). "In a certain sense the figure-ground problem is also an embedded figure problem. If a figure is to stand out relative to the ground on which it lies, it must be extracted. In order to extract a form from an embedding context, the individual must scan the context, focus his attention on the form and make the form serve as figure and the remainder as ground." (Solley and Murphy, 1960, p. 139). Solley and Sommer (1957) and Solley and Engel (1960) used the technique of tachistoscopic exposure of right-left profile faces which could be shown separately or interlocking to form a circle with a jagged middle line. They found that giving or taking away monetary rewards in connection with one or another of the profiles influenced the child's perception when they were shown together. Particularly between the ages of five and eight years, children tended to see the rewarded face as "figure" and the punished face as "ground." These investigations suggest that at least certain aspects of figure-ground perception are learned as a result of association with pleasant or unpleasant experiences.

Figure-ground perception played a prominent role in the early work in the diagnosis of organic brain damage (Werner and Strauss, 1941) and it remains an important part of present-day diagnostic test batteries such as the Ayres (1963) and the Frostig (1963). The diagnostic term "perceptually handicapped" is sometimes used in place of "brain-injured" and carries the strong implication of a major problem in figure-ground perception. Cruickshank and his co-workers repeated the Werner-Strauss procedures (recognition of a pictured object partially covered by a simple "ground" pattern after very brief exposure) and reported that cerebral palsy children of average IQ were significantly inferior to a control group in distinguishing the figure from the background (Dolphin and Cruickshank, 1951; Cruickshank, Bice and Wallen, 1957). Like Lehtinen before him, Cruickshank was primarily interested in the educational implications of such findings and evolved a teaching method largely dependent on the figure-background problem (Cruickshank *et al.* 1961). Surprisingly little effort has been made to replicate the early work with mentally retarded. Although Spivack concludes that "research in this area suggests that brain injury rather than retardation produces responses to background or intrusion of background in perception" (1963, p. 485), he quotes only one study which matched moderately retarded mongoloid subjects with an equally retarded brain injured group and *no* difference was found (Coleman, 1960).

The notion of figure-ground difficulties has been a popular one for explaining learning difficulties, particularly in the area of reading. On the face of it, it seems reasonable to say that a child does not "perceive" the "gestalt" of letters or words and therefore cannot read, but there is a danger of circular reasoning, that is, giving the phenomenon of failure to read another, fancier name. Clearly, letters and words are learned "figures." However, there is some research to suggest that the perceptual problem goes beyond the specific task of letter and word recognition. Elkind *et al.* used a modification of the hidden figures technique and found indeed that retarded readers were inferior in picking them out of the total matrix (1965). Silver, Hagin and Hersh review a number of studies which report that at least the beginning aspects of reading are closely related to perceptual abilities. They evolved special training for "stimulation of deficit perceptual areas" which included teaching for 1) accuracy of perception in visual, auditory, tactile, and kinesthetic modalities; 2) integration of perception from different modalities; and 3) verbal training to insure the transfer of perceptual abilities to language skills. On the basis of limited case history material, the authors concluded that "where perceptual deficits are first trained out, reading instruction at intermodal and verbal levels will have a better chance of success" (1967, p. 750). They interpret this as "enhancing neurophysiological maturation" in a critical period; the explanation as to why a given child should have the perceptual deficit is vaguely given as a function left behind in successive waves of maturation." A similar emphasis of remedial perceptual training has been advanced by Frostig (1961, 1963). She cites studies reporting perceptual difficulties in all forms of child psychopathology (learning problems, neurosis, psychosis, and brain damage, minimal or otherwise) and suggests that in remediation it is far more important to know the extent and nature of symptoms rather than initial cause. She suggests that "the development of visual-perceptual processes is the major function of the growing child between the ages of three and seven and that at this age level perceptual development becomes a most sensitive indicator of the developmental status of the child as a whole" (1963, p. 671). Accordingly her test of visual perception (consisting of 1) eye-hand coordination; 2) figure-ground perception; 3) perception of form constancy; 4) perception of position in space; and 5) perception of spatial relationships) is designed to evaluate these functions between three and nine years. She expresses the hope that perceptual training procedures instituted at the right developmental moment will benefit the child in more than perception. One would expect such special training to have a general beneficial effect on learning and behavior, not necessarily because of any complicated neurophysiological or maturational reason, but as a by-product of the social reinforcement from extra attention and experience of success.

It is worthwhile noting the lack of developmental research which crosses traditional boundaries. The work on stages in cognitive development showed the dramatic and sudden changes which occur around five years and it would be valuable to know how changes of this order relate to levels of perceptual-motor functioning. Is a certain quality in perceptual organization necessary for understanding the concept of conservation? In theory, it would seem that this cognitive concept would depend on a certain amount of "field independence" or ability to extract the figure from background context; however, there is no data. Research workers tend to remain within their own "cultures" as much as any representative from any social group.

The Problem of Attention

The study of perception cannot be divorced from consideration of the problem of attention, particularly in relation to the figure-ground problem. Nearly all theories of attention have stressed the selective aspects and some theorists have tried to explain the mechanism in terms of additional energization (Berlyne, 1951; Rapaport, 1951). Solley and Murphy propose that most acts of attending are conditioned along the lines of operant conditioning and describe an experiment with 9- and 10-year-old children which showed how they scanned a field until they found the object which had been rewarded in the experiment. They did not stop searching as quickly when they looked at a non-rewarding figure (1960). This concept is closely related to the idea of "set" as something which a) prepares and facilitates perception; b) excludes certain reactions as well as making possible certain others; c) is localizable in the organism rather than in the stimulus object; d) can have the character of intention or expectancy; e) can be voluntary or involuntary (Pronko, Ebert, and Greenberg, 1966, p. 66). When such "sets" are systematized into consistent foci of attention, they constitute the individual's "perceptual style," a term used almost interchangeably with "cognitive style." Such styles represent characteristic differences in the way that the individual remembers percepts (levelling-sharpening) (Gardner, 1962), and the way that he deploys attention in a stimulus field (scanning-focussing and constrictive-flexible) (Santostefano, 1964). These cognitive styles have in turn been linked with personality characteristics in a kind of interlocking chain where it is impossible to say where perception, intelligence, or personality begin and end. Although we can readily see how certain perceptual styles will improve cognitive functioning over time, the reverse is also true—accuracy of perception will depend on mental level. "It may be that inability to direct attention appropriate to the significant features of the environment is caused at least in part by an incapacity to understand the nature of the situation and to perceive its significant features (Vernon, 1966, p. 393)."

This last point is very important in relation to a large body of research that has been reported by Zeaman and House explaining the difficulties for retarded to learn visual discriminations on the basis of a deficit in attending to the relevant stimulus dimension. For the most part, they used moderately to severely retarded subjects in an institutional setting. Analysis of the learning curves for simple discrimination learning showed a prolonged preliminary period of chance-level responses followed by an accelerated curve of the same form as that shown by the normal learners. From this, they concluded that "the difference between fast and slow learning is not so much the rate at which improvement takes place, once it starts, but rather the number of trials for learning to start" (Zeaman and House, 1963, p. 162). They found that abrupt mastery of problems could be obtained by changing stimulus aspects of the situation and suggested that successful training of moderately retarded children could be achieved through the engineering of their attention. Their work is ingenious but the explanation seems to beg the issue. To know what to look for, or at, is no minor matter. Perception and selective attention is certainly involved in a reciprocal relation with mental development.

There is another aspect of attention which looms large in working with retarded children, namely, the holding of attention over a period of time—attention span versus distractibility. As far back as 1904, Kuhlman held the short attention span accountable for some of the retardate's difficulty in learning. However, attention span must be considered in relation to a particular task rather than an invariant characteristic of the individual. Measurements with normal children indicated a wide range from a few seconds to nearly an hour depending on the specific activity (Moyer and von Haller, 1955), and the recent work on hyperactivity with brain-damaged children suggests that this comes and goes as a partial function of the situation (Schulman, Kaspar and Throne, 1966). Given the external situation of the usual classroom demands, inability to get and hold attention is the common lament of special education teachers. Teacher efforts are usually indirect—improving the curriculum by using interesting materials, short periods of directed activity and frequent changes of task. Recently, two programs were reported which attempted to lengthen attention directly. Martin and Powers described experimental efforts to increase the amount of time spent engaging in a task by immediate reinforcement contingent on time spent (1967). In the individualized, artificial laboratory situation, they were entirely successful. The authors comment that in the classroom situation, many children receive more reinforcement, that is, more attention, when they leave their desk or in some way exhibit non-attending behavior so that extinction does not take place. This analysis in terms of operant conditioning has considerable validity, although one must also appreciate the realistic situation of the classroom teacher who perforce must intervene when a child is disruptive.

The second program was conducted in conjunction with a community nursery school and day care program via the mothers of 31 severely to moderately retarded children ranging in age from 3.5 to 7.8 years. The materials used were cut-outs of various forms and colors presented in progressively more complex arrangements. The child's task was to remove selected cut-outs so that it was necessary for him to scan the total field, select the appropriate forms and ignore the others. The training was done in daily 10-20 minute sessions for a period of four months. The experimental group showed a significant improvement in post-test compared to the control group, from which they concluded that "training in the developmentally early cognitive function, focal attention, generalizes to and promotes the effectiveness of higher functions. Such training by mothers renders the child's cognition more accessible to instruction by others" (Santostefano and Stayton, 1967, p. 741). This study raises some very interesting questions from a developmental standpoint. The authors found no correlation between IQ and amount of change in either group, but one would like to see the data re-analyzed in terms of mental age. These were young children (about 6 years old in the experimental group and about 5 years old in the control group) and with an average IQ of 54 and 50 respectively, the mental ages *could* range anywhere from 1 to 5 years.

In all the discussion of attention, whether theoretical, experimental, or practical, the writers have emphasized the importance of reinforcement of some nature. If we think only of the problem of attention for the moment, it seems that for retarded children "intrinsic motivation" (Hunt, 1963) or "competence motivation" (White, 1959) is not sufficient and supplementation from external sources is needed, but this is discussed at more length in the final section of this review.

Intersensory Integration

By and large, studies on perception and attention have focussed on one or another modality and have neglected intersensory organization, the capacity of the individual to deal in integrated ways with multimodal information. The outstanding exception is the sophisticated research program of Birch and Lefford who used a method of equivalence for assessing intersensory development (1963). The subjects (normal children aged 5 through 11) were asked to judge whether simultaneously paired stimuli were the same or different in shape. Presentations were visual-haptic (one form visible and the other hidden but available to touch); visual-kinesthetic (the second stimulus of the pair was provided by moving his arm through a path describing a geometric form); or haptic-kinesthetic. The data showed clearly that the ability to make the various intersensory judgments improved with age with the most marked improvement between ages 5 and 8 years. There was also a clear hierarchy of intersensory adequacy. The easiest task was judging equivalence in the visual-haptic pairs whereas any modality paired with the kinesthetic modality was much more difficult. Apparently being passively put through some invisible motions did not yield much information to the child, either because of the specific modality or because of his passivity.

There are many unanswered questions about the facilitating or distracting effects of concurrent double stimulation with regard to age level and specific modalities. The general idea that simultaneous stimulation of many senses is helpful in learning underlies some of the special reading techniques of Fernald (1943) and training for retarded proposed by Seguin (1866, 1907). With reference to our next topic, motor development, we can look at it in part as a kind of intersensory integration of visual and kinesthetic or proprioceptive stimulations.

Motor Development

More and more one encounters "sensorimotor" or "perceptual-motor" in hyphenated or one-word forms suggesting that any division between input and output is an artificial one. However, there are some classical studies describing developmental stages of motor behavior, particularly in the first two years of life. From motion picture studies, Ames (1937) delineated 14 stages in the development of creeping and crawling and the importance of this sequential progression has been reasserted by one of the special therapies to be discussed shortly. Shirley described the development of posture and locomotion in infants (1933) and Halverson identified 10 stages in the development of prehension (1931). Studies of this normative, descriptive nature were reported in the maturational era of child psychology when it was thought that growth changes and maturation of the neural and muscular systems, rather than environmental conditions or practice, determined the emergence of function. There have been efforts to develop a normative scale of motor development for older ages, mainly based on the Oseretsky Scales (Sloan, 1955; Cassell, 1949), but none have received widespread acceptance. Stott discusses some of the problems involved in the selection, administration, and scoring of motor test items. One problem is the practical one of space requirements. Cooperation and interest must be engaged, as in any test. And as the child grows older, the role of experience and training becomes increasingly important. Stott concludes that "Differences in previous learning present as great a problem in a motor test as they do in one of intelligence. It is doubtful whether such a test can ever be culture-free"(1966).

Despite the unsolved difficulties, everyone expresses the need for age norms for motor behavior. There is still a feeling that motor behavior reflects nervous system functioning in a special way that is important diagnostically. Again quoting Stott, "Motor co-ordination requiring very exact time-sequencing, reaction to exteroceptive cues and accurate muscle control, similarly demands a refinement of neural function, a moderate derangement of which produces noticeable effects. A test of motor impairment may consequently prove the best means by which a neurological factor in behavior disturbance may be demonstrated. Motor impairment can be due to physical malformation, injury, or debility as well as to neural dysfunction. The last cause is the most difficult to diagnose and is now of chief interest" (Stott, 1966, p. 523). Indeed, when one looks at the so-called "soft" neurological signs, one finds that the majority involve indicators of motor dysfunction such as poor visual tracking, clumsiness, poor balance, poor coordination, tremors and involuntary associated movements or what Oseretsky called "unwilled collateral movements" (Prechtl & Stemmer, 1962; Walton *et al.,* 1962). A major diagnostic difficulty is that many of these signs are normal for young age levels so that they must be evaluated in terms of age-appropriateness. Ayres has published a diagnostic test battery in which many of the items are modifications of standard neurological examination procedures but standardized for administration and scoring and with the provision of specific age norms. In four separate units (Ayres Space Test, Southern California Motor Accuracy Test, Southern California Figure Ground Test, and Southern California Kinesthetic and Tactile Perception Test), this battery has been administered to children in the age range from 4 to 10 years (1963, 1966, 1967). The scores are translated into standard deviation scores, and Ayres has approached the problem of interpretation through factorial analysis of these scores. She identified two major factors; one best identified as general perceptual-motor ability dominated by tactile, kinesthetic and motor functions and the second one, appearing primarily as visual perception (1966). Clinically, she proposed five clusters or syndromes, identified by the constellation of test scores (1967). Unfortunately, there is little test-retest data and no correlational analysis with MA or IQ even for those children suspected of having perceptual deficiencies because of learning or behavioral problems.

Diagnosis is further complicated when the child is mentally retarded. In his review of the research, Malpass (1963) concluded that there is a positive relationship between motor proficiency and mental ability for subjects of subnormal intelligence which did not appear to be true for subjects of average or better intelligence. This co-variance may be a sign that both areas of dysfunction represent organic brain damage; in Heath's studies of familial versus non-familial groups, he found low correlations between IQ and the Railwalking Test score in the former and high correlations in the latter (1942, 1953). In view of the interest in classifying the mentally retarded, it is surprising that this lead has not been followed up.

Motor skill is not a unitary factor and correlations between tests of motor ability are usually lower than between parts of IQ tests (Sloan, 1955). For this reason, it is necessary to look at some of the more important specific behaviors which have been loosely categorized as "motor" or "perceptual motor." Historically, the task which has attracted the greatest amount of psychological attention has been that of *copying designs*. Some form of this task is part of many tests—the Bender Gestalt, Stanford-Binet, WISC, and Frostig, to mention a few. Developmentally, there is a considerable time lag between the child's ability to discriminate and name forms and his ability to reproduce them in drawing (Maccoby and Bee, 1965). This might be explained on the basis of motor inadequacy or an inability to use perceptual information for the control and direction of action. In the same comprehensive study mentioned earlier (Birch and Lefford, 1967), children between the ages of 5 and 11 years were presented with four simple forms and asked to copy them 1) by freehand drawing; 2) with the help of a dot grid background; 3) with the help of a line grid background; 4) with the help of extra visual cues in the design; 5) by connecting dots arranged at the angle of the forms; and 6) by tracing. They found that the maximal rate of improvement of motor skill occurred between the ages of five and six years and that there was a consistent ordering of difficulty in terms of the availability of visual cues from tracing (the easiest), to connecting dots, to the dot and line grid backgrounds, and finally, freehand drawing on a blank page (the most difficult). Relating these findings to the findings on the visual perceptual tasks, Birch and Lefford reported a close association between skill in copying and visual-kinesthetic intersensory integrative ability. Recalling the nature of the kinesthetic stimulation used, it seems that if a child can interpret, in visual symbols, his movements when he has no control over them, he can also do the reverse, that is, translate visual symbols into the appropriately executed hand motions. This does not imply mutual dependency of any form: in fact, it seems more likely that at this level both skills are dependent on some central mediational process.

This contrasts with Ayres' view regarding the primacy of tactile functions in the development of motor skills. However, she is dealing with a simpler level of functioning. Her measures of tactile perception are 1) accuracy of localizing a touch stimulus on hand or forearm; 2) ability to discriminate one or two touch stimulations; and 3) ability to recognize a form drawn on back of hand (graphesthesia). Motor planning is measured by 1) tracing a line; 2) copying a postural position demonstrated by examiner; and 3) object manipulation. Using these measures, she found a close relationship between deficits in motor planning and tactile perception and concluded that "the continuous flow of tactile sensations, if meaningful, lay down in the brain the body scheme upon which all future motor planning is based" (Ayres, 1963, p. 223). However, if we pursue the matter further, it is apparent that most tactile stimulation originally stems from motor activity; much more touching is done as the result of reaching than as the result of being touched. This is what led Kephart to postulate that "all behavior is basically motor....Behavior develops out of muscular activity, and so-called higher forms of behavior are dependent upon lower forms of behavior, thus making even these higher activities dependent upon the basic structure of the muscular activity upon which they are built" (1960, pp. 35-36). This is reminiscent of Piaget's notion that one learns an object through one's action upon it. Clearly, there is a reciprocal spiralling relationship here; early diffuse motor behavior initiates tactile and kinesthetic stimulation which feeds back into the "afferent pool" for integration and direction of more and more specific, differentiated motor behavior.

Body Image and Laterality

In this discussion we are proceeding backwards from the standpoint of time in ontogenetic origin but forwards in terms of professional interest. It is only recently that primitive motor responses have been linked directly with higher cognitive functions, particularly by applied professions such as optometry, special education, physical and occupational therapy. The theoretical base for many of the special therapies to be discussed shortly rests in the never-never land between neurology and psychology and there has been virtually no research for the validation of the theoretical premises. What little research there is has been done to evaluate success in treatment.

Much of this work takes us back to motor behavior in the first two years of life and the development of body control and body image. Although body image has been the subject of much psychological writing, in the past it has been the representational aspect of body image, particularly as reflected in drawings, which has been of prime interest (Harris, 1963). In the present context, it is the motor base of body awareness with which we are concerned. Kephart asserts that the basic movement pattern out of which all other movement patterns must develop is that of posture and quotes a study of Kagerer (1958) who found that substantial and consistent correlations between activities designed to measure ability to move within a posture (flexibility) and achievement in school (first grade level). In comparing this with earlier, seemingly contradictory results, Kephart points out that "early studies in the area of posture have investigated the postural adjustment of the child while he was not moving. Present studies investigate his posture during the process of movement. The emphasis has swung from highly specific motor skills (which can be learned as splinter skills and have limited relationship to the activities of the total organism) to investigations of general movement patterns and the ranges involved in these general patterns" (Kephart, 1960, p. 41). From body movement, and the observation of such movement, the child acquires a body image; he learns where his body is, how much space it requires, and how to move it selectively. In Kephart's view, the body is the zero point, or point of origin, for all movements and perceptual understanding of outside objects will be disturbed if the body image is disturbed. Looking at mental development from his unique epistemological viewpoint, Piaget says the same: "Development begins by the construction of a multiplicity of heterogenous spaces (oral, tactile, visual, etc.) each of which is centered on the child's own body or perspective. Then, after a kind of miniature Copernican revolution, space finally becomes a general place that contains all objects including the child's own body"(Piaget, 1954).

One aspect of body image and body movements which occupies a major position with regard to higher psychological functioning is that of *laterality*. The child must become aware of the right and left sides of his own body in order to get a directional sense in space. The relative importance of factors which give him the right-left feeling of his body is a matter of dispute. The optometrists (and to some extent Kephart) emphasize the control of the eyes and the matching of eye movements with movement of outside objects, including his own hand movements. Ayres discusses the association between crossing the mid-line of the body (in eye or hand movements) and right-left discrimination and considers hand dominance to be part of the body-image problem. Much of our knowledge of the world begins with our knowledge of our own bodies. Visual space perception begins with the understanding of the spatial relations of ourselves. Early number concepts have a body reference. Without adequate knowledge of the body, a child is handicapped in learning number concepts, all processes involving visual and spatial perception, and all skilled motor tasks. It is quite possible that the emergence of hand dominance is dependent upon reaching a certain stage of development in the body scheme" (Ayres, 1961).

The lack of cerebral dominance, or mixed laterality, has been held responsible for a variety of intellectual defects since the original work of Orton (1928). Later investigators, particularly in the area of reading disability, questioned whether this factor alone could account for major learning difficulties. Part of the confusion probably comes from the fact that dominance is not a simple, yes or no, matter. On the contrary, there seems to be a continuum from those who have strong and consistent eye-hand-foot preference to those who alternate hands in carrying out a single activity if it requires crossing the midline of the body. Investigators looking at large numbers of children in public school settings are looking at the great middle group of "normal" variations whereas other investigators are reporting on clinically identified populations where one can see the extreme forms of mixed laterality, usually in combination with other signs of perceptual-motor dysfunction.

Special Therapies

There has been a wave of special therapies based on perceptual-motor training with various professional idiosyncrasies. The common denominator seems to be a reliance on the principle that "ontogeny recapitulates phylogeny" which is taken to mean that one must take the child back to the beginning and retrace the usual sequence of steps in early perceptual-motor development. Some of the therapies are trying to influence "basic neurophysiological integration." As one would expect, optometrists approach the problem with eye exercises, pointing out that visual perception is very early in the order of development (Getman, 1958). Doman and Delacato, with backgrounds in physical therapy and speech, try to "reach the brain itself by pouring into the afferent sensory system...all of the stimuli normally provided by his environment but with such intensity and frequency as to draw, ultimately, a response from the corresponding motor systems" (quoted by Freeman, 1967). A major part of their therapy is "patterning," that is, a regimen of passive movement exercises coupled with prescribed creeping and crawling exercises, which is designed to "pattern" the brain through its sensory pathways. The establishment of cerebral dominance through specific eye, hand, and foot exercises, positioning in sleep, and the cross-pattern creeping is a major objective. The controversy around this therapy has been particularly heated because 1) it is very time-consuming and rigorous; 2) it is presented as "curative" rather than "symptomatic;" and 3) it has been recommended as "good" for all children, normal or of any diagnostic description. As the theory is presented, the only test would seem to be a pragmatic one, that is, does enhancement of motor functions (by their techniques) result in improvements in other areas without specific attention. The original publication reported an uncontrolled study which yielded encouraging preliminary results (Doman *et al.* 1960) and three books have been published reporting on the relationship between reading, on the one hand, and dominance and neurological organization on the other (Delacato, 1959; 1963; 1966). There have been thoughtful and critical reviews, mainly on the basis of inadequacies of research design and misinterpretation of results (Brown, 1964; Wepman, 1964; Cole, 1964). Attempts to replicate the findings on an independent basis have yielded negative results with retarded readers of normal intelligence (Robbins, 1967) and weak support, if any, with trainable retarded children (Kershner, 1968). Although his samples were small (16 control and 15 experimental), Kershner's study was exceptionally well controlled. Every school day for a period of four months, two classes of trainable retarded children were subjected to a *total* curriculum of perceptual motor training, either of the specific nature recommended by Doman-Delacato or non-specific activities designed to achieve better rhythm, balance, coordination, and body image. Unfortunately, the two groups were significantly different from the outset in terms of Peabody Picture Vocabulary Test IQ (mean IQ was 40 for the experimental group and 62 for the control group). Results indicated that 1) creeping and crawling performance improves through participating in creeping and crawling exercises; 2) unpracticed perceptual motor skills improved equally in both groups; and 3) the PPVT IQ score increased to 52 for the experimental group and was essentially unchanged (but still higher than 52) for the control group. This would seem to support, in part, the Doman-Delacato assertions with respect to neurological organization and higher cognitive functions, but the author is cautious in drawing conclusions on the basis that the two groups were not matched and that the improvement may have been due to factors associated with initial group differences (for instance, regression to the mean). However, evidence of this sort, even with qualifications, makes replication an imperative. In the face of claims which are obviously exaggerated, it is easy to ignore the germ of truth.

The therapies which are to follow are all much less rigid than the Doman-Delacato, are more modest in claims, and more individualized in accordance with the functioning of the child. However, they all have in common the idea that training in basic perceptual and motor functions is a necessary prerequisite for higher cognitive functions, and furthermore, that such functions will be facilitated indirectly, that is, without direct remedial attention, once the perceptual motor foundation is thoroughly established. Kephart offers a large number of varied training activities in eye-hand coordination, form perception, general body exercises, and ocular control to be selected in accordance with the child's performance on a survey rating scale (1960). Barsch presents a "space-oriented approach" to learning with rhythmic and sensory motor activities derived from 9 movement areas (1967). Ayres' treatment proposals also are individually based but emphasize sensory stimulation to increase body awareness and "to normalize tactile and kinesthetic sensation." Unlike Kephart and Barsch (from the field of special education) and similar to Doman and Delacato, she feels that treatment is based "primarily on influencing basic neurophysiological integration, through control of sensorimotor behavior" (1963, p. 225). Frostig emphasizes perceptual training, but mainly in the area of visual perception, and says little about possible neurological base. One can see in all these therapies a direct line from theory (either neurophysiological or educational), to diagnostic test, to treatment which is derived from the observed deficits in the tests used.

Surprisingly little has been done in the way of follow-up or longitudinal study to assess the results of any of these perceptual-motor therapies. Most of the reported studies have evaluated the results over a short period of time, a year at most, and have used criteria very similar in kind to the training activities (Painter, 1966). A major question remains as to whether this kind of training is a direct lead into higher cognitive functions involving language, abstraction, concept formation, and academic skills or whether there is a gap between two levels or stages of development. It is interesting to note that so many kinds of studies place the maximum rate of improvement between the ages of 5 and 7 years. It would seem that major changes are taking place *simultaneously* in cognitive and perceptual motor functioning and one wonders if one really precedes the other. It is interesting to note that the current literature on early education stresses environmental enrichment and language stimulation in the preschool age period but says little about perceptual motor training as such. On the other hand, these special therapies which are attempting to reconstruct the normal development of the same age period de-emphasize language training as if this will follow as a matter of course. A great deal more information is needed to determine what forms of perceptual motor training are effective for whom. In terms of theory, it is also important to determine why it works. There is some indication that general physical education is intellectually beneficial (Oliver, 1958; Corder, 1966) and it may well be that teacher attention, interest and experience of success for the children are the significant variables. It may be of no consequence in practice (at least not immediately), but for building a coherent and consistent theory of normal cognitive development, it is imperative to tease out the critical variables.

Inhibition of Movement

Before we leave this field, some mention should be made of inhibitory mechanisms. As movement patterns become more skilled, superfluous movements drop out. Failure of inhibition results in either the collateral overflow movements which are regarded as "soft" neurological signs or a generalized pattern of hyperactivity. The counterpart in perception is the problem of attention; activity and attentiveness are, of course, related, if for no other reason than that the child must be able to sit still in order to concentrate. Several workers have offered perceptual explanations for hyperactivity. Because of the figure-ground disturbance, Strauss and Lehtinen saw the brain-injured child as driven hither and yon by his shifting attention to any and all sensory stimuli, relevant or irrelevant. Ayres relates increased motor activity to tactile defensiveness which she considers the result of deficit in tactile perception. "Tactile defensiveness consists of feelings of discomfort and a desire to escape the situation when certain types of tactile stimuli are experienced" (1964, p. 8). Thus, in the one theory, hyperactivity is the result of lack of differentiation and in the other it is occasioned by protective withdrawal. The importance of tactual stimulation has received some support from other quarters cited by Cromwell, Baumeister, and Hawkins, 1963). Gellner (1959) and Zaporozhets (1957, 1960) suggest that there is a sequence in relative primacy of the senses. At an early age, motor activity has a role in external-orienting and investigatory behavior. This foundation of tactual association serves as a basis for the later development of distance receptors such as vision and audition and the transition to verbal associations. The older child with fluent visual and verbal associations need not invoke his motor-touch system as much. In this view, the hyperactivity is explained on a positive need to touch rather than a pulling away from touch sensations. The idea that hyperactivity represents a fixation or regression to an early level is an attractive one, particularly when one observes that it is exacerbated under conditions of frustration or anxiety. If it were a symptom inherent in the nervous system, "organic driveness," (Kahn & Cohen, 1934) or in the perceptual system, one would expect it to be much more consistent under all conditions and throughout the age span than it in fact is.

Some research has been done with activity level and movement control in normal children. With a group of nursery school children of average and superior intelligence, Maccoby *et al.* (1965) found that their total level of general activity was *not* related to measures of intellectual proficiency but that the children's ability to inhibit motor movement on demand ("draw a line slowly" *was* related to measures of cognitive performance. This provides a good example of the interrelationship between personality and cognition. "If we agree that the primary importance of the activity dimension lies in the ability to inhibit activity when this is necessary for problem-solving, then when we study activity we are in the larger domain of impulse control, frustration tolerance and delay of gratification" (Maccoby, 1968, p. 195).

RELATIONSHIP OF LANGUAGE TO COGNITIVE FUNCTIONS

Without language, an individual will inevitably be stunted, both intellectually and emotionally. If he has no understanding of words, he can have only a hazy idea of what others are saying; he is forced to rely on facial expressions, vocal inflections, gestures, and situational clues. He cannot make reference to absent persons or things; he cannot tell another person what has happened; he cannot inquire about future events. He cannot state his complaints, his wishes, or his feelings, except in actions which can be easily misinterpreted. He has to do things rather than think thoughts. In the words of Church, "Language transforms experience first by creating new channels through which the human environment can act on the child....At the same time, the learning of language transforms the individual in such a way that he is enabled to do new things for himself, or to do old things in new ways" (1961, p. 95). It is generally accepted that a child's use of language is closely related to his intellectual level; so much so, in fact, that the common criticism of IQ tests is that they are "too verbal." From an operational point of view, tests of intelligence and language measures may present the same stimuli, evaluate the same responses, and classify the behavior on the same bases. With this identity in mind, Spradlin questioned if it might not be profitable to collapse "intelligence" and "language" into a single construct (1963). In brief, there is no argument regarding the fact that language serves as a necessary ingredient of higher cognitive functions such as abstract thought. The arguments revolve around issues regarding acquisition of language and effect of language on specific learning tasks.

Acquisition of Language

The origin of language is regarded as a greater or lesser mystery from Langer's broad statement that "Language is, without a doubt, the most momentous and at the same time the most mysterious product of the human mind" (1942, p. 103) to Skinner's concise explanation that "A child acquires verbal behavior when relatively unpatterned vocalizations, selectively reinforced, gradually assume forms which produce appropriate consequences in a given verbal community" (1957). Part of the mystery in language development comes from the nature of the interaction between environment and brain structure; nowhere else is this interaction so obvious. Brown and Bellugi (1964) offer a modern statement of the problem:

> *There must be some kind of distinctive mechanism, peculiar to the human brain which is appropriate to the processing of speech. One must somehow account for the fact that, when children have heard a lot of speech, they start to talk, whereas, if apes hear the same noises, they do not talk. A "language generator" must be built into the brain and set to operate independent of any natural language.... The language generator is either initially or through maturational processes primed to go off when suitable samples of speech are presented to it, and this has little to do with learning. (p. 113)*

Theories regarding cortical localization of speech functions, especially with reference to cerebral dominance, were discussed in the first section of this review; but in the present state of knowledge, we do not understand how cortical neurons are specifically adapted for processing language and why such neurons tend to congregate in particular parts of the cortex.

We do know that the environment must provide input of auditory stimuli. Concern about the language deficit in culturally deprived populations has stimulated a number of interesting studies on this point. Irwin had mothers of twenty-four children of lower socioeconomic status spend from l5 to 20 minutes a day reading stories to their children from the time the children were l3 months old until they were 30 months old. Compared to a control group of l0 children the experimental group showed a significantly higher frequence of vocalization by l8 months, and the differences became larger with increasing age (1960). It is unfortunate that this important and provocative study was not followed up to see if the experimental group retained an advantage in the functional use of language. A quite different approach was taken by Hess *et al.* . Hess and Shipman undertook to analyze the maternal influences on cognitive behavior of children as related to different social-class levels. Their project is based on the notion "that the mother can be viewed as a teacher, as a programmer of input, during the pre-school years and that mothers from different social-class levels will program or socialize the cognitive behavior of their children in different ways (1968, p. 91). The research focussed on three characteristics of mother-child interaction: imperative-normative ("you must not"); personal-subjective ("you should not"); and cognitive-rational ("you should, because...."). The research population was made up of 40 mother-child pairs (the child about 4 years old) from each of four socioeconomic groups; the techniques used were interviewing the hypothetical questions and observing the mother's style as she taught her child a specific task presented in the laboratory or worked on a collaborative task such as copying a design with the Etch-a-Sketch. Major differences were found in sheer volume of verbal output and the nature of control strategies with a larger percentage use of imperative responses by the mothers from the lower socioeconomic groups. The performance of the children showed similar social-class differences. These observations led to some very significant conclusions regarding the nature of verbal input in relation to social class and to learning behavior:

> *It appears that learning styles and information-processing strategies that the child obtains in these early encounters with his cognitive and regulatory environment may set limits upon the potential mental growth of the child....The cognitive environment of the culturally disadvantaged child is one in which behavior is controlled by imperatives rather than by attention to the individual characteristics of a specific situation, and one in which behavior is neither mediated by verbal cues which offer opportunites for using language as a tool for labeling, ordering, and manipulating stimuli in the environment, nor mediated by teaching that relates events to one another and present to the future (1968, p. 103).*

Although this study is not directly related to the relationship of input to the *initial* acquisition of language, it is directly related to the question of later use of language as a tool.

The problem of input has been considered in the Illinois Test of Psycholinguistic Ability, a diagnostic test which attempts to analyze the component parts of language functions following a rationale derived from Osgood (1957). In the ITPA, there are two basic modes of input (visual and auditory) and two basic modes of output (vocal and gestural). There are two levels of organization—the automatic sequential and the representational; and there are three psycholinguistic processes— decoding (input), association, and encoding (output). The battery of 9 tests was standardized on 700 children between 2½ and 9 years. Similar to the tests described in the section on perceptual-motor development, the ITPA has been used as the base for specific remedial language training with some success (Smith, 1962; Mueller and Smith, 1964). However, we have the same problem in evaluating "success," namely, it depends largely on the degree of similarity between the final criterion measurement and the activities in the intervening training program. What is not known is whether improvement in specific functions is generalizable or whether it provides a base from which the child can continue on his own.

Returning to the subject of initial acquisition of language, we have the problem of its relation to perceptual-motor antecedents and the old question of continuity or discontinuity in early development. Although the notion of stages, implying some discontinuity, is associated with Piaget's work, he emphasizes the point of *continuity* in the transition from the sensorimotor phase to the preoperational period ushered in by language. Sensorimotor intelligence deals only with the most concrete aspects of reality, but in its sixth, and last, stage, there is behavior indicative of representational thought—apparently without benefit of verbal symbols. The child of 18 months or so can reconstruct events which are not present in the perceptual field and he can figure out the consequences of various actions in his mind, without doing or seeing them, and then act appropriately as a result of this "thinking through.' It is at this stage that one would expect the sudden "insight" experiences which have been described for chimpanzees and other infrahuman organisms. Wallach (1963) has pointed out the irony that Piaget, a philosophically oriented European psychologist, should offer observational data to support the early statements of Watson and Skinner to the effect that thinking involves internalized behavior, and the irony is compounded by the fact that Freud also held a similar view that thought is "essentially an experimental way of acting." The question of the origin of thought has brought together some strange bedfellows.

Agreeing that thought precedes language and is closely linked with sensorimotor experiences, we have the question of the transformation of thought into spoken verbal symbols, the problem of output. Spoken speech is a collection of motor responses which have been differentiated out of the great medley of sounds which exist in the infant's repertoire of vocal play.* The questions are: 1) what was the process of differentiation; 2) how did they acquire communication value; and 3) how did they acquire meaning as signifiers? This brings us to the topic of reinforcement. Rheingold *et al.* demonstrated that the amount of vocalization of infants of 2 months (living in an institution) could be significantly increased by secondary social reinforcement from adult persons. Skinner reduced the problem to

---

*It should be recalled that our non-speaking ape has nothing like the repertoire of sounds possessed by the normal human infant and does not engage in the same kind of vocal play with tongue, lips, breath, and changes in pitch and volume.

principles of operant conditioning where certain spontaneously delivered sounds are selectively reinforced either because the mother shows pleasure (as in Rheingold's study) or because it is effective in bringing about a desired action. Mowrer suggests that at the first stage of language learning the child makes word-like sounds because *he* likes to hear them, not because of their social effectiveness. The child's preference and enjoyment of certain sounds comes from his association of vocalization with loving care: "When a child is lonely, frightened, hungry, cold, or merely bored, he can comfort and divert himself by making noises which have previously been associated with comfort and diversion" (1960, p. 700). In many ways this echoes earlier comments of Schilder: "Expressive movements may also be defined as action in the absence of an object, or as fundamentally incomplete action. Primitive language is, therefore, partly expressive movements and partly magic action. The onomatopoetic imitations in primitive languages are magic passes; by making the sounds of an object, I become that object and thereby obtain power over it. The beginnings of language clearly bear the marks of its need-character....I therefore consider language a partial action which appears when the action proper cannot be consummated" (1930; 1951, p. 528). Mowrer would add to this that by making the sounds of a person, the child becomes that person, through identification, and feels correspondingly reassured.

One of the strongest critics of the operant conditioning model for learning spoken language is Church and his comments are particularly relevant when we think of language as a signifier. He points out that passive language, or understanding, is usually ahead of active language, or speech, so that words are learned silently without opportunity for external reinforcement. When they are spoken, they are reinforced but some prior learning has taken place. Church adds that babbling does not proceed in a continuous way up to the moment of speech; to the contrary, the babbling and jargon of the infant may increase in volume and approximate the inflection of speech more closely, but this diminishes before real speech appears. Speech is *not* taught by the parents listening to catch a word sound and then responding with the appropriate word or action. On the basis of accumulating such chain associations, it would take forever to build up anything like the normal vocabulary of the two- year-old. It is impossible to understand the snowball effect of learning language without considering one, the role of learning sets and two, intrinsic motivation.

Moderately retarded and autistic children provide an excellent opportunity to study the processes involved in the acquisition of language. It seems probable that most of these children could acquire verbal responses by means of operant conditioning; if so, one could study the limitations of this method of learning. Even without specific training, it is not uncommon for autistic children to learn rote phrases, but language for communication remains seriously deficient because they have no sense of separate identity. They do not observe themselves and consequently cannot observe others or place themselves in the position of another person. With severely or moderately retarded children, the words they learn do not have the normal snowball effect because no learning set is established. Without consistent reinforcement, they are likely to lose their speech. This perhaps accounts for case histories which report that a child had a few single words which he then lost. If the initial words do not provide the springboard for further language learning, they are not sufficiently useful to be retained. It is probably not a sign of deterioration but a failure to go on to the next stage. In this connection, it is also interesting to compare the speech histories of Mongoloid children raised in institutions from birth with those living in their own homes. The marked advantage demonstrated by those living at home attests to the importance of identification and social reinforcement in language learning (Centerwall and Centerwall, 1960).

Effect of Language on Cognitive Learning

Assuming that the line from sensorimotor development to language is relatively continuous, what is the effect of possessing language skills on other forms of learning? Does the emergence of language constitute a genuine transformation for the child so that all subsequent behaviors are modified? In the words of information theory, has the human mind as a computer changed its data-processing characteristics? The first question would be the effect of language on perception and simple discrimination. Whorf has taken a strong position for linguistic determinism; perceptions can be no richer or more precise than language labels permit (1958). In studies of "acquired distinctiveness," the evidence seems to be against this hypothesis. Using adult subjects with different native languages, Lenneberg found that the capacity to discriminate hues was the same, even though the verbal labels indicated different cultural distinctions (Lenneberg, 1961). The situation may be different with young children. Spiker reviewed the experiments studying verbal factors in discrimination learning in preschool children and found that by and large, verbal labels had a facilitating effect (1963). The experimental design in these studies is first learning different verbal responses with the final criterion task involving a differential motor response. In this design, perceptual discrimination and verbal cues are learned simultaneously which is quite different from the Lenneberg study which relied on old knowledge, both perceptual and verbal.

By far the greatest work on the verbal mediation hypothesis has been done with more elaborate research designs involving transposition, reversal shifts, and concept attainment tasks. Kuenne (1946) hypothesized that possession of a verbal concept of the relation between two stimuli in a discrimination task ("bigger than," for instance) would facilitate transposition to a new discrimination involving the same principle with a new pair of stimuli, "near" or "far" from the original stimuli. She reported "two developmental stages as far as the relation of verbal response to overt choice behavior is concerned. In the first, the child is able to make differential verbal responses to appropriate aspects of the situation, but this verbalization does not control or influence his overt choice behavior. Later, such verbalizations gain control and dominate choice behavior" (l946, p. 488). In general, the results confirmed Kuenne's findings that preschool children have difficulty transposing the original learning to a new situation if the new stimuli are very different from the original (the "far" test) whereas for older children, the absolute difference does not matter as long as the same principle holds (Alberts and Ehrenfreund, 1951). However, there has been considerable argument as to whether transposition learning is a valid test of verbal mediation since far transposition has been elicited in supposedly nonverbal children. Rudel (1958) using children between 2l and 33 months of age obtained transposition on both far and near stimuli although this group required twice as much training on the initial discrimination as did the older, verbal group (34 to 45 months). In their review, Rebelsky, Starr, and Luria (1967) offer the cautious conclusion that "Transposition can be most readily mediated by verbalization but it can be mediated also by some mechanisms of a preverbal nature" (1967, p. 326).

Reversal and nonreversal shifts in discrimination learning has been another experimental method used to study the verbal mediation hypothesis. Simple reversal means that the child must learn that one answer is right and one wrong in the first situation and then reverse this in the second learning situation. A nonreversal shift means that the child must attend to a different stimulus cue in the second learning situation. According to a single unit, stimulus-response theory of learning, it would be easier for the child to learn to attend to a new stimulus cue than for him to reverse what he has once learned is "right." According to the mediation hypothesis, if the child has the idea that a certain aspect of the stimulus situation is important, he can look at either way to figure out "what's right." There is considerable evidence to indicate that reversal learning is indeed more difficult for younger subjects. Working with preschool and kindergarten children, the Kendlers found that older and brighter children were superior on the reversal condition and slightly inferior on the nonreversal shift (Kendler and Kendler, 1959; Kendler, Kendler, and Wells, 1960). Kendler *et al.* suggested that "there is a stage in human development in which verbal responses, though available, do not readily mediate between external stimuli and overt responses" (1960, p. 87), practically the same statement as the earlier one of Kuenne.

Many reviews have appeared regarding these and other experimental paradigms for evaluating the effect of language on non-language behavior using retarded as well as normal young children. Conclusions vary from one extreme to the other. Reese concludes that "there *is* a deficiency in mediation in young children, compared with older children" (1962, p. 507), but Rebelsky *et al.* are more cautious: "The specific hypothesis that the young child (usually taken to mean the preverbal child) is deficient in ability to mediate, and therefore will perform in experiments said to require verbal mediation, like infrahuman subjects rather than like older human subjects appears to be at best controversial. Early results on reversal shift, transposition, acquired equivalence of cues, and double alternation appeared to support the mediation-deficit hypothesis; but later work has uncovered conditions under which mediation deficit in preverbal children is not the rule" (1967, p. 328). Wolff (1967) offered a critique of discrimination reversal learning in humans. His arguments are too lengthy and technical to be briefly reviewed here, but he concluded that "the studies just reviewed offer *little* support for the position that verbalization is a crucial factor in the shift-learning process" and further that "the principal factors operating in the shift process in general are probably attentional in nature, as Zeaman and House have supposed, rather than verbal or perceptual as other investigators have sometimes implied" (1967, p. 403). Clearly, it is a controversy that is not dead and one which strikes at the center of various learning theories. Retarded subjects have been used frequently to try and settle this particular developmental issue but these studies have tended to confuse rather than clarify. One of the problems has been poor techniques for deciding whether a given child is or is not "verbal." Everyone agrees that spoken speech cannot be used as the criterion, but they are not clear about the measurement of "inner" speech.

Experimental studies of concept attainment stand somewhere midway between the discrimination studies discussed above and true language behavior. The ability to acquire and utilize concepts is one of man's most powerful tools. To the young infant, every situation is in some sense unique. In the course of development, the child manages to order his experiences into coherent categories by defining a given situation as a member of a larger unit. It is through the acquisition of concepts that the child learns to organize, understand, and react constructively to his environment. Concepts can be of any order of complexity and abstractness from the perceptual concepts of shapes and colors to the logical concept of conservation. Experiments in this area typically are sorting tasks or a succession of two or three stimuli presentations with a minimum of verbal instruction, and some form of reinforcement when the "right" one is chosen. The subjects are usually school age. Briefly, it has been found that ability to form concepts improves as the child gets older and that it is influenced by IQ (Hoffman, 1955; Zaslow, 1961; Osler and Fivel, 1961). Comparisons of matched mental age groups (one normal and one retarded) have reported conflicting results with Griffith *et al.* (1959) and Meyers *et al.* (1961) reporting differences for normal and *institutionalized* retarded subjects of like mental age, and Johnson and Blake (1960) finding no differences in concept attainment for groups drawn from regular and special public school classes.

In this context, we are particularly interested in the question of the *mode* of concept attainment. Paralleling the previous discussion, we find two major theories. The first is the S-R incremental model (Bourne and Restle, 1959) where the correct response to the concept exemplars is built up gradually on the basis of previous reinforcement of stimuli belonging to the same class. The second theory is that concept attainment is achieved not by simple S-R associations, but by mediational symbolic processes. A stimulus in a concept problem elicits an implicit response (or hypothesis) which in turn serves as a cue for the overt response. According to this view, concept attainment would occur suddenly when the correct mediator is selected, rather than gradually.

A number of studies reported by Osler and her colleagues indicate a positive relationship between concept attainment by mediation hypothesis and intelligence (Osler and Fivel, 1961; Osler and Trautman, 1961; Osler and Shapiro, 1964) when normal and superior subjects are compared. Marshall (1964) found the same relationship to hold true when normal and mildly retarded subjects (living at home) were compared. From this, she concluded that there is a continuum rather than two distinct models of concept attainment. "Earlier studies suggested that bright children attain concepts by the use of hypotheses or mediators. In comparison, average children rely on S-R associations and build up concepts gradually. It now appears that slow learners are even more dependent than average children on S-R associations and are less able to acquire concepts by means of hypotheses" (1964, p. 73). This provides one of the rare instances where comparisons were made throughout the entire range of intelligence and a continuum demonstrated. Another approach to assess the influence of language on concept attainment is to compare success in attaining two kinds of concepts, which are differentially favored by language, for instance, the concept of opposition which is more language relevant than the concept of "same" versus "different." Replicating an earlier study with deaf children (Furth, 1961), Milgram and Furth found that educable retarded children (mental ages between 5 and 9) were similarly handicapped and concluded that "the retarded performed more poorly in the discovery and application of a language relevant concept that was within their realm of comprehension, but performed as well as normals in solving problems where perceptual rather than verbal modes of solution were assumed to be more suitable" (1963, p. 739). When it is all added together, it is hard to escape the conclusion that retarded children have particular difficulty in using verbal symbols and that this interferes with their learning and problem solving behavior.

This has been considered sufficiently important to represent the major basis for "explaining" mental retardation by Luria. He speaks of two signaling systems, the first, composed of direct signals of reality, and the second, consisting of words, and suggests that retardation can be explained by underdevelopment of the second signaling system or failure in its effectiveness to regulate acts of behavior (1963). His experimental tasks are deceptively simple: "When the light appears, press the balloon" or "When the red light appears, press the balloon. Do nothing when the green light appears." He finds that even normal children cannot do the first task until around the age of 3-3½ years and not until 5-5½ years can the child regulate his behavior (positive and negative) according to the complete verbal instructions (1961). His explanation for the dissociation between verbal signals and motor responses is conceptualized in psychophysiological terms. He proposes that connections between stimuli not formed through verbal associations are extremely unstable and depend upon constant reinforcement. Without specifying the degree of retardation, age, or life experience of his subjects, Luria states that "oligophrenic" children use speech in an active, orienting role in only the most elementary problem situations and only in the first such experiments. When new problems are introduced and "the child must inhibit the previously coupled connections and orient itself in a new situation, the picture essentially changes: the previous verbal formulation, owing to the inertia of processes in the verbal system, persists, and speech, far from helping the child to orient itself in the new situation, even hinders the transition from its previous experience to the elaboration of new connections" (1963, p. 384).

With respect to the understanding of normal development, there is much more to learn about "the changing relation between verbal and nonverbal processes as children's mastery of language increases and on the evolution of the self-directive role of language" (Ervin and Miller, 1963, p. 135). In contrast to American studies of school-age children, Russian research has dealt more with preschool children, including mentally retarded children for comparative purposes. It is from the Russian work that distinct stages in the verbal control of behavior have emerged: language progresses from an auditory stimulus which acts as a trigger to semantic meaning which allows for generalization and mobility and concurrently it progresses from an external stimulus to an internal one. Although it is tempting to study the effect of language on learning as a unilateral problem, there is obviously a circular reaction involved when we recall the problems of acquiring language. As Roger Brown nicely pointed out in his description of "The Original Word Game" (1958), learning a word is a form of concept attainment. With relation to the development of relatively abstract concepts, Piaget feels that intellectual operations direct language acquisitions rather than vice versa (1967). It is certainly true that a problem is clarified by putting it into words, but this does not mean that it is the words which do the clarifying. Similar reasoning is involved with regard to the suggestion that "the learning of language is crucial to the ability to categorize one's self and one's acts and hence crucial to social and moral behavior" (Ervin and Miller, 1963, p. 138). Because limitation in the use of verbal symbols is the most ubiquitous deficit in mentally retarded individuals, to varying degrees, they can provide the acid test for many developmental issues in this particular field. However, we will be faced for a long time to come with the problem of the ultimate cause of this particular deficit. Luria's suggestion that it is due to "the very fact of the pathological inertness of the verbal system" seems to be little more than a rephrasing of the problem—words which do *not* serve to clarify.

SOURCES OF INDIVIDUAL DIFFERENCES

A comprehensive theory of cognitive functioning must account for the diversity of cognitive performance as well as the commonalities found among individuals. The spectrum of what might be looked at as individual differences is wide, including, for instance, variations in sequential development, preferred modes of processing information, cognitive styles, and so on. However, the characteristics which have attracted the greatest amount of research attention and caused the greatest concern have been differences in the rate and ceiling of cognitive development as measured by IQ tests. It has always been tempting to account for IQ differences in terms of opposing factors such as genetic versus environmental or organic versus functional. Although lip service is always given to the importance of interaction, professional workers tend to polarize around the physical or psychological factors in their efforts to determine the proportional contributions of each. Figure I is an effort to schematize the multiple factors which produce the end product of an intellectually achieving individual. Hopefully, this figure of concentric circles has some value for purposes of presenting issues, but it has two serious flaws. One, it may imply that

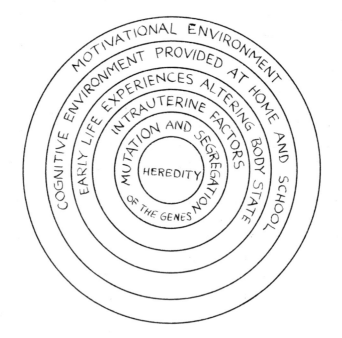

FIGURE 1
Origin of Differences in Cognitive Performance

the factors involved have a time-limited action in the development of the individual and then combine in an additive effect. To the contrary, these factors interact in a continuous, coextensive fashion throughout life. Second, the fact that the intervals are of equal size may imply that each subsequent factor contributes an equal amount of difference which is far from the truth in any given case. For instance, if we think of Down's syndrome as an example of genetic mutation, it certainly overshadows any other single factor in its influence on intelligence whereas under normal circumstances, the second circle has no effect. The factors indicated in Figure I will be discussed in relation to mental retardation rather than any other individual cognitive difference primarily because it is the most unwanted individual deviation and therefore the most studied.

Heredity and Mental Retardation

In times past, heredity was assumed to be the major determinant of intelligence, and environment had to prove its case. In the last ten years, the situation has reversed as represented by Sarason and Gladwin's statement that "it will be our thesis that a hereditary determinant of mental capacity must not be assumed to exist unless proven" (1958). Part of the reversal comes from broadening the concept of "environment" to include the prenatal and physical environment. Following his many studies relating social class, pregnancy, and birth histories to later psychopathology, including mental retardation, convulsive disorder, and learning disability, Pasamanick decided that there was no need to posit any hereditary basis of intelligence: "It is now possible to entertain a new tabula rasa theory hypothecating that at conception individuals are quite alike in intellectual endowment except for these quite rare hereditary neurologic defects. It appears to us that it is life experience and the sociocultural milieu influencing biological and psychological function which, in the absence of organic brain damage, makes human beings significantly different from each other" (1959, p. 318). This sentiment is in complete accord with the Russian position, briefly stated by Luria: "We contest the viewpoint— incompatible with modern medicine—which is included to deduce peculiarities of development from different inborn abilities. The assertion of some authors that a considerable part of the population is hereditarily 'subnormal'....can hardly be regarded as a worthy contribution to science" (1963, p. 369).

To assess the validity of these conclusions, it is necessary to take a look at the kind of facts which were originally used to establish the hereditary base of intelligence. The two major lines of evidence for inheritance factors are 1) family resemblances and 2) the normal distribution of IQ test scores. The correlational-type studies are reviewed by Gottesman (1963). Many of the studies suffer from a confounding of concurrent environmental factors, but Burt's report of individual intelligence test correlations for substantial samples of different degrees of sibship in London school children is impressive evidence for genetic factors (1958). He reported correlations of .843 for 2I pairs of identical twins reared apart to .252 for 287 unrelated children reared together. It is also interesting that the reported correlations for non-identical twins reared together, siblings reared together and siblings reared apart were all close (.526, .491, and .463 respectively). Honzik compared developmental trends with regard to mother-child resemblance in intelligence for children reared in their own homes and the children reared in foster homes reported by Skodak and Skeels (1949). For both groups there was no correlation between IQ's at age 2 years and any index of maternal intelligence, but by the age of 4 years, significant positive correlations of equal magnitude were found. No significant correlation was found between the child's IQ and foster mother's educational level. Honzik concluded that "the fact that the parent-child resemblance is no greater for children reared by their own parents and the further fact reported by Skodak-Skeels of no relationship between the children's mental test performance and the foster parents' ability suggest that the education of the parents *per se* is not an environmentally important factor and that the obtained parent-child correlations reflect individual differences which are largely genetically determined' (1957, p. 227). However, the same study can be used to demonstrate the beneficial effects of environment in that the mean IQ for the foster children was I06 compared to a mean IQ of 86 for their true mothers.

It is an undisputed fact that intelligence test scores tend to fall in the normal bell-shaped distribution curve when a sufficiently large number of individuals is tested. This fact, by itself, means little except that a large number of independent factors must be responsible. However, it assumes more meaning when compared with similar distributions for a great variety of physical measures, such as height and weight, where the genetic components are less controversial. In his review of genetic aspects of intelligent behavior, Gottesman explains that "The genetic hypothesis which fits the observed distribution of IQ scores is that biological factors based on polygenic effects are operating" (1963, p. 261). But he goes on to add the caution that "Other hypotheses are also possible which stress the additive effects of random environmental factors." Because of the impossibility of controlling the environment, it is difficult to prove the polygenic basis of inheritance of mental ability in human beings, but there is abundant proof of the existence of polygenic systems (and normal distribution curves for resulting characteristics) in work with animals (Fuller and Thompson, 1960).

Simply to posit polygenic inheritance is no explanation; geneticists ask the further question: What is it that is inherited in this fashion which explains differences in IQ's? Here one could review the prior discussions in this chapter with regard to differences in drive (intrinsic motivation), inhibition mechanisms, the various neurophysiological correlates and so on for possible candidates. In the present state of knowledge, it seems probable that there are differences in the inherent biological properties of man which account for some of the intellectual variance. Anderson points out that those traits which are influenced genetically by polygenes are more subject to environmental modification than are those characteristics controlled by a single genetic locus, but he cautions "at the same time we should not expect an infinite plasticity in response to differences in environment" (1964, p. 373). Anderson goes on to suggest that not all genetic combinations are equally susceptible to environmental influences and that it is possible that persons with unusually high or unusually low genetic potential may be more susceptible than those in the middle range which would be an interesting idea to explore further.

A Two-Group Approach to Mental Retardation

A number of writers have pointed out that the distribution of IQ scores has an excess of individuals at the very low end of the scale compared to expectancy (Roberts, 1952) and proposed that intelligence distribution be conceptualized in terms of two curves, one representing the "normal" distribution from ±3 standard deviations (IQ range approximately 50 to 150) with a second curve superimposed at the lower end with a mean IQ of about 35, ranging from zero to 70 (Zigler, 1966a). It is presumed that this second population is comprised of those retardates for whom there is an identifiable physiological defect. According to this notion, the great majority of mildly retarded individuals would represent the lower end of the normal continuum with many environmental and polygenic factors involved in causation whereas the great majority of the moderately and severely retarded would have a single major cause. An IQ of 50 is often taken as the line of demarcation, partly because this represents -3 standard deviations but also there is some empirical evidence in justification. Follow-up studies have shown that children testing under 50, at any initial age, stay in this general range with rare exceptions, although there is a great deal more fluctuation and variability in the later results for children initially testing above 50 (Oppenheimer, Tanguay and Smith).

This two-group approach revives a familiar diagnostic distinction between the familial or so-called "garden variety" mentally retarded and the "organic" (Sarason, 1953). In theory this remains a valid distinction, although it is often difficult to distinguish in an individual case. Also, it is important to keep in mind that neurophysiological differences may well be part of the polygenic inheritance affecting IQ, a point made by Kugel. He studied a group of 18 children who were diagnosed "familial" retarded on the basis of 1) socioeconomic background, 2) having one sibling or one parent who was mentally retarded, 3) having an IQ between 50 and 80, and 4) having no known organic cause. Mainly on the basis of an unexpectedly large number of abnormal electroencephalograms, he proposed that "a group of children who were originally regarded as having no neurological or neurophysiological basis for their retardation may in fact have such a basis for this, which indeed may be on an inherited basis" (1963, p. 210).

There are important implications for further research in the two-group approach. One would expect that differences of any kind, found in those mildly retarded representing the lower segment of the "normal" range, would also in a continuum with children of average and superior intelligence, perhaps even in a linear relationship. On the other hand, psychological or neurophysiological differences in the "clinical" group might well be discontinuous with the rest of the population. To some extent research investigators can assume that their populations of retarded subjects will be weighted towards one etiologic group or the other in terms of severity of the retardation, but more information than IQ and home versus institution should be provided. In community research, there is a general tendency to utilize slow-learning subjects from suburban areas because of ease of access and, in the very least, such studies should be replicated in culturally deprived areas before generalizing principles of retarded functioning. Although it is beside the purpose of this paper, the two-group approach also has implications for long-range community planning. In a presentation to the Secretary's Committee on Mental Retardation in HEW, Albee objected to the false hopes aroused by pleas to look for "major breakthroughs needed to bring significant reduction in the incidence of mental retardation" (MR 67, First Report to the President) and argued that "if most cases of deficiency are due to normal polygenic inheritance, a significant reduction in incidence cannot be anticipated." Albee suggested that we should redirect a significant proportion of our research efforts towards the development and evaluation of services and programs to maximize the limited potential of the mildly deficient and to do research on socially innovative opportunities for these people to be reasonably self-sufficient (1968).

Congenital Contributions to Intelligence

According to a classification diagram proposed by Cattell (1950), the term "congenital," which means present at birth, includes three components of biologically based behavior: heredity, mutant genes, and intrauterine environment effects—the innermost three circles in Figure I. Gene-based qualities biologically acquired from the parents are called hereditary and, in addition to the polygenic inheritance already discussed, major gene inheritance may modify intelligence as the by-product of metabolic dysfunction. Some ninety diseases have been identified as inborn errors of metabolism of fats, proteins, or carbohydrates, and most seem to be transmitted by means of an hereditable trait. The most famous of these in the field of mental retardation is phenylketonuria which is inherited when the individual is homozygous for the recessive genes involved. Since its discovery in 1934 (Folling), volumes have been published on its recognition, the hereditary mechanisms, the chemical reactions involved, and dietary treatment which is moderately successful in preventing retardation. However, it still is not understood how the brain is damaged by the phenylalanine metabolites which accumulate in phenylketonuria (Waisman and Gerritsen, 1964). The original hope that the pathology of phenylketonuria would shed light on the biochemistry of the normal brain has so far not been realized but still seems reasonable. Not all the inborn errors of metabolism result in retardation (although many do) and retardation results from some other recessive genes which are of a different order; for instance, one form of microcephaly is a rare disease inherited in the recessive fashion (Book, Schut, and Reed, 1953).

When we look at the second circle, we are considering changed genes in the germ cell due to spontaneous mutations or mutagenic agents which become part of the hereditary component for the next generation. The most important example is Down's syndrome, or Mongolism, which is associated with an extra chromosome (#21), usually as the result of non-disjunction in the formation of the ovum (Anderson, 1964). Again, the mechanisms whereby the extra chromosome leads to the multiple defects is by no means clear. Gottesman remarks that "among the most exciting outcomes of this particular discovery is the clue to the gene content of chromosome 21 and the possibility of chemical correction of the defect" and cites studies which suggest that perhaps mongols suffer from a disturbance of tryptophan metabolism and might be affected by a low amount of brain serotonin. This is a good example of levels of explanation in the scientific world; what is one man's explanation is another man's question.

There are other questions about Mongolism besides those regarding the reason for the non-disjunction and the nature of the biochemical effect, namely, the reason for the distribution of intelligence. Dunsdon, Carter and Huntley (1960) reported an upper limit of 70 IQ in their sample of 52 children with Down's syndrome (1960) but individual cases with higher IQ's have been reported and are known to the author. Attempts to relate IQ to physical or cytological differences have indicated no relationships. Some of the observed differences are attributable to the support and stimulation provided by the environment, but it seems logical that these differences might also reflect variations in hereditary potential and it is surprising that no one has correlated IQ's of Mongol children with IQ's of their parents. Experimental work with animals has shown that "whether or not an embryo exposed to a teratogen develops a malformation is determined, in part, by its genetic constitution" (Fraser, 1964), so one might reason that the biochemical effects of the extra chromosome would have differential effects depending on the other genes present.

The third congenital component is concerned with intrauterine environmental factors which affect fetal development without genetic alteration. Many of these have been described in the medical literature: German measles, radiation, toxoplasmosis, to mention a few (Fraser, 1964) and it would be inappropriate to embark on a lengthy discussion in this area. The medical factors, by and large, result in a recognizable clinical syndrome of which mental retardation is one symptom. From the point of view of psychology, some of the research on prenatal nutrition is more significant because the effects are more subtle and fall into the continuous distribution of IQ differences. Harrel *et al.* offered a dietary supplement to one group of pregnant women in low-income groups while a control group received placebos. When tested at the ages of three and four years, the offspring of the experimental group obtained a significantly higher mean IQ than did the offspring of the controls (1955). This is one of those studies which should be repeated but ethical considerations make one hesitate to deliberately deprive an unborn child of something which is probably good for him in the interest of science, but perhaps it could be reproduced with subhuman primates.

Constitutional Determinants of Intelligence

"Constitutional" has been suggested as the umbrella term to cover all that is physiological or somatic in the determination of intelligence, including the components discussed above plus any "alterations of body state by life experience" (Cattell, 1950). The nature of this "life experience" may be physically toxic or traumatic, occurring any time from birth onward. A list of possible perinatal and postnatal physical agents is provided in standard pediatric texts and discussed in some detail in the American Association on Mental Deficiency Nomenclature (Heber, 1959). Prematurity is given as one significant cause of mental retardation and stands in a peculiar relation between prenatal and postnatal factors with respect to time. In part, it is an effect of prenatal conditions rather than a cause per se. Nutritional and maternal health factors have been shown to contribute to gestation age and these in turn are related to socioeconomic status. The fact of the low birth weight and immature physiological state make the premature baby susceptible to infection and neonatal crises which are life threatening and potentially deleterious for later development in all areas: "perceptual-motor disturbance (as measured by the Bender-Gestalt), flaws in comprehension and abstract reasoning, perseveration trends, poor gross motor development, immature speech and impaired IQ significantly identify low birth weight children" (Weiner *et al*, 1965). Drillien found a greater percentage of her prematures in special schools for the handicapped or given special treatment in normal schools than would be expected on the basis of general school rates, and when prematures were compared to their siblings, they tended to be slower (1964). There has been a shift from viewing these relationships as only organically determined towards consideration of the special environment of the premature—after his birth. Recent writers on this subject have tended to attribute more of the intellectual and behavior problems to child rearing and the deprivations and distortions in maternal care which follow in the wake of premature birth. The interrelationships between prematurity and social class make it difficult to separate the factors involved. Wortis and Freedman compared 215 prematurely born babies with term children in the same economic status and found that the deprived environment apparently had a more depressing effect on the IQ's of the premature children (at 2½ years) than of the term children. They concluded that "infants who have a defective or vulnerable nervous system may be especially sensitive to poor environment, and disturbing factors may more readily elicit abnormal patterns of development in defective children" (1965, p. 65).

Two points about evaluating organic effects are worth special note. First, the sequelae of organic trauma are not determined solely by the nature, time, and severity of the illness, injury, or "risk" factor. C. Kennedy and Ramirez (1964) reported on monkeys who had been subjected to the same objective condition of risk (i.e. asphyxia early in life). Pathological examinations of the brain revealed differing amounts of damage, including some cases where there was none. When the animals were permitted to develop, their behavior was as varied as the anatomical findings, ranging from normal to massively disturbed learning and motor functioning. The effect of organic trauma, even on nervous tissue, is no more predictable than the effect of psychological trauma. The second point concerns the need for longitudinal studies to evaluate the effects of physical trauma. Such studies with children who have had measles, encephalitis (Meyer and Byers, 1952), or lead encephalopathy (Byers and Lord, 1943) show for some an immediate return to premorbid state after recovery from the acute phase and only later is it possible to detect the adverse effects of the illness when the child fails to regain the premorbid *rate* of development.

Although one usually thinks first of physical agents as altering the body state, the earlier discussion on neurophysiological correlates of learning should be recalled at this point. A number of the studies cited described measurable physiological differences in organisms raised in different kinds of environment—extremes of enrichment or impoverishment. One would suspect that environmental conditions would leave a physical mark only in the critical periods of early development, but this hypothesis has not been systematically tested.

Cognitive Environment

This has been touched on also in previous sections concerned with maturational hypotheses and the relation of experience in perceptual—motor and language development. Therefore, only a few additional studies will be mentioned. One of these is of special interest because it links environmental effect with genetic differences. Cooper and Zubek (1950) used two strains of rats, one known to be "bright" in maze learning and the other known to be "dull." The two groups were compared under three environmental conditions: enriched, normal, and restricted. When their error scores were compared, it was found that the bright rats were superior to the dull rats under normal conditions (as expected), but under enriched conditions, the dull rats performed almost as well, and under restricted conditions, the bright rats were depressed to the same level as the dull rats. The "good" environment did little to improve the bright rats and the "poor" environment had little effect on the dull rats. Gottesman interprets this study in terms of reaction range, that is, the range of variation which can be evoked by environmental circumstances in different genotypes, and mentions that heredity is the capacity to utilize an environment in a particular way. With reference to human potentials, Gottesman suggests that "it may be that eventual manipulation of the intelligence phenotype will be only a question of economics. Within the range of intelligence accounted for by a polygenic system, a great expenditure of effort may replace the effects of intelligence-enhancing genes" (1963, p. 273).

Another line of approach has been taken by those interested in the impact of different social environments on cognitive behavior. There is no need to review here the concepts and research related to deprivation and cognitive development (refer to Yarrow's chapter) or the research relating social class and intellectual achievement (Kessler, 1965). As mentioned before, the well-documented facts on these scores have led to a tremendous push for early education and the key principles are reviewed in a report of a Conference on Pre-School Education (Hess and Bear, 1968). However, attempts to delineate specific aspects of environment which operate as intervening variables to affect cognitive development have been relatively few. White points out that there is a tendency to equate the environments of lower class children with the barren environment of the institution as equally "depriving." In fact, the lower class infant lives in an environment which offers perceptual change and variety, tactual stimulation, and maternal company and affection—not at all like an institution. White raises the question that perhaps the lower class home is relatively satisfactory before the age of 3 years, that is, before the child has progressed enough in language to need the stimulation of complex structure which the lower class parent usually cannot model for him (1968). Freeberg and Payne reviewed the literature dealing with child rearing practices that influence cognitive development and concluded that the most compelling lines of evidence point to a critical role for verbal patterns established by the parents (1967). The previously quoted study by Hess and Shipman is an example of sophisticated research in this area. Hess questions whether the socioeconomically disadvantaged child can successfully be socialized or educated in isolation, that is, without involving the family and community reference group and suggests that perhaps we should attempt to educate families as a unit, a point of view which fits the author's bias (1968). However, at the present time, there are widely divergent preschool programs going on with the same purpose of enhancing cognitive development. A basic question is:

"to what degree is it important to stress information as against open-ended system engagements with reality dimensions?" (Fowler, 1968). Some groups aim for structured programs (Bereiter *et al,* 1965; Montessori, 1912; operant conditioners, Staats *et al,* 1964; social learning theorists, Vance, 1965), whereas the traditional nursery point of view has stressed open-system, creative play orientations. We have no data to compare the relative effectiveness of intervention at different ages in areas affected by education, nor do we know the most effective mode of interference. There is a unique opportunity to follow these children exposed to specialized training techniques, hopefully in a collaborative manner which will allow comparisons. Failure to do so will represent serious professional negligence.

Motivational Environment

The pre-school educators also have drawn attention to problems of providing motivation for learning and a second controversy revolves around the relative importance of external reinforcement (material or social) versus "intrinsic" motivation. Maccoby remarks that "in the history of the culturally deprived child, intrinsic reward for learning has often not been sufficient to overcome the elements in his experience that would lead him to avoid, or be afraid of, learning situations" (1968, p. 198), a remark which would seem to fit the mentally retarded as well. Observations of children from culturally deprived backgrounds indicate passivity, apathy and discouragement at early ages, compared to the active, optimistic and inquisitive behavior of young children raised in more favorable circumstances. Gray and Klaus analyzed the possible reinforcement differences related to social class, commenting that the over-worked, worried lower class mother has little time to respond in a differential way to her child's behavior and rewards the child for behavior which makes her life less burdensome on a day-by-day basis. Thus, it is likely that the child will be rewarded more for staying out of the way, inhibitory behavior, than for exploratory behavior, and his "natural" curiosity may die for lack of encouragement (1968). The difference in motivation has a cumulative effect, positive or negative, as the child gets older. Children with a high degree of aggressive achievement motivation tend to rise in IQ from early childhood to adolescence (Sontag, Baker, and Nelson, 1958), whereas those with a passive outlook tend to fall behind. Research on achievement motivation has been rather confusing because so much has been based on retrospective information and self-reports from parents (Crandall, 1963) and indices used to assess achievement motivation have varied from projective test data (Winterbottom, 1958) to concrete evidence of achievement. In their review, Freeberg and Payne state as a general principle that permissive-restrictive environments in the home and parental pressures for achievement "indicate some promise" for differentiating levels, as well as areas, of cognitive skill development, but the mechanics of transmission are not at all clear. The verbal patterns provided by the parents are important not only in terms of information processing, but also in terms of establishing reasons for external events and reasons for behavior. "The meaning of (cultural) deprivation would thus seem to be a deprivation of meaning in the early cognitive relationships between mother and child. This environment produces a child who relates to authority rather than to rationale, who may often be compliant but is not reflective in his behavior, and for whom the consequences of an act are largely considered in terms of immediate punishment or reward rather than future effects and long-range goals" (Hess and Shipman, 1968, p. 103). The nature of the identification model also must be considered. In their work in attempting to encourage postponement of gratification, Mischel and his colleagues were able to encourage delay by allowing the child to observe a model who chose delayed rather than immediate reward, or even by informing him that the model made delayed choices (Bandura and Mischel, 1965).

It seems clear that socially mediated motivational aspects of cognitive development become increasingly important as the child moves from infancy to school age, whether the reward is a material object provided by a person or social approval. In the contemporary preschools for culturally deprived, efforts have been made to offer reinforcement on a systematic basis. Usually this requires a high ratio of adults to children so that reinforcement is immediately available on an individualized basis. Gray and Klaus suggest starting with M&M's or sugared cereal, cuddling the child in the lap, and gradually moving on to more abstract and delayed rewards. Baer and Wolf assume that attention is the most pervasive and primitive form of social reinforcer and use teacher's attention in a systematic way so that the reward is clearly contingent on what the child does. They comment that this is nothing unusual or alien to nursery school teacher's professional behavior, an important point because reinforcements rarely work if they are elaborately contrived and foisted upon the teacher who then parcels out her attention in an unconvincing manner. Preschool educators are not alone in looking at the environment for its reinforcement properties. Baer and Wolf also describe a motivational plan with sixth grade children by which they earn tokens for achievement which are turned in for concrete rewards—trips, money, etc. The progress shown by these children is quite remarkable when compared with progress in the ordinary classroom situation where reinforcement is admittedly chancy and provides a blurred kind of feedback to the child (1968).

Robinson and Robinson give us a succinct summary of the general picture of what a motivational environment should include: "Our educated guess remains that high intelligence is fostered by warmth, support, and plentiful opportunity and reward for achievement and autonomy. Moreover, it is probably important to provide active, warm, achievement-oriented parental figures of both sexes after whom appropriate role patterns can be established" (1968, p. 51). We should keep in mind the reciprocal role between cognitive and social learning as phrased in

Bronfenbrenner's questions: "What role does social reinforcement or modeling play in furthering or impeding the transition from one stage of cognitive development to the next? Or, conversely, what part does cognitive development have in determining the child's susceptibility to social reinforcement or modeling?" (1963, p. 541). Some light on the second question might be provided by studying the growth of imitative behaviors in mentally retarded children. The fact that one often sees copying behavior which does not generalize to more global identifications indicates that there are cognitive requirements for learning a model.

Functional Analysis of Retarded Development

One learning theorist, Bijou, has made the concept of reinforcement a central point in explaining retarded behavior. In his view, the retarded individual is one who has a limited repertory of behavior as a consequence of the organism-environment interaction that constitutes his history. He allows that an individual with biological irregularities may have altered response capabilities, but he stresses the possibility that retarded development may result from inadequate reinforcement and discrimination histories. Reinforcements may be infrequent, insufficient, noncontingent on behavior, or even aversive for learning purposes (1966). Although this approach is attractive in terms of suggesting ways of modifying retarded behavior, one must consider the differences in the reinforcement needs of the retarded child. Under normal circumstances, he meets with less success so that reinforcement must be much more generous and very clearly understood by the child and yet it must be sincerely delivered. We are asking a lot of a parent when we want him to show enthusiasm for the diminutive achievements of his show developing child who is being obviously surpassed by his peers. The normal parent expects and wants more than the retarded child can give. In a paradoxical way, the task is made somewhat easier if the parent has known of the diagnosis from birth, as in the case of Down's syndrome. If, with this information, he has chosen to keep the child, his expectations are low and he may be agreeably rather than disagreeably surprised. This may account in some measure for the frequent observation that Mongoloid children are by and large more sociable and eager to please than equally retarded children of unknown cause.

This section has been a review of kinds of courses of differences in cognitive development: genetic, acquired physical, and environmental. This leads us to the final section dealing with the relationship of personality factors and cognitive performance, not so much in terms of environmental factors but rather how they interact within the individual.

INTERDEPENDENCE OF AFFECT AND COGNITION

Nature of Motivation

This topic has been subjected to exhaustive discussion and review; here we will touch on a few principles which are relevant to a theory of cognitive development. There seems to be agreement that there are two families, or systems, of motivation— one having to do with drive reduction and one to do with intrinsic motivation. Drives arise from lacks and deficits and, in their primary form, they are powerful and persistent internal stimuli which arouse the organism and promote activities that eliminate the deficit, thus reducing tension and restoring homeostasis. Secondary drives are learned in association with primary drive reduction. White (1960) and Hunt (1963), amongst others, have criticized learning theories which have made drive a necessary condition on the basis that learning can be demonstrated in the absence of painful stimulation, drive deficit, or drive reward. They point to the directed, selective, and persistent nature of child play and Piaget's observations that a child seeks opportunities to investigate his surroundings as evidence for a second system of motivation inherent in the organism's information processing and action. Hunt terms this "intrinsic motivation" and White speaks of "effectance" motivation. "Effectance is to be conceived as a neurogenic motive, in contrast to a viscerogenic one. It can be informally described as what the sensori-neuromuscular system wants to do when it is not occupied with homeostatic business. Its adaptive significance lies in its promotion of spare-time behavior that leads to an extensive growth of competence, well beyond what could be learned in connection with drive reduction" (1966, p. 303). Hunt relates intrinsic motivation to shifts of interest in infancy away from the familiar and towards the novel which has a measure of incongruity with what he already "knows." "At this point (in developmental epigenesis), circumstances with too little incongruity become boring and those with too much incongruity become frightening" (1966, p. 131).

Several times throughout this chapter, reference has been made to the possibility that mentally retarded and/or culturally deprived children are somehow different in respect to intrinsic motivation. This notion raises questions which could only be answered by naturalistic observations in the first months and years of life. Do retarded children show less curiosity and persistence in self-initiated play? Is there a difference in their preference for the familiar versus the novel? Do they encounter "failure" experiences in play so that they do not acquire the "feeling of efficacy" described by White? Unfortunately, or fortunately, it is hard to predict retardation in infancy and to find subjects outside of the institutional environment. However, there are ways of identifying the slow-developing child towards the end of the first year of life. If this "at risk" group could be observed carefully, without diagnostic commitment, some partial answers would be forthcoming. The few studies of play in young normal and retarded children (matched in mental ages in the range from 1½ to 2½) have indicated no differences in level, persistence, or flexibility (Hunt, 1965 and Ablon, 1967), but these have been done in experimental settings which do not allow free reign for preferences dictated by curiosity. Also, it should be noted that there is a cognitive component in the stimulation of intrinsic motivation; for instance, recognition of something as familiar or strange entails memory and prior organization processes. Perhaps the ordinary course of life events is mismatched for the retarded infant in that he is constantly exposed to so much incongruity that he is in a perpetual state of anxiety. The research by Fantz and his co-workers on shifts in visual preference in the first few months may give us the first line on early differences, not only in form perception, but also in preferences for novelty.

Motivational Theories Related to Mental Retardation

The major theorists have considered the motivational problems of retarded children at later ages and in relation to differences in life experiences. The work of Zigler and his co-workers was initiated by the original Lewin-Kounin formulation that retarded individuals were like normal younger children in having less cognitive differentiation but inherently different because of a "greater stiffness, a smaller capacity for dynamic rearrangement in the psychical systems" (Lewin, 1936). The Lewin-Kounin idea of "rigidity" did not refer to repetitious behavior as such, but rather to "that property of a functional boundary which prevents communication between neighboring regions." The original experiments used measures of satiation time on similar tasks and measures of interference in changing tasks. In the former, the retarded were more "rigid," that is, they continued longer at similar tasks, and in the latter, the retarded were less "rigid," that is, there was less carry-over effect from one task to another. In their further exploration of this hypothesis, Zigler found that differences in rigid behaviors between normal and retarded individuals of the same MA in instruction-initiated tasks could be related to differences in the subjects' motivation to comply with instructions rather than to differences in cognitive rigidity (1966b). In the original test of this hypothesis, Zigler, Hodgden, and Stevenson found that retarded subjects spent a significantly greater amount of time playing the games under conditions of experimenter support compared to nonsupport conditions, whereas the normal subjects did not (1958). A number of subsequent studies related the degree of perseveration to the degree of social deprivation, either length of time in the institution or social history factors leading to institutionalization. In addition, Zigler reported that institutionalized children of normal intellect are just as perseverative as institutionalized retardates and noninstitutionalized retardates are no more perseverative than noninstitutionalized children of normal intellect (Green and Zigler, 1962; Zigler, 1963). Stevenson and Fahel also found deprivation factors to be the crucial factors in determining the child's response to social reinforcement on a simple task (1961). Evidence for the deprivational aspects of institutionalization was noted as a tangential, but important, finding that the IQ's had decreased in a five-year period of institutionalization (Zigler and Williams, 1963). As a result of extensive work in this area, Zigler concluded "it is almost impossible to place too much emphasis on the role of overdependency in the institutional familial retarded and on the socialization histories that give rise to such overdependency. Given some minimal intellectual level, the shift from dependency to independence is perhaps the single most important factor necessary for the retardate to become a self-sustaining member of our society. It appears that the institutionalized retardate must satisfy certain affectional needs before he can cope with problems in the manner of those whose affectional needs have been relatively satiated" (Zigler, 1966, p. 150).

The Reinforcer Hierarchy

From the studies of the effects of social deprivation on perseverative behavior, Zigler and his colleagues went on to explore the effects of experimentally manipulated reinforcers on aspects of cognitive performance, particularly with reference to cognitive rigidity. In learning theory terms, for every child, there is a particular hierarchy of potency for various reinforcers, determined by 1) the child's developmental level; 2) the frequency with which these reinforcers have been paired with other reinforcers; and 3) the degree to which the child has been deprived of these reinforcers (Zigler, 1966). Differing reinforcer hierarchies have been investigated in relation to social class as well as IQ. Terrell, Durkin, and Wiesley (1959) found that middle class children did better on a discrimination learning task when an intangible rather than a tangible reinforcer was employed, while lower class children did better with the tangible reinforcer. Another study compared three groups, middle class, lower class, and retarded, matched for MA. in a concept switching task. The three groups were equal when a toy was the reward, but both the lower class and retarded groups were inferior to the middle class group when the only reinforcement was the information that the child was correct (Zigler and de Labry, 1962).

In between simple reports of "correctness" and a present of a toy or food, there are degrees of social approval and warmth, not only as meted out by the examiner, but also as received by the child subject. In Zigler's words, "the effectiveness of an adult as a social reinforcing agent for a particular child depends upon the valence that that adult has for the child" (1966b, p. 93). This issue has been followed up in a series of studies with children of normal intellect (Berkowitz, Butterfield and Zigler, 1965; Berkowitz and Zigler, 1965; McCoy and Zigler, 1965). Briefly these studies have manipulated pre-experimental contacts and then measured the experimenter's subsequent value as a social reinforcing agent in a boring satiation-type test with the expected results that prior positive contacts increase and prior negative contacts decrease the adult's effectiveness as a reinforcer. Zigler uses the disproportionate amount of negative adult contacts experienced by the retarded child to explain the characteristic initial wariness and "negative reaction tendency."

Zigler's discussions are in classical learning theory terms where the effectiveness of specific reinforcers depends on prior learning experiences, eventually reducible to a drive theory of learning. According to this approach, the effectiveness of attention and praise as reinforcers diminishes with maturity and is replaced by the reinforcement inherent in the information that one is correct (Beller, 1955; Zigler, 1963). Here one can see a point of disagreement which hinges on one's view regarding the nature of motivation. In Zigler's view, motivation is originally provided by drive reduction which is then associated with need-fulfilling persons, converted into a motivation for attention from such persons, and finally internalized as self-approval with the knowledge of correctness. In the view of Hunt, or White, this system of motivation develops alongside another system where there is pleasure, from the earliest age, in the "correct" answer because it "works"—it solves a self-imposed problem.

Expectancy of Failure

Another line of investigations has emanated from the social learning theory of Rotter who postulated that the occurrence of a behavior of a person is determined not only by the nature or importance of goals or reinforcements, but also by the person's anticipation or expectancy that these goals will occur (1954). The relation between failure expectancies and behavior in normal individuals has been documented by Atkinson (1958), Katz (1964), and Sarason *et al.* (1960). In his review of experiments with retarded subjects, Cromwell assumes that the retardate has a higher expectancy of failure and that this accounts for a characteristic style of problem solving which causes him to be more motivated to avoid failure than to achieve success. In summary, Cromwell states that retardates "1) enter a novel situation with a performance level which is depressed below their level of constitutional ability, 2) have fewer tendencies to be 'moved' by failure experience than normals, and 3) have fewer tendencies than normals to increase effort following a mild failure experience" (1963, p. 87). However, to date, the experimental work employing success-failure manipulations with retarded subjects (and/or normal) has yielded conflicting results. One source of inconsistency between theory and experimental findings may be that the laboratory situation with simple, immediate success or failure is not analogous to the accumulated effect of years of failure, ambiguously communicated to the retarded child. The effect of a failure experience in a single experiment is hardly comparable, but in the closer parallel of life provided by one study involving repeated failure over a period of time, retardates regressed in functioning and were unable to solve a problem which they had mastered before the experiment began (Zeaman and House, 1960).

Because of the confusion in results regarding the effects of success and failure when they were measured in relation to the reality of experimenter—defined goals, a redefinition was introduced. "Success is the attainment of goal under conditions where the individual attributes the attainment to his own effectiveness. Failure is the nonattainment of a goal under conditions where the individual attributes the outcome to his own lack of effectiveness" (1963, p. 62). Thus, a new construct, "locus of control," was born. This is a sort of hybrid concept, half cognitive style and half personality trait, having to do with the individual's characteristic way of explaining events, either as the outcome of his own behavior (internal locus of control, ILC) or as the result of the efforts of other people or of chance (external locus of control, ELC). The developmental assumptions were that ILC is more advanced: "As development proceeds, the child begins to note that he is often able to influence the outcome of events by his own actions. Therefore, as the child grows older, he is more likely to view many of his goal—directed experiences as being internally controlled. With the shift in the conceptualization of locus of control from external to internal there evolves, by definition, the ability of the child to categorize the outcomes of certain goal—directed behaviors in terms of success and failure" (Bialer, 1960, p. 3). This view contradicts some developmental observations made by Piaget (and also Freud) regarding the development of causality. Piaget has shown that the *first* explanations of outside events are made in terms of the child's own behavior as part of his characteristic egocentric thinking and the child's appreciation of the role of other people develops slowly, whereas his understanding of chance factors is even a later development. From these observations, there is a kind of primitive ILC which is based on magic and naivete which precedes ELC. The theoretical conflict might be resolved if Cromwell and Bialer gave some age references or qualified the locus of control construct in terms of external reality.

High incidence of failure experience, when appreciated by the child as of his own doing, would logically have the effect of getting him to look elsewhere for assistance. Lacking self-confidence, the retarded child will search for guidance and cues from his environment, using an "outer-directed" problem—solving approach. Again, we have Zigler to thank for some research investigations related to this concept. Green and Zigler (1962) found that, while normal children exhibited little tendency to do so, retarded children (noninstitutionalized more than institutionalized) terminated their performance on experimental games following a suggestion from the examiner. Turnure and Zigler (1964) carried out two later experiments which confirmed the outer—directed hypothesis in that retarded children showed more imitative behavior than controls of the same mental age and also learned more from incidental watching of someone else's performance on a puzzle task. Many times outer—directedness is reinforced for the retarded child because following a model leads to more success than relying on inner resources. Zigler suggests that this is generalized into characteristic environmental "scanning" which would give the appearance of distractibility, a common observation about retarded children. Consistent with his total theory, Zigler objects to the idea that distractibility may be inherent in the retarded child and offers the alternate explanation that it is learned behavior emanating from the unique experiential histories of retarded children.

Several points stand out when one looks over the foregoing research on motivational variables and cognitive performance. First, most of the research has related motivation to a qualitative aspect of cognitive performance with relatively little research concerned with changes in level of skill or proficiency. Second, this research on qualitative differences has been dominated by the theoretical issues of "learned" versus "inherent" behavior. The mental retardation is taken as a "given" (from where?) and subsequent differences are explained as secondary consequences. Third, the experimental paradigm has been to compare retarded and normal subjects, matched for mental age, with the recent addition of social class as a significant variable. It would be interesting to see if differences of the same order exist when average and superior subjects are compared or whether these relationships hold only in the presence of a significant deficit leading to visible failure as in the case of the retarded. Finally, in the manipulation of social variables, no one has investigated the emotional significance of the experimenter for the child. Zigler touches on this in his discussions of the meaning of adult companionship for the institutionalized child and his statement regarding the "valence position," but there has been no systematic exploration of parent—child interaction. It would be interesting to repeat some of these studies using the parent as the experimenter, an idea stimulated by Hess' recent work. Most parents could be trained to function as experimenters, although some investigators would certainly argue that there are many confusing and unknown variables in the previous parent—child history. However, these variables exist in any case and are in some measure displaced to the strange experimenter.

Anxiety in Relation to Cognitive Performance

Although anxiety is widely recognized as an important motivating force in behavior, research in this field has not been well coordinated. In some ways anxiety, or the desire to avoid and reduce it, is the major motivational component in behavior related to failure expectancy, outer—directedness, and so on. Although anxiety may be the common denominator for many varieties of so—called secondary drives and cognitive styles, some investigators, like Zigler, prefer to work with second—order behavior which can be directly measured rather than inferred. Anxiety is hard to define, difficult to measure operationally, and not easy to manipulate in a humane experimental situation. Evaluation of anxiety through the observation or ratings of others, or physiological measurement (Martin, 1961), proved disappointing and the concept was operationalized through the development of self-report questionnaires such as the Manifest Anxiety Scale (Taylor, 1953), the Children's Manifest Anxiety Scale, CMAS (Castaneda *et al.* 1956), the General Anxiety Scale, GASC, and the Test Anxiety Scale for Children, TASC (Sarason, 1960). Relying mainly on these measures, investigators have explored the ins and outs of anxiety as a drive in the modification of behavior. According to the drive approach to anxiety advanced by Spence (1956) and Taylor (1963), anxiety serves as a generalized energizer of behavior which arouses the organism to increased vigilance and readiness to learn. Supporting evidence came from the greater speed of establishing simple classical conditioned responses (e.g., defensive eyelid blinking) in subjects who scored high on the Taylor Manifest Anxiety Scale (Spence, 1964). In general, it seems that anxiety is beneficial in learning very simple tasks where little or no choice or verbalization is required from the subject. The situation, however, is reversed when it comes to learning more complex tasks. One explanation has been presented in terms of competing responses which are aroused in a complex learning situation and the fact that the increased drive provided by heightened anxiety tends to reinforce the dominant habit, whether or not it is correct.

Apart from theoretical considerations, research is quite consistent in showing that high anxiety is interfering on verbal tasks, tests of creativity, visual—motor tasks, etc., almost in direct relation to the complexity and difficulty of the task for the subject (Ruebush, 1963). Ruebush's comprehensive review of 24 studies relating measures of anxiety and scores on conventional intelligence tests indicated a "box score" of 19 studies reporting small to moderate negative relationships between anxiety and IQ, to 5 studies who failed to find a negative relationship. His "box score" for the relationship between anxiety and various educational indexes such as achievement test scores was 16 studies reporting a negative relationship, 3 reporting no relationship, and one lone study reporting a positive relationship. The notion of a curvilinear relationship has been supported by some studies (Cox, 1960), and it seems logical from clinical observation that extremes of high anxious or low anxious individuals (either "not caring" or denying any concern) will be handicapped in learning and achievement. One of the few investigations using a physiological measure of anxiety also supports a curvilinear relationship; Patterson *et al.* (1960) obtained interference with verbal learning in children who fell at either extreme on a skin-conductance measure of anxiety. Ruebush points out that past experiences of educational success and failure and learned ways of coping with such experiences play an important role in mediating the effects of anxiety and also mentions that several studies have obtained significant relationships between anxiety and measures which reflect a negative conception of the self or a tendency toward self-disparagement (1963), which brings us around full circle to the special situation of the mentally retarded individual.

Anxiety in Relation to Mental Retardation

In case one should wonder, Meyerowitz (1962) found more self-derogation for retardates in special and normal classes when compared with a control group. It seems clear that retarded individuals are either more anxious or have less effective coping mechanisms that normals (Zigler, 1966). Studies of young, mildly retarded children, living in their own homes, indicate some interesting differences when compared with normal groups matched in MA. Ablon found that retarded children with MA's between 18 and 30 months showed the same regression in play when separated from their mothers in an experimental play session, but the retarded children were more overwhelmed by the separation anxiety and less able to direct it in terms of verbal or purposive behavior to communicate their desire (1967). Polster, using a kind of picture—choice project test, found that young retarded children (Mean MA 3-9, Mean IQ 68.5) chose the face previously identified as showing fear with much more frequency than a matched group of average children (1967). This study was done in order to follow up Jersild's earlier work on developmental aspects of fear where he found a positive correlation between IQ and number of fears in *young* children and a definite shift from concrete to imaginary fears during the preschool period (1933). In her comparisons of younger and older retarded and normal groups, Polster found support for the second proposition in that there were significant differences between the average and retarded groups with regard to certain categories of fear-arousing stimuli. At both age levels, the retarded children scored significantly higher on fears of situations dealing with interpersonal relationships. At the older age level, the average children exhibited a significantly greater concern with fears of an imaginary and remote nature than the retarded children. In another way, this comes back to the greater dependency needs and outer-directedness of the retarded individual which influences both problem-solving behavior and source of anxiety.

Clinical Observations of Anxiety and Learning

When we deal with a construction so powerful as anxiety, it is clear that the usual experimental situation can be nothing but a pale shadow of the real life counterpart. Severe, chronic anxiety of ill-defined origin, and perhaps even misidentified by the sufferer as something other than anxiety, takes an inevitable toll when it persists over a long enough period of time. The effect may be simply economic, that is, that so much energy is needed to handle the anxiety that little remains for conflict-free mental activity. Or by the processes of displacement (in psychoanalytic terms) or generalization (in learning theory terms), functions involved in learning and achieving are connected with the nuclear conflict and become secondarily capable of producing anxiety and therefore must be avoided. Freud's original example had to do with fear of sexual knowledge, and the feelings and wishes associated with such knowledge. In his introduction to the case history of Little Hans, Freud stated that

"Thirst for knowledge seems to be inseparable from sexual curiosity" (1909, 1955, p. 9). Later psychoanalytic case reports indicated that inhibition of curiosity on *any* emotionally toned subject—sex, marital conflicts, antisocial escapades, alcoholism, serious illness—can have the same pervasive effect on learning (Hellman, 1954). It is not possible for the young child to compartmentalize his curiosity and restrict it only to "safe" subjects. However, even with this general knowledge, it is rare indeed for anyone to investigate the instruction and concept learning which takes place around topics of vital interest to the young child, and clinical diagnosis of a generalized learning problem rarely includes inquiry regarding interest or knowledge outside academic subjects.

Other neurotic anxieties can result in learning blocks, the dynamics of which are well described in a survey article by Weisskopf (1951). Although it is assumed that failure is anxiety—producing, it is possible in unusual situations to find that success may be anxiety—producing. Success may symbolize "growing up" with attendant apprehension about some aspect of the adult status as perceived by the young child. Some young children are anxious about success in relation to unresolved oedipal feelings where there are strong desires to "beat" out someone, projection of inner hostility so that it is imagined as fearful jealousy and retribution on the part of the "loser." In such situations, the defenses against anxiety may be quite effective and only when one tries to intervene with the child's maladaptive solution does the anxiety emerge. Such neurotic inhibitions can be contrasted with the high anxious child, identified by questionnaire methods, who is uncomfortable and distracted by fantasies or unhappy possibilities such as failure, disapproval, and so on. Granted that the original psychoanalytic formulations were overgeneralized from the atypical child, it is important to save the pieces since a complete theory must be capable of offering consistent explanations for pathological as well as normal cognitive development. The great difficulty in nomethetic style research is that individual differences are obscured. The psychology of the exception to the general rule deserves most meticulous attention.

Aggression and Learning

The subject of aggression and learning has barely been touched except in individual case reports. Part of the neglect comes from difficulty with definition of aggression. One of the earliest psychological definitions was presented by Dollard *et al.* as part of the frustration—aggression hypothesis in which aggression was "an act whose goal response is injury to an organism (organism—surrogate)" (1939). In essence, Kaufman agreed with this definition when he concluded that "no behavioral act as such can consistently be called aggression, unless inferences about intention or expectation regarding its outcome are made" (1965, p. 353). He felt that aggression must have an object (person) and the aggressor must expect that he can hurt the object. This raises all kinds of problems because what is seen as "hurtful" is highly subjective and may not, in fact, be so, or may be hurtful only in a psychological—symbolic sense. One might say that aggression should be interpreted only in the context of the accompanying feeling tone of anger, but there seems no way around the problem of subjectification. Other people have used "aggression" in a much broader sense, almost synonymous with "activity," following one dictionary definition of the verb "aggress" meaning to "step forward, to approach." Although this definition is too inclusive for most workers, it is easy to see how activity can be associated with aggression since the latter necessarily involves the former, in fantasy or action.

The emotional states of anger and fear are closely related. Similar factors are involved in their instigation and either emotion may accompany or give rise to the other. As Jersild has said, a child's anger is likely to involve him in conflict of a twofold nature: "conflict with others who object to his anger, or are threatened by it; and conflict within himself by reason of the fact that a healthy child's impulse to feel and express anger runs counter to other strong impulses, such as those connected with affection and fear" (1968, p. 367). The effects of anger on the body chemistry are not as clear-cut as those of anxiety, but the physiology is close. In anxiety, the body is made ready for fighting as well as for fleeing. The sharpest difference between the response of anger and the response of anxiety is the way the person feels. If he wants to attack, it is anger; if he wants to run, it is anxiety. Often he wants to do both, and experiences the resulting conflict as additional discomfort. From his review, Ruebush concludes that "in general, anxiety is negatively related to the direct expression of aggression toward others and positively related to indices of the presence of underlying conflict concerning aggression and to the expression of self-aggression" (1963, p. 501).

Although there are no research studies to be reviewed, there are many clinical observations and discussions regarding the relationship of aggression and learning (Kessler, 1966). In these instances, the inhibition does not stem as much from anxiety about knowing, fear of growing up or of competing, as from difficulties in the relationship with the teacher or adult person who wants the child to learn. Such a child may do quite well in "incidental" learning when he is left to his own devices and "intrinsic motivation," but does poorly in a socially mediated, structured learning situation. Sometimes this is described as "withholding": "The child could but just won't." Sometimes this is described as "passive aggression," where the child is outwardly compliant but inwardly resistant (Dudek and Lester, 1968). In the face-to-face encounter with an instructor, he smiles, agrees, but out of her or his presence, he throws off any influence and "just forgets." As the teacher says, "I just can't get through to him." Sometimes the passivity goes farther into withdrawal and the aggressive component is easier to detect. Nothing can be more aggressive than a child who consistently ignores your existence.

The possible sources of such pathological defenses against aggression are many. One mechanism is by displacement from an earlier situation where the parents emerged triumphant (for instance, coercive feeding or toilet training) but which left the child angry and with covert defenses for handling his aggression. There are many other possible reasons for a child to harbor angry feelings, and if these are not expressed in the relevant context, and if the parents set great store by intellectual performance, this can become the arena for a Pyrrhic victory for the child.

Other ways of looking at the origin of aggression involve social learning principles of identification and reinforcement. Bandura and Walters carried out a number of experimental investigations of aggressive behavior in children and assert that role model learning (or identification) is the most important single factor antecedent to the emergence of aggressive behavior in children, even more important than frustration or punishment and reward for aggressive responses (1963). Case histories of boys with pathological inhibition of aggression and associated learning problems support the same general hypothesis. Sperry *et al.* described family patterns which required a denial of hostile feelings toward the parents as well as giving in to someone else in order to receive parental approval. In one case, the child was required to give in to a retarded brother, but was not supposed to know that the brother was retarded. Another boy was warned never to argue with his father, but not told that his father had an ulcer. There was a family secret plus the requirement that hostility be repressed (1958). The case of Henry given by Kessler demonstrates the "foolish" behavior that can occur when any act even remotely suggestive of aggression must be avoided (1966). In Grunebaum's description of fathers of sons with neurotic learning inhibitions, there are many more examples of "learning" self-derogation, inhibition of aggression towards others, renunciation of ambition, through identification with the father (1962). Conflicts around aggressive behavior are particularly keen for boys and it is imperative in both clinical and experimental work to separate the boys from the girls in order to study the process of role model learning, and the relationships between dependency and aggression, anxiety and aggression, and learning and aggression.

The preceding remarks have dealt mainly with the negative effects of inhibited aggression on academic learning processes. We have some empiric evidence for the converse, namely, that overtly aggressive behavior, even too much, leaves the learning process relatively intact. Sperry *et al.* remarked that "the boys whose activity in school annoys the teacher and interferes with their work seem to us to be in a psychologically more favorable position eventually to achieve in school" (1958). Harris found that learning difficulties were associated both with extreme aggressiveness and submissiveness, but his data indicated that the overly aggressive "nonlearner" was brighter in IQ than the overly submissive "nonlearner" (1961). In their longitudinal study of "normal" children, Sontag *et al.* found that the "passive, infantile dependence pattern" led to a decreasing level of performance on the

Stanford—Binet, whereas "aggressive, self-reassuring mastery of tasks, competitive, independent pattern" led to progressively advanced performance (1955).

This brings us to the special situation of the mentally retarded child. We have discussed the experiential reasons for greater anxiety and the consequences in terms of the mobilization of defenses and coping mechanisms. However, there are equally good reasons for the retarded child to have a greater amount of aggression, particularly because of frustrations and disappointments, and at the same time to have fewer outlets for such feelings. First, the identification process is distorted, perhaps by the child's lack of perceptiveness, and certainly because it is not so enthusiastically fostered by the parents who do not like to see a retarded child as "just like himself." Second, the attitude of the parents toward aggressive behavior is altered by their knowledge that the child is retarded. With all their natural apprehensions about his future, they will try to safeguard his social acceptability by ensuring that he is "at least" very clean, kind, and polite. The question is whether such inhibitory behavior is achieved at the cost of some intellectual productivity.

CONCLUSIONS

Since this paper throughout has been a summary of literature and issues in various areas related to cognitive development, no attempt will be made to resummarize. Certain general research needs emerge:

1. Replication of experiments, especially those which are cited as "classics."Although replication is taken as a matter of course in the physical sciences, it does not enjoy the same prestige or urgency in the behavioral sciences. Replication would not only be beneficial for the advancement of psychological science, but also would provide a good vehicle for the education of the student and beginning research investigator.

2. Replication of research with subjects selected according to different, but carefully specified criteria. In general, the research literature is poor in the description of the subjects; particularly if they are retarded, there is a paucity of collateral information about their personality, social background, medical status, and functioning in areas other than those measured by the conventional IQ. Research comparing retarded with average subjects should be repeated across the total spectrum of mental abilities to identify genuine dichotomies, linear or curvilinear relationships.

3. Chaining of research, that is, using the same subjects who have been explored and identified in one research study as extremes or exceptions and exploring other parameters of cognitive functioning.

4. Naturalistic research, not only in terms of longitudinal natural histories, but to study interactional effects of environment and development, particularly in social learning.

5. Creative research which crosses over the "cultural" boundaries of specific research interests and theoretical orientations. Those interested in the role of verbal mediating processes should also look at role model learning; those interested in Piaget-oriented concept development should consider the nature of perceptual motor development; and so on.

Child development theorists would certainly identify different issues as of paramount importance in our present state of knowledge. In the author's opinion, the following stand out as holding promise:

1. Pharmacologic modification of learning. A sharp eye should be kept on what is going on in the investigation of the biochemistry and neurophysiology of learning. Although such work has been necessarily restricted to animal laboratories and it is premature to speculate on its import for human subjects, within the next decade one can anticipate some spill-over into the field of human learning. At such a time, the behavioral scientists must be ready with highly sophisticated research designs which isolate the separate bits and pieces of intellectual processes which coalesce into the totality of what we call "human learning." Logically, one can hope that chemical intervention will affect one or another of these "bits," for instance, attention, vigilance, short—term memory, or whatever, and such specific influences should be neither exaggerated nor lost in the complexity of human development.

2. Remedial and compensatory education in the modification of mental development. At the moment, there is a flurry of special education programs designed to alter the environment for the culturally deprived and other efforts designed to teach basic perceptual and motor functions for those who have specific deficits. It is imperative that the SE programs be thoroughly recorded and followed objectively for the sake of the light they can shed on areas of modifiability in cognitive development.

3. The question of drives and affects in learning. This topic has not drawn much attention to date, mainly for lack of appropriate experimental methods. Nevertheless, it is important to consider the

possibility of differences in intrinsic motivation (which brings us back to observations of infants in naturalistic settings) and also to examine the interrelationship of anxiety and aggressions (and the consequent defense mechanisms and coping styles) on mental development.

4. The "difference" hypotheses in mental retardation. Zigler has given us the particular challenge that the various differences observed between retarded and normal individuals, matched in mental age, can be interpreted in the light of differences in experiential history. Right or wrong, this is a most valuable hypothesis to pursue because of its heuristic value. Confirmation or refutation requires more particularization about early life experiences and research across the whole range of intelligence and at all levels of development. Are retarded children the same as their normal, mental age counterparts, or if not, when do they veer off from the slower but normal developmental patterns? What are the crucial juncture points where they part company? Do the patterns of similarities and differences hold for all degrees of mental retardation and all facets of early development, or only for some and only in the milder forms of retardation?

5. Stage theory of development. The author favors the developmental hypotheses of states where hierarchical transformation of cognitive processes take place and it would seem that investigation of "ceilings" in retarded children would shed light on this issue. With maximal educational and training efforts, are there ceilings in how far one can go with retarded children of different degrees of handicap? Such fixation points would be determined by limits in generalization and failure of the retarded child to escalate his benefits from one situation to another. If these points could be identified and understood, it must answer some of the questions regarding the nature of changes at the beginning of learning language and again in the age period between 5 and 7 years.

6. Two group hypotheses regarding the origin of mental retardation. This is another valuable hypothesis provided by Zigler. Research would probably utilize the paradigm of the early work of Werner and Strauss establishing the differentiation of the "exogenous" and "endogenous" forms of mental deficiency. Unfortunately, the value of this work was somewhat contaminated by over-enthusiastic efforts to utilize it in diagnosis and treatment. Closure was effected too soon. The paradigm should be revived with more sophisticated and cautious interpretation of the underlying neurophysiologic processes and also with greater awareness of experiential factors (such as institutionalization) in the

shaping of cognitive skills. Admitting our basic ignorance as to the ultimate neurological cause of intellectual functioning and differences, we still have the operational questions whether the mentally subnormal population is entirely and simply at the lower end of a continuum of intellectual ability which embraces the total population.

Finally, as we review the literature which has appeared in the last ten years, we must ask how well we have met the challenge presented in the publication of Masland, Sarason, and Gladwin. This most important book represents a point of demarcation of eras of interest in the mentally retarded. In their introduction of the survey of research on biological, psychological, and cultural factors in mental subnormality, the authors state, and this author would reiterate:

> *The challenge lies in the realization which we hope is clear in these reports that the more we know about mental subnormality, the more we will also know about normal intellectual processes. Study of the subnormal individual suggests subclinical organic deficits which contribute to variations in intellect within the normal range. Similarly, studies of learning in retarded children have important implications for understanding the development and structure of intellect in normals, and also focus our attention on an almost completely neglected subject, the kinds of intellectual skills which are actually needed to function in our culture, particularly outside of the school situation.*
>
> *These and other research prospects fill us with a real excitement as we contemplate the research future which lies ahead. We hope we have been able to communicate in our reports some of this excitement. (Masland, Sarason, and Gladwin, 1958, p. 7)*

References

Ablon, Gridth, COMPARISON OF THE CHARACTERISTICS OF THE PLAY OF YOUNG MILDLY RETARDED AND AVERAGE CHILDREN, WITH MOTHER PRESENT AND ABSENT, Unpublished doctoral dissertation, Western Reserve University, 1967.

Agranoff, Bernard W., "Molecules and memories," PERSPECTIVES IN BIOLOGY AND MEDICINE, 9: 13-22, 1966.

Albee, G. W., PRESENTATION TO THE SECRETARY'S COMMITTEE ON MENTAL RETARDATION. Department of Health, Education, and Welfare. March 5, 1968.

Alberts, E., and Ehrenfreund, D., "Transposition in children as a function of age," J. EXP. PSYCHOL. 41: 30-38, 1951.

Almy, Millie, Chittenden, E., and Miller, P., YOUNG CHILDREN'S THINKING. New York: Teacher's College Press, Columbia University, 1966.

Altman, J. and Das, G. D., "Autographic examination of the effects of enriched environment on the rate of glial multiplication in adult rat brain," NATURE, 204: 1161-1163, 1964.

Ames, L. B., " The sequential patterning of prone progression in the human infant," GENET. PSYCHOL. MONOGR., l9: 409-460, 1937.

Anderson, R. C., SHAPING LOGICAL BEHAVIOR IN SIX— AND SEVEN—YEAR—OLDS. Co-operative Research Project No. 1790A. Chicago: University of Illinois, 1964.

Atkinson, J. W., "Towards experimental analysis of human motives in terms of motives, expectancies, and incentives," In J. W. Atkinson (Ed.), MOTIVES IN FANTASY, ACTION, AND SOCIETY. Princeton, N. N.: D. van Nostrand, pp. 288-305, 1958.

Ausubel, David, THEORY AND PROBLEMS OF CHILD DEVELOPMENT. New York: Grune & Stratton, 1957.

Ayres, A. J., "Development of Body Schema in Children," AMER. J. OCCUP. THERAPY, 15: No. 3, 1961.

Ayres, A. J., "The development of perceptual—motor abilities: A theoretical basis for treatment of dysfunction," AMER. J. OCCUP. THERAPY, 17: 221-225, 1963.

Ayres, A. J., "Tactile functions—their relation to hyperactivity and perceptual motor behavior," AMER. J. OCCUP. THERAPY, 18: 6-11, 1964.

Ayres, A. J. "Interrelationships among perceptual motor functions in children," AMER. J. OCCUP. THERAPY, 20: No. 2, 1966.

Ayres, A. J., "Perceptual motor Dysfunction: Neurobehavioral Criteria," AMER. J.

ORTHOPSYCHIAT., 37: 405-406, 1967.

Baer, D. M. & Wolf, M. M., "The Reinforcement Contingency in Preschool and Remedial Education," In R. Hess & R. Bear (Eds.), EARLY EDUCATION. Chicago: Aldine, 119-130, I968.

Bandura, A., & Mischel, W., "Modification of self-imposed delay of reward through exposure to live and symbolic models," J. PERS. SOC. PSYCHOL., 2: 698-705, 1965.

Bandura, A., & Walters, R. H., SOCIAL LEARNING AND PERSONALITY DEVELOPMENT. New York: Holt, Rinehart, & Winston, 1963.

Barsch, Ray H., ACHIEVING PERCEPTUAL—MOTOR EFFICIENCY. Seattle, Washington: Special Child Publications, 1967.

Basser, L. S., "Hemiplegia of early onset and the faculty of speech with special reference to the effects of hemispherectomy," BRAIN, 85: 427-460, 1962.

Baumeister, Alfred A., "Problems in comparative studies of mental retardates and normals," AMER. J. MENT. DEFIC., 71: 869-875, 1967.

Baumeister, A. A., & Bartlett, C. J., "A comparison of the factor structure of normals and retardates," AMER. J. MENT. DEFIC., 66: 641-646, 1962.

Baumeister, A. A., & Hawkins, W. F., "Alpha responsiveness to photic stimulation in mental retardates," AMER. J. MENT. DEFIC., 71: 783-786, 1967.

Bayley, Nancy, "On the growth of intelligence," AMER. PSYCHOLOGIST, I0: 805-818, 1955.

Beilin, H., & Franklin, I. C., "Logical operations in area and length measurement: Age and training effects," CHILD DEVELPM., 33: 607-616, 1962.

Beller, E., "Dependency and independence in young children," J. GENET. PSYCHOL., 87: 25-35, 1955.

Belmont, J. M., "Longterm memory in mental retardation," in N. R. Ellis (ed.), RESEARCH IN MENTAL RETARDATION, Vol. I, New York: Academic Press, pp. 2I9-256, 1966.

Benjamin, R. M., & Thompson, R. F., "Differential effects of cortical lesions in infant and adult cats on roughness discrimination," EXP. NEUROL., I: 305-321, 1959.

Bennett, E. L., Diamond, M. C., Krech, D., & Rosenzweig, M. R., "Chemical and anatomical plasticity of the brain," SCIENCE, 146: 610-619, 1964.

Bereiter, C., & Engelmann, S., TEACHING DISADVANTAGED CHILDREN IN THE PRESCHOOL. Englewood Cliffs, N. J.: Prentice-Hall, 1966.

Bereiter, C., Osborn, J., Englemann, S., & Reidford, P. A. AN ACADEMICALLY ORIENTED PRESCHOOL FOR CULTURALLY DEPRIVED CHILDREN. Paper read at the Amer. Educ. Res. Assoc., Chicago, Feb., 1965.

Berkowitz, H., Butterfield, E. C., & Zigler, E., "The effectiveness of social reinforcers on persistence and learning tasks following positive and negative social interactions," J. PERS. SOC. PSYCHOL., 2: 706-714, 1965.

Berkowitz, H., & Zigler, E., "Effects of preliminary positive and negative interactions and delay conditions on children's responsiveness to social reinforcement," J. PERS. SOC. PSYCHOL., 2: 500-505, 1965.

Berlyne, D. E., "Attention, perception, and behavior theory," PSYCHOL. REV., 58: 137-146, 1951.

Bialer, I., & Cromwell, R. L., "Task repetition in mental defectives as a function of chronological and mental age," AMER. J. MENT. DEFIC., 65: 265-268, 1960.

Bijou, S., "A functional analysis of retarded development," In N. R. Ellis (Ed.), RESEARCH IN MENTAL RETARDATION, Vol. I. New York: Academic Press, pp. 1-20, 1966.

Birch, Herbert G. BRAIN DAMAGE IN CHILDREN: THE BIOLOGICAL AND SOCIAL ASPECTS. Baltimore: Williams & Wilkins, 1964.

Birch, H. G. and Lefford, A., "Intersensory development in children," MONOGR. SOC. RES. CHILD DEVELOPM., 28 (No. 89): 1-47, 1963.

Birch, H. G. and Lefford, A., "Two strategies for studying perception in 'brain damaged' children," In H. G. Birch (Ed.), BRAIN DAMAGE IN CHILDREN: THE BIOLOGICAL AND SOCIAL ASPECTS. Baltimore: Williams & Wilkins, pp. 46-60, 1964.

Birch, H. G. and Lefford, A., "Visual differentiation, intersensory integration, and voluntary motor control," MONOG. SOC. RES. CHILD DEVELPM., 32: No. 110, 1967.

Bloom, B. S., STABILITY AND CHANGE IN HUMAN CHARACTERISTICS. New York: Wiley, 1964.

Book, J. A. Schut, J. W., & Reed, S. C., "A clinical and genetic study of microcephaly," AMER. J. MENT. DEFIC., 57: 637-660, 1953.

Booth, David, "Vertebrate brain ribonucleic acids and memory retention," PSYCHOL. BULL., 68: 149-177, 1967.

Bourne, L. E., Jr., & Restle, F., "Mathematical theory of concept identification," PSYCHOL. REV., 66: 278-296, 1959.

Broca, Pierre Paul, Sub le Siege de la Faculte du Langage Articule avec deux Observations d'Aphemie (parte de la parole). BULL. SOC. ANAT., V. 6, August 1861.

Bronfenbrenner, U., "Developmental theory in transition," In H. W. Stevenson (Ed.), CHILD PSYCHOLOGY. NSSE Yearbook, Vol. 62, Part I. Chicago: University of Chicago Press, pp. 517-542, 1963.

Brown, J. R. Review of C. H. Delacato, "The Diagnosis and Treatment of Speech and Reading Problems," In NEUROL., 14: 599-600, 1964.

Brown, R. W. WORDS AND THINGS. Glencoe, Ill.: The Free Press, 1958.

Brown, R. W. & Bellugi, U., "Three processes in the child's acquisition of syntax," HARVARD EDUC. REV., 34: 133-151, 1964.

Burt, C., "The inheritance of mental ability," AMER. PSYCHOLOGIST, 13: 1-15, 1958.

Byers, R. K., & Lord, E. E., "Late effects of lead poisoning on mental development," AMER. J. DIS. CHILD., 66: 471-494, 1943.

Caldwell, B. M., "What is the optimal learning environment for the young child?" AMER. J. ORTHOPSYCHIAT., 37: 8-21, 1967.

Caldwell, B. M., & Richmond, J. B., "Programmed day care for the very young child—a preliminary report," J. MARRIAGE AND THE FAMILY, 26: 481, 488, 1964.

Cassell, R. H., "The Vineland adaptation of the Oseretsky Tests," TRAIN. SCH. BULL., 46 (Suppl.): 11-32, 1949.

Castaneda, A., McCandless, B., & Palermo, D., "The children's form of the Manifest Anxiety Scale," CHILD DEVELOPM., 27: 317-326, 1956.

Cattell, R. B., PERSONALITY. New York: McGraw-Hill, 1950.

Centerwall, S. A., & Centerwall, W. R., "A study of children with mongolism reared in the home compared to those reared away from home," PEDIATRICS, 25: 678-685, 1960.

Church, Joseph. LANGUAGE AND THE DISCOVERY OF REALITY. New York: Random House, 1961.

Clements, Sam D. MINIMAL BRAIN DYSFUNCTION IN CHILDREN. NINDB Monogr. No. 3. Washington, D. C.: U. S. Department of Health, Education, and Welfare, 1966.

Cole, E. M. Review of C. H. Delacato, "The Diagnosis and Treatment of Speech and Reading Problems," In HARVARD EDUC. REV., 34: 351-354, 1964.

Coleman, T. W., A COMPARISON OF YOUNG BRAIN—INJURED AND MONGOLIAN MENTALLY DEFECTIVE CHILDREN ON PERCEPTION, THINKING AND BEHAVIOR. Unpubl. doctoral dissertation, University of Michigan, 1960.

Cooper, R. M., & Zubek, J. P., "Effects of enriched and restricted early environments on the learning ability of bright and dull rats," CANAD. J. PSYCHOL., 12: 159-164, 1950.

Corder, O., "Effects of physical education on the intellectual, physical, and social development of educable mentally retarded boys," EXCEPTL. CHILD., 32: 357-364, 1966.

Cox, F. N., "Correlates of general and test anxiety in children," AUSTRALIAN J. PSYCHOL., 12: 169-177, 1960.

Crandall, V. J., "Achievement," In H. W. Stevenson (Ed.). CHILD PSYCHOLOGY. NSSE Yearbook, Vol. 62, Part I. Chicago: University of Chicago Press, pp. 416-459, 1963.

Cromwell, R. L., "A social learning approach to mental retardation," In N. R. Ellis (Ed.), HANDBOOK OF MENTAL DEFICIENCY. New York: McGraw—Hill, pp. 41-91, 1963.

Cromwell, R. L., Baumeister, A., & Hawkins, W. F., "Research in activity level," In N. R. Ellis (Ed.), HANDBOOK OF MENTAL DEFICIENCY. New York: McGraw—Hill, pp. 632-663, 1963.

Cruickshank, W. M., Bice, H. V., & Wallen, N. E., PERCEPTION AND CEREBRAL PALSY: A STUDY IN FIGURE BACKGROUND RELATIONSHIP. Syracuse, N. Y.: Syracuse University Press, 1957.

Cruickshank, W. M. Bice, H. V., & Wallen, N. E. A TEACHING METHOD FOR BRAIN—INJURED AND HYPERACTIVE CHILDREN. Syracuse, New York: Syracuse University Press, 1961.

Cruse, D. B., "The effects of distraction upon the performance of brain-injured and familial retarded children," In E. P. Trapp & P. Himelstein (Eds.). READINGS ON THE EXCEPTIONAL CHILD. New York: Appleton-Century-Crofts, pp. 492-499, 1962.

Delacato, C. H. THE TREATMENT AND PREVENTION OF READING PROBLEMS. Springfield, Ill.: Charles C. Thomas, 1959.

Delacato, C. H. THE DIAGNOSIS AND TREATMENT OF SPEECH AND READING PROBLEMS. Springfield, Ill.: Charles C. Thomas, 1963.

Delacato, C. H., (Ed.), NEUROLOGICAL ORGANIZATION AND READING PROBLEMS. Springfield, Ill.: Charles C. Thomas, 1966.

Dennis, W., "Causes of retardation among institutional children," J. GENET. PSYCHOL., 96: 47-59, 1960.

Deutsch, J. A., "Higher Nervous Function: The Psychological Bases of Memory," ANNUAL REVIEW OF PHYSIOLOGY. 24: 259-286, 1962.

Dingman, W., & Sporn, M. B., "The incorporation of 8-azaquanine into rat brain RNA and its effect on maze learning in the rat: An inquiry into the biochemical bases of memory," J. PSYCHIAT. RES., 1: 1-11, 1961.

Doll, E. A., "The essentials of an inclusive concept of mental deficiency," AMER. J. MENT. DEFIC., 46: 214-219, 1941.

Dollard, J., Doob, L., Miller, N., Mowrer, O., & Sears, R., FRUSTRATION AND AGGRESSION. New Haven: Yale University Press, 1939.

Dolphin, J. E., & Cruickshank, W. M., "The figure-background relationship in children with cerebral palsy," J. CLIN. PSYCHOL., 7: 228-231, 1951.

Doman, R. J., *et al.,* "Children with severe brain injuries," J. AMER. MED. ASSOC., 174: 257-262, 1960.

Drillien, C. M., THE GROWTH AND DEVELOPMENT OF THE PREMATURELY BORN INFANT. Baltimore: Williams & Wilkins, 1964.

Dudek, S. Z., & Lester, E. P., "The good child facade in chronic underachievers," AMER. J. ORTHOPSYCHIAT., 38: 153-160, 1968.

Dunsdon, M. I., Carter, C. O., & Huntley, R. M. C., "Upper end of range of intelligence in mongolism," LANCET, 2: 565-568, 1960.

Elkind, D., Larson, M., & Van Doorninck, W., "Perceptual decentration learning and performance in slow and average readers," J. EDUC. PSYCHOL.: 56: 50-56, 1965.

Ellis, Norman R. (Ed.), HANDBOOK OF MENTAL DEFICIENCY. New York: McGraw-Hill, 1963.

Ellis, Norman R., INTERNATIONAL REVIEW OF RESEARCH IN MENTAL RETARDATION. Vol. I. New York: Academic Press, 1966.

Ernhart, Claire B., *et al.,* "Brain injury in the preschool child: some developmental considerations, Part II, Comparison of brain injured and normal children," PSYCHOL. MONOGR., 77 (No. 11, Whole No.): 574, 1963.

Ervin, S. M., & Miller, W. R., "Language Development," In H. W. Stevenson (Ed.), CHILD PSYCHOLOGY, NSSE Yearbook, Vol. 62, Part I. Chicago: University of Chicago Press, pp. 108-143, 1963.

Fagan, Joseph F., "Short-term memory processes in normal and retarded children," J. EXP. CHILD PSYCHOL., 1968, (In Press).

Fantz, Robert L., "Pattern discrimination and selective attention as determinants of perceptual development from birth," In A. H. Kidd & J. L. Rivoire (Eds.),

PERCEPTUAL DEVELOPMENT IN CHILDREN, New York: International Universities Press, pp. 143-173, 1966.

Fantz, Robert L., & Nevis, Sonia, "Pattern preferences and perceptual-cognitive development in early infancy," MERRILL—PALMER QUART., 13: 77-108, 1967.

Fernald, G. M. REMEDIAL TECHNIQUES IN BASIC SCHOOL SUBJECTS. New York: McGraw—Hill, 1943.

Flavell, J. H., THE DEVELOPMENTAL PSYCHOLOGY OF JEAN PIAGET. New York: D. Van Nostrand Co., 1963.

Flexner, L. B., & Flexner, J. B., "Effect of acetoxycycloheximide and of an acetoxycycloheximide-puromycin mixture on cerebral protein synthesis and memory in mice," PROC. NAT. ACAD. SCI., 55: 369-374, 1966.

Folling, A., "Uber Ausscheidung von Phenylbrenztraubensaure in den Harn als Stoffwechselanomalie in Verbindung mit Imbezillitat," HOPPE SEYLER Z. PHYSIOL. CHEM., 227: 169, 1934.

Fowler, W., "The effect of early stimulation on the emergence of cognitive processes," In R. Hess & R. Bear (Eds.), EARLY EDUCATION. Chicago: Aldine, pp. 9-36, 1968.

Fraser, F. C., "Teratogenesis of the Central Nervous System," In H. A. Stevens & R. Heber (Eds.), MENTAL RETARDATION: A REVIEW OF RESEARCH. Chicago: University of Chicago Press, 395-428, 1964.

Fraser, M. S., & Wilks, J., "The residual effects of neonatal asphyxia," J. OBSTET. GYNAECOL. BRIT. EMP., 66: 748-752, 1959.

Freeberg, Norman E., & Payne, Donald T., "Parental influence on cognitive development in early childhood," CHILD DEVELOPM., 38: 65-88, 1967.

Freeman, R. D., "Controversy over 'patterning' as a treatment for brain damage in children," J. AMER. MED. ASSOC., 202: 385-388, 1967.

Freud, S. (1909), "Analysis of a phobia in a five-year-old boy," In J. Strachey (Ed. & Trans.), COMPLETE PSYCHOLOGICAL WORKS OF SIGMUND FREUD, Standard Edition, Vol. 10, London: The Hogarth Press, 5-149, 1955.

Frostig, M., "Visual perception in the brain-damaged child," AMER. J.

ORTHOPSYCHIAT., 33: 665-671, 1963.

Frostig, M., Lefever, D. W., & Whittlesey, J. R. B., "A developmental test of visual perception for evaluating normal and neurologically handicapped children," PERCEPT. MOT. SKILLS. 12: 383-394, 1961.

Fuller, J., & Thompson, W., BEHAVIOR GENETICS. New York: Wiley, 1960.

Furth, H. G., "The influence of language on the development of concept formation in deaf children," J. ABN. SOC. PSYCHOL., 63: 386-389, 1961.

Gaito, J., "A biochemical approach to learning and memory," PSYCHOL. REV., 68: 283-292, 1961.

Gaito, J., "DNA and RNA as memory molecules," PSYCHOL. REV., 70: 471-480, 1963.

Gaito, J. & Zavala, A., "Neurochemistry and learning," PSYCHOL. BULL., 61: 45-62, 1964.

GAP (Group for the Advancement of Psychiatry), PSYCHOPATHOLOGICAL DISORDERS IN CHILDHOOD: THEORETICAL CONSIDERATIONS AND A PROPOSED CLASSIFICATION. Report No. 62, Vol. 6. New York: GAP, 1966.

Gardner, R. W., "The development of cognitive structures," In C. Shearer (Ed.), COGNITION: THEORY, RESEARCH. PROMISE. New York: Harper & Row, 1962.

Gellner, L., A NEUROPHYSIOLOGICAL CONCEPT OF MENTAL RETARDATION AND ITS EDUCATIONAL IMPLICATIONS. Chicago: J. Levinson Research Foundation, 1959.

Getman, G. N., HOW TO DEVELOP YOUR CHILD'S INTELLIGENCE. Luverne, Minn.: privately printed, 1958.

Glickman, S. E., "Perseverative neural processes and consolidation of the memory trace," PSYCHOL. BULL., 1961, 58: 218-233, 1961.

Goldstein, K., "Die Lokalisation in der Grosshirnrinde," BETHES HANDB. D. NORM. U. PATHOL. PHYSIOL., 10, 1927.

Goldstein, K., AFTEREFFECTS OF BRAIN INJURIES IN WAR. New York: Grune & Stratton, 1942.

Goodenough, F. L., "The measurement of mental growth in children," In L. Carmichael (Ed.), MANUAL OF CHILD PSYCHOLOGY. New York: Wiley, pp. 450 ff., 1946.

Goshen, C. E., "Mental Retardation and Neurotic Maternal Attitudes," ARCH GEN. PSYCHIAT., 9: 168-175, 1963.

Gottesman, Irving I., "Genetic aspects of intelligent behavior," In N. R. Ellis (Ed.), HANDBOOK OF MENTAL DEFICIENCY. New York: McGraw-Hill, pp. 253-296, 1963.

Graham, F., *et al.*, "Development three years after perinatal anoxia and other potentially damaging newborn experiences," PSYCHOL. MONOGR., 76 (Whole No. 522): 1962.

Graham, F., *et al.*, "Brain injury in the preschool child: Some developmental considerations, Part I, Performance of normal children," PSYCHOL. MONOGR., 1963, 77 (No. 10, Whole No. 573): 1963.

Gray, S. W., & Klaus, R. A., "An experimental preschool program for culturally deprived children," CHILD DEVELPM., 36: 887-898, 1965.

Gray, S. W., & Klaus, R. A., "The early training project and its general rationale," In R. Hess & R. Bear (Eds.), EARLY EDUCATION. Chicago: Aldine, pp. 63-70, 1968.

Green, C. & Zigler, E., "Social deprivation and the performance of retarded and normal children on a satiation-type task," CHILD DEVELPM., 33: 499-508, 1962.

Griffith, B. C., Spitz, H. H., & Lipman, R. S., "Verbal mediators and concept formation in retarded and normal subjects," J. EXP. PSYCHOL., 58: 247-251, 1959.

Grunebaum, M., *et al.*, "Fathers of sons with primary neurotic learning inhibitions," AMER. J. ORTHOPSYCHIAT., 28: 98-111, 1962.

Halverson, H. M., "An experimental study of prehension in infants by means of systematic cinema records," GENET. PSYCHOL. MONOGR., 10: 107-286, 1931.

Harrell, R. F., Woodyard, E., & Gates, A. I., THE EFFECT OF MOTHERS' DIETS ON THE INTELLIGENCE OF OFFSPRING. New York: Bureau of Publications, Teachers College, Columbia University, 1955.

Harris, D. B. CHILDREN'S DRAWINGS AS MEASURES OF INTELLECTUAL MATURITY. New York: Harcourt, Brace & World, 1963.

Harris, I. D.,EMOTIONAL BLOCKS TO LEARNING. New York: The Free Press of Glencoe, 1961.

Heath, S. R., Jr., "Railwalking performance as related to mental age and etiological types," AMER. J. PSYCHOL., 55: 240-247, 1942.

Heath, S. R., Jr., "The relations of railwalking and other motor performances of mental defectives to mental age and etiological types," TRAIN. SCH. BULL., 50: 110-127, 1953.

Hebb, Donald O., "The effect of early and late brain injury upon test scores, and the nature of normal adult intelligence," PROC. AMER. PHIL. SOC., 85: 275-292, 1942.

Hebb, Donald O., ORGANIZATION OF BEHAVIOR. New York: John Wiley & Sons, Inc., 1949.

Heber, Rick, "A manual on terminology and classification in mental retardation," AMER. J. MENT. DEFIC. MONOGR. SUPPL., 64 (No. 2), 1959.

Hellman, I., "Some observations on mothers of children with intellectual inhibitions," PSYCHOANALYTIC STUDY OF THE CHILD, Vol. 9. New York: International Universities Press, 1954.

Hermelin, B., & O'Connor, N., "Short-term memory in normal and subnormal children," AMER. J. MENT. DEFIC., 69: 121-125, 1964.

Hess, R. D., & Bear, R. M. (eds.), EARLY EDUCATION. Chicago: Aldine, 1968.

Hess, R. D., & Shipman, V. C., "Early experience and the socialization of cognitive modes in children," CHILD DEVELPM., 36: 869-886, 1965.

Hess, R. D. & Shipman, V. C., "Maternal influences upon early learning: The cognitive environments of urban pre-school children," In R. Hess & R. Bear (Eds.), EARLY EDUCATION. Chicago: Aldine, pp. 91-104, 1968.

Hoffman, H. N., "A study in an aspect of concept formation, with subnormal, average, and superior adolescents," GENET. PSYCHOL. MONOGR., 52: 191-239, 1955.

Hofstaetter, P. R., "The changing composition of 'Intelligence': A study in T-technique," J. GENET. PSYCHOL., 85: 159-164, 1954.

Honzik, M. P., "Developmental studies of parent-child resemblance in intelligence," CHILD DEVELPM., 28: 216-277, 1957.

Hood, B. H., "An experimental study of Piaget's theory of the development of number in children," BRIT. J. PSYCHOL., 53: 273-286, 1962.

House, B. J., & Zeaman, D., "Position discrimination and reversals in low-grade retardates," J. COMP. PHYSIOL. PSYCHOL., 52: 564-565, 1959.

Hubel, D. H., & Wiesel, T. N., "Receptive fields of cells in striate cortex of very young, visually inexperienced kittens," J. NEUROPHYSIOL., 26: 994-1002, 1963.

Hunt, J. McV., "Motivation inherent in information processing and action," In O. J. Harvey (Ed.), MOTIVATION AND SOCIAL INTERACTION, New York: Ronald, 1963.

Hunt, J. McV., "Intrinsic motivation and its role in psychological development," NEBRASKA SYMPOS. MOTIVATION, Lincoln: University of Nebraska Press. 13: 189-282, 1965.

Hunt, J. McV., "Toward a theory of guided learning in development," In R. H. Ojemann & K. Pritchett (Eds.). GIVING EMPHASIS TO GUIDED LEARNING. Proceedings of a conference on guided learning, Educational Research Council of Greater Cleveland, pp. 98-160, 1966.

Hyden, H., & Egyhazi, E., "Nuclear RNA changes of nerve cells during a learning experiment in rats." PROC. NATL. ACAD. SCI., 48: 1366-1373, 1962.

Inhelder, B. LE DIAGNOSTIC DU RAISONEMENT CHER LES DEBILES MENTAUX. Nauchateli Delachaue Niestle, 1944.

Irwin, O., "Infant speech: effect of systematic reading of stories," J. SPEECH HEAR. RES., 3: 187-190, 1960.

Jersild, A. T. CHILD PSYCHOLOGY. Sixth Ed. Englewood Cliffs, N. J.: Prentice-Hall, 1968.

Jersild, A. T. Markey, F. V., & Jersild, C. L., "Children's fears, dreams, wishes, daydreams, likes, dislikes, pleasant and unpleasant memories," CHILD DEVELPM.

MONOGR., No. 12, 1933.

Johnson, G. O., & Blake, K. A., "Learning performance of retarded and normal children," SYRACUSE UNIVER. SPEC. EDUC. REHABIL. MONOGR., No. 5, 1960.

Kagerer, R. L., "The Relationship Between the Kraus-Weber Test for Minimum Muscular Fitness and School Achievement," Unpubl. Master's Thesis, Purdue University, 1958.

Kahn, E., & Cohen, L. H., "Organic driveness: A brainstem syndrome and an experience," NEW ENGLAND J. MED., 210: 748-756, 1934.

Katz, I., "Review of evidence relating to desegregation on the intellectual performance of Negroes," AMER. PSYCHOLOGIST, 19: 381-399, 1964.

Kaufmann, Harry, "Definitions and methodology in the study of aggression," PSYCHOL. BULL., 64: 351-364, 1965.

Kelleher, R. I., "Discrimination learning as a function of reversal and nonreversal shifts," J. EXP. PSYCHOL., 51: 379-384, 1956.

Keller, J. E., "The use of certain perceptual measures of brain injury with mentally retarded children," In E. P. Trapp & P. Himelstein (Eds), READINGS ON THE EXCEPTIONAL CHILD. New York: Appleton-Century-Crofts, pp. 485-491, 1962.

Kendler, H. H., & D'Amato, M. F., "A comparison of reversal shifts and non-reversal shifts in human concept formation behavior," J. EXP. PSYCHOL., 49: 165-174, 1955.

Kendler, T. S., & Kendler, H. H., "Reversal and non-reversal shifts in kindergarten children," J. EXP. PSYCHOL., 58: 56-60, 1959.

Kendler, T. S., & Kendler, H. H., & Wells, D., "Reversal and nonreversal shifts in nursery school children." J. COMP. PHYSIOL. PSYCHOL., 53: 83-88, 1960.

Kennard, M. A., "Reorganization of motor function in the cerebral cortex of monkeys deprived of motor and premotor areas in infancy," J.NEUROPHYSIOL., 1: 477-496, 1938.

Kennard, M. A., "Cortical reorganization of motor function: Studies on series of monkeys of various ages from infancy to maturity," ARCH. NEUROL. PSYCHIAT.,

48: 227-240, 1942.

Kennedy, C., & Ramirez, L. S., "Brain damage as a cause of behavior disturbance in children," In H. G. Birch (Ed.), BRAIN DAMAGE IN CHILDREN: THE BIOLOGICAL AND SOCIAL ASPECTS. Baltimore: Williams & Wilkins, pp. 13-26, 1964.

Kephart, N. C., THE SLOW LEARNER IN THE CLASSROOM. Columbus, Ohio: Charles E. Merrill, 1960.

Kershner, J. R., "Doman-Delacato's theory of neurological organization applied with retarded children," EXCEPTL. CHILD., 34: 441-450, 1968.

Kessler, Jane W., "Environmental components of measured intelligence," SCHOOL REVIEW, 73: 339-358, 1965.

Kessler, Jane W., PSYCHOPATHOLOGY OF CHILDHOOD. Englewood Cliffs, N. J.: Prentice-Hall, 1966.

Klausmeier, H. J., Feldhusen, J., & Check, J., AN ANALYSIS OF LEARNING EFFICIENCY IN ARITHMETIC OF MENTALLY RETARDED CHILDREN IN COMPARISON WITH CHILDREN OF AVERAGE AND HIGH INTELLIGENCE, Madison, Wis.: University of Wisconsin Press, 1959.

Krech, D., "Dynamic systems as open neurological systems," PSYCHOL. REV., 57: 345-361, 1950.

Krech, D. Rosenzweig, M. R., & Bennett, E. L., "The effects of environmental complexity and training on brain chemistry," J. COMP. PHYSIOL. PSYCHOL., 53: 509-519, 1960.

Kuenne, M. K., "Experimental investigation of the relation of language to transposition behavior in young children." J. EXP. PSYCHOL., 36: 471-490, 1946.

Kugel, R. B., "Familial mental retardation: Some possible neurophysiological and psychosocial interrelationships," In A. J. Solnit & S. A. Provence (Eds.). MODERN PERSPECTIVES IN CHILD DEVELOPMENT. New York: International Universities Press, pp. 206-216, 1963.

Kuhlman, E., "Experimental studies in mental deficiency," AMER. J. PSYCHOLOGY, 15: 391-446, 1904.

Langer, Susanne K. PHILOSPHY IN A NEW KEY: A STUDY IN THE SYMBOLISM OF REASON, RITE, AND ART. Cambridge, Mass.: Harvard University Press, 1942.

Lashley, K. S. BRAIN MECHANISMS AND INTELLIGENCE: A QUANTITATIVE STUDY OF INJURIES TO THE BRAIN. Chicago: University of Chicago Press, 1929.

Lenneberg, E. H., "Color naming, color recognition, color discrimination: A reappraisal," PERC. MOT. SKILLS, 12: 375-382, 1961.

Lewin, K. A DYNAMIC THEORY OF PERSONALITY. New York: McGraw-Hill, 1936.

Luria, A. R. THE ROLE OF SPEECH IN THE REGULATION OF NORMAL AND ABNORMAL DEVELOPMENT. New York: Pergamon Press, 1961.

Luria, A. R., "Psychological studies of mental deficiency in the Soviet Union," In N. R. Ellis (Ed.), HANDBOOK OF MENTAL DEFICIENCY. New York: McGraw—Hill, pp. 353-387, 1963.

Luria, A. R., RESTORATIONS OF FUNCTIONS AFTER BRAIN INJURY. Moscow: USSR Academy of Sciences Press, 1948. English translation, London: Pergamon Press, 1964.

Luria, A. R. HUMAN BRAIN AND PSYCHOLOGICAL PROCESSES. B. Haigh (Trans.). New York: Harper & Row, 1966.

McConnell, J. V., "Comparative physiology: Learning in invertebrates," ANNUAL REVIEW OF PHYSIOLOGY, 1966, 28: 107-136, 1966.

McCoy, N., & Zigler, E., "Social reinforcer effectiveness as a function of the relationship between child and adult," J. PERS. SOC. PSYCHOL., 1: 604-612, 1965.

McGaugh, J. L., Jennings, R. D., & Thompson, C. W., "The effect of distribution of practice on maze learning of descendants of Tryon maze-bright and maze-dull strains," PSYCHOL. REPORTS, 10: 147-150, 1962.

McPherson, Marian W., "Learning and mental deficiency," AMER. J. MENT. DEFIC., 62: 870-877, 1958.

Maccoby, Eleanor, "Developmental Psychology," ANNUAL REVIEW OF

PSYCHOLOGY, 15: 203-250, 1064.

Maccoby, Eleanor, "Early learning and personality: Summary and commentary," In R. Hess & R. Bear (Eds), EARLY EDUCATION. Chicago: Aldine, pp. 191-202, 1968.

Maccoby, Eleanor, & Bee, Helen L., "Some speculations concerning the lag between perceiving and performing," CHILD DEVELPM., 36: 367-377, 1965.

Maccoby, Eleanor, Dowley, E. M., Hagen, J. W., & Degerman, R., "Activity level and intellectual functioning in normal preschool children," CHILD DEVELPM., 36: 761-770, 1965.

Malpass, L. F., "Motor skills in mental deficiency," In N. R. Ellis (Ed.), HANDBOOK OF MENTAL DEFICIENCY. New York: McGraw—Hill, pp. 602-631, 1963.

Mannix, J. B., "The number concepts of a group of E. S. N. children," BRIT. J. EDUC. PSYCHOL., 30: 180-181, 1960.

Martin, B., "The assessment of anxiety by physiological behavioral measures." PSYCHOL. BULL., 58: 234-255, 1961.

Martin, G., & Powers, R. B., "Attention span: An operant conditioning analysis," EXCEPTL. CHILD., 33: 565-572, 1967.

Marshall, Joan M., CONCEPT ATTAINMENT IN AVERAGE AND SLOW LEARNING CHILDREN. Unpubl. doctoral dissertation, Western Reserve University, 1964.

Masland, R. L., Sarason, S. B., & Gladwin, T., MENTAL SUBNORMALITY. New York: Basic Books, 1958.

Meyer, E., & Byers, R. K., "Measles encephalitis: A follow-up study of sixteen patients," AMER. J. DIS. CHILD., 84: 543-570, 1952.

Meyerowitz, J. H., "Self-derogation in retardates and special class placement," CHILD DEVELPM., 33: 443-451, 1962.

Meyers, C. E., Orpet, R. E., Attwell, A. A., & Dingman, H. F., "Primary abilities at mental age six," MONOGR. SOC. RES. CHILD. DEVELPM., 27 (No. 1), 1962.

Milgram, Norman A., & Furth, Hans G., "The influence of language on concept attainment in educable retarded children," AMER. J. MENT. DEFIC., 67: 733-739, 1963.

Miller, J. G., "Information input overload and psychopathology," AMER. J. PSYCHIAT., 116: 695-704, 1960.

Miller, J. G., "Adjusting to overloads of information," In D. Rioch & E. Weinstein (Eds.), DISORDERS OF COMMUNICATION. Research Publications, ASSOC. RES. NER. MENT. DIS., 42: 87-100, 1964.

Montessori, M. THE MONTESSORI METHOD. New York: Frederick A. Stokes Co., 1912.

Mowrer, O. H. LEARNING THEORY AND THE SYMBOLIC PROCESSES. New York: Wiley, 1960.

Moyer, K. E., & von Haller, Gilmer B., "Attention spans of children for experimentally designed toys," J. GENET. PSYCHOL., 87: 187-201, 1955.

Mueller, M., & Smith, J. O., "The stability of language age modification over time," AMER. J. MENT. DEFIC.: 68: 537-539, 1964.

Neufeldt, Aldred H., "Short-term memory in the mentally retarded," PSYCHOL. MONOGR., 80 (No. 12, Whole No. 620), 1966.

Oliver, J., "The effects of physical conditioning exercises and activities on the mental characteristics of educationally subnormal boys," BRIT. J. EDUC. PSYCHOL., 49: 155-165, 1958.

Oppenheimer, S., Tanguay, Y., & Smith, E., A FOLLOW-UP STUDY OF EARLY IDENTIFICATION OF MILDLY RETARDED CHILDREN. In progress, at the Mental Development Center, Case Western Reserve University, Cleveland, Ohio.

Orton, S., "Specific reading disability: Strephosymbolia," J. AMER. MED. ASSOC., 90: 1095-1099, 1928.

Osgood, C. E., A BEHAVIORISTIC ANALYSIS OF PERCEPTION AND LANGUAGE AS COGNITIVE PHENOMENA. Cambridge, Mass.: Harvard University Press, 75-118, 1957.

Osler, S. F., & Fivel, M. W., "Concept attainment: I. The role of age and intelligence in concept attainment by induction," J. EXP. PSYCHOL., 62: 14-23, 1961.

Osler, S. F., & Shapiro, S. L., "Studies in concept attainment: IV. The role of partial reinforcement as a function of age and intelligence," CHILD DEVELPM., 35: 623-633, 1964.

Osler, S. F., & Trautman, G. E., "Concept attainment: II. Effect of stimulus complexity upon concept attainment at two levels of intelligence," J. EXP. PSYCHOL., 62:9-13, 1961.

Painter, Genevieve, "The effect of a rhythmic and sensory motor activity program on perceptual motor spatial abilities of kindergarten children," EXCEPTIONAL CHILD., 33: 113-116, 1966.

Pasamanick, B., "Research on the influence of sociocultural variables upon organic factors in mental retardation," AMER. J. MENT. DEFIC., 64: 316-320, 1959.

Patterson, G. R., Helper, M. E., & Wilcott, R. C., "Anxiety and verbal conditioning in children," CHILD DEVELPM., 31: 101-108, 1960.

Piaget, J., THE CONSTRUCTION OF REALITY IN THE CHILD. New York: Basic Books, 1954.

Piaget, J., SIX PSYCHOLOGICAL STUDIES. A. Tenzer (Trans.), D. Elkind (Ed.). New York: Random House, 1967

Pines, Maya, REVOLUTION IN LEARNING: THE YEARS FROM BIRTH TO SIX. New York: Harper & Row, 1967.

Polster, M. F., A STUDY OF EXPRESSED FEAR IN AVERAGE AND RETARDED CHILDREN OF THE SAME MENTAL AGE. Unpubl. doctoral dissertation, Western Reserve University, 1967.

Prechtl, H. F. R., & Stemmer, C. J., "The choreiform syndrome in children," DEVELPM. MED. CHILD NEUROL., 4: 119-127, 1962.

Pronko, N. H., Ebert, R., & Greenberg, G., "A critical review of theories of perception," In A. H. Kidd & J. L. Rivoire (Eds.), PERCEPTUAL DEVELOPMENT IN CHILDREN. New York: International Universities Press, pp. 57-78, 1966.

Provence, Sally, & Lipton, Rose C. INFANTS IN INSTITUTIONS: A COMPARISON OF THEIR DEVELOPMENT WITH FAMILY—REARED INFANTS

DURING THE FIRST YEAR OF LIFE. New York: International Universities Press, 1962.

Rapaport, D., ORGANIZATION AND PATHOLOGY OF THOUGHT. New York: Columbia University Press, 1951.

Rapin, Isabelle, "Brain damage in children," In Joseph Brennemann (Ed.). BRENNEMANN'S PRACTICE OF PEDIATRICS. Hagerstown, Md.: W. F. Prior Co., Inc., Vol. IV., Ch. 17, 1965.

Rebelsky, F. G., Starr, R. H., Jr., & Luria, Z., "Language development in the first four years," In Y. Brackbill, INFANCY AND EARLY CHILDHOOD. New York: The Free Press, pp. 289-360, 1967.

Reese, Hayne W., "Verbal mediation as a function of age level," PSYCHOL. BULL., 59: 502-509, 1962.

Reeves, Carol, "Cholinergic synaptic transmission and its relationship to behavior," PSYCHOL. BULL., 65: 321-335, 1966.

Rheingold, H. L., Gewirtz, J. L., & Ross, H. W., "Social conditioning of vocalizations in the infant," J. COMP. PHYSIOL. PSYCHOL., 52: 68-73, 1959.

Riesen, A. H., "Plasticity of behavior: Psychological aspects," In H. F. Herlow & C. N. Woolsey (Eds.), BIOLOGICAL AND BIOCHEMICAL BASES OF BEHAVIOR. Madison, Wis.: University of Wisconsin Press, 1958.

Robbins, M. P., "Test of the Doman-Delacato rationale with retarded readers," J. AMER. MED. ASSOC., 202: 389-393, 1967.

Roberts, J. A. F., "The genetics of mental deficiency," EUGENICS REV., 44: 71-83, 1952.

Robinson, Helbert B., & Robinson, Nancy M. THE MENTALLY RETARDED CHILD: A PSYCHOLOGICAL APPROACH. New York: McGraw—Hill, 1965.

Robinson, Helbert B., & Robinson, Nancy M., "The problem of timing in pre-school education," In R. Hess & R. Bear (Eds.), EARLY EDUCATION. Chicago: Aldine, pp. 37-52, 1968.

Roeper, A. & Sigel, I. E., "Finding the clue to children's thought processes," In W. W. Hertup and N. L. Smothergill (Eds.), THE YOUNG CHILD. Washington, D. C.: Nat. Assoc. for the Educ. of Young Children, pp. 77-95, 1967.

Rosenzweig, M. R. & Leiman, A. L., "Brain functions," ANNUAL REVIEW OF PSYCHOLOGY. 19: 55-98, 1968.

Rotter, J. B., SOCIAL LEARNING AND CLINICAL PSYCHOLOGY. Englewood Cliffs, N. J.: Prentice-Hall, 1954.

Rudel, R. G., "Transposition to size in children," J. COMP. PHYSIOL. PSYCHOL., 51: 386-390, 1958.

Ruebush, R. E., "Anxiety," In H. W. Stevenson (Ed.), CHILD PSYCHOLOGY. NSSE Yearbook, Vol. 62, Part I. Chicago, Ill.: University of Chicago Press, 1963.

Sackett, G. P., "A neural mechanism underlying unlearned, critical period, and developmental aspects of visually controlled behavior," PSYCHOL. REV., 70: 40-50, 1963.

Santostephano, S. C., "Cognitive controls and exceptional states in childhood," J. CLIN. PSYCHOL., 20: 213-218, 1964.

Santostephano, S. C., & Stayton, S., "Training the preschool retarded child in focusing attention: A program for parents," AMER. J. ORTHOPSYCHIAT., 37: 732-743, 1967.

Sarason, S. B., PSYCHOLOGICAL PROBLEMS IN MENTAL DEFICIENCY, 2nd Ed. New York: Harper, 1953.

Sarason, S. B., & Gladwin, T., "Psychological and cultural problems in mental subnormality: A review of research," GENET. PSYCHOL. MONOGR., 57: 3-289, 1958.

Sarason, S. B., *et al.*, ANXIETY IN ELEMENTARY SCHOOL CHILDREN. New York: Wiley, 1960.

Schachter, Frances F., & Apgar, Virginia, "Perinatal asphyxia and psychologic signs of brain damage in childhood," PEDIATRICS, 24: 1016-1025, 1959.

Schilder, P., "Studien zur Psychologie und Symptomatologie der Progressiven Paralyse," ABHENDL. NEUROL. PSYCHIAT. PSYCHOL. GRENZAEB., 58: 1-176, 1930.

Schilder, P., "Studies concerning the psychology and symptomatology of general paresis," In D. Rapaport (Ed. and Trans.), ORGANIZATION AND PATHOLOGY

OF THOUGHT. New York: Columbia University Press, pp. 519-580, 1951.

Schulman, J. L., Kasper, J. C. & Throne, F. M. BRAIN DAMAGE AND BEHAVIOR, Springfield, Ill.: Charles C. Thomas, 1965.

Seguin, E. IDIOCY: AND ITS TREATMENT BY THE PHYSIOLOGICAL METHOD. Albany, N. Y.: Brandow, 1866. New York: Columbia University Press, 1907.

Shirley, M. THE FIRST TWO YEARS: A STUDY OF TWENTY—FIVE BABIES. Minneapolis: University of Minnesota Press, 1933.

Silver, A. A., Hagin, R. A., & Hersh, M. F., "Reading disability: Teaching through stimulation of deficit perceptual areas," AMER. J. ORTHOPSYCHIAT., 37: 744-752, 1967.

Skinner, B. F. VERBAL BEHAVIOR. New York: Appleton-Century-Crofts, 1957.

Skodak, M., & Skeels, H. M., "A final follow-up study of one hundred adopted children," J. GENET. PSYCHOL., 75: 85-125, 1949.

Sloan, W., "The Lincoln-Oseretsky Motor Development Scale," GENET. PSYCHOL. MONOGR., 51: 183-252, 1955.

Smedslund, J. Articles I-VI, SCAND. J. PSYCHOL., 2: 11-20, 71-84, 85-87, 153-155, 156-160, 203-210, 1961.

Smith, J. O., "Group Language Development for Educable Mental Retardates," EXCEPT. CHILD., 29: 95-101, 1962.

Solley, C. M., & Engel, M., "Perceptual autism in children: The effects of reward, punishment, and neutral conditions upon perceptual learning," J. GENET. PSYCHOL., 97: 77-91, 1960.

Solley, C. M., & Murphy, Gardner. DEVELOPMENT OF THE PERCEPTUAL WORLD. New York: Basic Books, 1960.

Solley, C. M., & Sonmer, R., "Perceptual autism in children," J. GEN. PSYCHOL., 56: 3-11, 1957.

Sontag, L. W., Baker, C. T., & Nelson, V. L., "Personality as a determinant of performance," AMER. J. ORTHOPSYCHIAT., 25: 555-562, 1955.

Sontag, L. W., Baker, C. T., & Nelson, V. L., "Mental growth and personality development: A longitudinal study," MONOGR. SOC. RES. CHILD. DEVELOPM., 1958, 23 (No. 2), 1958.

Spence, K. W. BEHAVIOR THEORY AND CONDITIONING. New Haven: Yale University Press, 1956.

Spence, K. W. "Anxiety (drive) level and performance in eyelid conditioning," PSYCHOL. BULL., 61: 129-139, 1964.

Sperry, B., *et al.*, "Renunciation and denial in learning difficulties," AMER. J. ORTHOPSYCHIAT., 28: 98-111, 1958.

Spiker, C. C., "Verbal factors in the discrimination learning of children," In J. C. Wright & J. Kagan (Eds.), "Basic cognitive processes in children," MONOGR. SOC. RES. CHILD DEVELPM., 28 (No. 2): 53-71, 1963.

Spitz, Herman H., "Field theory in mental deficiency," In N. R. Ellis (Ed.), HANDBOOK OF MENTAL DEFICIENCY. New York: McGraw-Hill, pp. 11-40, 1963.

Spitz, Herman H., "The role of input organization in the learning and memory of mental retardates," In N. R. Ellis (Ed.), RESEARCH IN MENTAL RETARDATION. Vol. 2. New York: Academic Press, 1966.

Spitz, Herman H., "A comparison of mental retardates and normals on the distorted room illusion," AMER. J. MENT. DEFIC., 72: 34-39, 1967.

Spivak, G., "Perceptual processes," In N. R. Ellis (Ed.), HANDBOOK OF MENTAL DEFICIENCY. New York: McGraw-Hill, pp. 480-511, 1963.

Spradlin, J. E., "Language and communication of mental defectives," In N. R. Ellis (Ed.), HANDBOOK OF MENTAL DEFICIENCY. New York: McGraw-Hill, pp. 512-555, 1963.

Staats, A. W., *et al.*, "A reinforcer system and experimental procedure for the laboratory study of reading acquisition," CHILD DEVELOPM., 35: 209-231, 1964.

Stevenson, H. W. & Fahel, L., "The effect of social reinforcement on the performance of institutionalized and noninstitutionalized normal and feebleminded children," J. PERS., 29: 136-147, 1961.

Stott, D. H., "A general test of motor impairment for children," DEVELPM. MED. CHILD NEUROL., 8: 523-531, 1966.

Stott, L. H., & Ball, R. S., "Infant and preschool mental tests," MONOGR. SOC. RES. CHILD DEVELPM., 1965, 30: 1-151, 1965.

Strauss, A. A., & Lehtinen, L. E. PSYCHOPATHOLOGY AND EDUCATION OF THE BRAIN-INJURED CHILD. New York: Grune & Stratton, 1947.

Tanner, J. M., & Inhelder, B. (Eds.). DISCUSSIONS ON CHILD DEVELOPMENT. New York: International Universities Press, 1960.

Taylor, J. A., "A personality scale of manifest anxiety," J. ABN. SOC. PSYCHOL., 96: 64-70, 1953.

Taylor, J. A., "Drive theory and manifest anxiety," In M. T. Mednick & S. A. Mednick (Eds.), RESEARCH IN PERSONALITY. New York: Holt, Rinehart, & Winston, pp. 205-222, 1963.

Terrell, G., Jr., Durkin, K., & Wiesley, M., "Social class and the nature of the incentive in discrimination learning," J. ABN. SOC. PSYCHOL., 59: 270-272, 1959.

Teuber, Hans-Lukas, & Rudel, R. G., "Behavior after cerebral lesions in children and adults," DEVELOP. MED. CHILD. NEUROL., 4: 3-20, 1962.

Thompson, R., et al., "An analysis of the differential effects of ECS on memory in young and adult rats," CANAD. J. PSYCHOL., 12: 83-96, 1958.

Thompson, W. R., "The effects of prenatal and early postnatal experience," LESSONS FROM ANIMAL BEHAVIOR FOR THE CLINICIAN, 7: 10-17, 1962.

Thurston, D. L., Middelkamp, J. N., & Mason, E., "The late effects of lead poisoning," J. PEDIATRICS, 47: 413-423, 1955.

Turnure, J., & Zigler, E., "Outer directedness in the problem-solving of normal and retarded children," J. ABN. SOC. PSYCHOL., 69: 427-436, 1964.

Vance, B. J., "Social learning theory and guidance in early childhood," YOUNG CHILD, 21: 30-42, 1965.

Vernon, M. D., "Perception in relation to cognition," In A. H. Kidd & J. L. Rivoire (Eds.), PERCEPTUAL DEVELOPMENT IN CHILDREN, New York: International

Universities Press, pp. 391-406, 1966.

Waisman, H. A., & Gerritsen, T., "Biochemical and clinical correlations," In H. A. Stevens & R. Heber (Eds.), MENTAL RETARDATION: A REVIEW OF RESEARCH. Chicago: University of Chicago Press, pp. 307-347, 1964.

Walk, R. D., & Gibson, Eleanor, "A comparative and analytical study of visual depth perception," PSYCHOL. MONOGR., 75 (Whole No. 519), 1961.

Wallach, L., & Sprott, R. L., "Inducing number conservation in children," CHILD DEVELPM., 35: 1057-1072, 1964.

Wallach, M. A., "Research on children's thinking," In H. W. Stevenson (Ed.): CHILD PSYCHOLOGY. NSSE Yearbook, Vol. 62, Part I. Chicago: University of Chicago Press, pp. 236-276, 1963.

Walton, J., Ellis, E., & Court, S., "Clumsy children: A study of developmental apraxia and agnosia," BRAIN. 85: 603-612, 1962.

Weatherwax, J., & Benoit, E. P., "Concrete and abstract thinking in organic and non-organic mentally retarded children," In E. P. Trapp & P. Himelstein (Eds.), READINGS ON THE EXCEPTIONAL CHILD. New York: Appleton-Century-Crofts, pp. 500-507, 1962.

Weiner, G., *et al.*, "Correlates of low birth weight: Psychological status at six to seven years of age," PEDIATRICS, 35: 434-444, 1965.

Weisskopf, E. A., "Intellectual malfunctioning and personality," J. ABN. SOC. PSYCHOL., 46: 410-423, 1951.

Wepman, J. M. Review of C. H. Delacato, THE DIAGNOSIS AND TREATMENT OF SPEECH AND READING PROBLEMS, in Contemp. Psychol., 9: 351-352, 1964.

Werner, H., & Strauss, A., "Pathology of figure ground relation in the child," J. ABN. SOC. PSYCHOL., 36: 58-67, 1941.

White, B. L., & Held, R., "Plasticity of sensorimotor development in the human infant," In J. F. Rosenblith & W. Allinsmith (Eds.), THE CAUSES OF BEHAVIOR, 2nd Ed. Boston: Allyn & Bacon, 1966.

White, R. W., "Motivation reconsidered: The concept of competence," PSYCHOL.

REV., 66: 297-333, 1959.

White, R. W., "Competence and the psychosexual stages of development," In M. R. Jones (Ed.), NEBRASKA SYMPOSIUM ON MOTIVATION, Vol. 8, Lincoln: University of Nebraska Press, 1960.

White, S. H., "Learning," In H. W. Stevenson (Ed.), CHILD PSYCHOLOGY, NSSE Yearbook, Vol. 62, Part I. Chicago: NSSE, pp. 196-235, 1963.

White, S. H., "Age differences in reaction to stimulus variation," in O. J. Harvey (Ed.), FLEXIBILITY, ADAPTABILITY, AND CREATIVITY. New York: Springer, 1966.

White, S. H., "Evidence for hierarchical arrangement of learning processes," In L. P. Lipsitt and C. C. Spiker (Eds.) ADVANCES IN CHILD DEVELOPMENT AND BEHAVIOR, Vol. 2, New York: Academic Press, 187-216, 1965.

White, S. H., "Some educated guesses about cognitive development in the preschool years," In R. Hess & R. Bear (Eds.), EARLY EDUCATION. Chicago: Aldine, 203-214, 1968.

Whorf, B. L., "Language and Stereotypes," In E. Maccoby, T. M. Newcomb, & E. L. Hartley (Eds.), READINGS IN SOCIAL PSYCHOLOGY, 3rd Ed. New York: Holt, pp. 1-9, 1958.

Winterbottom, Marian, "The relation of need for achievement in learning experiences in independence and mastery," In J. Atkinson (Ed.), MOTIVES IN FANTASY, ACTION, AND SOCIETY. Princeton, N. J.: Van Nostrand, 1958.

Witkin, H. A., et al., PERSONALITY THROUGH PERCEPTION: AN EXPERIMENTAL AND CLINICAL STUDY. New York: Harper, 1954.

Wohlwill, J. G., & Lowe, R. C., "Experimental analysis of the development of the conservation of number," CHILD DEVELPM., 33: 153-157, 1962.

Wolff, Joseph L., "Concept-shift and discrimination-reversal learning in humans," PSYCHOL. BULL., 1967, 68: 369-408, 1967.

Woodward, Mary, "The behaviour of idiots interpreted by Piaget's theory of sensorimotor development," BRIT. J. EDUC. PSYCHOL., 29: 60-71, 1959.

Woodward, Mary, "Concepts of number in the mentally subnormal studied by

Piaget's method," J. CHILD PSYCHOL. PSYCHIAT., 2: 249-259, 1961.

Wortis, H., & Freedman, A., "The contributions of social environment to the development of premature children," AMER. J. ORTHOPSYCHIAT., 35: 57-68, 1965.

Zaporozhets, A. V., "The development of voluntary movements," In B. Simon (Ed.), PSYCHOLOGY IN THE SOVIET UNION. Stanford: Stanford Univ. Press, pp. 108-114, 1957.

Zaporozhets, A. V., DEVELOPMENT OF VOLUNTARY MOVEMENTS. Moscow: The Publishing House, Academy of Pedagogical Sciences, 1960.

Zaslow, R. W., "A study of concept formation in normals, mental defectives, and brain-damaged adults," GENET. PSYCHOL. MONOGR., 63: 279-388, 1961.

Zeaman, D., & House, B. J., "Approach and avoidance in the discrimination learning of retardates," In D. Zeaman, et al., LEARNING AND TRANSFER IN MENTAL DEFECTIVES. Progress Report No. 2, NIMH, USPHS, Res. Grant M-1099 to Univ. of Connecticut, pp. 32-70, 1960.

Zeaman, D., & House, B. J., "The role of attention in retardate discrimination learning," In N. R. Ellis (Ed.), HANDBOOK OF MENTAL DEFICIENCY. New York: McGraw-Hill, pp. 159-223, 1963.

Zigler, E., "Rigidity and social reinforcement effects in the performance of institutionalized and noninstitutionalized normal and retarded children," J. PERS., 31: 258-269, 1963.

Zigler, E., "Mental retardation: Current issues and approaches," In M. L. Hoffman & L. W. Hoffman (Eds.), REVIEW OF CHILD DEVELOPMENT RESEARCH, Vol. II. New York: Russell Sage Foundation, pp. 107-168, 1966a.

Zigler, E., "Research on personality structure in the retardate," In N. R. Ellis (Ed.), RESEARCH IN MENTAL RETARDATION, Vol. I. New York: Academic Press, pp. 77-108, 1966b.

Zigler, E., & deLabry, J., "Concept-switching in middle-class, lower-class, and retarded children," J. ABN. SOC. PSYCHOL., 65: 267-273, 1962.

Zigler, E., Hodgden, L., & Stevenson, H. W., "The effect of support on the performance of normal and feebleminded children," J. PERS., 26: 106-122, 1958.

Zigler, E., & Williams, J., "Institutionalization and the effectiveness of social reinforcement: A three-year follow-up study," J. ABN. SOC. PSYCHOL., 66: 197-205, 1963.

THE USES OF EXPERIENCE:
OPEN STATEMENTS, ILL-DEFINED STRATEGIES,
AND INTELLIGENT INFORMATION PROCESSING

Walter R. Reitman, Ph.D.

INFORMATION PROCESSING MODELS AND INVESTIGATIONS OF THINKING

In 1957, Newell, Shaw, and Simon published a description of the Logic Theorist, their first information processing theory of thinking. Incorporating strategies similar to those used by humans, this computer-programmed model solved problems only humans had solved before. It also generated behavior sequences resembling in many ways the behavior of subjects asked to think aloud as they worked through the same problems. Offering a new way of studying and accounting for complex thought processes, these early investigations attracted considerable attention within cognitive psychology and gradually gave rise to a substantial body of research applying computer simulation techniques to problems in pattern recognition, learning, and other areas as well as thinking.

The growing appreciation of the conceptual and methodological advantages of these new tools is easy to account for. They help make possible precise, objective definitions of the functions presumed to underlie extremely complex human activity. They permit construction of models in which that activity is represented directly and explicitly, as the behavior of a dynamic system purposefully analyzing, seeking, and manipulating objects and information to achieve its ends. Furthermore, such models are generative. They allow us to produce the behavioral consequences of a system of theoretical assumptions on a computer, and, consequently, to study the strict implications of a model in an exact and unambiguous way. Though some pertinent conceptual and methodological problems are not yet fully resolved (Reitman, 1965; 1966; 1967), it is clear that the existing body of work utilizing these concepts and techniques already constitutes an important methodological advance and a substantial contribution of our understanding of cognitive activity (Hunt, 1968; Newell and Simon, 1965; Reitman, 1965).

Most significant and influential of the efforts to generalize the model of thinking developed in the Logic Theorist is the work on the General Problem Solver (GPS: Newell and Simon, 1963; Ernst and Newell, 1967). GPS incorporates a very general conception of the means by which humans apply an integrated core of methods and strategies to a broad range of problems, it deals in detail with the problems of attention allocation as a function of complex hierarchical goal structures, it provides a detailed representation of mediating processes in cognitive activity, and it reflects very well the recursiveness of human thinking. But the organization of GPS and the structures and processes incorporated in the system also involve simplifications limiting its utility as a general theory at several important points. In particular, GPS in its present form does not deal with human thinking in areas involving large amounts of specific information; it so far has been restricted to problems specified in terms of well-defined objects, properties, and methods, hence is not necessarily applicable to thinking about ill-defined problems; and though Newell, Shaw, and Simon (1960) and others have considered how GPS might be made adaptive, present versions do not actually learn or improve with experience.

Note that remarks of this sort at best only characterize a particular class of theories at one stage in their development. It would be wrong to think such models incapable of significant extension and generalization. Quite the contrary: there is every reason to anticipate development of information processing models that describe how humans solve ill-defined problems and how they use and learn from their experience in doing so. The purpose of this paper is to discuss some of the problems involved and to describe work under way whose long range goal is just such a more general theory of thinking.

The Informational Context of Thinking.

Scientific thinking typically takes place against a rich informational background, which may be more or less well organized. In some fields, the social and behavioral sciences for example, as the recent National Research Council (1967) report on COMMUNICATION SYSTEMS AND RESOURCES IN THE BEHAVIORAL SCIENCES points out, scientists must work in complex, diffusely structured informational contexts. The bodies of knowledge they have available:

> ...change rather rapidly and lack general and widely accepted definitions and principles. A large part of knowledge in the social and behavioral sciences is an assortment of empirical generalizations, hypotheses, hunches, descriptive phrases, uninterpreted sentences, and the like. Organization of information is frequently found in propositional inventories or encyclopedia-like outputs.
>
> Future behavioral science theories are unlikely to consist simply of a few touchstone principles. Comprehensive theories, it should be expected, will evolve out of conscious syntheses of thought and research with repeated reorganization of past conceptualizations and findings.....

Even work in the natural sciences typically requires an extended knowledge base. Jauncey (1946) describes a classic case, a sequence of experiments deriving from

Becquerel's observation that after having been kept for several days in the darkness of a closed drawer, a thin button of a uranium compound fastened to the outside of a holder containing an unexposed photographic plate left an impression on the plate when it was developed. The data actually available to us give little information on Becquerel's thought processes at that point, and so there is little chance of accounting in detail for the resulting investigations of radioactivity. Had we, however, the detailed thinking aloud data we now know how to collect, and were we to attempt such an account, it surely would require representations of the knowledge Becquerel brought to the problem, including facts about closed drawers, light, photographic plates, and the as yet imperfectly specified properties of uranium, as well as processes capable of manipulating such extended bodies of information in thinking. Since present models of thinking have been explored only in limited, simply structured information contexts, and since the specific routines they employ typically presume such structures, the explanatory power of this class of theories with respect to thinking in complex informational environments remains to be determined. The studies described below of strategy systems operating in an on-line information system context relate directly to this problem.

Open Statements, Open Strategies, and Ill-defined Problems

The results of a series of previous studies of thinking (Reitman, 1964; 1965) underscored the importance of one basic property of the problems and objects of thought: In general, the things we think about are given in open statements rather than in well-defined or fully specified form.

To see what this property involves, consider one example discussed in some detail in Reitman (1965). The problem is to design a vehicle that will propel itself. The individual trying to solve this problem discovers that in order to do so he must pose and solve subproblems having to do with properties and processes not explicitly given in the original problem. He must, for example, determine the source of energy, and he must evolve some basic assumptions about the organization of the system. Is the energy source to be connected to the locomotor mechanism as in an automobile, or a jet aircraft; or should a living system like the horse be taken as a model? Though none of these considerations may be referred to in the problem as given, solving the problem requires the locating and working out of such ill-defined aspects. The decisions made in doing this are a major determinant of subsequent thinking and of the end result. In sum, because the problems humans deal with often are posed in ill-defined form, a good deal of human problem solving activity is a matter of discovering and closing constraints left open in problem statements. At times deliberately, at other times without being aware of it, the problem solver regularly must close gaps in the specifications he works with.

Open statements and consequent ill-definedness are not restricted to thinking and problem solving. They are a general feature of human information processing. Even in simple sentences, much is left to be filled in by the listener. Consider such injunctions or questions as "Please move your car" or "Find a good man for the job." It is up to the listener to figure out where the car is to be moved to when, or to determine what "a good man" is to mean in the context of this particular request. Numerous examples in other areas of human information processing are given by Neisser (1967), who uses ill-definedness as a basic concept throughout his discussion of perceptual and cognitive phenomena.

It is easy to suggest why so much of human activity involves open, ill-defined statements. The brain stores and has the ability to utilize large amounts of information. With respect to that stored information, detailed new information often would be redundant. Open statements enable us to avoid that redundancy in perceiving, communicating, and thinking. It is inefficient for an intelligent system communicating with others or with itself over time to specify objects and ideas fully if their properties are readily filled in or inferred as needed from information already available. Similarly, why specify a new object or idea in detail if it can be indicated simply by naming some already stored schema together with properties or modifications peculiar to the new instance (Woodworth, 1938; de Groot, 1965).

Note also that the use of open statements separates out important properties from the temporary or local ones, the ones that vary with the situation. It allows a strategy to fit many different situations without explicit specification of the values of these local variables. It also simplifies preservation of the invariant aspects of strategies over time.

It is one thing to suggest a rationale for the openness we find in human thinking, problem solving, and cognitive activity generally. It is quite another to account in detail for the mechanisms that mediate the use of open statements, enabling man to work with minimal cues and to adapt stored information to new situations. In particular, it is important to realize that existing models of thinking and problem solving do not in general deal with these aspects of human activity. Present versions of the General Problem Solver, for example, presume that all objects, operators, and properties are well-defined. That is, each is given completely and in full detail. When an operation in GPS is not applicable in a particular situation, it is because input conditions associated with the operator are not satisfied. It is never because the operation itself is ill-defined. Yet many human strategies, for example those Polya (1954; 1957) discusses, are in fact non-operational. That is, they involve open constraints which must be closed before the strategies can be carried out. In such cases, part of the human problem solving process involves operations on these incompletely specified strategies in order to realize them in forms permitting their application in the situation at hand.

Problems of this sort do not arise in existing problem solving models, which seldom are required to make plausible assumptions, to fill in gaps, or to construct something from incompletely specified information. As a result, such systems have little to say about how humans cope with problems defined with minimal cues and requiring for their solution intelligent inference from background knowledge.

We have noted that one of the long range goals of the present work is development of a system capable of using ill-defined strategies to solve ill-defined problems. It may be objected that, after all, if we are going to get a computing system to solve these problems, the procedures for solving them will in some sense certainly have to be well-defined. If the computer does not have enough information to carry out the appropriate operations, then those operations will not be carried out. Conversely, if the computer solves a problem, then in what sense can the problem or the procedures involved in solving it be termed ill-defined?

We certainly would agree that if any system, artificial or natural, can solve a problem, it must have had enough information to do so. But there are widely varying ways in which that information may have been stored, obtained and used. At one extreme, a problem may come preclassified, or in a form easily classified by the problem solving system. The system thus may be able to use a procedure keyed to solving problems of this class. At the other extreme, however, the information may be stored diffusely throughout the system, distributed over its varied experiences, ideas, concepts, and intuitions, so that "the procedure for solving this particular problem" is effectively coextensive with the total experience of the system. That is, there is nothing like a single strategy, rule, procedure, or system of procedures capable by itself of solving the problem. In this light, the notion of ill-definedness may be viewed as having to do with how discreet, delimited, and self-contained individual strategies for solving particular problems are. If the requisite information exists only as bits and pieces of rules and experience, then we must explain how under these conditions an intelligent problem solving system goes about coming up with problem solution. How can a network of information and problem solving strategies most of whose elements are ill-defined (in the sense of being inoperable by themselves) be organized so as to achieve such results?

In sum, we might want to say that any system capable of solving a problem has well-defined procedures for solving that problem. But where the set of procedures is coextensive with the full intelligence and information contained in the system, the major focus of interest is the organizational arrangements that enable so diffuse a system to solve problems.

214

The Uses of Experience

In the models we are developing, problems, objects, and strategies all may involve open statements. Such models must be able to adapt and develop available objects and operators if they are to function successfully. Consequently these models also provide a framework for investigating the ways in which human thinkers learn and improve their performance with experience.

The previous experience of a skilled problem solver affects his present thinking in many different ways. It provides data, facts, and concrete examples. These may serve to guide searches, to indicate discrepancies, and as raw material for models, strategies, and higher level abstractions generally. To be useful, this background has to be accessible, capable of making contact with present activity. To some extent this may be accomplished by deliberate attempts at integration (see, for example, Polya, 1957); strategy systems of the sort described below would appear to provide a useful framework for analyzing the means by which this integration is achieved. But such deliberate efforts to integrate material by associating it with preexisting conceptual structures are by no means the whole story. To see why, consider the following group problem solving protocol reported by Gordon (1961). The group

> ...was faced with the problem of inventing a dispenser which could be used with various products from glue to nail polish. The dispenser was to be in one piece without a top to be removed and replaced with each use. These specifications meant that the mouth of the dispenser had to be designed to open for dispensing and to close tightly after use. Group members directed themselves to a new way of thinking about the problem. Among the mechanisms which were brought to bear on the problem was Direct Analogy. The group asked itself what actions in nature operated the way the dispenser must in order to satisfy the conditions imposed by the problem.
>
> A: A clam sticks its neck out of its shell...brings the neck back in and closes the shell again.
>
> B: Yeah, but the clam's shell is an exoskeleton. The real part, the real anatomy of the clam is inside.
>
> C: What difference does that make?
>
> A: Well, the neck of the clam doesn't clean itself...it just drags itself back into the protection of the shell.

D: What other analogies are there to our problem?

E: How about the human mouth?

B: What does it dispense?

E: Spit...the mouth propels spit out whenever it wants...Oh, oh. It isn't really self-cleaning...you know, dribbling on the chin.

A: Couldn't there be a mouth which was trained so that it wouldn't dribble?

E: Maybe, but it would be contrived as hell...and if the human mouth can't keep itself clean with all the feedback in the human system. . . .

D: When I was a kid I grew up on a farm. I used to drive a hayrack behind a pair of draft horses. When a horse would take a crap, first his outer...I guess you'd call it a kind of mouth, would open. Then the anal sphincter would dilate and a horse ball would come out. Afterwards, everything would close up again. The whole picture would be as clean as a whistle.

E: What if the horse had diarrhea?

D: That happened when they got too much grain..but the horse would kind of wink a couple of times while the anal mouth was drawn back...the winking would squeeze out the liquid...then the outer mouth would cover the whole thing up again.

B: You're describing a plastic motion.

D: I guess so...could we simulate the horse's ass in plastic?

Later the particular Synectics group working on the dispenser problem built a product which operated almost exactly as described by the above analogy.

The overall flow of this problem solving session is not too difficult to grasp. The group members are trained in specific strategies for making use of experience, and they apply these strategies quite deliberately. What gives pause are the twin problems of 1) representing the total mass of experience, expecially non-verbal experience, that humans appear able to store; and 2) inducing retrieval methods that could account for human ability to access that experience appropriately. With repect to these problems, the work described below is at best propadeutic, in the sense that once the on-line system and the models we are working on have been completed it then may be possible to ask how one might extend such systems in the right direction.

MODELING THE STRATEGY SYSTEMS OF SCIENTIFIC THINKING

Having considered some of the basic problems motivating the present investigation, we now briefly outline some of the specific phenomena we are concerned with and the framework we have developed for dealing with them.

The basic data are verbal protocols collected and analyzed by means of the usual procedures employed in information processing studies (e.g., Newell and Simon, 1961). The subject is a working scientist requested to think aloud as he works. What he says is tape recorded and then transcribed. In most cases the subject works alone. Occasional protocols also have been taken from pairs of subjects who regularly work together in an effort to utilize conversations between co-workers as a source of data. The protocols are taken over substantial time periods while the subject is working at current real problems of his own choosing to provide data on thinking under conditions approaching those of natural work settings. We want to see how people think when they are trying their best to solve problems that are important to them and suited to the strategies they have developed in previous work.

The data collected to date display many instances of what the skilled problem solver can do with his experience. Of these, the following cases presently are of particular interest.

There are situations in which the thinker retrieves some quite specific situation, experiment, argument, etc., that appears to embody a method or strategy relevant to the present problem. In working with this material, however, the thinker interprets it quite loosely, and modifies it to suit local conditions of the present problem. The specific experience is transformed, abstracted into a more open form, by means of as yet incompletely specified strategies for distinguishing important variables and conditions from unimportant details.

Another frequent open situation is one in which some condition, requirement, or constraint on the thinker's goal is specified in open form. That is, some information about the form of the constraint is given, but the exact nature of the test that will determine whether the constraint has been satisfied appears to be left open, as something which the system will have to fill in later based on criteria to be determined at that time. A test or operation may be specified in terms of some aspect of what it is to accomplish, but without identifying any particular test. Since any operation is likely to have multiple effects on the problem structure, it is evident that the system will have to select among possible tests, or devise new tests, taking into consideration the varied effects upon the problem structure at the point at which the test actually is applied.

Still another frequently encountered open information structure is the strategy that consists not of a sequence of steps and operations, but of clues or hints about what one might want to do, or the kinds of steps one might want to follow. Often there appears to be no explicit specification of the conditions that will determine which of the several possible procedures or desired states one ought to try to obtain; occasionally not even an order of application is indicated.

In sum, the strategies a skilled problem solver uses and the statements he makes in analyzing or describing a problem for himself or for communication to others with comparable skills presume both intelligence and information for their effective use. Just as a good cook knows how to modify general instructions to take account of local variations in humidity and in the quality and consistency of his ingredients, so the skilled problem solver stores and interprets his knowledge and strategies as open information structures, an arrangement that presumes a high level of flexibility and intelligence at the time at which they are utilized.

The preliminary framework we now are using as a basis for analyzing our data is as follows. All strategies are treated as schemes, as in GPS. As the illustration that follows demonstrates, however, the strategy schemes employed here differ from those of GPS in several important respects. They generally involve open statements which must be closed before the strategies become operational; they are more numerous; and they are continuous with the other elements of the system's knowledge structures. Thus knowledge of what to do in any particular situation is more diffusely organized, more intimately connected with general experience.

These differences imply corresponding differences in mode of operation. If we look at a flow chart for a GPS method (Newell and Simon, 1963), we see that each method consists of a set of interrelated calls on subroutines such as "match A to B to find difference D." The specific operations that realize such a routine may vary with the task at hand. The way one matches objects in symbolic logic is not necessarily the way one matches objects in some other area. This in itself is not a source of new problems in GPS, however. The specific operation is determined *a priori*, by the particular task environment context. In GPS, furthermore, the statement of a problem is in terms of unambiguous referent objects and operations. This generally is not true for problem statements in the present system. Faced with the request to "find a good man for the job" it first may be necessary to determine what "the job" involves, what "a good man" should be taken to mean in this context, and what specific operations might be employed to "find" him. In short, in going from an initial open statement to operations that can be carried out, the system we envisage must set up and solve new problems involving background information not actually given in the problem as stated.

To convey some idea of how this general scheme is intended to operate, we outline the working of the executive and then give a specific example. Strategies are realized by an interpreter similar in conception to that used in the Argus program (Reitman, Grove, and Shoup, 1964). Its rules of operation in very general terms are these. Presented with a strategy specified with respect to available primitive operations, with all parameters well-defined, the interpreter carries out the strategy. Presented with a strategy in which these conditions are not met, for example a strategy in which some of the parameters are open, the interpreter generates a subproblem involving the closing of some parameter (the filling in of some open statement). If this new problem is accepted, the interpreter searches for a strategy that might be used to solve it. If such a strategy is found, the interpreter attempts to carry it out. If no such strategy can be found, or if the strategy involved is itself non-operational, because it involves open statements, the interpreter may return with a new problem. Thus the system is recursive in its overall structure. The organization of behavior depends upon a network of ill-defined strategies realized by an interpreter which can operate both on task objects and on the strategy schemes themselves. Or in other words, our results take the form of a system of strategies which has "the ability to turn round upon its own 'schemata' and to construct them afresh" (Bartlett, 1932).

The components of the strategy network are a great many interconnected functions such as: **VARY; FIND SIMILAR ELEMENT; INDUCE GENERALIZATION; FIND SIGNIFICANT PROPERTIES; TEST CONJECTURE; COMPARE;** and **RETRIEVE INSTANCE**. Since each such function is defined in open statements, it differs from a GPS method scheme in that it generally is non-operational when called. The following example illustrates how interpretation of the strategy system proceeds.

Assume the system has a problem and so far has not been able to find an immediate solution procedure for it. The **FIND SIMILAR ELEMENT** function is called. Since the antecedent element is a problem, the value of **ELEMENT** is set to be **PROBLEM**. The value of **SIMILAR** remains open, however. If the function is to be carried out, **SIMILAR** must be closed. This creates a new subproblem. If accepted, the system may call the **FIND SIGNIFICANT PROPERTIES** function. This function takes the properties of the current **PROBLEM** as input. If it succeeds, **SIMILAR** is now closed and **RETRIEVE INSTANCE** is called with specifications taken from the closed **FIND SIMILAR ELEMENT** function.

Should **RETRIEVE INSTANCE** fail, a call to **VARY** may result. The **VARY** function must be closed, in this case by selection of some properties (attribute-value pairs) from those now associated with the **FIND SIMILAR ELEMENT** function. After calling upon a function that retrieves from memory alternative values for those attributes, **VARY** returns a new set of specifications differing in one or more properties from those previously associated with the **FIND SIMILAR ELEMENT** function. A call to the **RETRIEVE INSTANCE** function using these new specifications now perhaps may succeed. If so, the element retrieved will be a new problem similar in its significant properties to the problem the system started with. Should this new problem prove soluble, the system may be able to apply the solution scheme to the original problem. If the solution scheme does not apply, the system may be able to modify the scheme, using the **VARY** function again, so as to produce a related scheme that does work.

As this example illustrates, the strategies underlying the data we are working with are highly interconnected. The **VARY** function, for instance, enters among others into strategies for retrieval, conjecture testing, generalization, and local improvement or optimization (compare the "hill climbing" strategy discussed in Minsky, 1963). Many of these functions may be called upon in turn in the course of closing and carrying out **VARY** in some particular case.

Numerous details of the present formulation remain to be worked out. One of the main purposes of the on-line facility we are constructing is to provide both the additional detailed strategy data we require and also a context in which to evaluate implementations of the strategy system formulation. From the results so far, however, it seems reasonable to regard the general formulation we now have as a good first approximation to the strategy systems humans actually employ.

AN ON-LINE FACILITY FOR THE STUDY OF SCIENTIFIC THINKING

The foregoing discussions are based on tape recorded protocols collected in something close to a normal working context. For several reasons, however, it is desirable to investigate thinking in an on-line situation. This section describes our present on-line research facility and the contribution we expect it to make.

The basic idea is to develop (in stages) an increasingly intelligent computer support system for an individual scientist or for small groups working with textual information. This system will provide him with information storage and retrieval facilities augmented by access to a large net of associations between text items and between words describing those text items. The system will use information about the user, about the subject matter stored, and about the current working context, to allow the user to communicate with the system quickly, efficiently, and eventually in ill-defined terms. That is, the system eventually will be able to make plausible inferences about what the scientist wants and about the best way of getting it. When in doubt, it will ask pertinent questions. The system is to have the capacity for learning (or being taught) more and more about its users and about the subject matter, and about how the user wants to communicate with it. As a long-range goal, we plan to work toward a system that is increasingly trainable, adaptive, able to change its own problem solving strategies, make better inferences, and in general improve the speed, efficiency, and payoff of communication as man and system increasingly "understand" one another better.

Hardware Configuration.

The system we are using to study the information processing activity of thinkers functioning with on-line access to the storage and processing capabilities of large computers is based on The University of Michigan's on-line IBM 360/67 system. Special hardware components include a large volume data storage device, the IBM 2316 disk pack (25 million character capacity), and a CCI 30 display terminal. The disk pack provides economic and efficient storage of the data generated by the project. The CCI display serves as the system terminal for scientists working as subjects. The device can display up to 800 characters of text at a time and its keyboard provides a variety of useful editing facilities.

First Stage of Software Development.

The first-stage information storage and retrieval system serves four functions. It provides a useful working facility for our scientist subjects. It facilitates the investigation of how scientists think when working in a rich informational context. It is a first step towards an artificial intelligence system capable of sophisticated man-machine communication and information utilization and retrieval, as discussed below. And finally the facility also provides the necessary basis for our efforts to model and simulate the operation of ill-defined strategy systems.

To meet these needs, the first-stage system must satisfy several requirements. In particular, it must be able to handle large quantities of complexly interrelated data; it should permit their organization, reorganization, and utilization in a flexible fashion, with a minimum of trouble to the user; and it must make possible recursive searches of the resulting data base. The main features of the system we use to implement to satisfy these requirements are as follows.

The TRAMP system (Ash, 1968) serves as the basic software for setting up and searching the information structures associated with the text units to be stored and retrieved. This system is an extension of The University of Michigan's UMIST interpreter (TRAC) which provides an associative data structure and relational operations. That is, it stores information about the properties of objects of any sort (text materials, etc.) as attribute-value pairs. TRAMP uses hash coding algorithms which permit data to be stored and retrieved as flexibly as is possible with the commonly used list and string processing languages, and it also is faster and more efficient than systems based on list or string search. Memory access time is substantially independent of the size of the data space. These speed and efficiency considerations become increasingly significant as we begin working with the large data bases our subjects generate.

The user of this first-stage system is able to store units of texts (notes, plans, summaries of published materials, etc.) and associated descriptions of their properties and interrelations. He can indicate sub- and super-set connections, synonyms, and similar relations among the terms he uses to describe his materials. Since TRAMP permits definitions of new relations either as undefined primitives or in terms of existing relations, the user will be able to add further relations as he needs them.

Text is retrieved and questions answered by recursive search through the associative structure defined by these interconnected properties and relations. The TRAMP system in its present form allows the use of such interconnections and of logical combinations of properties and relations in defining retrieval requests. Any properties associated with text items can be employed in making searches. The user can specify searches in terms of such details as the date on which an item was entered or used, comments he may have made on the importance or value of the item, and any indications he may have given of the particular problem context associated with the entry.

The initial system soon also will handle a variety of data management and housekeeping problems associated with the system flexibility we wish to achieve. It will be able to accept interleaved commands, thus enabling the user to halt work on one problem temporarily, begin work on some other problem, and later come back if he chooses. Low value information, as indicated by user feedback, will be retrieved only when specifically requested. The changes in associative structure involved in copying, combining, modifying, and rearranging items will be taken care of for the most part automatically. The system will be able to provide counts of the number of items that satisfy a particular retrieval request, to order the outputs in terms of the user's prior assessments of the importance of the individual items, and, on request, to generate samples from the set of items so as to enable the user to redefine or respecify his request in terms of properties associated with the items he finds most useful. We also plan to implement procedures whereby the system can report encounters with information previously evaluated as important in the course of searching for new information. In effect, the system will be able to interrupt an ongoing search with a comment such as: "By the way, item X is involved here. Are you interested in examining the connection?"

A system with these properties is within the present state of the art, and it should be useful enough to our scientist subjects to encourage them to take advantage of it. Thus it will enable us to build up a sufficient information base to proceed with the subsequent stages of system development. That is, it will enable us to collect the requisite detailed data on human problem solving in a rich informational context and permit us, using the information thus obtained, to gradually increase the capability of the system and its match to the working characteristics of the intelligent human problem solver employing it.

Subsequent Software Development.

As is evident from discussions such as Licklider's (1965), a great deal of intensive effort is being devoted to the development of increasingly more useful and powerful software systems. Though the system just outlined here should prove a useful instrument in its own right, its main significance is in the context of the present study of scientific thinking. Its function is to provide a basis for further research on the strategy systems humans use. To the extent that further development of the system also contributes significantly to software development, it will do so by taking advantage of the results obtained from these investigations. The importance to further software development of research aimed at improving our understanding of human information processing is emphasized in the recent National Research Council (1967) report on COMMUNICATION SYSTEMS AND RESOURCES IN THE BEHAVIORAL SCIENCES.

> The scientist makes progress in his line of inquiry by adding new information to existing knowledge in ways that suggest more powerful explanatory principles and point to fruitful hypotheses for additional research. Very little is known, however, about the cognitive process by which this is accomplished. Since the facilitation of inquiry is the ultimate purpose of a scientific information system, it would be useful to learn: (a) how scientists in different specialties organize existing knowledge and use it as the basis for seeking information; (b) how information (either in digested form, as in documents, or in raw form, as in data archives) can best be "packaged" to meet scientists' needs. Studies directed to these questions might suggest ways of indexing and classifying information to complement association patterns *in the minds of scientists*, and to develop more efficient information "packages."

The subsequent software developments we envisage will proceed hand in glove with what we discover through use of the initial system about the ways in which scientists use information. In particular, given the results already obtained regarding the importance of open statements in communication and thinking, we will want to work toward a system increasingly capable of accepting such communications, making plausible inferences, and filling in information left out. In basing software development on theoretical constructs inferred from detailed observations of how working scientists think and use information, we are in effect asking how an artificial intelligence system might be made gradually to take over some of these functions, and in so doing provide a more efficient and powerful tool for human problem solvers working in an on-line context.

The issues involved here already have been discussed in terms of the theory of human thinking underlying the research. It may be useful, however, to examine them as they apply to research on artificial intelligence and advanced software systems.

A major limiting factor in present on-line information processing systems is the rate and information content of human inputs. A user can type only so fast. Anything that permits him to convey more in a message of a given length increases the utility of the system to him. Our concern here is with software developments that would enable the system to take advantages of redundancies with respect to already stored information about content or process so as to minimize the amount of new information the human being must communicate each time he calls upon the system.

To see what might be accomplished along these lines, consider how we might enable a system to take over and carry out as a single unit the steps of some search and retrieval strategy a human user might apply. We noted above that the initial software system we plan to provide will permit the user to request a count of items satisfying some general description (e.g., "experiments on memory"). If the number of items is large, he may then request a sample from the set. After he has examined this sample, he may ask to see the properties associated with the items in the sample most relevant to his present purpose. Then, drawing on this property information, he may formulate a new, better specified request to obtain further items having similar descriptions. The data collected in the previous phase of our work contain many examples of such progressive redefinition as a function of interaction with the materials being worked on. The strategy just outlined also is closely related to the basic operating procedure Norman (1967) postulates in his model of human information retrieval.

Use of this strategy with the initial software system requires four interchanges with the system. Any improvement that decreased this number without debasing the quality of the results would improve its utility to the user. It might be possible to cut the number of interchanges in half by adding an option such that for any request which would retrieve a number of items exceeding some parameter the system automatically returns a count and a sample. The user then need only indicate which items are relevant and the system at the point returns further items with similar descriptions.

To make explicit the relation between a software option of this sort and the underlying theoretical framework, imagine the on-line system replaced by a human assistant. In response to the scientist's initial request, the assistant provides a sample of descriptions of items. The scientist circles those he is interested in and returns them with a new request for "some more like these." To comply with the new request, the assistant must close the gaps in the open statement; he must infer what "like" is to mean operationally in this context. And this is what the system option also must do.

We cannot be sure in advance that such an option is feasible. It assumes we will be able to specify for the system appropriate ways of working with the properties and interrelations users associate with items. But experience with how individual users employ the first-stage system will furnish the data needed to undertake the development of such an option. We can examine the records of first-stage requests and the corresponding thinking-aloud protocols to determine the properties and relations used and the ways in which they are employed. There will be ample opportunity to test and improve the adequacy of the option by comparing the results obtained with those the user secures using the four-step sequence. In effect we take advantage of the fact that since the initial system provides only low level primitive operations, the user must make the organization of his higher order strategies explicit in the course of using these operations to achieve his ends. Thus the on-line setting should provide much more finely detailed data on the organization of these aspects of human thinking than those secured in a non-interactive situation. It will provide many more overt behavioral points of contact with what the individual thinker is doing. Given these, it becomes that much easier to induce the structure of individual strategies and the ways in which they interrelate. In short, the very results obtained with the first-stage system should prove a rich source of ideas for further software development.

The retrieval option just discussed is one of several procedures we plan to implement once we have the necessary first-stage data. It should indicate the general direction work on subsequent software development will take. In particular, it illustrates the close relation between work on practical software problems and the study of the strategy systems of users. Present day software has made significant progress in reducing the amount of explicit input required, through use of implicit default settings. These permit the user to omit parameter specifications in cases in which some constant value the system then fills in is adequate. The developments we are proposing go one step further. They will enable the system to close open constraints by using already stored process and content information to fill in values of variables. Thus they will permit the user to call larger strategy units with fewer commands and, consequently, reduce the number of explicit information interchanges needed to achieve the desired result.

The analysis of basic problems underlying the software developments proposed here is closely related to that of several investigators in the computer sciences now attempting to develop more powerful information storage and retrieval systems. See for example Thompson's (1963) treatment of "semantic disengagement" and "extrinsic knowledge." Thus it is reasonable to expect that investigations of how humans solve these problems quite likely will generate other new concepts leading to improvements in the power of artificial intelligence systems.

Evaluation of strategy system models.

The on-line facility just described will facilitate investigation of scientific thinking in several ways. The previous section discussed its use as a substantially self-correcting tool for discovering how working scientists organize and use the materials they work with. The system also will contribute to the evaluation of the resulting strategy system models.

The ultimate role of the system in this regard is as a vehicle for simulating strategy systems operating on a realistic data base. Earlier we noted that present information processing models have yet to be tested in rich and complexly organized informational contexts. One of the by-products of use of the on-line system will be such a data base. As we make progress in discovering and encoding the strategies users employ, the data base the users generate will make it possible to test the inferred strategies by simulating them in a realistic context. Taken together, the data base and the system's housekeeping facilities thus amount to a convenient general purpose medium that can be used to facilitate evaluation of competing models of the strategy systems of users.

The on-line system also should prove a useful evaluation aid well before detailed simulation is feasible. Since strategies are represented as schemes to be interpreted, they can themselves be stored within the data base even before they are operational. This will make it possible for the user to request information about the steps the system would propose in response to some problem, and that in turn should yield useful feedback about the match between inferred strategies and those the user actually would select in that situation. Such a procedure has other uses as well. In particular, it should serve as a valuable pedagogical tool for on-line instruction of students in the use of problem solving strategies appropriate to a given problem context.

CONCLUSION

Information processing models have contributed a great deal to our understanding of cognitive processes. This paper describes the motivation, methods, and theoretical structure of research within this framework having as its goal extensions of present concepts of thinking and intelligent information processing. It also discusses an on-line information retrieval system serving both as a research facility and as a vehicle for studies of artificial intelligence, and it considers some of the relations between natural and artificial intelligence as they appear in the light of the basic theoretical concepts underlying the present work.

Most investigators working in these domains will agree that all of us are a long way from the artificial intelligence system and the models of natural intelligence we are trying to achieve. There may yet prove to be, as some philosophers argue, aspects of natural intelligence so remote from what can be conceived and incorporated in our present representations that all such enterprises are doomed from the start. If so, there probably is no better way to establish the point than to assume the contrary and see how far we get.

I would like to acknowledge the very helpful comments on an earlier draft of this paper provided by John Brown, Richard Sauvain, John Thomas, and Alan Weintraub, and the support received under U.S.P.H.S. Grant MH-12160 for the work described here.

References

Ash, W. Tramp. "CONCOMP Project", Unpublished manuscript, The University of Michigan, 1968.

Bartlett, F. C. REMEMBERING. Cambridge, England: Cambridge University Press, 1932.

de Groot, A. D. THOUGHT AND CHOICE IN CHESS. The Hague: Mouton, 1965.

Ernst, G. W., & Newell, A. "Generality and GPS", Unpublished manuscript, Carnegie-Mellon University, 1967.

Gordon, W. J. J. SYNECTICS. New York: Harper & Row, 1961.

Hunt, E. "Computer simulation: artificial intelligence studies and their relevance to psychology", In P.R. Farnsworth, M. R. Rosenzweig, & J. T. Polefka (Eds.), ANNUAL REVIEW OF PSYCHOLOGY. Vol. 19: 135-168, 1968.

Jauncey, G. E. M. "The early years of radioactivity" AMERICAN JOURNAL OF PHYSICS, 14: 226-241, 1946.

Licklider, J. C. R. LIBRARIES OF THE FUTURE. Cambridge: The M.I.T. Press, 1965.

Minsky, M. "Steps toward artificial intelligence", PROCEEDINGS OF THE IRE, 49: 8-29, 1961. Reprinted in E. A. Feigenbaum & J. Feldman (Eds.), COMPUTERS AND THOUGHT. New York: McGraw-Hill, pp. 406-450, 1963.

National Research Council, Division of Behavioral Sciences, Committee on Information in the Behavioral Sciences. COMMUNICATION SYSTEMS AND RESOURCES IN THE BEHAVIORAL SCIENCES. Publication 1575. Washington, D. C.: National Academy of Sciences, 1967.

Neisser, U. COGNITIVE PSYCHOLOGY. New York: Appleton-Century-Crofts, 1967.

Newell, A., Shaw, J. C., & Simon, H. A. "Empirical explorations of the logic theory machine", PROCEEDINGS OF THE WESTERN JOINT COMPUTER CONFERENCE, 11: 218-230, 1957.

Newell, A., Shaw, J. C., & Simon, H. A. "A variety of intelligent learning in a general problem solver," In M. C. Yovits & S. Cameron (Eds.), *Self-organizing systems.* New York: Pergamon Press, pp. 153-189, 1960

Newell, A., & Simon, H. A. "Computer simulation of human thinking," *Science,* 134: 2011-2017, 1961.

Newell, A., & Simon, H. A. "GPS, a program that simulates human thought ", In H. Billing (Ed.), LERNENDE AUTOMATEN. Munich: Oldenbourg, 1961. Reprinted in E. A. Feigenbaum & J. Feldman (Eds.), COMPUTERS AND THOUGHT. New York: McGraw-Hill, pp. 279-293, 1963.

Newell, A., & Simon, H. A. "Programs as theories of higher mental processes", In R. W. Stacy & B. Waxman (Eds.), COMPUTERS IN BIOMEDICAL RESEARCH. Vol. II. New York: Academic Press, pp. 141-172, 1965.

Norman, D. A. "Attention and retention", Unpublished manuscript, University of California, San Diego, 1967.

Polya, G. PATTERNS OF PLAUSIBLE INFERENCE. Princeton, N. J.: Princeton University Press, 1954.

Polya, G. HOW TO SOLVE IT. Garden City, N. Y.: Doubleday Anchor, 1957.

Reitman, W. R. "Heuristic decision procedures, open constraints, and the structure of ill-defined problems", In M. W. Shelly & G. L. Bryan (Eds.), HUMAN JUDGMENTS AND OPTIMALITY. New York: Wiley, pp. 282-315, 1964.

Reitman, W. R. COGNITION AND THOUGHT. New York: Wiley, 1965.

Reitman, W. R. "The study of heuristics", In A. de Groot & W. R. Reitman (Eds.), HEURISTIC PROCESSES IN THINKING. Moscow: "Nauka" (Science) Publishing House, pp. 44-53, 1966.

Reitman, W. R. "Modeling the formation and use of concepts, percepts, and rules", In L. Lecam & J. Neyman (Eds.) PROCEEDINGS OF THE FIFTH BERKELEY SYMPOSIUM ON MATHEMATICAL STATISTICS AND PROBABILITY. Vol. IV. Berkeley: University of California Press, pp. 65-79, 1967.

Reitman, W. R., Grove, R. B., & Shoup, R. G. "Argus: an information-processing model of thinking", BEHAVIORAL SCIENCE, 9: 270-281, 1964. Reprinted in P. C. Wason (Ed.), THINKING AND REASONING. West Drayton, Middlesex, England: Penguin, 1968.

Thompson, F. B. "The semantic interface in man-machine communication", TEMPO, September 1963, General Electric Company, Santa Barbara, California, Contract Nonr-4l0l(00), Office of Naval Research.

Woodworth, R. S. EXPERIMENTAL PSYCHOLOGY. New York: Holt, 1938.

CONCEPTUAL THINKING IN YOUNG CHILDREN
AS A FUNCTION OF AGE AND
SOCIAL CLASS BACKGROUND

Herbert Zimiles, Ph.D.

Although the variable of socio-economic status has traditionally served as a basic dimension for organizing and categorizing descriptive data in the social sciences, relatively little progress has been made in understanding why this factor tends to be so influential. In the area of cognitive development, for example, it has long been recognized that children's performance on the Stanford— Binet as well as most other measures of intellectual aptitude are highly correlated with their socio-economic status; this relationship was sufficiently prominent to stimulate efforts to develop so-called culture—free tests. Yet relatively little effort has been expended toward diagnosing the nature of the relationship between socio-economic status and intellectual functioning—of delineating the character of the differences between groups that have been found, and identifying the factors which mediate this relationship.

The sudden surge of interest in the educational needs of disadvantaged children has served to sharply intensify the study of psychological development as it is affected by socio-economic factors, particularly in the area of cognitive functioning. Most attention has been directed toward the analysis of the intellectual functioning of deprived Negro children, but numerous studies have also examined other ethnic groups among the poor—white, Puerto Rican, Indian and Mexican, for example. For many investigators, the most expeditious method of conducting this work has been through comparative studies of middle-class and disadvantaged groups. This methodological stance is often favored because the variables of the cognitive domain are so ill-defined, and their methods of assessment so primitive, that absolute measurement is simply not possible. It is feasible to make comparative judgments of differences between groups, to examine one group of children in relation to another. In the absence of a suitable frame of reference, a full, meaningful, non-relativistic description of an isolated group is virtually impossible to achieve. So much more is known, in both informal as well as formal terms, about the intellectual characteristics of middle-class children, that it is sensible to use this group as a reference point while exploring the intellectual functioning of disadvantaged children.

Furthermore, it should be noted that most educational techniques and programs have been devised for use with middle-class children, and the bulk of most teachers' professional experience has been with middle-class children, so that the exposition of the intellectual skills and educational needs of disadvantaged children has to be made to educators in terms of their framework of experience and theory; recommendations for the education of disadvantaged children can be made more understandable if they are described in terms of the departures they require from already established modes of analysis and practice. While there are a number of self-evident advantages to studying Negro disadvantaged children in relation to characteristics of middle-class Negro children, rather than middle-class white children, so that comparisons are based on differences in social class structure, thereby avoiding invidious racial comparisons, middle-class Negro children are often not available in sufficiently large numbers for study purposes. Perhaps more important, if the purpose of a comparative study of the disadvantaged Negro child is to compare the characteristics of his intellectual functioning with those which tend to prevail in the schools, and with those about which most is known, then it is the white middle-class child who should serve as a reference point.

The present study has followed the latter position; it has compared the intellectual functioning of Negro disadvantaged five- and six-year-old children with that of white middle-class children of the same age. More specifically, it has examined the influence of a set of variables on conservation of number performance in three groups of five- and six-year-old children of white middle-class, Negro disadvantaged, and Jewish parochial school backgrounds. It was originally designed to study the role of several stimulus attributes of the conservation procedure as well as the influence of two antecedent factors—the child's differentiation ability and his ability to tolerate delay of gratification—on conservation of number performance. The stimulus attributes which were studied involved a comparison of the difference between conservation of equivalence and conservation of difference, and examination of the effect of homogeneity and heterogeneity of the objects to be conserved, the size (large and small number) of the aggregates to be conserved, and the meaningful-neutral dimension of the objects. The overall findings with regard to these variables have been reported elsewhere (Zimiles, 1966, 1967); it should be noted that the aforementioned factors did not interact with ethnicity or social class in their effect upon conservation of number. The present paper deals with a comparison of performance of the three diverse groups of children on several of the measures employed in the study.

METHODS AND PROCEDURE

Subjects

The sample consisted of 146 boys, 72 kindergarten children and 74 first graders, comprising three groups: a) 50 predominantly white, middle-class children selected from two public schools in a middle-class neighborhood; b) 48 Negro, underprivileged children selected from a public school in a slum neighborhood; and

c) 48 children of predominantly lower-middle-class background randomly selected from two orthodox Jewish parochial schools. The first two groups afforded a comparison between white middle-class and Negro disadvantaged children; the third provided a sample of children raised according to stern, traditional moral and religious precepts which required rapid socialization in narrowly defined spheres, and expected early mastery of symbolic systems so that scholarly religious training could begin. Each of the three groups was equally divided between kindergarten and first-grade children, except for the white middle-class group where there were 24 kindergartners and 26 first graders.

Tests

The tests are described briefly below; a fuller description is published elsewhere (Zimiles, 1966):

Conservation of Number

Six conservation of number trials were given in which the stimulus characteristics of the items varied systematically in counter-balanced fashion from trial to trial. Conservation performance was scored according to whether S passed or failed the six trials, or performed in mixed fashion, *i.e.* passing on some trials and failing on others.

Conservation Pictures

This test consisted of 11 cards each of which contained two rows of paper seals of familiar objects arranged so that they presented a conflict between spatial and numerical cues, as they do in the final phase of the conservation of number problem. (See Figure 1 for a schematic presentation of the Conservation Pictures Test.) The test was scored according to the number of items that were answered correctly.

Differentiation Tasks

Picture-Vocabulary Test: A 12-item test in which each item presented pictures of three objects that belonged to the same class, but could be differentiated from one another in terms of some more specific referent, *e.g.*, one item presents three pictures of balls and S is asked to identify the baseball. The number of items answered correctly constituted the test score.

Children's Embedded Figures Test (CEFT): Patterned after Gottschaldt's early work, this test was developed by Karp and Konstadt (1963). A raw score based on 25 items was obtained for each child.

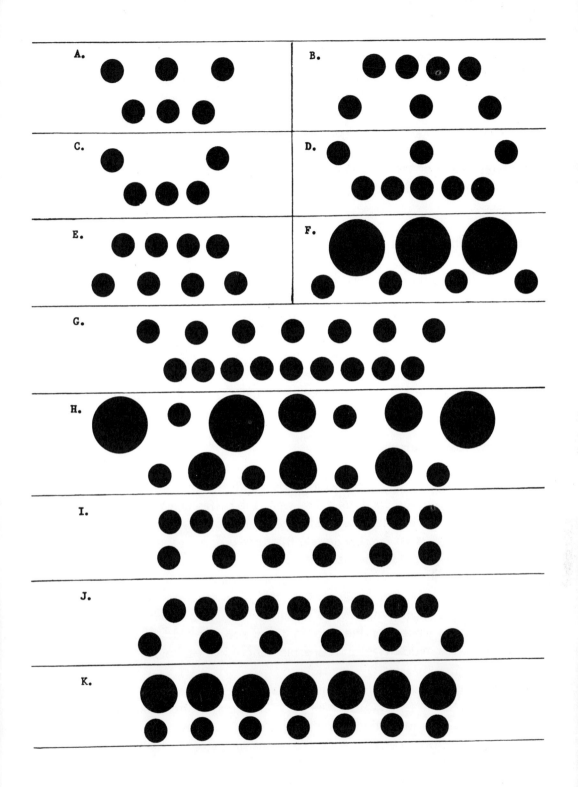

FIGURE 1

Schematic Presentation of Conservation Picture Items

Differentiation between age and height: * A set of photographs depicting a younger but visibly taller person standing next to an older but shorter person were presented to *S*, who was asked on some trials to indicate which person was taller and on others which person was older. Performance was scored according to whether *S* failed no items, one item, or more than one item.

Differentiation of the self: The child's drawing of a person was scored according to Harris' revision of Goodenough's early work (1963). Raw scores rather than IQ units were used.

WISC Vocabulary Test

Raw scores based on Wechsler's scoring (1949) criteria were obtained for each child.

RESULTS

The results are presented in Table 1 for each of the three contrasting groups at each of the two age levels, thereby facilitating a comparison of social class-ethnic differences in relation to differences in age. This permits examination of whether differences resulting from ethnicity exceed differences attributed to age.

Conservation of Number

The results of the six conservation trials indicate that in both age groups, the disadvantaged groups performed less well; the difference between them and their more privileged age-mates was much greater among the six year olds than among the fives. There was great overlap among the three groups at the five-year level, whereas among the six year olds, the disadvantaged group trailed markedly. Among the white middle-class and parochial school groups, a sharp rise in performance from the kindergarten to the first-grade level is discernible, whereas only modest differences between these age groups were found among the disadvantaged groups. The distribution of scores for the disadvantaged six year olds is hardly distinguishable from the white middle-class and parochial school five year olds.

Another distinctive feature of these data is the frequency of mixed conservation performance. The tendency to pass some conservation items and to fail others may be interpreted as indicating a transitional state midway between nonconservation and conservation, or, as an index of consistency, as behavior which from one viewpoint at least may be considered to be more aberrant or maladaptive than the consistent failure to conserve. This response pattern occurred with much greater

---

*Other differentiation items—between depth and width, thickness and length, height and width—were answered correctly by all the children and were therefore excluded from the data analysis.

TABLE 1

Summary of Group Performance on Conservation and Differentiation Tests and Related Measures

Subject Group	Conservation of Number Performance			Conservation Pictures Test Mean Score	Differentiation Scores						WISC Vocabulary Test Mean Score
					Picture Vocabulary Test Mean Score	CEFT Mean Score	Draw-a-Person Test Mean Score	Age-Height: Differentiation No. of Ss Answering (0, 1, >1) Items Incorrectly			
	+	Mx	−					0	1	1	
Experiment I											
Kindergarten (5.3-6.3 yrs.)											
Middle Class	8	9	7	8.08	11.48	8.17	15.14	15	3	6	16.52
Disadvantaged	5	11	8	6.71	9.77	6.41	12.57	13	7	4	11.91
Parochial	9	7	8	7.58	8.13	7.22	13.57	9	2	13	11.70
First Grade (6.3-7.3 yrs.)											
Middle Class	18	6	2	9.58	11.52	12.64	18.16	21	5	0	20.64
Disadvantaged	8	12	4	8.96	11.18	9.05	20.62	16	2	6	15.82
Parochial	17	1	6	10.00	9.67	8.67	14.78	10	1	13	13.92

235

frequency among the disadvantaged groups; it was found least often among the Jewish parochial school children.

Conservation Pictures

The Conservation Pictures findings show a similar trend, but the differences in mean score between the two age groups is not as large, nor is the discrepancy between the disadvantaged group and the other two groups as great. In addition, it may be observed that the mean Conservation Pictures score of the six-year-old disadvantaged group is somewhat greater than that obtained by the five-year-old white middle-class and parochial school groups.

Insofar as there is a difference in pattern between the conservation of number performance and the Conservation Pictures scores, it is attributable to the fact that most of the Conservation Pictures items could be solved by virtually all the children. The differences found among the groups are attributable to a few very difficult items. Only items E, G, H, I, J (see Figure 1) presented substantial difficulties to even the younger groups, *i.e.*, were failed by more than 30% of the children. The data clearly indicate that spatial cues do not invariably override numerical cues. For nonconserving as well as conserving five year olds, the first few simple Conservation Pictures items were almost always answered correctly despite the fact that these items presented a conflict between spatial and numerical cues, *i.e.*, the longer rows of objects were not more numerous. The problems became more difficult when larger aggregates were introduced (*e.g.*, items G-J), or when equivalent numbers of items (rather than different numbers) were presented in rows of unequal length (*e.g.*, item E). Although Conservation Pictures scores correlated substantially with conservation of number performance (r= .42 for kindergartners and r= .43 for first graders), the most difficult items were frequently failed by conservers as well. Some of the Conservation Pictures items were passed by virtually all the children (*e.g.*, items A, C, D, F) while others were failed by most of the five year olds (*e.g.*, items E, G, H). Thus it would appear as though it is the nature of the conflict between numerical and irrelevant cues, not the mere presence of the conflict, which determines its role in the conservation situation. The data (particularly that obtained from items G and J) suggest that the potence of irrelevant spatial cues is determined by a combination of factors—the length and density of the rows and the magnitude of the numerical discrepancy between the aggregates.

The age difference between the kindergarten and first-grade groups sharply differentiated performance on the more difficult Conservation Pictures items. Only a small number of children from the older parochial school and middle-class groups failed even the more difficult items; only two of the five items which troubled the kindergartners, items G and H, posed difficulties for the older groups as well. An equally sharp difference between the kindergarten and first-grade disadvantaged groups was found, but their trailing position in relation to the other groups remained. The performance of the first-grade disadvantaged group closely resembled that of the middle-class and parochial school kindergarten children. Thus it may be concluded that performance on the more difficult Conservation Pictures items changes markedly during the child's sixth year, and that the performance of disadvantaged first graders closely resembled that of middle-class and parochial school kindergartners.

Vocabulary

The results of the WISC Vocabulary Test indicate a consistently superior score among the middle-class children in both age groups. As expected, all groups perform substantially better at the older age levels; the smallest improvement was found among the Jewish parochial school children where their bilingual educational program (Hebrew was the primary language and English secondary) would be expected to contribute less to the development of proficiency in English. In both age groups the parochial school children ranked last, although the largest gap among the different groups is that between the middle-class children and the others. The middle-class kindergarten children out-performed the first-grade parochial school children by a large margin and performed slightly better than the first-grade disadvantaged group.

The results of the Picture Vocabulary Test present essentially the same picture as that of the WISC Vocabulary Test except that these data are marred by the low ceiling of the test, a factor which appears to have prevented the middle-class first graders from outdistancing the remaining groups. Otherwise, the pattern of scores followed closely upon those obtained with the WISC Vocabulary. Here too, the parochial school groups ranked last, and the performance of the middle-class kindergarten children surpassed that of the first-grade disadvantaged and parochial school children.

Embedded Figures Test (CEFT)

The CEFT findings indicate that the middle-class group performed best at both age levels. The largest difference between kindergarten and first-grade performance was found in the middle-class groups and the smallest difference in the parochial school children. On this task, the mean scores of all three first-grade groups exceeded those of the highest scoring kindergarten group.

Differentiation between age and height

The results of this test suggest that social class-ethnic difference were more influential than age differences. Although this was a relatively easy task for middle-class and disadvantaged children at the five- as well as the six-year level, many items were failed extensively by the parochial school children of both age groups. The performance of the middle-class group was highest at both age levels but differed only slightly from the disadvantaged group. The middle-class kindergartners performed slightly less well than the disadvantaged first graders, while both the middle-class and disadvantaged kindergarten groups performed markedly better than the first-grade parochial school children.

Draw-a-Person

The results of this measure of nonverbal intelligence and self-differentiation suggest an interaction between ethnicity and age. The disadvantaged group ranked last among the kindergarten children but first among the first graders. The lagging position of the first-grade parochial school group was substantial; their mean score was surpassed by that of the middle-class kindergarten group.

DISCUSSION

The data of this study bear on performance of three groups of children from varied social class, ethnic, and experiential backgrounds at age five and six on a set of diverse cognitive tasks. In accordance with expectations based on the findings of previous studies, the middle-class children's performance was uniformly high. The group of Jewish parochial school and disadvantage children performed in more irregular fashion relative to the front-running middle-class groups. The performance of the Jewish parochial school group on the conservation of number and Conservation Pictures tasks was on a par with that of the middle-class children. They were able to observe the invariance of numerical relationships in the face of transformations of the spatial arrangements of sets of objects; they were not prone to be influenced by misleading spatial cues in the judgment of numerical relationships. At the same time, they were markedly deficient, relative to the other two groups, in their ability to distinguish between differences in height and differences in age among pictures of people standing adjacent to each other. This anomolous behavior may be attributable to the difficulty these children may have had in understanding the terms pertaining to relative age and relative height. Other data indicate that these bilingual children scored lowest on the two vocabulary tests as well, attesting to their lack of mastery of English. Their scores on the remaining tasks—the Draw-a-Person and the Children's Embedded Figures Test—were also relatively low, particularly those obtained from the first-grade group. Unless sampling factors account for the differences between the kindergarten and first-grade parochial school groups, the data suggest that these children begin to fall behind increasingly in several areas of cognitive functioning, probably as a result of the uniqueness of their school program. It is interesting to observe, however, that the factors associated with performance on the conservation tasks are not similarly affected; this aspect of cognitive functioning remains sturdy despite apparent declines in skills which would appear to be associated with numerical reasoning and logical analysis. The data suggest that abilities can, indeed, be compartmentalized during the developmental levels that were studied.

With the exception of the Draw-a-Person Test, the mean scores of the disadvantaged Negro groups consistently trailed those of the middle-class children. In the case of conservation, the Embedded Figures Test, and the age-height differentiation test, the first-grade disadvantaged children scores slightly above the middle-class kindergarten children, whereas the middle-class kindergarten group performed slightly higher on the two vocabulary tests than did the first-grade disadvantaged children. Thus, on several different tasks, there seems to be close correspondence between the performance of six-year-old disadvantaged children and five-year-old white middle-class children. The exception to this pattern is the high score achieved by the disadvantaged first graders on the Draw-a-Person Test. The drawing data are consistent with those obtained by other investigators; they present an important mystery to unravel regarding the cognitive status of the Negro disadvantaged child. What are the unique features of the figure drawing task which produce this pattern of successful performance; what do these data reveal about the cognitive strengths of the disadvantaged child?

Obviously, the data provided by this study are but a fragment of the mass of information required to conduct an analysis of the cognitive status of the disadvantaged child. Although there is ample evidence that disadvantaged children perform less well than their middle-class counterparts on most intelligence and achievement tests, a comprehensive delineation of the nature of these differences in cognitive functioning as well as of their antecedents is not yet forthcoming.

Lesser, Fifer and Clark (1965) have recently provided impressive evidence that ethnic variation produces distinctive patterns of mental ability, and that social class variation within the same ethnic group affects the level of intellectual functioning but not the overall pattern of abilities. Their findings are sufficiently provocative to warrant more extended empirical validation and theoretical analysis. However, it should be noted that some of the most dramatic features of their results stem from the variance they obtained in language functioning, variance which is in large measure attributable to the fact that two of the four ethnic groups with which they worked—Puerto Rican and Chinese—were from bilingual cultures, so that the most marked patterning of skills that were found were highly predictable.

Scholnick, Osler and Katzenellenbogen (1968) compared discrimination learning and concept identification in middle-class and lower-class five-year-old white children. Social class differences were found to be associated with WISC IQ scores and discrimination learning performance, but were not found to be a significant factor in the concept tasks that were employed.

A first-level theoretical analysis of this problem was recently made by Jensen (1968), who proposed that most tests of intellectual ability assess two types of mental process, Level I and Level II. Level I processes are for the most part associative, whereas Level II involve more complex operations, according to Jensen. His data suggest that Level I functioning is not strongly associated with socio-economic background, whereas Level II is highly correlated with the socio-economic factor.

Toward achieving an explanation of the nature of cognitive differences between children varying in ethnicity and social class, it is suggested that the strategy of investigation employed in the present study be followed. That is, ethnic or social class differences should be studied in groups of children spanning a given age range. It is a useful device to compare children of diverse experiential backgrounds within a developmental framework. Thus it is important to study children at contiguous age levels, and to find cognitive tasks on which performance changes markedly during the age range represented in the sample, because such transition points help to identify the course and pattern of cognitive growth. One of the first questions to be answered is whether differences in social class or ethnicity merely produce variations in the rate of cognitive development but do not affect the sequence and pattern of this development, or whether significant experiential variation will alter the pattern of cognitive growth itself—the nature of the skills that evolve, and the sequence of their development. The results of this study tentatively suggest that it is the latter which is the case. If this be so, then the next step is to identify the distinctive patterns associated with prominent variations observable among groups of children developing in our society.

This study was supported by the Cooperative Research Program of the Office of Education (Project No. 2270). The author wishes to acknowledge the valuable assistance in data collection and analysis provided by Harvey Asch, Ernest Drucker and Anne Gordon.

References

Harris, D. B. CHILDREN'S DRAWINGS AS MEASURES OF INTELLECTUAL MATURITY: A REVISION AND EXTENSION OF THE GOODENOUGH DRAW-A-MAN TEST. New York: Harcourt, Brace & World, 1963.

Jensen, Arthur R. PATTERNS OF MENTAL ABILITY AND SOCIOECONOMIC STATUS. Presented at the Annual Meeting of the National Academy of Sciences, Washington, D. C., April 24, 1968.

Karp, S. A. & Konstadt, Norma L. MANUAL FOR THE CHILDREN'S EMBEDDED FIGURES TEST. Brooklyn: Cognitive Tests, 1963.

Lesser, G. S., Fifer, G. & Clark, D. H. "Mental Abilities of Children from Different Social-Class and Cultural Groups," MONOGRAPHS OF THE SOCIETY FOR RESEARCH IN CHILD DEVELOPMENT, 30: 4 (No. 102), 1965.

Scholnick, Ellen Kofsky, Osler, Sonia F. & Katzenellenbogen, Ruth. "Discrimination Learning and Concept Identification in Disadvantaged and Middle-Class Children," CHILD DEVELOPMENT, March 1968.

Wechsler, D. WECHSLER INTELLIGENCE SCALE FOR CHILDREN. New York: Psychological Corporation, 1949.

Zimiles, Herbert. "The Development of Conservation and Differentiation of Number," MONOGRAPHS OF THE SOCIETY FOR RESEARCH IN CHILD DEVELOPMENT, 31: 6 (No. 108), 1966.

Zimiles, Herbert. "Cognitive Functioning and Tolerance for Delay in Gratification." Presented at Annual Meeting of the Society for Research in Child Development, New York City, March 29-April 1, 1967.

CULTURAL VARIATIONS IN COGNITIVE SKILLS

Jacqueline Goodnow, Ph.D.

In recent years there has been a considerable increase in studies conducted with children who are not from the same cultural background as our usual middle-class *S*s. The backgrounds have varied, sometimes being pre-literate societies, sometimes cultures that are literate but still of a village type, and sometimes milieus that are urban and educated but not Anglo-Saxon in tradition or style.

My aim is not to provide an extensive review of these studies. Rather, I hope to use some illustrative studies as a way of asking some general questions, questions about the nature of cross-cultural variations and their implications for our ideas about how intelligence develops and how differences in skills arise.

We may start with the question: Why be interested in children from other cultures? It is often said that different cultures provide some ready-made variations in environment that would be impossible to produce in the laboratory or in a planned experiment. This is true, but it is also true that we are not as yet skilled in specifying the critical points of difference between one environment and another, critical, that is, for the performance we have in mind. As a result, it is often difficult to interpret results in any fine way, to know what the environmental conditions are that give rise to the similarities and differences we find. How much of a problem this represents depends, of course, on the state of our knowledge. There are times when we have so little data that all is grist to the mill, and times when we need data of a particular type in order to advance. At our present state of knowledge, however, the problem is large enough to give a special point to questions about what one can learn from cross-cultural studies that cannot be learned in other ways.

In a broad sense, each cross-cultural study provides a piece for a developmental puzzle. The puzzle lies in accounting for the fact that we change as we grow older, that at 2, 5, 20, and 40 we are not identical when it comes to remembering, classifying, or problem-solving. The fact that we change with age is easy to observe. What is difficult is answering those perennial questions: Just what is the difference? And how does it come about?

For this general puzzle, cross-cultural studies can supply pieces we did not have before, variations in method we did not think were possible or significant, upsets in relationships we had come to think of as constant. As in all puzzles, of course, the pieces are not all equally valuable at any one time, and on occasion we have to set a piece aside until we reach a point where it can be fitted in.

From the puzzle point of view, the biggest difficulty with cross-cultural studies has been the lack of overlap between pieces: each study a new culture, and, very often, a new task. Now we are a long way from being able to plan for critical points of overlap between cultures; i.e., we do not know as yet how to match culture X and culture Y on the features that affect performance Z, or on all the features save one. Overlaps between tasks, however, can be planned, and such overlaps are much to the fore in a number of recent cultural studies. To give some examples:

Segall, Campbell, and Herskovits (1966) have gathered results from a wide variety of cultures, using the same visual perception tasks throughout. Their results have been so intriguing that other psychologists, like Jahoda (1966) have been taking the same tasks to still more cultural groups, trying to pin down just what produces the variations in performance.

A group with a Harvard core has used the same classification task with children from several settings: Boston, Senegal, Alaska, urban and rural Mexico. This is the work of Olver and Hornsby, Greenfield, Reich, Maccoby and Modiano, all branching out from the Harvard Center of Cognitive Studies (Bruner, Olver, & Greenfield, 1966).

Vernon (1965, 1966) has used the same extensive battery of tasks with several samples of 11-year-old boys: English, West Indian, Canadian Indian, and Eskimo. In a rare step, he has as well made ratings on a number of environmental variables and is attempting a set of direct relationships between the environmental differences and the patterns of test performance.

Lesser, Fifer, and Clark (1965) have given the same tasks to lower and middle class American children with varying ethnic backgrounds: Chinese, Negro, Jewish and Puerto Rican. Class variations, it turned out, lowered the level of performance but not the pattern of abilities; ethnic differences varied the pattern.

The last example is a group of people who have come to overlap through no deliberate intent on their part, but through a shared interest in tasks developed by Piaget and his colleagues. It is this group I shall emphasize. It offers some nice overlaps in several respects: in the sample of tasks, the sample of Ss, the environmental variable, and happiest of all, in some of the results.

The group of studies has the following points in common:
   1. Two or more tasks have been used. This similarity is critical, since

what is often most informative for the developmental puzzle is not the absolute level of performance so much as ·the relationship among performances.

2. Some of the tasks have been the same. In particular, at least one of the tasks has been a Genevan conservation task; i.e., a task where a change is made in the perceptual appearance of an object and the child is asked whether there has been a change in some invariant quality like weight or length.

3. On the environmental side, the studies have all been strongly concerned with variations in the amount and quality of schooling.

To run through the list quickly, the set of studies includes three where the children have had no formal schooling or practically none: studies by Siegel and Mermelstein (1965) with Negro children in Prince Edward County, Virginia; by Magali Bovet* with Algerian children; and by myself in Hong Kong. In addition, there are two studies by psychologists primarily interested in the difference between types of schooling: by Peluffo (1962, 1964, and personal communication), working in Italy with children coming up to the urban North from southern villages, and by Vernon (1965) comparing English schoolboys with West Indian schoolboys.

What has come out of these overlapping pieces?

1. As we move away from a technological society there is not any overall lag or retardation across tasks, but rather what Vernon has called a series of "peaks and troughs". Some tasks shift their difficulty level more than others.

2. Fortunately, there is some consistency to the tasks that stand up well throughout. If we list tasks in terms of the extent to which performance changes as we shift away from our traditional *S*s, some of the conservation tasks appear at the top of the list as showing either no change or the least degree of change. Only some of the conservation tasks are sturdy in this sense, namely the tasks for amount, weight, volume, and surface, but not tasks for the conservation of length (Vernon, 1965) or time and speed (Bovet).

3. Again fortunately, there is the beginning of the consistency in the tasks not handled so well outside the traditional group. This

*All references to the work of Magali Bovet are based on personal communication.

consistency is harder to define, but in a rough fashion they seem to be predominantly tasks where the child has to transform an event in his head, has to shift or shuffle things around by some kind of visualizing or imaging rather than by carrying out an overt series of changes. The spatial or perceptual aspect of these tasks comes as something of a surprise. It used to be thought that "disadvantaged" groups would be most handicapped on verbal or abstractive tasks and that imaging or spatial-type tasks would be the fairest. This seems not to be so, and a division of tasks into "verbal" and "non-verbal" seems not to be the most fruitful that could be made.

The three results warrant some special attention. They provide a set of focal points for looking at cross-cultural variations, both in terms of the way they parallel the results of other studies and in terms of the problems and implications they bring with them.

The first result—no overall lag but a diffential shift—has its parallels in several studies. To span a time range, Nissen, Machover and Kinder pointed out in 1935 that children in French Guinea gave varying performances on a number of tasks. They were, for instance, much closer to Western norms in reproducing a sequence of moves made by a tester (touching a set of cubes) than in reproducing designs. Recently, this kind of effect has been taken further by results showing that differential patterns of skill are more likely to occur among children of similar formal schooling with differences in ethnic background than with differences in schooling than with differences of class or ethnic background (Goodnow, 1963), or differences in intelligence (Goodnow & Bethon, 1966).

Whenever such differential shifts are found, they challenge assumptions we may hold about general factors underlying performance. It is easy to assume that tasks with the same difficulty level, especially if they have some surface similarity, are based on the same abilities and processes, or on a general and unitary intelligence. This assumption requires a closer look when we find the tasks we work from do not necessarily hang together. From the particular set of studies cited, for example, one would become cautious about assuming "conservation" to be a skill more general than it is content-specific. Equally, the closer look may need to be at some of our global descriptions of environments. In recent years, for example, there has been a great deal of interest in "amounts of stimulation", in searching for an "optimal amount" that will neither "under-stimulate" nor "over-stimulate". To this pattern of search, differential shifts are a reminder that "stimulation" is a variable constantly in need of definition and specification, in terms of kind as well as amount. The critical factors may equally well turn out to be some specific experiences.

The second and third results—areas of agreement on the skills that unite and divide children from different backgrounds—are the ones that help most towards specifying what kind of experience leads to what kind of skill. They are the points from which we can start a sharper analysis of just what it is that a task demands and a society provides. These analyses are, for me, the heart of cross-cultural studies, and some examples of them form the major body of this paper.

PINNING DOWN DIFFERENCES IN SKILLS

Matches between the features of a task and the features of an environment may well start from an analysis of tasks, either by asking what it is that some tasks have in common or what it is that gives rise to uneven performances. Typically, the focus is either on the content of the task or on the operation that is to be carried out. One may start, for example, from the fact that the scores of Negro children on a number of intelligence tests are by and large lower than those of middle-class white children, and set up the hypothesis that the difficulty stems from the content, from varying degrees of familiarity with the words used and the objects portrayed. Alternately, one may look not so much to features of the material as to what the child has to do with the material, the operation he is asked to carry out. This is the direction taken in the suggestion that poorly schooled children have particular difficulty with tasks calling for some kind of imaged change in material. And finally, one may look for the solution in some interaction between content and operation: children from a particular background may well be able to carry out a particular operation with one kind of material but not with another.

From any direction, it is never easy to specify and prove just what it is about a task that makes it easier for children of some cultures than for others. But the effort is critical if we are to make any meaningful connections between skills and experiences. For a particular example, I would like to turn to the data that suggests the importance of "imaged transformations". I have suggested that children with little schooling may be especially handicapped on tasks calling for imaged changes, for transformations that have to be carried out in the head. In stressing this kind of difference among groups, I am not alone. Vernon (1965, 1966) has suggested a similar kind of task area in his stress on an "imaging" factor, affecting performance on a number of perceptual-spatial tasks. Vernon looks to an environmental variable other than schooling, namely the extent that the background is, for boys, purposeful, planful, and male-oriented. For the moment, the important thing is the stress on a common area as highly vulnerable to group differences, whatever its source. Despite the common stress, however, neither "imaging" nor "imaged transformations" nor "mental shuffling" is a definitive description of what underlies the vulnerable tasks, and I would be the first to admit that these identifications of the vulnerable area are tentative.

To give a closer look at an identification in terms of "imaged changes" I shall take two sets of results. The first set comes from a combination of some Hong Kong data with some American data gathered by Gloria Bethon and myself. The second set is drawn from Vernon's work with West Indians. From these results and the nature of the tasks they are based on, others may draw hypotheses different from the one presented here. Whatever the hypotheses, the overlap in results is striking enough and rare enough to call for some detailed attention.

Figure I presents data adapted from Goodnow and Bethon (1966). There are three groups of boys, all 11 years old. One group is Chinese with little or no schooling. The other two are American schoolboys, with known levels on an intelligence test, the California Test of Mental Maturity. The median for the group labelled "dull" is 81, with a top of 88; the median for the group labelled "average" is 111, with a top of 120.

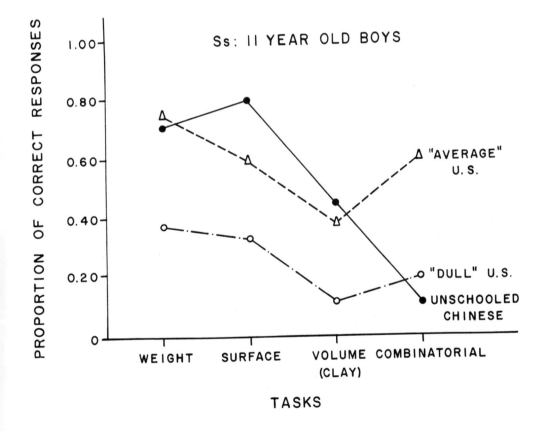

FIGURE 1

Patterns of task difficulty Ss varying in nationality, schooling, and intelligence (adapted from Goodnow & Bethon, 1966).

The interesting features to these results are:

I. First of all, the pattern or order of difficulty is the same for the dull and the average American groups. We can eliminate the possibility that any change in pattern with a non-schooled group is the result of a simple drop in general intelligence.

2. On the first three tasks there is very little difference between the Chinese group and the average American group. These tasks are all conservation tasks. The first is the well-known task for conservation of weight, with two pieces of clay. The second—conservation of surface—is perhaps less well-known. The child starts with two equal pieces of green paper, each one a grassy field with a cow on it. The child agrees that one cow has as much to eat as the other, and then the experimenter starts putting down 12 houses on each field, one on each field at a time. In the end the two fields look quite different, with the houses on one arranged in two rows of six, and the houses on the other scattered widely. Again the child is asked if one cow has as much to eat as the other. The fourth task is conservation of volume, with displacement of water. (Two balls of clay are shown to displace equal amounts of water. Then, with one ball changed to a pancake-shape, comes the question: What about now? Do both push the water up by the same amount, or does one push the water up more than the other?)

3. The only task on which the Chinese boys fall below the "average" Americans is the Genevan task of combinatorial reasoning. The child has to make pairs of colors, repeating no pairs and omitting none. He starts off with practice on three colors, then on four colors, and he is helped to get all pairs. Finally, he is asked to work with six colors. The heart of the request is that he figure out something in advance. He is asked to try and figure out a trick or a system that will make the task easy, will help him to repeat none and omit none. The task is scored for the presence of a systematic approach to the problem, and this is what the unschoooled group had trouble with. A number of them ended with 15 pairs, and some of them became aware that they had to have the same number of each color, but they relied a great deal on moving the pieces around physically, shifting them from here to there in actual movements and then looking at the moved-around pairs.

My first hypothesis for these results (Goodnow, 1962) was that there might be something special to conservation tasks in general. But that hypothesis is set aside by Vernon's (1965) results with conservation of length, and by Magali Bovet's results with conservation of time: both conservation tasks but both poorly handled in contract with conservation of amount. For the combinatorial task, I had the feeling that the trouble was in the request to work it out in advance, in the head, so to speak; but one task provided a poor base to work from. The result in itself seemed a stable enough one, in that Peluffo (1964) also found the combinatorial task harder than conservation of volume for rural but not for urban school children in Sardinia.

A much wider base was offered by Vernon's (1965) results. I have taken out some of his West Indian results to illustrate again a pattern of strengths and weaknesses, and to show how they raise again a theme of mental rather than physical shuffling of material. Figure 2 shows the material selected.

In one of those happy overlaps, Vernon was also working with boys around 11. In his case the Ss were schoolboys aged 10½ to 11, one group Jamaican, the other English. And he had used some of the same tasks as were given in Hong Kong:

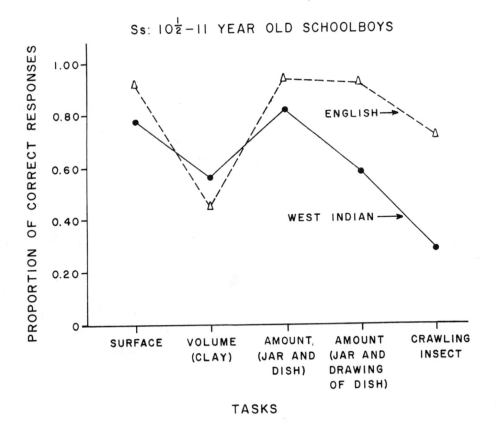

FIGURE 2

Patterns of task difficulty for English and West Indian schoolboys (adapted from Vernon, 1965).

conservation of surface, with the cows in the fields, and conservation of volume with water displaced by two balls of clay. On neither of these tasks, as Figure 2 shows, was there a difference between the two groups. What is more, the absolute levels of performance on these two tasks by all four groups of boys (American, English, Chinese, and Jamaican) do not vary widely. All the scores on the volume task, for example, are between 40% correct and 60% correct at this age level.

Both the third and fourth tasks selected from Vernon (1965) ask about conservation of amount with liquids. The third task starts with two transparent jars, half filled with water. The child adjusts them until they are equal. Then the experimenter presents a small dish and says, "Now I'll pour mine into this dish. Have we the same, or have you more, or less than me? On this task, the two groups were equal. On the fourth task, however, the Indian group falls well below the English group, even though the task seems to involve only a minor change. The tester now uses one tall jar and the drawing of a dish, and asks: "If I poured the water from this bottle into this dish, would there be more water in the dish than in the bottle, or less, or the same?"

The difference between the two forms of the amount task may be simply a difference in content. It has often been said that children from less technological societies have trouble with drawings and diagrams. The difficulty could also be a combination of content and operation. The child not only has to cope with a drawing rather than an object—a difference that should not faze schoolboys too greatly—but he must also imagine the water transferred from bottle to dish, without the benefit of first adjusting for himself the level in two jars or of seeing the experimenter actually pour all the water from the jar to the dish.

That the difficulty may lie in the operation as much as in the content is suggested by some other tasks used by Vernon. One of these is shown in Figure 2—the task of the crawling insect. Vernon showed the child a circle 2½ inches in diameter and said, "Here's a drawing of a jar on its side. I'm going to draw a little insect on top." The drawing shows a clear head and tail, with the head pointing left. "Now," says Vernon, "the insect starts walking round the outside edge, like this. You draw for me what he would look like when he gets round to here." "Here" is a dot on the bottom rim of the circle. If we ask how many Ss draw the insect with his head pointed correctly, the answer is 71% of the English group and 28% of the West Indians.

Again the task seems to have two parts to it. The child must attend to direction or orientation as a critical part of a drawing and he must make a transformation in his head. Orientation in a drawing does appear to be a feature that is made salient by learning. McFie (1961), for example, points out that student nurses and boys entering high school in Uganda were very different from English *S*s in their attitude towards orientation in copying designs or on the Kohs Block Test, so that on the first encounter with tasks inversions and rotations were common.

Paying inadequate attention to direction may be part of the Jamaicans' difficulty. There is as well, however, the need to image the reversal in position, and it seems to be this part of the task that links it with the poorer Jamaican performance on two further tasks. On one of these, the child is shown a string of cards, each containing a number, so that what he sees is 3 2 5, or 2 8 4 9 3. He is asked, "What is the biggest number you could make with these?" He is not allowed to shift the cards around by hand. On this task, the English and the Jamaican schoolboys are again widely apart: 86% and 58% respectively with three numbers, 73% and 32% with five numbers. The two groups are equally apart on a last task, where they have to think through some left-right relationships. The tester places a pencil, a penny, and an eraser in a line, and asks such questions as : "Is the rubber to the left of the penny or to the right? Is the rubber to the left of the pencil or to the right?" With six questions like these 61% of the English schoolboys make no errors, but only 30% of the West Indians.

No one of these tasks is conclusive in itself, but taken together they suggest that one of the sharpest differences among cultural groups may lie in tasks where the child has to carry out some spatial shuffling or transforming in his head, without the benefit of actually moving the stimulus material around. This suggestion, we may add, is in line with a recurring comment on a differnce in task approach among groups with varying degrees of formal schooling in the Western sense. *S*s with less formal schooling often impress their highly educated observers as making greater use, even excessive use, of action and direct manipulation of material. This kind of comment has been made for non-Western groups by Maistriaux (1955), McFie (1961), and Richelle (1966), and for Western adults by Hanfmann (1943).

I have looked at the role of "transformations in the head" in some detail for several reasons. There is a need for working hypotheses in comparing cultural groups, and differences in "imaging" or "imaged transformations" have now appeared often enough and with enough specificity to qualify as a promising working hypothesis (cf. Vernon, 1965, 1966; Goodnow and Bethon, 1966; Goodnow, 1968). And as we come closer to such specific skills, we may begin to ask more sharply whether there are experimental differences that might match the differences in skill. I do not wish to suggest, however, that the picture is in any way final. Very recently to hand, for example, is the first major statement of Vernon's results with Canadian Indians and Eskimos (Vernon, 1966). Both groups were surprisingly weak on conservation tasks, perhaps, as Vernon suggests (1966, p. 192), because of linguistic factors. (Vernon's *S*s were all tested in English, a language more familiar to the Jamaican than to the Canadian *S*s; Goodnow's Chinese *S*s were tested, through an interpreter, in their own

251

dialect). Whatever the explanation for the poor conservation performance, the surprise still remains of a good performance by the Eskimos especially, on most of the perceptual-spatial tasks. On these, the Eskimos were close to the English norms. This kind of result means that good spatial or imaging performances can occur without high-level schooling, a result that sharpens and spices considerably the question of what kinds of experience help in producing particular kinds of skill.

MATCHING SKILLS TO EXPERIENCE

Suppose for a moment that varying degrees of skill in mental shuffling or in imaging transformations do account for the recurring performance differences we have noted among several cultural groups. This would represent one of the two aims in cross-cultural research: pinning down the nature of a difference in skill. The other aim is to tie the difference in skill to a difference in experience. How could it come about that the children in our usual samples have developed some kinds of imaging skills more fully than the children in some other groups have? And how is it that there is so much less variation in performance on tasks like the conservation of amount?

At this point, we must lean to some extent on conjecture, and on some general points in the literature on spatial skills. To start with, we may note that "spatial" skills—often imaging skills—seem to be a highly variable area of performance in general. Piaget, for example, rarely comments on a great deal of variability in the age at which a child can master a task, but it is for a spatial task (predicting the flat shape of a folded or rolled piece of paper) that he notes a considerable effect from specific experiences: "The child who is familiar with folding and unfolding paper shapes through his work at school is two or three years in advance of children who lack this experience" (Piaget & Inhelder, p. 276). And Sherman (1967) has recently argued that many of the sex differences on cognitive tasks stem from the stress on spatial visualization in the tasks, visualization that girls, because of sex-typed activities, are poorly prepared for. It seems unlikely, then, that there will be any simple or single explanation of how differences arise in skills at mental shuffling or transforming. In a broad sense, the explanations that have been suggested can be placed into two groups, one emphasizing the role of general attitudes, the other stressing more specific experiences.

An example of a general factor is Vernon's argument for a relationship between performance on perceptual-spatial skills and the degree of purposefulness and planning shown in the home (cf. Vernon, 1966). Vernon points out that the relationship is yet to be fully tested. It seems quite reasonable, however, to expect that a general readiness to stop and plan ahead would make a considerable difference to tasks where premature action can lead to difficulties that are hard to undo (as in many mazes), or where there is a premium on a systematic approach to a task (as in the Genevan task of combinatorial reasoning). In fact, Richelle (1966) considers the reluctance to "inhibit action" as the chief cause of poor scores by a large group of Congolese children of many of Rey's performance tasks.

Even if a child has the readiness, however, to stop and think ahead, he needs the tools to do so. It is here that specific experiences would appear to be most critical. Such experiences have often been pointed to. Vernon (1966), for example, mentions the training that Indian and Eskimo children have in tracking and in locating objects spatially. Porteus (1931) felt that tracking helped some primitive peoples achieve a better performance on his mazes, and Havighurst, Gunther and Pratt (1946) considered that experience in drawing and painting played a similar role for the Draw-a-Man task. These identifications of critical experience are highly plausible, but two things are needed. One is some *a priori* identification; the other is some clear demonstration of a difference in skill between two groups selected to vary in terms of some specific experience.

Price-Williams' (1968) recent study of conservation of amount is a case in point. From the Mexican town of Tlaquepaque he selected boys with two kinds of family background. One group came from pottery-making families; the other from non-pottery-making families of a similar social class. Out of several conservation tasks, the former group is significantly better on only one: conservation of amount with clay. Price-Williams is currently conducting a replication of this kind of study. Whatever its outcome, his study is a nice example of the kind of research needed to make explicit and testable any matches between experiences and skills.

Even given demonstrated matches between experiences and skills, we shall still have to ask how the specific experiences can give rise to the skill we have in mind. How, for example, do certain past actions or experiences lead on to skill in thinking a problem through in one's head, without benefit of some reminding or testing action? One of the general effects of repeated and varied actions may be an atmosphere in which magical explanations do not easily survive. Beyond this, past actions may provide an "action model", a pragmatic model that serves as a landmark, reference point, or mnemonic device for pinning down a relationship and holding it in mind. An example of this comes from a Chinese boy explaining conservation of weight. He pointed out that sometimes when he bought rice it came in a bag like this ⟨bag shape⟩ and sometimes it came in a bag like this ⟨bag shape⟩ , but it was always the same weight: he knew because he had carried them.

Another function actions may have is to provide the opportunity for translating a problem into terms other than actions. For a translation from actions to some map of relationships, we may simply need a fair amount of practice. This is, for example,

253

the argument Mandler (1954) makes for maze-learning: *S*s at first find their way through a maze mostly by feel and in terms of a sequence of actions. With more and more practice, however, they begin to have some kind of mental map of how the maze might be laid out. The same sort of learning seems to occur in mastering the layout of a new city. It takes a considerable amount of actually going to places and actually consulting a map before we have some independent picture of how things are arranged, clear enough to realize that such and such a street ought to be able to provide a detour if a familiar path is blocked. I am not suggesting that this translation into units that can be mentally shuffled around takes place automatically. Part of it must depend upon a certain amount of general practice in "mapping things out", a certain amount of learning to drop unessential details out of the mapping.

That translation with "maps" does not take place automatically is suggested by some actual maps—drawn maps—gathered by Dart and Pradhan (1967) from Nepalese children. Even for a familiar route, these children gave maps that marked places by pictures rather than points, where the path reflected more the sequence of actions than a set of relationships. They were, comment Dart and Pradhan, essentially "like a string of beads, list(ing) in correct sequence the places we should pass through without giving any clues as to distance, trail intersections, changes of direction, and so on" (1967, p. 653). One can find such directions outside of Nepal, but at least we are usually aware that there is another kind of map, and by and large the difference between cultures is not in complete presence and complete absence, but in frequencies of occurrence and in the content to which an idea or a principle is applied.

I have suggested so far that in order to move from a physical to a mental shuffling of objects and events, we may need practice with actually moving the objects around, or seeing them move, and we may need general practice in mental shuffling and mapping. To close the argument, we may turn back briefly to the shared and unshared skills described earlier.

For the argument to be reasonable, we would have to argue that most cultures provide the practice and the pragmatic models needed for judgments of properties like amount, weight, surface and displacement of water—or at least that practice for these judgments is more widespread among cultures than is practice for judging properties like length or time. That seems feasible. Amount and weight especially seem to be areas that meet Price-Williams' criteria (1961, 1962) for good task performance: a variety of actions for practice and a high value placed on the accuracy of judgment.

We would also have to argue that cultures differ more among themselves in the practice they provide in mental as against physical shuffling. That also seems feasible. There are almost certainly culture and class differences in attitudes towards impulsive or unnecessary action, in the number of times that a child is told: "You didn't have to do it that way, or you didn't have to ask me that; you could have worked it out." Formal schooling is very likely to be another source of differences in restraints on unnecessary or impulsive action, and of differences in the amount of time spent constructing things, putting them together and taking them apart, or matching a drawn shape—often schematic—against the memory of an object. There is a world of difference, as McFie (1961) points out, between the American or British middle-class child who has played with "shapies" and jig-saw puzzles, and the child who has few construction toys, or toys at all, and who sees few diagrams or schematic representations of things. The Nepalese children referred to, for example, "use no other kind of map; they do not use drawings or spatial representation at all (except for records of land ownership, which does not change very frequently), and the lack of spatial models may be very natural" (Dart and Pradhan, 1967, p. 653). Vernon's Eskimo boys, however, are a reminder that "familiarity with the spatial products of white civilization" (1966, p. 193) is not a necessary condition for developing spatial skills and that the road to a set of nicely specific ties between skills and experiences is likely to be a long one.

One last remark needs to be made about ties between skills and experiences. If the ties are likely to be so specific, how is it that so often one cultural group is poorer than another on a large number of tasks? And is the overall goal to be simply a long list of specific ties? For such questions, Ferguson (1954, 1956) offers a provocative argument. There is, he argues, considerable transfer among skills, and the lack of one which normally opens the road to developing several others can easily create a picture of generally lower performance. If we can ever identify such cornerstone skills, or firm hierarchies of skills, then the task of describing how differences in skill develop is likely to become much easier.

A substantial part of this paper was presented at the meetings of the American Psychological Association, September, 1967.

References

Bruner, J. S., Olver, R., & Greenfield, P. M. STUDIES IN COGNITIVE GROWTH. New York: Wiley, 1966.

Dart, F. E., & Pradhan, P. L. "Cross-cultural teaching of science", SCIENCE, 155: 649-656, 1967.

Ferguson, G. "On learning and human ability", CANAD. J. PSYCHOL., 8: 95-112, 1954.

Ferguson, G. "On transfer and the abilities of man", CANAD. J. PSYCHOL., 10: 121-131, 1956.

Goodnow, J. J. "A test of milieu differences with some of Piaget's tasks", PSYCHOL. MONOGR., 76 (No. 36) (Whole No. 555): 1962.

Goodnow, J. J. "Problems in research on culture and thought", In J. Flavell & D. Elkind (Eds.), FESTSCHRIFT FOR PIAGET. Oxford University Press. In press.

Goodnow, J. J. & Bethon, G. "Piaget's tasks: The effects of schooling and intelligence", CHILD DEVELOPMENT. 37: 573-582, 1966.

Hanfmann, E. "A study of personal patterns in an intellectual performance", CHARACTER & PERSONALITY, 9: 315-325, 1941.

Havighurst, R. J., Gunther, M. K., & Pratt, I. E. "Environment and the Draw-a-Man Test: the performance of Indian children", J. abn. & soc. Psychol., 41:50-63, 1946.

Jahoda, G. "Geometric illusions and enviroment: A study in Ghana", BRIT. J. PSYCHOL., 57: 193-199, 1966.

Lesser, G. S., Fifer, G., & Clark, D. H. "Mental abilities of children from different social groups and cultural groups", MONOGR. OF SOCIETY FOR RESEARCH IN CHILD DEVPM., 30 (Whole No. 102) : 1965.

McFie, J. "The effect of education on African performance on a group of intellectual tests", BRIT. J. EDUC. PSYCHOL., 31: 232-240, 1961.

Maistriaux, R. "La sous-evolution des noirs d'Afrique. Sa nature - ses causes - ses remedes", REVUE DE PSYCHOLOGIE DES PEUPLES, 10: 167-189, 397, 456, 1955.

Mandler, G. "Response factors in human learning", PSYCHOL. REV., 61: 235-244, 1954.

Nissen, H. W., Machover, S., & Kinder, E. F. "A study of performance tests given to a group of native African Negro children", BRIT. J. PSYCHOL. 25: 308-355, 1935.

Peluffo, N. "Les notions de conservation et de causalite chez les enfants prevenant de differents milieux physiques et socio-culturels", ARCHIVES DE PSYCHOLOGIE, 38: 75-90, 1962.

Peluffo, N. "La nozione de conservazione del volume e le operazioni di combinazione come indici di sviluppo del pensiero operatorio in soggetti appartenenti ad ambienti fisici e socioculturali diversi", RIVISTA DI PSICOLOGIA SOCIALE, 11: 99-132, 1964.

Piaget, J., & Inhelder, B. THE CHILD'S CONCEPTION OF SPACE. New York: Norton, 1967.

Porteus, S. D. THE PSYCHOLOGY OF PRIMITIVE PEOPLE. New York: Longmans Green, 1931.

Price-Williams, D. R. "A study concerning concepts of conservation of quantities among primitive children", ACTA PSYCHOLOGICA, 18: 297-305, 1961.

Price-Williams, S. D. "Abstract and concrete modes of classification in a primitive society", BRIT. J. EDUC. PSYCHOL., 32: 50-61, 1962.

Price-Williams, S. D. & Gordon, W. "Manipulation and conservation: A study of children from pottery-making families in Mexico", Unpublished Paper.

Richelle, M. "Etude genetique de l'intelligence manipulatoire chez des enfants africains a l'aide des dispositifs de Rey", INTERNATL. J. PSYCHOL., 1: 273-287, 1966.

Segall, M. H., Campbell, D. T., & Herskovits, M. J. THE INFLUENCE OF CULTURE ON VISUAL PERCEPTION. New York: Bobbs-Merrill, 1966.

Sigel, I. E., & Mermelstein, E. "Effects of nonschooling on Piagetian tasks of conservation", Paper presented at APA meeting, September, 1965.

Sherman, J. A. "Problem of sex differences in space perception and aspects of intellectual functioning", PSYCHOL. REV., 4: 290-299, 1967.

Vernon, P. E. "Environmental handicaps and intellectual development", BRIT. J. EDUC. PSYCHOL., 35: 1-12, 117-126, 1965.

Vernon, P. E. "Educational and intellectual development among Canadian Indians and Eskimos", BRIT. J. EDUC. PSYCHOL., 18: 79-91, 186-195, 1966.

CONCEPT STUDIES IN DISADVANTAGED CHILDREN

Sonia F. Osler, Ph.D.

That children raised in disadvantaged environments suffer from multiple intellectual handicaps has been amply documented in recent years. The handicaps range from low scores on tests of mental ability (Anastasi, 1958; Dreger & Miller, 1960; Lesser, Fifer, & Clark, 1965) to poor reading (Feldman & Weiner, 1964), immature use of language (Deutsch & Brown, 1964; Jensen, 1963; John, 1963), and constricted conceptualizations (Siller, 1957). Two factors are said to account for these deficits: a) inadequate or inappropriate stimulation and b) a low level of motivation for learning.

In an effort to compensate for the cognitive deficits of disadvantaged children, various types of enrichment procedures have been employed. These have included perceptual and linguistic training, exposure to a more varied environment, and greater involvement of parents in the education of their children. Intervention has in most cases been based on the general assumption that any form of enrichment is better than none and that the more types included, the better. This has been called the philosophy of total enrichment (Blank & Solomon, 1968). Although benefits resulting from such procedures have been observed in many cases, the duration of improvements is often short lived.

It seems reasonable, therefore, to start with the assumption that before adequate plans for intervention can be designed it is necessary to determine more precisely how environmental deprivation is translated into inadequate cognitive function. At present it is not known, for example, whether the lower achievement scores of disadvantaged children represent an informational deficit brought about by restricted exposure to relevant experiences; or whether they represent more basic deficits in the capacities for abstraction and learning; or whether they are the result of inadequate motivation, or possibly a combination of all these factors. Distinctions as to the variables associated with poor achievement have theoretical importance for the understanding of developmental processes and practical importance for the planning of effective intervention procedures.

This paper will be concerned with the learning capacity of the disadvantaged child. While an extensive literature exists on the comparative *achievement* of disadvantaged children and their more privileged counterparts, investigations designed to determine the relative *learning* capacity of these two populations are scarce. In most instances impairment in learning ability is inferred from the depressed achievement scores. However, evidence from several *laboratory* studies in which learning scores were the dependent variable has shown that frequently children from disadvantaged environments achieve scores indistinguishable from those of middle class children.

258

Rohwer (1967), for example, found no difference between children of varied social class membership in rate of learning paired associate tasks, while Zigler and deLabry (1962) and Spence and Segner (1967) obtained equivalent learning scores in discrimination learning. In view of these findings and the importance of obtaining systematic data on learning, concept learning in lower class children was investigated. Since a number of investigators had reported that disadvantaged children are especially handicapped in conceptual behavior, it was anticipated that performance deficits would be found in this population when complex concept problems were employed. The general plan of the work was to manipulate task variables and experimental procedures in order to discover some of the underlying processes differentiating the performance of the two populations.

The research to be described was concerned with three problems: a) to compare the performance of lower and middle class children on inductive concept learning tasks, b) to compare the capacity of these two populations for utilizing instructional aids, and c) to study their capacity for transferring knowledge gained in one type of problem to the solution of other problems. The investigations relating to the first two questions were performed in collaboration with Dr. Ellin Kofsky Scholnick.

EXPERIMENT I*

The experimental task was a complex inductive concept attainment problem which will be described below in greater detail. It was hypothesized that low status children would show a learning deficit and that this deficit might be due to inadequate prior experience in inductive problem solving and in discriminating the stimulus attributes. Consequently, training tasks were devised to provide both types of experiences. Half the children in each social class received experience in discrimination learning prior to working on the concept problem. Because middle class children were more likely to have had these types of experiences outside of the laboratory, it was anticipated that the laboratory training would be of greater benefit to the lower class subjects. A training by social class interaction was therefore predicted. To recapitulate, not only was an initial quantitative difference in performance expected, but it was anticipated that the training procedure would be more effective in improving the performance of lower class than middle class children.

One hundred ninety-two 5- and 8-year-old children participated in this investigation. The subjects were drawn equally from two areas of Baltimore to assure maximum social class differentiation. The principal wage earners in the families of the lower class children were in the semiskilled or unskilled occupations or were unemployed. In contrast, the fathers of the middle class children held professional or executive

*This work has been reported in Scholnick, Osler and Katzenellenbogen, 1968.

posts. The status difference between the two groups was confirmed by the mean IQ scores obtained on the WISC, which were 88 and 111 respectively. In order to select two groups of subjects who were typical in ability of their social class, only children whose IQ's were within one standard deviation of the mean IQ of their groups participated in the study. Thus the lower class children ranged in IQ between 75 and 101 and the middle class range was 102 to 123.* All subjects were Caucasian.

An inductive concept problem was presented to each child who was tested individually. The subject was required to learn the correct response for each of a group of stimuli consisting of pictures of geometric figures which varied in form (circle—square), color (blue—red), size (large—small), and number (one or two identical figures). The stimuli were projected individually on a small screen below which two levers were located. For each stimulus the child was required to press one of the levers. A correct response was reinforced with a marble. In order to solve the problem it was necessary for the subject to learn which of the stimulus dimensions was relevant and to associate each value of the dimension with one of the levers. For example, he might be required to learn that the color of the stimulus was the important feature, and that blue stimuli gave marbles when the right lever was pressed, and red when the left lever was pressed. He would in this case have to ignore the shape, size and number dimensions, as they would be irrelevant for solution. Each of the dimensions was relevant for an equal number of subjects. The procedure was terminated after 160 trials or earlier if the subject attained the criterion of 30 correct responses in a block of 32 trials.

The problems were of two levels of difficulty suitable to the two subject ages. The eight-year-olds worked on the four-dimensional problem described above consisting of 16 different stimuli, while the five-year-olds worked on a three-dimensional problem consisting of eight different stimuli. The number dimension did not appear in the eight-stimulus set.

The children received verbal instructions and were then allowed to work on an illustrative problem before attempting the concept learning task. Following the illustrative problem, half the subjects proceeded to the concept attainment problem (untrained group); the other half of the children received, in addition, training in discrimination learning (trained group). The latter training was designed to fulfill two functions: a) to familiarize them with the stimulus dimensions used in the concept problem and b) to provide experience in inductive problem solving. The discrimination learning tasks utilized the same lever pressing procedure described above. The stimuli, however, were unidimensional, each dimension being one of those used in the concept task. For example, one required discrimination was between a large black circle and a small black circle. Obviously, size was the relevant

*The scores of the middle class children were curtailed slightly at the lower end to prevent overlap between the two social class groups.

260

cue here. Following this problem, others were presented to the same subject until each of the stimulus dimensions included in the concept task had been used singly in a discrimination learning problem. Each problem was presented for 100 trials or terminated earlier if the subject gave 16 correct responses in a block of 17 trials. Training in discrimination learning was introduced in order to determine its effect on concept attainment; and, more particularly, to determine the extent to which the two populations would profit from this experience.

The results were analyzed separately for the discrimination and concept learning problems. Since one of the major aims of this investigation was to observe the effects of discrimination learning on concept attainment, a subject who failed to attain criterion in any of the discrimination learning problems was dropped from the experiment. In the disadvantaged group it was necessary to drop 13 subjects (ten 5—year—olds and three 8—year—olds) because of failure on one of the discrimination problems, while in the middle class group no child failed to complete successfully all the training problems (X^2 = 8.72, df =1, p < .01). We can conclude, therefore, that disadvantaged children show a performance deficit in simple discrimination learning. The deficit seems to be more substantial at age five than at age eight.

The concept learning data were analyzed in terms of mean errors and in terms of the number of children who attained criterion. These data are presented in Tables 1 and 2. As both analyses yielded consistent results, only the error data will be discussed.

An analysis of variance of the error scores at each age level revealed a highly significant main effect for training (F age 5 = 24.45, df = 1/84, p < .001; F age 8= 13.84, df = 1/80, p < .001) and a significant training by dimension effect for the 5-year-olds (F = 10.17, df = 2/84, p < .001). The subjects who had had the benefit of discrimination learning made approximately 40 percent fewer errors than the group without training. The analysis of the interaction revealed that the size dimension was much easier in the trained group than the other dimensions. This was probably due to the similarity between the size stimuli in the training and concept conditions. Contrary to expectations, social class was not a significant source of variance. Although the lower class 8-year-olds in the untrained condition made approximately 23 percent more errors than the 8-year-old middle class children, the difference was not large enough to be significant at the .05 level. Following training both lower class groups surpassed the corresponding middle class groups, but again the differences were not significant.

Separate analyses were made of the performance of subjects who had failed to achieve criterion. In a previous investigation it had been found that young children who fail to solve concept problems frequently engage in perseverative behavior, such

TABLE 1
Mean Errors in Concept Attainment

Experiment I

Group	Untrained Subjects Relevant Dimension					Trained Subjects Relevant Dimension				
	Color	Form	Size	Number	Mean	Color	Form	Size	Number	Mean
5 year olds:										
Lower Class	65.1	41.0	57.0		54.4	30.0	63.6	6.4		33.3
Middle Class	47.6	70.0	42.2		53.3	43.9	62.2	13.0		39.7
Mean	56.4	55.5	49.6			37.0	62.9	9.7		
8 year olds:										
Lower Class	52.3	59.8	69.0	38.0	54.8	16.2	38.3	11.8	26.2	23.1
Middle Class	15.0	66.7	53.8	42.8	44.6	39.0	37.5	8.8	32.5	29.5
Mean	33.6	63.2	61.4	40.4		27.6	37.9	10.3	29.4	

Note: The N per cell is 8 for the 5-year-old subjects and 6 for the 8-year-old subjects.

TABLE 2
Number of Subjects who Attained Criterion as a Function of Age, Training, and Social Class

Experiment I

	Age			
	5 years		8 years	
	Untrained	Trained	Untrained	Trained
Lower Class	10	17	10	19
Middle Class	10	15	13	19

as responding to position cues or irrelevant stiumulus dimensions (Osler & Kofsky, 1965). The performance of the subjects who had failed to attain criterion in the present investigation was also analyzed for perseverative patterns. It was found that failing subjects from lower and middle class populations did not differ in the type of perseverative strategies employed. These data are shown in Table 3. In summary, it appears that lower and middle class children performed equally well on the concept learning task and that both groups showed equivalent transfer effects from discrimination learning to concept attainment.

The results on concept learning in the two social classes were puzzling, as they were not only at variance with the predictions but also with the general belief of other investigators. Some thought was, therefore, given to possible confounding factors in the experiment. The suggestion that the problem might have been too easy to reveal social class differences was dismissed because only 45 percent of the children who had had no prior experience in discrimination learning attained criterion.

A reexamination of the experiment suggested that two features of the design may have served to reduce possible social class differences in performance. One of these was the method of subject selection and the other was the manner of instructing the children. It will be recalled that only those subjects whose IQ's were within one standard deviation of their population means were accepted into the study. This method of subject selection was used in an effort to obtain groups that were typical of the two social classes. In effect, however, the method of subject selection excluded children with very low and very high IQ's. As there is some evidence to suggest that subjects at the extremes of the IQ distribution may be the ones that account for social class differences in performance (Siller, 1957), it is possible that the absence of differences in the present investigation was related to the relatively narrow IQ range of the populations studied.

Another feature of the experimental design which may have reduced social class differences was the method of instructing the subjects. To avoid the possibility that the younger children would misunderstand verbal instructions (especially the lower class children), an illustrative problem was presented to all subjects. While this procedure was effective in clarifying the task, in retrospect it appeared possible that the illustrative problem may have had a differentially facilitative effect on the lower class children. This supposition was based on prior experimental evidence suggesting that children of superior intelligence can provide their own self instructions in the course of problem solving, while children of lower intelligence are more dependent on cues provided by the experimenter. Osler and Weiss (1962) found that performance differences in concept attainment related to IQ were most apparent under minimal instructional cues. In that study it was shown that for subjects of above average intelligence performance on concept attainment problems was

TABLE 3
Strategies Pursued by Subjects Who Failed to Attain Criterion

Experiment I

Group	N	Relevant Dimension	Irrelevant Dimension	Position	Alternation	Random
5-year-olds:						
Lower Class	21	0	9	3	11	1
Middle Class	23	3	6	1	11	4
8-year-olds:						
Lower Class	19	0	4	2	9	4
Middle Class	16	0	1	1	7	8

Note:-The subjects were considered to have employed a given strategy if their response to a cue was more consistent than would be expected by chance ($p < .001$). There are instances in which the total number of subjects adopting a strategy will exceed N because some subjects adopted more than one strategy.

TABLE 4
Mean Errors as a Function of Social Class, Instructions, and Relevant Dimension

Experiment II
Relevant Dimension

Group	Form	Color	Number	Size	Mean
L-C[a]	78.2	74.4	29.7	76.8	64.8
M-C	49.2	59.3	46.3	69.2	56.0
L-P	63.2	46.5	37.8	55.2	50.7
M-P	46.9	45.2	10.7	65.1	42.0

[a]The first letter in group designation refers to social class, lower or middle, while the second letter refers to experimental condition, C or P.

equivalent under two types of instructions differing in specificity. In contrast, children of average intelligence were aided when instructions were increased in explicitness. It seemed as if the more intelligent children were capable of defining the experimental task more effectively than the less intelligent children. Another line of evidence consistent with this finding comes from the work of Kendler and Kendler (1962). They have shown that intellectual growth is associated with increasing ability to supply verbal mediators that facilitate problem solving. On the basis of the two types of evidence, it now seemed likely that the instructional aids provided the subjects may have obscured possible social class differences in learning by reducing the need for verbal self instructions. In order to obtain direct evidence on these two admittedly *post hoc* hypotheses, a second investigation was conducted.

EXPERIMENT II

The experimental procedure was similar to that described above. However, subject selection within each social class was random with respect to IQ, and two types of instructions were used. One group (P group) received the same instructions as the untrained group in Experiment I. These instructions included a verbal statement and an illustrative problem. The second group (C group) received no illustrative problem, but only verbal directions to try to find out which handle to press for each stimulus in order to win the marbles. Only 8—year—old children were included in this investigation, but in all other respects the population was similar to the subjects used in the previous experiment. There were 192 subjects divided into 16 groups formed by the orthogonal combination of two social classes, four relevant dimensions and two types of instructions. Each of the 16 groups consisted of 12 subjects.

One aim of the investigation was to determine whether a condition in which the subject was required to define the task for himself would present more of a challenge to a lower class than middle class child. As in the first experiment, an interaction effect was anticipated. This time the interaction was expected between type of instruction and social class membership. The second aim of the experiment was to determine the effect of selecting subjects without regard to IQ.

And now for the results. Table 4 shows the mean errors within each group. An analysis of variance resulted in two significant main effects: Instructions ($F = 11.98$, $df = 1/176, p < .001$) and social class ($F = 4.60, df = 1/176, p < .05$). There was, however, no interaction effect, as the illustrative problem facilitated performance equally at both social class levels. This finding does not, therefore, throw any light on the results obtained in Experiment I, as in the present investigation social class differences in performance prevailed under both treatment conditions.

Another way of evaluating the effect of the illustrative problem is to compare the lower class P group with the middle class C group. Under these conditions the social class differences in error scores disappear. In fact, the lower class mean error score in the P group is smaller than the middle class mean error score in the C group, but the difference is not reliable. In essence this finding tells us that the initial difference between the two social classes can be eliminated by providing the lower class child with some practice on the type of performance to be expected from him. Whether the illustrative problem serves merely to clarify the experimental procedure or whether it provides, in addition, information on the problem solving process, is not altogether clear at this point. From a practical point of view, the introduction of the illustrative problem seems to constitute one form of effective intervention in eliminating the performance gap between lower and middle class children.

We turn now to considering the effect of random subject selection. To evaluate this effect, the performance of the P group was compared with the performance of the untrained subjects in Experiment I, as the experimental conditions were identical for both groups. An examination of the data in Tables 1 and 4 for the 8-year-old children shows that for the lower class subjects the error scores in the two investigations were 54.8 and 50.7 and for the middle class children the error scores were 44.6 and 42.0 respectively. It is obvious that these figures represent a nearly perfect replication of results in the two investigations. The change in the method of subject selection in Experiment II did not, therefore, produce significant changes in the error data.

How, then, can the difference in the statistical effects between the two experiments be reconciled? It will be recalled that in Experiment I there was a 10-point difference between the two untrained 8-year-old groups. This difference is of the same order of magnitude as those reported in Experiment II. Thus the difference in statistical effects is apparently a function of the larger number of subjects per group used in Experiment II.

To recapitulate, the work described up to this point leads to two main conclusions: a) Lower class children show a deficit in discrimination learning and concept attainment. This deficit places the mean of the lower class group approximately .4 standard deviations below the mean of the middle class children. b) However, the disadvantaged child is capable of profiting from instructional aids and can generalize skills obtained in solving simple problems to the solution of more complex problems. The ability to generalize raises important questions concerning the kind and amount of training required by the disadvantaged child to optimize his performance on concept attainment problems. In order to assess the relative effectiveness of several training procedures on the two populations another experiment was performed.

EXPERMENT III

The subjects in this experiment were 208 kindergartners selected in the manner described in Experiment I. The aim of the study was to evaluate the transfer effects from two training procedures to concept attainment. One type of training was designed to familiarize the subject with the attributes of the stimulus set used in the concept problem (stimulus differentiation) and the other was designed to provide experience in problem solving (inferential training). These two procedures individually and combined, together with two control groups, resulted in five treatment groups. The experimental procedure for the first four groups started with the presentation of an illustrative problem. The five groups are described below.

1. Stimulus differentiation (S)

The subjects were presented with three discrimination learning problems. The two stimuli used in each of the problems differed in one of the dimensions which later appeared in the concept task. The problems were similar to those used in the trained group of Experiment I. For each problem the subject was required to learn to associate the appropriate lever with each of the two stimuli. Initially, as each stimulus was presented the experimenter showed the child how to respond. After several demonstrations, the subject was required to respond without help until he gave 10 correct responses in a block of 11 trials. The maximum number of trials allowed for each problem was 64. The object of this procedure was to provide the child with experience in discriminating the stimulus attributes without at the same time including practice in problem solving. The stimuli used in this and subsequent training groups are shown in Table 5. The problems were presented in a counterbalanced order, with the dimension which was to be relevant in the concept problem always appearing second in the sequence.

TABLE 5
Stimuli Used in
Discrimination Learning Tasks

Experiment III
Group

S and SI	I
black circle and black square	pumpkin and flower
red triangle and blue triangle	coat and clock
large orange star and small orange star	dog and wagon

2. Inferential training (I)

The children in this group were presented with three discrimination learning problems which they were required to solve without assistance. The stimuli consisted of pairs of pictures of common objects such as a clock and a coat. These problems were intended to provide experience in problem solving without at the same time exposing the subject to the stimulus attributes used in the concept problem.

3. Stimulus differentiation and inferential training (SI)

This group combined the experiences of the first two groups by using the problems of group S and requiring that the subject solve them without assistance from the experimenter, as in Group I.

4. Control with illustrative problem (P)

This group was given no experience in discrimination learning, but proceeded directly from the sample problem to the concept problem.

5. Control without illustrative problem (C)

This group received only verbal instructions prior to working on the concept problem.

Some subjects in groups S, I, and SI failed to solve the discrimination learning problems on their own. Since more of these subjects came from the lower class group, dropping these children from the experiment might have raised the possibility of a bias in subject selection. To avoid a possible bias, the subjects who were failing to attain criterion in the discrimination problems were given assistance by the experimenter until they attained solution. In most instances the assistance was minimal, consisting of one or two corrections or demonstrations by the experimenter.

The concept problem presented to each subject consisted of a eight—stimulus set combining two values of form, color, and size. The procedure was the same as described in Experiment I, except that only form or color were used as relevant dimensions. Size was always irrelevant.

The five treatment groups, two social classes, and two relevant dimensions constituted the three variables combined into 20 experimental groups. Every group consisted of ten subjects except the C groups which consisted of 12 subjects each, making a total of 208 subject.

Tables 6 and 7 present the mean errors per group in discrimination learning and concept attainment. The data were analyzed separately for the two types of problems. The figures show that the lower class children made approximately twice as many errors on the discrimination learning problems as did the middle class children. Five of the lower class children required assistance in solving discrimination problems, while only one middle class child required such assistance. Had this additional aid not been forthcoming, the differences between the two social class groups might have been even larger. An analysis of variance of error scores resulted in two significant main effects: social class (F = 4.80, df = 1/114, p < .05) and type of training (F = 7.89, df = 2/114, p < .001). Similarly, the analysis of the concept attainment data resulted in two significant main effects and, in addition, one significant interaction. The main effects were again social class (F = 10.10, df = 1/188, p < .005) and training (F = 4.99, df = 4/188, p < .001), and the interaction effect was between training and relevant dimension (F = 4.22, df = 4/188, p < .005). Once again there was no interaction between social class and training.

A breakdown of the training effect revealed that there was no reliable difference between the three trained groups, S, I, and SI, nor between the two control groups, P and C. A comparison of the pooled data of the trained groups with the pooled data of the control groups yielded a significant difference (t = 4.10, df = 188, p < .001).

To summarize, the lower class children quite clearly showed a deficit in discrimination learning and concept attainment, but the transfer effects from the several forms of training were equivalent in the two social classes.

Three aspects of the results require discussion. First, does the equivalent performance of the three trained groups allow us to conclude that stimulus differentiation and inferential training are equally effective in facilitating concept

TABLE 6
Mean Errors in Discrimination Learning
as a Function of Social Class and Training

Experiment III

Social Class	Training Group		
	S	I	SI
Lower	1.7[a]	3.4	5.7
Middle	0.8	1.8	3.6

[a]Each figure represents the mean of three scores obtained on 20 subjects.

TABLE 7

Mean Errors in Concept Attainment as a Function of Social Class, Relevant Dimension and Training

Experiment III

Social Class	Relevant Dimension	Training Group					Mean
		S	I	SI	P	C	
Lower	Color	35.6	60.4	50.8	65.6	72.2	57.5
	Form	59.7	4.0	46.6	67.2	63.1	48.7
	Mean	47.6	32.2	48.7	66.4	67.7	
Middle	Color	28.3	35.8	41.4	33.0	62.9	41.1
	Form	42.4	29.2	30.6	47.9	38.2	37.7
	Mean	35.4	32.5	36.0	40.4	50.6	

Note: N per cell in all groups except C is 10. In the C groups N is 12.

attainment? Unfortunately, a retrospective evaluation of the S training procedure leaves some doubt about the nature of that experience. It will be recalled that originally it was intended that the S procedure familiarize the subject with the stimulus attributes but *not* provide inferential training. However, since the subjects were required to attain the criterion of 10 correct responses in a block of 11 trials, following the initial help by the experimenter, it is likely that some inferential training did occur. It is certainly not easy to eliminate that possibility, especially in view of the equivalent scores of the S and SI groups. Because of the ambiguity in the nature of the S training, the results do not allow for the evaluation of the effect of stimulus differentiation alone on concept attainment. On the other hand, the equivalent performance of the I and SI groups demonstrates clearly that inferential training without stimulus differentiation is as beneficial as inferential training with stimulus differentiation. It can be concluded, therefore, that once inferential training is provided, there is no advantage in supplementing it with stimulus differentiation.

The failure of the C and P groups to differ was puzzling because the same two conditions in Experiment II produced significant differences in results. The two studies differed in the ages of the children who participated. In the present investigation the subjects were five years old, while in the former they were eight years old. It is possible that the younger children were not as capable as the older ones of generalizing from the illustrative problem to the concept problem. The data in Experiment I also show transfer of training effects to be smaller for 5—year—old than for 8-year-old subjects

The investigation of transfer effects under the five experimental conditions employed in Experiment III was undertaken for two reasons. First, it was thought that by breaking down the concept attainment process into two components, stimulus differentiation and inductive inference, useful information might be obtained on the role of each component in concept attainment. Second, the employment of lower and middle class populations allowed for the comparison of transfer effects within and between each population. The between class comparisons seemed particularly useful in determining whether lower class children were capable of generalizing to the same extent as middle class children.

With respect to the first point, the information is not complete because of the ambiguity of the S training condition discussed above. So far as the second point is concerned, the data clearly show that lower class children can generalize to the same extent as middle class children.

GENERAL SUMMARY AND DISCUSSION

The evidence gathered from the three experiments can be summarized in two statements. First, lower class children show a deficit in discrimination learning and concept attainment. Second, there is no difference in the way lower and middle class children profit from instructional cues and generalize from discrimination learning to concept attainment. There remains the question of conceptualizing the results into a meaningful theoretical framework.

It will be recalled that initially these investigations were undertaken in an attempt to specify the characteristics of the learning deficit of disadvantaged children. The three experiments were designed to evaluate the role of several pretraining procedures in concept attainment. It was anticipated that the experimental treatments would differentially facilitate the performance of lower class children, and that by observing the specific effects of the treatments on the two populations, some aspects of the learning deficit of disadvantaged children could be specified. It turned out, however, that improvements associated with the experimental procedures were uniform across the two social classes. As a consequence, the original disparity between the two populations remain unchanged after training was incorporated into the procedure.

There is, however, another way of comparing the performance of the two populations and this was suggested in Experiment II. Instead of analyzing the data in terms of scores obtained by both groups *either* before *or* after training, one could ask how effectively a given form of intervention applied to lower class children *reduced* their *initial* learning deficit. To answer this question it was necessary to compare the scores of the trained lower class children with the scores obtained by the middle class children before training. When the data in Experiments II and III were analyzed in this fashion, the differences between the two social classes disappeared.

What are the implications of these findings? In the first place, it has been shown that deficits in concept learning exhibited by lower class children can be eliminated by providing enriched instructions or experience in discrimination learning. Whether this implies that the deficits stem from insufficient experience in problem solving is another matter. Before such a conclusion could be accepted it would be necessary to test the effects of a variety of other treatments, such as experience in providing verbal labels, perceptual differentiation, etc. Until then it can only be concluded that experience in problem solving is one effective means of eliminating deficits in concept attainment.

The second finding, which was not anticipated at the beginning of the work, is that transfer effects were of equal magnitude in both social class groups. As a result, the initial disparity in performance between the two populations was also apparent after training. It is interesting to speculate what the effects of additional training would have been, and, particularly, under what circumstances, if any, the difference between the two populations could have been totally eliminated, even when both had an equivalent amount of help. That problem remains to be investigated. On the basis of the present data, it is clear that a variety of methods for equalizing concept learning in the two social classes exist, provided that the enrichment procedures are applied to the lower class children exclusively.

The work described in this paper was supported by funds from the Institute of Child Health and Human Development, Grant No. HD 754, the National Science Foundation, Grant No. GB 7827, and by the Grant Foundation, New York City.

References

Anastasi, A. DIFFER. PSYCH. (3rd Ed.) New York: McMillan, 1958.

Blank, M., & Solomon F. "A tutorial language program to develop abstract thinking in socially disadvantaged preschool children." CHILD DEVELOP., 39: 379-389, 1968.

Deutsch, M. & Brown, B. "Social influences in Negro—White intelligence differences." J. OF SOC. ISS., 20: 24-35, 1964.

Dreger, R. M., & Miller, K. S. "Comparative psychological studies of Negroes and Whites in the United States." PSYCH. BULL., 57: 361-402, 1960.

Feldman, S., & Weiner, M. "The use of a standardized reading achievement test with two levels of socio—economic status pupils." J. OF EXPER. ED., 32: 269-274, 1964.

Jensen, A. R. "Learning ability in retarded, average, and gifted children." MERRILL-PALMER QUART., 9: 123-140, 1063.

John, V. P. "The intellectual development of slum children: some preliminary findings." AM. J. OF ORTHOPSYCH., 33: 813-822, 1963.

Kendler, H. H., & Kendler, T. S. "Vertical and horizontal processes in problem solving." PSYCH. REV., 69: 1-16, 1962.

Lesser, G. S., Fifer, G., & Clark, D. H. "Mental abilities of children from different social—class and cultural groups." MONOG. OF THE SOC. FOR RES. IN CHILD DEVELOP., 30 (No. 4), 1965.

Osler, S. F., & Kofsky, E. "Stimulus uncertainty as a variable in the development of conceptual ability." J. OF EXPER. CHILD PSYCH., 2: 264-279, 1965.

Osler, S. F., & Weiss, S. R. "Studies in concept attainment, III: Effect of instructions at two levels of intelligence." J. OF EXPER. PSYCH., 54: 38-44, 1963.

Rohwer, W. D., Jr. Cited in A. R. Jensen, SOCIAL CLASS, RACE, GENES AND EDUCATIONAL POTENTIAL. (Address delivered to the Annual Meeting of the American Educational Research Association) New York City, February 17, 1967.

Scholnick, E. K., Osler, S. F., & Katzenellenbogen, R. "Discrimination learning and concept identification in disadvantaged and middle—class children." CHILD DEVELOP., 39: 15-26, 1968.

Siller, J. "Socioeconomic status and conceptual thinking." J. OF ABNOR. AND SOC. PSYCH., 55: 365-371, 1957.

Spence, J. T., & Segner, L. L. "Verbal versus nonverbal reinforcement combinations in the discrimination learning of middle— and lower—class children." CHILD DEVELOP., 38: 29-38, 1967.

Zigler, E., & deLabry, J. "Concept-switching in middle—class, lower—class, and retarded children," J. OF ABNOR. AND SOC. PSYCH., 65:267-273, 1962.

THE ETIOLOGY OF MENTAL RETARDATION
THE DEPRIVATION MODEL *

Leon J. Yarrow, Ph.D.

Our theories and our implicit assumptions about the etiology of mental retardation in the past have had very significant implications for preventive and therapeutic programs. For a long time the emphasis on the biological and genetic determinants of mental retardation, and the belief in the irreversibility of the behavior patterns symptomatic of retardation resulted in concentration on custodial care.

We have now moved a long way from this simple biogenetic orientation regarding the significant etiological factors in retardation. In the 1964 report of the President's Panel on Retardation, it was explicitly stated that "our best estimate... is that of the five and one-half million retarded persons in the U.S. over four and one-half million have no known pathological anomalies... Since the great majority of mentally retarded persons present behavioral disabilities independent of demonstrable pathology of the central nervous system, behavior modification techniques are the only form of treatment or intervention available at this point in our knowledge... The Task Force believes that functional mental retardation is often related to cultural deprivation in our city slums, in our depressed rural areas, and in other subcultural conditions. Should this prove to be the case, the vast majority of mental retardation may be ameliorable, preventable or modifiable by finding ways of stimulating desired behavioral patterns." (p. 3)

This conclusion may be somewhat overoptimistic. The evidence regarding environmental influences on level of intellectual functioning is not unequivocal. However, during the past 25 years there has been an accumulation of evidence from diverse sources that adds up and is compelling in its general consistency. Moreover, there have been great strides in the development of systematic theories of cognitive growth, with greater clarity about the determinants of various aspects of cognitive functioning. In order to utilize this new knowledge and theory effectively in programs for prevention and treatment, we need to establish some links between theoretical concepts and practical aspects of programming. A coherent systematic framework for formulating research questions and for experimenting with programs is needed.

It is evident that the old simplistic formulation regarding the relative importance of heredity or environment is no longer meaningful in the light of current knowledge

* Based on address presented to the American Academy of Mental Retardation, Denver, Colorado, May 16, 1967. I am especially indebted to Dr. Judith Rubenstein for help in organizing the literature and for her many constructive suggestions.

and concepts. As a geneticist, Gordon Allen has pointed out, "According to modern genetics, heredity determines for each quantitative trait and for each individual a probably bell-shaped distribution of potentialities, called a norm of reaction. Most people end up near the middle of their respective curves, but exceptional early environments can realize potentialities far above or far below a person's ordinary expectancy. The curve provided by the genes is, more precisely, a scale of probabilities. The highest probabilities, near the center of the scale, correspond to the environments he is most likely to encounter...

"For every person, individually, heredity fixes an IQ corresponding to each possible environment, but the choice of environments is immense, and is being expanded by medical and social progress. A person whose bell-shaped curve centers at the moron level is likely to have potentialities reaching up into the normal range, and it is the future task of medicine and psychology to find the rare environments or treatments that correspond to these high potentials" (Allen, 1958).

The etiology of mental retardation should be seen in the broader perspective of the determinants of a wide range of variations in intellectual and cognitive functioning. Presumably similar principles govern the development of cognitive differentiation and the expression of behaviors that are components of intellectual functioning at both ends as well as in the middle of the continuum. Similarly, with regard to environmental influences, it is conceptually most meaningful to consider "deprived" environments, "optimal" environments and "enriched" environments in terms of common concepts. From this perspective I should like to consider several major systematic issues regarding environmental influences on intellectual development. One issue centers around the definition of the parameters of the environment. Another issue concerns the interaction between environmental influences and organismic factors, i.e., constitutional characteristics, sensitivities and vulnerabilities. A third issue has to do with the degree of specificity of relationships between variations in environmental inputs and specific aspects of cognitive functioning. A fourth important issue concerns the mechanisms through which environmental influences operate.

Conceptualizing Environmental Influences

The research data on early environmental influences come from many and diverse sources. A major share come from studies of children and adults who have been subjected to extremely depriving conditions in infancy and early childhood as a result of placement in poor institutional environments. More recently, we have begun to look at a broader range of home environments, to analyze the antecedents of normal variations in early cognitive - intellectual development. Other data on environmental influences, of which there has been an increasing amount in recent years come from "enrichment" studies, in which there have been attempts to undo the effects of early deprivation or to prevent these effects in infants and young children who are especially vulnerable (Skeels and Dye, 1939; White and Held, 1964). Finally, there now exist a large body of findings from more controlled experimental studies of animals who have been deprived of various kinds of sensory and social stimulation (Bronfenbrenner, 1968).

Much of the early research on institutionalization referred to a global, undifferentiated entity as the antecedent of the cognitive deficits and personality deviations found in children and adults with a history of institutionalization. In recent years, we have begun to place the concept of deprivation within a broader perspective of psychological theory (Ainsworth, 1962; Casler, 1961; Yarrow, 1961, 1965; Bronfenbrenner, 1968). Deprivation can be conceptualized in terms of inadequacies or distortion in maternal care, inadequate or inappropriate stimulation from the inanimate environment. These deprivations may be a consequence of many different environmental circumstances. Deprivation is frequently an aftermath of separation from the mother; it may also occur in intact families because of maternal inadequacy or general environmental impoverishment, associated with social or economic factors. If deprivation is to be placed in a systematic context, these phenotypically diverse conditions must be related to more general theoretical concepts. On the most basic level, these diverse and complex events can be organized in terms of concepts related to stimulation, and concepts related to the conditions under which stimulation are provided, i.e., the learning conditions—the kinds of reinforcements and contingencies associated with varied kinds of stimulation. These basic concepts which serve to organize analysis of the human as well as the inanimate environment can be further differentiated in terms of more specific environmental parameters which can be experimentally manipulated.

Stimulation

In order to analyze differential effects of stimulation on specific aspects of cognitive and personality development, it is useful to distinguish several classes of stimulation: sensory, affective, social.

Sensory Stimulation

The importance of adequate sensory stimulation for the development of cognitive abilities in young children has been well-documented. Data from experimental studies on animals involving restriction in stimulation can be integrated meaningfully with data on infants and young children in institutions. The findings of developmental retardation in children who have been exposed to institutional environments are paralleled by findings of sensory impairment in animals deprived of stimulation. Among the significant dimensions of stimulation that have been identified are intensity, variety, complexity, and distinctiveness. It is likely that there are optimal levels on all of these dimensions. Clearly, the specification of "optimal" levels is complex since it is an interactional concept. What is optimal with regard to intensity, the degree of complexity, the amount of stimulation per time unit, the distinctive cue-value of a stimulus in a total environmental complex probably depends upon individual differences in thresholds, and also varies significantly at different developmental levels.

For the very young child, stimuli have important evocative functions. They arouse him, they direct and focus his attention on the external environment; they elicit approach or avoidance responses. For stimuli to be effective in eliciting responses and maintaining behavior, it would appear to be essential that they be of appropriate intensity, above the child's threshold of awareness, but not so intense as to be physiologically disruptive or painful. Thus, overstimulation, or stimulation of too great intensity may be comparable to deprivation in the sense that it may arouse protective defenses in the child, in effect elevating his sensory thresholds.

In considering the effects of early stimulation and of early stimulus deprivation, we need to give systematic attention to the modalities of stimulation. The limited data that exist suggest that there may be differential effects of deprivation in given modalities at different developmental periods. For instance, Harlow's research on infant monkeys emphasized the important role of tactile contact during the earliest months of life. His subsequent studies indicated that tactile stimulation became less significant at later developmental periods (Harlow, 1961).

The importance of variety in stimulation has been increasingly emphasized in recent years, both from a neurophysiological orientation as well as from a psychological-behavioral perspective. Central to Piaget's concept of differentiation of schemata is the notion of a gradation of variation in the properties of stimuli. Stimuli that vary on a number of dimensions enable the child to develop and consolidate concepts through the processes of assimilation and accommodation. It is likely that monotonous unvaried stimulation leads to habituation so that a given level of stimulation or a given degree of complexity loses its evocative power.

In much of the literature, several aspects of human stimulation have not been clearly distinguished—affective stimulation, social stimulation and affectional interchange. Moreover, affective stimulation has usually been confounded with intensity of emotional involvement between mother and child. It is likely that these aspects of stimulation do not show a simple pattern of covariation, and one might assume that their impacts on the infant are quite different. It seems theoretically meaningful to distinguish the characteristic level of expression of positive or negative feelings from the sustained quality of affectional relationship.

Social stimulation has been defined in various ways. Usually it is restricted to a particular class of responses provided by a social being, such as being visually present, smiling, giving verbal stimulation or response. In attempting to develop a systematic conceptualization of environmental influences, it is useful to analyze the human environment along dimensions similar to the inanimate environment, i.e., in terms of the amount, quality, and intensity of stimulation in different sensory modalities. In addition, there are dimensions distinctive to the human environment: the affective and affectional characteristics of social interaction; the level or depth of relationship with caretakers and other significant persons; the extent of individualized sensitivity to the child; the behavioral and personal characteristics of caretakers and peers as indentification models; the consistency and predictability of the behavior of caretakers; and the continuity of significant people. The most important and distinctive characteristics of the social environment, as distinguished from characteristics of the inanimate environment, are the active, the mediational, and responsive functions, particularly the capacity for contingent responsiveness. An important aspect of the human caretaker's behavior involves bringing the child in contact with appropriate material and objects, manipulating situations and creating experiences to elicit appropriate intellectual and personal-social responses. A most significant aspect of the mediational function is the buffering or regulatory activity. The mother can enhance or reduce the intensity of stimuli by regulating the ways in which the child comes into contact with stimuli. When these functions are not adequately handled, the environment can be considered depriving. If the young child is not protected adequately from a bombardment of stimuli, or from inappropriate or excessive stimulation, he is likely to develop behavior patterns that interfere with attentional processes. In our research on the relationship between early maternal care and infant characteristics at six months we found that the variable showing the highest relationship to IQ at six months was stimulus adaptation, $(r = .85)$, (Yarrow, 1963).

Perhaps the most important characteristic of the social environment is its capacity for contingent responsiveness—a basic condition for learning. Recent research has emphasized the deviant learning conditions in institutions in terms of the relationship between the behavior of the child and the responses of caretakers. David and Appell's (1961) analysis of an institutional environment in France and Provence and Lipton's research in the United States document the randomness of caretaker's responses in these settings.

Selective responsiveness is the basis for very important learning in the child. If an appropriate or desirable behavior pattern, e.g., smiling, vocalizing, is reinforced by the caretaker, these patterns are strengthened and become part of the learned repertoire of the child. In addition to providing conditions for learning appropriate behavior, this kind of interaction provides the bases for the child's acquisition of the response patterns involved in the development of reciprocal relationships with people.

Finally, an individualized affectional relationship with a person to whom the child has special meaning serves as a model for acquiring new behavior patterns, serves to reduce anxiety that interferes with the child's capacity to become oriented to and attend to relevant environmental stimuli.

As we have indicated, most of our information about the effects of environmental deprivation in humans has come from studies of infants and young children who have been exposed to depriving institutional environments. In analyzing closely the characteristics of very poor institutional settings, it becomes clear that the deficiencies and distortions in development often found in institutionalized infants and children can be related to specific dimensions of these environments. Conversely, a number of studies have indicated that it is possible to create in institutional settings conditions that foster adequate intellectual and personality development.

In brief, poor institutional environments are characterized by many kinds of sensory deprivation, by lack of opportunities to practice emerging skills, by lack of meaningful contact with significant adults, by lack of affective stimulation, by lack of appropriate and contingent responses to the child's exploratory, verbal and social behavior.

In considering the impacts of these conditions, we can postulate effects on different functions and at different levels of organization: on the behavioral level and on the neurophysiological and neuroanatomical levels. The effects of these deprivations become evident early. Infants and young children exposed to early environmental impoverishment begin to show developmental disturbances very early—a general retardation in developing language functions, deviations in motor development, and a variety of social and personality disturbances.

In the studies of children in institutions, general developmental retardation reflected in depressed developmental test scores is a consistent finding. Although the evidence is not conclusive, differences in the degree of retardation found seem to be related directly to the degree and kinds of stimulation provided. All aspects of development are not equally affected; the kinds of developmental retardation found seem to be related quite directly to the characteristics of the environment.

It is clear that language is one of the most basic functions, underlying the development of simple discrimination processes, as well as complex thinking and reasoning. This function is apparently most vulnerable to early deprivation experiences. Data from a variety of sources attest to the vulnerability of verbal stimulation and the early precursors of language, as well as to indices of later linguistic capacity, e.g., vocabulary, sentence length, complexity and structure.

A number of studies, some in recent years, and others almost twenty years ago document clearly the relationship between language stimulation and the development of specific linguistic functions. Brodbeck and Irwin (1946), and more recently Haggerty (1959), Provence and Lipton (1962) show the dampening effects of early institutionalization on emerging language functions. Rheingold, Gewirtz and Ross (1959), and Weisberg (1963) have demonstrated the extent to which the rate of vocalization in young infants is susceptible to experimental control. Hess and Shipman's (1965) work show the effects of language styles of the mother on the preschool child's functional use of language. Studies now underway by E. Schaefer (1968) with fifteen to thirty-six-month-old infants are demonstrating the effects of simple language stimulation on the development of verbal capacities in children from disadvantaged environments.

Provence and Lipton (1962) point to the close interdependence of language and other aspects of cognitive and personal-social development. They noted differences as early as two months between family and institutionalized infants in sheer amount of vocalization, as well as in the type and quality of vocalization. Most significant with regard to future social and personality development is their finding of retardation in the development of the functional use of language by the end of the first year. In the last of the first year they found"...virtually non-existent...the repertoire of sounds through which the average baby by this time expresses pleasure, displeasure, anger, eagerness, anticipation, gleefulness, and excitement." These infants had not developed specific differentiated vocal signals to communicate their needs; and by one year there were no specific words.

The data from various studies are not consistent with regard to the extent to which motor functions are affected by early deprivation experiences. In general, the studies on motor development suggest that those skills which seem to be primarily dependent on the maturation of the neuromuscular apparatus tend to develop normally under conditions of relative deprivation; whereas there is retardation in those skills which are dependent on environmental stimulation and opportunities for practice.

Provence and Lipton (1962) suggest that there are some early deviations in motor development in institutionalized infants which may have significant implications for social and personality development. The earliest difference noted in the second month was in the reaction to being held. The institutionalized infants did not make appropriate postural adjustment—they did not adapt their bodies to the arms of the adult; they were not pliable or "cuddly." They also noted in these deprived infants several kinds of motor deviations considered derivatives of psychic drives, i.e., a diminished impulse to reach out toward people and objects, "a significant impairment of the ability to use the motor skills to seek pleasure, avoid unpleasure, to initiate a social interchange, to exploit the environment for learning and to express feelings." Another significant finding was the disturbance in the capacity to modulate motor impulses to produce smooth motor movement. Perhaps this deviation is an early precursor of the hyperactivity syndrome found so commonly in older children with a history of early deprivation. (There are similar findings in animals who have been subjected to early stimulus-deprivation.)

With regard to social responsiveness and the development of interpersonal relationships, a number of studies have found retardation and a variety of distortions in infants and young children in institutional settings. Among the characteristics found are: a generalized lack of responsiveness to people and lack of social initiative; sometimes a general blandness or undifferentiated amiability; a low incidence of customary playful activities, and, most significantly, a lack of rudimentary imitative behavior, such as peek-a-boo, pat-a-cake. A conspicuous finding in older children is a lack of social sensitivity manifested by an inability to respond discriminatively to different kinds of emotional expression. Also frequently found is a lack of social discrimination indicated by failure to show normal differentiating responses to strangers and familiar caretakers, and the absence of normal anxiety towards strangers at the expected developmental points.

Finally, there are many indications of the lack of development of a sense of trust as shown by specific expectations, particularly expectations of gratification, from specific persons. These characteristics seem to be precursors of more serious disturbances in later life in intellectual and personal-social functioning. The most significant disturbances in older children are in interpersonal relationships. Relationships tend to be shallow; while at the same time there may be indiscriminate and insatiable demands for affection and attention. An absence of normal identification behavior patterns may in turn result in failure to develop normal patterns of goal-directedness and positive achievement orientation, normal impulse control, and normal guilt or anxiety about antisocial behavior.

These studies highlight a number of very basic functions essential to cognitive development which are impaired by early environmental deprivation in humans—attentional processes, activity level, language skills, and motivation for achievement. The developing apathy and generalized unresponsiveness to all kinds of stimulation found in institutionalized infants means that the thresholds for environmental stimulation of all kinds are raised. These infants become deficient in one of the basic capacities required for learning—attentiveness to stimuli. Several studies in recent years give evidence of direct relationships between specific aspects of maternal stimulation and early development of normal infants in homes. Several aspects of maternal behavior were found (Yarrow, 1963) to be highly related to infant developmental status—amount of physical contact, amount of social stimulation, the extent to which the infant was provided with stimulation appropriate to his developmental level. More recently Rubenstein (1967) provides clearcut data on the relationship between maternal stimulation and the infant's visual attention to objects, and his exploratory behavior with objects. She also found a significant relationship between maternal attentiveness and amount of vocalization to objects.

Animal research on deprivation

The experimental work with animals gives more precise evidence of direct relationships between specific kinds of sensory deprivation and impairments in functioning. Perhaps the most significant contribution of the animal studies has been the emphasis on the importance of the developmental stage at which deprivation occurs—the evidence for the critical period hypothesis. Much of the research has been on visual deprivation, ranging from gross absence of light to varying degrees of deprivation of patterned stimulation. There has been some research with primates on tactile and social stimulation.

With regard to light deprivation, several studies (Riesen & Aarons, 1959; and Baxter, 1966) have found that animals reared in darkness from earliest infancy show significant impairment in visual functioning in later life. The kinds and the timing of visual deprivation were found to be very significant with regard to the degree of visual impairment and the extent of reversibility. For example, Riesen (1965) found different effects on later visual functioning of deprivation in patterned visual stimulation, as distinguished from diffuse light. Cats deprived of patterned stimulation during the first eight weeks were unable to discriminate between a moving and a stationary visual stimulus, whereas they were able to discriminate light intensities. A contrast group exposed to normal patterned stimulation was able to make the appropriate discriminations at eight weeks. The animals completely deprived of visual stimulation were unable to discriminate either light intensities of moving and stationary objects. The importance of the timing of visual deprivation is emphasized in another study. Cats reared in normal laboratory environments for the first five months of life, and then exposed to five months of darkness were able to learn to discriminate between moving and stationary objects.

With regard to deprivation in other modalities, rats placed in environments in which bodily movement was restricted were significantly inferior in maze learning capacity than animals raised in an environment providing adequate opportunities for free movement.

Prescott (1968), in reviewing the literature, has postulated that adequate somesthetic stimulation during the early months of life may be crucial for the development of basic attentional processes and the personal-motivational characteristics essential for adequate intellectual functioning. He cites the evidence from a number of animal studies on the relationship between somesthetic deprivation and hypersensitivity and hyperexcitability. He suggests that these behavior patterns are similar to those commonly found in mentally retarded children. The pattern of hyperactivity and hyperexcitability frequently found in institutionalized children and associated with somesthetic deprivation in animals obviously interferes with the child's ability to focus on, attend to and discriminate among stimuli.

In general, the data suggest that the earlier the deprivation the more severe the impairment in functioning. It is likely, however, that there are critical periods for different kinds of stimulation or deprivation. There may be different periods during infancy at which tactile, somesthetic, visual or auditory stimulation may be most significant. It is likely, too, that the characteristics of the stimulus, in any of the modalities, are highly significant. For example, the degree of perceptual complexity required for a stimulus to have an effective impact may differ at different developmental points; and conversely, a given degree of stimulus complexity may be adequate at one developmental period and "depriving" at another.

Characteristics of lower class environments

In recent years there has been an increasing number of investigations which have provided detailed descriptions of the patterns of parent-child interaction as well as the general aspects of environmental stimulation provided in American lower class families. It is striking to see the basic similarities, in a conceptual sense, of these family environments and deprived institutional environments. In the past we have talked grossly about social class differences but only recently have we begun to take a more dynamic view of social class, involving awareness of the differing behavioral requirements for parents in lower class settings and of effects on parental behavior of the psychological concomitants of material deprivation and the constant exposure to high levels of stress, and the essential unpredictability of daily living.

Chilman (1968) has summarized the findings from many studies on the kinds of psychological deprivations for children associated with economic deprivation. Middle and lower class families differ on a number of dimensions significant for cognitive development. As contrasted to the future orientation and goal commitment of the middle class, lower class families tend to be oriented to the present. As distinguished from a "self-confident positive, trustful approach to new experiences," lower class families tend to have a "keep out of trouble, alienated, distrustful approach to society outside of the family," and to be suspicious and fearful of new experiences. In these families, as noted earlier, there is "limited verbal communication, a relative absence of subtlety and abstract concepts, a physical action style." As compared to the "rational, evidence-oriented attitudes" of the middle class, lower class families tend to have fatalistic, personalistic attitudes and to indulge in magical thinking. They also tend to have "low self-esteem, little belief in their own coping capacity" and to assume a basically passive orientation.

The current studies of Hess and Shipman (1965) in focusing on the characteristics of the linguistic environment in homes of low socio-economic status point up some of the more proximate variables which consitute "cultural deprivation." Their findings emphasize the importance of the language environment throughout early childhood, not only for the development of language skills per se but for a variety of cognitive functions. Among the most salient dimensions of deprivation in lower social class homes are a basic lack of cognitive meaning in the mother-child communication system and the exercise of controls which emphasize pre-determined solutions and which provide few alternatives for choice. The modes of control in the lower class environments were characterized as status-oriented, with a sharp definition of authority roles, demanding blind compliance, and restricting alternatives, as distinguished from the person-oriented middle class modes which are more individualized in responses to the child, and which encourage the child to try alternative ways of carrying out instructions. In contrast to the restricted language patterns of lower class mothers, middle class mothers showed more elaborated language patterns. These styles of maternal care were associated not only with retardation in cognitive functions, but with various motivational deficiencies, and an approach to cognitive tasks characterized by impulsivity, a lack of planfulness. These children Hess *et al.* described as being oriented to the immediate situation, and showing little future directedness.

These modal attitudes, orientations and child care patterns would appear to be related to the high incidence of impaired intellectual functioning, inconsistent behavioral controls, and low achievement striving found so frequently in this population. Lower class families are not, however, an undifferentiated mass, all of whom show these characteristics to the same degree. In fact, Pavenstedt (1965) emphasizes the differences between stable low income families and very low-lower class socially disorganized families. Related to these environmental differences, were significant differences in cognitive and personality characteristics of the children from these two types of lower class families.

Enrichment studies

Significant information regarding environmental influences on cognitive development has come from "enrichment studies" which have attempted to undo or reverse the effects of earlier deprivation. Most recently there have been a few preventive studies which have provided enrichment experiences to infants and young children especially vulnerable to deprivation effects. These essentially experimental investigations have ranged from controlled limited variable studies to broad demonstration projects in which a great number of variables have been manipulated simultaneously.

The studies in recent years have essentially confirmed the findings of the classical investigations in the 1930's at the Iowa Child Welfare Research Station (Skeels, et al., 1939; Wellman, 1932). Skeels and his co-workers found that progressive intellectual deterioration, commonly found in retardates placed in poor institutional environments, could be reversed by the introduction of stimulating experiences tailored to the developmental level of the children, as well as by the introduction of more individualized relationships. The gross IQ changes found in several enrichment studies of preschool children vary greatly, from 28 IQ points in the Skeels studies to 5 points (Gray and Klaus, 1965). These findings are impressive, however, since in all of these studies, the IQ scores of the control subjects consistently dropped.

A few recent studies have demonstrated striking effects with very young infants of specific types of stimulation. For example, White (1964) introduced extra tactile stimulation to institutional infants beginning at six days of age and continuing during the first month of life. Between one and three months of age, the children were given both special kinesthetic stimulation and visual enrichment. The visual enrichment consisted of simple natural types of stimulation, e.g., suspending special toys over the cribs, providing patterned sheets and bumpers. He found that the infants given these kinds of stimulation showed advanced visually directed reaching and increased visual attentiveness.

Casler (1961) studying the effects of special tactile stimulation for very young infants, found improvement in general intellectual functioning as measured by the Gesell Test. At a later age (7 to 18 months) encouragement in manipulation of objects was associated with increased IQ scores on the Cattell Test.

Santostefano (1967) found marked improvement in the test performance of retarded preschool children following carefully planned training in focal attention by their mothers.

On the crucial question of the long-term effects of "enrichment" or special stimulation during infancy and early childhood there are almost no data. Skeels (1966) is one of the few investigators who has reported a follow-up into adulthood of the "retarded" children given special stimulation in the preschool years. He found dramatic differences in the general life adaptations of those adults who had been provided enriched experiences during infancy compared with the control cases. All 13 cases from the experimental group were self-supporting; their educational and occupational status compared favorably to the U.S. Census figures for 1960. On the other hand, 8 of the 12 cases in the control group were still in institutions for the retarded.

These studies point up some of the salient dimensions of early environmental influence. They also emphasize the importance of the timing of specific kinds of experiences, and the necessity for an appropriate "fit" between the types of experience and the developmental level of the child. Similar principles hold for reparative as for preventive programs. We can assume that the degree of reversibility will be related to the age of the child and the type and degree of impairment or deficit.

Conclusions

Our concepts and theories about the nature of intellectual functioning are still rather crude. Advances in understanding the etiology of mental retardation will be dependent on more adequate conceptualization of the cognitive processes underlying intellectual functioning, and the interactions between intellectual performance and motivational and personality factors. We need more precise and differentiated information on the motivational factors that influence all aspects of information processing—attending, perceiving, discriminating stimuli, and making appropriate responses to these discriminations.

It is essential, too, that we look in a more differentiated way at environmental influences. We need to begin to refine and analyze the significant environmental variables which are prepotent at different points in early infancy, and throughout early childhood. We need to be able to define accurately various levels and patterns of stimulation in all of the modalities. Most important is precise analysis of the conditions under which stimulation is provided, especially the reinforcement contingencies. We need to attempt to analyze complex environments in terms of these basic concepts.

We no longer argue about *whether* environmental influences are significant or even *which* is more potent—genetic or environmental factors. We have begun to formulate more differentiated questions. Our questions must be in the form of refined statements of complex relationships, i.e., relationships between specified developmental outcomes and specific environmental variables acting on an organism with given sensitivities or vulnerabilities at specified developmental periods.

Increased clarity on a theoretical level with regard both to cognitive functioning and to the nature of the early environment and the modes of interaction between organismic and environmental factors is essential if we are to have any measure of success in developing practical programs to prevent, mitigate and undo the effects of environmental deprivation on intellectual functioning.

References

Ainsworth, Mary D. THE EFFECTS OF MATERNAL DEPRIVATION: A REVIEW OF FINDINGS AND CONTROVERSY IN THE CONTEXT OF RESEARCH STRATEGY. In Public Health Papers #14, World Health Organization, Geneva, 97-165, 1962.

Allen, Gordon. PATTERNS OF DISCOVERY IN THE GENETICS OF MENTAL DEFICIENCY. Amer. J. of Mental Deficiency, 62 (No.5):847, 1958.

Baxter, B. L. EFFECT OF VISUAL DEPRIVATION DURING POSTNATAL MATURATION ON THE ELECTROENCEPHALOGRAM OF THE CAT. Exper. Neurol., 14:224-238, 1966.

Brodbeck, A. J., & Irwin, O. C. THE SPEECH BEHAVIOR OF INFANTS WITHOUT FAMILIES. Child Development, 17:145-156, 1946.

Bronfenbrenner, U. EARLY DEPRIVATION IN MAMMALS AND MAN. In G. Newton and S. Levine (Eds.) Early Experience and Behavior: The Psychobiology of Development. Springfield: Thomas, 1968.

Casler, L. MATERNAL DEPRIVATION: A CRITICAL REVIEW OF THE LITERATURE. Monographs of the Society for Research in Child Development, Serial No. 80, 26 (No. 2) 1961.

Chilman, Catherine S. POOR FAMILIES AND THEIR PATTERNS OF CHILD CARE: SOME IMPLICATIONS FOR SERVICE PROGRAMS. In Dittman, L. (Ed.) New Perspectives on Early Child Care. New York, Atherton Press (In press), 1968.

David, Myriam, & Appell, Genevieve. A STUDY OF NURSING CARE AND NURSE-INFANT INTERACTION. In B. M. Foss (Ed.) Determinants of Infant Behavior, New York: Wiley, 121-141, 1961.

Gray, Susan W., & Klaus, R. A. AN EXPERIMENTAL PRESCHOOL PROGRAM FOR CULTURALLY DEPRIVED CHILDREN. Child Development, 36:887-898, 1965.

Haggerty, A. D. THE EFFECTS OF LONG-TERM HOSPITALIZATION OR INSTITUTIONALIZATION UPON THE LANGUAGE DEVELOPMENT OF CHILDREN. J. Genetic Psychol., 94: 205-209, 1959.

Harlow, H. F. THE DEVELOPMENT OF AFFECTIONAL PATTERNS IN INFANT MONKEYS. In B. M. Foss (Ed.) Determinants of Infant Behavior, New York: Wiley, 75-88, 1961.

Hess, R., & Shipman, V. EARLY EXPERIENCE AND THE SOCIALIZATION OF COGNITIVE MODES IN CHILDREN. Child Development, 34, (No. 4):869-886, 1965.

Pavenstedt, Eleanor. A COMPARISON OF CHILD-REARING ENVIRONMENTS OF UPPER-LOWER AND VERY LOW-LOWER CLASS FAMILIES. Amer. J. Orthopsychiatry, 35:89-95, 1965.

President's Panel on Mental Retardation. REPORT OF THE TASK FORCE ON BEHAVIORAL AND SOCIAL RESEARCH. William I. Gardner (Ed.) U. S. Department of Health, Education and Welfare, March, 1964.

Prescott, J. EARLY SOMESTHETIC DEPRIVATION AND BEHAVIORAL EXCITABILITY: ISSUES IN CRITICAL PERIODS OF DEVELOPMENT. Unpublished Manuscript, 1968.

Provence, Sally, & Lipton, Rose. INFANTS IN INSTITUTIONS. New York, International Universities Press, Inc., 1962.

Rheingold, Harriet, Gewirtz, J., & Ross, H. SOCIAL CONDITIONING OF VOCALIZATIONS IN THE INFANT. J. of Comp. Physiol. Psychol., 52:58-73, 1959.

Riesen, A. H. EFFECTS OF EARLY DEPRIVATION OF PHOTIC STIMULATION. In S. F. Osler & R. E. Cooke (Eds.) The Biosocial Basis of Mental Retardation. Baltimore: Johns Hopkins Press, 1965.

Riesen, A. H., & Aarons, L. VISUAL MOVEMENT AND INTENSITY DISCRIMINATION IN CATS AFTER EARLY DEPRIVATION OF PATTERN VISION. J. Comp. Physiol. Psychol., 52:142-149, 1959.

289

Rubenstein, Judith. MATERNAL ATTENTIVENESS AND SUBSEQUENT EXPLORATORY BEHAVIOR IN THE INFANT. Child Development, 38 (No. 4):1089-1100, 1967.

Santostefano, S., & Stayton, S. TRAINING THE PRESCHOOL RETARDED CHILD IN FOCUSING ATTENTION: A PROGRAM FOR PARENTS. Amer. J. of Orthopsychiatry, 37:732-743, 1967.

Schaefer, E. INTELLECTUAL STIMULATION OF CULTURALLY DEPRIVED INFANTS. Oral presentation at the National Institute of Mental Health, Bethesda, Md., April, 1968.

Skeels, H. M. ADULT STATUS OF CHILDREN WITH CONTRASTING EARLY LIFE EXPERIENCES. Monographs of the Society for Research in Child Development, Serial No. 105, 31 (No. 3), 1966.

Skeels, H. M., & Dye, H. B. A STUDY OF THE EFFECTS OF DIFFERENTIAL STIMULATION ON MENTALLY RETARDED CHILDREN. Proceedings and Addresses of Amer. Assn. on Mental Deficiency, 54 (No. 1):114-136, 1939.

Skeels, H. M., Updegraff, R., Wellman, B. L., & Williams, H. M. A STUDY OF ENVIRONMENTAL STIMULATION: AN ORPHANAGE PRESCHOOL PROJECT. G. D. Stoddard (Ed.) University of Iowa Studies in Child Welfare, 40 (No. 4), 1938.

Weisberg, P. SOCIAL AND NONSOCIAL CONDITIONING OF INFANT VOCALIZATION. Child Development, 34 (No. 2):377-388, 1963.

Wellman, Beth L. THE EFFECTS OF PRESCHOOL ATTENDANCE UPON THE IQ. J. Exper. Education, 1:48-69, 1932-33.

White, B. L., & Held, R. M. OBSERVATIONS ON THE DEVELOPMENT OF VISUALLY-DIRECTED REACHING. Child Development, 35:349-364, 1964.

Yarrow, L. J. CONCEPTUAL PERSPECTIVES ON THE EARLY ENVIRONMENT. J. of Amer. Academy of Child Psychiatry, 4(No. 2), 1965.

Yarrow, L. J. MATERNAL DEPRIVATION: TOWARD AN EMPIRICAL AND CONCEPTUAL RE-EVALUATION. Psychological Bulletin, 58 (No. 6):459-490, 1961.

Yarrow, L. J. RESEARCH IN DIMENSIONS OF EARLY MATERNAL CARE. Merrill-Palmer Quarterly of Behavior and Development, 9 (No. 2):101-114, 1963.

A REVIEW AND PERSPECTIVE ON THE THINKING OF DEAF PEOPLE*

Hans G. Furth, Ph.D.

Part I

RESEARCH WITH THE DEAF: IMPLICATIONS FOR LANGUAGE AND COGNITION

Deaf people who are deprived of linguistic experience during the formative years seem to provide a unique opportunity to psychologists concerned with the language-cognition relationship. Empirical studies of deaf people's performance on nonverbal cognitive tasks were reviewed. Deaf were found to perform similarly to hearing persons on tasks where verbal knowledge could have been assumed a priori to benefit the hearing. Such evidence appears to weaken a theoretical position which attributes to language a direct, general, or decisive influence on intellective development. The poorer performance of the deaf on some tasks is parsimoniously attributed to either lack of general experience which is no longer manifest by adulthood or to specific task conditions which favor linguistic habits.

One of the most intriguing problems which falls within the domain of the psychological investigator is the relationship of language to cognitive or intellective development. In general, psychologists have not critically examined this relationship and have been content with speculative or anecdotal evidence. It was James (1890) who remarked that it mattered little in which medium thinking was going on and he quoted biographical recollections as evidence that thought processes were developed in a deaf person before English had been learned. Somewhat later Binet and Simon (1905) made similar inferences from Helen Keller's and Laura Bridgman's outstanding achievements in spite of their being both blind and deaf from early childhood. Reliable empirical studies, however, on the proposition that development of language and of thinking are relatively independent processes were lacking. Under the impact of behaviorism and the modern approaches to verbal learning and verbal mediation on the one hand and the stress on oral language learning of deaf children

*Writing of Part I was aided in part by Grants 198=T and RD 704, Part II by Grant 1484-S from the United States Rehabilitation Services Administration. Part I is taken from PSYCHOLOGICAL BULLETIN, Vol. 62, No. 3, September 1964, pp. 145-164 and is reprinted by permission of THE PSYCHOLOGICAL BULLETIN and the American Psychological Association.

**Thanks are expressed to N. A. Milgram for helpful collaboration in the preparation of this paper and to J. Youniss and R. Dowling for critical reading of the manuscript.

on the other hand, the opposite proposition has been implied, if not explicitly stated. It is easy to find quotations similar to the following in almost any modern psychological account of cognitive development:

> Skill in concept formation is closely linked to the acquisition of language, particularly to labelling. After he has learned the names or labels applied to objects or events, a child is likely to react in the same way to all stimuli having the same labels. This is known as verbal mediation or mediated generalization. Numerous experiments demonstrate that such mediation is of paramount importance in concept formation, problem solving, thinking and learning (Mussen, 1963, p. 37).

At another point, Mussen, citing as partial evidence research of Soviet psychologists, suggests that language gradually "becomes the most important mediator and regulator of behavior (p. 45)."

With regard to the deaf, the above mentioned observations of James and Binet were actually exceptions to the majority of past and present opinions of lay and professional people in a twofold sense. First, the deaf persons mentioned were certainly not average and were cited more to show what is possible than what commonly happens. Secondly, the authors who quoted them sought empirical illustration for their viewpoint on the relative independence of language and thinking. In contrast to this viewpoint writers on deaf people generally tended to consider these two phenomena quite closely related. The view that the deaf child or adult is cognitively different from and inferior to the hearing person even in nonverbal complex learning tasks because he lacks the free use of language is not only congruent with the common notion of a deaf and dumb person, but seems also in accord with more sophisticated ideas about the deaf. Moreover, it is still common to cite deficient verbal performance of the deaf as evidence for their conceptual deficiency, although it should be rather obvious that the use of verbal tasks with deaf persons is less a test of their intelligence than of their verbal skill.

It seems therefore appropriate to review experimental studies on the nonverbal cognitive functioning of deaf people, both for the general reasons by which psychologists study any special group within human society and for special theoretical implications about language and thinking. As an introduction there follows first some preliminary remarks about the life history of deaf people and classifications of terms relative to language and thinking. The main body of this article reviews studies involving complex learning tasks which can be considered closely related to conceptual ability and intelligence. Afterwards two sections on memory and visual perception complete the survey of nonverbal cognitive studies.

Finally, the author proposes a tentative theoretical position about the influence of language on intelligence and considers further implications from the reviewed studies of the deaf as well as additional suggestive evidence from language learning of hearing children.

SOME OBSERVATIONS ABOUT DEAF PEOPLE

As the deaf person is perhaps the least known and understood of persons with a physical handicap, it is hardly surprising that little attention has been paid to him by scientists who were expressly concerned with language and cognition. It is, however, the considered judgment of this author that no investigator in this area of interest can afford to neglect the presence of persons in our society who have been minimally exposed to the linguistic environment during their developmental period and who appear to go about the business of living—apart from relatively minor social idiosyncrasies—in much the same way as other persons.

Most deaf people have been born to hearing parents. Young deaf children not only do not know the spoken language of their society, but in general, the level of verbal or gestural communication in which they are able to engage with their parents, teachers, and peers is of the most primitive and limited kind. Only after they enter special schools for the deaf do they receive consistent instruction in language, by reading and writing, and by lip reading and speaking. If one observes these children in the primary grades, one concludes that their ordinary life and play are not strikingly different from that of other children their age. They are apparently normal children growing up in a society and culture which is intimately bound up with language despite the fact that they themselves have had minimal direct exposure to the all-pervading linguistic environment. A number of questions, it would seem, are raised as the behavioral scientist observes these children. How has language deficiency affected the cognitive development of these children? Have they organized their experiences on meaningful perceptual and conceptual bases? Do they manifest the beginnings of logical reasoning? Can they recall things, observe relevant aspects of a whole, and can they form theoretical judgments?

As for the deaf adult, we may notice that they use formal signs, gestures and manual spelling to converse with each other. A typical male adult may be employed as a semiskilled worker on an assembly line, be married to a deaf wife, and have hearing children. His mastery of English is quite poor, with reading level not above Grade 3; and his speech and lipreading are so limited as to be of little functional value on their own. Note that in contrast to hearing people with a similar reading level, Grade 3 written English constitutes the ceiling of this deaf person's comprehension of language. The conventional sign language, which is customarily not taught in schools for the deaf, is usually acquired during later childhood informally from other deaf people and it is used rather effectively for various social purposes. Deaf adults, who are as thoroughly "at home" in English as any hearing person, either lost their hearing after the establishment of language or do not have so serious a hearing loss as to be justifiably classified among the deaf, or finally, they are rare exceptions.

For all practical purposes, the typical deaf person, whether child or adult, is a language-deficient person both in his present functioning and in his past experience. Even though we may accept the conventional sign language of the deaf as a "true" language and the adult deaf may employ it for everyday communication, it still remains true that only some deaf children of deaf parents—a small minority of all deaf people—learned these signs before age 6. This peculiar status with respect to language makes the deaf a unique experimental subject for clarifying the influence of language on cognition.

MEANING OF TERMS

Definition of some terms used thus far is already overdue. *Language* refers to the living language as heard and spoken in our society. Knowing a language means mastery of a particular language so that its structure and ordinary vocabulary are implicitly understood and employed by a person. In this sense a 4-year-old child knows his mother's tongue and so does an adult who has an IQ of 40. Deaf persons are called deficient in language precisely because they do not have readily available a verbal medium in which they can communicate.

While overt language or mastery of language is easily defined, the term language is sometimes used in a sense in which it is difficult to observe its presence or even clearly conceptualize its meaning. Covert or *inner language* is a case in point. It is quite difficult to observe and it is even more difficult to define. It can mean—and really should mean nothing else but—silent verbal language. However, at times, the term inner language is used to cover practically the whole domain of cognitive or symbolic behavior and then it is obviously impossible to use it as an explanatory scientific construct.

Terms like *concept* and *symbol* are highly ambiguous and potentially confusing. Language behavior may coincide with conceptual and symbolic behavior, but not necessarily. A person pronouncing nonsense words or words in a language unknown to him engages in verbal but not in symbolic behavior. A child may understand the word "sufficient" as a verbal symbol within a restricted verbal context but have a very inadequate concept of its meaning. On the other hand, one may have an adequate concept of what is expressed by the word "money" yet be unable to define it in verbal terms.

The term intelligence has never been satisfactorily defined so as to find broad acceptance among psychologists, but it is obviously related to conceptual and symbolic behavior. *Intelligence* is here understood as the ability to perform complex learning tasks. These tasks are commonly concerned with discovering a relevant aspect of the total stimulus situation or with behavior controlled by a rule which may be symbolized and verbalized through a generalized concept.

While it is readily admitted that in everyday life verbal language is usually connected with behavior covered by the above terms, two points should be equally obvious. First, language can be conceptually separated from intelligence; secondly, in cases where language is given an explanatory or indispensable role in intellective development, such a position amounts to a major theoretical assumption. It is here suggested that any theory of cognition which invokes language as an explanatory variable should be tested against the behavior of deaf children and adults.

CONCEPTUAL TASKS WITH ABSTRACT MATERIAL

An overview of the majority of studies is presented in Table 1 in the order in which they are discussed in the body of the article. The sections correspond to headings in the text and are there explained. Besides giving the age level of subjects employed in the studies, the last two columns of Table 1 indicate the nature of the task and the relative performance of deaf and hearing subjects. It should be noted that by the term "nonverbal" studies nothing is implied but the minimal use and requirements of verbal behavior in instruction, performance, or as criterion of success.

Nonverbal conceptual tasks can be conveniently classified into those employing relatively meaningless artificial materials, such as geometrical designs, blocks, etc., and those which use meaningful material, familiar from everyday life for which verbalization may be readily available. The stimulus material of the first group is referred to as "abstract" insofar as relevant stimuli are treated as isolated dimensions in distinction from the latter group which treats stimuli as concrete objects. In both these situations the emphasis of the experiment may be on the discovery aspect or on the use a person makes of a principle he is assumed to know. These rough distinctions will allow a more orderly presentation of research by starting with concept discovery studies employing abstract material and proceeding to tasks emphasizing concept shift and transfer.

Concept Attainment

Studies under this heading have as a major task requirement the discovery of a relevant principle (i.e., a concept) according to which success can be achieved. Templin (1950) employed the Brody Nonverbal Abstract Reasoning Test together

TABLE 1
Nonverbal Cognitive Studies with the Deaf

Task and age	Author	Performance of deaf compared to hearing subjects	
		Not inferior	Inferior
Conceptual-abstract			
Attainment			
10-20	Templin, 1950	Classification	Analogies
5-7	Oléron, 1957	Spatial	Alternation
7-12	Furth, 1961a	Same, Symmetry	Opposite
4-7	Oléron, 1962	Same, Different	Strategies
16	Kates, Yudin, & Tiffany, 1962	Strategies	
7-17	Stafford, 1962		Discovery
8-13	Ewing, 1942; Oléron, 1949; Seifert, 1960		1938 Matrices
4-12	Smith, 1952; Farrant, 1964	1947 Matrices	
Transfer			
8-15	Hoefler, 1927; McAndrew, 1948; Oléron, 1951		Shifting
8-12	Rosenstein, 1960	Shifting	
5-7	Oléron, 1957	Transposition	
5, 7, 13	Russell, 1964; Youniss, 1964	Reversal shift	
6, 9	Furth & Youniss, 1964	Reversal association	
6-8	Vincent, 1957		Transfer
Adult	Furth, 1963a	Concept level	Mediated transfer
Adult	Furth, 1964a	Transfer disjunction	
Conceptual-concrete			
Sorting			
6-12	Heider & Heider, 1940	Color sorting	
16, Adult	Kates et al., 1961, 1962	Object sorting	

Knowledge of classes

Age	Reference		
8	Vincent, 1959		Classification
8, 12	Rosenstein, 1960	Classification	Classif., 8 yrs.
8, 16	Furth & Milgram, 1965	Classif., 16 yrs.	
6-14	Furth, 1963b	Concept control	

Piaget-type

Age	Reference		
5-8	Borelli, 1951	Seriation	
7-17	Oléron & Herren, 1961; Furth, 1964b		Conservation
8	Bradshaw, 1964		Transitivity

Practical intelligence

Age	Reference		
6-12	Chuillat & Oléron, 1955		Manipulatory
5-7	Oléron, 1957; Seifert, 1960	Manipulatory	

Memory

Age	Reference		
7-12	Blair, 1957	Nonspan	Span
14, Adult	Olsson & Furth, 1966	Design span	Digit span
8-11	Doehring, 1960	Spatial	
6-12	Furth, 1961b	Rote, 6-10 yrs.	Rote, 11-12 yrs.

Visual perception

Age	Reference		
8-10	Myklebust & Brutten, 1953	Organicity-type	Organicity-type
7-10	McKay, 1952; Hayes, 1955; Larr, 1956	Gestalt laws	
8, 14	Furth & Mendez, 1963		

with other tasks which used a verbal procedure to test hypotheses about the influence of deafness or residential schooling on reasoning in children. The Brody test was divided into classification and analogy subtests. On the classification problem, subjects had to identify one of five figures which did not belong; on the analogy items, they had to select from multiple-choice alternatives the figures which did not belong; on the analogy items, they had to select from multiple-choice alternatives the figure which had a relationship to the third figure analogous to that of the second to the first. With chronological age ranging from 10 to 20 years, and with an N of 106 and 56 for the main comparisons of residential and day schools, respectively, hearing and deaf groups were matched on a one-by-one basis. Templin found no differences between hearing and deaf subjects on the classification task, but on the analogy task the deaf were below the hearing, particularly the residential deaf. The interpretation of this latter result is somewhat shaky because of the uncertainty that the severely deaf understood the instructions. Templin (1950) believed that the results, in general, indicated equality of reasoning ability between deaf and hearing "as long as the general type of reasoning measured is one with which the subjects are familiar."

Oleron of France is one of the few psychologists to show a continuing interest over the years in the cognitive development of deaf children and in theoretical implication for the language-cognition relationship. In 1957 he published a major monograph which examined deaf children's performance on nonverbal types of cognitive tasks which were hypothesized as possibly benefiting from language. In Chapter 4 of this monograph, Oleron (1957) reported his observation with 33 deaf children, aged 4-7, on tasks of what he called temporal and spatial order. The temporal task was a double and a triple alternation problem on which the deaf were about 2 years behind hearing children. On the discovery of a spatial order no difference between deaf and hearing children emerged. From these results, Oleron argued in a post hoc fashion that alternation tasks probably require use of symbols (i.e., language) to a greater degree than do spatial-order tasks although there was no a priori reason to assume that one task required symbols less than the other.

Furth (1961b) studied the attainment of three concepts with the expectation that lack of language would not handicap deaf children in discovering the principles of Sameness or Symmetry but would do so in attaining and using the concept of Opposition. Results supported the expectation: on the first two concepts no consistent difference emerged, while on Opposition, deaf were poorer than hearing children at all age levels, 7 through 12. Deaf children's inferiority on one specific concept was predicated upon the assumption that verbal language by the constant use of opposites gives the hearing children an advantage over the deaf. This seemed an appropriate example of what Vygotsky (1962) called pseudoconcepts, created through linguistic usage. By this is meant behavior, mostly verbal, which gives the impression of mastery of a certain concept, but which under close scrutiny turns out to be mainly determined by frequent linguistic associations. Thus, a child may use the word "sufficient" in many correct contexts but when urged to distinguish "full" from "sufficient" he may reveal his relative ignorance of the mature concept. In the same way it is not likely that the 7-year-old children of this experiment really mastered the concept of opposite, but it is more reasonable to suppose that their test performance was helped by thorough familiarity with their mother tongue.

Consistent with the above results was a study by Oleron (1962) reporting no appreciable differences between deaf and hearing children on learning tasks based on the concepts of Sameness or Difference. Comparing performance of 38 deaf and 38 hearing children, aged 4-7, with stimulus-discrimination objects of shape, object, color, weight, size or speed, Oleron observed that from age 5 onward a majority of both groups of children succeeded.

Kates, Yudin, and Tiffany (1962) studied attainment of conjunctive concepts by 30 seniors at the Clarke School for the Deaf. The deaf seniors were paired in two ways with hearing controls: on IQ and age or on IQ and scholastic achievement. The materials were cards illustrating various combinations of four attributes grouped in an orderly or random fashion and six concepts were chosen as focus cards for six different problems. Deaf and hearing subjects were found to proceed by use of similar strategies and no other differences emerged from among a great number of comparisons made except that deaf subjects took more time in making a first choice.

Stafford (1962) paired 29 deaf students, aged 6-17, with hearing controls and presented them with 12 nonverbal discovery problems in increasing order of complexity. Unfortunately the study is not reported in sufficient detail. The summarized results mention superiority of hearing subjects on number of problems solved and trials to criterion per problem solved except that the older deaf required less trials than the hearing successful subjects.

Three investigations in three different countries used Raven's 1938 Progressive Matrices individually on a large number of deaf students: Ewing and Stanton (1943) in England, Oleron (1949, 1950) in France, and Seifert (1960) in Germany. Only Ewing used a hearing control group while the others relied on Raven's tentatively established norms. All three investigators found that only a small percentage of subjects (between 6 and 11%) fell into the two above-average categories (25% expected) while between 15 and 27% were in the lowest subnormal category (5% expected). Ewing explained part of these findings on the basis that schools for the deaf invariably have more subnormal children than normal schools from which defective children are more commonly excluded. While Oleron considered the results as evidence for a developmental retardation in deaf children, Seifert pointed out that after age 12 the deaf seem to make up to a great extent for the developmental retardation shown at earlier ages.

Smith (1952) presented the Colored Progressive Matrices to all younger pupils (N=28, age 4-10) enrolled at a school for the deaf and found that they performed similar to published norms; but the 30 older pupils, tested on the adult version of the test, showed a lower mean score than the norms. Farrant (1964) compared 120 deaf or hard-of-hearing subjects between the ages of 8 and 12 with a hearing control group on a battery of tests which also included the Colored Progressive Matrices. In his factor-analytic treatment of the data, the author observed that the deaf were retarded on all verbal tests and on some tests of figural reasoning but they were not different from the hearing on the Raven test.

Concept Transfer

The ability to classify same objects successively under two or three different aspects has long been regarded as a mark of intelligent, abstract behavior. In particular, rigidity in shifting was considered indicative of aphasic or general cognitive dysfunction. Four studies have been directly concerned with the problem whether nonspeaking deaf people are in this one respect of rigidity alike to aphasic patients. Hoefler (1927) presented the Weigl Sorting Test to 30 deaf school children and observed that only four shifted spontaneously from one sorting category to another. McAndrew (1948) in a restructuring situation employed various degrees of social pressure to have his subjects, ranging in age from 9 to 15 years, change their previous principle of classification. Only 4 out of 24 deaf students changed while all the normals easily succeeded in doing so. Oleron (1951, 1953) worked with a somewhat older age group (mean age 15) and gave training trials with blocks and transfer trials with drawings. Differences between deaf and hearing were not as marked as with the two former investigators. Yet more hearing subjects shifted spontaneously to a third sorting on the transfer task but the deaf responded easily to suggestion, hence there were few total failures to shift on their part. The order of shifting, object, color, number, was predominant among the hearing but no one order was characteristic for the deaf. Oleron interpreted the deficiencies in terms of a lack of subordination of perceptive elements to conceptual aspects. These characteristics were thought to be due to general lack of linguistic habits and not at all related to any aphasiclike rigidity.

Rosenstein (1960) employing the Wisconsin Card Sorting Test with 8-12 year old deaf children found no differences at all between his 60 deaf and 60 hearing control subjects as measured by total errors, number of concepts attained, or perseverative errors. Other investigators cited in this and subsequent sections also used shifting as part of their experimental procedure insofar as any transfer design requires shifting. They likewise failed to observe any particular shifting difficulty in deaf subjects.

In Chapter 3 of his monograph, Oleron (1957) reported on transposition tasks which he gave to deaf children since a number of earlier studies had suggested that language ability may be a decisive determinant in such tasks. Transfer tasks were devised for size alone, size with form changed, weight and speed. On the first three tasks no differences were observed between the performances of 4-7 year old deaf and hearing children. On the speed task, results were inconsistent with the deaf, apparently poorer in one but better on a second measure. In spite of the small number of subjects, Oleron's major conclusion was that attainment and use of relation is not adversely affected by deafness and its concomitant language deficiency.

In order to fit complex learning processes into a behavioristic model verbal mediation has been postulated as a crucial variable. It was suggested that verbal mediation was related to the performance of reversal as compared to nonreversal learning on the grounds that presence of a mediator facilitated reversal but absence made reversal more difficult than nonreversal shift. Insofar as the mediator is conceptualized as verbal in nature, deaf as compared to hearing children may be handicapped on tasks in which verbal mediation is presumed to operate because of this impoverished linguistic experience. The following two studies tested the reversal-nonreversal paradigm with deaf children. Russell (1964) replicated a reversal study of Kendler and Kendler (1959), and Youniss (1964) employed and extended design of two shift stages. In both studies there were no differences between hearing and deaf children on reversal shift performance. The conclusion to be drawn here from these studies would suggest that mediated behavior is not to be too readily identified with verbal behavior, and that lack of early linguistic experience does not retard such behavior (cf. Youniss & Furth, 1963).

Within a different context, Furth and Youniss (1964) studied paired—associate learning of color and colored objects under reversed and control condition in 6- and 9-year-old children. For example, in the reversed condition, subjects had to learn such associations as "fire truck-white" and "refrigerator-red"; while in the control condition, "blue" and "brown" were substituted for "white" and "red" respectively. It was observed that hearing but not deaf subjects' performance was significantly worse in the reversal condition. Far from being "perceptually bound" the deaf apparently paid less attention to the color of the objects and hence were not as much hindered when the natural colors were reversed as were the hearing.

Michele Vincent (1957), another French investigator who has published several psychological articles on deaf children, gave deaf children, aged 6-8 years, the task of discovering successively three different principles of sorting and finally a series of mixed items without correction as measure of transfer of the previously learned principles. The main results showed that deaf children were about 1 year behind hearing children: They performed more poorly on the discovery task of attaining color and size while disregarding form and on the final transfer task. However, they were not considered to exhibit special difficulties in the shifting aspect of the task. Vincent interpreted her results in Piaget's framework and pointed out that language should not be considered the exclusive way of passing from perceptive to intellectual processes even though as a habit it may facilitate this transition.

Doehring (1960a) presented some observations on color-form attitudes of deaf as compared to hearing children. His hearing subjects ranged in age from 4 to adult years and he found, against expectation, that age had no appreciable influence on the proportion of form-preferred choices on a color-form task in which either choice could reasonably be made. At the 8-year level there were 58% form choices for hearing boys and 66% for girls, while only 36% and 53% of form-preferred choices, respectively, were registered by deaf subjects.

Furth (1963a) performed a transfer experiment which had a bearing on linguistic habits and level of concept attainment. College students made four different kinds of shifts after a first concept-attainment task involving a disjunctive concept. It was found that performance on the second task was in direct relation to a possible verbalization of a rule for the first task; yet if the nature of the disjunctive concept had been mastered during the first task, any of the four subsequent shifts would have been equally easy. Only one shift did not benefit from the verbalization and, in fact, the performance of the hearing college students on this shift was poorest. Deaf college students were equal to hearing students on this shift; they were, however, poorer on the other three shifts presumably because the deaf did not benefit from linguistic habits. Where linguistic habits did not help, namely, on the fourth task, the hearing students showed a level of concept attainment not above that of deaf students.

To test the hypothesis that experience may be a sufficient determinant for the development of intellectual capacities and that deaf adults may have made up their possible initial experiential deficiency by simply living an adolescent and adult life, Furth (1964a) devised a series of nonverbal transfer tasks which were aimed at incorporating the following three controls deemed necessary for use with deaf adults; completely nonverbal procedure, initial training to assure understanding of instruction, and performance of some logical operation which differentiates adult persons of above and below average intelligence. Two sorting tasks were designed and were presented as eight conceptual problems. Problems 6 and 7, the critical problems, were shift tasks in which already familiar elements were sorted into various conjunctive and disjunctive combinations. On such tasks the more intelligent hearing group performed better than the less intelligent group. Apparently, intelligence was related to the ability to benefit on the critical problems from the foregoing training tasks. The comparison of deaf and hearing control groups showed remarkable similarity in terms of trials to criterion, number of errors, or proportion of successes. It should be added that this study for the first time employed deaf adults aged 20-50 years who constituted a sample of typical noncollege working people.

CONCEPTUAL TASKS WITH CONCRETE MATERIAL

There are four sections under this heading. Common to these is the use of stimulus material that is familiar from everyday life and in this sense the stimulus situation can be called concrete. The first two sections deal with free sorting and with knowledge of classes, respectively, the third is devoted to problems taken from Piaget's investigations and finally the last section deals with problems of practical intelligence.

Sorting

Heider and Heider (1940), as some investigators before and after them, considered the possibility that deafness affects cognitive behavior in a way typical of aphasic patients. Interest in this question is understandable and is bound to come up repeatedly because of the exterior similarity of speech and language defect in deafness and aphasia and because of the presence of the poorly diagnosed multiple-handicapped child in schools for the deaf. Heider and Heider required deaf and hearing children at various age levels to select from many blocks to different hues those that were similar to certain standard colors. On such a task, aphasic subjects typically select only an exact match and reject similar hues as being different. The deaf children in this experiment performed in an opposite fashion, that is, they selected a wider band than hearing controls, a result which is more related to a younger chronological age. However, differences in number of instances chosen, although fairly consistent over all age levels, were small and permitted an assertion that the performance of the deaf children was quite similar to hearing subjects and quite incongruent with aphasic behavior.

Kates, Kates, Michael, and Walsh (1961) and Kates, Kates, and Michael (1962) employed the Goldstein-Scheerer Sorting Test, a task which was also originally designed to probe into cognitive processes affected by aphasic conditions. The authors, as before (Kates, Yudin, and Tiffany, 1962), worked with a matched sample of deaf seniors and two control groups and an additional group of adult alumni from the Clarke School for the Deaf. While the authors' main concern was a comparison of nonverbal and verbal classificatory behavior and some expected differences were found in verbal performance, no differences were observed on nonverbal performance. In this respect the deaf categorized familiar objects at a level comparable to their peers under free and more structured sorting conditions and they manifested as much flexibility and acceptable range of choices. Generalization from these results is only limited by the fact that the deaf subjects were a select group and uniformly well above average ability and linguistic achievement as compared with the average deaf person.

Knowledge of Classes

These studies were nonverbal versions of the familiar Similarity test of the type: "In which way are—and—alike?" Vincent (1959) obtained norms for young children on a task in which they had to group familiar objects and afterwards were required to verbalize the reason for their choice. When she observed the grouping behavior of 8-year-old deaf children she found their performance on the level of 6-year-old hearing children. Rosenstein (1960) employed a paired-associate procedure of three lists of five pictures each, illustrating five different concepts. Attainment of concepts was inferred by improved performance on Lists 2 and 3. Deaf and hearing subjects showed similar improvement and the author considered these together with earlier mentioned results as evidence that deaf children do not consistently exhibit conceptual restriction or reduced ability to think abstractly. Furth and Milgram (1965) reported on a picture similarity task with 8- and 16-year-old deaf subjects in comparison with normal and in addition subnormal subjects who also verbalized to it and were given the task in verbal form. The nonverbal task of interest to this discussion had 20 different problems. On each problem a subject had to select three out of seven pictures presented that shared a common attribute. The younger deaf children were found to make more errors than their hearing 8-year-old peers with their performance being comparable to that of 6-year-old children while the deaf adolescents succeeded as well as their counterparts. The authors, relying on evidence from the results with the subnormal group, suggested as probable source for their deficient classificatory behavior not lack of language but rather the experiential restriction of deaf children's early life resulting from the lack of language. Results with the older group were cited as additional demonstration that no lasting conceptual deficit was present in deaf children.

In order to observe classificatory behavior under the control of one concept, Furth (1963b) collected normative data on a pictorial choice task of which the major source of difficulty was the consistent selection of two pictures illustrating the part-whole concept in spite of the presence of other reasonable choice possibilities. The term "verbal control" has often been employed in connection with increased cognitive control of the growing child (cf. Luria, 1957; Mussen, 1963). If a readily available language influenced controlled behavior, deaf more frequently than hearing children should make more incorrect, perceptually-bound choices. Comparison of the performance of deaf and hearing subjects over all age levels revealed, however, a close correspondence between their scores. Moreover, results indicated that over an age span of from 6 to 14 years intelligence contributed significantly to a better performance of hearing subjects on the part-whole task, age contributed to a smaller degree, and success in verbalizing the concept hardly at all. Since presence versus absence of the verbal label on this and other conceptual tasks was observed to be irrevelevant to success, the author suggested "conceptual control" as a more appropriate and more inclusive term for a performance which is under the control of an internal principle rather than verbal control.

Piaget-Type Tasks

Piaget's theoretical model of cognitive development and his basic biological position on intelligence as being rooted in overt action would suggest that the growth of intelligent, logical operation is not dependent on but rather reflected in language behavior. In line with this reasoning, it could be predicted that deaf would not differ from hearing children with respect to the age of which logical operations emerge. Within such a theoretical framework, Michele Borelli Vincent (see Borelli, 1951) tested children of between 5 and 8 years in half-year steps on their ability to place first manikins and then sticks along a size continuum and finally to place the matching elements of both series in correspondence under various conditions. Success on such tasks was considered by Piaget as an indication that the child is beginning to use the number concept in a logical manner. Vincent observed only a slight retardation of about 6 months in her deaf subjects, as compared to hearing subjects. She concluded that these deaf children exhibited no fundamental difference in logical elementary capacities and that the beginnings of logical operations are largely independent of language. She speculated further that probably with operation at a more formal level of logical thought these conclusions may not hold.

Deaf children's performance on some of Piaget's familiar conservation problems was tested by Oleron and Herren (1961). Rightly arguing that deaf children were handicapped if language was part of the experimental procedure, the authors devised a series of pictures which were learned by their subjects, designed to serve as equivalents of the verbal responses "heavier," "same," "lighter" for the conservation of weight and "more," "less" for the conservation of volume. After training with these pictures, the age at which 50% of hearing succeeded on the weight problem was 8.5 and with the quantity of liquid problem was 10.5. Corresponding age levels for deaf subjects were about 6 years later. While Oleron admitted that the retardation of 6 years need not be taken in an absolute sense he believed that Piaget's theory does not emphasize sufficiently the role of language in the emergence of logical behavior, particularly in the subordination of perceptual to conceptual conditions.

As the possibility existed that the use of pictorial symbols introduced an extraneous difficulty for deaf subjects which was mainly responsible for Oleron's results, Furth (1964b) replicated the conservation experiment. He modified the pretask procedure by training his subjects first to express a judgment of equal weight by a horizontal hand movement and indicate judgment of heavier by moving downward the hand holding the heavier object. Two clay balls were used, transformed before their eyes, and put back into their hands. The lowering of the hand on the critical trials indicated a wrong judgment since the object was merely the transformation of a former object. After observing responses of 8-year-old deaf children it was discovered that their final performance was not like 8-year-old hearing children in Grade 3 but more like 6.5-year-old children in Grade 1. A qualitative investigation of failures, however, revealed that many more 8-year-old deaf children made hesitant and inconsistent responses than 6-year-old hearing children. This was interpreted as a possible clue that the older deaf children felt uncomfortable about the response and were really closer to the correct solution than a mere summary of failures of successes would indicate. Evidence from other sources (Goodnow, 1962; Lovell & Ogilvie, 1961) is cited which corroborates the view that kind of experience with the physical world rather than language or formal training determines in part the age at which children pass from a perceptual to a logical judgment on many Piaget-type experiments.

Bradshaw (1964), in a study of inferential reasoning of size relation, used nonverbal methods with hearing and deaf children, aged 6 and 8 years. His procedures were divided into preoperational and two concrete-operational tasks. The results demonstrated that the older hearing children differed from the younger on the latter but not the former tasks, and that the 8-year-old deaf children performed more like 6-year-old children on the sequential but were equal to their peers on the simultaneous operational task. The author pointed out that the average inferiority of the deaf group may have been associated with their lower socioeconomic status.

Practical Intelligence

Chuillat and Oleron (1955) reported the results of a series of six experiments based on a standardized test of practical intelligence by Rey. They observed that tasks which were easy to solve for hearing children, aged 6-7, were difficult or insolvable even with help from the experimenter for the deaf school children in an age range from 5 to 12. Such a striking inferiority in practical intelligence was not replicated in a second study (Oleron, 1957, Ch. 2) in which deaf children, aged 5-7, solved a manipulatory problem quantitatively and qualitatively very much like hearing children of their age. While Oleron in explaining the first results had recourse to factors such as understanding of instructions, personal initiative and language habits in structuring a task, the present finding seemed to him to contradict a rigid theory which linked language and practical intelligence.

Seifert(1958) observed that a sample of 80 deaf children were as skilled as their hearing peers in manual dexterity in cutting out figures and bending wires according to a given copy.

TASKS OF MEMORY

Blair (1957) compared the performance of two groups of 53 deaf and hearing children, aged 7-12, on visual tasks of immediate memory: Knox Cube, memory for design, object location, and four different span tasks. Only overall mean scores were presented with age levels collapsed. While the two groups did not differ on object location, deaf subjects were superior on Knox Cube and memory for design but consistently inferior to hearing subjects on the span tasks. The author suggested that such a performance pattern may be characteristic for the deaf child's visual memory as a compensatory effect for his auditory deficiency. Doehring (1960b) failed to observe any notable difference between hearing and deaf children, aged 8-11, on a memory task for spatial location under various conditions of delay, interference, and exposure times.

Olsson and Furth (1966) tested adolescent and adult subjects on visual span tasks and observed the following results: on visual nonsense figures, deaf and hearing subjects, in general, performed alike on simultaneous and successive presentation of nonsense figures; on visual digits, however, deaf subjects were poorer than hearing subjects at both age levels. Moreover, when recall of figures of low and high associations was compared, deaf subjects against expectation improved as much as hearing subjects on high association figures. This similarity between deaf and hearing subjects with figures of high and low association value would seem to demonstrate that a deficient memory performance on the part of the deaf cannot simply be due to their verbal deficiency. Otherwise one would have expected that a high verbal association value would be of less facilitation to deaf than to hearing subjects. The differences in the performance on digits were interpreted as manifesting the particular effects of continual practice of hearing individuals to a much greater degree than deaf persons in recalling digits (e.g., telephone).

Naffin (1959) mentioned pertinent research published in German journals and books for teachers of the deaf. This research, Naffin noted, demonstrated a marked superiority of the deaf child's visual memory in certain specific situations which were characterized by a perceptual poverty or simplicity.

Furth (1961b) presented a paired-associates task with four visual color stimuli and two motor responses. A comparison of total errors yielded no differences on this rote performance between hearing and deaf children aged 7-10, but superiority of hearing subjects aged 11 and 12.

TASKS OF VISUAL PERCEPTION

Myklebust and Brutten (1953) used a series of visual perception problems: marble board, figure-ground, pattern reproduction and perseveration. These tasks like others mentioned earlier, originally designed to observe behavioral disturbances in brain damage, were employed to investigate the possibility of organicity-like disturbances in deaf children. The authors reported that their deaf subjects, aged 8-10, performed significantly different from their hearing controls on a number of tasks: they made more errors in reproducing marble patterns present before their eyes, in two out of five problems they required more exposure time to succeed in reproducing patterns of dots, and a greater number of deaf subjects gave background rather than foreground responses in one out of five items in the object series and three out of five items in the design series. No statistical differences between deaf and hearing groups emerged on reproduction of line patterns and on perseverative after-effects with an ambiguous figure. The authors concluded that the results supported their initial hypothesis of an organismic disturbance due to sensory deprivation in deaf children and that their perceptual inferiority is related to an impairment in abstract functioning.

In view of these striking differences and sweeping implications it seemed important to replicate the above study. Larr (1956) performed this task with two independent groups of 25 deaf students each from the lower grades of two different schools for the deaf. The deaf groups were paired with a normal and subnormal control group. Larr's results showed that the deaf subjects performed equally well on marble board reproduction. On the figure-ground task a greater proportion of deaf subjects gave background references than did either control groups. Such findings seem to weaken the evidence for a general perceptual disturbance in deaf children, particularly since two more investigations (Hayes, 1955; McKay, 1952) also reported results not in agreement with those of Myklebust and Brutten.

Furth and Mendez (1963) studied visual perception of figures which illustrated some of the major principles of gestalt. Deaf and hearing subjects at two age levels (9 and 16 years) performed, in general, alike except that younger but not older subjects were inferior to hearing subjects on two problems which called primarily for a discriminatory as opposed to a global approach.

DEAF PERSON'S PERFORMANCE ON COGNITIVE TASKS

The above summarized studies of deaf people's nonverbal cognitive performance do not provide a unified picture; in each topic discussed conflicting results were found. Some of the factors which may be responsible for this lack of agreement are rather obvious. Nonverbal procedures which are not uniformly understood by subjects—noncognitive motivational or emotional characteristics, feelings of insecurity in a problem situation with no verbal explanation, and other factors—may interfere with good cooperation. There is finally the ever present personal bias of the investigator who either expects or does not expect to find differences in performance between deaf and hearing subjects and who according to this expectation selects the problems and methodological procedures. However, if these things are taken for granted as part of any human endeavor, there remains a considerable number of studies in which deaf subjects performed quite similarly to hearing subjects. These empirical results would be evidence for the assertion that the cognitive development and functioning of deaf people—outside of the realm of language—is not different from hearing people.

One cannot ignore, however, these studies in which deaf subjects performed below the standard of hearing peers. Where such reported differences are reliable, the investigator is left with the task of explaining these deficiencies. In some cases, differences were expected and directly related to lack of linguistic experience (Furth, 1961b) and in some others this relationship was only observed post facto (Furth, 1963a, Olsson and Furth, 1966).

In other studies the relationship between lack of language and present inferior performance of deaf subjects was more a matter of speculation than of observation (e.g., Furth, 1964b; Oleron, 1951, 1957; Vincent, 1959). The danger of coming up with untestable hypotheses and of circular reasoning is rather obvious in the latter situation. Concerning the retarded performance of deaf children, even on some nonverbal tasks, Ervin and Miller (1963) cautioned wisely that other than linguistic factors, such as a great proportion of psychologically or mentally abnormal or brain-damaged children in a deaf sample, may affect the results. They imply that one should be wary about inferring some direct or indirect effect of language when other variables could just as easily or better explain an average deficiency with a deaf sample.

In line with this reasoning the present author has on different occasions (Furth, 1961a, 1964b; Furth & Milgram, 1965) proposed that lack of language experience may have a retarding effect on the individual child indirectly via lack of sufficient cognitive stimulation and motivation. This possibility is more than mere speculation since it is common knowledge among workers in the field that deaf children rarely enjoy cognitive stimulation and social-emotional acceptance equal to hearing children (cf. Levine, 1960). Deaf children are, in fact, usually neglected children in some respects. After making this concession to language, it is suggested that this unfavorable set of environmental circumstances is remediable. A possible change in overall educational attitude could encourage the early use of nonverbal cognitive stimulation and learning and thus could largely compensate for deficient linguistic skill. Such a hypothesis can be subjected to experimental testing, although the difficulty of executing this design is not underestimated.

An explanation of experiential deficiency would thus seem to be a parsimonious one in understanding the results of a number of cognitive studies, particularly those in the sections on Knowledge of Classes and Piaget-Type Tasks which reported a lag of 1 or 2 years between deaf and hearing young children. The fact that with increasing age less or no difference was observed by several investigators (Furth & Mendez, 1963; Furth & Milgram, 1965; Seifert, 1960), or that with improved controls previously reported differences were no longer manifest (Rosenstein, 1960; Larr, 1956), or that deaf adults who were not skilled in language performed as well as hearing adults on classification tasks involving rather difficult conjunctive and disjunctive concept shifts (Furth, 1964a), would appear to lend additional support to the suggested explanation.

With the studies in which deaf subjects performed at a level of hearing peers, the above mentioned argument of Ervin and Miller may be turned around and one would seem to have empirical reasons for stating that, at least, linguistic skill or deficiency is not an important determinant of the particular task at hand. While such studies may not be particularly enlightening as to deaf people's intellectual functioning, they may be helpful in clarifying the status of some hypothetical constructs related to language, such as verbal mediation, symbol and concept formation, concrete and abstract behavior, etc. Rosenstein (1961), discussing the literature on cognitive research in deaf children, has highlighted some of the confusion which stems from lack of a clear terminology. Some of these points have been briefly touched upon during the discussion of specific research, for example, on transposition (Oleron, 1957), reversal (Youniss, 1964), conceptual control (Furth, 1963b), logical operations (Borelli, 1951), verbal association (Olsson & Furth, 1966).

IMPLICATION FOR THE RELATIONSHIP OF LANGUAGE AND INTELLIGENCE

By generalizing the results of the studies summarized above the applying them to a theoretical position on the influence of language on intellective development, the following is suggested: (a) Language does not influence intellectual development in any direct, general, or decisive way. (b) The influence of language may be indirect or specific and may accelerate intellectual development: by providing the opportunity for additional experience through giving information and exchange of ideas and by furnishing ready symbols (words) and linguistic habits in specific situations.

From this position it should follow that persons, deficient in linguistic experience or skill (a) are not permanently or generally retarded in intellectual ability, but (b) may be temporarily retarded during their developmental phase because of lack of sufficient general experience and (c) they may be retarded on certain specific tasks in which available word symbols or linguistic habits facilitate solution.

When the question is raised: "How do deaf persons think if not in language?" the person asking the question may understand by language any kind of symbolic or communicative behavior and thinking may include for him any internal activity related to intelligent behavior. However, language and intelligence are here taken in the specific sense in which they were first defined. Since there is general agreement that most of the learning studies reviewed could not be solved in the absence of symbolic activity, successful performance on these tasks by deaf persons implies an efficient functioning of a symbolic system other than verbal. If the above question is then modified to read "What kind of symbols do deaf people use?" the author is doubtful that this kind of question lends itself to an empirical answer. A search for explanation of conceptual behavior in terms of symbols may lead closer than is realized to the impasse of the early introspectionists who were looking for the elements which make up thinking.

In general, it should be understood that the social and cultural aspects of language have been taken for granted throughout this discussion and no speculations about the role of language in creating and transmitting a culture are made.

It is quite possible, for instance, that a deaf person may act in a way which seems unintelligent to a hearing person, but the reason for his action may be in the deaf person's different kind of experience and information on which he premises his action. By the same token, it may well be that only by extensive perusal of verbal material a person can be motivated and become directly interested in some specific intellective pursuits. Finally, it would be absurd to deny that hearing people commonly employ language to express and communicate intelligent acts overtly and often use some form of language internally when searching for an intelligent understanding of a given situation. In all these cases, however, language seems to play a subsidiary role to intelligence proper, a role which the reviewed studies indicate could in some instances be taken over by symbol-like structures.

It may be necessary to clarify more precisely what is implied by the term "the indirect influence of language" since Oleron (1957) employed a similar phrase with a somewhat different meaning. For Oleron, language is directly supposed to further and train intellectual experience, for example, by saying a "brown bookcase" the child is led to perform the intellectual operation of abstracting the concept of "brownness" form the concept of "bookcase" and by constant use of such linguistic habits which separate a noun from an adjective he develops a corresponding intellectual habit. According to Oleron, language makes an essential contribution by helping the person to transcend the perceptual order and by giving habitual training in intellective habits and symbolic techniques, even if it is not the main determinant of intellective development. Although the distinction may appear subtle, in our discussion the notion of an indirect linguistic influence is used in a different sense.

Our position refers to the human person in his interaction with the environment—which is called experience—as being responsible for intellective development. A hearing child through language may simply have more opportunity to interact with or meet the environment. Language thus affords opportunity for more experience, but it is not considered a primary or necessary factor in developing intellective habits. In other words, an intellective habit is not thought to presuppose or have at its base a linguistic habit. If it were otherwise, would it not follow that people, deprived of language during the formative years, would remain permanently crippled in intellectual development? Would one not also expect that usage and comprehension of language structure is closely associated with intelligence?

Obviously more refined and sophisticated research with deaf people is desirable to extend the empirical evidence available thus far. Even more important is the quest for other than verbal models to help the psychological investigator understand intellective functioning. A close study of children's nonverbal cognitive development would be most desirable. The reason for stressing the attribute "nonverbal" is simply that if we direct our attention to manifestations of "verbal intelligence" we already preempt the question about the relationship of language and intelligence. Even Piaget (1962) in a recent review of his position admits "that the root of logical operation lies deeper than the linguistic connections, and that my early study of thinking was centered too much on its linguistic aspect (p. 5)."

Where the above theory mentions persons deficient in linguistic experience or skill, other than deaf persons are clearly in mind. Mentally retarded, culturally deprived, speech impaired, and some emotionally disturbed people may all show the specific indirect results of language deficiency. Wepman (in press) and Eisenson (1963) explicitly pointed out that aphasia should regarded as a linguistic and not a general cognitive handicap. Lenneberg (1962) presented a case study of an 8-year-old child who had never talked but, in general, understood language and performed on psychometric tests according to his age level, a rather obvious and not too rare instance which demonstrated at least that active speech is no prerequisite for mastery of language and normal cognitive development. Milgram and Furth (1963), replicating the above-cited results with Same, Symmetry, and Opposition (Furth, 1961b) on mentally retarded, suggested that retarded persons can be considered as linguistically deficient over and above their general mental age level.

As a final and complementary body of evidence for the general position of the relative independence of language and intellective development correlations between intelligence and language measures from different authors (Goda & Griffith, 1962; Harrell, 1957; Templin, 1957; Winitz, 1959) were examined. Based on combined results of 746 persons from 5 to 21 years of age the *r* for IQ and Sentence Complexity was a weak .16 and based on *N*=426 the *r* for IQ and Sentence Length was an equally unimpressive .19. Similarly Burt (1949), reviewing the results of several studies, pointed out that there seems to be general agreement among factor analysts that verbal ability is independent of so-called "higher mental processes," such as generalization, abstraction, judgment, and reasoning.

Three additional points may be added, one that hearing children of quite low mentality learn to master the basic structure of their mother tongue at a functional level. Secondly, there is the observation that the learning of foreign languages is not substantially related to measures of intelligence (Carroll, 1962).

Finally, there is increasing evidence that training in verbalizing particular task variables does not, as such, appreciably improve a conceptual performance (Beilin & Franklin, 1962; Wohlwill & Lowe, 1962). In those cases where verbalization did seem to help, inspection of the procedure usually shows that verbalization did more than merely provide words. For example, in Gagne and Brown (1961) all groups were supplied with appropriate verbal terms, but the group which emerged as best learners was guided in using the terms in varying contexts. Thus, this group differed from others not so much in verbal as in conceptual training. Perhaps this is what Gagne implied when he stressed the importance of what has been learned in a situation in contrast to how it has been learned, that is, whether verbally or nonverbally.

In summary, then, the reported investigations seem to emphasize as legitimate the distinction between intellective and verbal skills. The ability for intellective behavior is seen as largely independent of language and mainly subject to the general experience of living. Various sources of empirical evidence confirm the theoretical position that just as language learning is not closely related to intellectual endowment so intellective performance is not directly dependent on language.

References

Beilin, H., & Franklin, Irene C. "Logical operations in area and length measurement: Age and training effects." CHILD DEVELOPM., 33: 607-618, 1962.

Binet, A., & Simon, T. "Methodes nouvelles pour le diagnostic du niveau intellectuel des anormaux." ANNEE PSYCHOL., 11: 191-244, 1905.

Blair, F. X. "A study of the visual memory of deaf and hearing children." AMER. ANN. DEAF, 102: 254-263, 1957.

Borelli, Michele. "La naissance des operations logiques chez le sourd-muet." ENFANCE, 4: 222-238, 1951.

Bradshaw, D. H. A STUDY OF INFERRED SIZE RELATIONS USING NONVERBAL METHODS. Unpublished doctoral dissertation, Catholic University of America, 1964.

Burt, C. "The structure of the mind: A review of the results of factor analysis." BRIT. J. EDUC. PSYCHOL., 19: 176-199, 1949.

Carroll, J. B. THE PREDICTION OF SUCCESS IN INTENSIVE FOREIGN LANGUAGE TRAINING. Pittsburgh: Univer. Pittsburgh Press, 1962.

Chulliat, R., & Oleron, P. "Sur le development de l'intelligence practique chez les enfants sourds." ENFANCE, 8: 281-306, 1955.

Doehring, D. G. "Color-form attitudes of deaf children." J. SPEECH HEAR. RES., 3: 242-248, 1960a.

Doehring, D. G. "Visual spatial memory in aphasic children." J. SPEECH HEAR. RES., 3: 138-149, 1960b.

Eisenson, J. "Aphasic language modifications as a disruption of cultural verbal habits." ASHA, 5: 503-506, 1963.

Ervin, Susan, & Miller, W. H. "Language development." YEARB. NAT. SOC. STUD. EDUC., 62: 108-143, 1963.

Ewing, A. W. G., & Stanton, D. A. G. "A study of children with defective hearing." TEACHER DEAF, 41: 56-59, 1943.

Farrant, R. H. "The intellective abilities of deaf and hearing children compared by factor analyses. " AMER. ANN. DEAF, 109: 306-325, 1964.

Furth, H. G. "Influence of language on the development of concept formation in deaf children." J. ABNORM. SOC. PSYCHOL., 63: 386-389, 1961a.

Furth, H. G. "Visual paired-associates task with deaf and hearing children." J. SPEECH HEAR. RES., 4: 172-177, 1961b.

Furth, H. G. "Classification transfer with disjunctive concepts as a function of verbal training and set." J. PSYCHOL., 55: 477-485, 1963a.

Furth, H. G. "Conceptual discovery and control on a pictorial part-whole task as a function of age, intelligence, and language." J. EDUC. PSYCHOL., 54: 191-196, 1963b.

Furth, H. G. "Conceptual performance in deaf adults." J. ABNORM. SOC. PSYCHOL., 1964, 68, 1964a.

Furth, H. G. "Conservation of weight in deaf and hearing children." CHILD DEVELPM., 34: 143-150, 1964b.

Furth, H. G., & Mendez, R. A. "The influence of language and age on gestalt laws of perception." AMER. J. PSYCHOL., 76: 74-81, 1963.

Furth, H. G., & Milgram, N. A. "The influence of language on classification: A theoretical model applied to normal, retarded, and deaf children." GENET. PSYCHOL. MONOGR., 72: 317-351; 1965.

Furth, H. G., & Youniss, J. "Color-object paired-associates in deaf and hearing children with and without response competition." J. CONSULT. PSYCHOL., 28: 224-227, 1964.

Gagne, R. M., & Brown, L. T. "Some factors in the programming of conceptual learning." J. EXP. PSYCHOL., 62: 313-321, 1961.

Goda, S., & Griffith, B. C. "Spoken language of adolescent retardates and its relation to intelligence, age, and its relation to intelligence, age, and anxiety." CHILD DEVELPM., 33: 489-498, 1962.

Goodnow, Jacqueline J. "A test of milieu effects with some of Piaget's tasks." PSYCHOL. MONOGR., 76(36, Whole No. 555), 1962.

Harrell, L. E. "A comparison of the development of oral and written language in schoolage children." CHILD DEVELPM. MONOGR., No. 22, 1957.

Hayes, G. A STUDY OF THE VISUAL PERCEPTION OF ORALLY TRAINED DEAF CHILDREN. Unpublished master's thesis, University of Massachusetts, 1955.

Heider, F. K., & Heider, Grace M. "A comparison of color sorting behavior of deaf and hearing children." PSYCHOL. MONOGR., 52 (1, Whole No. 232): Ch. 2, 1940.

Hoefler, R. "Ueber die Bedeutung der Abstraktion fuer die geistige Entwicklung des taubstummen Kindes." Z. KINDERFORSCH., 33: 414-444, 1927.

James, W. PRINCIPLES OF PSYCHOLOGY. New York: Holt, 1890.

Kates, S. L., Kates, W. W., & Michael, J. "Cognitive processes in deaf and hearing adolescents and adults." PSYCHOL. MONOGR., 76(32, Whole No. 551), 1962.

Kates, S. L., Kates, W. W., Michael, J., & Walsh, T. M. "Categorization and related verbalizations in deaf and hearing adolescents." J. EDUC. PSYCHOL., 52: 188-194, 1961.

Kates, S. L., Yudin, L., & Tiffany, R. K. "Concept attainment by deaf and hearing adolescents." J. EDUC. PSYCHOL., 1962, 53: 119-126, 1962.

Kendler, Tracy S., & Kendler, H. H. "Reversal and nonreversal shifts in kindergarten children." J. EXP. PSYCHOL., 58: 56-60, 1959.

Larr, A. L. "Perceptual and conceptual ability of residential school deaf children." EXCEPT. CHILDREN, 1956, 23:63-66, 1956.

Lenneberg, E. H. "Understanding language without ability to speak: A case report." J. ABNORM. SOC. PSYCHOL., 65: 419-425, 1962.

Levine, Edna S. THE PSYCHOLOGY OF DEAFNESS. New York: Columbia Univer. Press, 1960.

Lovell, K., & Ogilvie, E. A. "A study of the conservation of weight in the junior school child." BRIT. J. EDUC. PSYCHOL., 1961, 31: 138-144, 1961.

Luria, A. R. "The role of language in the formation of temporary connections." In B. Simon (Ed.), PSYCHOLOGY IN THE SOVIET UNION. Stanford: Stanford Univer. Press, 1957.

McAndrew, H. "Rigidity and isolation: A study of the deaf and the blind." J. ABNORM. SOC. PSYCHOL., 43: 467-494, 1948.

McKay, E. B. AN EXPLORATORY STUDY OF THE PSYCHOLOGICAL EFFECTS OF SEVERE HEARING IMPAIRMENT. Unpublished doctoral dissertation, Syracuse University, 1952.

Milgram, N. A., & Furth, H. G. "The influence of language on concept attainment in educable retarded children." AMER. J. MENT. DEFIC., 67: 733-739, 1963.

Mussen, P. H. THE PSYCHOLOGICAL DEVELOPMENT OF THE CHILD. Englewood, N. J., Prentice-Hall, 1963.

Myklebust, H., & Brutten, M. "A study of the visual perception of deaf children." ACTA OTO-LARYNGOL., STOCKHOLM, Suppl. No. 105, 1953.

Naffin, P. "Die psychologischen Voraussetzungen der Erziehung des taubstummen Kindes." In H. Hetzer (Ed.), PAEDAGOGISCHE PSYCHOLOGIE. Gottingen, Germany: Hogrefe, 1959.

Oleron, P. "Etude sur les capacites intellectuelles des sourds-muets." ANNEE PSYCHOL., 47-48: 126-155, 1949.

Oleron, P. "A study of the intelligence of the deaf." AMER. ANN. DEAF, 95: 179-195, 1950.

Oleron, P. "Pensee conceptuelle et langage: Performances comparees de sourds-muets et d'entendants dans des epreuves de classement multiple." ANNEE PSYCHOL., 51: 89-120, 1951.

Oleron, P. "Conceptual thinking of the deaf." AMER. ANN. DEAF, 98: 304-310, 1953.

Oleron, P. RECHERCHES SUR LE DEVELOPPEMENT MENTAL DES SOURDS-MUETS. Paris, France: Centre National de la Recherche Scientifique, 1957.

Oleron, P. "Le developpement des reponses a le relation identite-dissemblance: Ses rapports avec le langage." PSYCHOL. FRANC., 7:4-16, 1962.

Oleron, P., & Herren, H. "L'acquisition des conservations et le langage: Etude comparative sur des enfants sourds et entendants." ENFANCE, 14: 203-219, 1961.

Olsson, J. E. & Furth, H. G. THE INFLUENCE OF LANGUAGE EXPERIENCE ON VISUAL MEMORY SPAN. Unpublished master's thesis, Catholic University of America, 1966.

Olsson, J. E. & Furth, H. G. "Visual Memory Span In The Deaf." AM. J. PSYCH. 76: 480-84, 1966.

Piaget, J. COMMENTS ON VYGOTSKY. Cambridge: Massachusetts Institute of Technology Press, 1962.

Rosenstein, J. "Cognitive abilities of deaf children." J. SPEECH HEAR. RES., 3: 108-119, 1960.

Rosenstein, J. "Perception, cognition and language in deaf children." EXCEPT. CHILDREN, 27: 276-284, 1961.

Russell, J. REVERSAL AND NONREVERSAL SHIFT IN DEAF AND HEARING KINDERGARTEN CHILDREN. Unpublished master's thesis, Catholic University of America, 1964.

Seifert, K. H. "Untersuchungen zur Frage der Kompensation auf dem Gebiet des Handgeschicks." Z. EXP. ANGEW. PSYCHOL., 5: 465-490, 1958.

Seifert, K. H. "Erfahrungen mit dem Progressive Matrices Test bei taubstummen Kindern." Z. EXP. ANGEW. PSYCHOL., 7: 255-290, 1960.

Smith, D. I. "A survey of the intelligence and attainments of a group of deaf children." BRIT. J. PSYCHOL., 22: 71-72, 1952.

Stafford, K. "Problem-solving ability of deaf and hearing children." J. SPEECH HEAR. RES., 5: 169-172, 1962.

Templin, Mildred C. THE DEVELOPMENT OF REASONING IN CHILDREN WITH NORMAL AND DEFECTIVE HEARING. Minneapolis: Univer. Minnesota Press, 1950.

Templin, Mildred C. CERTAIN LANGUAGE SKILLS IN CHILDREN. Minneapolis: Univer. Minnesota Press, 1957.

Vincent, Michele, "Sur le role du langage a un niveau elementaire de pensee abstraite." ENFANCE, 10: 443-464, 1957.

Vincent, Michele. "Les classifications d'objets et leur formulation verbale chez l'enfant." PSYCHOL. FRANC., 4: 190-204, 1959.

Vygotsky, L. S. THOUGHT AND LANGUAGE. Cambridge: Massachusetts Institute of Technology Press, 1962.

Wepman, J. M. "Five aphasias: A concept of aphasia as a regressive psycholinguistic phenomenon." PROC. ASS. RES. NERV. MENT. DIS., V. 42, Baltimore: William & Wilkins, 1964.

Winitz, H. "Relationships between language and nonlanguage measures of kindergarten children." J. SPEECH HEAR. RES., 2: 387-391, 1959.

Wohlwill, J. T., & Lowe, R. C. "Experimental analysis of the development of the conservation of numbers. "CHILD DEVELPM., 33: 153-167, 1962.

Youniss, J. "Concept transfer as a function of shifts, age, and deafness." CHILD DEVELPM., 35: 695-700, 1964.

Youniss, J., & Furth, H. G. "Reaction to a placebo: The mediational deficiency hypothesis." PSYCHOL. BULL., 60: 499-502, 1963.

Part II

ADDITIONAL NONVERBAL RESEARCH WITH DEAF SUBJECTS

Since publication of the above review a number of new studies in the general area of nonverbal learning in deaf subjects have been reported. It seems that psychologists are slowly beginning to realize the opportunity offered by the presence of linguistically deficient persons by means of which one can test theories about the influence of language on thinking. As an illustration of the increasing popularity of this approach, seven studies with the deaf were reported in a single recent volume (1966) of a leading child psychology journal, CHILD DEVELOPMENT.

Table 2 lists 32 studies in the order in which they are summarized in this section. The table affords an overview and is similar, though not identical, in arrangement to Table 1 of the preceding section. The studies are grouped into five subsections, starting with tasks of Rule discovery and Logical thinking, followed by Piaget-type tasks, Memory tasks and ending with Perceptual tasks. In response to criticisms or misunderstandings, additional clarifications concerning the notion of linguistic deficiency are presented at the end of the present review.

Rule discovery

1) Blank and Bridger (1966) tested 24 deaf and 24 hearing children, age 3-4, on a concept discovery and transfer task in which the relevant cue was the presence or absence of stimulation (light or vibration). In median trials to criterion no difference was observed between deaf and hearing children. In a second experiment performances of 19 hearing and 13 deaf children, age 5-6, on a successive discrimination task with visual and tactual conditions were compared. The relevant cues were the number concepts "one" and "two." Again, there were no differences in performance, except that deaf children in both experiments showed greater facility in handling tactual material than did hearing children. The authors concluded that deaf children, although deficient in general language, succeeded "not because they had a non-language concept," but rather "because they have been taught and have learned to utilize the symbol."

2) Pufall and Furth (1966) studied double alternation in deaf and hearing children in an age range of from four to nine years (N=12 at each level). They employed a series of tasks which tested for generalization and stability of the acquired principle. At age four and again at ages seven and nine there were no differences between the groups, while hearing children were somewhat better than deaf children at age five on acquisition and at age six on transfer.

3) Two experiments were reported by Youniss and Furth (1966b, pp. 9-13) in which eight-year-old deaf children were found to perform comparably on a simple discrimination learning task in which the relevant cue and the location of response were spatially separated. At age six, however, deaf children were not able to benefit from instructions to attend as did hearing children. With a somewhat more complex cue pattern no differences at either age level emerged. A third experiment reported by Youniss and Furth (pp. 16-18) concerned temporal discontiguity in an acquisition and reversal task that included familiar labable stimuli as well as nonsense figures. The major results were as follows: 1) Reversal performance was easier for the nine-year-old children than for the younger group (age 6, 7); 2) the condition of five-second delay between presentation of stimuli and response had no systematic effect; 3) for younger children, both hearing and deaf, familiarity of stimuli made reversal more difficult; 4) hearing and deaf children performed alike. These three studies taken together suggest that the processes which bridge spatial and temporal discontiguity, are effectively similar in linguistically deficient and linguistically competent children.

4) In order to test the hypothesis that verbal mediation may facilitate reversal Andre (1964) observed seven- and 12-year-old hearing and deaf children (N=96). The results showed that a greater proportion (about 75%) of older than younger children (about 54%) chose reversal, but the main hypothesis was contradicted by two facts. The linguistically deficient deaf children performed consistently like the hearing controls and reversal performance occurred as frequently with those hearing subjects who were able to verbalize correctly as with those who verbalized incorrectly.

5) O'Connor and Hermelin (1965) observed a series of tasks that were intended to be visual-spatial analogies of operations required in linguistic competence. These tasks were: 1) Ordering or seriation, 2) rule discovery involving both sight and touch, 3) immediate memory and 4) perceptual matching. Besides psychotic and imbecile experimental groups, aphasic, deaf and normal control groups, age 10-11 (N=12), were employed. These three control groups succeeded equally well on all tasks. It was concluded that capacity to manipulate signs and symbols is not dependent on speech or verbal comprehension and that consequently the logic of thinking and the competence in verbal expressions develop relatively independently.

6) Additional data on deaf children's performance on Raven's Standard Progressive Matrices were provided by Goetzinger, Wills and Dekker (1967). They reported a mean of 33.3 (with a significant increase to 36.0 at retesting after three months) at a mean age of 13½ (N=96), an apparent lag of 1½ to 2 years compared to the published norms. When 60 deaf children, around 18½ years of age were tested, two interesting results emerged. First, the Raven's Score was now 45.1, within normal limits, and secondly, the reading level of the older groups indicated less than a six

TABLE 2

Additional Nonverbal Studies with Deaf Subjects

TASK AND AGE	No	Author	Performance of deaf compared to hearing subjects	
			Not inferior	Inferior
Rule Discovery				
3-6	1	Blank & Bridges, 1966	Cross-modal transfer	
4-9	2	Pufall & Furth, 1966	Double alternation at 4,7,9 yrs.;	at 5,6 yrs.
6-9	3	Youniss & Furth, 1966b	Spatial and temporal discontiguity	
7-12	4	Andre, 1964	Reversal shift	
11-5	5	O'Connor & Hermelin, 1965	Visual rules	
11-19	6	Goetzinger et al, 1967	Matrices at 18½ yrs;	at 13½ yrs.
15-19	7	Michael & Kates, 1965	Social concepts	
Logical Thinking				
9	8	Furth, 1966a	Logic symbols	
16-20	9	Furth & Youniss, 1966	Symbol use;	Symbol discovery
10-14	10	Youniss & Furth, 1968		Symbol use
11-15	11	Ross, 1966	Probability guesses;	at 11-13 yrs
Piaget-type				
5-8	12	Youniss & Furth, 1965	Transitivity	
5-8	13	Youniss & Furth, 1966a	Transitivity	
4-12	14	Piaget, 1966	Conservation	Quantity of liquid
9-16	15	Furth, 1966a		Quantity of liquid

No.	Age	Reference		
16	6-9	Youniss, 1967		Seriation
17	8-12	Robertson & Youniss, 1968	Anticipatory images	

Memory

No.	Age	Reference		
18	6, adults	Lantz & Lenneberg, 1966	Color	Recognition strategies
19	7-10	Youniss & Furth, 1966b		Pictorial
20	9-16	Rozanova, 1966	Span	
21	11-15	Ross, 1968		
22	18-19	Goetzinger & Huber, 1964	Design	
23	9-13	Furth, 1964a	Combinatorial	
24	6½, 10½	Furth & Pufall, 1966	Combinatorial at 10 yrs,	at 6 yrs.

Perceptual

No.	Age	Reference		
25	17	Odom & Blanton, 1967	Combinatorial	
26	4-6	Oleron & Gumusyan, 1964		Pictorial recognition
27	6-11	Yashkova, 1966		Figural reversal
28	11-16	Gozova, 1966	Recognition;	Drawing of figures
29	7-12	Suchman, 1966	Color preference	Form preference
30	8-18	Carrier, 1961	Color-weight association	under 12 yrs.
31	5½-10	Costa et al, 1964	Visual RT	
32	Adult	Stoyva, 1965	EMG and REM	
33	Adult	Furth, 1961	Size-weight illusion	Bimodal RT

months superiority over the younger group. The authors inferred from these results that lack of experience and not linguistic deficit could best explain the poor performance of the younger age group.

7) Michael and Kates (1965), with a selected sample of 20 deaf seniors from the Clarke School and two hearing controls, according to age and scholastic standing, found that there were no notable differences between the groups on a discovery task which required the identification of familiar social attributes. The test material consisted of 32 picture cards portraying social situations with different affect, sex, age, or clothing. The task was to discover the pictures that were correct instances of a given "focus" picture. It was concluded that the deaf subjects in this sample manifested an equally mature social attitude as the controls.

Logical Thinking

8) Chapter XIV of Furth (1966a pp. 215-222) described a teaching demonstration of logical thinking, based on symbolized concepts of classes and logical connectives. Three groups of 16-, 13-, and 9-year-old deaf children participated. After four days of teaching even the youngest deaf children succeeded in some symbolic-conceptual situations. A follow-up study, not yet reported, indicated that the performance of the ten deaf children in the youngest age group was quite comparable to a class of 11 hearing peers. Here are the results in terms of mean errors for each logical operation, showing in parenthesis first the errors of the deaf, followed by the errors of hearing children: Part I, Negation (.4, .5); Conjunction (1.1, 1.6); Simplification (1.1, .2); Disjunction "simple" (.6, .8), "exclusive" (1.7, 1.5), "addition" (1.8, 1.6); Part II, Disjunction (1.2, 1.4), Conjunction (1.2, 1.4); Conjunction, 1 Neg. (.7, .6); Conjunction, 2 Neg. (.3, .9); Negated Conjunction (1.2, 1.2); Negated Disjunction (1.7, 1.6). The Center for Research in Thinking and Language at Catholic University is now continuing the application of this "symbol logic" method in the field of education proper both with hearing and deaf grade school children.

9) The above method was derived from an experimental procedure, first devised by Furth and Youniss (1966) to test logical thinking by means of a series of symbol cards (containing logical symbols for affirmation, negation, conjunction, and exclusive disjunction) and a series of instance cards illustrating specific colors or forms that corresponded or did not correspond to the symbolized expressions of the symbol card. A subject had to learn the use of the symbols by repeated matching of a symbol and an instance. The authors first established that performance on the Symbol Use task correlated with standard measures of intelligence in a non-college sample of young adults; then they tested deaf young persons from a state school and found their performance quite similar to the average hearing group. While this finding confirmed previous studies on logical thinking in which linguistically

deficient persons did as well as hearing subjects, these same deaf persons who succeeded on Symbol Use were found to fail on a Symbol Discovery task which was comparatively easy for 13-14 year-old hearing youngsters as reported in greater detail by Youniss and Furth (1964).

As the acquisition task on Symbol Discovery did not by itself require learning of the meaning of the symbols, success on Symbol Discovery could only be achieved if subjects took the initiative in discovering the meaning of the logical symbols. It is in the discovery aspect of thinking that the deaf subjects apparently failed. Following the suggestion that experiential deficiency may result in lack of intelligent initiative or motivation, the authors sampled a rural population of a lower socio-economic strata and observed that the performance of the rural sample was similar to that of the deaf sample: they were equal to controls on Symbol Use, but failed on Symbol Discovery. Such results seem to confirm the proposition that a deaf person's failure on nonverbal tasks of thinking is less related to linguistic deficiency as such than to lack of a stimulating social and experiential environment.

10) Continuing in the line of the two previous investigations, Youniss and Furth (1967) trained 24 deaf, 24 hearing culturally deprived (American Indians) and 24 control young adolescents in five sessions of logic learning. After training they were tested on their ability to identify newly introduced drawings as true or false instances of symbolic concept statements. On the more complex concepts, deaf and Indian children were inferior to the control middle-class children; on simpler concepts no differences emerged. The authors distinguished between a concrete operational and formal operational level of using logical symbols and inferred that the deaf and Indian children alike manifested the debilitating influence of long-term experiential deprivation on intellectual development.

11) Ross (1966) compared hearing (CA 7-15) and deaf children (CA 11-15) on a probability task in which children were required to guess the outcome of objectively varying odds. While younger deaf children were found to be slightly poorer, the older ones, though still linguistically deficient, caught up with the hearing children. It was hypothesized that "direct exposure to and commerce with probability situations affords sufficient opportunity for the attainment of probability competence even in the absence of concomitant improvement in linguistic skills."

Piaget-Type Tasks

12) Youniss and Furth (1965) investigated by nonverbal means the manifestation of the logical principle of transitivity (A > B; B > C; therefore A > C). Employing an inclined plane they first taught the child that a ball of color A would push down a

ball colored B, but not vice versa, and similarly that ball B pushed down a third ball C. Subsequently, a comparable proportion of deaf and hearing children of age eight to nine predicted that ball A would push down ball C, while hearing children with CA 5-6 showed no preference for any particular prediction. This performance was interpreted as indicative of the spontaneous logical order which older, but not younger children, impose on a neutral event.

13) A second study (Youniss and Furth, 1966a) explored the former issue further by introducing size as an added irrelevant dimension so that in the congruent condition a smaller ball would push a bigger ball. In both cases, however, the color of the ball was the critical variable. Using hearing children in Kindergarten, Grade 1 and Grade 3, it was found that "transitive" predictions were made by the older children irrespective of perceptual congruency, but the youngest age group performed according to a logical pattern only when size was congruent with logical grouping. Deaf children, comparable in age to children in Grade 3, made in general more errors but, as far as logical grouping was concerned, they performed like the hearing children. Both this and the former study were interpreted as supporting Piaget's theory of development of concrete-operational thinking as largely independent from the absence or presence of linguistic competence.

14) Piaget (1966) reported the results of a pilot developmental study carried out by F. Affolter. Twelve to 26 deaf children at various age levels were employed for each task and tested with a clay ball for judgments of conservation. Similar to controls, a successive order of attainment occurred in deaf children regarding substance (8 years), weight (9 years) and volume (11 years). These results presented a slight retardation compared to a control group using the same procedure; however, in conservation of surface and volume area there was a greater difference (10½ vs. 8½ years for surface). Finally, only conservation of quantity of liquid manifested a substantial retardation of about three years (11½ years). Piaget concluded in these words: "The deaf children manifest a retardation in operativity that is not overly notable and the differences of retardation...are due rather to the procedures by which the problem is communicated. While there may exist a certain global retardation probably due to linguistic deficiency, the role of language seems to consist more in stimulating general intellectual activity and in facilitating social mobility rather than in bringing about the structures of operations."

15) Similar results and conclusions were reported by Furth (1966a pp. 121-124; pp. 155-158) on judgment of conservation of amount of liquid with deaf, control and culturally deprived children. The results indicated a considerable time lag between the hearing and the deaf; so much in fact, that performance could not be taken as a valid manifestation of intellectual level in the deaf group. These were the results. On a logical operation which Piaget and others report as mastered by the age of seven,

deaf children did not generally succeed until age 16, children in a rural area until age 11 and hearing controls until age nine. Furth suggested that these discrepancies are due primarily to a factor of discovery which strongly influences success on Piaget's task.

16) A series of investigations were reported in Youniss and Furth (1966b, pp. 32-40) and in Youniss (1967) concerning spontaneous logical rules imposed by the child in handling concrete material. The tasks were Seriation, Correspondence, Reverse correspondence, Sorting and resorting, Multiple seriation and Multiple classification. In a comparison of the performances of deaf children, age 6 to 9, with hearing controls a considerable lag in spontaneous logical behavior was observed. With additional task-information and demonstration and logical performance of deaf children approximated the level of hearing children. On the basis of these and other studies it was hypothesized that "with deaf children in the age range sampled there is often-times a discrepancy between intellectual capability and performance;" in other words, for some reason deaf children did not readily utilize logical operations that were otherwise shown to be available.

17) Additional confirmation on the operative similarity between deaf and hearing children is provided by Robertson and Youniss (1969) in a developmental study that utilized some of the more recent techniques of Piaget. The authors observed children's knowledge of horizontality of water level and projection of shadows at two age levels (8-9 and 11-12). The tasks included anticipation, demonstration, re-test and generalization, in this order. The 16 deaf children at each age level were strikingly similar to their controls, with younger performing consistently poorer than older children. Only on anticipation of shadows did the younger deaf children show a slight retardation.

Memory

18) The division of the color continuum is commonly recognized to be a more or less arbitrary affair, determined largely by social transmission. It is therefore of particular interest to observe whether linguistically deficient deaf children differ from controls on a task that requires discrimination of a particular color. Lantz and Lenneberg (1966) carried out such an investigation, using deaf and hearing subjects as ages six and at college age. The principal task was to recall among 43 comparison colors, arranged in a circular array, two particular hues which were first presented followed by a five second interval. Recognition performance was better for adults than for children and for younger hearing as compared to younger deaf children. Communication accuracy was also measured for the hearing and the older deaf groups and positive correlations were computed between recognition and communicability. Both deaf groups were found to differ somewhat in pattern of

recognition errors over the color spectrum. From these data the authors concluded that color categorization develops somewhat differently in deaf children and that the late acquired linguistic skill facilitates recognition without basically modifying the original patterning of colors.

19) Four pilot studies to explore strategies in recognition memory were reported by Youniss and Furth (1966b, pp. 19-25). The procedure consisted of presentation of nine drawings arranged in a 3 x 3 matrix and to point to three of the drawings. The child's requirement was to name three either immediately or after a ten second delay when the nine drawings were again shown, but each drawing appeared in a different position than in the original matrix. The performance of deaf children, age 7-10, was compared to control children. It was observed that the recognition scores of deaf children were somewhat below that of hearing children; moreover increasingly with age hearing children pointed to the three drawings in correct order particularly when familiar (hence labable) objects were involved. A final experiment included pre-exposure to facilitate attention to the two-dimensional relation of the matrix, from smaller to bigger and from lighter to darker. Under these conditions the scores of all, particularly of deaf children, improved and deaf-hearing differences became negligible. Insofar as deaf children were found not to employ as effective strategies as did hearing children they demonstrated inferior recognition performance. The readily induced effect of training seemed to indicate that this inferior recognition was not due to a deficit in intellectual structure but to a lack of spontaneous utilization of strategies.

20) Rozanova (1966) reported two experiments on the pictorial memory of deaf children. In experiment 1 partial and whole pictures were first presented and had to be reproduced after ten minutes. Younger deaf children (age 9-10) were found to perform more poorly than hearing controls; the deficiency was more marked in the partial condition and disappeared with age, resulting in no differences at age 15-16. In a second experiment deaf and hearing children (ages 8, 10 and 12) were shown 16 pictures of familiar objects and had to recognize them 20 minutes later within a set of 80 cards including some similar "trick" cards. Younger age and deafness were found to affect memory performance adversely. Still on the same task, after a further interval of ten minutes, two or three cards at a time were shown to the child, including incorrectly chosen pictures. In this condition deaf children corrected their mistakes as well as hearing children.

21) In a test of memory for a span of nine binary (+, -) symbols, Ross (1968) presented patterned series (alternating symbols with the insertion of a run of three identical symbols) and unpatterned series (alternations and doubles in random sequence). Deaf and hearing children at the ages tested (11, 13, 15) did not differ in terms of errors. Both groups performed better on the patterned series and at the same time showed longer runs of errors primarily in this series. A second test was

made with deaf and hearing children at age 15 using 3-symbol and 4-symbol series nine items long. Although fewer items were retained than with binary series, results were similar between deaf and hearing children for both patterned and unpatterned series.

22) Goetzinger and Huber (1964) matched 30 hearing and 30 deaf youngsters on age (14 to 18) and tested them on memory-for-design (Benton Visual Retention Test). On immediate reproduction both groups were similar, both being somewhat worse with a 5-second than with 10-second presentation. But on 10-second presentation, followed by 15-second delay, hearing children experienced no decrement in their performance due to delay; deaf children, however, performed worse, particularly when the delay condition came first. The authors suggested that verbalization may have benefited the hearing in memorizing the design when a delay was interspersed between presentation and reproduction.

23) Two studies were reported in which recognition of the particular presentations of a sequence was crucial for success; for instance, the subject had to make four different responses to the four three-unit stimuli: ABB, AAB, BAA, BBA. It was hypothesized that this skill implicitly underlies linguistic competence. In both studies three groups of subjects were employed: control, deaf and sensory-aphasic children. In the first study (Furth, 1964a) a visual analogue of a linguistic sequence, consisting of nonsense figures, was employed. The deaf group (mean age 10) performed similarly to the hearing group, both in simultaneous and successive presentation, and somewhat better than the aphasic group.

24) A second study (Furth and Pufall, 1966) did not uphold the suggested inferiority of aphasic children. On the visual task the younger hearing impaired children performed somewhat below the controls on successive sequences but the older performed alike; on the simultaneous condition no differences were noted. For hearing children auditory successive presentation was consistently easier than visual presentation. The inferior results of the hearing impaired group were linked to general lack of linguistic skill insofar as natural speech may afford training in the ability to master sequentially presented combinations.

25) In a similar vein Odom and Blanton (1967) hypothesized that deaf children may have difficulty remembering the temporal order of unfamiliar material because as a rule sequential information is not a relevant dimension of their linguistic experience. Groups of deaf children about 17 years old and two hearing control groups (one equated on age, the other of age 11 equated on reading achievement) were shown 20 pairs of letters (PL) or of nonsense forms (PN), in successive (SUC) or simultaneous (SIM) conditions. The sequential order of the two elements within these pairs followed the rule that five elements were always in the first place, while

five others were always in the second place. Subsequently a recognition task was given which included new combinations of the familiar elements. Some of the new combinations were according to the above rule, others were reversed. It was expected that deaf subjects would be less prone to make recognition errors due to sequential rule learning (systematic errors) than errors of sequential reversal (reversal errors). In terms of overall results deaf subjects' performance fell between the two control groups: they correctly identified 14.9 pairs (versus 15.7 and 14.1 for the two hearing groups) and made 3.1 systematic errors (versus 3.4 and 3.3) and 1.7 reversal errors (versus 1.1 and 2.0). In particular, compared to their age controls, the deaf subjects were equal in correct recognition on the SUC tasks and somewhat poorer on the SIM tasks; they made more reversal errors on PN SUC and PL SIM (similar to the younger hearing), in the other two conditions their error performance was alike. While some statistical tests in part confirmed the superiority of the hearing children in recognizing sequences and in making systematic errors, the overriding substantive result appears to be the striking similarity of linguistically deficient deaf children and hearing children in acting on implicit rules pertaining to sequence order.

Perceptual Tasks

26) Oleron and Gumusyan (1964) employed a perceptual task of embedded figures (Poppelreuter Test) and tested 28 deaf and 28 hearing children at ages four to six. The children had to choose from a series of individual drawings those objects or geometric designs which they recognized in the composite picture of superimposed drawings. With a scoring system that rewarded correct choices and penalized wrong choices, deaf children were consistently somewhat poorer; however, only the five-year-olds (on the meaningful figures task) emerged significantly poorer in statistical comparison. As the deaf appeared perceptually inferior, not only on meaningful (hence nameable) objects, but also on geometric designs (for which names were not available to the hearing children), the authors suggested that linguistic skill may facilitate the establishment of an interior symbolic habit which intervenes in the perceptual recognition of the environment.

27) Yashkova (1966) published a report on deaf children's ability to make reverse drawings of geometric figures. Nine to 11 year-old deaf children were found to be as good as hearing controls, while at younger age levels deaf children were somewhat retarded. Additionally the author reported a general improvement following instructions in generalized methods of figure reversal. Self-discovery appeared to be the most valuable method which became notable with hearing children from five years on, with deaf children, however, only from eight years upward.

28) Spatial notions of deaf children, grades 5 to 10, were investigated by Gozova

(1966). In a recognition task young children were provided with a draft of a three-dimensional form which they had to find among a number of other similar forms. Older children had to recognize an object by its draft in three projections and then make a drawing of it. The observed similarity of performance on the first task suggested that spatial notions are normally developed in deaf children while the observed retardation on the second task indicated to the author a lack of attentive and detailed thinking on the part of older deaf children.

29) As an extension of earlier work by Doehring on color-form attitude, cited in Part I, Suchman (1966) replicated Doehring's test on 36 hearing and 36 deaf children with a mean age of 10. She observed that 86% of the hearing and only 33% of the deaf children preferred form, while only 14% of hearing and 67% of deaf children preferred color. Subsequently these same children manifested a similar difference in discriminative accuracy: hearing had higher accuracy scores for form than deaf children and conversely deaf were better than hearing children for color discrimination. On a third task, discrimination learning, hearing excelled over deaf children on the form test while on the color learning task both groups were equal. On the basis of these data Suchman viewed the color preference of deaf children as an acquired habit of categorization that is more adequate vis-a-vis color cues than form cues.

30) Carrier (1961) investigated a question related to the one asked by Lantz and Lenneberg (1966) as well as by Suchman (1966). He found that hearing children over a wide age range (6-18 yrs.) showed a significant tendency to judge a black cube heavier than a white cube of similar size and material. The converse, that white is judged as lighter than black, was also observed, although to a lesser degree. In a comparison of other colors, yellow was reacted to like white, while blue and red elicited no systematic weight reaction. The experimental procedure was essentially nonverbal and included a training session with a balance and weights. Deaf children over age 12 performed consistently similar to controls, but younger deaf children, below age 10, failed to manifest systematic color-weight associations. Subsequently Carrier observed that hearing children rated color-words in a weight hierarchy with black as heavy and white as light. The author suggested on the basis of these results that color-weight associations are primarily mediated by general linguistic experience rather than the specific fact that in English the word "light" combines the two elements of the weight-color association in one word.

31) Costa, Rapin, and Mandel (1964) investigated reaction time (RT) to visual, auditory, and paired (visual and auditory) stimulation in a group of 30 children with communication disorders and 28 control children of mean age 8 years. It was established that visual RT was similar in both groups and that positive reinforcement improved performance on successive days. For controls auditory RT was shorter

than visual, and paired RT was still shorter than auditory RT. In deaf children, however, paired stimulation had no facilitating effect.

32) It has long been held that with deaf persons who habitually use manual means of communication one can readily observe finger electromyography (EMG) movement, analogous to something like internal verbalization. Moreover, rapid eye movements (REM) have recently been found associated with dreaming. Consequently Stoyva (1965) investigated whether in deaf adults REM during sleep would be related to EMG to a significant degree. On the basis of two experiments during sleep, one with seven deaf adults who habitually use manual finger spelling and the other with six deaf and six hearing controls, the following results were established. In deaf persons REM, but not EMG, was associated with dreaming; EMG activity during REM periods in deaf was similar to hearing adults and during non-REM periods there was a high degree of overlap between deaf and hearing groups. These findings by means of modern electrical techniques seem to challenge the former view that linked finger EMG to image activity in deaf persons.

33) Finally, it may be of interest to report here that Furth (1960) found deaf adolescents to be equally subject to the size weight illusion as hearing peers. Moreover, deaf, like hearing subjects, could be trained to overcome in a large measure the illusion and to show the permanent effect of training on a trial a week later.

Conclusions

The Bulletin article (Furth, 1964b) reprinted in Part I of this chapter, was criticized by Marion Blank (1965). She considered that Furth presented inadequate evidence for stating that thinking can develop without the benefit of language and she pointed out that many deaf are well trained in language and thus cannot be considered linguistically deficient. Clarifications on these and other critical points were incorporated in a book in which Furth (1966a) presented a more comprehensive treatment of his view from a theoretical angle. This view is closely patterned after Piaget's developmental theory (Furth, 1966c). Insofar as Piaget states categorically that language is not a constitutive element of logical thinking, it is intriguing to consider that the evidence collected in this review provides as strong empirical support as can be reasonably expected for his theory. However, to accept the evidence two things are required; namely, to understand 1) the nature of a deficiency experiment and 2) the notion of linguistic deficiency.

When it is stated that deaf persons are linguistically deficient, this does not mean that they are lacking in general symbolic ability or that they are ignorant of any and all English words. Most deaf persons in our society know some English words or phrases; but admittedly the most vital aspect of the living language is not single words but the structure of the language, the syntax into which single words are fitted to form meaningful sentences. If language influences thinking, it must do so mainly through its structure; it is precisely with this general structure that no hearing child has any difficulty and the vast majority of deaf children have very great difficulties.

Commonly the fact is overlooked and comes as a surprise to many that the majority of people born deaf, even though they spend ten to fifteen years in schools with almost single-minded emphasis on language learning, do not have competence in the natural language of their society. For understandable reasons this fact is usually not broadcast and with the exception of one normative study by Wrightstone, Aronow and Moskowitz (1963) which omits comparisons with hearing norms, only summarizing statements to this effect by educators of the deaf can be gleaned from the literature.

Concerning an appropriate criterion of linguistic competence for the deaf, comprehension of fourth-grade reading as measured by present standarized tests may be suggested, since our interest does not center on speech or lipreading as such. Reading tests below grade four sample only a fragmentary aspect of language and there should be general agreement that knowing a few words and isolated phrases does not constitute linguistic competence. Significantly, the standardizing study of Wrightstone *et al.* (1963) based on an imposing norming total of 5,824 deaf pupils between the ages 10½ and 16½, demonstrated strikingly that their average reading achievement stops short at grade three. On the Metropolitan Elementary Reading Test the youngest age group (CA 10½ - 11½, N=654) had a mean raw score of 12.6, barely above the chance level of 11, while the upper age group (CA 15½ - 16½, N=1075) achieved a mean of 21.6; the respective SDs were 8.14 and 9.51. In terms of national hearing norms, as Furth (1966b) has shown, this means that the mean score over a span of five years increased from a grade equivalent of 2.8 to grade 3.6, never reaching the mean raw score of 25 for beginning grade four.

Moreover Furth (1966b) computed that hardly 10% of the total sample scored above grade 4, a reading level that experts consider to fall within "functional illiteracy." It stands to reason that the poor reading performance of deaf school children cannot be relegated to any of the usual types of reading difficulty. A slow reader is rightfully assumed to be quite competent in the language in which he has reading difficulties. Not so with deaf persons. In this case reading level is almost uniquely determined by competence in language and therefore reflects that competence.

Here, then, is quantified evidence that only a small percentage of deaf persons is at all comparable to hearing persons in being "at home" in the conventional language of the society. In other words, apart from notable exceptions, the difference in linguistic skill between persons born profoundly deaf and hearing persons is not merely relative or statistically significant, but it is as great and nearly as absolute as the difference in level of hearing. At one extreme there are hearing youngsters steeped from earliest childhood in the conventional language; at the other extreme, there are deaf youngsters who during the early formative years of their life have no ready-made symbol system available. On this crucial fact rests the present author's interpretation of the reviewed studies on various aspects of nonverbal learning in deaf persons.

There remains to add that a conventional gestural language is only available to deaf children born of deaf parents, a very small percentage of the deaf population. Hence it is literally true that most deaf children grow up during the early formative period of life without any viable language. The significant fact is precisely that in spite of not having been provided with a conventional symbol structure, deaf children construct their own symbols as they are needed for the development of thinking.

A second important point is a comprehension of what can and what can not be demonstrated by means of a deficiency experiment. If an organism without a certain factor fails on a given task, one cannot conclude that the factor is directly related to the task since other uncontrolled influences may be at work. But if he succeeds on a given task, one can infer conclusively that the missing factor is not a prerequisite for the task. As a consequence the fact that on nearly half the tasks reviewed above deaf subjects were somewhat retarded is by far less conclusive than the fact that on so many tasks they were equal.

During the recent International Congress of Psychology, Furth (1966d) summarized his view on thinking and language which is contrary to most traditional schools of thought. Another participant in this congress, Neal O'Connor (1966) reported that he had conducted a number of studies which seemed to demonstrate the importance of speech on thinking tasks. Yet, he continued (p. 38), the recent "findings...force on me the somewhat unwelcome conclusion as far as I am concerned that whatever effect auditory deprivation may have on speech, it cannot be said to have a strong effect on reasoning capacity."

The recent work in deafness has produced further confirmation of the implications presented in the first section of this article. The thinking processes of the deaf appear substantially similar to hearing persons and must be explained without recourse to language. This interesting fact implies that the current emphasis in psychology on basing the growth of intelligence mainly on verbal factors is unquestionably inadequate. As a general method, a nonverbal approach may be a fruitful one for an objective study of thinking and for an adequate appraisal of the function of the conventional language in the development of thinking.

References

Andre, J. (Abstract) "Reversal-shift behavior and verbalization in two age groups of hearing and deaf children." AM. PSYCH. 19: 561, 1964.

Blank, M. "The use of the deaf in language studies: a reply to Furth." PSYCH. BULL., 1965, 63: 442-444, 1965.

Blank, M., & Bridger, W. H. "Conceptual cross-model transfer in deaf and hearing children." CHILD DEVELOP. 37: 29-38, 1966.

Carrier, E. O. "The influence of language in the color-weight associations of hearing and deaf children." SC. ED. RES. REP., Harvard Graduate School of Education, 1961.

Costa, L. D., Rapin, I., & Mandel, I. J. "Two experiments in visual and auditory reaction time in children at a school for the deaf." PERCEP. MOT. SKILLS, 19: 971-981, 1964.

Furth, H. G. "Sequence learning in deaf and hearing children." J. SPEECH HEAR. DIS., 1964, 29: 171-177, 1964a.

Furth, H. G. "Research with the deaf: implications for language and cognition." PSYCH. BULL. 62: 145-164, 1964b.

Furth, H. G. THINKING WITHOUT LANGUAGE: PSYCHOLOGICAL IMPLICATIONS OF DEAFNESS. New York: Free Press, 1966a.

Furth, H. G. "A comparison of reading test norms of deaf and hearing children." AM. ANNALS OF THE DEAF, 1966, 111: 461-462, 1966b.

Furth, H. G. "Langage et pensee operatoire: consequences tirees des etudes des sourds adultes." BULLETIN DE PSYCHOLOGIE, 1966, 19: 673-676, 1966c.

Furth, H.G. "Development of thinking in the deaf: implications for the relation of thinking and language." In Boskis, R. M., & Meshcheryakov, A. I. (Eds.) MENTAL DEVELOPMENT AND SENSORY DEFECTS. Symposium 33, pp. 49-61, Moscow, International Congress of Psychology, 1966d.

Furth, H. G., & Pufall, P. B. "Visual and auditory sequence learning in hearing-impaired children." JOURNAL OF SPEECH AND HEARING RESEARCH , 9: 441-449, 1966.

Furth, H. G., & Youniss, J. "The influence of language and experience on discovery and use of logical symbols." BRIT. J. PSYCH., 56: 381-390, 1965.

Goetzinger, C. P., & Huber, T. G. "A study of immediate and delayed visual retention with deaf and hearing adolescents." AM. ANNALS OF THE DEAF, 109: 293-305, 1964.

Goetzinger, C. P., Wills, R. C., & Dekker, L. C. "Non-language I.Q. test used with deaf pupils." THE VOLTA REVIEW, 69, 500-506, 1967.

Gozova, A. P. "Spatial notions of deaf school children." In Boskis, R. M., & Meshcheryakov, A. I. (Eds.) SENSORY DEFECTS AND MENTAL DEVELOPMENT. Symposium 33, pp. 119-125, Moscow, International Congress of Psychology, 1966.

Lantz, D., & Lenneberg, E. H. "Verbal communication and color memory in the deaf and hearing." CHILD DEVELOP., 37: 765-780, 1966.

Michael, J., & Kates, S. L. "Concept attainment on social materials by deaf and hearing adolescents." JOURNAL OF EDUCATIONAL PSYCHOLOGY, 56: 81-86, 1965.

O'Connor, N. "Sensory defects and mental development." In Boskis, R. M., & Meshcheryakov, A. I. (Eds.) MENTAL DEVELOPMENT AND SENSORY DEFECT. Symposium 33, pp. 30-48, Moscow, International Congress of Psychology, 1966.

O'Connor, N., & Hermelin, B. "Visual analogies of verbal operation." LANG. AND SPEECH, 197-207, 1965.

Odom, P. B. & Blanton, R. L. "Rule learning in deaf and hearing subjects." AM. N. PSYCH., 1967, 80: 391-397, 1967.

Oleron, P., & Gumusyan, S. "Analyse perceptive et langage: application d'une epreuve de Poppelreuter a des enfants sourds et entendant." PSYCHOLOGIE FRANCAISE, 1964, 9: 47-60, 1964.

Piaget, J. "Surdi-mutite et conservations operatoires." In ETUDES D'EPISTEMOLOGIE GENETIQUE, Paris: Presses Universitaires de France. No. 20: 61-64, 1966.

Pufall, P., & Furth, H. G. "Double alternation behavior as a function of age and language." CHILD DEVELOP., 37: 653-662, 1966.

Robertson, A., & Youniss, J. "A developmental study of anticipatory visual imagery in deaf and hearing children." CHILD DEVELOP. in press.

Ross, B. M. "Probability concepts in deaf and hearing children. " CHILD DEVELOPMENT, 37: 917-928, 1966.

Ross, B.M. "Sequential visual memory and the limited magic of the number seven." J. EXP. PSYCH., in press, 1969.

Rozanova, T. V. "Pictorial memory of deaf children." In Boskis, R. M., & Mescheryakov, A. I. (Eds.) MENTAL DEVELOPMENT AND SENSORY DEFECTS. Symposium 33, pp. 103-114, Moscow, International Congress of Psychology, 1966.

Suchman, R. G. "Color-form preference, discriminative accuracy and learning of deaf and hearing children." CHILD DEVELOP, 37: 439-452, 1966.

Stoyva, J. M. "Finger electro-mygographic activity during sleep: its relation to dreaming in deaf and normal subjects." J. ABNORM. PSYCH., 70: 343-349, 1965.

Wrightstone, J. W., Aronow, M. S., & Moskowitz, S. "Developing reading test norms for deaf children." AMERICAN ANNALS OF THE DEAF, 108: 311-316, 1963, and TEST SERVICE BULLETIN, No. 98, Harcourt, Brace and World, 1962.

Yashkova, N. V. "Intellectual reversibility formation in deaf and in normal children." In Boskis, R. M., & Meshcheryakov, A. I. (Eds.) MENTAL DEVELOPMENT AND SENSORY DEFECTS. Symposium 33, pp. 135-139, Moscow, International Congress of Psychology, 1966.

Youniss, J. "Psychological evaluation of the deaf child: observations of a researcher." THE EYE, EAR, NOSE AND THROAT MONTHLY, 46: 458-464, 1967.

Youniss, J., & Furth, H. G. "Attainment and transfer of logical connectives in children." J. ED. PSYCH., 1964, 55: 357-361, 1964.

Youniss, J., & Furth, H. G. "The influence of transitivity on learning in hearing and deaf children." CHILD DEVELOP., 36: 533-538, 1965.

Youniss, J., & Furth, H. G. "Prediction of causal events as a function of transitivity and perceptual congruency in hearing and deaf children." CHILD DEVELOP. 37: 73-82, 1966a.

Youniss, J. & Furth, H. G. "Spatial and temporal factors in learning with deaf children: an experimental investigation of thinking." VOCATIONAL REHABILITATION ADMINISTRATION REPORT RD-1305-S, 1966b.

Youniss, J., & Furth, H. G. "The role of language and experience on the use of logical symbols." BRIT. J. PSYCH., 58:435-443, 1967.

THE DEVELOPMENT OF CONCEPTIONS
OF PSYCHOLOGICAL CAUSALITY

Martin Whiteman, Ph.D.

An understanding of psychological causality refers to the cognition of intentions and feelings as behavioral causes. Such cognitions were assessed by interviewing children with respect to their understanding of the motivations of a child in a number of story situations (M. Whiteman, 1967). Each of seven stories exemplified in rudimentary form a different mechanism of adjustment, i.e., displacement, wishful dreaming, projection, regression, repression, rationalization, and denial.

In the displacement story, for example, the child (if she were a girl) was asked to explain the behavior of Jane in the following episode.

"There was once a little girl named Jane. One day her mother promised that Jane's favorite dessert, ice cream, would be served at supper. But Jane's mother forgot to buy the ice cream, and so there wasn't any ice cream for dessert. Jane didn't say anything to her mother about the ice cream. After supper Jane went to play with her dolls and did something she never did before. She spanked her dolls. Why did she spank her dolls?"

In the wishful dreaming story Jane sees a girl riding a bicycle on T.V. and subsequently dreams that she herself has obtained one. In the projection story Jane, who doesn't like to share her toys with other kids, asserts that another child whom she's going to see for the first time wouldn't want to share her games and toys either. In the regression story Jane, not feeling well, acts like her baby brother—talking baby talk, wanting to suck her baby brother's bottle, wanting to be held by her mother. In the repression story Jane keeps forgetting to tell her mother about gloves she has lost though she does tell her friends. In the rationalization story Jane says she's not going to eat some spinach because it makes you fat, though she does like to eat fattening foods like ice cream and candy. In the denial story Jane, who wants very much to go to a party, claims, once she falls sick, that she really never wanted to go.

As adults, we are continually making inferences about others' underlying motivations. It becomes therefore a pertinent developmental problem to explore how and when such inferences are learned. The use of these rudimentary paradigms of the mechanisms of adjustment has three advantages—their informality, their indirection, and their theoretical relevance. With respect to their informality, the mechanisms **per se** are not formally taught in school. Therefore their understanding should show relatively limited relation to factors associated with scholastic achievement or opportunity. Indirection refers to the point that the underlying motivations of feelings suggested in the stories are not simply isomorphic miniatures of overt behavior as might be exemplified in the inference—"He acted angry because he felt angry." Typically in these stories, the underlying intent or motive has a direction different from the ostensible direction of the behavior itself. When a person displaces, rationalizes, or projects, he is doing or saying one thing but intends and feels something quite different. Allowance is therefore made for a developmental subtlety of interpretive nuance. From the viewpoint of theoretical relevance the mechanisms of adjustment themselves have become an accepted part of the conceptual language of psychologists. They are no longer rooted in purely psychoanalytic frameworks but are also based in self- and behaviorally-oriented personality theory (Hilgard, 1949; Shaffer and Shoben, 1956) and even have relevance to social psychological conceptions of a cognitive consistency stripe (Abelson, 1959). Therefore, how the naive psychology of the child approaches or approximates our own technical conceptions becomes an interesting subject for exploration. Heider (1958), in his analysis of naive psychology, has noted our tendency to refer evanescent and complex behaviors to more permanent, invariant, and simplifying dispositions. The other person's intentions comprise a major species of such attributed dispositions. The study of the development of such intentional attributions thereby becomes part of the broader study of how our world is perceived as more stable as our explanations become more dispositional.

DEVELOPMENTAL TRENDS: RELATED LITERATURE

In a broad sense, cognition of psychology causality might include the tendency to refer physical events as well as personal behavior to underlying motivations and feelings. The inclusion of physical events makes it possible to trace three developmental trends.

THE ALLOCATION OF PURPOSE OF PERSONS

The first of these trends involves the progressive stripping away of ideas redolent with purpose and feeling from explanations of physical realities. Heinz Werner (1948) posits that the child's perception tends to be physiognomic. Inanimate objects seem to be permeated with inner life, as is the human physiognomy. For Werner, the young child's mental life has a strongly syncretic quality, so that perceptual activity is fused with those sensory-motor and emotional processes that mediate physiognomic interpretation. Growth involves therefore the differentiation among, and the organization of such primordially joined psychical systems as perception, cognition, emotion, action; thus leading to the attenuation of syncretically-based physiognomic tendencies.

The early work of Piaget (1960a, 1960b) on causality has also stressed the young child's animistic strain. However, Piaget sees the animistic decline in the older child as one aspect of a more general differentiation between an earlier pre-causal and a later causal stage. In this distinction, he has specified a number of pre-causal modes of thought, most of which involve what he calls the adherences of subjective schemata—involving life, consciousness, purpose and inner force—to external phenomena. The thinking of the pre-causal child (under 7-8 years) is dominated by any or all of nine cognitive modes—motivational thinking, finalism, phenomenistic causality, participation, magical causality, artificialistic causality, animistic causality and dynamic causality. The progressive diminution of imputations of feeling and consciousness to inanimate objects is described in the following Piagetian stages: In the first stage, all things are considered conscious, for example, a table would feel pain if it were broken. In the second stage, things that can move are conscious, for example, the sun and moon. A further delimitation comes in the third stage when only things that can move of their own accord are deemed conscious, for example, the wind, or as in the case of one child, the streams because they feel they are flowing. Finally consciousness is reserved only for animals and people.

A body of investigation has arisen in the attempt to test Piaget's hypotheses regarding the development of the child's causal conceptions. Some investigators (Deutsche, 1937; Huang, 1943; Jones & Arrington, 1945; Klingberg, 1957) have disputed Piaget's differentiation of pre-causal and causal levels on theoretical, empirical, and methodological grounds. The substance of these claims is: a) that children's intellectual development is continuous rather than salutatory, b) that experience plays a more dominant role in cognitive development than Piaget is willing to assign, c) that there is greater specificity in children's thought than the Piaget notion of global stages suggest, and d) that the clinical interview, with its unstandardized format, is an unreliable or biasing factor. More favorable to Piaget's views are the cross-cultural studies of Dennis and Russell (1940) who found evidence of the existence of pre-causal thinking among the Zuni and Hopi, and of Havighurst and Neugarten (1955) who found a plethora of animistic thinking among children in ten American Indian tribes. Probably the most intensive investigation of Piaget's causal theories is that of Laurendeau and Pinard (1962). The latter studied 500 Canadian children ranging from four to twelve years with a carefully designed questionnaire dealing with the concepts of dream, life, the origin of night, the movement of clouds, and the floating and sinking of objects. They report a definite developmental progression similar to Piaget's but comprising three rather than two stages—a pre-causal stage, a stage where causal and pre-causal thinking are combined, and stage of causal thought.

The theories of Piaget and Werner are strongly cognitive in nature. They both stress the child's intellectual difficulties in differentiating actions and movements which are purposive and personal from those which are impersonal and physical. Piaget's concept of egocentricity, in which he feels animistic thought is rooted, is a cognitive construct, underscoring the child's inability to differentiate his own from others' viewpoints.

Such conceptions are in contrast to those of a more dynamic type which relate animistic thinking to emotional and motivational factors. Freud (1931) has stressed the importance of what he calls the "omnipotence of thought" in the animistic practices among primitive people. By means of such practices, anthropomorphic forces are controlled or placated. He traces this omnipotence of thought ontogenetically to an earlier psycho-sexual state of narcissism, whereby the infant is able to arrogate to himself magical powers because of a libidinal fixation upon the self. This is primary process thinking; thinking dominated by the peremptory urges of id drives. Besides the condensations, symbolizations, and hallucinatory wish-fulfillments, which are hallmarks of primary process thinking, the later ego analysts (e.g., Arlow and Brenner, 1964; Hartmann, 1964), would also stress the more primitive ego defenses against id drives, e.g., the displacements and projections of subjective volitions and anxieties upon an objective world.

There are undoubtedly points of rapprochement between the cognitive and dynamic approaches, but their lines of cleavage cannot be ignored. The two approaches are of course rooted in quite different theoretical systems. But besides the dynamic and cognitive difference described above, there is another perhaps more basic divergence. The dynamic formulation is one variant of what might be called "transfer theories" of animism, i.e., the child transfers to the outside world impulses, desires, feelings that he experiences in himself. The sequence is basically a) some knowledge of one's own inner psychological nature, and b) the attribution of such a nature to outer objects. By contract, the cognitive theories are more "dissociation" theories. The sequence of events is a) a confusion between outer and inner phenomena, a confusion that is more maturationally that dynamically determined, and b) a differentiation—cognitive in nature, social and maturational in etiology—between the purposive attributes of people and the impersonal causality of things.

THE DIFFERENTIATION BETWEEN PURPOSE AND BEHAVIOR

A second developmental trend is the cognitive differentiation between outer behavior and inner feeling and intention. Piaget (1932) has distinguished between objective and subjective responsibility. In the former, the child assigns blame on the basis of the outer behavior with relatively little focus upon the intentions and purposes of the actor. Thus, the child who is in the earlier stage of objective responsibility will consider more blameworthy the person whose acts are most damaging or have the most ill effects—despite the excellent intentions of the actor.

He will deem as of lesser culpability the person whose behavior does not produce negative consequences— despite the ill intentions. In short, the younger person tends to ignore inner motivational conditions in favor of outer behavioral consequences. Kohlberg's reviews (1963, 1964) of the research findings attests to the general validity of this developmental generalization. He has noted that objective responsibility qualifies as a genuine developmental dimension. By this he means a dimension whose values change regularly with age in groups varying in cultural milieu, social class or religion. Environmental factors may accelerate or delay the appearance of the more mature stage of responsibility. However, they do not interfere with the occurrence of the successive stages of the sequence. For example, Caruso's study (1963) has shown that fully 87% of a sample of Belgian school children attain the stage of subjective responsibility at the age of 9-l0 years as compared to 46% at the 6—7 year level.

It should be stressed that the idea of a developmental dimension is not inconsistent with the possibility of other factors, either intrinsic or extrinsic, contributing independently to variation in intentionality. Consider I.Q. as exemplifying an intrinsic factor. P. Whiteman and Kosier (1964) have shown that *within* each of their age groups (7—8, 9—10, 11—12 years) there are significant shifts with increased I.Q. toward choices indicating greater subjective responsibility.

A more extrinsic independent variable is afforded by experimental treatments designed to affect performance in intentionality within particular age groups. Crowley (1968) trained first graders through presentation of pairs of moral judgment stories. Each pair highlighted differences in intentionality, but the consequences were kept constant. He found that the training groups received significantly more mature scores on the posttraining test of subjective responsibility than did the control group which had received no training. Bandura and McDonald (1963) also successfully induced change in children's responses to stories tapping objective and subjective responsibility. The change was in the direction of the model's behavior. Models demonstrating objective responsibility made "subjective" children emit more objective responsibility responses. The modeling of subjective responsibility preferences produced a shift in the "objective" children to more subjective responsibility choices.

A basic issue is whether the effectiveness of the experimental treatments in the Bandura and McDonald, and Crowley studies is an embarrassment to Piaget's stage theory of morality. Bandura and McDonald, in consistency with a social learning approach, see the ready modifiability of intentionality as impinging on the utility of Piaget's theory. Insofar as the latter stresses slow, sequential development the experiments highlight conditions under which "development" is rapid and, on occasion, regressive. Turiel (1966, 1968) (and Crowley is in agreement) disputes this interpretation, pointing out that Piaget's theory is concerned with a broadly conceived heteronomous vs. autonomous orientation. The latter comprises a number of dimensions, only one of which is objective and subjective responsibility. From this viewpoint, the experimental conditions have successfully produced what is probably a transient change in relatively specific responses rather than permanent change in a broader underlying structure. However, an empirical test is needed; one which involves determining whether induced change in intentionality generalizes to the other Piagetian dimensions of morality, e.g., fixity of rules, absolutism of value, immanent justice.

Aside from its susceptibility to extrinsic and intrinsic factors, the developmental dimension of objective—subjective responsibility is open to interpolation and extrapolation. As for interpolation, Heider (1958) has noted the theoretical possibility, at least, of an intermediate stage between objective and subjective responsibility. In this stage, responsibility is assigned to the person who should have tried harder or attempted to know more, or should have been more careful or concerned, and so on. The person is blamed neither for damaging consequences nor for specific, bad intentions, so that neither intentionality nor effect comprise criteria for culpability. One would expect this stage to be associated with age ranges between seven and ten, *i.e.,* after the decline of objective responsibility and before the onset of full subjective responsibility, but the evidence remains to be gathered.

The work of two Israeli investigators (Breznitz and Kugelmass, 1967; Kugelmass and Breznitz, 1968) has highlighted an extrapolation of the intentionality in moral judgment. Studying a sample of over a thousand Israeli children, they have found a steady increase on the intentionality score from ages 11-17, with a relatively rapid period of acceleration from ages 14 through 17.

THE DEVELOPING COMPLEXITY OF PURPOSE

A third trend involves the development of conceptions of psychological causality from more simple to more complex levels. There are several dimensions of complexity operative here. Heider (1958) has specified two criteria by means of which the "naive psychologist" might distinguish between personal causality (or perceived intentionality) and physical causality: a) local cause, that is, a perceived source of the observed instrumental behaviors, and b) equifinality, or the perceived convergence of the various behaviors upon one particular end or goal. Heider's analysis focuses therefore upon three aspects of cognized intention: a) a source of behavior, b) the goals or ends of behavior, and c) the instrumental and equifinal actions. Using this framework we can trace three developmental trends in the conceptions of psychological causality.

There is first of all an increased awareness with age of the relativity of the *source* of the intention. Thus Lerner (1937) studied the responses of 112 boys aged 6—13 to an item, calling for the grasp of perspectives of different individuals in the same social situation. He found that the older children were able to give more relativistic and situation specific judgments, i.e., were able to differentiate feelings and/or behavior in accordance with the shifts in the status quo of the actor. Feffer (1959) developed a role taking test (RTT) calling for the ability to decenter perspectives from one actor to another. Feffer and Gourevitch (1960), studying children from ages 6—14, and Sullivan and Hunt (1967), working with children aged 7—11, found that the older children had greater facility for this social decentering. In Flavell's study (1966), children from grades 2—11 were given the choice of either removing a dime from one cup or a nickel from another while the experimenter (**E**) was out of the room. The **E** was then to choose which of the two cups was empty and which contained a coin—either the nickel or the dime. Flavell found that the choice of most of the younger children, grades 2—6, was guided by their assessment of **E**'s motives with respect to the game materials, stating for example, that **E** would choose the dime cup because he would get much more money if he guessed correctly. This attribution is basically rooted in the child's own desires for the larger coin. The older children however, were influenced additionally by the possibility that the **E** might have a different intentional viewpoint, that he might be attempting to assess the children's own motives. An older child might hypothesize, for example, that **E** might think the child is trying to fool him. The older children's ability to differentiate their own motivational perspective from that of the experimenter indicates their enhanced ability to accommodate to varying sources of intention.

With respect to the cognition of *goals*, there is increased complexity and symbolization. Gourevitch and Feffer (1962) using the RTT, have noted that older children, 10-13 years, cited a significantly greater number of external reinforcers, *e.g.*, pleasurable objects, material goods, than younger children, 6—9 years. Gollin (1958) had children and adults write opinions of the actions of a boy shown in four filmed situations. Three groups were studied (mean ages of 11, 14, and 17). There was a steadily increasing number of motivational inferences with increased age. Besides these quantitative differences in a sheer number of rewards of motives postulated, there is also a qualitative shift toward less concrete and more internalized goals. Gourevitch and Feffer (1962) found that the goals described by adults were much more symbolic (*e.g.*, generalized esteem and self-actualization) than those of the children's groups. Similarly, Kohlberg (1963a) has reported age associated with more internalized and generalized conceptions of what others' goals should or should not be. At the youngest levels, it is punishment by another which is defined as bad; at a second stage, immorality is related to more general disapproval by others or censure by legitimate authorities; while at a third stage, actions which are bad are identified with community disrespect or self condemnation.

The *instrumental* behaviors are more clearly perceived with increasing age. Thus Gollin (1958) in the experimental situation described above, found that among the older age groups there was a much more concerted attempt to account for contradictory behavior by postulating an underlying motive. These diverse behaviors then, are seen more clearly by the older groups as belonging to a family of equifinal actions rather than as discrete behaviors, each having its discrete underlying motive.

Concomitant with the changes specified above in the realm of psychological causality, there are a number of changes in the area of conception of physical objects. An integrating concept is the ability to decenter. Thus, for Piaget (1960) the intuitive child of 4–7, as contrasted with the concrete operational child (ages 7–11), has difficulty decentering from a focus on a limited aspect of the situation, obviating therefore the possibility of a coordination among several viewpoints. In the conservation of liquid substance, there is a focus upon one salient element, *e.g.*, the height to which the water is poured rather than a coordinate attention to the decreased width. In class inclusion problems, there is a centering on one attribute of the object with a consequent inability to see the object as simultaneously belonging to two classes, each defined by separate but coexisting attributes. For example, the child may not realize that an object can be both brown and wooden. Therefore he does not grasp that in an array of wooden blocks, only some of which are brown, that there are more wooden than brown ones. Similarly, difficulties in cognition of transitivity might stem from the fact that the child cannot see this middle–sized stick as simultaneously smaller than one, but longer than another.

An interesting question is whether decentering ability is general enough to produce significant associations between items of diverse content—physical and interpersonal. The research evidence is equivocal. Feffer and Gourevitch (1960) found a significant relation between decentering of physical objects, as manifested by conservation of substance and interpersonal decentering, as measured by RTT. On the other hand, Sullivan and Hunt (1967) failed to find consistent relations between objective and interpersonal decentering among their seven and nine year old groups, though the association was significant among the 11–year–olds.

SOME PROBLEMS AND RESEARCH FINDINGS

The above discussion suggests a series of problems related to conceptions of psychological causality, in the narrower sense of comprehension of the simplified paradigms of the defense mechanisms. These problems deal with 1) the question of age differences, 2) the relation between development of conceptions of psychological causality and the decline of animistic tendencies, 3) the relation between conceptions of psychological causality and indices of objective decentering, *e.g.*, performance on conservation problems, 4) the relation between conceptions of psychological causality and the development of more mature moral judgments based on the actor's intentions rather than on behavioral effects, 5) the role of more general intellectual and/or linguistic abilities, *e.g.*, mediating age differences on psychological causality and measures of intentional responsibility, 6) whether ethnic-class differences are associated with variation in conceptions of psychological causality.

Some of these problems have been explored in two studies reported earlier (M. Whiteman, 1967); some in a recently completed study (M. Whiteman, Lukoff, and Breining, 1968), and some in an ongoing project.

PREVIOUS RESEARCH

The two earlier studies have been concerned with:
I) Exploration of differences in conceptions of psychological causality between children at the intuitive age (5-6 years) and children at the concrete operational level (ages 8-9).

As noted above, Piaget has emphasized that the transition from the earlier to the later state implies a decentering of the more perceptually salient and changeable aspects of objects to their more stable and conceptual dimensions. It was felt therefore that a similar shift may occur in the cognition of interpersonal behavior, whereby emphasis may change from a centering upon the more overt behaviors to the less salient underlying motivations.

2) The study of intellectual differences with respect to conceptions of psychological causality.

3) The study of the relation between conception of psychological and physical causality, with specific focus on the development decline in animistic tendencies.

The first study involved 42 children; 21 kindergarten children matched by sex and I.Q. with 21 third graders. The second study comprised 70 children; 36 of whom were in kindergarten, 34 in the third grade. All children were Negro or Puerto Rican and drawn from two schools in the Harlem area of New York City.

The major findings of these two studies were as follows:

I) In each of the two studies, a Motivation Index was constructed from cumulated weights assigned to categorizations of the stories exemplifying the mechanisms of adjustment. These indices were quite susceptible to age differences. In both studies some 90% of the five to six year old children fell below the median score of the third graders.

2) An Animism Scale was constructed based on a series of questions originally constructed by Laurendeau and Pinard (1962). The child was asked whether each of 21 objects was alive. The score on the Animism Scale was the number of correct responses given by the child.

The Motivation Index was not significantly related to the Animism Scale. The independence of these two scales suggests a considerable independence in the rate and timing of development for the individual child of his conceptions of physical and psychological causality. The two indices of causal conception were not related despite the significant association of each to the age—grade variable. The older children were more sophisticated with reference to the Motivation Index and less "animistic".

3) The relation between age and conceptions of psychological causality (as assessed by the Motivation Index) was stronger than the relation between age and conceptions of physical causality (as assessed by the Animism Scale). For children who were homogeneous in Motivation Index Score, the relation between age and animism score ceased to be significant. However, the reverse was not true; the relation between age and the Motivation Index was still highly significant even among a group of children who were homogeneous in Animism Score.

4) In the first study, higher I.Q. was associated with higher scores on the Motivation Index. The I.Q. differences on the Motivation Index was significantly sharper among the girls than among the boys at both age levels, and stronger among the third graders as compared to the kindergarten children. However, these significant differences with respect to I.Q. were not obtained in the second study.

CURRENT RESEARCH

A recently completed study (M. Whiteman, Lukoff, and Breining, 1968) represents an extension of the preliminary studies into a number of different areas.

A first aim was the exploration of the relation between age and conceptions of psychological causality within an older age range. In the previous study the stories were too difficult even for many of the older children. It was considered desirable to extend the age range studied in order to determine whether there is continued growth in this ability beyond the upper eight-year-old level of the previous study.

A second aim was to determine whether age differences on the psychological causality measures were merely a reflection of broader cognitive and linguistic differences. Put more operationally—would age differences vanish if developmental differences on cognitive or linguistic variables were controlled?

A third aim was the exploration of the relation between conceptions of psychological causality and measures of conservation. In the preceding study, the differentiation between Piagetian stages was made on the basis of chronological age rather than behaviorally, and a direct study of the problem is indicated.

A fourth aim was the exploration of the relation between the growth of conceptions of psychological causality and the decline in what Piaget has conceptualized as objective morality, *i.e.*, the basing of moral judgments on the consequences of an act with relatively little consideration of the motivations and purposes of the actor. One would expect the growth of understanding of psychological causality to parallel the growth of moral judgments based on the other's intentions and purposes rather than on the sheer effect of his action.

Subjects

The subjects were 55 children, predominantly white and male, and ranging from eight through eleven years. This group comprises a complete count of the children in this age range living in a residential institution at time of testing. Because of the sectarian nature of the institution, nearly all of the children were Jewish. It should be pointed out that many of these children were placed because of emotional disturbance in a context of familial instability.

Procedure

The battery included a) seven psychological causality stories, b) six sets of stories dealing with Piaget's distinction between objective and subjective conceptions of responsibility, c) a measure of verbal conceptualization, the Similarities scale of the children's Wechsler, and d) items dealing with conservation of weight, mass, and number.

In order to achieve some standardization of the interview and to control for linguistic and memory differences, a series of probes was devised for each of the psychological causality stories. The more indirect probes were administered first and were followed up by the more direct probes if the indirect ones were unsuccessful in yielding a suitable response. The responses to each story were analyzed for the separate elements that made up the defense mechanism in question. Thus in the case of the displacement story, there were three elements that were categorized separately. These elements included a) whether the child recognized the deprivation associated with the ice cream disappointment, for example, "She didn't get what she was promised," b) whether there was an expression of appropriate emotion, *e.g.*, feeling sad or bad at loss of the ice cream, and c) whether the spanking of the dolls was seen as a displacement of anger, *e.g.*, "Because she didn't get any ice cream and she was mad and she had to take it out on the dolls." The overall percentage of agreement between independent coders was 88, with 80 as the lowest percent agreement for any one element. Based on the study of the intercorrelations among the story categories, a composite index was formed by cumulating scores from five of the seven stories dealing with psychological causality. These were the stories dealing with displacement, regression, repression, rationalization, and denial. The wishful dreaming story was omitted because of its limited range—most of the children got the point of it. The projection story was omitted because of its low degree of relationship with the other stories. For most of the stories included in the index, the children received credit for an element if the response was correct spontaneously, or followed an indirect probe. The median contingency coefficient expressing the relation between the score on a story and the total score was .55 with a range from .46 to .65. This index will be referred to as the Motivation Index.

The stories dealing with objective versus subjective responsibility were adapted from those presented by Piaget (1932). Piaget's stories fell into three major areas—clumsiness, stealing, and lying. Two sets of stories from each area were selected. For example, in the clumsiness area the objective responsibility story described a child who had inadvertently broken 15 cups while the subjective responsibility story described one who had broken only one cup, but whose intention was to obtain some forbidden jam. Under the stealing heading, an objective responsibility story dealt with a child who stole "a big loaf of bread" to help a poor friend as compared to another child, exemplifying a subjective responsibility theme, who stole a small crayon—but for herself. In connection with the lying rubric, a boy who tried to be helpful caused a man to lose his way and was compared with another child who tried to mislead a man who, however, did not get lost. Scoring criteria were based on a suitable rationale for selecting as least culpable the child whose negative behaviors were extenuated by more positive intentions. The overall percentage of agreement between independent coders was 96, with no story below 93%. A composite index was formed based on cumulated scores from the six Piaget morality stories. The median contingency coeffiecient expressing the relation between the score on a story and the total score was .50 with a range from .31 to .59. This index will be referred to as the Subjective Responsibility Index. Within each of the two batteries—the psychological causality and the moral judgment—the stories were presented in random order and the responses tape recorded.

Three types of conservation problems were used—conservation of weight, mass, and number. Research by Lovell and Ogilvie (1960, 1961) had indicated that the conservation of weight presented a more difficult task than conservation of mass or substance and was therefore a more appropriate task for this age group. In each of these problems the child was presented with a standard and a comparison stimulus. Care was taken to have the child perceive both the standard and comparison as equivalent either in weight (a scale balance was used), or in mass, or in number—depending upon the problem. The comparison stimulus was then altered. In the case of the weight and mass problems, where the stimuli with plasticine balls, the comparison stimulus was elongated. In the case of the number problem, where the stimuli were rows of **M and M** candies, the comparison row of candies was stretched out and made less dense. The child was then questioned as to whether the two stimuli were now the same or different in the relevant attribute. If the child was able to conserve on the most difficult conservation task (weight), he was given a score of 3. If he failed this task, he was assigned a score of 2, 1, or 0 depending on whether he had conserved on two, one, or none of the remaining tasks.

Results

Age differences and psychological causality.

Table 1 indicates a significant relationship between age and score on the Motivation Index. None of the eight, nine, or ten-year-olds were able to score at the highest levels of the Motivation Index, *i.e.*, to get the point of at least four of the five stories. However, 44% of the 11-year-olds were able to obtain scores in this range.

An analysis of covariance, partialing out the language measure, reveals that the age differences are still significant (P < .05). This failure of the verbal conceptualization measure, the Similarities test, to account for the age differences is due mainly to its lack of significant association with the Motivation Index. However the language

TABLE 1

Age as Related to Motivation Index Score

Motivation Index Score	Age in Years			
	8	9	10	11
4,5	0	0	0	11
2,3	3	7	8	9
0,1	3	4	5	5

$X^2 = 16.60$, DF = 4, p < .01

(Age categories 8-9 collapsed for adequate theoretical frequencies.)

measure was significantly associated both with age and with the Subjective Responsibility Index (P < .05, P < .01 respectively) attesting to its ability to make significant differentiations within this group.

Conservation and psychological causality.

An analysis of variance indicates a significant relation between conservation performance and the Motivation Index (see Table 2). The highest scoring conservers received a significantly higher mean on the Motivation Index than those who failed to conserve in at least one of the conservation tasks (means of 2.65 and 1.56 respectively).

TABLE 2

Analysis of Variance of Motivation Index as Related to Conservation Performance

Source	Sum of Squares	DF	Mean Square	F
Conservation				
Groups	13.51	1	13.51	7.58*
Within Groups	94.52	53	1.78	
Total	108.03			

*P < .01

Table 3 reveals that of the 16 who failed to conserve on at least one of the conservation tasks, only one was able to score at the upper level of the Motivation

TABLE 3

Motivation Index Score as Related to Conservation Measure

Motivation Index Score	Conservation Score			
	0	1	2	3
4,5	0	0	1	10
2,3	0	4	2	21
0,1	1	5	3	8

X^2 = 7.44, DF = 2, P < .05
(Conservation scores 0,1,2 combined for adequate theoretical frequencies.)

Index, that is, to get the point of at least four out of the five stories. In the highest scoring conserver group, more than five times this proportion were able to score at the higher levels on the Motivation Index. An analysis of covariance, controlling for age, revealed that the conservation differences on the Motivation Index was still significant (P < .05).

Subjective responsibility and psychological causality.
The Motivation Index, derived from the psychological causality stories, was significantly related at the .01 level to the Subjective Responsibility Index. It can be seen from Table 4, that of the 11 children scoring high on the Motivation Index (getting the point of at least four stories), seven scored in the highest range on the Subjective Responsibility measure (getting at least five of the six stories correct). By contrast, only one of the 17 children scoring low on the Motivation Index was able to score high on the Subjective Responsibility measure. Analyses of covariance, controlling for age and for differences on the language measure, revealed that this relation between the psychological causality and the subjective responsibility measures was still significant at the .01 level. The Similarities and conservation measures show different patterns of association with the Motivation and Intentional Responsibility indices. The conservation, but not the verbal conceptualization measure, is significantly related to the Motivation Index. On the other hand, it is the Similarities test but not the conservation measure which is significantly associated with the Subjective Responsibility Index.

DISCUSSION

Bringing together the findings from these three studies suggests the following: Our first developmental trend is the allocation of purpose to people and its conceptual divorce from things. In line with this general trend, we have found that the decline of animism and the development of psychological causality both occur during the

TABLE 4
Relation between the Motivation and Subjective
Responsibility Indices

Subjective Responsibility Index Score	Motivation Index Score		
	0,1	2,3	4,5
5,6	1	13	7
3,4	9	9	4
0,1,2	7	5	0

$X^2 = 13.72$, DF = 4, P < .01

ages 5-6 to 8-9. These two developments however take place with some degree of independence in the individual child. This implies that the more differentiated development of ideas of intention and feeling as cause of personal behavior shows a limited relation to the stripping away of ideas of purpose from physical events. A given child may attribute purpose only (or mainly) to people. He may not, however, have a differentiated view of such purpose. Another child's thinking may be more animistic, but at the same time his thinking about people's motives may be more subtle, complex, indirect, abstract. Part of the explanation may lie in the variables of mental and chronological age. The decline of animism seems more related to mental age; the growth of conceptions of psychological causality more to chronological age. Thus, selecting children who vary in chronological age, but have similar mental ages, tends to eliminate differences in animism, but not in conceptions of psychological causality; controlling for animism level still leaves the relation between chronological age and psychological causality a significant one. The failure to replicate significant relations between I.Q. and Motivation Index is also consistent with this interpretation. There is the suggestion here then, that nonintellective aspects of chronological age differences may contribute to differences in conceptions of psychological causality. In the preliminary studies, the children were of economically and socially disadvantaged backgrounds. Here "psychological mindedness" on the part of the parents would tend to be minimized because of educational limitations and because stringent economic demands leave little time for parental elaborations on or explanation of motivational realities (Hess and Shipman, 1965). Indeed the very language the parents use in these strata, as pointed out by Bernstein (1961), tends to be relatively weak in causal nuance, abstract connotation, or emotional labeling. Time, however, brings continued exposure to adult conceptions and formulations of motivation. Hence the pronounced age differences.

A second developmental trend discussed above was concerned with growth in the complexity of motivational conceptions. Our evidence indicates a progressive growth in the conceptions of the mechanisms of adjustment. From the viewpoint of our discussion the difficulty experienced by the younger children is quite understandable. The goals of the behavior described in the stories tend to be abstract rather than tangible environmental entities. These goals may involve self-protection or self-defense as for example in the displacement, rationalization, and denial stories. Secondly, the behaviors as instrumental activities are indirect; they have a detour like quality, *e.g.*, the child hits the doll but really means to punish the mother; the child says she doesn't want to go to the party but really wants to go. The overt behavior masks an inward intention and the differentiation of the two is no mean conceptual task. Third, with respect to the source of the intention, the child subject must be able to take the varying viewpoints of Jane in her various encounters described in the stories. Jane is embedded in different social contexts in the various stories and different motivations appropriate to these contents are being demanded.

Though there are strong differences between the concrete operational children and the intuitive children, the evidence of the more recent study suggests that a grasp of most of the stories is associated with children at a still older age level. Thus the finding of a kind of spurt occurring among the eleven-year-olds would suggest perhaps an acceleration in these abilities as the child approaches the Piagetian stage of formal operations, beginning at about ten or eleven years old. This would be consistent with Piaget's notion of the psychological underpinning for formal operations insofar as these situations require a relatively high level of abstraction in conception of goal, an imagined possibility of viewpoint, and a dissociation of hypothetical intention from the empirical data of behavior. There is congruency also with the findings of Flavell (1966), Gollin (1968), Gourevitch and Feffer (1952), and Kugelmass and Breznitz (1968) that motivational understanding reaches a kind of flowering during the period of formal operations beginning at about eleven years.

However we do not have any direct evidence that the age differences *merely* reflect the development of broader cognitive skills. Controls on language development and on ability to conserve, two facets of cognitive growth, indicate the age differences on our measure of cognized psychological causality still obtain. The study of significant sociocultural, interpersonal and emotional experiences which accompany growth in this area of cognized intentions would be an interesting next step.

Our findings also indicate the cognition of psychological causality does show a significant relation to the conservation measures. The finding that this relation exists despite control on age suggests the possibility of a more general ability to decenter which may be operative within the age levels studied and which may span physical and behavioral content. These results parallel those of Feffer and Gourevitch (1960) who found significant relations between physical and interpersonal measures of decentering (conservation of substance and RTT). Whatever the nature of the underlying ability, it seems to operate more as a necessary than as a sufficient condition. The failure to conserve tends to preclude success on the psychological causality stories much more than conservation attainment guarantees it. It may be that our measures of conservation are too unreliable, are not difficult enough, or that we require independent assessment of formal operations before success on the psychological causality stories can be more accurately predicted.

A third developmental trend cited above dealt with the differentiation between purpose and behavior as exemplified in the development of subjective responsibility, or intentionality as a basis for moral judgment. Our findings indicate that cognition of psychological causality is related to Piaget's concept of intentional responsibility. The controls on age and language development suggest the possibility of a more intrinsic relationship, namely that cognition of intention may be causally related to cognition of intentional morality. A sensitivity to people's feelings and intentions may be a precondition to the use of such awareness in evaluating others. Of course the reverse may be true—a morality which stresses intention may stimulate a perceptiveness of intention. The former possibility is perhaps more appealing, particularly in view of the finding of Crowley (1968) that experimental training in perceiving the intentionality aspect of moral judgment problems results in increased readiness to make judgments based on subjective responsibility. If Crowley's training procedures induces a sensitivity to motivation that is analagous to the "naturally" increased intentional awareness of those scoring high on the Motivation Index, a causal direction is suggested. But interpretive problems aside, we are currently attempting to replicate these findings with larger and more normative samples.

This research was supported by a grant from the National Institute of Child Health and Human Development (No. HD 02574-02). The assistance of Judith Lukoff in the collection and analysis of some of the findings presented here is gratefully acknowledged. Kimberly Breining served as an interviewer in one of the studies. Thanks are extended to Dr. Jack Adler, Mr. Irving Rabinow, and Mr. Paul Steinfeld of the Jewish Child Care Association for their cooperation.

References

Abelson, Robert P. "Modes of resolution of belief dilemmas." CONFLICT RESOLUTION, 3: 343-352, 1959.

Arlow, J. A. & Brenner, C. PSYCHOANALYTIC CONCEPTS AND THE STRUCTURAL THEORY. New York: International Universities Press, 1964.

Bandura, A. & McDonald, F. J. "Influence of social reinforcement and the behavior of models in shaping children's moral judgments." JOURNAL OF ABNORMAL AND SOCIAL PSYCHOLOGY, 67: 274-281, 1963.

Bernstein, B. "Social class and linguistic development: a theory of social learning." In A. H. Halsey, J. Floud, C. A. Anderson (Eds.) EDUCATION, ECONOMY, AND SOCIETY. New York: Macmillan, 288-314, 1961.

Breznitz, S. and Kugelmass, S. "Intentionality in moral judgment: developmental stages." CHILD DEVELOPMENT, 409-479, 1967.

Caruso, I. H. "La notion de responsibilite et du justice immanente chez l'enfant." ARCHIVES DE PSYCHOLOGIE, V. 29, 1943, No. 114. Cited in Kohlberg, L. "Moral development and identification." CHILD PSYCHOLOGY, The Sixty-second Yearbook of The National Society for the Study of Education. University of Chicago Press, 227-332, 1963.

Crowley, P. M. "Effect of training upon objectivity of moral judgment in grade school children." JOURNAL OF PERSONALITY AND SOCIAL PSYCHOLOGY, 3: 228-232, 1968.

Dennis, W. & Russell, R. W. "Piaget's questions applied to Zuni children." CHILD DEVELOPMENT, 11: 181-187, 1940.

Deutsche, J. M. "The development of children's concepts of causal relations." Minnesota: UNIVERSITY OF MINNESOTA INSTITUTE OF CHILD WELFARE MONOGRAPHS, 1937.

Feffer, M. H. "The cognitive implication of role taking behavior." JOURNAL OF PERSONALITY, 27: 152-168, 1959.

Feffer, M. H. & Gourevitch, V. "Cognitive aspects of role taking in children." JOURNAL OF PERSONALITY, 28: 383-396, 1960.

Flavell, J. H. "The development of two related forms of cognition: role taking and verbal communication." In Kidd, A. H. and Rivoire, J. L. (Eds.) PERCEPTUAL DEVELOPMENT IN CHILDREN, New York: International Universities Press, 246-271, 1966.

Freud, S. TOTEM AND TABOO. New York: New Republic, Inc., 1931.

Gollin, E. S. "Organizational characteristics of social judgments: a developmental investigation." JOURNAL OF PERSONALITY, 26: 139-154, 1958.

Gourevitch, V. & Feffer, M. H. "A study of motivational development." JOURNAL OF GENETIC PSYCHOLOGY, 100: 361-375, 1962.

Hartmann, H. ESSAYS ON EGO PSYCHOLOGY; SELECTED PROBLEMS IN PSYCHOANALYTIC THEORY. New York: International Universities Press, 1964.

Havighurst, R. J. & Neugarten, B. L. "Belief in immanent justice and animism." In Havighurst, R. J. (Eds.), AMERICAN AND WHITE CHILDREN: A SOCIO—PSYCHOLOGICAL INVESTIGATION. Chicago: University of Chicago Press, 1955.

Heider, F. THE PSYCHOLOGY OF INTERPERSONAL RELATIONS. New York: Wiley and Sons, 1958.

Hess, R. D. & Shipman, V. C. "Early experience and the socialization of cognitive modes in children." CHILD DEVELOPMENT, 36: 869-886, 1965.

Hilgard, E. "Human motives and the concept of the self." AMERICAN PSYCHOLOGIST, 4: 374-382, 1949.

Huang, I. "Children's concepts of physical causality: a critical summary." JOURNAL OF GENETIC PSYCHOLOGY, 63: 71-121, 1943.

Jones, F. N. & Arrington, M. G. "The explanation of physical phenomena given by white and negro children." COMPARATIVE PSYCHOLOGY MONOGRAPHS, Vol. 18 (No. 5), 1945.

Klingberg, G. "The distinction between living and not living among 7 to 10-year- old children, with some remarks concerning the so-called animism controversy." JOURNAL OF GENETIC PSYCHOLOGY, 90: 227-238, 1957.

Kohlberg, L. "The development of children's orientations toward a moral order." I. "Sequence in the development of moral thought." VITA HUMANA, 6: 11-33, 1963a.

Kohlberg, L."Moral development and identification." In Stevenson, H. W. (Ed.) CHILD PSYCHOLOGY. THE SIXTY—SECOND YEARBOOK OF THE NATIONAL SOCIETY FOR THE STUDY OF EDUCATION. Part I. Chicago: University of Chicago Press, 227-332, 1963b.

Kohlberg, L. "Development of moral character and moral ideology." In Hoffman, M. L. and Hoffman, L. W. (Eds.) REVIEW OF CHILD DEVELOPMENT RESEARCH. V. 1, New York: Russell Sage Foundation, 383-431, 1964.

Kugelmass, S. & Breznitz, S. "Intentionality in moral judgment: Adolescent development." CHILD DEVELOPMENT, 39: 250-256, 1968.

Laurendeau, Monique. CASUAL THINKING IN THE CHILD. New York: International Universities Press, 1962.

Lerner, E. "The problem of perspective in moral reasoning." AMERICAN JOURNAL OF SOCIOLOGY, 43: 249-269, 1937.

Lovell, K. and Ogilvie, E. "A study of conservation of substance in junior high children." BRITISH JOURNAL OF EDUCATIONAL PSYCHOLOGY, 30: 109-118, 1960.

Lovell, K. and Ogilvie, E. "A study of conservation of weight in junior school children," BRITISH JOURNAL OF EDUCATIONAL PSYCHOLOGY, 31: 138-144, 1961.

Piaget, J. THE MORAL JUDGMENT OF THE CHILD. New York: Collier Books, 1962. (First published in 1932.)

Piaget, J. THE CHILD'S CONCEPTIONS OF PHYSICAL CAUSALITY. Paterson, New Jersey: Littlefield, Adams & Co., 1960a. (First published in 1930).

Piaget, J. THE CHILD'S CONCEPTION OF THE WORLD. Paterson, New Jersey: Littlefield, Adams & Co., 1960b. (First published in 1929.)

Piaget, J. THE PSYCHOLOGY OF INTELLIGENCE. New York: Harcourt Brace, 1960c.

Shaffer, L. F. & Shoben, E. J. THE PSYCHOLOGY OF ADJUSTMENT. Cambridge, Mass.: The Riverside Press, 1956.

Sullivan, E. V. & Hunt, D. E. "Interpersonal and objective decentering as a function of age and social class." JOURNAL OF GENETIC PSYCHOLOGY, 110: 199-210, 1967.

Turiel, E. "An experimental test of the sequentiality of developmental stages in the child's moral judgments." JOURNAL OF PERSONALITY AND SOCIAL PSYCHOLOGY, 6: 611-618, 1966.

Turiel, E. (In press) "Developmental processes in the child's moral thinking." In P. Mussen, J. Langer, and M. Covington (Eds.) NEW DIRECTIONS IN DEVELOPMENTAL PSYCHOLOGY. Holt, Rinehart and Winston, 1968.

Werner, H. COMPARATIVE PSYCHOLOGY OF MENTAL DEVELOPMENT. Chicago, Illinois: Follett, 1948.

Whiteman, M. "Children's conceptions of psychological causality." CHILD DEVELOPMENT, 38: 143-156, 1967.

Whiteman, M., Lukoff, J. R., & Breining, K. DEVELOPMENT OF CONCEPTIONS OF PSYCHOLOGICAL CAUSALITY. Paper presented at the meeting of The Eastern Psychological Association, Washington, D. C., April, 1968.

Whiteman, P. H. & Kosier, K. P. "Development of children's moralistic judgments: age, sex, I.Q., and certain personal—experimental variables." CHILD DEVELOPMENT, 35: 843-850, 1964.

SOME RECENT TRENDS IN THE STUDY
OF SOCIAL JUDGMENT *

Melvin Manis, Ph.D.

When I was first asked to participate in today's symposium, I readily agreed, feeling that it was an excellent opportunity to honor a man I admire for his diverse and imaginative contributions to social psychology. As is so common in these matters, however, as I started to prepare my talk, I felt increasing anxiety, wondering just what I should say. One possibility, that I dismissed as being excessively historical for an audience of this sort, was a talk which simply outlined some of Professor Sherif's more important contributions, perhaps concluding with a paean of praise for the man's work and for the man himself. While my comments will include many of these ingredients, I would mainly like to focus on some recent developments in the study of social judgment that have emerged in the years following Sherif and Hovland's pioneering work (1952, 1961).

First, I would like to call your attention to some promising methodological developments. An outstanding example, is, of course, Professor Sherif's introduction of the own-categories technique for the assessment of attitude and ego involvement (1965). Through this procedure, the respondent is not characterized simply in terms of a preferred *point* on the attitude continuum; instead, attention is also drawn to his latitude of acceptance, his latitude of rejection, and perhaps most importantly, the range of items to which the respondent is *indifferent*.

Professor Sherif and his co-workers have called particular attention to the systematic manner in which extremity of attitude is related to the respondent's latitudes of rejection and indifference. They have repeatedly shown that people with extreme views on an issue typically *reject* more items than do those who are relatively uncommitted; moreover, the extremist is indifferent to relatively *few* items, when compared to subjects who favor the neutralist position.

These data have been generally interpreted as evidence that a wide latitude of rejection and a narrow latitude of indifference may be regarded as indicators of personal involvement with the issue at hand. Additional support for this position, derived from a rather different methodology, has been provided by Zimbardo (1960). In Zimbardo's study, subjects read a fictitious case history concerning a juvenile delinquent; they then responded to a series of opinion statements regarding

*Talk prepared for presentation at the Division 8 symposium in honor of Muzafer Sherif, APA Convention, 1966, New York City. All statements are those of the author and do not necessarily represent the opinions or policy of the Veterans Administration.

the relative importance of the youth's background vs. his personal responsibility for the crime he had committed. Involvement was heightened for half the subjects by leading them to believe that their responses were a good indicator of their basic personalities, social values, and outlook on important life problems. The remaining subjects, who were presumably less intensely involved, were informed that the case was too short to learn much from their reactions. The results indicated that the involved group rejected more opinion statements as being unacceptable than did their less involved classmates. Thus, as predicted from the own-category formulation, heightened ego involvement was accompanied by an increased readiness to reject statements that conflicted with the respondent's views.

There is yet another study using a rather different methodological approach that I believe is relevant to this discussion. In this study, Alice Eagly and myself (Eagly and Manis, 1966) presented a group of junior high school students with two messages, both of which argued that teen-agers should be more strictly controlled. One message contended that delinquency among teen-age boys could be reduced if they were provided with stricter rules, while the other held that mothers should strictly control their daughters' clothing selections, so as to prevent unwise choices. As you may have anticipated, these views were somewhat discrepant with the initial attitudes of our subjects.

The subjects' task was to rate the two experimental messages with respect to *fairness* and *writing style;* they were also to rate the authors' *personalities,* and were to indicate how *well-informed* they appeared to be. In analyzing the results, we assumed that the girls in our sample would be quite involved in the issue of clothing selection and rather less concerned with the problem of delinquency among teen-age boys. In contrast, we assumed that this involvement pattern would be reversed for the boys.

Our data were consistent with the underlying assumptions of the own-categories procedure. That is, in responding to these experimental messages, both of which challenged their beliefs, our subjects reacted more negatively when the topic was *involving,* than they did when they were relatively *uninvolved;* moreover, this negative reaction was *not* attributable to attitude differences between the boys and girls in our sample.

The studies cited above constitute a set of three converging operations which jointly support the assumption that increases in ego involvement enhance the likelihood that divergent attitude stands will be rejected as unacceptable.

While this assumption may warrant still further investigation, I would like to think that we have now reached a stage in this research where we can subtly measure ego-involvement through the own-categories procedure, and then investigate the impact of this variable upon *other* aspects of behavior. For example, in Zimbardo's study, he found that subjects whose views changed toward the beliefs that were ostensibly favored by their friends, tended to be people with a broad latitude of acceptance and a narrow latitude of rejection. Presumably, these were people who were relatively uninvolved in the experimental topic, and hence most amenable to persuasion. Unfortunately, however, this aspect of the study was reported in rather abbreviated terms, and it is possible that the obtained results were critically influenced by initial attitude differences between those who changed and those who did not. Nevertheless, a start has been made and I would hope to see further studies in which individual differences in response to persuasion attempts are related to performance on the own-categories procedure.

I find Professor Sherif's work on latitudes of acceptance and rejection particularly interesting in its assumption that the attitude continuum is *not* smoothly homogenous, as is sometimes implied in discussions concerning "distance" in a hypothetical space. That is, the own-categories approach postulates points of discontinuity, such that some regions of the continuum are qualitatively different from others. I find this idea intuitively appealing. For example, I suspect that if I am mildly positive with respect to a given issue, I will probably react less favorably to a message espousing a mildly negative point of view, than to a message that is equally divergent with my own position, but in a *positive direction*. Note that this example, if it has general applicability, would suggest that the individual's latitude of acceptance may often be asymmetric. That is, acceptance of another's views may be relatively rare, when he favors statements that are "beyond" the neutral point, with respect to the respondent's *most preferred* stand.

There is yet another type of discontinuity that often appears in attitude studies, although to my knowledge, it has rarely been explicitly treated in the literature. I am referring here to the inconsistency of the average subject's behavior when he is asked to check all the items with which he agrees, or finds acceptable. Given such an instruction, a subject may, for example, endorse items that fall in categories 1, 3, and 6 on a 15 point scale, thereby establishing a latitude of acceptance extending from category 1 to category 6. Note, however, that our subject has not endorsed *all* the items within this range—he has excluded items in categories 2, 4, and 5. How should this be interpreted? There are several possibilities that seem worthy of exploration.

One interpretation, of course, would be that the obtained inconsistency simply represents a random error component, meaning that S's failure to endorse all the in-range items is mainly due to chance factors. While this is possible, I personally find the conclusion rather unsatisfactory, particularly when we recognize that this pattern of inconsistent endorsements is, in many (or most) studies, far more common than is consistency.

Ignoring the error interpretation for the moment, we might consider the possibility that our items are not unidimensional, but instead, vary in several ways. In this case, the failure to endorse items that seem in-range with respect to evaluation may reflect the fact that these items are out-of-range with respect to some other, unknown, factor. For example, the items might vary in both evaluative significance and in sophistication of expression; an item with acceptable evaluative properties might not be endorsed because of its verbal crudity.

There is yet another possibility that I would like to mention, mainly because it leads to some unexplored aspects of attitude research. Here I am speaking of the possibility that inconsistent endorsements, such as described above, may meaningfully reflect something about the respondent's familiarity with the topic, or his commitment to a particular stand. In short, it is possible that discontinuities in endorsement may be attributable to some characteristic of the *respondent*, rather than being the logical consequence of a multidimensional item domain. Or perhaps these two accounts are complementary, for it may be that the subject's apparently inconsistent endorsement pattern reflects his *personal* view that the items vary in *several* ways, a possibility that may not have been noted by his more consistent colleagues. In any event, I feel that discontinuities in endorsement are a common occurrence that warrant more intensive study.

I would now like to turn to another type of methodological innovation that has, I believe, interesting possibilities for the future; here I am referring to the recent shift *away* from an exclusive emphasis on the method of equal-appearing intervals that characterized the early studies of social judgment. As has often been noted, rating scale methods that rely on absolute judgments suffer from a certain degree of ambiguity, due to our inability to establish the fact that the various response categories have the same significance from one subject to the next. For example, if we find that a given item is rated as "extremely pro-fraternity" by one subject, and "moderately pro-fraternity" by another, it may nevertheless be contended that our two subjects *interpreted* the item similarly, but that the experience which was labelled as "extreme" by one may simply have been labelled "moderate" by the second. An alternate formulation would hold that the item was actually *perceived* differently by the two respondents.

In an attempt to deal more effectively with this problem, two relatively recent studies have used methodologies that lead, I believe, to less equivocal results. In one study, Ager and Dawes (1965) investigated attitudinal effects upon social judgments, using a paired comparison technique. Their respondents were presented with several pairs of statements regarding the virtues and limitations of science, and were instructed to indicate which statement of each pair was more favorable to science. All pairs were composed of items that were relatively close together on the evaluative continuum. The results revealed a systematic tendency for the subjects' performance to deteriorate when they were responding to item pairs drawn from the side of the continuum that they opposed. That is, in responding to item pairs whose components were proscience, subjects who were themselves favorable to science made fewer errors (relative to a consensus ordering) than did those who were antiscience; the reverse trend appeared on item pairs that were antiscience in tone.

These data suggest that the relationship between attitude and social judgment does not hinge upon the equal intervals methodology. Previously reported results cannot, therefore, be attributed exclusively to differences between the labelling behavior of the groups being compared. Note however, that these results support previous findings in only the most general sense; they do not, for example, provide a detailed mapping of assimilation and contrast effects. Instead, the main finding might be termed a *perspective effect*. That is, the average subject finds it simpler to discriminate between attitude statements that roughly parallel his own views, as compared with his relative *inability* to discriminate between attitudes at the opposite side of the continuum.

A recently completed experiment in our laboratory provides another example of the way in which social judgments may be studied without undue reliance on the rating scale methodology. This study (Manis, 1966) was concerned with the operation of context effects in a communication setting. As demonstrated in numerous experiments on social and psychophysical judgments, judgmental responses to a given stimulus are partly determined by the total array of stimuli to which the respondent has been exposed, and not solely by the stimulus that he is judging at a specific point in time. Most typically, this contextual influence is manifested in an apparent contrast between the stimulus being judged, and those judged previously. For example, in rating the disorganization and eccentricity implied by various vocabulary definitions, subjects whose main experience has been with "high-pathology" definitions usually rate "midscale" items as being *less eccentric* than do those provided with a predominantly "low-pathology" context (Campbell, Hunt, and Lewis, 1957).

Despite the replicability and generality of this effect, the results of such an experiment may be interpreted either in *perceptual* terms or in *semantic* terms. Thus, the perceptual interpretation holds that the context affects the *subjective impressions* elicited by the various definitions, while the semantic view is that the context has no influence upon the subject's perception, but merely influences the *verbal labels* that he uses to describe his subjective impressions.

Figure 1 depicts these alternative explanations; it is important to emphasize that both accounts are completely consistent with the observation that the verbal judgments elicited in such an experiment typically contrast with the bulk of the subject's judgmental experience. The upper diagram depicts this effect as resulting from a *perceptual* shift, while the bottom assumes a *semantic* effect.

In discussing this problem, Donald Campbell and his associates (1958 a, b) have suggested that semantic shifts in the meaning of the available response alternatives may largely result from the rather vague and novel response language that the experimenter provides; this vagueness may inadvertently encourage the subject to interpret the various response alternatives so that they will be maximally compatible with the range of stimuli that is presented to him.

As I see it, the issues raised by experimentally induced context effects may have important implications for the study of verbal communication. In many communication settings, the receiver's main task is to infer the referent that the speaker had "in mind" when he constructed his message; thus, as in the method of

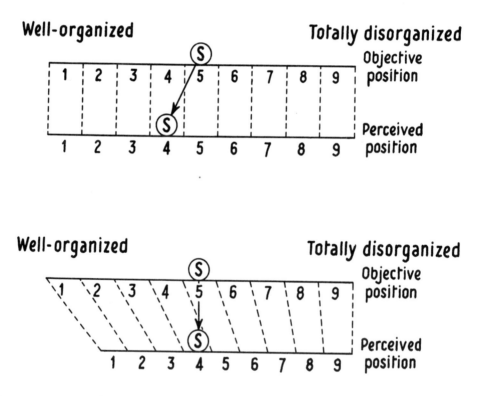

FIGURE 1

Two conflicting interpretations for the phenomenon of context-induced contrast effects. The top part of the drawing is based on an assumed perceptual effect, while the bottom depicts a semantic effect (see text).

single stimuli, the message (stimulus) must be placed into one of several categories, each category representing a different referent. If extreme contexts lead to true perceptual displacements, then it should be possible to affect the receiver's choice from a set of potential referents, even if the available alternatives are reasonably familiar and unambiguous. In brief, if a perceptual process is indeed involved, it should be possible to affect the listener's "understanding" of an incoming message by presenting it in contrasting contexts.

To test this hypothesis, subjects were presented with a series of written statements, each describing an actor's portrayal of an emotional state. The subjects were also given the eleven photographs that had been used to elicit these descriptions, and were instructed to indicate the picture (referent) that was being described in each message. To assess the impact of contextual factors upon the subjects' choices, one group was presented with descriptions of emotional states that were predominantly *unpleasant*, while another was given mainly *pleasant* descriptions; a third group responded to an unbiased mixture of both pleasant and unpleasant descriptions. In addition to these *context stimuli*, all *S*'s were also given 12 descriptions of emotions that were essentially *neutral* will respect to pleasantness-unpleasantness; these latter descriptions, which were presented intermittently, served as *test stimuli*.

Figure 2 shows the results of the experiment. The vertical axis represents the rated pleasantness of the photographs which were selected as referents for the successive test messages. It is quite clear that there is a consistent contrast effect. That is, subjects assigned to the pleasant context select less pleasant referents for the test messages than do those assigned to the unpleasant context, with the unbiased group generally falling between these two extremes.

I find these data particularly encouraging in demonstrating that context effects may be obtained without reliance on a rating scale methodology; moreover, these results were obtained in a situation where the meaning of the various response categories seems relatively stable and unambiguous. It is also interesting to note that these effects can apparently be obtained without any special "tuning," for our subjects were not instructed to focus attention on any particular dimension. It is likely, however, that the relative salience of the pleasantness dimension in descriptions of emotion may have been important here.

Having compeleted this brief excursion into the domain of social judgment, where do we now stand? While I am not given to outbursts of unbridled scientific optimism, and feel disinclined to alter my longstanding bias in this regard, nevertheless, I am encourage by the diversity of experimentation in this domain. I am also heartened by occasional reports of parallel results that have been obtained by investigators using diverse methodologies. It is only through the successful

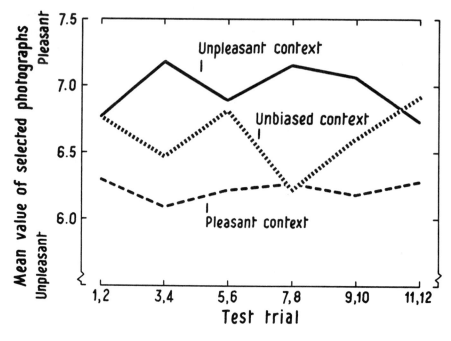

FIGURE 2

The effects of extreme contexts on *S*'s response in the matching task.

demonstration of converging operations that we can rise above the limitations of any particular method, and hopefully further our understanding of the judgmental process.

In conclusion, I would like to express my gratitude and admiration for Professor Sherif, both for his pioneering efforts, and because of his continuing interest and important contributions to this active domain of investigation.

References

Ager, J. W. and Dawes, R. M. "The effect of judges' attitudes on judgment." JOURNAL OF PERSONALITY AND SOCIAL PSYCHOLOGY, 1: 533-538, 1965.

Campbell, D. T., Hunt, W. A. and Lewis, N. A. "The effect of assimilation and contrast in judgment of clinical materials." AMERICAN JOURNAL OF PSYCHOLOGY, 70: 297-312, 1957.

Campbell, D. T., Hunt, W. A., and Lewis, N. A. "The relative susceptibility of two rating scales to disturbances resulting from shifts in stimulus context." JOURNAL OF APPLIED PSYCHOLOGY, 42: 213-217, 1958.

Campbell, D. T., Lewis, N. A., and Hunt, W. A. "Context effects with judgmental language that is absolute, extensive, and extra-experimentally anchored." JOURNAL OF EXPERIMENTAL PSYCHOLOGY, 55: 220-228 (6), 1958.

Eagly, Alice J. and Manis, M. "Evaluation of message and communicator as a function of involvement." JOURNAL OF PERSONALITY AND SOCIAL PSYCHOLOGY, 3: 483-485, 1966.

Hovland, C. I. and Sherif, M. "Judgmental phenomena and scales of attitude measurement: Item displacement in Thurstone scales." JOURNAL OF ABNORMAL AND SOCIAL PSYCHOLOGY, 47: 822-832, 1952.

Manis, M. CONTEXT EFFECTS IN COMMUNICATION. Unpublished manuscript.

Sherif, Carolyn W., Sherif, M., and Nebergall, R. E. ATTITUDE AND ATTITUDE CHANGE. Philadelphia: W. B. Saunders Company, 1965.

Sherif, M. and Hovland, C. I. SOCIAL JUDGMENT: ASSIMILATION AND CONTRAST EFFECTS IN COMMUNICATION AND ATTITUDE CHANGE. New Haven: Yale University Press, 1961.

Zimbardo, P. G. "Involvement and communication discrepancy as determinants of opinion conformity." JOURNAL OF ABNORMAL AND SOCIAL PSYCHOLOGY, 60: 86-94, 1960.

EXPERIMENTS ON TEACHING PIAGETIAN
THOUGHT OPERATIONS

G.A. Kohnstamm

Guided learning needs, among other things, a theory of cognitive development. As Piaget's theory is at the moment very much *en vogue* in Anglo-Saxon countries, the question of whether his theory can serve this purpose arises. I think this impossible for several reasons. Most of these reasons I cannot prove with *hard* facts, but they must be evident to anyone reading Piaget's books with a critical and educational mind. I shall begin by mentioning these reasons. Then I shall discuss some general characteristics of Piaget relevant learning experiments. The analysis of these characteristics will provide many issues relevant to experimental work on guided learning in general. One of the underlying reasons is that Piaget never really has been interested in education, although the name of his institute may have made many think so. This name "Institut des Sciences de l'Education" is misleading and redolent of the many misleading cues Piaget has introduced in his experiments for young children. Piaget's "school" is not interested in education either. When in Geneva in May 1965 several of Piaget's co-workers told me that " only Pierre Greco was interested in education". One of Piaget's former assistants, Professor Hans Aebli wrote me: "It seems to me that 'the Genevans' don't want to see the possible learning processes since their starting point is Rousseau's conception of development in which education and learning occupy a very moderate position". Now Aebli was a "brilliant" schoolteacher himself (Piaget's own qualification) and seriously tried to make Piaget's theory fruitful for school education. This can be read in a book by him published in 1951. In spite of the fact that he is not really interested in education Piaget now and then creates the impression that his theory is relevant to it. For instance Eleanor Duckworth begins her "Piaget rediscovered"* by writing "Everybody in education realizes that Piaget is saying something that is relevant to the teaching of children". And a little later she writes "Contrary to the view most often attributed to him, he (Piaget) maintains that good pedagogy *can* have an effect on this (intellectual) development".

What does Piaget consider good pedagogy? To understand this we might just mention, without going into details, the fact that in Piaget's theory *action* plays the first violin and language the second, the conductor being a tendency to the mind to strive towards equilibrium.

Although his early books have been criticized for their "verbalism" Piaget has come way back from his initial accentuation of language. Today "verbal thinking seems to

---

*First paper in PIAGET REDISCOVERED, a report on the Conference on Cognitive Studies and Curriculum Development, March 1964. Ripple and Rockcastle, (Eds.), School of Education, Cornell University.

him marginal to real thinking which, even though verbalized, remains until about eleven to twelve years of age centered upon action".* I quote from the very significant remarks Piaget made while at the Cornell conference.**

> Words are probably no short-cut to a better understanding...The level of understanding seems to modify the language that is used, rather than vice versa...Mainly, language serves to translate what is already understood; or else language may even present a danger if it is used to introduce an idea which is not yet accessible.

Language being a necessary evil the truly pedagogic adult should keep his mouth shut, except for asking the child diagnostic questions. It seems as if there is a Piagetian rule which says: as soon as the adult starts speaking the child stops his active handling and operational thinking and becomes a passive machine, waiting for atomistic S-R connections to be stamped in. Instead, the child should be active himself, handling his material environment as much as possible, discovering by induction the laws governing the physical world and by deduction the laws of logic and mathematics. The child should be allowed free play and the good pedagogue should provide him with the playthings.

At the Cornell conference Piaget said: "The teacher must provide the instruments which the children can use to decide things by themselves. Children themselves must verify, experimentally in physics, deductively in mathematics. A ready-made truth is only a half-truth". And also: "A teacher would do better not to correct a child's schemas, but to provide situations so he will correct them himself".

And what are we to make of Piaget's respect for pedagogics when reading the next statement made at the same conference? "The best idea I have heard from a pedagogue at the International Bureau of Education in Geneva was made by a Canadian. He said that in his province they had just decided every class should have two classrooms—one where the teacher is, and one where the teacher isn't".

If that is the best thing a pedagogue can tell Piaget it seems very strange to me that the educators present at those conferences did not protest in their papers against Piaget's view regarding their role in developing the child's mind.

Let me make it clear that I consider Piaget's theory beautiful and his lifelong work a masterpiece. Especially his theory with regard to children up to about two years of age gives, I think, a good explanation of cognitive growth. But to say that his theory

*Preface by Jean Piaget to CAUSAL THINKING IN THE CHILD, by M. Laurendeau and A. Pinard, 1962.

**p. 5 of the mentioned report.

can serve as a frame of reference when educating the minds of children of school age is quite a different matter. Another thing which I must be clear about is that my purpose is *not* the acceleration of what in Piaget's theory develops "spontaneously".

Although this might seem so from my experimental work, trying to teach "preoperational" 5-year-olds an insight characteristic of the operational level, it is not my intention to hasten the intellectual development of children living in culturally rich environments. The thing I want to demonstrate with these experiments is that there are ways of helping a child to solve new problems which are sound from a pedagogical and yet impossible from a Piagetian point of view. By demonstrating a possible acceleration I intend to show that the theory is wrong, not that we should strive towards this acceleration. Before continuing I must stress one final thing: I am not an opponent of free play and of the various activities the child may wish to fill his days with, even in school. I am not an advocate of techer-centered didactics, the child listening with folded arms. Not only did I myself enjoy Montessori schools from the age of 4 to 18 but I love also my own children most when they are amusing *themselves*; exploring their environment when very young and constructing their own play-world when a little older.

Of course spontaneous acting upon their environment is very good for children; it may stimulate growth the way Piaget describes that. But this does not have to imply a minor role for the immense stimulating force of language! Why can we not have it both ways—activity *and* language, inextricably mingled? In fact, more people are doing research on the interrelation between language and cognitive development than on the interrelation between activity and cognitive development. To give only two examples, the Russians, although with a deplorable accent upon verbal conditioning, and the Center for Cognitive Studies at Harvard. From these investigations one day an educationally useful psychology of cognitive development may be expected. Why did Piaget find it necessary to discard the role of language? What is wrong with an adult helping a child with words and guiding actions to behave in a new way?

If an adult helps a child to overcome his perceptual centerings upon wrong cues by teaching him to use mediational tools like new strategic combinations of words and actions, and teaches him to *use* these new tools (not only to recite them rote-fashion, as Piaget's school interprets any form of verbal learning) why should that necessarily imply the learning of a "half-truth", a "quasi-notion" or a "pseudo-concept"? Because it is not based upon action? Why not? Can not the adult with the help of words teach the child to act himself?

The distinction between "language" and "actions" is as artificial as Piaget's closely related distinction between learning and development.*

*See Cronbach's paper in the above mentioned report on the Piaget conference.

We now turn to a short review of the general characteristics of learning experiments expressly designed to accelerate the acquisition of Piagetian operations. The general opinion about these learning experiments is that they have had "remarkably little success in producing cognitive change" (Flavell, 1963; see also Huttenlocher, 1965). However true that may be, I do not believe this to be caused mainly by the way thinking develops in the minds of the subjects—as described and explained in Piaget's theory—but above all by the nature of the chosen didactics.

Let us begin with the end, the quality of the acquired learning results. The newly acquired behavior patterns should be tested for their quality. When the experiments are done with preoperational subjects in order to see if they can reach an operational behavior pattern in a certain field this quality should be "operational" in the Genevan sense of the word, at least as far the Piagetian demands for quality seem reasonable. But what is reasonable? Piaget himself has often discussed these criteria, and most recently at the Cornell conference. There he said that the acquired behavior should be 1) lasting, 1) transferable and 3) fundamentally different from the pre-experimental level of behavior.

As to the first criterion, which we shall name *durability,* Piaget's opinion is that "if a structure develops spontaneously, once it has reached a state of equilibrium, it is lasting, it will continue throughout the child's entire life". Since a research worker cannot wait all that long for durability testing, mostly periods of between one week and half a year are used. Piaget said in Cornell: "what remains two weeks or a month later?" It goes without saying that in his eyes the longer the period between training and the last post-test the better for the qualification of the acquired behavior.

Although I have used this criterion myself I do not think it to be a very important one. Why is it necessary for the child to remember without further training or repetition? The learned behavior usually bears no relation to daily life, so the child will only very seldom *use* the newly acquired "operation". In Piaget's theory the postulated underlying structure develops *because* of the need for the child to use it in daily practice. The fact that he is able at some time to solve the Piagetian problems in a so-called "clinical" experiment proves that the underlying structure has been developed. But what if this postulation of a gradual developing system of underlying structures were false? And what if the child one day solves the problem because in fact: 1) he has learned in daily life to use language to such a level as to be helpful in handling misleading perceptual cues (see Wohlwill's Cornell paper); 2) he structures his thought at the very moment of being confronted with the necessity of doing so (Aebli, 1963)? If this explanation were truer than Piaget's, remembering without further reinforcement would be a less important criterion for the quality of the acquired behavior. Therefore, the criterion of durability presupposes that

Piaget's theory is true. This makes it a doubtful criterion when testing the theory.*
The second criterion of **transfer** or **generalization** is a widely accepted criterion for
the quality of a learning result. Here too: the more the better. But exactly, how much
transfer is needed in a Piagetian quality test? The answer can only be either
theoretical and vague or empirical, based upon examples of Genevan experimental
practice.

The Piagetian theoretical answer is heavily loaded with the presupposition of the
truth of Piaget's theory about the organization of the mind in "structures
d'ensemble". If for instance Pascual-Leone and Bovet (1966) try to refute my
experimental results (Kohnstamm, 1963) by saying that I did not prove that the
subjects, after having learned behavior *a* were automatically able to perform
behavior *b, c* and *d* all related to the same underlying structure S, they presuppose
that this structure S actually exists and is really responsible for the existence of a
so-called "grouping of operations". Greco (1959) noticed this to be a presupposition
and as a result has not used a theoretically derived transfer test in checking the
quality of his experimental results.

The same presupposition underlies the view that a good check on the operational
character of a learned action of conservation (of weight for instance) is testing the
subjects for transitivity, because conservation and transitivity are closely knit
together, at least in Piaget's theory (Smedslund, 1961). But apart from Piaget's
theory one can of course apply transfer tests on the grounds of the general idea that
an acquired notion has more insight-quality if it can be transferred to new problems.
For example Greco, while studying the possibility of teaching children the inversion
of the order of three elements *a b c* into *c b a,* when the tube in which these elements
were fixed (upon a rod) was rotated 180°, and the inversion of inversion (*a b c* again)
after two rotations of 180°, checked the quality of the acquired notion by testing
for correct colutions in a) 3, 4 and 5 rotations (the same apparatus), and b) the
inversion of order of elements fixed upon a rotating disk (different apparatus). He
invented these tests because they seem reasonable, not because they necessarily
follow from Piaget's theory of groupings of operations.

With all Piaget relevant learning experiments it has been difficult to invent
reasonable transfer tests without leaning too much on as yet unproven assumptions
of underlying unity. The reason seems to be that many Piagetian tasks are so bound
up with a very specific material situation. In experiments using verbal materials or
verbal concepts which can be applied in many pictorial or imaginative situations the

---

*Let us note in passing that this postulation of Piaget's theory causes concepts like "remembering",
"forgetting", "brushing up one's memory" etc. to play no role of importance in his books nor in his many
experiments. Either the child has developed a structure or he has not yet done so. If he has, he possesses it for
his entire life. Could a theory which neglects the many problems of memory be of much value for education?

problem is easier to solve. Kreezer and Dallenbach for instance (1929) had no difficulty in finding really new items for transfer after they had taught their subjects to use the relation of opposition. The same applies to the experiments we did on teaching children to name similarities and differences between two verbally presented stimuli, as is done in the Stanford-Binet Intelligence test (Kohnstamm, 1965).

Anyway, a transfer may be "near" or "far". To give an example: In Beilin's experiment (1965) children were taught conservation of *length* and *number*. Beilin considered a "far" test of transfer the generalization to conservation of *area*, and a "near" test of transfer the generalization to a series of length and number items which differed only in color from the learning items.

A transfer may be too near to be significant, or too far. If it is too far it is an unreasonable test of the quality of the learned concept or operation. As far as I know nobody has criticized Kreezer and Dallenbach for not having checked if their subjects were able to solve immediately, and without further training, problems of naming the whole when only a part was given, although the chances are good that in a hypothetical Piagetian theory on verbal thinking the part-whole relation and the relation of opposition would be members of one "grouping" with an identical underlying structure.

There are other problems relating to the criterion of generality. One is the question of whether it is necessary for a child to be able to solve the transfer test immediately and without any help at all, or if he may be helped a little. In my opinion the idea of no help at all presupposes the existence of the above mentioned underlying wholes. In practice most experimenters allow some trials for the child to become accustomed to the situation. But how far may one go putting the child on the right track and directing his attention to the analogy with the problems taught?

I will not linger over the criterion of the difference between pre-test and post-test behavior, because this difference is implicit in the above mentioned difference between training and transfer, the child being trained to change his pre-test behavior into a qualitative different post-test behavior.

In Piaget's publications another criterion is often mentioned, that of *necessity*. If the child feels that the newly acquired response *must* be right because it follows necessarily from the premises a Piagetian will be satisfied. The trouble with this criterion is that one must place a lot of trust in what the child says after being asked why he gave the (correct) answer. Together with all other kinds of *verbal explanations* the child may give, this criterion is reminiscent of the time that Piaget was criticized for taking the child too much at his words. It is my opinion though, that additional use may be made of the child's verbal explanations in testing the quality of his acquired notions. For instance the way Smedslund categorized the explanations of his subjects into symbolic, symbolic-logical, perceptual and ambiguous seems useful. If one takes the precaution of testing for interjudge reliability, verbal explanations may serve as a good criterion.

Gestalt psychologists have attached much weight to the *suddenness* of the breakthrough of *Insight* as against the gradual rise in number of correct answers in a process of conditioning. Greco used this argument in demonstrating that what his subjects learned was no simple S-R connection and so did Morf (1959) although less detailed, and Kohnstamm (1963, 1965). In Gestalt theory Insight always came spontaneously and was originally limited to sudden mental restructurings in the perceived situation. The concept comes close to "discovery" and as with the latter the question may arise of whether insights should be acquired spontaneously or if one may be helped with them. It is my opinion that any teacher who can demonstrate a distinct moment of qualitative change for the better in his pupil's responses has the right to suppose that insight has occurred as a consequence of his didactics. The criterion seems very useful too as an argument in discussions about Piaget relevant learning studies, although Anglo-Saxon research workers have not made much use of it as yet.

The same is true for a criterion which has been used only intuitively as yet: the *ease* of the learning process. It is important to know how much energy a child (and the experimenter) needs to reach a certain level of behavior. An easy victory is suspected to be of less value than a difficult one! I have the impression that I did not make clear in my article on the teaching of inclusion problems that some children had great difficulty in learning to solve the problems. With them, it was very hard work for both experimenter and child. Perhaps, if my Genevan critics, Magali Bovet and Pascual-Leone, had themselves experienced this situation of real struggle, with the adult guiding the child, they would not have thought the children passive, "reading" with ease the ready-made solutions from the facilitated situations. But I myself experience this same impression (lack of significance because the training requires so little energy) from other Piaget relevant learning studies, e.g. the study of Wohlwill and Lowe (1962) in which the subjects were not confronted with any real problem and consequently developed no solutions.

There is another important group of criteria which may be named *resistance*. If a child has learned to behave in a new way characteristic of a higher level of development the depth of understanding can be tested by trying to lead him astray. Smedslund's "resistance to extinction" belongs to this group as well as the resistance to a verbal counter-suggestion as used by Wallach and Sprott (1964).

376

Counter-suggestions are very typical of Piaget's way of testing children, and one of the main arguments Bovet and Pascual-Leone have against my experimental results is that I did not try to confuse my subjects after having taught them to resist the misleading perceptual cues so characteristic of all Piagetian situations. In future research I shall also use this criterion albeit not without having first taught my subjects in a different task that their teacher (E) may sometimes try to mislead them too. Only after having accustomed a young child to the idea that this stranger (E) sometimes systematically tries to mislead him, a resistance-test seems a good criterion of the quality of understanding. If not, the timid child may fall back on the old answers, which E deftly suggests to be correct, while the self-confident child resists. Variables of personality or child-adult interaction should not interfere with the testing for quality of cognitive growth.

Of the above mentioned criteria, *durability, generality, verbal explanations* (including "necessity"), *suddenness* of transition from incorrect to correct answers in the learning process, *ease* and *resistance*, suddenness and ease are criteria which cannot systematically be introduced in a post-test. They are properties of the learning process. The other criteria are properties of the acquired learning result. As such they may be subsumed under a last and encompassing criterion, that of comparing the behavior of the young learners with the "spontaneous" behavior of a control group of older children. In the Piaget relevant learning studies only Greco has used this criterion in a systematic way. A problem is, however, how much older the older children should be. Although this criterion is a very important one we shall not linger over it here.

Still other criteria are conceivable, but have not as yet been used in Piaget relevant learning studies. In fact I am thinking of a very nice new criterion but I shall have to do some research before knowing for sure if it is really a good one.

Now we turn to the different learning methods as used in Piaget relevant learning studies. Most Piagetian problems seem to resist being solved by simply reinforcing the correct answers of the subjects (Smedslund, Wohlwill and Lowe, Beilin). Periods of free play with the materials seem equally insufficient to bring about in a relatively short time the necessary understandings. (Greco, Morf) The barriers being difficult to overcome other experimenters have tried to give different kinds of aid: from material hints to verbal rule instruction.

To start with the latter, simply telling the child the verbal rule leading to the correct solution seemed relatively successful in one experiment (Beilin) but not in another (Greco). It is the kind of verbalism Piaget is most opposed to because it is so isolated from action. Beilin told the subjects of one of his experimental groups each time they gave a wrong answer: "Whenever we start with a length like this one (E points) and we don't add any stick, but only move it, it stays the same length even though it looks different. See, I can put them back the way they were, so they haven't really changed". This rule was given upon each incorrect answer in two training sessions, lasting about 40 minutes each, and consisting of 36 similar items of conservation of length.

From a methodological point of view it is understandable that the experimenter always repeated the rule in the same form. From an educational point of view, however, it would be more interesting to be less rigid with the verbal composition of the rule, and to adapt it to the special needs of the child and the moment in the learning process.

Still other investigators tried to make their subjects construct the right solution by bringing them into a state of cognitive *conflict*. So Smedslund, referring to the theories of Festinger and Berlyne, created situations which might induce cognitive conflict in the subject but which would not provide him with any feedback as to whether his judgments were right or wrong.

This procedure of studying several possible learning factors *separately* is typical for most of the Piaget relevant learning studies. Each experimental group being treated with only one method at the same time the investigators hope to discover which factors are responsible for cognitive growth. For reasons of experimental elegance these experimenters avoid using differnt kinds of aid at the same time as much as possible. Understandable as this may be from a methodological point of view it prevents us from concluding that since teaching thought operations to preoperational children has had rather limited success this teaching is useless. In our experiments, in which our purpose was *not* to test several possible factors *apart*, but to reach an operational learning result *by any means* the teaching was pretty successful.

Our learning method was a very flexible combination of training sub-operations (e.g. counting an comparing counted numbers), confronting the child with his own contradictions, making him use verbal rules to resist the misleading perceptual cues inherent in the problems, making his solution more stable and flexible by helping through many different settings of the same problem, while at the same time discussing matters verbally with him and giving positive and negative reinforcements at that.

Sloppy from a methodological point of view, adapting strategies to the special needs of the individual child, repeating items when necessary, our 5-year-olds learned to behave in a way definitely better than 5-year-olds should behave according to Piagetian standards.

We started by explaining to the children how to solve the problems in their easiest form and increased the complexity of the problems only after they had shown signs of understanding with the easy ones. This is a very common didactic principle which, strangely enough, has not been applied by other experimenters in the field. Pascual-Leone and Bovet write in their critical article that "facilitating" procedures like beginning with the easiest form of a problem, may easily lead to quasi-insights because it allows for a less operational solution of the problem.

This is a typical example of how alien Piaget's school is to educational practice. In fact these authors are of the opinion that if facilitating factors have been introduced in the learning process the learning result is ipso facto devoid of a truly "operational" character. It appears to be very difficult for many experimental psychologists to think of the possibility of making the child a very active problem solver by guiding him verbally and motivating him with "external" reinforcements and "internal" conflicts at the same time.

Trained as a psychologist myself I remember the strange feeling of guilt when I started guiding my subjects in solving the problems they could not solve spontaneously; it was against the rules of diagnostic testing and experimenting which prescribe a strictly neutral attitude for the psychologist and only allow some examples to be given. Our learning method is neither objective nor standardized, and therefore bad from the methodological point of view. It certainly is, but the method works and eventually could help in bridging the gap between psychology of cognitive development and education.

Of course the experimenter should assume the typical neutral attitude while in the post-test sessions. Here he should strictly avoid guiding the child, just as the teacher in school does during exams. An exception could be made for the first examples of a new kind of problem introduced to test for the generality of the learned operations. My Genevan critics have rightfully pointed out the fact that I have only tested for transfer within different *materials*, including purely verbally posed problems, and that I should have changed the problem itself, because it might be conceivable that familiar problems (belonging to the same Piagetian family of a structure d'ensemble) did not profit from the training. They also purport to attach little value to the fact that my subjects were able to solve the problems again after periods of three weeks and six months since noncognitive habits formed by conditioning can also be very stable. In this respect they contradict Piaget's words (Cornell paper) and Greco's practice.

Interpreting the acquired learning results as Greco's "quasi-notions" they demand additional tests, including resistance to counter-suggestions, verbal explanations, and "farther" transfer tests. In a new book (Kohnstamm, 1967) I have discussed these problems more thoroughly, thereby including new experimental evidence from both a Canadian replication study and a new study by myself.

The discussions of the consequences of learning results acquired in experiments expressly designed to test Piaget's theory of how children learn new operations (gradual, coordinating interiorized action into a system of reversible operations) will certainly continue for several years. As I have tried to show in this article these discussions will be highly relevant for any theory of how children acquire new insights, and especially for a theory of guided learning.

Summary

These are statements read by the author at the 18th International Congress of Psychology, Moscow 1966, in the symposium "Learning as a Factor in Mental Development" organized by G. S. Kostyuk and N. A. Menchinskaya.

A difference of opinion still exists regarding the influence of training upon the speed at which mental development takes place and the form taken by it. If one imagines a line with on one side the optimistic and on the other side the pessimistic viewpoint, I find myself in a moderately optimistic position. The moderately pessimistic viewpoint is not very well represented in this symposium. It was better represented in the symposium organized by Inhelder and Galperin. In my opinion, the Genevan school of Piaget is on the pessimistic side as regards the possibility of helping intellectual development to take place in a way different from the so-called spontaneous development. Both sides have sustained their positions with the outcomes of learning experiments. The outcomes of the Genevan experiments are reported to be of small significance, those of the optimists are reported to be of great significance.

Much depends on the learning methods used by the experimenters. The Genevan learning methods can be termed "weak" methods, "laissez-faire" methods. This is in accordance with Piaget's theory, in which the child and his *material* environment form a sort of autonomous unit, more or less independent of a pedagogical interaction between the child and his *social* environment: parents, other children, teachers. It is therefore understandable that experimenters employing "stronger" learning methods, which can be termed directive teaching methods, in which there is a teacher who tries to reach the best possible results with the children, have obtained far better results.

Learning results obtained in this directive way are not highly esteemed by the Genevan school. One of the criteria demanded by this school is that children who have been taught a certain operation should be able to generalize automatically to other operations belonging to the same logical structure. But what if these logical structures do not exist? In my opinion the real existence of something similar to these networks of operations has never been proved. Therefore the criterion of transfer to other operations is based on theory, not on facts.

In my opinion, the groupings of logical operations postulated by Piaget and his school do not exist. The results of teaching experiments in which operations are formed in relative isolation — no transfer to other problems — are more in accordance with a conception of the mind of a child as a rather loose organization, in which all sorts of operations can be set up on request, with or without help from a teacher, and dependent upon the age of the child and his general level of intelligence, of which language constitutes the main component.

A most important point of view is brought forward in Aebli's contribution to this symposium. This is that the operations necessary to solve a certain problem are formed for the first time at the moment when the child is confronted with a problem. This means that specific operations do not take shape *gradually, outside* the experimental situation, as is held by the Genevan school. The results obtained in our own experiments sustain Aebli's view.

References:

Aebli, H. DIDACTIQUE PSYCHOLOGIQUE. APPLICATION A LA DIDACTIQUE DE LA PSYCHOLOGIE DE JEAN PIAGET, DELACHAUX ET NIESTLE, 1951. (In German: Psychologische Didaktik, Klett, 1963.)

Aebli, H. UBER DIE GEISTIGE ENTWICKLUNG DES KINDES, Klett, 1963.

Beilin, H. "Learning and operational convergence in logical thought development," J. EXP. CHILD PSYCHOLOGY, 4, 1965.

Flavell, J. H. THE DEVELOPMENTAL PSYCHOLOGY OF JEAN PIAGET, Van Nostrand, 1963.

Greco, P. L'APPRENTISSAGE DANS UNE SITUATION A STRUCTURE OPERATOIRE CONCRETE. Vol. VII of Etudes d'Epistemologie Genetique, P.U.F., 1959.

Huttenlocher, J. "Children's intellectual development." REV. OF ED. RESEARCH, Vol. XXXV, No. 2, 1965.

Kohnstamm, G. A. "An evaluation of part of Piaget's theory," ACTA PSYCHOLOGICA, Vol. XXI, No. 4/5, 1963. Reprinted in CURRENT RESEARCH ON PIAGET'S THEORIES (Sigel and Hopper, eds.) Holt, Rinehart and Winston, 1967.

Kohnstamm, G. A. "Developmental psychology and the teaching of thought operations," PAEDAGOGICA EUROPAEA, EUROPEAN YEARBOOK OF EDUCATIONAL RESEARCH. Elsevier — Westermann, 1965.

Kohnstamm, G. A. PIAGET'S ANALYSIS OF CLASS INCLUSION: RIGHT OR WRONG? Mouton, The Hague, Paris, 1967.

Kreezer, G. and Dallenbach, K. M. "Learning the relation of opposition". AMER. J. PSYCHOL., 1929 (41)

Morf, A. "Apprentissage d'une structure logique concrete (inclusion) Effets et limites", Vol. IX of ETUDES D'EPISTEMOLOGIE GENETIQUE, P.U.F., 1959.

Pascual-Leone, J. and Bovet, M. C. "L'apprentissage de la quantification de l'inclusion et la theorie operatoire." ACTA PSYCHOLOGICA, No. 25, 1966.

Smedslund, J. "The acquisition of conservation of substance and weight in children," I - VI, SCAND. J. PSYCHOL., Vol. 2, 1961.

Wallach, L. and Sprott, R. L. "Inducing number conservation in children." CHILD DEVELOPMENT, 35, 1964.

Wohlwill, J. F. and Lowe, R. C. "An experimental analysis of the development of the conservation of number." CHILD DEVELOPMENT, 33, 1962.

EXPERIMENTAL-LONGITUDINAL METHODS AND RESPRESENTATIVE BEHAVIOR SAMPLING IN STUDYING COGNITIVE LEARNING

Arthur W. Staats, Ph.D.

In the present paper there are several general points I would like to make of a methodological sort, in addition to providing a summary description of my learning approach and supporting research results. To begin, I would like to suggest that we need to develop methods of research and a research rationale that begin to deal experimentally with samples of actual cognitive development. This simple statement involves a number of issues which will have to be spelled out individually.

First, by the term experimental is meant the manipulation of variables which *produce* the behavior under consideration. In this sense test situations and traditional longitudinal study, while they are important areas of research and yield important types of information, are not experimental in nature. Thus, for example, presentation of a problem situation to a child and observation of his response either in a standardized test situation or in developmental research will not be considered as experimental. The behavior is not *produced* in such study. What the variables are that determine whether or not the child will display the behavior are not the subject study. In any case the behavior could have been learned in the child's past experience, or the behavior conceivably could have a biological basis.

This situation is not changed when (1) children of different age levels are put in the same problem situation and their behaviors are observed and compared, or (2) when a child is observed over a long period of time. Age (or time) is not a determining variable in itself--providing only an opportunity for unknown learning and biological determining variables to occur. While important information may be yielded by age comparisons on some task, it cannot be concluded from such studies what the determining conditions were. Such research actually deals with observations of behavior, not the experimental manipulation of conditions which produce the behavior.

Thus, typical developmental research ranging from the mental test movement, through the work of people like Gesell, to the modern study of cognition by individuals like Piaget must be considered in terms of what the observations can produce and what they cannot. Such research may make observations of important behaviors in children, and in the manner in which such behaviors develop over time. However, they do not provide information concerning what the basic learning (or possibly biological) principles are which give rise to the behaviors. Such studies are thus descriptive, not experimental. It should be noted that the findings of such

383

descriptive research are very much culturally bound, at least to the extent that learning variables are involved in the child's cognitive development. That is, they do not tell us what the child *could* learn under maximal learning conditions, but only what children typically acquire under the learning conditions generally imposed by the culture. Thus, developmental and longitudinal research, while contributing important and productive observations of significant human behaviors, will leave us with lacunae in our knowledge of the conditions which determine the development of the child's behavior, including his intellectual skills.

This gap in our knowledge, it is suggested, will not be reduced by typical research in experimental psychology either. (Since the study of biological processes has not produced information on conditions that can be altered to produce cognitive skills, the description here will refer only to experimental studies of learning.) The essence of basic experimental research in learning, human and animal, is to manipulate a determining variable--for example, reinforcement versus no reinforcement. This is ordinarily done employing groups of subjects so that extra-experimental variables can be controlled by randomization. That is, one randomly selected group will be subjected to the experimental conditions and the other randomly selected group will not. Any differences between the groups will be a function of the experimental manipulation, over and above the random differences between the groups. This type of research is thus experimental in the manipulative sense.

This methodology has been used to isolate clearly the basic laws of learning. In this quest it has been necessary to simplify the events under study as much as possible to gain as much control as possible of extraneous, interfering variables. Thus, this type of research has involved simple samples of the environment (stimuli), a light, a bell, a food pellet, and the like; simple samples of behavior, salivation, a bar press, a key peck, and the like; employing simple samples of living organisms, rats, dogs, pigeons, and the like.

The use of groups in such research, to randomize conditions which cannot be controlled directly, places certain restrictions upon the research. These restrictions become important when one moves from the study of basic, and thus simple, principles to the circumstances of complex human learning. That is, when large groups of subjects are employed it is not possible to spend a great deal of research time on each subject. However, when investigators have begun to *extend* to the human level the principles found in basic experimental work, they have traditionally employed the same methodology. Even when studies are conducted on such seemingly complex behaviors as concept formation, verbal problem solving, reasoning, communication, and so on, the tasks and behaviors studied have been relatively simple--ones the subjects can display in a very short period of time. The use of groups prevents the study of a learned behavior which is acquired only over a long period of training--that is, if detailed observations are going to be made. The resources required for detailed, long term observations of groups would be exorbitant in beginning the study of some complex human behavior. The use of group designs in traditional experimental methodology thus has severe limitations when one wishes to study complex human behaviors which are only acquired or changed over long periods of time during which time a great many learning trials occur.

There has, of course, been long term experimental research conducted in the field of education which also uses group research designs. The use of groups again is to control extra-experimental variables through randomization. Such research has been concerned with complex stimulus presentations and complex behavioral skills. However, this research has not made detailed observations upon either the stimulus (educational) materials or the complex behaviors which are learned. Traditionally, one teaching method, unanalyzed in terms of basic principles, is compared to another unanalyzed teaching method. The subjects' behavior is likely to be observed only during two brief periods, one before the training is commenced and the other at the end of the period of training. The specific effects of the materials upon the behavior are not studied, but only a gross over-all effect. This method, thus, makes it impossible to test specific aspects of the complex stimulus materials—and thus basic learning principles cannot be discovered in such research, nor can basic principles be tested in such research. Theories of cognitive learning which could be used as a framework for continued research and steady improvement of theory and teaching methods as a consequence have not been products of such research.

A newer variety of this approach has been the study of programmed instruction. This movement was at first considered as an application of learning principles. As such one would expect that research in this area would be concerned with an analysis of teaching materials in terms of learning principles and include the experimental test of the efficacy of the principles and of the materials based upon the learning analyses. This had not been the case, primarily because the learning approach involved (i.e., B. F. Skinner's) is non-analytical. The field of programmed instruction has thus differed by very little from traditional methods of development of educational materials. Almost entirely the principles involved in developing programmed instruction materials are that the items of instruction should advance in small steps so that the students can successfully respond to the items. There is also a rationale which indicates that being correct on an item is reinforcing.

As an example of the weaknesses of the approach it may be indicated that the important topic of reinforcement in cognitive learning has not even been suggested as a crucial area of exploration. Thus, being "correct" was assumed generally to be an adequate reinforcement for children by Skinner and his associates. Actually, as the author has indicated (Staats, 1964; Staats and Butterfield, 1965; Staats and Staats, 1963; Staats, et al., 1962, 1964) great variations exist in what constitutes reinforcement for children. The fact of the matter is that being correct and moving on to the next item are by no means universally reinforcing for children or adults. For young children such consequences have little durable reinforcing value. For culturally-deprived, retarded, emotionally disturbed children, such consequences are also not reinforcing. Actually, such events are not reinforcing for the very children who have problems of cognitive learning. The fact of the matter is that "motivational" (reinforcement) variables are crucial to the child's cognitive development. We need systematic, experimental study of such variables in the context of long term, arduous, complex learning tasks. Programmed instruction has provided no guidelines in this respect and has no rationale to lead to the necessary research.

Moreover, because there are not stimulus-response analyses of the stimulus materials used in the child's cognitive training, we have obtained no new conceptions of cognitive learning from the field of programmed instruction. Programmed instruction does not provide an analysis, for example, of what reading is, nor a basic theory for analyzing and evaluating methods of training children to read. Although there are programs for teaching children to read they have been composed from existing methods, and have no more theoretical justification than those methods. The same thing is true in the *various* areas in which we have programmed instruction materials. While programmed instruction materials may in certain cases provide an improved format for instruction, program development is strictly an applied activity.

Furthermore, research in programmed instruction has not led to methodological innovations. Rather it has utilized traditional educational research designs. One group of subjects is given programmed instruction materials, another group is given different materials. The groups are observed (tested) before and after and the methods compared. There is no detailed observation of the course of learning in either case, and thus no test of basic learning principles. Such research, as described, has not even varied reinforcement variables to any significant extent. It is thus suggested that neither the development of programmed instruction materials, nor the test of such materials in traditional educational research designs, will produce theoretical understanding of cognitive learning and function which is of a general nature.

The above discussion has been concerned with research methodologies which we have had at our disposal. An equally important topic concerns some additional, and basic, conceptions of the strategy by which we seek an understanding of human behavior. That is, in addition to the weaknesses in the research methods of traditional experimental psychology for the study of cognitive behavior, there has been an underlying strategy that is at fault. The underlying conception has led us to be content with experimentation which is at fault because the samples of behavior dealt with are not representative of the actual human behaviors in which we are interested. The faulty conception is a carry over from some of the mentalistic approaches prominent in the history of experimental psychology.

These points may be elaborated as follows. There is a marked tendency, even among researchers who are oriented along learning lines, when investigating some aspect of complex human behavior, to utilize the theory already existent in that area of study—in contrast to following a pure behavioral approach. Thus, as one example Dollard and Miller (1950) utilized the concepts of psychoanalysis to a large extent in analyzing personality and psychotherapy, rather than making a pure learning analysis. The same is true in other areas. As the author has already described (Staats, 1966, 1967, 1968) learning people who have experimented with concept formation or problem solving, as other examples, have tended to use previous categorizations of behavior as well as the traditional experimental tasks based upon those categorizations rather than to use samples of actual human behaviors. Somehow the abstract term *concept formation* for example, seems more fundamental or basic, less applied, than a term like reading or counting. However, there is nothing more basic about the study of an artificial sample of problem solving, concept formation, perception, or what have you, in comparison to actual repertoires of cognitive learning. In either case what makes the study basic is the extent to which basic principles are involved in the theoretical or experimental investigations. The use of precise and well controlled experimental methods in conjunction with "faculty psychology" concepts--which is actually the combination many studies in academic experimental psychology employ--constitutes an unproductive strategy which produces findings that are not basic and not applied. That is, such studies are not derived from or related to basic principles and are thus not basic, and yet the findings have no extensions to problems of human behavior and thus cannot be applied. It is time that we expect studies of complex human behavior to demonstrate one or the other characteristic, or both.

The author (Staats, 1967, 1968) has already suggested that psychology in general has followed what may be called a "category-underlying process approach" rather than a "representative behavior sample and S-R analysis approach." This notion may be elaborated a little in indicating the first step in the latter research strategy. The primary suggestion is that much of the research in psychology today is inadequate in its inception. That is, most present day research deals with experimental tasks (behaviors) that are trivial. This is done because it is assumed that it is the mental process underlying the task that is important. Thus, this approach in essence suggests that *any* task will reflect the workings of the underlying process. For example, the researcher following this orientation feels that any particular problem task taps internal problem-solving ability as well as any other problem, or that copying a diagonal taps the process involved in copying nature in fine art (Olson, 1967), or that any task of identifying categories of stimulus items constitutes a case of concept formation, or that any change of behavior through language typifies communication, and so on.

If, on the other hand, one does not accept the assumption involved--that of an implicit determining process for every behavioral category--then the experimental task becomes all important as *representative* of some universe of actual behaviors. From this conception we are not satisfied with just any task--selection of the task is a central part of the research. It is suggested that we need to accept this approach. We must in any case specify a universe of significant human behavior and select for study a representative sample of the universe. We must dispense with our idealized conceptions of human behavior and the artificial experimental tasks we construct on the basis of the conceptions. Before discussing a more appropriate research strategy, several examples will be given of the errors that the "category-underlying process strategy" produces.

First, the categorization approach leads one to treat as different behaviors that are actually, in principle, the same. The same behaviors are frequently discussed as different under the names of communication, meaning, perception, attitudes, motivation, and so on. Use of one label ordinarily restricts interest in the study to investigators working within that particular category. Studies done under one label are not related to those done under another.

In addition, many times behaviors are discussed as though they were the same, although different learning principles are involved in each case. Using communication as example again, it has been suggested (Staats, 1964, 1968) that classical conditioning and instrumental conditioning principles are involved in communications acts–as well as various S-R mechanisms. Categorization schemes that suggest a unitary process narrow the scope of our considerations. For this reason it is necessary to promulgate a "pluralistic" approach to many areas of human behavior.

Furthermore, our classificatory system and its related assumption of underlying, unitary, psychological processes has led us astray in another direction. Because it is felt that the *underlying* process is primary, studies which utilize this research strategy are considered basic and general. On the other hand, studies that pointedly attempt to study the behavior itself—even when the behaviors are more significant—are considered as applied and of far lesser value. If it was not because of the error in basic strategy, there would be no reason to consider a relatively trivial experimental task, such as sorting a deck of cards to classify stimuli, as generally typical of concept formation while relegating the learning of letter reading or initial number skills to a less "basic" role--in a direct reversal of reality. The opinion (based on the category--underlying process approach) that dealing with actual human behavior is unscientific is entirely unfounded. As already suggested, the study should be considered to be basic to the extent that we investigate or employ basic principles and methods. In the present view there are three levels of basic study in the field of learning--those that deal directly with the higher-order (more basic) conditioning principles, those that deal with the derived S-R mechanisms, or those that employ these principles in the study of human behavior. All relate to the basic theoretical structure. When the concern is with human behavior, in the third level of study, the closer the sample of behavior is to an actual human behavior the greater the basic value of the study.

At any rate, it is suggested that psychology is ready to deal with samples of actual human behavior using the methods and principles of the basic science. It is felt that more psychologists must begin their research efforts by looking to actual human behaviors for samples they wish to investigate, rather than looking to the categories of the past and the limitations of the presently used experimental tasks that enjoy popularity. (See Staats, 1967, for a more complete discussion.)

Thus, it is suggested that we need research which deals with representative samples of actual human repertoires--not some idealized conception of what must take place within the individual. The research must be based upon detailed theoretical analysis of the S-R events involved. If that is not the case the research cannot be related to the basic principles. Furthermore, it is suggested that the research must begin with simple samples of the universe of behaviors. In this manner the basic principles may be tested in the context of the behavior. Although the first steps must deal with samples of simple aspects of the behavior, we must advance in the research to where we are dealing with larger and larger (more complex) chunks of the behavior. This should be done with detailed, explicit, analysis of the behavior and observations of the process of learning. Finally, the principles and analyses verified through this experimentation, as well as the procedures developed, should be capable of extension to dealing with the actual, functional, learning of the cognitive skills. Thus, it should be possible within this strategy to contribute to the solution of human problems of learning as well as to build a scientific conception.

The strategy of this type of research demands long-term, longitudinal study which is experimental in the sense that learning principles and procedures are manipulated to produce the behavior under study. These demands dictate changes in research methodology. It is not possible to depend upon short-term group studies and statistical analyses, upon observations (or tests) of behavior which do not manipulate determining variables, or upon non-analytic applied studies.

This introduction raises the issues. The present paper will not resolve them--space limitations will not permit this. Thus, for example it will not be possible to present full stimulus--response analyses of the cognitive learning to be discussed herein, or to more fully discuss the methodological problems. The author has made a more complete account (Staats, 1968). The present paper will only characterize some of the work that has been commenced to deal with some of the problems that have been raised and to begin to suggest some of the types of information we need in the study of cognitive learning.

It was with this rationale in mind that I began the experimental study of samples of actual cognitive skills. The universe of behaviors of concern to this study has been language including such samples as number skills, writing, and reading. The latter area has received detailed attention in this work, and will be singled out for discussion herein. One of the aspects of reading acquisition involves instrumental discrimination learning in which the written verbal stimulus becomes the discriminative stimulus and controls the appropriate vocal response. Although the principle is simple, even a cursory analysis reveals that the learning task is extremely long-term and arduous. The number and subtlety of the discriminations the child has to acquire indicate the great complexity of the task.

Thus, we must consider motivational or reinforcement factors as of central importance to this type of learning. Because of the difficulty of the learning task and the length of time it takes to acquire the reading repertoire, we must expect that it will require a system of rewards that is strong. The behaviors of attending in class and responding as directed, the behaviors involved in being a good pupil, must be maintained for a long and arduous period. Without reinforcement these basic behaviors will not be maintained in good strength, and then educational learning will cease.

It was on the basis of this type of analysis that the author began the systematic study of learning variables in the context of early cognitive development--especially the acquisition of reading. The first step was to create a laboratory situation to verify the applicability of the general analysis and to begin the development of methods to work with this type of behavior and with the population of subjects involved. The first study to be reported will summarize this development.

The aim of the beginning aspect of the learning analysis of reading was to construct a laboratory procedure within which reinforcement principles could be studied objectively with young children over long periods of time, where the verbal stimuli were presented in a controlled manner. The reading stimulus materials devised for the first experimental work were selected to fulfill certain criteria. While the task was chosen to be a reading task, to produce good laboratory control the materials were selected to be as simple and as homogeneous as possible. Since words and sentences are of different lengths and difficulty, single vowels and consonant-vowel pairs were selected. In devising this reading learning task attention was also directed to a preliminary analysis of the learning to be achieved, that is, to what reading acquisition is and the type of stimulus discriminations which must be made and the responses which have to be controlled. This analysis, as will be discussed, by no means solves the problems of learning to read, but it does begin to confront them. Many investigators concerned with reading have pointed out that in the English language the same letter stimuli often must come to control different speech sounds when the letters are in different contexts. The letter *a* is responded variously to, as in *father, fate, fast,* and so on. One stimulus must thus come to elicit several responses depending upon the context in which it occurs. This represents a complex type of learning. Although there are some general consistencies or rules according to which the stimuli of context can come to control the correct one of the several responses, there are many exceptions, and even the consistencies of context form a very complex learning task.

There have been various suggestions for overcoming such problems in the training of reading, for example, (1) the English spelling may be altered and new symbols introduced, but this may make the transfer to normal English spelling quite difficult; or (2) in order to retain the actual English spelling, the system may deal with only a limited number of words, not including the many exceptions; however, this limits the generality of the learning.

The stimuli used in the present study were such that they might later be used in the study of some of these problems. The research method retains the letters used in English. However, a different identifying mark appears in conjunction with the letter for each different sound the letter must come to elicit, for example, *a* controls the "a" response in *father,* and *a* controls the "a" in *fate.* As a result, each letter with its symbol (when necessary) controls only one response, a method consistent with a preliminary behavior analysis of the learning involved. Once the child acquires such a letter repertoire he should be able to read any word including these letters. As the learning progresses, and the context stimuli have come to assume control over the correct response, the supplementary identifying stimuli could be eliminated gradually from the reading materials.

In addition, to obtain good experimental control, an apparatus was constructed in which the phonetic letter stimuli could be displayed systematically. The apparatus is schematized in Figure 1. The stimulus presentation apparatus consists of the panel with four plastic covered windows. One of the windows is centered above the other three. Pressure on any of the plastic covers activates microswitches which lead to various experimental contingencies.

FIGURE 1

The laboratory apparatus for the experimental study of reading behavior. The child is seated before the center panel within easy reach of the various manipulanda which are involved in the reading response sequence. Letter stimuli appear in the small plexiglass windows in front of the child whenever he activates the pushbutton on the table before him. If a correct reading response sequence then occurs, the marble dispenser located at the child's near-right drops a marble into a tray positioned at its base. To the child's left is an open bin in the Universal Feeder cabinet into which are delivered trinkets, edibles, or pennies, whenever the child deposits a marble in the funnel located atop the marble dispenser. A marble may also be "spent" for toys displayed at the child's far right. Whenever the plexiglass tube beneath a boy is filled with marbles the child receives that toy. An intercom speaker at the child's left allows his vocal behavior to be monitored from outside the experimental chamber. The light at the top of the center panel was not used in this study. From Staats, A. W., 1964.

The verbal stimuli are presented to the child in a discrimination procedure. The top stimulus is "matched" by one of the three stimuli in the bottom row of windows. The task of the child is to select the stimulus that matches the one in the top window. In the procedure the stimuli are presented, and the experimenter, who is not visible to the child, "names" the top stimulus. The child must repeat the name—read the stimulus—and then press the plastic cover over the top window. Then he must select the matching stimulus from among the bottom windows, press the plastic cover, and again "name" the phonetic stimulus. When this response occurs, and the match is correct, the child is automatically and immediately reinforced. If the child correctly "names" the stimulus before the experimenter does so, that is, "anticipates" the correct name, reinforcement immediately follows—it is then not necessary to go through the matching task.

The development of the apparatus was found to be crucial in insuring that only the correct behavior is learned. For example, the apparatus insures that the attentional responses of the child are under experimental control; he must be looking at the visual verbal stimulus while emitting the response. The apparatus also insures that errors in performance are not rewarded—for example, to eliminate "guessing" the electronic control was designed so that an error requires repetition of the task from the beginning. Reinforcement is thus contingent only on a correct response.

A problem with the study of child learning over long periods of time has also been with construction of a reinforcer system that will maintain voluntary participation (see Long, Hammack, May and Campbell, 1958). Children cannot, of course, as in laboratory studies with animals, be deprived of food for long periods of time and kept at reduced body weight, so that research may be conducted. And we cannot normally use the withdrawal of aversive stimulation as a source of reinforcement. One of the things we see on the basis of naturalistic observation, however, is that tokens, like money, become excellent reinforcers for people—even without states of deprivation of primary reinforcers. Taking this tip from everyday life, a reinforcer system following the same principle was developed by the author in 1959. This consisted of tokens backed up by various items which the child had previously selected. The token reinforcement system has since been used by the author and others in a number of studies, with various modifications.

In the experimental situation being described, each time a correct response is emitted a token, a marble, is ejected from the tube into the dish in the right corner of the table in front of the child, as shown in Figure 1. The tokens are backed up by reinforcers of different value, the difference in value determining the number of tokens that must be accumulated before the tokens may be exchanged for the reinforcer. One class of reinforcers, the small edibles and trinkets, may be exchanged for the token on a 1:1 ratio. Small toys are exchanged for 10 tokens, larger toys (or toys of higher quality) for 35 tokens, yet larger toys for 80 tokens; and the largest toys for 150 tokens. None of the toys are expensive; each token averages about one cent in value.

In the procedure, the child selects a number of toys from a large class of each value, before he commences the training program. A toy from each class is then hung in the experimental room (see Figure 1), each above a plastic tube. The size of the plastic tube indicates the number of tokens required to obtain the reinforcer. The child may thus "work" for any of the back-up reinforcers; he may obtain an edible or a trinket by depositing the token in the funnel shaped opening in the right upper corner; he may consecutively deposit 10 tokens in the smallest plastic tube and obtain the reinforcer above it, as with the other plastic tubes also; or he may work for several different back-up reinforcers at the same time.

The child can thus use his tokens to obtain four different classes of toy reinforcers (or trinkets or edibles) that are available to him. As soon as he obtains a toy, another that he has previously selected from the same class is placed on display so that he always has a choice among four "for which to work," plus the trinkets-edible mixture.

After the child has been trained to use the apparatus and to make the phonetic character discriminations, which took ordinarily two of the 20 minute training sessions, the reading procedure proper was begun. The child could press a door-bell type of button in front of him. That would bring on the next phonetic character which would appear in the top window. The experimenter (who was invisible to the child) would say the name of the character, and the child would repeat the name. This would turn on lights of the bottom windows and activate the switches connected to the plastic covers of the windows. In one of the bottom windows would be the same character as in the top window, the other two windows containing foil characters that differed either in the diacritical mark or in the consonant or vowel letters. The child would have to select the matching stimulus in the bottom window and press its plastic cover and say the character's name again. If the selection was incorrect a buzzer would ring and the lights in the window would go out, and the child would have to begin by pressing the door-bell type button again.

If the child's response was correct in all aspects, a marble-reinforcer would be delivered. The mechanism would then be turned off until the child had deposited the marble in one of the possible alternatives and had put away any back-up reinforcer that he might have received. Each correct response was recorded automatically with standard cumulative recording equipment. That is, the record consisted of a pen that moved from left to right at a constant speed. Thus, time constituted the baseline of the diagrams representing the child's rate of reading performance. Each time the child made a response, the pen would take a graduated step upwards. Thus, the more rapidly the child responded the more steeply would the line slope upwards. The steepness of the slope of the line thus indicates how rapidly the child is reading. Markers were also used to indicate when the child was reinforced with a marble and when he received a back-up reinforcer, as well as what it was. These cumulative records constituted the main results of the first studies that are to be summarized.

The next step in the experimental analysis of reading acquisition was to test the combined apparatus and procedure. While each phase of developing the laboratory facility involved pilot work, it was important to determine whether the entire system would maintain the child's behavior for a long enough period of time to study significant variables in the learning process, to see if the stimulus materials and apparatus produced control of attentional responses, to establish the feasibility of cumulative recording, and to note the sensitivity of the records, and so on. The learning curves of two children run for 40 daily twenty-minute training sessions under conditions of continuous reinforcement will be presented (Staats, et al., 1964). The first child's record is one of great consistency following the preliminary training sessions (see Figure 2). For this child the tokens appeared to immediately constitute strong and invariant reinforcers. That is, this child customarily deposited his tokens in the tubes for the larger toys, which meant that several times his behavior was maintained for as many as three daily sessions with no back-up reinforcers--only tokens. The second child's working behavior in the reading training was more variable, including pauses of various intervals (see Figure 3), with consequent changes in the child's rate of reading as indicated by the varying steepness of slope of the record.

The preceding study indicates by the length and quality of the children's participation that the reinforcer system was effective. That is, although it is usually difficult to get pre-school children to attend to a task and work arduously for long periods of time, when this behavior was reinforced as in the present study the behavior was well maintained. It should be remembered that voluntary participation in the training was in competition with free play since that is what the children would otherwise have been doing. Thus, the reinforcement system appeared to be very effective.

In addition, the apparatus for the presentation of the verbal stimuli appeared to function well. On the phonetic characters the child had not yet learned he received two learning trials per reinforcement. That is, he looked at the stimulus in the top window and said its name and then found the same stimulus in one of the bottom windows and said its name again, this being followed by reinforcement. The

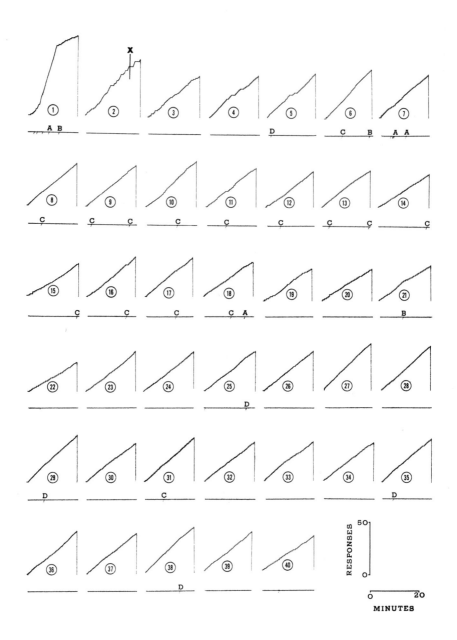

FIGURE 2

Cumulative records by sessions for Subject ... 1. Responses made prior to point **X** in Session 2 are those occurring during various pretraining phases. Point **X** marks the beginning of the actual reading task. The slash marks located on the line below each curve represent the presentation of various back-up reinforcers. **A** indicates that a $.10 toy was exchanged for 10 marbles; **B** marks the presentation of a $.35 toy in exchange for 35 marbles; the child's exchange of 80 marbles for a toy is denoted by a **C;** **D** marks the exchange of 150 marbles for a toy; unlettered slash marks indicate that the child deposited a marble for some item from the Universal Feeder. From Staats, et al., 1964a.

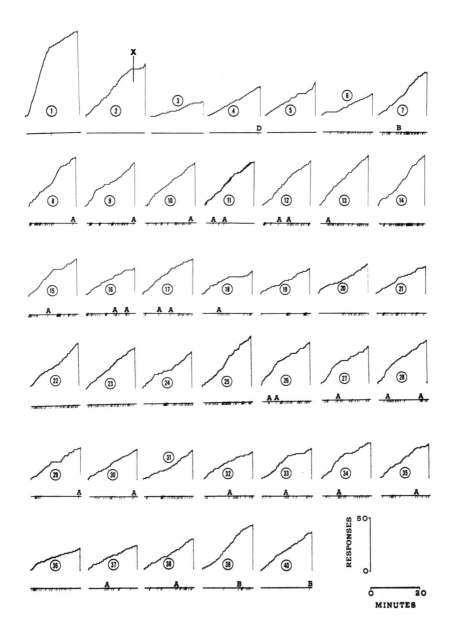

FIGURE 3

The cumulative records by sessions for Subject . . . 2. The sequence of pretraining tasks occurs until point **X** at which time the reading program was introduced. The occurrence of back-up reinforcers is indicated below each curve as on the previous subject's records. From Staats, et al., 1964a.

apparatus and procedure also worked effectively in now allowing incorrect responses to be reinforced.

In addition, the recording apparatus worked effectively. The child's moment to moment responding could be recorded. When the child was reading the phonetic stimuli rapidly this was shown by the steeper slope of the curve. Thus, the results for these children indicated that the various procedural developments were functional in producing a laboratory situation within which to study the complex human learning of a reading repertoire. Long-term studies now appeared to be possible as each of these two children emitted about 1,500 reading responses in the 40 days of training.

Although this study demonstrated the effectiveness of the use of the reinforcement system in maintaining arduous learning behavior of the children, it did not do so in a manipulative fashion. That is, the reinforcement was not manipulated during the study to see the effect that its presence and absence would have on the behavior of the children. This would be necessary to more firmly show the importance of this variable in the original learning of small children.

Thus, the next step in the systematic analysis of reading was to use the laboratory facility to begin to assess variables important to the acquisition of reading. As part of this, also, there was the need to test the extent to which the facility was well enough controlled to be sensitive to the manipulation of important independent variables.

An important variable needing more systematic study concerns reinforcement conditions, including the schedule of reinforcement. We know from more basic studies that certain schedules of reinforcement will produce better working behaviors than others. On a practical level of dealing with children's learning, can we improve the rate of response by reinforcement scheduling variables when complex learning is involved? Related to this is also a second goal of improving the reinforcer system. That is, it would be advisable to minimize the delivery of reinforcers to prevent satiation. Anything which postpones satiation can be considered to increase the effectiveness of the reinforcer system, and intermittent reinforcement would reduce reinforcer expenditure.

The next study (Staats, et al., 1964), using additional children, was oriented towards these questions. Two different schedules of reinforcement were applied to each of my subjects, and rates of response under each schedule were compared. The procedure was that of discrimination learning: the child was reinforced in one manner under one room-light condition, and in another manner under another room-light condition. These light-reinforcement conditions were alternated during each training session in a manner which has been referred to as a multiple schedule (Ferster and Skinner, 1957; Orlando and Bijou, 1960).

The first child was run under continuous reinforcement for one light condition and under extinction--no reinforcement--for the other light condition. We would expect a discrimination to develop such that the reading behavior would occur under the appropriate light condition, but much less so under the other light condition. That is what occurred. The records are shown in Figure 4. Each reinforcement condition is depicted as a separate component after which time the recording pen resets to the baseline. By the sixth session the discrimination begins to form and thereafter becomes even more pronounced. We clearly see how stimulus conditions (in this case the light) which are correlated with response-contingent reinforcement can assume control over the working behaviors of the child. That is, when the light came on which was correlated with reinforcement, the child immediately began responding more rapidly. When the light condition changed, reading behavior deteriorated. The dramatic nature of the discrimination is shown even more clearly in Figure 5, where the responses under each reinforcement condition are pieced together so that the two performances can be compared to each other over the 30-session training period. The records of the next two children to be described will also be of this latter type.

The second subject was run in a similar manner under continuous reinforcement and variable-ratio reinforcement--in the final training sessions the variable-ratio schedule had reached an intermittency of one reinforcer for an average of five responses. Higher rates of response were produced under the intermittent schedule--using, of course, fewer reinforcers (see Figure 6). The third child's results include responding under continuous reinforcement and variable interval reinforcement where the first response the child made after an average of 2 minutes had passed was reinforced. As would be expected, the child's reading response rate was lower under the variable-interval condition than under continuous reinforcement (see Figure 7).

These studies show clearly the importance of reinforcement in the context of this important type of learning. When the child is reinforced his participation is enthusiastic, interested, hardworking. When reinforcement for the behavior is not forthcoming the child's reading learning becomes desultory, disinterested, and other behaviors occur which are antithetical to learning. That is, the child when under the no-reinforcement condition would "fool around" in various ways, for example, spin on the stool and sing and so on—behaviors like those we typically see in the classroom.

In addition, finer reinforcement principles were demonstrated. That is, it was possible to increase the vigor of the children's reading behavior through the use of

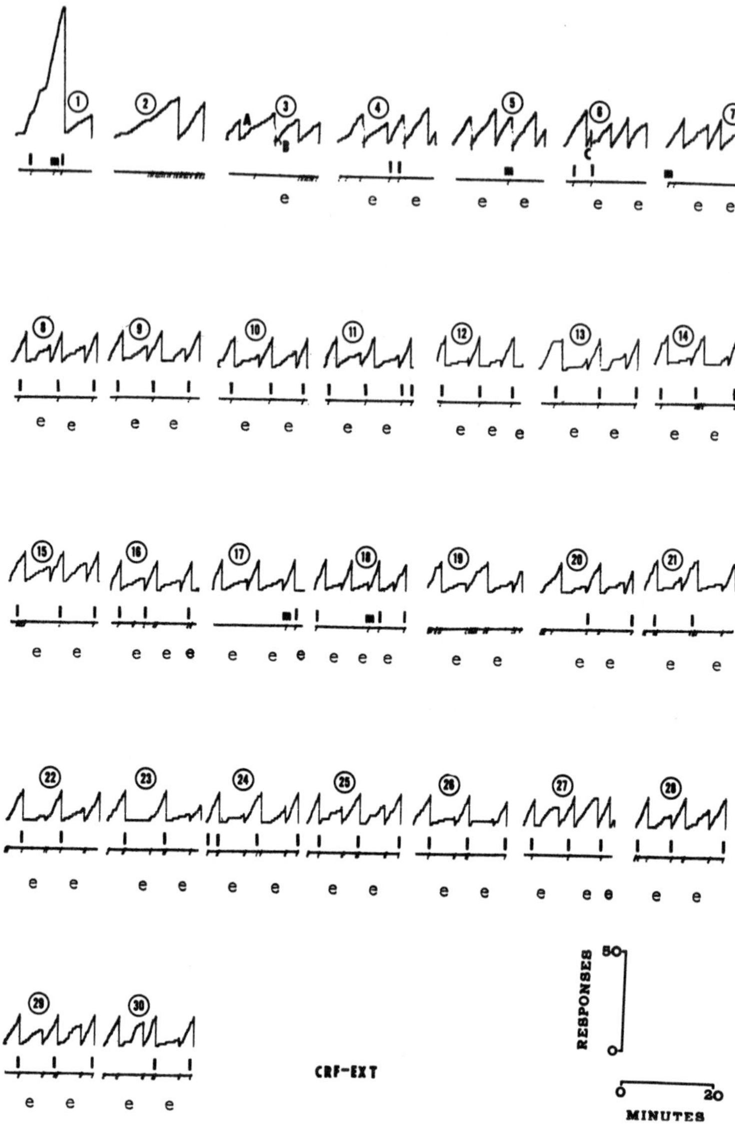

FIGURE 4

The thirty daily session records for the multiple continuous reinforcement-extinction (*mult* CRF-EXT) subject show the reading response rates for the various experimental conditions. Responses prior to point *A* occurred during the pretraining phases of the study. At this point the reading program was introduced under CRF. Beginning with Session 4 each 20-minute reading session commenced with a CRF component which then alternated with EXT conditions as the results show the child demonstrates a high rate of response under the reinforcement condition. The rate comes to immediately decline when the light changes and the child is in the extinction condition, as indicated by the letter *e* below each extinction period. The even marker on the line below each record indicates the delivery of a back-up reinforcer: *1* notes the exchange of 10 marbles for a $.10 toy, *o* notes the presentation of a $.35 toy in exchange for 35 marbles, and unlettered even marks indicate the exchange of 1 marble for an item from the Universal Feeder. From Staats, et al., 1964b.

400

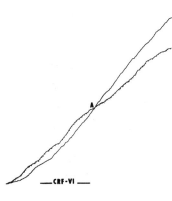

CRF-VI

FIGURE 5

Composite record for the *mult* CRF-EXT subject. In order to make a comparison between an *S*'s response rates for the two experimental conditions the records for reinforcement schedules were separated and recombined to yield an individual curve for each condition according to daily session sequence. All records commence with the introduction of the reading program. The composite records for the four *S*'s response rate. Figure 7 shows that for the *mult* CRF-EXT *S* the EXT rate was initially the higher rate, but at point *A* it declined and crossed the CRF curve. The CRF response rate was relatively rapid and stable throughout the experiment. From Staats, et al., 1964b.

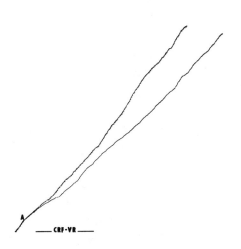

CRF-VR

FIGURE 6

Composite record for the multiple continuous-variable ratio reinforcement (*mult* CRF-VR) subject. The VR curve (shown with slash marks on the record) was initially lower than the CRF curve. However, from point *A* on the record, at which point it becomes the lower of the two curves. From Staats, et al., 1964b.

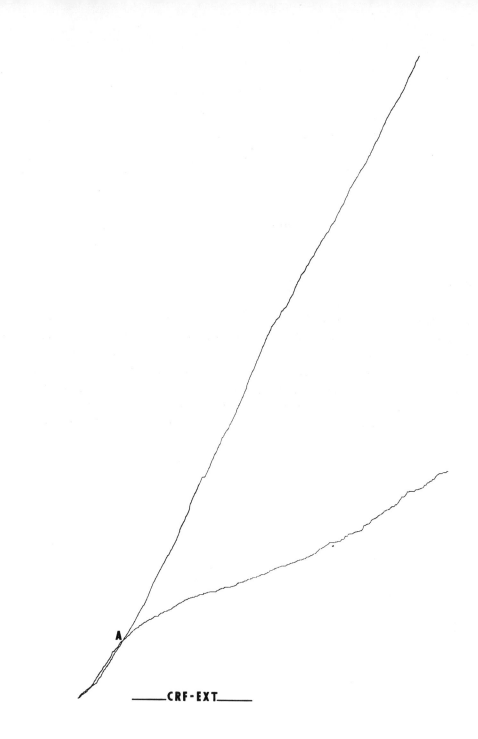

FIGURE 7

Composite record for the multiple continuous-variable ratio reinforcement (*mult* CRF-VI) subject. The VI curve (with slash marks) is depicted above the CRF curve until point *A* on the record, at which point it becomes the lower of the two curves. From Staats, et al., 1964b.

partial or intermittent reinforcement schedules. Contrary to common sense notions some intermittent schedules produce more rapid responding than does continuous reinforcement. This was evident with the children engaged in a reading task. The finding has strong implications for practical procedures of training since intermittent reinforcement can allow one to reduce the number of reinforcers given, thus reducing satiation while increasing performance. These variables need further study in the context of applications to actual educational learning where motivational conditions are crucially important. Before dealing with some of those problems, an extension of the basic laboratory for the study of retarded children will be briefly mentioned.

That is, the basic laboratory procedures have been tested and further developed for use with mentally retarded children; 2 educable retardates and 4 trainable retardates, including 2 mongoloid children. The children used in the study ranged in age from 7 years and 3 months to 10 years and 8 months. The children's mental ages ranged from 3 years and 2 months to 6 years and 5 months; the IQs from 36 to 67. Each child's participation in the study was well maintained by the reinforcer system. However, the more retarded children tended to use their marble tokens to obtain immediate reinforcement. That is, the marbles were deposited largely for the trinkets and edibles, rather than the toys which took longer to earn.

Another large difference among the children that appeared was in the quality of the children's attentional and working behaviors. Stipulation of these behaviors was made possible in the study by recording the time the children spent in the different aspects of the task. That is, the amount of time the children spent in the phonetic character discriminations were timed, as was the time spent in handling the reinforcers, as well as the time after putting the reinforcer away until the button was pressed to bring on the next card. The latter two periods were actually a measure of the time the child spent "fooling around." One of the major reasons for poor performance in several of the retarded children was in the poor quality of some of the children's work behaviors. The result suggested that further study be made of the possibility of improving these behaviors through training. The observation indicated this type of improvement would have aided the learning of some of the children.

In addition, there were differences in the length of time it took to train the children to use the apparatus. For normal children of 4 years of age, only two training sessions are required. In the present study the educable retardates took 2 or 3 times as long. However, thereafter they performed the reading task even more rapidly than have normal 4-year old children. In general, the more retarded the child, the greater the length of the training required to use the apparatus and to make the phonetic symbol discriminations. This was seen to be the case because of poor language development. The result was the necessity to directly train the children to the complex task rather than use the more usual verbal instructions. The most retarded child, a mongoloid retardate with a mental age of 3 years and 2 months, required special materials and a long period of training. However, this child had no spontaneous speech repertoire at the beginning of training, and it was necessary to train the child to make an appropriate verbal response to 10 pictures before the training in the reading task could begin.

One of the most important findings was that *all* of these children could make the discriminations involved in the task. A cumulative record of the letter reading responses of one trainable retardate is given in Figure 8. As the Figure shows the reading response rate of this child with an IQ of 50 was very adequate. It should be remembered that the stimuli involved were letters with diacritical marks and that the discriminations were much more difficult than those involved with ordinary letters. The results thus suggested that the difficulty in training retarded children to read does not involve the inability to make the visual discriminations, although such a defect has previously been suggested as causative (House and Zeaman, 1960).

The study gave a number of other suggestions. One was that the laboratory apparatus and procedure provided a situation in which the complex learning of retarded children could be objectively studied over a long period of time. A next step should be to attempt to train these types of children to actual repertoires to find out the specific types of difficulty involved. As the results suggested many of these children will probably turn out not to have special learning problems. The problem would seem to lie in the unfortunate learning circumstances they have encountered, for example, in the inadequacies of the sources of reinforcement for maintaining good attentional and working behaviors. For one thing, as is quite evident throughout this project of study, when there are not adequate sources of reinforcement, attention and working behaviors are not maintained in young children—and learning then ceases. Furthermore, once a child falls behind in the learning of his cognitive skills he enters a vicious cycle. Since his skills are poor he receives little reinforcement for the learning behavior and thus the behavior becomes even weaker resulting in additional cognitive deficit.

In any event, the basic principles of reinforcement in the context of cognitive learning may be considered to have been supported in these laboratory studies. The results and the preceding analysis, however, open up further lines of study in the systematic analysis of this type of learning. The next study, conducted by the author and his associates (Staats, et al., 1962), will indicate not only that reinforcement is important in maintaining the attentional and working behaviors of the child, but also that reinforcing these behaviors results in the actual learning of a

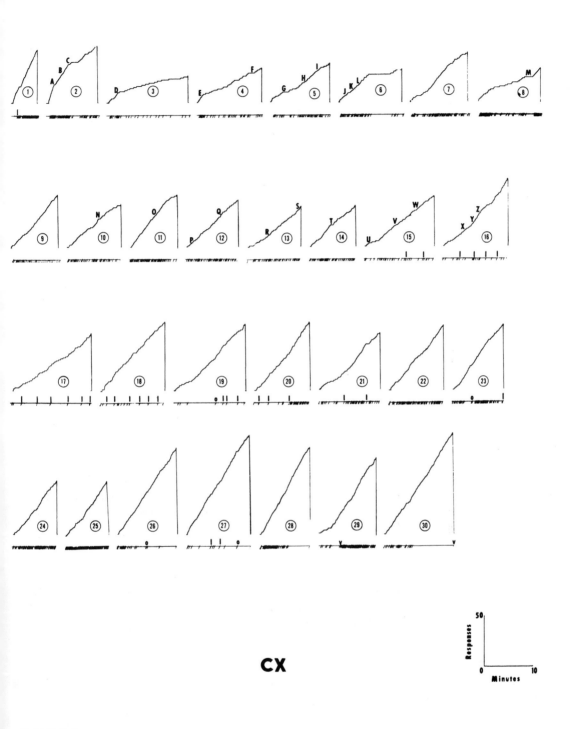

CX

FIGURE 8

Cumulative record of the reading responses of a retarded child with an IQ of 50. From Staats, 1968.

reading repertoire. This study is a step on the way to transposing the findings in the laboratory study of reading to actual procedures for training children to read.

For this study a small group of words was arranged in a program in which words were presented singly as well as in sentences and in short paragraphs. The child was prompted to say a word as he looked at it, and was reinforced with small edibles, trinkets, or tokens backed up by small toys. Eight 40-minute training sessions were presented to the children and the number of new words the children learned to read was tested after each training session.

Three four-year-old children were introduced to the training without extrinsic reinforcement--they were given social reinforcers (i.e., approval) but not the other reinforcers. This was continued until the child requested discontinuance of the activity, which was only 15 minutes for two of the children and 15 minutes into the second session for the other child. At this point reinforcement was instated and in each case the child's reading behavior was strengthened and maintained for the remainder of the training. The records of these children are shown in Figure 9. These children acquired respectively 16, 17, or 18 word reading vocabularies in the eight training sessions.

Three other children were given the opposite treatment. That is, they were started under the reinforcement condition and after two training sessions were switched to no-reinforcement condition and after two training sessions were switched to the no-reinforcement. As the figure shows they learned words readily under reinforcement, but when it was "cut off," their learning behaviors extinguished. After three or four sessions of no-reinforcement each child requested discontinuance of participation and the condition was then changed to reinforcement. In two cases the reading behavior was re-conditioned, and learning "picked up" again. The records of these children are presented in Figure 10.

The results of this study support and extend the findings of the previously described studies. That is, when the attentional and working behaviors of the children in the reading task were reinforced these behaviors were maintained in good strength. Without such reinforcement, however, the behaviors weakened and other competing behaviors that were not relevant to the task became relatively stronger. Furthermore, when the attentional and working behaviors of the children were strong they learned new reading responses rapidly, the converse was true when the behavior was not reinforced. The observations of the children's behavior in the learning situation as well as the recorded results indicated that basic to learning to read are the minute-to-minute attentional and working behaviors of the child. When the child attends to the material and works at a high rate, he rapidly learns to read. The major variation in learning seems to be a function of these basic behaviors.

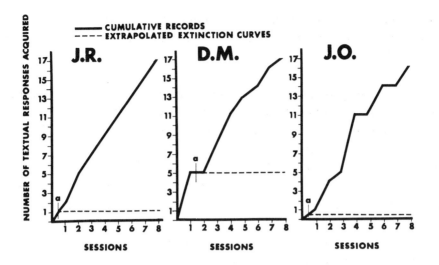

FIGURE 9

The curves shown here were generated under a beginning period of no "extrinsic" reinforcement. When *S* would no longer remain in the experimental situation, reinforcement was instated as indicated by the mark on the curve. The dotted line commences at the point *S* would no longer remain in the experiment, and indicates the curve which would have resulted if reinforcement was not introduced. From Staats, et al., 1962.

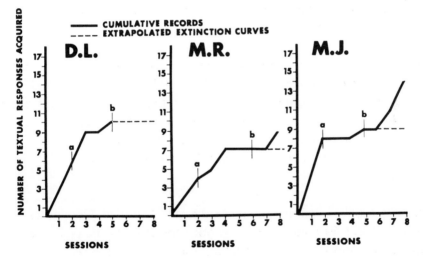

FIGURE 10

For these *S*'s, the first condition included reinforcement which was discontinued at the point of the first mark on the curve. When *S* would no longer remain in the experimental situation, reinforcement was reinstated, as the second mark on the curve indicates. The dotted line commences at the point the *S* would no longer remain in the experiment and depicts the curve which would have resulted if reinforcement was not reinstated. From Staats, et al., 1962.

Thus, it would appear that under more appropriate conditions of reinforcement, even very young children are capable of sustained work activities and can learn complex verbal skills.

The next step in applying principles from the learning model to a significant human behavior would be to conduct long-term studies in which children were actually trained to a reading repertoire. The author's work in this direction has followed two paths. One major goal has been to study in detail the process of the original learning of reading. Actually, the author had begun working on this long term project with his young daughter while the other studies were being conducted. The procedures developed in this study have more recently been generalized to other pre-school children, and the methods of study further developed (see Staats, 1968). It is only possible to briefly mention some of the general results in the present paper, after which the second goal, the study of the learning process involved in remedial reading problems, will be summarized.

The procedure and reinforcing system used in the study of the original learning of reading were adaptations of the laboratory apparatus and procedure described in the first study presented in the present paper. However, rather than the phonetic characters the children were first trained to read the upper and lower case alphabets, and then they were trained to read single words which were later combined into words and sentences. In addition, the children were given training in being able to pronounce letters phonetically.

The children involved in this research varied in age from 2- 5-year-olds. A few results may be summarized for one of the children. He was a 5-years and l-month-old boy at the time the study commenced. His Stanford-Binet IQ was 90, and he came from a working-class family with an average income. He was considered by his parents to be difficult to control and to train, and to learn more slowly than his siblings. The parents were concerned about his behavior problems and how he could adjust to school.

In the study it took 37 training sessions averaging less than 15 minutes each, for a total of 8 hours and 49 minutes, to introduce the child to the procedures and train him to the upper- and lower-case alphabets through "t." In 5 hours and 49 minutes of additional training, in 11 training sessions, the child was taught to individually read 21 new words. In this period he also learned to read these words in a number of different sentences and short stories (paragraphs).

In the 7 months of training in which this boy voluntarily participated, before the author terminated the study, he learned a number of additional significant aspects of a reading repertoire. (It is noteworthy to point out that his parents used cessation of the training as a threat with which to control the child's behavior which indicates how positive the training was to the child.) One of these types of training which is also a more formal study in itself, will be summarized. The study indicates that in addition to research on the motivational aspects of reading acquisition, the experimental methods and learning principles may also be used to investigate *methods* of training reading within the context of the extension of basic leaning analyses.

In learning to read it is necessary that single letters and other parts of words (syllables) come to control phonetic (part word) responses. In order to sound out a new word in reading new material, the child must be able to respond to the letter and syllable units with a correct sequence of vocal unit responses, the sequence then completing the word response.

This type of repertoire could be trained in different ways. For example, Bloomfield (1961) has suggested that unit reading repertoires come about in a way that can be seen as an example of a type of concept formation, only more complex. Using the present procedures as examples, it would be expected that if the child was presented with the letter stimuli *d, g, l, k, n,* and *w* each in combination with each of the vowels *a, e, i, o,* and *u*--the various combinations being presented--and was trained to read such syllables, the *single* stimuli involved in each **combination** would come to control the appropriate response *unit* involved in each total response. That is, the *d* would come to control the "duh" vocal response, the *a* the "aye" response, and so on. The present experiment actually only concerned the acquisition of the consonant vocal sounds (consonant concepts) under the control of the consonant letters. The learning of the consonant responses (phonemes) under the control of the consonant symbols (graphemes) was tested by teaching the child to respond to two new vowels, *y* and *a.* The new vowels were then combined with the consonants and presented to the child. These constituted novel syllables. If the consonant "concepts" had been learned, these new syllables should be read correctly.

In contrast another way that a phonetic reading repertoire could be developed would be to directly train the child to respond to the unit letter stimuli with unit vocal responses, rather than to use the above described concept formation type of presentation. That is, the child would be directly trained to give a specific vocal response to each letter. Presumably, then, when two such stimuli were presented together in a new combination the result would be the sounding out of a novel sequence of responses. That is, in the present study the test was made by combining two of the syllables the child had already learned to read separately, *da* and *gy,* to see if the two stimuli would control the novel reading response, *DAGY.*

Let me first begin by describing the establishment of grapheme-phoneme reading units through the concept formation training procedure. At the time the phonetic training began in the present study, the child had already learned to read the vowels: a "aye," e as "ee," i as "eye," u as "oo" (actually, this required additional training since the child had previously learned to pronounce the letter "you"), and o as "oh." In the phonetic training the a was first combined with the consonants to yield da, ga, la, ka, na, and wa. These syllables were presented in random order. The child was prompted to make the appropriate vocal response while looking at the character and was reinforced when he had done so. These characters were presented until the child had read each of the 6 four consecutive times without error. The same process was then repeated with the other vowels in combination with the same consonants. When this was finished for all of the vowels, the total procedure was then repeated twice more to the same criterion level. The child's performance on this task is shown in Table 1.

The Table shows for each of the three presentations of the five vowels the number of trials necessary to reach the criterion as well as the number of errors made on the consonant involved. Thus, it takes 54 trials to learn the "consonant-a" syllables on their first presentation with 7 consonant errors occurring. That is, in 54 learning trials the child could read da, ga, la, ka, na, and wa, when presented in random order. The number of consonant errors increases with the next consonant-vowel series, the consonant-i series. This would be expected from what is known about

TABLE 1

Learning The Consonant Concepts

Consonants with the Vowels	FIRST PRESENTATION TO CRITERION		SECOND PRESENTATION TO CRITERION		THIRD PRESENTATION TO CRITERION	
	Number of Trials	Number of Consonant Errors	Number of Trials	Number of Consonant Errors	Number of Trials	Number of Consonant Errors
a	54	7	114	9	36	0
i	108	16	66	4	36	0
e	90	12	36	1	42	1
u	138	15	36	0	30	0
o	42	4	42	0	36	0
Totals	432	54	294	14	180	1

retroactive inhibition. That is, presentation of the consonant-*a* series has a negative transfer effect upon the subsequent learning. By the time the consonant-*e* series is reached the errors begin to fall. However, more trials are necessary to reach criterion for the consonant-*u* series. It is possible this increase in errors is influenced by the vowel *u.* That is, the child had just been trained to make a new response to this vowel (the "oo" sound rather than the name of the letter) and this probably contributed to the complexity of the learning involved here.

In any event by the time the consonant-*o* series is reached, the errors have decreased markedly. Again, however, this may reflect the ease of learning the vowel involved. In the second presentation of the consonant-*a* series the effects of retroactive inhibition may be clearly seen. More errors are made on the consonants in the second presentation than in the first presentation. At this point it is clear the concept learning is incomplete. Nevertheless, the number of errors continues to decrease with the presentation of the other consonant-vowel series. By the time the third presentation of the various consonant-vowel sets occurs, the child is making almost no errors on the consonants. At this point it would seem that the consonant letter stimuli had come to control the correct vocal responses, that is, that the consonant "concepts" had been formed.

This was tested for generality by training the child to read two new vowels, *a* as "ah," and *y* as "ee." If the concept formation had actually taken place then the consonants when in combination with new vowel stimuli should still control the correct consonant responses. This possibility was tested in the following manner. The child was first trained to read the new vowel, *ã* by presenting the letter singly and prompting the child to say the correct sound, this being followed by reinforcement. The sound of the *a* was "ah." The card was presented in this manner until the child read it correctly 3 times. Then the new vowel was paired with each of the consonants to yield *dã, gã, lã, dã, nã,* and *wã.* These characters were randomly presented 5 times each for a total of 30 trials (to the same criterion of 4 consecutive errorless completions of the 6 sets of characters). This procedure was completed for the new vowel *y* also. In both cases the results showed almost perfect transfer of the concept consonants. There was only one error with the *a* series and one with the *y* series.

In addition to these aspects of the study, exploration was also made of the possibility that the direct type of phonetic training that has been described can effectively produce general training that results in the child's ability to sound out words. This was done in the following manner. As a consequence of the training the child had already undergone he had a syllabic reading repertoire. In the present phase of the study two syllables were presented together to see if the child would then read them in sequence, thus in essence sounding out a novel bi-syllabic word.

This was done in the following manner. First, all the *a* syllables were presented for review to the criterion of two consecutive errorless performances on all the syllables (*da, ga, la, ka, na,* and *wa*). This was then done for the syllables containing *y*. At this point the test for the novel behavior of reading the two together was made.

This was done by presenting *da* on a card followed in four spaces by *gy*. The experimenter placed a finger under *da.* Then the experimenter pointed at the *gy.* The same thing was repeated using another card on which the two syllables were separated by only 3 spaces. On the next card the syllables were separated by only 2 spaces, on the next by one space, and finally a card was presented on which *dagy* was typed.

The results showed clearly that a new, original, response may be emitted upon the basis of past learning. That is, although the reading responses had been learned separately, when the syllables *da* and *dy* were combined into a two-syllable "word" no errors were made. In fact, when the *dagy* card was presented for the first time, as well as in its representations, the child responded with the novel two syllable response before the experimenter could point to the two syllables in series. The same results were obtained for the *da* and *dy* syllables.

Several other items are of interest in the results of this specific experiment. The training and test of the hypotheses in this study consumed 32 training sessions. The sessions were held 5 days a week and thus extended over a period of more than 6 weeks. The training sessions averaged 15.8 minutes in length. During this period of training the child's attentional and working behaviors were maintained in good strength by the reinforcer system. During this time he made 1,420 reading responses for which he received the equivalent of about $13.45 in toys.

The results indicated that a process analogous to a learning conception of a type of concept formation may take place in the acquisition of reading. A part response of a total response that was reinforced in the presence of part of a total stimulus (*da*) would come under the control of that part of the total stimulus (*d*) even when the part stimulus was combined with a new stimulus (as in *dy*). Thus, the control of a unit vocal response ("duh") by a unit reading stimulus (the *d*) occurred and would transfer to new circumstances. The procedures are analogous to linguistic type methods in teaching reading. The study thus involves an analysis of the way in which a reading repertoire may be acquired, and suggests that this complex type of discrimination learning in children may be systematically studied in the laboratory. Actually, the study represents the first experimental investigation of linguistic reading teaching procedures. It shows in the controlled situation that grapheme-phoneme reading units can be learned from whole-word presentations.

In addition, the manner in which original behavior can occur was also indicated by the results of the study. That is, responses separately trained to separate stimuli will occur together in a novel combination when the separate stimuli occur together. This principle has been used by the author (Staats and Staats, 1963) to describe aspects of novel sentence generation, as well as social, scientific, and mathematical reasoning. The present results give support to the contention that behavior may be learned, yet under appropriate stimulus circumstances can occur in *novel* forms. In the context of reading learning, it was shown that reading units learned in the concept formation (linguistic) procedure were functional. The reading units could be "employed" by the child in learning new "words" by "sounding out" the units in succession. The possibility of studying basic S-R principles and procedures in the context of significant, functional, behaviors was again demonstrated.

In general, the results with the other children similarly substantiated the principles and methods of the approach in the context of this important, functional behavior. For example, the experimental procedures were applied to 12 4-year-old culturally deprived children in a research-treatment classroom. The three cognitive repertoires of reading, writing, and number skills were dealt with over a 7 month period. It is not possible to detail the results. However, they supported the previous findings that (1) 4-year-old children are capable of voluntary cognitive learning of an accelerated type when reinforcement principles are utilized (the children advanced from a mean IQ of 100.9 to 112.3, and mean readiness achievement at the second percentile to the twenty-eighth percentile as compared to children 1 1/2 years older), (2) it was possible to experimentally study the S-R principles involved in cognitive learning of a complex, long-term kind. It may be concluded that the principles and methods may be applied to the study of this type of behavior in pre-school children. Although the various indications cannot be given here, it was evident that this type of study would provide us with what has not heretofore been available, namely an analysis of what reading is and how it is learned. While these studies by no means complete the research that is necessary, the outlines of the analysis of this type of behavior can now be extracted, and implications for further research and practical applications can be shown (see Staats, 1968).

The other line of the extension of the basic principles and methods of research has involved the study and treatment of children with special problems of learning. These are examples of what has come to be called "behavior modification." However, in the present case the study is of long duration and deals with a complex repertoire. The first study to be described dealt with a single subject. After verification of the principles and method with the single subject replication studies were conducted with additional subjects and additional instructional-technicians.

The boy, who was a juvenile delinquent (the study was terminated when the boy was sent to a reform school), was given 40 hours of reading training which involved 70 training sessions extending over a period of 4½ months. During the training this child made more than 64,000 word reading responses and earned token-reinforcers worth about 20.31 dollars. He received specific training on 761 words that he did not know. Later tests indicated that he had learned and retained 431 of these words. To further evaluate the results of the training, this child was given reading achievement tests prior to the study, approximately in the middle of the study, and at the end of the study. The results of these tests are shown in Figure 11. The first point on the curve was a measurement obtained by use of the Developmental Reading Test giving a total score of reading achievement showing that S was performing at the grade 2 level. After 45 reading training sessions, S's performance on the California Reading Test showed a gain to the 3.8 grade level. By the end of the training, after 25 additional training sessions, S had advanced to the 4.3 grade level. As the graph shows, when the child's rate of progress is plotted with his regular school training as a comparison, his rate of learning in the experimental procedures shows a considerable acceleration.

Another indication of the general effect of the reading training came from the child's performance in school, both in school achievement and deportment. The period of reading training coincided with a school term. The boy received passing grades in all subjects at the end of the semester: a C in physical education, a D in general shop, a D in math. It should be emphasized that these grades represent the first courses that this child has *ever* passed, and thus his finest academic performance. Furthermore, S began to behave better while in school. The boy had always been a behavior problem in school, and this continued into the period during which S received reading training. As Figure 12 shows, during the first month of the training S committed 10 misbehaviors that resulted in the receipt of demerits. These behaviors were as follows: disturbance in class (which occurred twice), disobedience in class (5 times), loitering (twice), and tardiness. In the second month he was given demerits for scuffling on the school grounds and also for creating a disturbance. In the third month he was given demerits for cutting math class and for profanity in class. As the figure shows, however, no misbehaviors occurred in the fourth month, or in the half month after this until the conclusion of the school term.

The results of this study strongly supported the analysis of reading acquisition in terms of the learning theory, as did the findings that had already been obtained with younger children. Through the use of an adequate reinforcement system this child who had always been a behavior problem in school came to learn rapidly. His attentional and working behaviors were well maintained by the reinforcement and

414

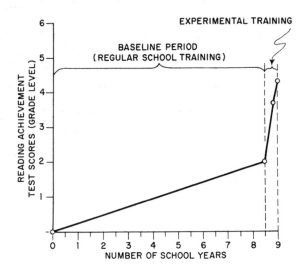

FIGURE 11

Reading-achievement test scores of the culturally-deprived delinquent child as a function of 8½ years of school training and 4½ months of experimental training. From Staats and Butterfield, 1965.

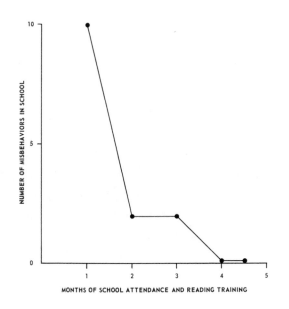

FIGURE 12

Number of official misbehaviors of the delinquent child in school as a function of months in experimental training. From Staats and Butterfield, 1965.

various measures of his achievement indicated good progress. The effects seemed also to be general. The boy reported that he liked to read better and that he liked his classes better. His grades were the best that he had ever gotten. In addition, his misbehaviors decreased (Staats and Butterfield, 1965).

This study again demonstrates an aspect of the experimental-longitudinal research methods that are being proposed. That is, after the exploration of the major learning principles in controlled laboratory circumstances study was extended to the more complex task of dealing with an actual problem of cognitive learning. The procedures were first worked out and tested with one subject. Following this a study was set up to replicate and extend the findings with additional subjects, in the manner followed in dealing with the original learning of reading. Thus, the reading procedures used with the juvenile delinquent were applied to 18 junior high school children. These included underachievers, children who were in classes for the educable mentally retarded, as well as children who constituted emotional or behavior problems (see Staats, Minke, Goodwin, and Landeen, 1967).

The first study, as well as the earlier studies, suggested that when an adequate motivational (reinforcement) system is employed, along with training materials which are specified, it is possible to administer effective training procedures employing instructional-technicians who are not highly trained. Thus, in the study with the juvenile delinquent the training procedures were administered by a probation officer. In the extension of these findings the "motivated learning" treatment procedures were administered by adult volunteers, who had no special training, and by average high school seniors who were literate. Essentially the same behavioral results were shown. The 18 children attended well and worked hard. During the 4½ months, which involved about 38 hours of training, they made many reading responses (a mean of about 94,000 single word reading responses). During the period of learning, moreover, the rate of the children's reading responses accelerated. This occurred even though the amount of reinforcement per reading response (ratio of reinforcement) was cut to 1/4 of its original level. Results indicated that the children were presented with a mean of 593.5 words that they did not know. In a long-term test of retention 70.9 per cent of these words were remembered when individually presented. The children received a mean of 22.29 dollars in reinforcers for their reading and learning behavior.

Last year this work was further extended to an additional 32 children in an experimental group, with 32 children in a control group. The children were Negro, residents of a ghetto area in Milwaukee, Wisconsin, and constituted problem learners of different types. The instructional-technicians were from the same population--one group of instructional-technicians was made up of literate high-school students, as in the preceding study. Half of the experimental subjects, however, were treated by instructional-technicians recruited through the employment office. They were employed full-time in the training of the problem children under the supervision of a teacher who had been trained in the "motivated learning" treatment procedures. Training for the instructional-technicians required about 3 hours.

Again, the results corroborated the findings of the earlier studies. The children worked well and learned accordingly. The results are not yet analyzed. However, preliminary inspection of the results suggests that besides the behavioral indices of the children's progress, the experimental group made significantly better progress as measured by achievement tests, grades, deportment, and attendance. These findings have positive implications for improving remedial educational practices; for upgrading employment for unemployed, culturally-deprived, adults who are literate or who can become literate; as well as for the learning theory and research methodology being tested.

Conclusions

These, however, are extensive topics and await a more complete presentation. The summary here does not constitute a full analysis of reading. Actually, only a part of the acquisition process has been described in brief. And only a part of the total learning model has been used. A more complete analysis of the complex behavior included under the term reading must draw more fully from the learning model (see Staats, 1968).

This summary of research on reading acquisition is presented, however, as a demonstration of the importance of the learning theory for dealing with complex human behavior, actually of various types. It is capable of producing not only theoretical understanding but also research suggestions as well as methods for actual application. It should be emphasized that the analyses stemming from the approach and from the experimental methods described herein are capable of *dealing* with problems of behavior--not merely diagnosing the problem of behavior, or of attributing its cause to personal defect. Theories of human behavior and its problems that are based upon test data, for example, ordinarily do not yield methods of specific treatment of the behavior problem. While testing is important for its diagnostic value, tests and test theory have not been as valuable in providing means for treatment of the problem. It is for this reason, in part, that it is suggested that learning analyses of behavior, and learning methods of treatment, have so much potential.

It is also suggested that a set of learning principles applied to problems of human behavior in the way described has all the attributes of a classical theory. That is, the basic principles have been systematically established in laboratory controlled experiments. These are the most general laws. The manner in which the basic principles combine to form more complex stimulus-response constellations has also been suggested (Staats, 1968) Both of these constitute the higher-order principles (or laws or axioms) of the theory. Each time an analysis is made of a new human behavior, it constitutes a lower-order hypothesis derived from the theory. Confirmation of the hypothesis through empirical study has the effect of verifying the specific hypothesis as well as the theoretical body from which the hypothesis derives. The studies that have just been cited on reading constitute both the confirmation of a specific hypothesis as well as more general support of the learning theory from which the hypotheses were drawn.

Thus, this suggests that the extension of learning principles to an aspect of significant human behavior, in addition to its practical value, also serves to develop the learning theory of human behavior. It may be suggested that already the theory has more systematic experimental support than other approaches. Further progress in the development of such a learning theory will rest upon projects such as the present one. This will have to involve various areas of behavior, for the greater the number of various behaviors sampled the more general the theory. It is suggested, however, that the theoretical body now has hypotheses and methods for the study of and treatment of various aspects of human behavior.

It may also be suggested that the progress of the research on reading that has been summarized herein contains a general strategy with which to investigate various aspects of human learning. To begin such research, the investigator who is familiar with the basic principles must first analyze the behavior in which he is interested in the terms of the S-R principles. This must include explicit statement of the observable behavior of interest. This task is usually easier to accomplish when dealing with the behavior when it is originally being acquired, that is in its simplest form. Thus, for example, it would be difficult to make an explicit statement of the behaviors involved in being a mathematician. It is much easier, however, to specify the behaviors involved in counting as well as how these behaviors are learned. (See Staats, 1968). When the simple behaviors are well understood, more complex forms can be studied. Even in its simple forms, however, significant human behaviors usually involve complex constellations of stimuli and responses. Nevertheless, the analysis of the behavior is basic to the research that follows and cannot be done ambiguously or in a simple minded manner. Ordinarily a full analysis of a significant behavior will require an integration of classical and instrumental learning principles as well as an indication of their interaction. Most human behaviors involve more than one behavior principle, or more than one type of response.

In addition to systematic analysis of the behavior involved, it will be necessary to include observations of the variables involved in the acquisition of the behavior.

Thus, one may have to explore the effective reinforcers involved, or absent, as well as other stimulus conditions effecting learning.

The next step in the extension of an integrated learning approach many times appropriately involves a "demonstrational" study. This means testing some of the main principles of the analysis in the context of the behavior of interest. For example, is reinforcement actually important in the acquisition and maintenance of the behavior involved? In any event, I have found that in this type demonstrational study one begins to learn more about the behavior and the subject population which is involved--and one may get ideas pertinent to more systematic study of the behavior.

The next step is to make a more systematic attempt to explore the principles involved in the acqustion, maintenance, or change in the behavior under study. Additional variables may be tested at this time—reinforcement schedules, discriminative stimulus control, or what have you. At this stage of the long-term study of a behavior problem, the attempt may be made to achieve better experimental control perhaps through the development of improved procedures or apparatus. If the behavior under study is complex, as most significant human behaviors are, it can be expected that short-term group studies will not suffice. Procedures will have to be worked out in which the behavior can be studied over a long period of time. We have to distinguish the modification of what are actually relatively simple behaviors or classes of behavior from the modification of more complex behaviors. It is stimulating to us, and a momentous step, to extinguish temper tantrums, or mold walking versus crawling, or teach going to bed at night without fuss. But we have to realize what the nature of this progress in learning extensions is, as well as the task that lies ahead. These are impressive demonstrations of the relevance and applicability of learning priciples to the treatment of behavior problems. However, we can't expect to bring an autistic child to high level educational achievement, or even good communication and good language behavior in reasoning through a short-term procedure. There are many behaviors—the original acquisition of speech, the acquisition of reading, the development of complex social behaviors, work behaviors, so-called mental retardation, and so on—which are acquired (or are not acquired) only over a period of many years. We must expect that is will take years to change or institute those behaviors even under good training procedures.

Nevertheless, we must begin the study of such complex human behaviors--as well as the more simple ones. But a belief that the operant shaping of a simple behavior in a short time indicates that all behaviors will fall into place this way, or that the major problems have been solved, is unrealistic. Although it would be expected on the basis of our findings that the principles hold from rat to man, the repertoire to be acquired by man is fantastically complex. The task of establishing long term procedures of training with which to deal with *problems* of complex human behavior lies largely ahead.

So, the learning approach appears to be tremendously productive--but there is much to do. Which brings us to the final step in the extension of learning to the solution of practical problems of behavior. Based upon my research on representative samples of cognitive learning, I would conclude that when one works over a period of years with the same problem of training behavior, first in demonstrational studies, then in other systematic studies, he learns a great deal about what can be done about some of the problems involved in modifying the behavior in the benign way. With this experience he is better prepared to begin research on actual practical problems. I had, for example, prior to actually training a child to read, very well worked out schemes for the procedure to be used, based upon my past research. At the present time, based upon my research, I have a full and detailed learning theory of reading (and language in general) on which to base new research and treatment methods.

For solving actual problems, thus, the simple knowledge of basic learning principles will not provide adequate background. Many learning theorists occupied solely with basic problems will confess quite frankly that they would not have the foggiest notion of how to help solve human problems involving learning, for example, how to train a child to read. I think the preceding steps I've outlined, on the other hand, will provide knowledge for approaching various practical problems of behavior, in quest of general solutions. Furthermore, the research conducted in this endeavor is an essential part of elaborating and verifying the basic principles and thus the basic science of learning.

The suggestion, then, is that it is important for investigators to become interested in the systematic and detailed study of a type of significant human behavior and continue with the study of the behavior over a long period of time, extending their progress in the extension of learning principles as far as possible towards the solution of practical problems. This suggestion would obtain far less than universal support, however, either from many of the prominent people in the psychology of learning, or many people involved in the various applied areas dealing with human problems. It is felt that it is time for a change in both of these opinions.

The objections of experimentalists in the field of learning to application of learning principles and methods stems, it may be suggested, from a misconception of what science is and does. These individuals many times see the status of a science as emerging only from laboratory precision and control, and mathematical theory. This is certainly true, in part. However, the paraphernalia that smack of science, for example, elaborate apparatus and the use of mathematics may unfortunately be seen to be the heart of science. The applied areas, lacking these accoutrements of science, at least in the realm of complex human behavior, may be seen as an entirely separate type of endeavor. This is a superficial analysis, however, and leads one to erroneously denigrate applied versus basic research.

It is true that in psychology the methods and principles of the practitioner have almost always been derived in ways other than through laboratory research. Thus, there actually has been a true separatism between basic and applied work--with little overlap. However, it is suggested that this is an artificial separation, a result of the previous lack of development of relevant principles and methods in the basic science. When the relevance of learning procedures and methods has been demonstrated in an area of human behavior it will be possible for the practitioner to use them and in so doing the applied and basic fields will draw closer together.

It should also be added and stressed that the high stratus of a science is reached when its methods and principles receive verification in the events of the real world. Although we revere laboratory apparatus and elaborate theoretical endeavors, we do so largely because they have produced methods and principles that make better predictions about the real world and enable us to manipulate the real world--better than the methods and principles produced by other types of study. A type of verification of a science, when its principles are relevant to events of the real world, involves the extent to which the principles of the science improve upon non-scientific conceptions. One of the avenues of support of a theory of learning, thus, is the extent to which its principles and methods can deal in an improved fashion with actual problems of human behavior. It is suggested that extension of learning principles into the area of human behavior will prove to be one of the most important avenues for producing verification and generality of the principles.

Another resistance to the extension of laboratory derived learning principles into the realm of human problems comes from the ranks of practitioners concerned with those problems. This resistance has also had its rational basis. That is, learning approaches were for a long time restricted to dealing with simple organisms, simple situations, and simple behaviors. During this period it was quite correct for the practitioner to conclude that "brass-instrument" experimentalism had nothing to offer him in his task of dealing with complex human behavior. As a consequence, most practitioners' knowledge of learning approaches has remained limited to a few basic principles and experimental procedures. This state of affairs has persisted since the traditional course in learning theory contributes little to an understanding of human behavior. However, this state of affairs is changing. There are now materials in the area of learning, as the present paper illustrates, that are relevant to practical problems of behavior. See the author's outline of a learning theory of human behavior (Staats, 1964, 1968; Staats and Staats, 1963). It is suggested that the learning theory is now more useful to the practitioner than are the various nonexperimentally derived theories of human behavior that are now more generally accepted. The practitioner who converts to a learning approach, it may be suggested, will have an advantage in his practice, and he will have an opportunity to contribute to a general scientific framework.

It is also suggested that the extension of learning principles and methods to the study and treatment of human behavior problems, and thus to the verification of an integrated-functional learning conception of human behavior, is occurring at an ever accelerating rate. Great advancements lie directly ahead. In this task, because the general method of the approach is based upon the manipulation of observable independent and dependent variables, the method should have advantages characteristic of other sciences—one of which is their "self-corrective" nature. That is, when working with observable events, it is evident when something has been accomplished and when it has not, where principles hold and where they do not, where development is still necessary, and so forth. Thus, to the extent that learning approaches to behavior modification, for example, are based upon a set of experimentally established principles, a development consistent with that occurring in other applied sciences can be confidently predicted.

Preparation of this paper was supported in part by the Educational Research and Development Center of the University of Hawaii.

References

Bloomfield, L. "Teaching children to read." In Bloomfield, S. and Barnhart, C. L. LET'S READ: A LINGUISTIC APPROACH. Detroit: Wayne State University Press, 196I.

Dollard, J., and Miller, N. E. PERSONALITY AND PSYCHOTHERAPY. New York: McGraw-Hill, 1950.

Ferster, C. B., and Skinner, B. F. SCHEDULES OF REINFORCEMENT. New York: Appleton, 1957.

House, B. J. and Zeaman, D. "Visual discrimination learning and intelligence in defectives of low mental age." AMER. J. MENT. DEFIC.,65: 51-58, 1960.

Long, E. R., Hammack, J. T., May, F., and Campbell, B. J. "Intermittent reinforcement of operant behavior in children." J. EXP. ANAL. BEHAV., 1: 315-339, 1958.

Olson, D. R. FROM PERCEIVING TO PERFORMING THE DIAGONAL. Paper presented at the annual meetings of the American Psychological Association, Washington, D. C., 1967.

Orlando, R. and Bijou, S. W. "Single and multiple schedules of reinforcement in developmentally retarded children." J. EXP. ANAL. BEHAV., 3: 339-348, 1960.

Staats, A. W. LEARNING, LANGUAGE, AND COGNITION. New York: Holt, Rinehart and Winston, 1968.

Staats, A. W. CATEGORIES AND UNDERLYING PROCESSES, OR REPRESENTATIVE BEHAVIOR SAMPLES AND S-R ANALYSES: OPPOSING STRATEGIES. Paper presented at the annual meetings of the American Psychological Association, Washington, D. C., 1967.

Staats, A. W. "An integrated-functional learning approach to complex behavior." In Kleinmuntz, B. (Ed.) PROBLEM SOLVING. New York: Wiley, 1966.

Staats, A. W. HUMAN LEARNING (Ed.). New York: Holt, Rinehart and Winston, 1964.

Staats, A. W. and Butterfield, W. "Treatment of nonreading in a culturally deprived juvenile delinquent: An application of learning principles." CHILD DEVELOP-MENT. 36: 925-942, 1965.

Staats, A. W., with contributions by Staats, C. K. COMPLEX HUMAN BEHAVIOR. New York: Holt, Rinehart and Winston, 1963.

Staats, A. W., Finley, J. R., Minke, K. A., and Wolf, M. Reinforcement variables in the control of unit reading responses. J. EXP. ANAL. BEHAV., 7, 139-149, 1964.

Staats, A. W., Minke, K. A., Goodwin, W., and Landeen, J. Cognitive behavior modification: "Motivated learning" reading treatment with a subprofessional therapy-technician. BEHAV. RES. THERAPY, 5, 283-299, 1967.

Staats, A. W., Staats, C. K., Schutz, R. E., and Wolf, M. The conditioning of testual responses using "extrinsic" reinforcers. J. EXP. ANAL. BEHAV., 5, 33-40, 1962.

Staats, A. W., Minke, K. A., Finley, J. R., Wolf, M., and Brooks, L. O. A reinforcer system and experimental procedure for the laboratory study of reading acquisition. CHILD DEVELOPM., 35, 209-231, 1964.

423

TESTS FOR THE EVALUATION OF EARLY CHILDHOOD EDUCATION: THE CINCINNATI AUTONOMY TEST BATTERY (CATB)*

Thomas J. Banta, Ph.D.

"Curiosity, one of the deepest of human traits, indeed far more ancient than mankind itself, was perhaps the mainspring of scientific knowledge in the past as it still is today." . . .George Sarton

"There are children playing in the street who could solve some of my top problems in physics, because they have modes of sensory perception that I lost long ago.". . .J. Robert Oppenheimer

"It is in our IQ testing that we have produced the greatest flood of misbegotten standards. Unaware of our typographic cultural bias, our testers assume that uniform and continuous habits are a sign of intelligence, thus eliminating the ear man and the tactile man.". . .Marshall McLuhan

While educators have adequate tests for early childhood intelligence (for example, the Stanford-Binet or the Peabody Picture Vocabulary) the focus of such tests is on the appropriate, the conventional, and the quick response. The tests which make up the Cincinnati Autonomy Test Battery (CATB) were designed to measure autonomous functioning in problem solving.

The word "autonomy," as it is used in the context of the CATB, refers to *self-regulating behaviors that facilitate effective problem solving.* My conviction is that these are not abilities which the child is forced or pressured into developing, but those abilities which the child enjoys developing in the process of his individually chosen work and play. The CATB measures *curiosity, exploratory behavior, persistence, resistance to distraction, control of impulse, reflectivity, analytic perceptual processes, and innovative behavior.* Each test emphasizes a separate aspect of self-regulating behavior relevant to good problem-solving strategies.**

All these factors are ready for further spontaneous development at age three, barring unfortunate home experiences. In addition, these factors can be influenced by prekindergarten educational efforts. The job for the future is to track down the ways in which prekindergarten education works, and *which kinds* of educational

*I am deeply grateful for the extraordinary help I have had in developing these tests. Mrs. June Sciarra, in her wisdom and patience with my theorizing, and Miss Jean Jett, in her skill and tolerance for my unreasonable work demands, should get full credit for keeping this entire research program moving forward. I can't thank them enough.

**Such strategies for adults have been delineated by the mathematician G. Polya (1945) in his book, HOW TO SOLVE IT. He presents ingenious verbal and cognitive strategies that, I argue, presuppose the arousal and sustenance of curiosity motivation and other self-regulating behaviors already developing in early childhood.

practice are most effective. The CATB is a step in this direction. My paper (Banta, 1966), "Educating Children for Adulthood," describes the philosophical basis of autonomy in education, and human development. (See also Banta, 1964, 1967).

The tests are administered individually. Great care has been taken to select testers who have worked extensively with young children. The testing procedure takes about one hour and requires sustained attention to the child, as well as complicated manipulations of test materials, stop-watch, and scoring that must be thoroughly mastered. The need for verbal comprehension is minimized in the tests in order to avoid penalizing children from homes where the opportunity to become skilled at following oral directions has not existed. All the tests focus on the child's behavior in problem-solving situations.

Effective problem solving does not necessarily mean the achievement of correct solutions to conventional problems, but rather the development of behaviors which are useful in a world that presents problems demanding creative as well as conventional solutions. It may be much more important for early childhood education to be concerned with the care and nurturance of these emerging tendencies than to be concerned only with conventional answers to conventional problems. Our job is to specify the tendencies objectively so that systematic educational research can be carried out with such goals of education in mind, along with the goals implicit in conventional intelligence tests.

John Holt, in his recent book, HOW CHILDREN FAIL (1964), put the issue nicely: "The true test of intelligence is not how much we know how to do, but how we behave when we don't know what to do" (p. 165). Because the three- and four-year old child is beginning to deal with a world full of entirely new problems and is learning to cope with novel challenges, our research is directed toward the understanding of "how we behave when we don't know what to do."

Criteria for selection of particular tests and test materials were: (a) relevance to autonomy theory, (b) relevance to later childhood and adulthood, (c) emphasis on behavioral rather than oral responses, (d) attractiveness of the materials to children, (e) minimal verbal demands on the child, both in instructions and responses, and (f) checks on the child's comprehension of instructions so that low scores will not be the result of not having caught on to the task.

The present tests are concerned with the *ways* in which a child solves a problem, not just his ability to perform a task "correctly." Some of the tests are by design so easy that all children can solve them, yet provide invaluable behavioral data which are analyzed for the child's style of approach to problems. Other tests are designed so that no children are able to perform satisfactorily in terms of the "correct" solution to the problem as defined by adults, and this enables us to measure each child's ability to cope with difficult problem situations. Still other tests are designed so that *some* children can solve them. These tests measure the children's *ability* to utilize specific problem- solving strategies.

The CATB, in its present form, provides test scores on fourteen basic variables. The following brief definitions give an idea of the range of behaviors assessed which are relevant to autonomous functioning.

DEFINITIONS OF AUTONOMY VARIABLES

Curiosity: Tendency to explore, manipulate, investigate, and discover in relation to novel stimuli.

Innovative Behavior: Tendency to generate alternative solutions to problems.

Impulse Control: Tendency to restrain motor activity when the task demands it.

Reflectivity: Tendency to wait before making a response that requires analytic thinking, when the task demands it.

Incidental Learning: Tendency to acquire information not referred to in the instruction stimuli.

Intentional Learning: Tendency to acquire information specified in the instructional stimuli.

Persistence: Attention to a problem with solution-oriented behavior where the goal is specified.

Resistance to Distraction: Persistence, with distracting stimuli present.

Field Independence: Tendency to separate an item from the field or context of which it is a part.

Task Competence: Ratings of tendency to deal effectively with problems of many kinds.

Social Competence: Ratings of ability to work comfortably with adults.

Kindergarten Prognosis: Ratings of ability to do well in conventional kindergarten.

Curiosity Verbalization: Tendency to talk to self or tester about a novel object while exploring it.

Fantasy-Related Verbalization: Tendency to engage in fantasy, expressed while exploring a novel object.

GENERAL THEORETICAL BACKGROUND

Ideas which have aided development of the CATB are found in diverse literature from the areas of personality, cognition and perception. There is a significant trend in each of these areas toward interest in aspects of what I call autonomous functioning, aspects especially concerning the style with which persons approach problems. The common element in these various perspectives can be stated briefly as interest in respects in which human functioning is not completely determined by internal impulses or conflicts (e.g., by compulsions, hostility, sex drive, guilt) or by external constraint (e.g., persuasion, punishment, oppression, deprivation). Hartmann's (1939) concept of the "conflict-free spheres of the ego" comes closest to summarizing this idea; his concept supports the view that ego functioning can be reality oriented, and that while much behavior and much mentation are overdetermined internally and externally, there are numerous facets of functioning which are "reality syntonic," enabling man not only to adapt to the average demands of living, but also to innovate--to find alternative ways of behaving and thinking.

Relevant examples of research and theory in the areas of cognition and perception are: Werner's (1948) mental development and the ontogenesis of abstraction; Dember & Earl's (1957) analysis of exploratory, manipulatory, and curiosity behavior; Guilford's (1959) divergent thinking; Lois Murphy's (1962) coping style; Kagan, Moss, & Sigel's (1963) analytic style; Kagan's (1965) impulsivity-reflectivity; Mendel's (1965) novelty seeking tendency; Wallach & Kogan's (1965) modes of thinking; Witkin's (1965) field independence; and Bruner's (1966) coping and defending.

Examples from the study of personality are: Anna Freud's (1936), Hartmann's (1939), and Rapaport's (1960) ego autonomy; Allport's (1937) functional autonomy; Erikson's (1950) early stages of development including basic trust, autonomy, initiative, and industry; White's (1960) competence motivation; Christie & Lindauer's (1963) personality structure and response style; and Angyal's (1965) autonomy-heteronomy dimension.

The autonomously functioning person uses fantasy, imagination, and impulse to aid his problem-solving attempts (see, e.g., Hilgard's [1962] "impulsive vs. realistic thinking" or Kris' [1952] "regression in the service of the ego.") He also uses persistent effort, reflective thinking, and impulse control when tasks or situations demand it. In other words, the autonomous person has access to both primary and secondary processes (Hilgard, 1962). This ability to switch from one level of functioning to another is discussed by Hartmann under the heading of "systems of regulation" in his 1947 paper, "On rational and irrational action."

Since "systems of regulation" are self-regulating systems, it should be clear that this kind of autonomous functioning is not *random* functioning, independent of all internal and environmental events. Autonomous functioning has direction, and that direction is provided by perceived problems, tasks, and goals. In this sense, Hebb's (1949) notion of "sustained purposeful behavior" and "autonomous central processes," along with Morgan's (1959) concept of "central motive state" deal from a physiological point of view with known facts of problem-directed behavior such as attention and persistence.

Hunt's (1961) excellent review of the major contributions of Piagetian theory, computer simulation of problem solving, and neurophysiological bases of intelligence concludes with the following statements. "...In the light of these theoretical considerations and the evidence concerning the effects of early experience on adult problem solving in animals, it is no longer unreasonable to consider that it might be feasible to discover ways to govern the encounters that children have with their environments, especially during the early years of their development, to achieve a substantially faster rate of intellectual development and a substantially higher adult level of intellectual capacity. Moreover, inasmuch as the optimum rate of intellectual development would mean also *self-directing interest and curiosity and genuine pleasure in intellectual activity* promoting intellectual development properly need imply nothing like the grim urgency which has been associated with pushing children" (p. 363, emphasis supplied). Hunt's review thus concludes on a theme which is both optimistic and humane.

Human beings are capable of organizing their tendencies in a pattern of goal-directed behavior which is self-sustained, and centrally motivated. These organizing tendencies are readily seen in the play behavior of children from about 18 months onward. Piaget's earliest period of development, the sensori-motor period, can be interpreted as a developmental preparation for organized behavior and problem solving. The infant moves from sensory and reflex control toward organization of reflexes and self-control. Imagery, object constancy, and means-ends relationships are achievements of the sensori-motor period. For Piaget, these achievements are precursors of pre- operational thought and more sophisticated cognitive behavior; for autonomy theory, these developments are preparation for self-directed and sustained purposeful behavior.

It should now be apparent that a multiplicity of determinants interact to produce autonomous functioning, and that autonomous functioning is itself complex. For this reason the CATB was developed to measure autonomy, not as a unitary dimension, but as a construct with multiple manifestations. Furthermore, these multiple manifestations of autonomy are not conceived in a static way. The test situation demands that the child shift to adaptive responding, which may be at odds with conventional responding in some cases. For these reasons the test battery becomes more valuable when viewed as an autonomy profile or pattern, rather than a single total score. I will return to the problem of unidimensionality again at the end of this section. Before that, I take up the question of the relation between autonomy and other current concepts and points of view. I will deal with them in the following order: (1) conventional intelligence, (2) creativity, (3) cognitive styles, (4) dependence and independence behaviors, and (5) the developmental orientations of Anna Freud and Erik Erikson.

Conventional intelligence. While intelligence measured by the usual IQ indices is in some degree relevant to effective problem solving, IQ is by no means the only determinant of effectiveness and may eventually be demonstrated to be a relatively weak factor. It is predicted that the relation between CATB scores and IQ will be low and will provide evidence of discriminant validity (Campbell & Fiske, 1959). Curiosity motivation, exploratory behavior, and innovative behavior for example, are not reflected in IQ scores, yet are important for problem solving. Problem-solving strategies that are based only on appropriate, quick, and conventional responses leave something to be desired in many problem-solving contexts.

As a supplement to the numerical reporting of IQ, the astute and sensitive clinician, when using IQ tests, many times reports on the kinds of variables the CATB is explicitly testing for. There are many incidental bits of information in IQ testing which a good clinician will capture. The CATB does this more directly and more objectively through intentional selection of test materials which will reveal clinically-relevant cognitive and behavioral *processes,* which are equally important as the *contents* of intelligent functioning (e.g., Tuddenham, 1962, pp. 518-519).

Creativity. Creativity is typically assessed by evaluating the *productive* aspects of behavior; creativity is manifested by the unique quality or unusual products of a person's behavior. Autonomy too, is concerned with productive aspects of behavior, but it is conceptualized more broadly. In addition to productive modes of behavior, autonomy includes passive and reflective modes. For example, reflectivity, impulse control, and analytic thinking, all of which require *inhibition* of certain responses, are seen as relevant to autonomy because these processes, while they do not directly produce novel or unusual responses, do enhance the possibility of effectiveness in relation to some problems.

Getzels & Jackson (1962) and more recently Wallach & Kogan (1965) have argued that educational emphasis on conventional intelligence may penalize the person who is creative. While such studies have been concerned with children somewhat older than the prekindergartner, it is important to keep in mind the kinds of testing operations which are feasible for later follow-up research. As Wallach & Kogan (1965) comment, "It is most unlikely that the thinking processes examined in the present volume emerged full-blown at the fifth grade level. . . .It would be of great interest to know, of course, how far below the fifth grade level the observed differentiation between intelligence and creativity can be maintained" (p. 322). Some of the CATB tests should shed light on this question.

Cognitive styles. Research that has had a direct bearing on the selection of testing procedures in the CATB is that of Kagan (1965) and Witkin (e.g. 1962, 1965). Their work on reflectivity and field independence, respectively, has been borrowed upon for use in the CATB by simplifying and extending their testing procedures downward for work with younger children.

Kagan's emphasis on the capacity to behave reflectively is here viewed as a valuable aid to effective problem solving. Reflectivity is a manifestation of autonomous functioning in the sense that the person must be "free" to withhold the inappropriately quick response. Kagan's Matching Familiar Figures (MFF) test was ingeniously designed to benefit the reflective subject and to penalize the child who habitually makes the quick, premature response in picking the matching figure.

Witkin's excellent studies of field independence have resulted in three measurement procedures: the rod and frame test, the body adjustment test, and the embedded figures test (EFT). The common element in the three procedures is the ability of the subject to perceive a component in the visual field independently of the context in which it is embedded. This "decontextualizing" process is viewed as a manifestation of autonomy in that the person must be "free" to perceive components of the world in an analytic way. The autonomous person's perceptions are not over-determined by the context in which he is attempting to function effectively. This concept of field independence is related in interesting ways to learning processes. For example, it has been shown that field independent persons are better at incidental learning tasks (Witkin, et al., 1962, pp. 141-142). This result affirms our conviction that autonomous factors are present in the field independence procedures; the field independent subject is "free" to perceive aspects of a learning task which are not central to that task.

From the point of view of autonomy theory, it is assumed that impulsivity and field dependence need not be learned, or if they are learned in some sense, such learning takes place very early. Reflectivity and field independence, on the other hand, are capacities which must be developed. Once developed, the child can supposedly function in impulsive *or* reflective ways and in field dependent *or* field independent ways. The autonomous person has the ability to **shift** from one mode of responding to another, as discussed earlier in relation to Hartmann's "systems of regulation." An alternative possibility, however, is that persons may develop distinct styles of perception and cognition, but not the ability to shift from one to the other.

A person high on field independence would not be autonomous if the possibility of field-dependent functioning were not available to him. For example, the clear, analytic mind does not facilitate certain kinds of aesthetic perception. Approaching a painting or a poem by dissecting it into components, while interesting, is not the same as appreciating the piece of art as a "complete" object or pattern. An analytical approach to classical ballet is certain to reveal striking regularities and relationships, but such field-independent behavior inhibits successful enjoyment of the full configuration of the dance. It is somewhat like trying to make love while simultaneously recording the systolic blood pressure of one's lover.*

A provisional assumption, however, is that both reflective and field- independent styles do not exclude the possibility of shifting to impulsive or field-dependent styles. This assumption awaits direct research examination. The most thoroughgoing theoretical treatment of this kind of shifting ability is found in Werner's (1948) COMPARATIVE PSYCHOLOGY OF MENTAL DEVELOPMENT, pages 234 to 298, where he emphasizes the "primitive" and inflexible nature of early forms of thinking in contrast to the more flexible processes which are available at later stages of development.

Dependence and independence behaviors. In addition to perceptual and cognitive "independence," the research literature also contains reference to *social* forms of "independence" and "dependence." The excellent review by Hartup (1963) provides a good reference point for examining this problem in relation to autonomy. For a definition of dependence, Hartup suggests that ". . .the term covers a wide variety of behaviors, all of which are directed toward the satisfactions derived from contact with or nurturance from other people" (p. 333). As for independence, Hartup notes that "Frequently, the term independence denotes simply the absence of dependence." Reference is made to Beller's (1955) and Heathers' (1955) insistence that independence is more than the absence of dependence, and that it refers also to achievement-striving and self-assertion. Beller's and Heathers' view is closer to autonomous functioning if self-regulated shifting from dependent to independent behaviors can be added to this more positive conceptualization of independence.

In the three-year-old child, much dependent behavior is necessary and helpful to positive development. Lois Murphy (1962), emphasizing aspects of functioning in

---

*Non-analytic or field-*dependent* behavior is not all bad. There are many good examples from the field of aesthetic perception. An excellent description of field-dependent functioning is given by John Cage, the composer of experimental music, in his book titled *SILENCE* (1961). He points out that " . . . one may give up the desire to control sound, clear his mind of music, and set about discovering means to let sounds be themselves rather than vehicles for man-made theories or expressions of human sentiments" (p. 10). From another point of view, Eugene Herrigel, in *THE METHOD OF ZEN*, emphasizes the inadequacies of the analytic style of perception: "A person who judges in this manner, who isolates things both from himself and from one another, breaking up the whole, is no longer a 'seer' but an observer, who stands outside the picture and experiences the observed as an opposite. He does not feel one with what he sees, he is addressed by things as if from the outside, and in turn questions them so that they shall answer" (p. 53). The virtues of non-analytic behavior have likewise been described by psychoanalysts (e.g., Kris, 1952; Shafer, 1958). For example, Kubie (1967) asks, "How can we equip our children, our students, our patients with the tools that they will need in life without destroying that free play of preconscious processing and of the derived creative imagination which they will need if they are ever to be able to use the tools which they acquire?" (p. 97).

early childhood, notes that ". . .the capacity to seek help when it is needed is related to other active coping operations and to autonomy as well" (p. 227). Both independence and dependence must be available to the child for autonomous functioning. Dependence facilitates transmission of cultural values and learning from adults, while independence and self-assertion facilitate achievement of personal goals and personal identity.

In Hartup's (1963) review of the literature, his decision was to ". . .place greater emphasis upon dependent than upon independent behavior because the literature relating to the development of the latter is not extensive" (p. 334). One of the reasons that the literature is not extensive is that concepts like independence, initiative, self-direction and the like are only awkwardly managed by most current theory and methodology. Many experimental psychologists find it unappealing to deal with concepts that do not reduce variability in behavior. Autonomy and some forms of independence are such concepts; they implicitly deal with self-direction, choice-making, and variability. Contemporary experimental approaches show little interest in self-direction; they tend to deny that subjects have choice-making capacities; and there is expressed regret when variability appears in the data. Such predilections do not lead to an "extensive literature" on the determinants and effects of independence behaviors.

A recent exception to this experimental trend, however, is found in the work of Schoenfeld, Harris, & Farmer (1966). They make the point that "Where once it was regarded and treated as a form of experimental 'noise' reflecting a lack of experimental control, response variability in a single organism under stable experimental conditions is now well recognized as a legitimate behavioral measure or dependent variable in behavioral studies" (p. 551). This is an important theoretical comment. One might say that the behaviorists have been committed to using elaborate experimental procedures to eliminate novel or variable behavior from the repertoire of the subjects they have studied. The reason why one must go to such lengths might well be that variability in behavior is inherent in the very organisms they have studied.

Developmental theories of Anna Freud and Erik Erikson. Anna Freud's (1965) concept of developmental lines is helpful in thinking about the kinds of assessment procedures the CATB is directed toward. In particular, the developmental line she calls "from the body to the toy and from play to work" is especially relevant. Briefly these stages are: (1) play as an activity yielding erotic pleasure, involving the mouth, fingers, vision, and the child's and mother's skin (with no clear distinction between the two from the infant's point of view); (2) the transfer of the child's concerns with his and his mother's body to some transitional object (Winnicott, 1953) such as a blanket, a toy, or a rug; (3) transition to more indiscriminate liking for soft toys offering security; (4) fading out of interest in soft toys except at bedtime and increasing use of toys in the service of gratification through fantasy play and displaced and sublimated feelings; (5) fading out of the immediate gratification of fantasy and displacement to increased pleasure in the finished product, in task completion, and competent problem solving. Anna Freud points out the importance of these developments for successful performance in school, as Buhler (1935) has argued. The Montessori method is also cited as relevant to this stage. Anna Freud (1965) observes that "In this nursery school method the play material is selected so as to afford the child the maximum increase in self-esteem and gratification by means of task completion and independent problem-solving, and children can be observed to respond positively to such opportunities almost from the toddler stage onward" (p. 81).

Anna Freud's Stage (6) deals with change from the ability to play into the ability to work. Work involves the ability to carry out preconceived plans, sacrificing immediate pleasure with maximum pleasure allocated to the outcomes of activity. This involves the ability to control, inhibit, or modify impulsiveness in play so that constructive and positive use may be made of materials. Needed, also, is emphasis on the reality principle rather than the pleasure principle. Putting aside the pleasure principle is regarded as "essential for success in work during latency, adolescence, and in maturity" (1965, p. 82).

It is Anna Freud's stages (5) and (6) which are most clearly manifested in "good" performances on the CATB, although it should not be overlooked that there is an underlying assumption of adequate social competence in relating to the tester and the new situation. This relation between social competence and task competence is more explicitly given in Erikson's (1950) second stage of Autonomy vs. Shame and Doubt, which is preceded by the stage of Basic Trust vs. Basic Mistrust. These early stages are viewed as complex interactions of both social and task competencies and securities which pave the way for later stages involving Initiative and then Industry. These latter two stages of Erikson's appear to be directly parallel with Anna Freud's stages (5) and (6).

The CATB's conceptual focus on behaviors that facilitate effective problem solving finds much in common with Anna Freud and Erik Erikson. The methodological commitment is that their theoretical orientation, based on clinical analysis, can be readily translated into objective assessment procedures.

Unidimensionality. James Lumsden (1961, 1962) and I (Banta, 1962, 1963) had a short debate about the necessity for unidimensional tests, and my position now, as it was then, is that complex tests must be used to get at complex variables, an instance of which is the concept of autonomy with its multiple manifestations. Theories of autonomous functioning, reviewed above, are of heuristic value for devising tests to assess autonomy's many dimensions. Each test in the battery has been developed for theoretical reasons, which will be reviewed, test by test, in the next section. The intercorrelations of tests in the battery are regarded as information about the relations among indicators of autonomous functioning. Tests in the CATB were never expected to intercorrelate highly, and in fact they have not been found to do so uniformly, although some tests do relate closely to others on a predictable basis.

TEST THEORY AND TEST DESCRIPTIONS

CURIOSITY: TASK INITIATION AND CURIOSITY BOX
The pioneering work of Montgomery (1951a, 1951b, and 1952) on the exploratory drive led to the conclusion that ". . .a novel stimulus situation evokes in an organism an exploratory drive which motivates exploratory behavior" (1953, p. 129). Similar early conclusions were drawn by Harlow (1950), Hebb (1949), and Dashiell (1925). This is the underlying assumption behind each of our own explorations with Task Initiation and the Curiosity Box. Not all preschool children manifest the same degree of exploratory drive, and the reasons for this presence or lack is complexly determined by social anxieties, immaturity, fear of novel stimuli, separation anxiety, and paucity of encounters with what Winnicott (1953) has called "not-me" objects.

From the very start of our own work with young children, we have found variations all the way from complete withdrawal (and consequently no learning through exploration), to thoroughgoing involvement with novel objects such as those represented in these two tests resulting in a rather full and satisfying encounter with the environment.

It is not hard to see how these tendencies relate to the development and maintenance of autonomous functioning of the child. Autonomous, active exploration is an important precursor to later problem-solving strategies. Many helpful naturalistic descriptions of this process are provided in Chapter 2 of Lois Murphy's WIDENING WORLD OF CHILDHOOD (Murphy, 1962). The chapter is titled, "Children Encounter Newness." Her first example of a child absorbed by the environment, self-assured, and ready to explore in autonomous ways, was summarized as follows: "Here is a little boy who moved into the new situation warmly and spontaneously, quickly orienting himself by his own alert, widely ranging observation, and supplementing his own grasp by asking questions to clarify things further" (p. 27). We have seen this kind of child in our own testing. He is typically middle or upper class. We also have found many children who do not touch, do not manipulate, and do not visually explore our test materials, although our trained testers have gone to considerable lengths to make the setting comfortable, pleasant, and non-threatening. Most noticeably lacking among lower class children is the important strategy of "asking questions to clarify things further." This is not only a matter of poor verbal ability. More important is the implicit *assumption* made by the child as to what role the adult plays in relation to his explorations. It is clear that many of our upper class children assume that the adult *owes* them an explanation or a clarification of the situation and the test materials: "What is this for?" "Did you make this?" "Will you make one for me?" "What do you do with this thing?" The lower class child typically makes no such assumption and makes little if any effort to get the adult tester to contribute meaning or structure to his own experience.

The task of test construction was to devise standardized procedures and objective scoring methods to describe these differences in approach. Valuable information about the child's approach toward novel objects is gained in a short time. The Task Initiation test takes two minutes, the Curiosity Box takes five minutes of testing.

Task Initiation Test. Before the child enters the room, small, smoothly-sanded, softly colored wooden figures are arranged on the testing table as shown in Figure 1. When the child is brought in, he is seated in front of the miniature figures. The tester takes her seat on the other side of the table, starts her stopwatch, and busies herself with paper work--deriving age of child from birth date, writing name and date on the test protocol, etc. Nothing is said to the child about the figures before him. The tester waits one minute for the child to inspect the figures, pick them up, or begin talking fantasy with the figures. If no initiative occurs within this minute, the tester puts the toys away and begins the next test. If the child does begin play, the tester observes for an over-all two minute period in preparation for rating task initiation behavior.

For Task Initiation, ratings are based on the following definitions. Examples are also given below.

> *Rated 1: No initiation.* No initiation--child sat looking at objects while tapping his feet on the floor.
> *Rated 2: Minimal contact.* As child sat down he knocked giraffe over. Reached out hesitantly to stand it up and then withdrew. No further contact with materials.
> *Rated 3: Initiation with minimal involvement.* Child started as soon as she sat down. Put all objects flat on the table. Picked up one at a time and looked at it. Stopped and looked at the examiner.
> *Rated 4: Initiation with high degree of involvement.* Began as soon as she sat down. Arranged everything in a row--put bridges end to end and placed animals on bridges. Lined up others at end of bridge--walked each one across. Was very involved.

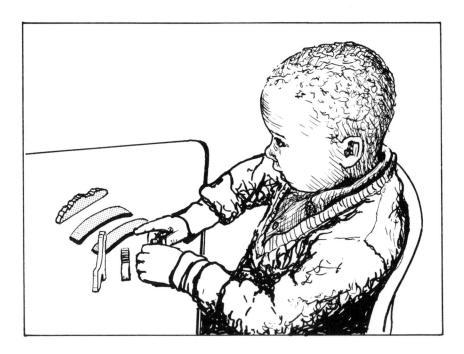

FIGURE 1

Task Initiation figures as they appear to the child entering the testing room (above); child initiating play with figures (below).

Curiosity Box Test. The Curiosity Box (Figure 2)[*] is placed on the table in front of the child as the tester says "Here is something for you to play with." The tester then takes a seat behind the child, somewhat to the left, so as to improve the observation perspective and to remove obvious social distractions from the range of view of the child.

The internal structure of the box is shown in Figure 3; the left compartment with the colorful designs in it is lighted; the middle compartment is completely dark and the horse can be reached only through an aperture covered by a rubber gasket, while the right-hand compartment is accessible through the latched lid.

The tester presents the box in an inviting way, and takes an observation position to the left and behind the child. The observation period is five minutes, unless the child does not explore or manipulate the box within the first three minutes. The termination procedure is as follows: If the child does not touch the box during the first two minutes, the tester says "This is for you to play with," and simultaneously

* I want to thank Mr. Raymond Starr for his innovation and help in designing the present Curiosity Box, and we both owe a great deal to Miss Jean Jett who developed earlier cardboard models and tested them with great patience and superior powers of observation.

FIGURE 2

Child manually exploring the Curiosity Box. This response (moving the chain lock) would be scored as manipulatory exploration. Note that the tester is seated to the left and behind the child during the test.

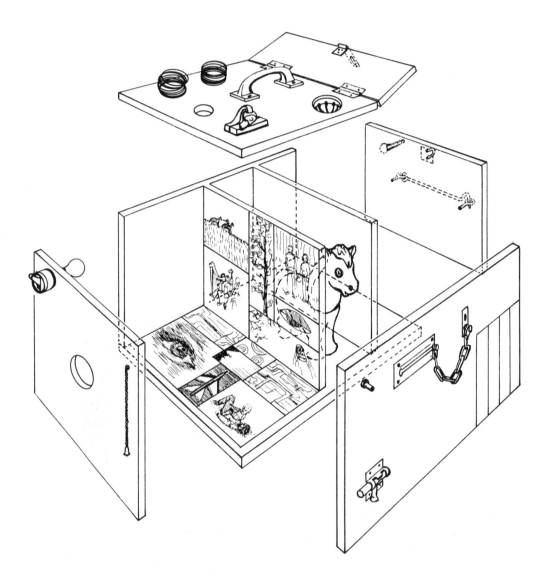

FIGURE 3

Exploded view of the Curiosity Box. Pictures in the left compartment are colorful designs. Outside surfaces are brightly painted (top--green, front--green, right end--red, left end--orange, back--yellow, lid on top right--bronze).

the tester manipulates the chain lock and bolt on the front side of the box. If the child does not touch the box for one minute after the prompt, the Curiosity Box is removed.

The observation form is reproduced in Figure 4. The major observational division is between "Activity" and "Verbalization." Under Activity, we have designated a variety of forms of exploratory behaviors; in each .5 minute interval the class of behavior observed is circled. At least one item in the Activity record must be circled in every time period. If two behaviors are related to one another, an additional line is drawn between the circles to indicate that they occurred simultaneously. The "Verbalization" observations will be discussed later in relation to Curiosity Verbalization and Fantasy- Related Verbalization.

Curiosity Box scores are based on observations of (a) manipulatory exploration, (b) tactual exploration, (c) visual exploration, (d) movement--subject, and (e) movement--box. Each of the five categories of exploration is defined specifically in relation to aspects of the box. *Manipulatory exploration* refers to the child's attempt to move objects or parts of the box--pulling the bolt back, working door hinge back and forth, opening lid, attempting to turn a screw. *Tactual exploration* refers to mild forms of "surface exploration" of the box or parts of it, with little or no attempt to move them--fingering the links of the chain, rubbing the sandpaper strips on the front of the box. *Visual exploration* is defined in relation to a specified set of behaviors. Not all visual exploration is scored here. Passive, detached observation is excluded. Only obvious behavioral movement is taken as an indication of a visual exploration. The apertures on the left side and on top of the Curiosity Box were designed so that if a child were to look in from a distance of several inches, nothing much could be seen in the designs and pictures appearing in the lighted chamber of the box. Thus the child, if he is to actively explore, must move his head from side to side or circularly in order to scan the designs within the box. More passive visual exploration is not scored, but signs of active visual interest do apply to this category--looking through hole in door hinge, looking into part of Curiosity Box closed off by a hinged lid, looking in cracks of box.

Movement-subject is scored when the child moves bodily to get in better position to observe or touch or manipulate (see Figure 2). The use of the large skeletal muscles in the service of active exploration is interpreted as an indication of good investigative tendencies--leaning around to see another side better, standing up to look at back of box or see into the box from the top. *Movement--box* is scored when the child moves, or attempts to move the box in order to see better or in order to get at a part of the box--sliding the box on the table, tipping it, turning it around.

One point is given for each .5-minute segment in which each of the five categories

CURIOSITY BOX SCORE SHEET

Time	Manip. Explor.	Tact. Explor.	Visual Explor.	Other	Move.- Subject.	Move.- Box	Quest. &/or Comment	Fantasy	Quest. &/or Comment	Fantasy
.50	me	te	ve	other	m-s	m-b	q &/or c	fan.	q &/or c	fan.
1.00	me	te	ve	other	m-s	m-b	q &/or c	fan.	q &/or c	fan.
1.50	me	te	ve	other	m-s	m-b	q &/or c	fan.	q &/or c	fan.
2.00										
Prompt	me	te	ve	other	m-s	m-b	q &/or c	fan.	q &/or c	fan.
2.50	me	te	ve	other	m-s	m-b	q &/or c	fan.	q &/or c	fan.
3.00	me	te	ve	other	m-s	m-b	q &/or c	fan.	q &/or c	fan.
Term										
3.50	me	te	ve	other	m-s	m-b	q &/or c	fan.	q &/or c	fan.
4.000	me	te	ve	other	m-s	m-b	q &/or c	fan.	q &/or c	fan.
4.50	me	te	m ve	other	m-s	m-b	q &/or c	fan.	q &/or c	fan.
5.00	me	te	ve	other	m-s	m-b	q &/or c	fan.	q &/or c	fan.

FIGURE 4

Observation and scoring form for Curiosity Box.

440

occurs. If a child were involved in all five types of exploration in every .5-minute observation segment, his total Curiosity Box score would be 50. High scores thus represent active exploratory behavior.

CURIOSITY VERBALIZATION AND FANTASY-RELATED VERBALIZATION
In the course of testing children with the Curiosity Box, we have been impressed with the fact that many children augmented their sensori-motor exploratory experiences with talk of their own. We have very little theory to guide us in this area of spontaneous verbalization, but it appeared that many children showed good signs of self-directed and self-sustaining exploration, particularly when they supplemented their visual, tactual, and manipulatory behavior with spontaneous curiosity verbalization. Sometimes they supplemented their explorations with fantasy-related comments.

These observations are given some support in Werner's (1948) emphasis on development in terms of *hierarchic integration;* accordingly, the more the verbal domain is coordinated in a supplementary way with sensori-motor behavior, the greater the opportunity for organized self-regulation. Piaget (1936, 1937), similarly, describes the sensori-motor period in terms of *circular reactions* which progressively facilitate the coordination of reflexes, then facilitate the coordination of means-ends sequences in exploratory behavior.

Development leads to coordination of verbal behavior with sensori-motor exploration. Since sensori-motor activity obviously precedes verbal skills and conceptual development, it is tempting to say that the correlation between exploratory activity and verbalization is due primarily to sensori-motor factors. However, it might well be that, once curiosity verbalization emerges in development, it becomes *directive,* rather than simply *supplementary* to ongoing sensori-motor exploration. This possibility awaits systematic empirical investigation.

Because of these informal observations and because of these theoretical considerations, we have derived scores based on the children's behavior while exploring the Curiosity Box. Curiosity Verbalization and Fantasy-Related scores are taken from the observation record shown in Figure 4. The last four columns are divided into "box-related" and "other," and each of these is further subdivided into "questions and/or comments" and "fantasy." Observation of many testing sessions has suggested that Curiosity Verbalization is best indicated by the occurrence of behavior classified as box-related questions and/or comments, in the first of the four observation columns. Here the children talk about the material they are exploring: "How does this work?" "Who made this?" "The light doesn't go off," or "There's something in there," are questions or comments frequently observed in this category of Curiosity Verbalization.

In Fantasy-Related Verbalization, children sing or hum, talk about Bat-man "flying in there," or they may talk about themselves: "Have you ever been to the Bahamas?" "What's your name?" or "What are you writing there?" Thus our category of "Fantasy" is much broader than most definitions which typically include some reference to symbols, images, wish fulfillment, and the like. Our decision is to go ahead on a trial basis, examining the interrelations of this with other variables, pending fuller evaluation of this variable as more data become available.

The scores derived from the first column which defines Curiosity Verbalization, range from zero to ten. The scores derived from the remaining columns which define Fantasy-Related Verbalization, can range from zero to thirty, since there are ten observation periods and three columns.

INNOVATIVE BEHAVIOR: THE DOG AND BONE TEST
Most tests of creative behavior involve production of variable responses. The format for assessing creativity is usually a fixed problem which admits of many solutions. Typically, these are verbal tests, however, and one of our major commitments is to test children without placing an undue burden on verbal skills. For a child of three or four, creativity in the form of innovative behavior must be assessed by sensori-motor methods; this after all, is the young child's mode of operation, and this, we feel, is where he can best express his creative ability.

The Dog and Bone test invites the child to play a game of "getting the dog to his bone" by various routes. The child is shown two paths the dog might take to get to his bone; then he is asked to find another way for the dog to get to his bone. If the child repeats a pathway used in the two demonstrations, or if he repeats one of his own previous pathways, he is given no credit. Only novel responses are scored. The autonomous child should be able to find a number of ways to do this simple task. He should be responsive to alternatives and be able to generate new ones, rather than perseverate in fixed ways.

The Dog and Bone test does the assessment job quite satisfactorily, is easy to administer, and takes less than ten minutes. Another approach through operant conditioning of some simple forms of response variability has been demonstrated using rats as subjects, by Schoenfeld, Harris & Farmer (1966), but this involved rather elaborate equipment and time-consuming experimental procedures. Our present goal becomes that of efficiently finding out just how much variability a three- or four-year old child can produce, and eventually to evaluate the factors--school, family, community--in his past experience which have enhanced or inhibited this tendency.

The tester places the board shown in Figure 5 with the red and white "houses" affixed, in front of the child, and points to the houses saying, "These are houses." Then the tester picks up the toy dog and shows it to the child saying, "What is this?" The tester pauses long enough to give the child a chance to respond, "dog." If child does not say "dog" the tester tells him it is a dog. After placing the dog as indicated in Figure 5, the tester holds up the bone for the child to see and says, "This is the doggie's bone. The doggie likes to chew his bone." The bone is then placed on the board near the edge closest to the tester between the two houses.

At this point the tester demonstrates two paths by which the dog can get to his bone. Tester says, "One way he can get his bone is to come up this way." Tester first demonstrates by following a straight path with his finger as in Figure 6a. Then, demonstrating the second possible path, tester says, "And another way he can go, is around this way," as shown in Figure 6b. This last instruction is given with emphasis on the phrase, *"around this way,"* at the point at which the path turns most acutely around the house on the child's lower left. This is important since it carries the burden of communicating the concept "another way" to the child.

The tester then goes on, saying, "Now *you* take the doggie and find *another* way for him to get his bone." Tester encourages the child to pick up the dog. As the child

FIGURE 5

Child seated in front of Dog and Bone Board.

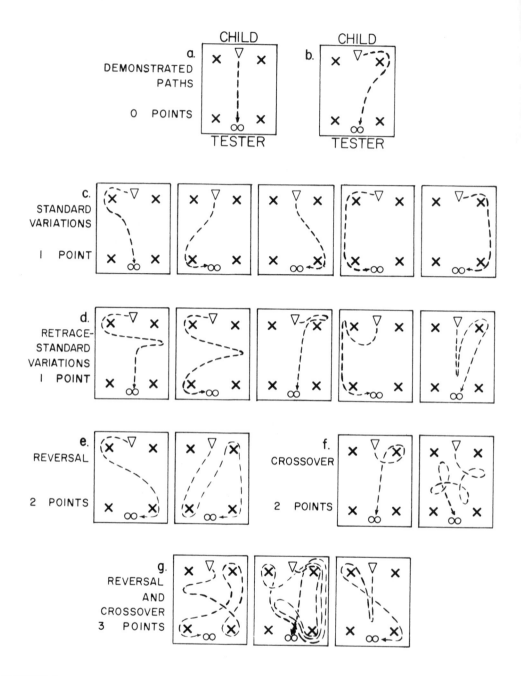

FIGURE 6

(a) First demonstrated path in Dog and Bone test; (b) second demonstrated path; (c) all possible standard variation paths, each scored one point (all innovative responses are scored on first occurrence only); (d) all possible retrace standard variations, which are minor variations from the standard paths, each scored one point; (e) examples of reversal paths (more are possible) scored *two* points; (f) examples of crossover paths, scored two points; and (g) examples of reversal and crossover paths, each scored *three* points.

gets the dog to the bone, tester diagrams the path. The score sheet resembles Figure 6. Children move the dog slowly enough so that the diagram can be made while the child is responding.

After each path is made by the child, the tester says, "Now find *another* way for him to get his bone." The child is asked in this way to make ten responses, and the exact route the child uses is recorded each time. Scoring is done after testing is completed.

On any one trial the child can get zero, one, two, or three points. Only innovative, non-repeated paths are scored. A zero score is assigned if the child repeats one of the demonstrated lines or if he repeats one of his own previous paths from dog to bone. There are five standard variations that appear frequently, and are basically simple paths between dog and bone. *Standard variations* are shown in Figure 6c, and each is worth 1 point the first time it appears.

Occasionally, a child will use a path which is very similar to one of the *standard variations,* adding a small retrace to the path. Some examples of these are depicted in Figure 6d as *retrace standard variations.* Such patterns are scored as novel responses the first time they occur and are scored 1 point.

Two criteria are used beyond these one-point patterns: 1) a *reversal* of direction in a pathway, and 2) a *crossover* in a pathway. Examples of *reversals* and *crossovers* are given in Figure 6e and f. The rationale for assigning two points to these paths is that they are more complex and indicate that intentional mental operations are at work. Some children begin a clockwise churning motion, for example, and the number of such turns is merely a reflection of continuous motoric output; such a pathway is repetition of a single idea. But when the child terminates this process and reverses his direction, we infer that an intentional change of response patterning, or innovative behavior has in fact occurred.

Finally, three points are assigned a response which is *both* a *reversal* and a *crossover.* Examples of these are shown in Figure 6g.

In addition, some children move the dog over the tops of the houses in a hopping motion. These moves are diagrammed as usual, and scoring for novel over-the-house patterns is done in the same way as the more typical responses: one point for over-the-house variations that resemble the standard variations or retrace standard variations; two points for a reversal or a crossover pathway; and three points for both a crossover *and* a reversal in the same pathway. If, on two trials, a pathway is identical except for an over-the-house move, we have *not* scored the second of such pathways as a novel one.

The total score, then, is based on a sum of scores assigned to each of the ten responses and ranges between zero and 30. One hour of scoring-practice and brief familiarization with the above rules, resulted in a correlation of .95 between the trainee and a skilled scorer. Another hour of practice improved agreement to .98. Highly experienced scorers show an inter-rater correlation of .996. About 30 protocols per hour can be scored after one or two hours' practice.

REFLECTIVITY-IMPULSIVITY: THE EARLY CHILDHOOD MATCHING FAMILIAR FIGURES TEST (EC-MFF)

The Matching Familiar Figures test is designed to evaluate the child's ability to control impulsive responding, when the task demands reflectivity. The tendency for the child to behave reflectively when confronted with uncertainty, rather than to behave impulsively, is an important aid in maintaining autonomy. A reflective disposition, when the task demands it, permits more information processing on the part of the child, and theoretically should provide a sound defense against irrational action based upon inadequate information or impulsive forces. The original form of the test devised by Kagan was used in a study of first grade children (Kagan, 1965), and was found to be related to accurate word recognition, a task demanding reflectivity under conditions of uncertainty. Evidence for the relation of MFF to other indicators of reflectivity is provided in Kagan, Rosman, Day, Albert & Phillips (1964). These authors also discuss the possible relation between reflectivity and problem solving: "The child who does not reflect upon the differential validity of several solution possibilities is apt to implement mentally the first idea that occurs to him. This strategy is more likely to end up in failure than one that is characterized by reflection" (p. 35).

We have re-designed the test for use with lower class children, ages three and four, and refer to the test as the Early Childhood Matching Familiar Figures test (EC-MFF) to distinguish it from Kagan's test which was designed for later childhood. In addition, the EC-MFF materials were designed to assess social-motivational components in reflectivity. Half the figures to be matched are social in character (matching a test line drawing of a face with its counterpart embedded in an array of other faces); the other half of the figures are non-social or geometric designs (matching a test figure like an airplane or a car).

Since the matching of stimuli is difficult for some three to six year old children, we have developed some very simple training pictures in order to help the child understand what is expected of him without relying heavily on verbal instructions.

The tester opens the notebook containing the first pair of training figures. The tester points to a single picture of a striped circle on the child's left and says, "Look at this picture." The tester then brushes her hand lightly and slowly over the two circles on

446

the opposite page as she says, "Find the one on this page that is just like this one." As she ends the sentence with the words "this one" she again points back to the page with the single striped circle on it. When the child makes a choice by pointing to one of the circles, the tester corrects if necessary, or verifies the correct response by saying, "Yes, this one is round (indicating with gestures the roundness of the circle) and has lines across it, and *this* one is round and has lines across it."

The tester turns the page to the second training pictures, and uses the same words and gestures as in the first training pictures. The tester corrects if necessary, but does not verify if the child makes the correct choice in this case. Once the tester is satisfied that the child grasps the instructions, she proceeds with the same instructions and the same gestures for all twelve test pictures. Examples are presented in Figure 7.

Kagan, et al., (1964) report the use of timed latencies correlating negatively with error scores; that is, the quicker the response, the higher the probability of error, and with older children, this appears to be a stable finding. Our experience with three and four year olds, however, does not support this; the child may take a long time to make a response because he is distracted, or is fantasying, or is talking with the tester. For this reason, EC-MFF reflectivity scores are based on correct responses only, and latency data are omitted from scoring. This has considerably simplified the administration and scoring of the EC-MFF. Scores range from zero to twelve; a high score indicates reflectivity.

FIELD INDEPENDENCE: THE EARLY CHILDHOOD EMBEDDED FIGURES TEST (EC-EFT)

Perceptual field independence has been measured by the Embedded Figures Test (EFT) devised by Witkin (1950) for adults. In 1963 Karp & Konstadt published the Children's Embedded Figures Test (CEFT) standardized on ages 5 through 12. The CEFT has also been used with preschool children (Maccoby, Dowley, Hagen, & Degerman, 1965), but these children had an extremely high average IQ. We have found the CEFT too difficult for three year old lower class children. For this reason we have devised a simpler form with less verbal material in the instructions and with thorough checks on comprehension. We have designated this test the Early Childhood Embedded Figures Test (EC-EFT) and have developed it for use with lower class Negro children, culturally deprived Spanish-American children, as well as white upper class children.

The field independent person ". . .tends to experience his surroundings analytically, with objects experienced as discrete from their backgrounds. The person with a more field-dependent way of perceiving tends to experience his surroundings in a relatively global fashion, passively conforming to the influence of the prevailing field

447

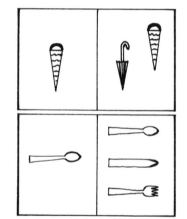

TRAINING

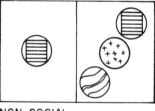

NON-SOCIAL

SOCIAL

FIGURE 7

Child pointing to correct alternative in the Early Childhood Matching Familiar Figures test (EC-MFF). Examples of training pictures, social figures, and non-social figures used in the EC-MFF are presented below.

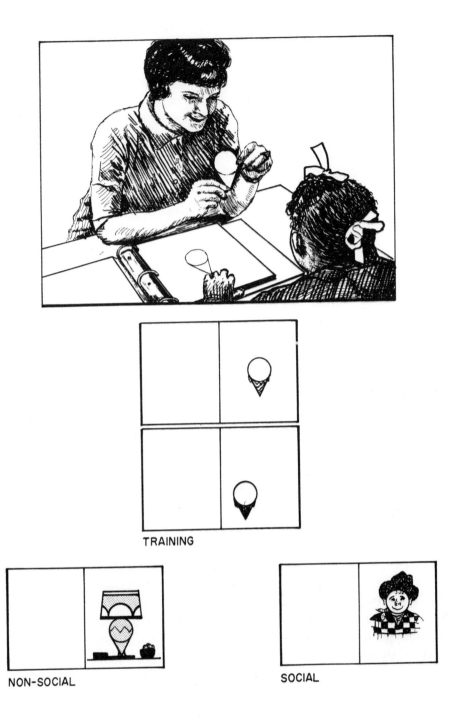

TRAINING

NON-SOCIAL

SOCIAL

FIGURE 8

Training period for Early Childhood Embedded Figures Test (EC-EFT). The tester is establishing the cone as the figure to be identified. Examples of training pictures, social figures, and non-social figures used in the EC-EFT are presented below.

or context" (Witkin, Dyk, Faterson, Goodenough, & Karp, 1962, p. 35). It is expected that the autonomous person can perceive in a field-independent way when the task demands it, particularly in view of the many correlated findings cited by Witkin, et al., which suggest that the field independent person: (a) is less susceptible to influence in social groups (Rosner, 1957; Crutchfield, 1957); (b) is likely to show an "active attitude" expressed in TAT responses (Witkin, et al., 1962, p. 180), posture (Witkin, et al., 1962, p. 182), and in style of dreaming (Eagle, 1959); and (c) is likely to have come from parents who let their children set their own standards (Witkin, et al., 1962, p. 353).

The figure to be located in the embedded context of EC-EFT stimuli is in the shape of a cone, as shown in Figure 8. Three training pictures are used to assess comprehension and readiness to perform the task. The first training picture is identical with the cut-out cone figure; the second training picture is only slightly embedded by line drawing of dripping ice cream and a cross-hatching on the cone; the third training picture has still more lines on it and is placed in the lower left corner of the page. Fourteen test pictures, embedding the "cone", for example, as sun setting between mountains, a lamp base, a cowboy's face and scarf (see Figure 8), and complex geometric designs, are used to assess field independence.

Training. In order to ensure readiness to perform the task, the training instructions must be adapted, within limits, to the needs of the individual subject. The tester must permit the child to work with the training pictures until it is apparent that he comprehends what is expected of him. Flexible use of the training instructions will ensure a more accurate measure of the child's ability to overcome embeddedness. When the training has been completed, however, it is necessary to adhere to the verbatim instructions to ensure uniformity of procedure on the test pictures.

A cut-out cone figure is presented and the child is asked, "What is this?" If the child's response is something other than *cone* or *ice cream cone,* tester pursues the question until both agree that it looks like an ice cream cone. If the child says, "It's a ball," tester may say, "The top part looks like a ball, but there is a brown point down here. What does this whole thing look like?" Tester should point to the parts of the cone as they are mentioned in the dialogue because gestures as well as words help clarify the instructions. If the child turns the cone point upward, for example, and says, "It's a clown's hat," tester may say, "It could look like a clown's hat if it pointed up this way, but if we turn it around like this it looks like something good to eat. Doesn't it look like an ice cream cone?" The child usually agrees that it is an ice cream cone.

The cut-out cone figure is *always* placed on the table to the tester's left with the *point of the cone toward the child.* The first training picture is presented. Tester says, "There is a picture of an ice cream cone on this page just like our ice cream cone. You take our ice cream cone and put it on top of the picture of the ice cream cone." During the verbal instructions tester places her hand first over the cut-out cone figure and then over the training picture, the gesture coinciding with the instructions. Tester gives any assistance necessary to obtain accurate placement of the cut-out figure. With appropriate gestures and comments, it is pointed out that the point and the top of the ice cream cone must coincide with those of the picture, and that the point of the cone is down. After the cut-out cone figure has been adjusted so that it is exactly aligned with the picture of the cone, tester may say, "Good. See how it fits right on top of the picture? See how the ice cream cone points toward you? Look how our ice cream cone covers the picture of the cone."

The second training picture is presented. Tester says, "There is a picture of a cone on this page just like our cone. (Note: Words *ice cream* are dropped from the instructions.) Put our cone exactly on top of the picture of the cone." Tester again gestures to demonstrate appropriate placement of the cut-out figure.

The third training picture is presented. Tester says, "Put our cone exactly on top of the cone on this page." Placement gestures are eliminated, but any necessary help is given to ensure comprehension of proper vertical orientation of the cone figure. After presentation of the three training pictures, standardized testing procedures are strictly adhered to, and no further help is given.

Testing. The test pictures are numbered one to fourteen. Tester places the cut-out cone figure to tester's left, *pointing toward the child,* prior to the presentation of each test picture. If the subject picks up the cut-out figures after he has placed it on the test picture, tester gently removes it from his grasp, places it in proper position before presenting the next test picture. After the test picture is presented, tester uses these exact words: *"Put our cone on top of the cone on this page."* After the child places the cone, tester reinforces the response by quietly saying, "Um-hum." This procedure, using the exact words, "Put our cone on top of the cone on this page," is repeated for the fourteen test pictures.

There are no time limitations for EC-EFT. The time allowed for each test picture will depend upon tester's assessment of the behavior of the child being tested. The pacing of the presentation of the test pictures should be compatible with the child's rate of response. The child who is slow-moving and reflective will require a slower pace than the distractible, impulsive child who requires a quick change of scene in order to maintain interest. The goal of the testing is to obtain the best assessment of the child's ability to overcome embeddedness regardless of these individual differences.

Responses to each of the 14 test pictures are scored 1 or 0. A score of 1 is given when the cut-out model is placed within ½ inch of the embedded figure. It is assumed that a ½ inch error margin allows for placement error which may result from inadequate muscle control. On the other hand, when *any portion* of the cut-out model is *more than ½ inch* away from the embedded figure, it is assumed that the child has not perceived the embedded figure and a 0 score is given. Scoring judgments can be made quickly and accurately with practice. EC-EFT total score is based on the number correct, therefore, the scores range from 0 to 14.

MOTOR IMPULSE CONTROL: THE DRAW-A-LINE SLOWLY TEST

Part of autonomous behavior may be characterized by the ability to control and restrain impulsive action, *when the task demands it.* Such motor impulse control ability is self-regulated--the autonomous person should be able to use impulse control when appropriate, but not be dominated by generalized inhibition. A good measure has been devised by Hagen & Degerman, and has been used in a study by Maccoby, Dowley, Hagen, & Degerman (1965); the findings of this study was one of the reasons the present measure of motor impulse control, the Draw-a-Line-Slowly test, was adopted for the CATB. Maccoby, et al., asked preschool children to draw a line very slowly. This and other measures of inhibition of movement ("walking slowly" and "moving a truck slowly") were found to correlate with Binet IQ scores.

The Binet implicitly requires that the child inhibit impulsive movements and distractions, and thus can be taken as one indication of task-appropriate inhibition. This interpretation is given further support in that a measure of *general* activity level correlated very nearly zero with the Binet IQ's. Thus the common element in both IQ problem solving and the impulse control measure was task-appropriate inhibition, not generalized inhibition reflected in low activity level. As Maccoby, et al., point out, "The successful problem solver, then, probably does not engage in less total bodily activity over an extended period of time; he merely modulates or regulates his activity, so that expressive activity is inhibited during crucial points of problem-solving where it might constitute an interference..." (p. 763). This reasoning ties in very closely with the present definition of autonomy as self-regulating behavior which facilitates effective problem solving. Many problems are like the IQ performance, and many more kinds of problems which demand reflectivity, delay of gratification, or inner language and thought require that the person establish inner control before effective solutions are possible.

At the start of the Draw-a-Line-Slowly test the tester gives the child a crayon. The tester takes a crayon of a different color and places an 8½" x 11" paper on the table before the child. The tester says, "I'm going to draw a line *real fast.*" As the tester says "real fast," she draws a line very quickly (*toward* the child, from top to bottom of the page). The tester then goes on to say, "Now you draw a line *real fast*--right

here" (showing the child where to begin the line, pointing to the top of the page).
The purpose of the fast line is to give meaning to the words "fast" and "slow," by
getting the child to make a response, equivalent to the meaning of the words in this
context.

The tester turns the paper over and says, "Now watch what I'm going to do." The
tester begins to draw a line slowly, and continues talking. "I'm going to draw a line
verrrry sloowly. . .very slooowly. . .just as sloooowly as I can." While saying this, the
tester does draw a line very slowly; the wording and the pauses in the speech of the
tester paces the line drawing at about 20 to 25 seconds for an 8-inch line. This is
about twice the time taken by the average child to draw a similar line. To
summarize, the slow line is begun by the tester immediately after saying, "Now
watch what I am going to do." The drawing of the line ends with the 20-25 second
speech.

After drawing this slow line, the tester tells the child, "Now you draw a line just as
slooowly as you can" (and she shows the child where to begin the line, at the top of
the page). The stopwatch is started when the child begins to draw. The time taken to
draw the line is recorded in hundredth's of a second. A watch with a re-start
mechanism is desirable, since some children lift their crayon, pause, and begin again.
These intervals are not timed. The time taken to draw the line is recorded, and a
second sheet is presented to the child.

The second slow line sheet, unlike the first has two large X's on it. The X's are made
with one-inch crossed lines. The distance between the center of the X's is 8". These
X's are helpful in guiding the response of the child, but pretesting has shown that
they tend to distract children when present on the training page. Therefore, we have
omitted them until the second slow line. At this point the tester presents the paper
with the X's and says, "Now I want you to draw a line from here to here, just as
slooowly as you can." The tester indicates where the line is to be drawn by slowly
running her finger from the top X to the bottom X. The tester then points to the
top X and says, "Start here." The line drawn is timed again. The time is recorded.

The tester now presents a third sheet, also designated with two X's. The same
instructions are used with the addition, "I want you to draw a line from here to
here--this time *even slooower* than the last time. Start here." The time is recorded.

Since not all children draw a straight line, and not all children draw a line 8" long,
the length of line must be taken into account in scoring impulse control. We measure
the length of line with a device for calculating distances on maps. The device is
calibrated in quarter-inches; however, we interpolate the measures in decimal
fractions. The impulse control score is calculated as a rate measure--length of line,

divided by time in hundredths of a second; the higher the rate, the lower the motor impulse control. After rate for each line is computed, the three "slow instruction" rates are averaged for a total score.

INCIDENTAL AND INTENTIONAL LEARNING:
FIND-THE-COLOR-GREEN TEST

We have developed a test for two kinds of learning. One kind of learning reflects ability to master a task set by an adult for the child; this is called *intentional* learning. Another kind of learning reflects the ability of the child to learn things *other than* those which the child is told to learn; this is called *incidental* learning, the learning of aspects of the problem incidental to the main task.

Postman's (1964) review of theory and data on short-term memory and incidental learning, makes several points that help in understanding the operations we have invented for studying these features of learning in very young children. He makes the point that both intentional and incidental learning "are concerned with basic capacities and dispositions which the learner brings to the experimental situation and which determine the initial reception and immediate storage of information" (p. 145). It is these dispositions brought to the situation in both kinds of learning that interest us from the point of view of autonomy. Many types of problem solving demand a rather broad attention span, a receptivity to many incidental features of the components of the problem. The stimulus array in any given problem situation may conceal the critical, but incidental, elements necessary to problem solution. Thus it becomes important that the child develop receptivity to incidental cues, as well as concentration on and controlled attention to other cues. The autonomous child should be able to function both as an "intentional learner" and as an "incidental learner."

Postman contends that these two kinds of learning are not qualitatively different but that they simply define the extremes of a dimension; incidental learning is just like other learning except that the instructions or the subject's set do not prepare him for the test of performance. Postman cites McGeoch to support the view that the two kinds of learning do not constitute a dichotomy. McGeoch's ideas are worth noting: ". . .much of the learning which goes on with no overt instructions is, nonetheless, influenced by implicit instructions and sets. . .certainly it cannot be said with any conclusiveness that there are experiments in which implicit sets have not operated; but, more than this, probability is on the side of the hypothesis that all of the results [in incidental learning] have been determined by set" (1942, p. 304). This may be interpreted to mean that set is involved in all learning. There is also the further implication that set itself is learned. It is this latter implication that concerns us in relation to autonomy. If sets can be acquired, then the "incidental learning set" may be learned and this expression of autonomous behavior may be

454

amenable to educational intervention. Part of education's effects manifest themselves in the kinds of set individuals take toward the world, and more specifically, toward problem-solving situations.

In the Find-the-Color-Green test, the tester places the closed notebook with the stimulus pictures in it on the testing table, along with a small piece of paper. The tester says, "I'm going to teach you something about this color green." She makes a mark with a green crayon on the small piece of paper. The green matches the green which appears on the stimulus materials. The tester, while opening the notebook, then says, "We're going to look at some things in this book." The child is shown the first page. Tester says, "Find the color green on this page." The child points to the part of the picture which is colored green, as shown in Figure 9. The tester helps the child do this if there appears to be confusion about what is expected.

The tester then proceeds in the same way, saying, "Find the color green on this page," as each page is turned. When all pages have been turned, the free recall training portion of the test begins. This is important because a free recall response is fairly demanding on the three and four year old child in terms of the cognitive difficulty implicit in producing labels of pictures not immediately present. The following brief training procedure is used.

The tester turns back to the first picture (one of three training pictures at this point), and asks, "What is this?" *All* labels given to pictures by the children are accepted, even if "wrong" by adult standards. Using the label the child gave for the first picture, the tester says, "Yes, the (table) is one of the things you saw with green on it in this book." The next picture is presented and the child is asked, "What is this?" After the child responds, the tester says, "Yes, the (house) is *another* thing you saw with green on it in this book." This is repeated for the third training picture (the apple) and the tester closes the book. The tester gives extra training if necessary to be sure the child understands that he is to label the entire picture, and not just the part colored green.

The tester then asks, "Now tell me something else you saw with green on it in this book." The book is pointed to and the tester's hand rests on top of the closed notebook. The stopwatch is started. If the child does not respond for .15 minute, the tester gives *one* prompt: "Tell me something *else* you saw with green on it in this book." No other prompts are given during the test portion of the procedure. After each response, whether it is relevant or irrelevant, the tester says, "Tell me something else you saw in this book." The stopwatch is reset after each response.

The testing is terminated 1) if the child does not respond for .30 minute, 2) if the child gives three irrelevant responses, 3) if the child repeats any two responses which

TRAINING

TESTING

FIGURE 9

Child pointing to the color green in Find-the-Color-Green test of incidental and intentional learning. Examples of training and testing pictures for the Find-the-Color-Green test are presented below.

he has already given, or 4) if the child terminates by saying "That's all," or "I don't know."

The next phase of this test serves two purposes. It permits us to check on the child's ability to label each picture when it is in front of him, and secondly, it serves as an intentional learning sequence, with practice at labeling each of the pictures. The tester re-opens the notebook and says, "What is this?" After each response, the tester says, "Um-hmm." A similar procedure is used for each picture.

A check is placed in the center column of the record form if the child uses one of those labels. If the child uses a different label (e.g., call the car a "machine" or the dog a "wolf"), his response is written under the label listed.

At this point, intentional recall is tested. Again the recall is preceded by training. Using the labels the child used on the three training pictures, the tester says to the child, "One of the pictures you saw with green on it in this book was this (table). You saw this (house) and this (apple)." The tester then closes the book and asks, "What else did you see with green on it in this book?" No prompts are given in this portion of the test. After each response, the tester says, "What else did you see?" The same termination procedures used in incidental learning are used in this recall test. The same recording procedures are used, this time in the right column of the record form, designated "post-familiarization recall."

Before calculating scores on incidental and intentional learning, the tester must review the child's responses. For example, if "dog" were labeled "wolf" both on incidental recall *and* on post-familiarization recall, this is counted as a correct response.

The incidental recall score is the total number of correct responses corresponding to the ten test pictures. Similarly, the intentional learning score is the total number of correct responses made during the post-familiarization recall procedure. Scoring for both tests range between 0 and 10.

PERSISTENCE AND RESISTANCE TO DISTRACTION: THE REPLACEMENT PUZZLE TEST

The problem of persistent attention has had a long and interesting history in psychology. An excellent review of the literature was written by Shacter in 1933. In it she argued that deficits in attention account for many problems experienced by school children. Tilson (1929) surveyed seven child guidance clinics in five different cities and listed the types of problems which were referred. Between the ages of one and five, 53 types of problems were identified, and the ninth most frequent was "restlessness" designating instability of attention. The educational import of attention was underlined in 1908 by Burnham and by Tichener. Burnham is quoted by Shacter as stating that, "The development of habits of attention. . .is quite as important for the prevention, as restoration for the cure, of nervous and mental defects" (p. 528). Tichener in that same year argued for its general importance for psychology as well as its specific educational relevance: ". . .the intrinsic tendency of psychology to deal with attention in the large has been further strengthened by the practical importance of attention, its importance of educational regard. . .Here, if anywhere, a sound psychology (of attention) might be of immediate service to the responsive teacher" (p. 182).

Comparable enthusiams for the importance of attention has not been present until recently, when it emerged in another form: the study of observation responses, the orienting reflex, and need for variation in stimulation. Recent research and theory is summarized in Berlyne (1960), Fiske & Maddi (1961), Bakan (1966), Fowler (1965), and most elegantly by the theoretical work of Dember & Earl (1957). Most of this work has been confined to the laboratory, the animal laboratory at that, and no research exists on the outcomes of different educational techniques in relation to children's attention.

The Replacement Puzzle, shown in Figure 10, is an adaptation of a test developed

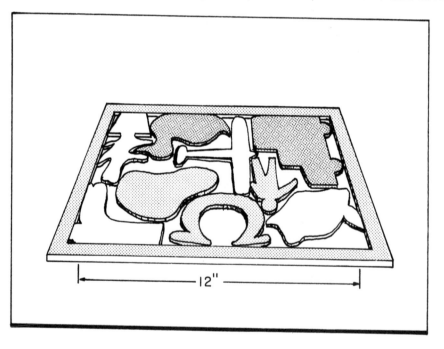

FIGURE 10

Replacement Puzzle used to measure persistence and resistance to distraction. Puzzle is shown from child's point of view during training.

by Keister (1943). Our emphasis is on how involved the child becomes in attaining a solution during a period when no distractions are present other than those inherent in the situation--furniture, tester, testing equipment. The puzzle can be solved in only one way. The pieces are constructed so that a solution is very improbable in a two-minute period. During these two minutes the child is observed for indications of task-oriented behavior carried out in an independent and persistent fashion. At the two-minute mark, the tester introduces four toy blocks with the words, "You may play with these, or you may finish putting the pieces back in flat." For the next minute, the child's persistence is observed, this time with the distractor blocks present.

Our concerns here, as elsewhere in the test battery, are in terms of the structures and dispositions within the child. Some children respond to, and some children ignore the distracting materials. Thus the stimulus cannot account for either attention or distractibility in the present setting, since stimulus factors are held constant for all children. In a sense we are concerned with what one might call "Persistibility-and-Distractibility," which are complementary tendencies and abilities that have developed within the child.

Considerable time is spent by the tester to insure that the child understands the goal of the puzzle so that all children are clear as to what is expected of them. The test scores reflect, then, the way in which the child reacts to a situation demanding attention and resistance to distraction. The autonomous child, one expects, has these elements of self-control in his behavioral repertoire. Such behaviors facilitate a wide variety of effective problem solving strategies.

The puzzle is placed on the testing table as shown in Figure 11. (Later in the procedure the puzzle is rotated 180°, just before the child starts to work.) The tester says, "I want you to look at how flat all these pieces fit into this tray. This looks something like a puzzle, but there are spaces between the pieces. (Tester rubs the tray in several different spaces between the figures.) Some of these pieces come out. The 'boy' comes out. (Tester lifts the boy out of the tray and holds the piece up before the child.) When we put it back in, it can't rest on another piece. (Tester replaces it in the tray, on top of another piece, so that it is not in flat.) It must lie flat. (Tester puts it in flat.) That's very important. Now you try. (Tester sees to it that the child understands how to put the piece back in flat, correcting the child if necessary.) Now rub your hand across here (across 'boy' and all adjacent pieces) and feel how flat it is."

Words in the above instructions are continuously accompanied by gestures and movements. Most importantly, the child is involved in the instructions--picking up pieces, replacing them, and rubbing his hand over the surface of the puzzle. "Getting

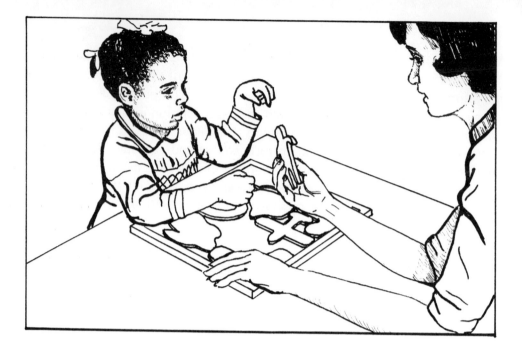

FIGURE 11

Training period for Replacement Puzzle. Tester is stressing that all pieces must be made to lie flat.

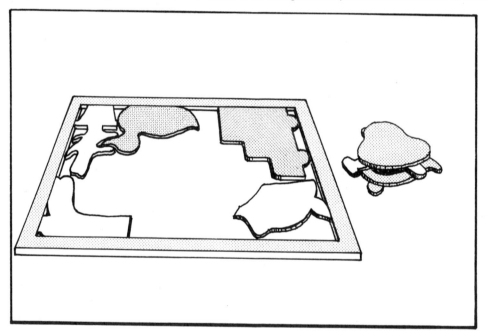

FIGURE 12

Replacement Puzzle as it appears to the child after the removal and standardized placement of the detachable pieces. Board is then rotated 180°.

the pieces to lie flat" is the goal of the puzzle, and the child's understanding is mediated by the sensori-motor experience of actually touching the puzzle to verify what "flat" means. Such sensori-motor interpretation of the instructions is necessary.

The instructions continue. "I'm going to take some of the pieces out. (Tester removes "horseshoe" and "boy" placing the horseshoe on top of the boy at the *child's left,* then removes the "plane" and "pear" placing them in that order on top of the other two pieces. Tester now rotates the tray 180°). Now you put the pieces back into the tray." The puzzle now appears to the child as in Figure 12.

At this point the stopwatch is started and recording is begun; observations are recorded every one-third minute. Prompting is permissible, but must always be limited to the words, "Put all the pieces in flat," in response to requests for help, wandering away from task, looking up as if finished, or requesting approval.

Occasionally a child completes the puzzle within the two minute limit. The pieces are removed, and the tester says, "Put them back in again for me." The scoring is continued as before. When two minutes have elapsed, tester places the four "distractor" blocks, shown in Figure 13, on the table just to the *child's right.* Tester

FIGURE 13

Distractor blocks used with Replacement Puzzle to measure child's persistence after a distraction has been introduced.

then says, "You may play with these if you want to, or finish putting the pieces back." The child is given one minute to continue with the puzzle or to play with the distractor blocks. After one minute, tester terminates test by asking, "Would you like me to help you put these back?" and puts the puzzle back together.

An observation record is shown in Figure 14. In every .33-minute segment, all items which describe the child's behavior are circled. At least one item will be circled in every time segment. If two categories appear simultaneously (e.g., the child uses the distractor blocks *in* the puzzle frame) tie the two circles together with a line. This occurs only with non-goal-directed activity.

Two scores are derived from each protocol: Persistence, based on the first two minutes of activity; and Resistance to Distraction, based on the final minute of activity with distractor blocks present. The scoring will be described separately for each period of activity.

During the first two minutes, goal-directed behavior is scored two points for each .33-minute period; while non-goal-directed behavior and other behavior is scored minus one point for each .33-minute period it appears. A constant of +12 is added to eliminate negative scores. With six .33-minute periods, the maximum score is 24 (*all* goal-directed activity, *no* non-goal-directed or other activity); and the minimum score obtainable is 0 (*no* goal-directed activity, and *all* non-goal-directed activity).

During the last minute, while the distractor blocks are present, the goal-directed behavior is scored three points for each .33-minute period; and non-goal-directed behavior, other behavior, and block-directed activity are each scored minus one point for each .33-minute such behaviors appear. A constant of +9 is added to eliminate negative scores. Thus, with three periods, the maximum score obtainable is 18 (*all* goal-directed activity); and the minimum score obtainable is 0 (*no* goal-directed activity, and *all* non-goal-directed activity).

TASK COMPETENCE, SOCIAL COMPETENCE, AND KINDERGARTEN PROGNOSIS: POSTTEST RATINGS

Task Competence and Social Competence scales theoretically correspond to the distinction between task roles and social roles in problem solving groups (Bales, 1958). The assumption is of course that children may differ in their competence in handling the demands of these two kinds of roles early in their development. Bales, in his studies of group problem solving, has found that persons who become "task specialists" are not likely to become "social-emotional specialists."

Doing well on tasks, and doing well in social interaction, can thus be viewed as two unrelated skills. The degree of relationship between social and task competence, however, is a matter of theoretical contention. As White (1960) has pointed out,

REPLACEMENT PUZZLE TEST
SCORE SHEET

Time	Activity			Prompt	Blocks	Puzzle or Block Related		Verbalization		Other
	Puzzle - Goal Direct.	Puzzle-non Goal Direct.	Other			Ques. &/or Comments	Fantasy	Ques. &/or Comments	Fantasy	
.33	pgd	pngd	other	P		q &/or c	fan.	q &/or c	fan.	
.66	pgd	pngd	other	P		q &/or c	fan.	q &/or c	fan.	
1.00	pgd	pngd	other	P		q &/or c	fan.	q &/or c	fan.	
1.33	pgd	pngd	other	P		q &/or c	fan.	q &/or c	fan.	
1.66	pgd	pngd	other	P		q &/or c	fan.	q &/or c	fan.	
2.00	pgd	pngd	other	P		q &/or c	fan.	q &/or c	fan.	
2.33	pgd	pngd	other	P		q &/or c	fan.	q &/or c	fan.	
2.66	pgd	pngd	other	P		q &/or c	fan.	q &/or c	fan.	
3.00	pgd	pngd	other	P		q &/or c	fan.	q &/or c	fan.	

FIGURE 14

Observation and scoring form for Replacement Puzzle.

competence "....applies to interactions with people as well as to dealings with inanimate environment" (p. 104). White says that "Sense of social competence may well be the more important of the two. . . ." (p. 104).

The interrelation of social skills and task skills is reinforced in the epigenetic theory of Erikson (1950). The resolution of the problem of basic trust vs. basic mistrust precedes the child's management of more task-related achievements implied in his next three stages involving autonomy, initiative, and industry. Developmentally there is a mutual facilitation; autonomy, initiative, and industry have their basis in the solution of social problems of the child such as separation anxiety, loss, and "confidence." Erikson added a footnote to his Chapter 7, "Eight Ages of Man," in his revised and enlarged edition of CHILDHOOD AND SOCIETY, in which he pointed out that "...some writers are so intent on making an *achievement scale* out of these stages that they blithely omit all the 'negative' senses (basic mistrust, etc.) which are and remain the dynamic counterpart of the 'positive' ones throughout life" (pp. 273-274). If one examines the content of the "negative" senses of each stage, it is readily apparent that these are heavily weighted with problems of social competence: shame and doubt, guilt, and inferiority. The social strengths of the child may thus be related to good task performance since the "ages of man" are progressing toward a stage of "integrity," not isolated skills and strengths. If the child is bogged down in his social-emotional coping, this will inevitably be reflected in his task competence. Thus we feel it necessary to assess the relation between these two aspects of autonomous functioning, task competence and social competence.

The rating scales, shown in Figure 15, were adapted for operationalizing these theoretical concerns. They originally appeared in the Stanford-Binet Record Booklet, Form L-M (1960). Thus the assessment of task and social competence can be made in the context of the Binet and CATB settings for comparison purposes.

In addition, we have included a "Kindergarten Prognosis" scale, intended as an estimate of the child's ability to cope with a conventional kindergarten situation. This scale should be thought of in relation to a kindergarten where classes are large, programs are structured, and children are encouraged to conform. This rating is designed to get at the tester's opinion of the child's chances for success in a typical kindergarten on an all-round basis, rather than on the basis of separate skills. Any elaboration of the specific factors underlying this prediction can be recorded in the "comment" section at the bottom of the page.

The ratings must be done immediately after the child has been tested. Impressions fade rapidly and testing many children results in considerable difficulty in recalling the specific behavior of individual children. The ratings are each based on a five point scale shown in Figure 15, with weights assigned as follows: "Optimal" five

SOCIAL COMPETENCE RATING

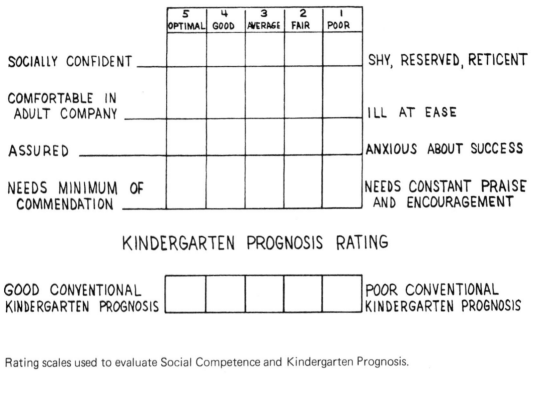

	5 OPTIMAL	4 GOOD	3 AVERAGE	2 FAIR	1 POOR	
SOCIALLY CONFIDENT						SHY, RESERVED, RETICENT
COMFORTABLE IN ADULT COMPANY						ILL AT EASE
ASSURED						ANXIOUS ABOUT SUCCESS
NEEDS MINIMUM OF COMMENDATION						NEEDS CONSTANT PRAISE AND ENCOURAGEMENT

KINDERGARTEN PROGNOSIS RATING

GOOD CONVENTIONAL KINDERGARTEN PROGNOSIS						POOR CONVENTIONAL KINDERGARTEN PROGNOSIS

Rating scales used to evaluate Social Competence and Kindergarten Prognosis.

TASK COMPETENCE RATING

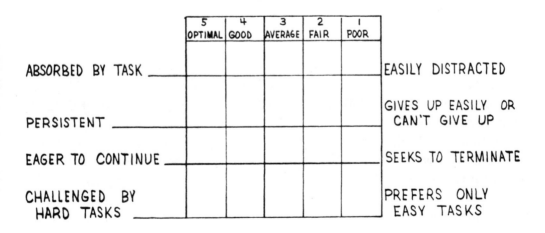

	5 OPTIMAL	4 GOOD	3 AVERAGE	2 FAIR	1 POOR	
ABSORBED BY TASK						EASILY DISTRACTED
PERSISTENT						GIVES UP EASILY OR CAN'T GIVE UP
EAGER TO CONTINUE						SEEKS TO TERMINATE
CHALLENGED BY HARD TASKS						PREFERS ONLY EASY TASKS

FIGURE 15

Rating scales used to evaluate Task Competence. Child is rated from one to five along each dimension; score is based on sum of ratings for each variable.

points; "Good" four points; "Average" three points; "Fair" two points; and "Poor" one point. Most ratings will fall in the "Good," "Average," or "Fair" columns. The better a child's behavior is in relation to a given scale, the closer to "Optimal" should his rating be. Very few children show "Optimal" behaviors and very few children show "Poor" behaviors. Each rating is based only on the child's test performance; the ratings should be thought of as general summaries of the overall tendencies throughout the testing. For example, the first rating ranges from "Absorbed by task" to "Easily distracted." If the child was *rarely* absorbed by *any* test in the battery and was *very* easily distracted throughout the testing, an X would be placed in the column labeled "Poor." If the child worked *very* well on all tasks and was *not at all* distracted, an X would be placed in the column labeled "Optimal."

Scores for task competence are computed as a sum of ratings on the dimensions depicted in Figure 15. Both ends of the rating continuum are specified, and the ratings reflect the degree to which the child showed these capacities during testing only.

Thus the four scales for Task Competence and the four scales for Social Competence, when totaled, range from five to a maximum of twenty. The Kindergarten Prognosis scale is a single global rating ranging from one to five.

RESULTS AND DISCUSSION

These findings are reported as products of "research in progress." They should be viewed as tentative. It is hoped that other investigators will soon take up the challenge to correct our current appraisals of reliability, validity, and the meaningfulness of the present approach to autonomous functioning in young children.

Reliability
In Anna Freud's (1965) NORMALITY AND PATHOLOGY IN CHILDHOOD, the point is made that "There is in childhood no stable level of functioning in any area at any time" (p. 122). This provides a considerable challenge from the point of view of anticipating significant reliability coefficients for young children's performances on the CATB. Our view is that this question must be put to empirical test.

We obtained three kinds of reliability information: (a) test-retest reliabilities based on one-month and two-month intervals, (b) internal consistency coefficients, and (c) inter-rater correlations for test results which had to be coded.

Over 300 children have been tested from lower class as well as upper class areas of

Cincinnati. All children were between three and six years, and almost all reliabilities reported were derived from lower class Negro children's responses. The data are based on six studies, done over a two-year period; thus we typically have more than one estimate of each reliability for each test. This is an important feature of our research strategy, since assessing reliability with different groups under different conditions, and at different times of the year, with different testers, insures that our reliability estimates are not an artifact of special test conditions, a particular tester, or unique populations of children.

Our goal has been to develop short and efficient tests. We hope that even small samples of behavior in these areas, with good testers and good test procedures, will prove to be stable and internally consistent. Reliability coefficients may be affected by test length, or by limited range of scores. These factors may be operating, but we have proceeded on the assumption that they are not of major importance in most of these measures of the problem-solving *process,* unlike the role played by age factors in conventional intelligence measures of *content.* We expect a large "range of talent" within the limits of the ages of three and six for our process variables.

All available data are reported. If a child failed to complete a particular test, that score is not included in the reliability estimate; however, other tests which he did complete are included in the reliability data. One reliability study permitted retesting 100% of the children over a one-month test-retest interval; the other study permitted retesting only 68% over a two-month test-retest interval. A summary of reliabilities is presented in Table 1.

The mean of all test-retest reliabilities was .50; this distribution ranged from .82 for the Dog and Bone test for Innovative Behavior down to a -.07 for the Resistance to Distraction test. The mean of the internal consistency coefficients was .62; this distribution ranged from .94 for the Dog and Bone test and .91 for the Curiosity Box, down to a .16 for Incidental Learning. Inter-rater correlations averaged .96; the highest obtained, .996, was based on rater agreement on Dog and Bone scoring and lowest obtained was a .83 derived from the Persistence ratings.

As we anticipated, some tests proved to be consistently high in reliability, while others revealed little evidence of stability or consistency. We were rather surprised, however, to find that *those tests which allowed the child the most freedom of response showed consistently the highest reliabilities:* the Dog and Bone test (innovative behavior), the Curiosity Box, and Task Initiation (curiosity motivation). Tests which involved instructions for the child to behave in a certain way tended to be less stable and less internally consistent. This was just as true for upper class children as for lower class children.

TABLE 1

Summary of CATB Reliability Coefficients

Test	Test-retest reliability coefficients		Internal consistency reliability coefficients		Inter-rater reliability coefficients	
	N	r	N	r	N	r
Innovative Behavior						
Dog and Bone Test	33	.73**a	33	.76**c	42	.996**
	32	.82**b	48	.94**c		
Curiosity						
Curiosity Box	Not available		83	.91**d	--	--
Task Initiation	33	.76**a	--f	--f	33	.96**
Puzzle Boards	Not available		27	.77**d	--	--
Impulse Control						
Draw-a-Line-Slowly	33	.43*b	32	.72,.66,.69**e	30	.90**
	33	.41*a	74	.55,.47,.80***e		
Field Independence						
EC-EFT	Not available		34	.48**c	--	--
	Not available		84	.59**e	--	--
Intentional Learning						
Picture Recall	32	.60**b	118	.40**c	--	--
Incidental Learning						
Find-the-Color-Green	32	.27b	118	.16c	--	--

Reflectivity EC-MFF	Not available	62	.37**[c]	--	--
Persistence Replacement Puzzle	Not available	84	.33**[d]	--	--
Resistance to Distraction Puzzle plus Distractor Blocks (narrative ratings)	33	-.07[b]	--	49	.98**
Task Competence Posttest Ratings	34	.39*[b]	63	.82**[c]	--
Social Competence Posttest Ratings	34	.60**[b]	63	.66***[c]	--
Kindergarten Prognosis Posttest Ratings	34	.55**[b]	--	--	--

[a] One-month test-retest interval.
[b] Two-month test-retest interval.
[c] Odd items vs. even items.
[d] Odd-numbered time intervals vs. even-numbered time intervals.

*Significant beyond the .05 level.
**Significant beyond the .01 level.

[e] Correlations among the three lines drawn. Correlations presented in following order: line 1 vs. line 2, line 1 vs. line 3, and line 2 vs. line 3.

[f] Not applicable; for example, task initiation scoring is based on ratings of narrative recordings written out by the tester—since there is only one rating, no internal consistency r's are possible.

The test for Innovative Behavior, the Dog and Bone test, proved to be highly successful in terms of test-retest stability as well as internal consistency, with no correlation lower than .76. The theoretically derived scoring procedures showed almost perfect agreement between independent scorers (.996).

All estimates of reliability for Curiosity were high, ranging from .76 to .91. On Task Initiation, behavior was rated on a four-point scale; inter-rater reliability was .96, a highly satisfactory degree of agreement. Test-retest data on the Curiosity Box have not been obtained yet using the scoring format described in the previous section. Such data are available, however, for the earlier form, a rating derived from the tester's narrative descriptions which were written during the testing itself. This two-month test-retest correlation was .50. These narrative ratings provide a conservative estimate of reliability, and we feel confident that the new scoring procedures will improve recording accuracy and eliminate errors of recording observations and subsequent rater judgment.

Impulse Control measures based on three lines drawn "as slowly as you can," showed modest test-retest stability in the .40's. These estimates were calculated from average rates of drawing the three lines by each child. Inter-rater reliabilities were necessary since the measurement of length of line drawn is crucial to computing the inches/.01 minute rates. The inter-rater agreement of .90 was lower than we expected and this was traced to the fact that occasionally the map measuring device was not always reset to exactly zero, thus introducing measurement error into the calculations for length of line.

We have not used the Field Independence measure, EC-EFT, in a test-retest reliability study to date. Internal consistency coefficients, averaging .54, were disappointing, but this may be due to restrictions in range of abilities; both coefficients were based on lower class samples. These reliability estimates may prove to be too conservative.

For a ten-item picture-recall test, the Intentional Learning stability was fairly good, with a value of .60. The odd-even correlation of only .40 is no doubt the result of the fact that average scores for "odd" items were less than one and "even" scores averaged less than two, not allowing much variation.

Incidental Learning test-retest coefficients were not high; a two-month interval produced a correlation of only .27. This is a difficult test for these children both upper and lower class, and, like other tests of ability in the battery showed more homogeneity of variance than the process tests.

Data on the Reflectivity test are sparse. Internal consistency was only .37 and should be improved upon. We have not used the test in a stability study yet, although a one-year test-retest study will be completed after this chapter is published.

The Persistence measure, with the new rating forms described in the previous section, has not been used in a test-retest study yet. The old narrative rating procedure, however, provides a conservative estimate of a two-month test-retest reliability of .34; this was a six-point rating done after testing based on narrative descriptions written by the tester. Interrater reliability for this was .83. The new rating forms should provide better stability.

Resistance to Distraction based on a one-minute sample of behavior showed no stability whatever when data consisted of ratings of tester descriptions, even though the ratings had good inter-rater reliability of .98. The one-minute sample may be too brief, or it may be that "distractibility" is inherently difficult to assess by efficient testing methods. An analysis of the test procedure showed that lower class children who tended to be distractible *before* the distractor blocks were introduced continued to be distracted afterward; upper class children, however, were persistent before the blocks were offered, then *they too* turned toward the blocks. This latter form of "distractibility" was in part a function of their attention to the tester as someone they responded to more effectively, and whom they appeared to trust more. We think that they were not distracted, but were attending to the new materials placed before them by the tester; the tester and her concerns had greater value for the upper class child. Nevertheless, it is an important enough variable theoretically, to pursue further. Experimental work is now under way to get at the Resistance to Distraction variable more effectively.

The four-item rating scale for Task Competence was moderately stable, .40. By comparison, we were surprised that the four-item scale for Social Competence had a test-retest two-month stability of .68. This suggests that even within a highly task-oriented testing situation, Social Competence can be diagnosed reliably. Internal consistency, however, was higher for Task Competence (.82) than for Social Competence (.68). This is entirely understandable; the social variable may be more complex, and may be more difficult to infer from task-oriented responding; whereas, the task variable is easily inferred from the task-oriented responding. There is no statistical reason necessitating that the complex test be less stable than the homogeneous test.

The one-item Kindergarten Prognosis rating was moderately stable over a two-month period (.47). It cautions, however, that such opinions are not perfectly stable and that even with experienced testers who have been teachers, these opinions should be regarded with caution.

Test Intercorrelations

Two studies of the intercorrelations among CATB variables have been completed. Both samples were made up of lower-class Negro children between the ages of three and six. The first study was done in 1966; the second study was done in 1967. The latter study represents the latest form of the tests used and is representative of relationships found in the earlier study. The results from the second study are presented in Table 2. The product-moment correlations were based on a sample of 84 children in prekindergarten classrooms located in an all-Negro community.

The average of the correlations in Table 2 was only .15. Yet, of the 66 correlations, 43% were significant beyond the .05 level. This clearly nonrandom distribution of correlations along with the meaningful pattern of relationships relative to each variable discussed below, is encouraging with respect to test validity.

It is the mutual meaningful relations among the variables which is helpful to understanding these new tests. As Campbell (1960) describes this point, "Validation, when it occurs, is symmetrical and equalitarian" (p. 548). All tests used provide validation evidence to some extent, and no test is to be regarded as an infallible criterion. Therefore, each test will be reviewed briefly in relation to other tests in the battery, not only to check on expected significant relationships, but also to examine evidence of **discriminant** validity (Campbell & Fiske, 1959), "...the requirement that a test not correlate too highly with measures from which it is supposed to differ" (Campbell, 1960, p. 548).

CURIOSITY: TASK INITIATION. The highest correlation with Task Initiation was with Curiosity Box activity (.39), along with Curiosity Verbalization (.52), and Fantasy-Related Verbalization (.34), both of which were derived from Curiosity Box protocols. In light of the prediction that these measures were indicators of the curiosity variable, this was highly relevant validity information. There was a significant negative correlation with the Intentional Learning scores (-.22) and this very likely reflects some degree of interference with learning because of impulsiveness manifested in the Task Initiation behavior. This interpretation is given support in that Task Initiation correlates slightly negatively with the Impulse Control measure (-.16); Impulse Control also correlates with Intentional Learning (.31, at the .01 level).

Further validity support is given in that Task Initiation correlated significantly with Task Competence (.24), but not Social Competence (.02).

CURIOSITY: CURIOSITY BOX. As pointed out above, Curiosity Box, Task Initiation, and Curiosity Box Verbalization scores showed good convergent validity; these were the highest correlations for Curiosity Box also. Close behind, however,

TABLE 2

Product-Moment Correlations Among Fourteen CATB Variables

	1 Task Init.	2 Cur. Box	3 Dog Bone	4 EC-EFT	5 Imp. Cont.	6 Int. Learn.	7 Inc. Learn.	8 Persist.	9 Resist. Distract.	10 Task Comp.	11 Soc. Comp.	12 Kind. Prog.	13 Cur. Verb.
1. Curiosity: Task Initiation	--												
2. Curiosity: Curiosity Box	39**	--											
3. Innovative Behavior: Dog and Bone test	06	11	--										
4. Field Independence: EC-EFT	13	04	21	--									
5. Impulse Control: Draw-a-Line-Slowly	-16	-01	23*	07	--								
6. Intentional Learning	-22*	16	33**	07	31**	--							
7. Incidental Learning	-03	-01	11	09	12	45**	--						
8. Persistence	-12	-03	06	28*	28*	15	-18	--					
9. Resistance to Distraction	-11	-20	-18	25*	27*	-04	-09	07	--				
10. Task Competence Ratings	24*	-05	10	52**	25*	27*	19	45**	51**	--			
11. Social Competence Ratings	02	37**	26**	27*	17	22*	25*	-06	00	44**	--		
12. Kindergarten Prognosis Rating	-13	22*	18	31**	31**	27*	33**	26*	23*	71**	70**	--	
13. Curiosity Verbalization	52**	48**	-01	14	05	-06	06	-20	-14	-01	53**	23*	--
14. Fantasy-Related Verbalization	34**	31**	10	10	-03	-07	-03	-14	-16	-06	38**	08	55**

*Significant beyond the .05 level.
**Significant beyond the .01 level.

Note.--Decimal points have been omitted. N's are based on all available data. Eighty-four children were included in the study, but due to the fact that not all test scores were available for every child, N's varied from 79 to 84.

was the highly significant relation to the Social Competence Rating (.37). It is evident that the child, in this situation, is permitted to express social skills and social needs, even though the tester is seated behind the child and offers no reward for social interaction. Thus the tester is given greater opportunity to observe the child's social skills on this test than on others where social skills are "submerged," as it were, in the task at hand.

Both Curiosity measures correlated well with one another (convergent validity) and relatively lower with other measures in the test battery (discriminant validity). Thus it appears that curiosity behavior at this age level does not facilitate solutions to problems that demand impulse control and sustained attention. This generalization must be tested in other settings and with other samples of children and other curiosity tests.

INNOVATIVE BEHAVIOR: THE DOG AND BONE TEST. The highest correlation for the Dog and Bone test was with Intentional Learning (.33). It should be kept in mind that if there is any relation at all with another variable, the Dog and Bone test is very likely to show it, since most of the test variance is reliable variance. Since the Intentional Learning test is dependent, more than any other test, on verbal skills, one might suspect that it is this factor which the two tests have in common; some children, surely, get low scores on both tests because of comprehension factors. This must be checked empirically of course, but the percent common variance for the two tests ($.33^2$ = 11%) would appear to be a fair estimate of the verbal comprehension component of the Dog and Bone test. The interpretation is strengthened by the correlations with EC-EFT (.21) and Impulse Control (.23), both of which involve verbal comprehension, although not as much as the Intentional Learning variable.

The remaining significant correlation with Social Competence (.26) gives support to the notion put forth by Wallach & Kogan (1965) that the social psychological context of the testing situation is relevant to the production of creative solutions to problems. This finding was not due to halo effect. Ratings of *Task* Competence correlated only .10 with Innovative Behavior shown in the Dog and Bone test.

Since no other measures of innovative behavior were used, convergent validity cannot be evaluated. The evidence above indicates that the Dog and Bone test however, measures some elements of behavior common to EC-EFT, Impulse Control, and Intentional Learning performance. Additionally, the Dog and Bone test does *not* correlate with the Curiosity measures (Task Initiation, .06; and Curiosity Box, .11). The pattern of correlations then, suggests that innovative behavior indicated by this test contains a great deal of specific variance; the reliabilities, it will be remembered, were very high, yet the correlations with other tests were only modest.

FIELD INDEPENDENCE: EC-EFT. EC-EFT is a demanding task; it is businesslike, demands attention, persistence, and task motivation; this was reflected in the Task Competence ratings (.52), while correlating only .27 with *Social* Competence ratings. The high correlation with Task Competence thus mutually supports validation for both measures. In addition, performance on the Persistence variable and the Resistance to Distraction variable was found to correlate .28 and .25, respectively.

It is noteworthy that the testers' Kindergarten Prognosis ratings correlated highly with the Field Independence measure (.31). This should be interpreted with caution in light of the fact that Kindergarten Prognosis is highly related to the Social Competence measure (.70) as well as the Task Competence measure (.71). It may well be that EC-EFT performance gives evidence of good Kindergarten adjustment, but this cognitive functioning is embedded in a network of relationships involving social and task factors. Disentangling these theoretically distinct variables is a job for future research.

IMPULSE CONTROL: DRAW-A-LINE-SLOWLY TEST. Impulse Control entered into the performance of a number of CATB variables. In order of magnitude of relationship, they are: Intentional Learning (.31), Kindergarten Prognosis (.31), and Persistence (.28), all at the .01 level; and Resistance to Distraction (.27), Task Competence Ratings (.25), and Innovative Behavior (.23), all at the .05 level. Social Competence correlated only .17, showing evidence for discriminant validity for this highly task-oriented test. These findings taken together, suggest that Impulse Control is an important developmental variable affecting a variety of behaviors relevant to problem-solving ability.

The Draw-a-Line-Slowly test is directed toward assessment of inhibition of motor responses; the very modest relation to the EC-EFT measure (.07) suggests that Field Independence, as measured by the embedded figures procedure, is to some degree independent of motor impulse control. This lack of relationship was also noted by Maccoby, et al., (1965) in a sample of preschool children, using the Karp & Konstadt CEFT measure. The implication is that impulse control training will have little effect, by itself, on increasing analytic perceptual skills.

INTENTIONAL LEARNING: FIND-THE-COLOR-GREEN TEST. Intentional Learning was most highly related to Incidental Learning (.45). Significant relations between these two variables have been reported by Plenderleith & Postman (1956) for college undergraduates; they reported a correlation of .26 (p < .01) between intentional and incidental learning. Since the two CATB scores are derived from the same test materials, and since the two tests are adjacent to one another in the test battery, it is likely that the correlation is inflated beyond the Plenderleith &

Postman correlation due to shared "method" variance (Campbell & Fiske, 1959) rather than a pure relationship per se. The finding substantiates the fact that intentional-incidental learning abilities correlate in early childhood as well as in college populations.

Intentional Learning also correlated well with Innovative Behavior (.33) and with Impulse Control (.31). These two variables, in turn, correlated significantly with one another, as noted earlier. This is an interesting triad, in that it provides evidence that conventional behavior involved in intentional learning and impulse control is not incompatible with unconventional and creative responding involved in innovative behavior at this age.

It should be noted that Task Initiation correlated negatively (-.22) with Intentional Learning, which supports the interpretation that Intentional Learning is better for those children who do not tend to initiate behavior on their own.

Intentional Learning showed low but consistently significant relations to the three tester ratings. Only slight discriminant validity is shown in that Task Competence correlated higher (.27) than Social Competence (.22), although the difference is not significant. This relationship will be cross-checked in subsequent studies.

INCIDENTAL LEARNING: FIND-THE-COLOR-GREEN TEST. Unlike Intentional Learning scores, the Incidental Learning scores did not relate significantly to other test scores (with the exception of Intentional Learning, discussed above). It did relate significantly to the Kindergarten Prognosis rating (.33) beyond the .01 level, and probably reflected the tester's sensitivity to the child's management of a difficult task. Social Competence correlated .25 while Task Competence fell short of significance ($r = .19$).

Incidental Learning was expected to correlate significantly with the EC-EFT measure as was reported by Witkin, et al., (1962, p. 142) for 10-year-olds. This correlation turned out to be only .09, far below significance. At least two factors may explain this paucity of validity support: a) the test itself may be invalid for this age level, or b) the low reliability along with the difficulty level and consequent restrictions on range of scores may thus have attenuated the correlations. We prefer to think that the latter factor is responsible for the lack of validity evidence found at this point, and we are proceeding to simplify the task and improve its reliability.

PERSISTENCE: REPLACEMENT PUZZLE TEST. Persistence scores showed a very high relation to Task Competence (.45), as would be expected. This is given good discriminant validity support in that *Social* Competence was unrelated to the Persistence scores (-.06). In addition, Kindergarten Prognosis, while correlating at the .05 level (.26), was not as high as the directly relevant Task Competence ratings.

The correlations with EC-EFT (.28) and Impulse Control (.28), significant at the .01 level, are consistent with the idea that both these measures involve persistent task-oriented behaviors. By contrast, variables *not* involving these kinds of behaviors did *not* show significant correlations with the Persistence measures: Curiosity, Innovative Behavior, and Social Competence. This picture of good discriminant validity as well as good convergent validity is somewhat marred by the low and non-significant correlations with Intentional and Incidental Learning. However, these two tests have validity problems of their own which were discussed above, and should probably not be weighted heavily in the validity evaluation of the present test.

RESISTANCE TO DISTRACTION: REPLACEMENT PUZZLE TEST. The pattern of correlations for Resistance to Distraction is almost identical to that obtained for Persistence. Since these two tests are scored similarly and are basically two approaches to measuring persistence, it is understandable that they relate in highly similar ways to outside variables. Task Competence, as expected, showed the highest relationship to Resistence to Distraction (.51), and was less strongly related to Kindergarten Prognosis (.23). The EC-EFT (.25) and Impulse Control (.27) measures correlated significantly at the .05 level. Discriminant validity, shown in low correlations with non-task-oriented variables, paralleled very closely with that found in the Persistence correlations.

TASK COMPETENCE AND SOCIAL COMPETENCE: POSTTEST RATINGS. Both Task and Social Ratings showed high correlations with each other (.44) and with performance on a number of other tests in the battery. The possibility that halo effect was operating in producing high ratings on both of these variables is not tenable in view of the fact that each rating correlates with predictably different tests. For example, Task Competence correlates with Task Initiation (.24), but not Curiosity Box (-.05), while Social Competence relates to Curiosity Box (.37) but not Task Initiation (.02). In addition, Task Competence relates *higher* than Social Competence on other task-oriented variables: EC-EFT, Impulse Control, Persistence, and Resistance to Distraction. This is particularly striking on Persistence (.45 vs. -.06) and Resistance to Distraction (.51 vs. .00). The *reverse* was true for the less task related variables of Curiosity Verbalization (-.01 vs. .53) and Fantasy-Related Verbalization (-.06 vs. .38).

Both Task and Social Competence ratings correlate very highly with Kindergarten Prognosis (.71 and .70, respectively). This finding is consistent with the idea that both social roles and task roles are useful in group experiences, but in view of the relatively lower correlation *between* Task and Social Competence (.44), it is not likely that both can be handled well by all children. This is commensurate with Bales' theory of incompatibility of task roles and social roles (Bales, 1958).

KINDERGARTEN PROGNOSIS: POSTTEST RATINGS. The highest correlations for Kindergarten Prognosis were discussed in the Task Competence and Social Competence section, above. These correlations (.71 and .70, respectively) are undoubtedly enhanced by the shared method variance involved in any rating procedure. This of course does not affect the *relative* levels of correlation among ratings themselves.

Correlations, in order of magnitude (for non-rating-type measures) were: Incidental Learning (.33), EC-EFT (.31), Impulse Control (.31), Intentional Learning (.27), Persistence (.26), Resistance to Distraction (.23), Curiosity Verbalization (.23), and Curiosity Box (.22). It is very important to note that these variables connote task-orientation, obedience, and self-control in the "dutiful child" sense of good behavior. While Curiosity Verbalization and Curiosity Box performance depart somewhat from this picture, they are the lowest of the seven significant correlations, but more important theoretically, the Curiosity Box is an *explicitly* permissive test situation; the tester tells the child, "Here's something for you to play with." Task Initiation, on the contrary, demands initiative on the part of the child, without direct adult support, and the correlation was not only non-significant, but was negative (-.13). Innovative Behavior also was not significantly related to Kindergarten Prognosis (.18). It is tempting to speculate that the "good" conventional kindergarten child is dutiful, hard-working, controlled, and analytic, but lacks initiative, self-direction, and innovative solutions to problems.

REFLECTIVITY: EC-MFF. The Early Childhood Matching Familiar Figures test was not used in the study summarized in Table 1, but was used in an earlier version of the test battery. In that earlier study, correlations significant at the .01 level were: EC-EFT (.49), Intentional Learning (.48), Kindergarten Prognosis (.48), Task Competence (.44), Incidental Learning (.43), Social Competence (.40), and Impulse Control (.37). One other variable, the Karp and Konstadt CEFT, correlated at the .05 level (.27). These are higher correlations than those found for other variables reported, and this evidence suggests that Reflectivity may be central to the task-oriented measures in the test battery.

In terms of the discussion in the previous section, EC-MFF predictably correlated very highly with Kindergarten Prognosis (.48), providing additional evidence that the good kindergarten child is controlled and inhibits impulses successfully. In this test, such impulse control leads to good solutions to problems demanding a degree of reflectivity. The implication, then, is that the child who can control impulses need not be thought of as an inhibited child. Judging from evidence presented by

Maccoby (1965), this is a safe statement in that children with good impulse control did well on the Binet, but were not necessarily inactive or inhibited in free play. One is still left with the picture that, when given instructions to work on a problem, the "good" kindergarten child appears to be obedient and controlled, rather than curious, exploratory, and innovative.

CURIOSITY VERBALIZATION AND FANTASY-RELATED VERBALIZATION. These two variables correlated .55 with one another, the highest relationship that was obtained for each variable. This would suggest that they are measuring the same factor, and the pattern of relations with other tests in the battery supports this interpretation. In general, Fantasy-Related Verbalization does not correlate as highly with other tests as does Curiosity Verbalization, but the over-all pattern is very similar.

The two verbalization variables related highly significantly to the curiosity measures, Curiosity Box activity (.48 and .31) and Task Initiation (.52 and .34). This set of high correlations supports the notion that curiosity and exploratory behavior are supplemented by spontaneous verbalization. In fact, the two verbalization scores correlated in very much the same way that Curiosity Box activity correlated with other tests.

This close relationship between exploration, curiosity, and verbalization is consistent with the hierarchic integration hypothesis of Werner and with the circular reaction hypothesis of Piaget which were discussed earlier. Piaget's notion that, in infancy, what is heard becomes something to look for; what is seen becomes something to reach for, may now be extended to a higher level of functioning in early childhood: what is explored becomes something to talk about, which provides a mutually supporting feedback loop. Exploring leads to verbalization and verbalization leads to more exploring.

A suggestion of how this comes about and is maintained is provided in the very high correlations with the Social Competence variable (.53 and .38). The testers saw the children who verbalized freely while exploring the Curiosity Box as relatively high on the following Social Competence rating scales: socially confident, comfortable in adult company, assured, and need minimum of commendation. This leads to an hypothesis that curiosity and exploratory behaviors are facilitated by good adult-child relationships; without security in the social-emotional sphere, curiosity is stifled. The child who is shy and unexpressive in social relationships may well be the child who is shy and unexpressive of curiosity in relation to new and novel objects. By contrast, this would appear to be in no way handicapping to the child in the Task Competence area, since the testers ratings on Task Competence were unrelated (-.01 and -.06) to the spontaneous verbalization variables or to Curiosity Box activity

(-.05). In addition, the correlations between the verbalization scores and the other more task-oriented variables in the battery ranged from -.20 to .14, averaging only -.03. Similarly, Curiosity Box activity correlations ranged from -.20 to .16, with an average of .00.

One must conclude from this that curiosity and exploratory behavior,, with its supporting spontaneous verbalizations is independent of task performance where goals are clearly spelled out, impulse control is demanded, and obedience to instructions is expected. The job of early childhood education is to maintain both of these useful forms of problem-solving strategy. The autonomous child should be able to adapt to effective coping with both kinds of situations, and with imaginative planning, the prekindergarten curriculum should be able to enhance and maintain effective functioning in both areas.

Score Distributions

Means, standard deviations, and ranges of all CATB scores are presented in Table 3.

TABLE 3

CATB Means, Standard Deviations, and Ranges*

	Variable	$\overline{X}$	σ	N	Possible Range	Obtained Range
1.	Task Initiation	1.58	.98	83	1-4	1-4
2.	Curiosity Box	13.83	10.22	84	0-50	0-32
3.	Innovative Behavior	4.80	3.80	84	0-30	0-22
4.	EC-EFT	8.36	2.88	84	0-14	1-13
5.	Impulse Control	.69	.39	84	>0	.10-2.51
6.	Intentional Learn.	2.81	1.75	84	0-10	0-7
7.	Inc. Learning	1.48	1.30	84	0-10	0-5
8.	Persistence	20.70	4.02	84	0-24	10-24
9.	Resistance to Distraction	10.73	5.28	80	0-18	3-18
10.	Task Competence	12.17	2.57	84	4-20	4-17
11.	Social Competence	11.96	2.46	84	4-20	4-18
12.	Kindergarten Prog.	3.00	.66	84	1-5	1-4
13.	Curiosity Verb.	1.88	3.05	84	0-10	0-10
14.	Fantasy-Related Verb.	.51	1.16	84	0-30	0-6
15.	Reflectivity	4.20	1.89	71	0-8	1-8

*Data on variables one through fourteen are computed from the 1967 study in an all-Negro community. Data on variable fifteen were based on the 1966 study in a Negro ghetto and Negro public housing area.

When comparing with data derived from other populations, it should be remembered that these data were derived from a population of lower-class Negro children living in an all-Negro community. The children had been in prekindergarten for approximately six months.

Not all distributions are normal. This is particularly true of the curiosity variables, Task Initiation, Curiosity Box, Curiosity Verbalization, and Fantasy-Related Verbalization. Examination of the frequency distributions reveals that these variables are platykurtic, very nearly bimodally distributed. This is supported by tester observations that children behave in an all-or-none manner in relating to the curiosity materials. It is as though there were a decision point at which the child begins activity, exploring, touching, manipulating, investigating, or he sits back apathetically unable to initiate this kind of behavior.

Innovative Behavior scores, using the Dog and Bone test, were positively skewed. Eighty percent of the scores fall in the range zero to six; the remaining 20% fall in the range seven to twenty-two.

The Impulse Control scores were symmetrically distributed with the exception of only two extreme scores of 1.87 and 2.51.

Intentional and Incidental Learning scores were quite low, averaging only 1.48 and 2.81, respectively, out of possible scores of 10. Difficulty level of this test is probably too high, particularly with respect to Incidental Learning, where 27% of the children scored zero. Only 12% scored zero on Intentional Learning.

All other variables appear to be symmetrically distributed and approximately normal.

Correlations with Stanford-Binet IQ
Seventy-six of the children tested in the CATB intercorrelations study, described in the last section, were tested with Form L-M of the Stanford-Binet. IQ testing was done under the auspices of the county school board during the same interval in which CATB testing was done. The mean IQ for this population was 94; the range was from 67 to 128, with an SD of 12.45.

The CATB-IQ correlations are presented in Table 4. The average of these correlations is .20, non-significant. The distribution of correlations, however, is clearly non-random, with seven of the fourteen CATB scores correlating beyond the .05 level of confidence.

Social Competence on the CATB was the highest correlation with IQ, while Task

TABLE 4

**Pearson Product-Moment Correlations between
Fourteen CATB Variables and
Stanford-Binet Scores (Form L-M)[a]**

Test	r
Social Competence Ratings	.37**
Field Independence: EC-EFT	.33**
Kindergarten Prognosis Rating	.31**
Innovative Behavior: Dog and Bone test	.31**
Impulse Control: Draw-a-Line-Slowly	.24*
Intentional Learning	.23*
Curiosity Verbalization	.23*
Fantasy-Related Verbalization	.22
Curiosity: Curiosity Box	.20
Incidental Learning	.19
Task Competence Ratings	.17
Curiosity: Task Initiation	.04
Persistence	.02
Resistance to Distraction	-.10

* Significant beyond the .05 level.
**Significant beyond the .01 level.

[a]All N's=76 with the exception of Task Initiation (N = 75) and Resistance to Distraction (N = 72); the former was due to an error in recording, the latter was due to the fact that four children solved the puzzle and therefore could not be presented with the distractor blocks.

Competence on the CATB was one of the lowest correlations. The high IQ child then, appears socially competent on CATB testing, but does not appear to be more competent on the kinds of behaviors required in handling the variety of CATB tasks. Thus, it is the socially competent Negro child who also shows relatively good IQ test performance.

In addition, the higher the IQ: a) the better the analytic ability shown on the EC-EFT, b) the better the prediction for conventional kindergarten behavior shown on Kindergarten Prognosis ratings, c) the better the impulse control, and d) the better the intentional learning performance. Each of these scores reflect "good behavior," obedience to instructions, and capability in carrying out instructions.

By contrast with the above significant correlations, neither of the Curiosity scores were systematically related to IQ. This does not mean that curiosity behaviors penalize the child's performance on the IQ test, but that *curiosity behaviors share little, if anything, with conventional IQ performances.*

Like Curiosity measures, Persistence and Resistance to Distraction show no common variance with the IQ performance. This is explained by the fact that the IQ test procedures and materials combine to maintain the interest of the child, if at all possible, throughout the testing situation. Our Persistence and Resistance to Distraction procedures, on the other hand, rely on the internal resources which "the child brings with him" to the testing situation.

Terman and Merrill (1960) point out that, in IQ testing," ...it becomes the examiner's task to keep the child encouraged and confident by liberal praise and by taking advantage of every bit of curiosity shown. When attention lags, it is often possible to stimulate curiosity by the promise of interesting material to come. When the usual methods to secure motivation are ineffective it is sometimes helpful to promise a reward, such as the privilege of playing with specified toys, or returning to his home" (p. 54). A good IQ tester will terminate testing if the child is highly distractible, or if he doesn't maintain good attention to instructions. In CATB testing, such attention and motivation factors underlying persistence or distractibility are viewed as *variables* to be assessed, rather than as *parameters* of the testing situation to be controlled.

Innovative Behavior, measured by the Dog and Bone test, correlated significantly with IQ performance. It will be recalled from the earlier discussion of test intercorrelations, that the Dog and Bone test also correlated significantly with Impulse Control, Intentional Learning, and Social Competence; these three variables, in turn, were related to IQ scores. To the extent, then, that the Dog and Bone test demands some impulse control, some verbal comprehension (as was hypothesized in the last section), and some degree of social competence, *some* of its variance should be shared with IQ test performance. As was pointed out before, the Dog and Bone test is highly reliable, as is IQ; consequently, these two measures, more than any others, stand an excellent chance of correlating highly if they share anything at all in common. It remains as a research task for the future to demonstrate that another independent measure of Innovative Behavior correlates higher with the Dog and Bone test than with IQ, before a clearer interpretation of the relation between these two variables can be made. For the present, it is a tenable interpretation that Innovative Behavior does correlate with IQ, but that it is largely due to the pattern of impulse control, verbal comprehension, and social competence involved in IQ and Dog and Bone test performances.

Summary

This has been a report of efforts to develop new tests for young children. These tests were devised so that they reflect separate aspects of autonomous behavior; that is self-regulating behavior that facilitates effective problem solving. Theoretical relations to conventional intelligence, creativity, cognitive style, and developmental psychology in general, have been examined. The variables, in addition, have been chosen so that they are relevant to later childhood and adulthood; so that they make minimal verbal demands on the child; and so that comprehension of instructions by the child can be evaluated prior to assessing each child's tendencies. Attention to these kinds of details has certainly helped persons interested in assessing early childhood education see the relevance of the CATB to their work.

Reactions to our efforts have been most encouraging. CATB research is now under way in California, Colorado, Florida, Georgia, Michigan, Minnesota, New York, Ohio and Washington. Other research has begun on a cross-cultural basis in Central America, Greece, and Uganda. In 1968-1969 I will initiate research at Makarere University College (Kampala, Uganda) to study social psychological variables affecting CATB performance.

Future research will focus on four kinds of problems: (1) cross-cultural comparisons, (2) evaluation of known curriculum practices (see Banta, 1967, in press), (3) development of alternate forms of the present tests, and (4) experimental research on factors affecting each variable. Our experimental research is now concentrated on the role of the adult-child nurturance bond and its effect upon self-sustained and self-directed curiosity behavior in young children.

I hope that our work will influence educational practice and child rearing practice, without sacrificing the precision of good research design. I have written about this strategy at greater length in my paper, "Two Voices of Psychology and the New Psychologist" (Banta, 1967b). One voice is that of the experimental laboratory, the other voice is that of the laboratory-in-community. If the new psychologist is hearing voices these days, it is probably these two. I trust that this system is not one of schizophrenia, but one of healthy adaptation to the real world. Let us hope that both our assimilative and our accommodative processes are up to this important challenge from the community and the laboratory.

References

Angyal, A. NEUROSIS AND TREATMENT. New York: Wiley, 1965.

Allport, G. W. The functional autonomy of motives. AMERICAN JOURNAL OF PSYCHOLOGY, 50:141-156, 1937.

Bakan, P. (Ed.), ATTENTION. New York: Van Nostrand, 1966.

Bales, R. F. Task roles and social roles in problem-solving groups. In Eleanore E. Maccoby, T. M. Newcomb, & E. L. Hartley (Eds.), READINGS IN SOCIAL PSYCHOLOGY. New York: Holt, 1958. Pp. 437-447.

Banta, T. J. Critical note on unidimensional tests. PSYCHOLOGICAL REPORTS, 11:449-450, 1962.

Banta, T. J. Non-unidimensionality and validity. PSYCHOLOGICAL REPORTS, 12:146, 1963.

Banta, T. J. Autonomy in an absurd society. UNIVERSITY OF DENVER MAGAZINE, 2:10-15, 1964.

Banta, T. J. Educating children for adulthood. YOUNG CHILDREN, 21:272-280, 1966.

Banta, T. J. Existentialism, morality, and psychotherapy. THE HUMANIST, 27:44-48, 1967

Banta, T. J. Two voices of phychology and the new psychologist. OHIO PSYCHOLOGIST, 13:6-11, 1967.

Banta, T. J. Research on Montessori and the disadvantaged. In R. C. Orem (Ed.), MONTESSORI AND THE SPECIAL CHILD. 1967, in press.

Beller, E. K. Dependency and autonomous achievement striving related to orality and anality in early childhood. CHILD DEVELOPMENT, 28:287-315, 1957.

Berlyne, D. E. CONFLICT, AROUSAL, AND CURIOSITY. New York: McGraw-Hill, 1960.

Bruner, J. S. On coping and defending. In J. S. Bruner, TOWARD A THEORY OF INSTRUCTION. Cambridge, Mass.: Harvard University Press, 1966.

Buhler, Charlotte & Hetzer, H. TESTING CHILDREN'S DEVELOPMENT FROM BIRTH TO SCHOOL. New York: Rinehart, 1935. Originally published in German in 1932.

Burnham, W. H. Attention and interest. AMERICAN JOURNAL OF PSYCHOLOGY, 19:14-18, 1908.

Cage, J. SILENCE. Cambridge, Mass.: MIT Press, 1961.

Campbell, D. T., & Fiske, D. W. Convergent and discriminant validation by the multitrait-multimethod matrix. PSYCHOLOGICAL BULLETIN, 56:81-105, 1959.

Campbell, D. T. Recommendations for APA test standards regarding construct, trait, or discriminant validity. AMERICAN PSYCHOLOGIST, 15:546-553, 1960.

Christie, R., & Lindauer, Florence. Personality structure. In P. R. Farnsworth, Olga McNemar, & Q. McNemar (Eds.), ANNUAL REVIEW OF PSYCHOLOGY, Palo Alto: Annual Reviews, Inc., 1963. Pp. 201-230.

Crutchfield, R. S. "Personal and situational factors in conformity to group pressure." Paper read at 15th International Congress of Psychology, Brussels, 1957.

Dashiell, J. F. A quantitative demonstration of animal drive. JOURNAL OF COMPARATIVE PSYCHOLOGY, 5:205-208, 1925.

Dember, W. N., & Earl, R. W. Analysis of exploratory, manipulatory, and curiosity behaviors. PSYCHOLOGICAL REVIEW, 64:91-96, 1957.

Eagle, Carol J. "An exploratory study of the relationships between cognitive and perceptual styles and drives and defenses in differing states of awareness." Unpublished study cited in Witkin, et al., 1962. p. 184.

Erikson, E. H. CHILDHOOD AND SOCIETY. New York: Norton, 1950.

Fiske, D. W., & Maddi, S. R. Functions of varied experience. Homewood, Illinois: Dorsey Press, 1961.

Fowler, H. CURIOSITY AND EXPLORATORY BEHAVIOR. New York: MacMillan, 1965.

Freud, Anna. THE EGO AND THE MECHANISMS OF DEFENSE. New York: International Universities Press, 1946. Originally published in German in 1936.

Freud, Anna. NORMALITY AND PATHOLOGY IN CHILDHOOD. New York: International Universities Press, 1965.

Getzels, J. W., & Jackson, P. W. CREATIVITY AND INTELLIGENCE. New York: Wiley, 1962.

Guilford, J. P. Three faces of intellect. AMERICAN PSYCHOLOGIST, 14:469-479, 1959.

Harlow, H. F., Harlow, Margaret K., & Meyer, D. R. Learning motivated by a manipulatory drive. JOURNAL OF EXPERIMENTAL PSYCHOLOGY, 40:228-234, 1950.

Harlow, H. F. Learning and satiation of response in intrinsically motivated complex puzzle performance by monkeys. JOURNAL OF COMPARATIVE AND PHYSIOLOGICAL PSYCHOLOGY, 43:289-294, 1950.

Hartmann, H. Rational and irrational action. In ESSAYS ON EGO PSYCHOLOGY. New York: International Universities Press, 1964. Originally published in PSYCHOANALYSIS AND THE SOCIAL SCIENCES. Vol. 1. New York: International Universities Press, 1947.

Hartmann, H. EGO PSYCHOLOGY AND THE PROBLEM OF ADAPTATION. New York: International Universities Press, 1958. Originally published in German in 1939.

Hartup, W. W. Dependence and independence. In H. W. Stevenson (Ed.), CHILD PSYCHOLOGY. Chicago: University of Chicago Press, 1963. Pp. 333-363.

Heathers, G. Emotional dependence and independence in nursery school play. JOURNAL OF GENETIC PSYCHOLOGY, 87:35-57, 1955.

Hebb, D. O. ORGANIZATION OF BEHAVIOR. New York: Wiley, 1949.

Herrigel, E. THE METHOD OF ZEN. New York: McGraw-Hill, 1960.

Hilgard, E. R. Impulsive vs. realistic thinking: an examination of the distinction between primary and secondary process. PSYCHOLOGICAL BULLETIN, 59:477-488, 1962.

Holt, J. HOW CHILDREN FAIL. New York: Dell, 1964.

Hunt, J. McV. INTELLIGENCE AND EXPERIENCE. New York: Ronald Press, 1961.

Kagan, J., Moss, H. A., & Sigel, I. E. Psychological significance of styles of conceptualization. In J. C. Wright, & J. Kagan (Eds.), Basic cognitive processes in children. MONOGRAPHS OF THE SOCIETY FOR RESEARCH IN CHILD DEVELOPMENT, 28:73-112, 1963.

Kagan, J., Rosman, B. L., Day, D., Albert, J., & Phillips, W. Information processing in the child. PSYCHOLOGICAL MONOGRAPHS, 78 (Whole No. 578), 1964.

Kagan, J. Reflection-impulsivity and reading ability in primary grade children. CHILD DEVELOPMENT, 36:609-628, 1965.

Karp, S. A., & Konstadt, Norma L. MANUAL FOR THE CHILDREN'S EMBEDDED FIGURES TEST. Brooklyn, N. Y.: Cognitive Tests, 1963.

Keister, Mary E. The behavior of young children in failure. In R. G. Barker, J. S. Kounin, & H. F. Wright (Eds.), CHILD BEHAVIOR AND DEVELOPMENT. New York: McGraw-Hill, 1943, Pp. 429-440.

Kris, E. PSYCHOANALYTIC EXPLORATIONS IN ART. New York: International Universities Press, 1952.

Kubie, L.S. The utilization of preconscious functions in education. In E.M. Bower & W. G. Hollister (Eds.), BEHAVIORAL SCIENCE FRONTIERS IN EDUCATION. New York: Wiley, 1967.

Lumsden, J. The construction of unidimensional tests. PSYCHOLOGICAL BULLETIN, 58:122-131, 1961.

Lumsden, J. In defense of unidimensionality. PSYCHOLOGICAL REPORTS, 11:832, 1962.

Maccoby, Eleanore E., Dowley, Edith M., Hagen, J. W., & Degerman, R. Activity level and intellectual functioning in normal preschool children. CHILD DEVELOPMENT, 36:761-770, 1965.

McGeoch, J. A. THE PSYCHOLOGY OF HUMAN LEARNING. New York: Longmans, Green, 1942.

McLuhan, M. UNDERSTANDING MEDIA: THE EXTENSIONS OF MAN. New York: McGraw-Hill, 1964.

McLuhan, M. & Fiore, Q. THE MEDIUM IS THE MASSAGE. New York: Bantam Books, 1967.

Mendel, Gisela. Children's preferences for differing degrees of novelty. CHILD DEVELOPMENT, 36:453-465, 1965.

Montgomery, K. C. "Spontaneous alternation" as a function of time between trials and amount of work. JOURNAL OF EXPERIMENTAL PSYCHOLOGY, 42:82-93, 1951 (a).

Montgomery, K. C. The relationship between exploratory behavior and spontaneous alternation in the white rat. JOURNAL OF COMPARATIVE AND PHYSIOLOGICAL PSYCHOLOGY, 44:582-589, 1951 (b).

Montgomery, K. C. A test of two explanations of spontaneous alternation. JOURNAL OF COMPARATIVE AND PHYSIOLOGICAL PSYCHOLOGY, 45:287-293, 1952.

Montgomery, K. C. Exploratory behavior as a function of "similarity" of stimulus situations. JOURNAL OF COMPARATIVE AND PHYSIOLOGICAL PSYCHOLOGY, 46:129-133, 1953.

Morgan, C. T. Physiological theory of drive. In S. Koch (Ed.), PSYCHOLOGY: A STUDY OF A SCIENCE. Vol. 1. New York: McGraw-Hill, 1959. Pp. 644-671.

Murphy, Lois. THE WIDENING WORLD OF CHILDHOOD. New York: Basic Books, 1962.

Piaget, J. THE ORIGINS OF INTELLIGENCE IN CHILDREN. 2nd ed. New York: International Universities Press, 1936.

Piaget, J. THE CONSTRUCTION OF REALITY IN THE CHILD. New York: Basic Books, 1937.

Polya, G. HOW TO SOLVE IT. Princeton, N. J.: Princeton University Press, 1945.

Postman, L. Short-term memory and incidental learning. In A. W. Melton (Ed.), CATEGORIES OF HUMAN LEARNING. New York: Academic Press, 1964. Pp. 145-201.

Rapaport, D. On the psychoanalytic theory of motivation. In M. H. Jones (Ed.), NEBRASKA SYMPOSIUM ON MOTIVATION. Lincoln, Nebraska: University of Nebraska Press, 1960. Pp. 173-247.

Rosner, S. Consistency in response to group pressure. JOURNAL OF ABNORMAL AND SOCIAL PSYCHOLOGY, 55:145-146, 1957.

Sarton, G. A HISTORY OF SCIENCE: ANCIENT SCIENCE THROUGH THE GOLDEN AGE OF GREECE. New York: Wiley, 1952.

Schafer, R. Regression in the service of the ego: the relevance of a psychoanalytic concept for personality assessment. In G. Lindzey (Ed.), ASSESSMENT OF HUMAN MOTIVES. New York: Rinehart, 1958. Pp. 119-148.

Schoenfeld, W. N., Harries, A. H., & Farmer, J. Conditioning response variability. PSYCHOLOGICAL REPORTS, 19:551-557, 1966.

Shacter, Helen S. A method for measuring the sustained attention of preschool children. JOURNAL OF GENETIC PSYCHOLOGY, 42:339-369, 1933.

Terman, L. M., & Merrill, Maud A. STANFORD-BINET INTELLIGENCE SCALE RECORD BOOKLET--FORM L-M. Boston: Houghton Mifflin, 1960.

Tichener, E. B. FEELING AND ATTENTION. New York: Macmillan, 1908.

Tilson, M. A. Problems of preschool children. TEACHER'S COLLEGE CONTRIBUTIONS TO EDUCATION, No. 356, 1929.

Tuddenham, R. D. The nature and measurement of intelligence. In L. Postman (Ed.), PSYCHOLOGY IN THE MAKING. New York: Knopf, 1962. Pp. 469-525.

Wallach, M. A., & Kogan, N. MODES OF THINKING IN YOUNG CHILDREN. New York: Holt, 1965.

Werner, H. COMPARATIVE PSYCHOLOGY OF MENTAL DEVELOPMENT. New York: Science Editions, 1948.

White, R. W. Competence and the psychosexual stages of development. In M. H. Jones (Ed.), NEBRASKA SYMPOSIUM ON MOTIVATION. Lincoln, Nebraska: University of Nebraska Press, 1960. Pp. 97-141.

Winnicot, D. W. Transitional objects and transitional phenomena. INTERNATIONAL JOURNAL OF PSYCHO-ANALYSIS, 34:89-97, 1953.

Witkin, H. A. Individual differences in ease of perception of embedded figures. JOURNAL OF PERSONALITY, 19:1-15, 1950.

Witkin, H. A., Dyk, R. B., Faterson, H. F., Goodenough, D. R., & Karp, S. A. PSYCHOLOGICAL DIFFERENTIATION. New York: Wiley, 1962.

Witkin, H. A. Psychological differentiation and forms of pathology. JOURNAL OF ABNORMAL PSYCHOLOGY, 70:317-336, 1965.

THE COGNITIVE CURRICULUM:
A PROCESS-ORIENTED APPROACH TO EDUCATION

Martin V. Covington, Ph.D.

Introduction

The growing recognition that one of the primary goals of education is the identification and the nurturing of productive thinking potential portends a revolution in educational practice. As part of the more general renaissance in educational thought, this unique trend holds a number of implications for educational planners. It will, among other things, serve to focus attention on the means by which the student arrives at and creates understanding. Indeed, the last decade has seen the instigation of a number of attempts to develop curricular materials which strengthen directly the processes underlying productive thinking. However, despite the enormous potential value of such undertakings, the concept of cognitive process as applied in the class room and as conceptualized in the laboratory is typically inadequate to the task of fostering truly productive students. All too often such developments are open to a host of criticisms which are prompted in large part by the seeming artificiality of many of the mental skills taught, the contrived nature of the instructional procedures used, and the lack of evidence that such training has more than a transient impact on regular classroom behavior. The basic difficulty is that teaching for productive thinking is typically an afterthought, an exercise which is essentially "grafted" on to more traditional curricular practices. Consequently, before the student can derive maximum benefits from a strong "process-oriented" approach to education, it will be necessary to develop a curriculum model which has as one of its fundamental objectives the fostering of intellectual processes in their own right, a goal which must be fully integrated and coordinated with other more traditional objectives, such as mastery of content and assimilation of cultural values.

The purpose of this paper, then, is to outline briefly the nature of a cognitive curriculum: to indicate its long-range educational goals and the pedagogical techniques for implementing these goals as well as to suggest some of the social, educational and psychological justifications for this approach to teaching.

Preliminary Definitions and a Statement of Educational Objectives

Before proceeding, a definition of the concept of "process" is necessary along with a statement of the educational objectives of a cognitive curriculum. The term "process" as used here refers to a set of inferences about the workings of the mind—the mental skills, strategies, attitudes and cognitive styles basic to the effective

491

management of thought. These inferences involve psychological concepts such as incubation and intuition; mental skills such as idea generation and question asking; and cognitive styles which include, among others, resistance to premature closure, persistence in the face of recurring frustrations, and a propensity for reflectivity. In a closely related sense, "process" also refers to those methods and techniques which the community of scholars have found useful and even necessary in the structuring and accumulation of knowledge. These include such intellectual concepts as the notion of cause and effect, the role of evidence and proof, and the interaction of variables as well as certain intellectual postures, like skepticism and objectivity. For present purposes, the concept of "process" both in the psychological and in the intellectual-academic sense may be distinguished from subject-matter content. Here "content" refers to the facts, theories, beliefs and generalizations which are the end-products of long and complex sequences of psychological and intellectual operations.

Given these broad definitions, the ultimate objective of a cognitive curriculum is to foster productive thinkers—individuals who in adulthood will fulfill their unique capacities for intellectual innovation and who possess a habitual willingness to question and to speculate about the *how* and *why* of things and events. The principal means to achieve such ultimate goals is the strengthening of those cognitive processes and attitudes which promote the productive thinking act, independent of a given subject-matter discipline.

It should be noted, of course, that the goal of a self-guiding and original intellect is not unique to a cognitive-curriculum model. Indeed, this vision is shared in common with virtually all modern curricular systems, including the more traditional content-centered approaches. The essential difference between various approaches lies not so much in the goals sought as in the means to achieve these goals. In this regard the unique contribution of a process approach is the *directness* with which it undertakes to foster these behavioral objectives. More specifically, the strategy of a process-oriented curriculum is to teach for a number of cognitive skills fundamental to all innovative thinking, and then to show the student how such generalized operations can be applied in a number of specific subject-matter areas. Succinctly put, the primary "content" of a cognitive curriculum is the thought process itself!

In contrast, a content-centered approach by its very nature is obliged to devote a large proportion of its effort to presenting the basic facts, theories and generalizations which comprise the structure of each subject-matter discipline. It is not surprising then to find proponents of this approach often arguing that productive thinking is highly dependent upon the depth and breadth of knowledge possessed by the student and that the primary responsibility of education is to present accumulated knowledge from a number of subject-matter domains in such a manner as to promote intellectual innovation and productivity.

It is obvious that while these two approaches represent somewhat different emphases, they are nevertheless complementary. For example, research has consistently shown (and naturally so) that the more well-informed and knowledgeable an individual, the more productive will be his thinking. At the same time we know that a large store of information alone is not sufficient to permit the fullest expression of the individual's capacity for productive thought.

A Specific Curriculum Comparison

The unique characteristics of a cognitive-curriculum approach to education can perhaps best be indicated by contrasting it with other existing curricular systems. However, we shall not attempt to draw comparisons with approaches which stand in obvious and clear opposition. For example, we would gain little from contrasting a cognitive approach with that of the time-honored "copy-book" method of achieving content mastery with its focus on rote learning, since virtually all other present curricular reforms *also* differ in marked ways from this venerable educational archetype. Rather, we shall examine one curricular strategy which shares a number of characteristics in common with the cognitive approach, most notably the vital role played by considerations of process. If some valid distinctions can be made here, then the nature of a cognitive curriculum will stand in sharper relief than might otherwise be possible.

The specific example in question is the "discovery-learning" method (Suchman, 1960, 1961). Although both this approach and the cognitive-curriculum model rely on and indeed owe their uniqueness to a process-orientation, the crucial distinction to be drawn lies in the respective roles played by process. In the case of "discovery-learning", the primary focus is on an acquisition and understanding of subject-matter content. Typically this is achieved through direct inquiry and consequent discovery by the student of the generalizations, laws and principles of a particular discipline. Here, in essence, process serves as a vehicle for the mastery of subject-matter content.

In contrast, the principal aim of a cognitive curriculum is to teach mental operations and strategies as an end in themselves, not merely as vehicles to a destination, but themselves a key destination. It is hoped that by strengthening the child's cognitive repertoire he will be more able and willing to explore and structure the *unknown* rather than to discover what is *already known,* that is, what has previously been agreed on by subject-matter experts and pre-structured in advance for efficient learning and retention.

The differences in what a student actually learns when he is instructed in the art of searching for prearranged structure as contrasted to learning to create his own structure may seem inconsequential and unimportant, especially in the context of normal day-to-day classroom routine. Yet these differences become quite important when viewed form the perspective of the ultimate goal of fostering self-guiding, self-activating adult thinkers. At the risk of overstating the case, perhaps the essential difference between the "discovery-learning" method and the "cognitive-dominated" approach is that in the former instance the student practices *learning-to-learn*, whereas in the latter case the student practices *learning-to-think*.

Let us explore further this last statement. Paradoxically, the greatest potential limitation of the "discovery-learning" approach for fostering innovative thought arises chiefly from one of its presumed pedagogical strengths, namely the effectiveness with which content can be mastered, understood, and retained. More specifically, it cannot be assumed that techniques which make for efficient learning and retention will also be most effective in fostering innovative use of what is learned. For example, since "discovery-learning" focuses primarily on a specialized intellectual quest—the discovery and understanding of prearranged regularities—there is a danger that only a limited set of cognitive strategies will be strengthened, principally those dealing with inquiry and question-asking operations. Crucial as these operations are, they nonetheless represent only a part of the total repertoire of skills and dispositions necessary to innovative thought. Moreover, searching for prearranged structure tends to promote a dependence on external authority. The student may come to rely excessively on the teacher to oversee and to monitor his progress during the act of discovery, to point out his mistakes, and to indicate when he has reached an adequate level of understanding. Such a dependency is antithetical to productive thought, where typically the creator must rely on his own initiative to decide what course of investigation is most fruitful, to recognize his own errors, and to judge when he has accumulated enough evidence or sufficient ideas to complete his search. Furthermore, there is the potential danger that a student may learn to engage in personal intellectual inquiry only when an external authority (teacher) provides an invitation in the form of a clearly defined, well-structured set of circumstances. Again, such a disposition is contrary to one of the essential features of the productive mind—an inveterate, spontaneous searching for problems, paradoxes and dilemmas and the imposing of solutions in spite of complex and even chaotic conditions. In this regard, the cognitive-curriculum approach, as we shall see, deliberately confronts the student with complex, untidy yet manageable tasks which permit extensive practice in dealing with disarray.

Since the purpose of the foregoing discussion was to illuminate the nature and purpose of the cognitive-curriculum model rather than to draw comparisons at the expense of the "discovery-learning" approach, it should be noted with emphasis that the intent was not to suggest that the use of process in the service of content mastery is improper. Indeed, it is a perfectly valid procedure and judging from recent research a beneficial technique in terms of increasing retention and of stimulating student enthusiam toward the act of learning (Kersh, 1958; 1962). Nor was the purpose of the previous remarks to suggest that the "discovery-learning" approach cannot incorporate additional techniques to implement more directly the overall goal of fostering self-initiating independent thinkers. It is to this point—the specification of additional pedagogical techniques and procedures—that we now turn.

Specific Pedagogical Techniques

In order to have any reasonable hope of attaining the ambitious educational objectives set out above, it is imperative that the maturing student come to regard the act of using his mind in productive pursuits as a highly useful and personally rewarding enterprise. This obvious but crucial observation stands as the central consideration in all curricular decisions made from the cognitive point of view. The fostering of such positive attitudes depends on the long-range continuance of a number of pedagogical conditions, including the following: 1) that a willingness to engage in intellectual activities be strengthened as a life-style in its own right. One means of promoting such a disposition is to lead the student to realize that self-improvement in intellectual functioning is possible; 2) that cognitive skills be taught which do *in fact* make the student more intellectually effective than he would otherwise be. This increases the likelihood that he will encounter progressively more successes in the productive use of his mind; 3) that these skills possess enduring utility not only for dealing with current problem topics but for those intellectual complexities of unknown character which will occur in the unforeseeable future as well. This assures that the individual will not lose enthusiasm for the intellectual quest simply because what he learned in school no longer serves as an adequate basis for productive thought.

These last two considerations, taken together, point to the most fundamental difficulty facing the development of a cognitive curriculum—determining which skills and strategies to teach (and in what order and in what combinations) to achieve the long-term objectives of a self-directing thinker. In large part such pedagogical decisions can be made only after identifying the kinds of adult behavior ultimately desired. Once such an analysis is accomplished, the desired behaviors—no matter how complex or how far removed from the student's present capabilities—can be reduced to their basic skill components. It is these cognitive components which hopefully can be strengthened progressively in the student by direct educational means.

In this connection, although the processes of human thought are as yet not well understood, psychology nevertheless has made some fruitful beginnings in explaining those factors which facilitate and inhibit productive thought (Duncker, 1945; Luchins, 1942). Moreover, a good deal is known both from formal laboratory research (Crutchfield, 1963; MacKinnon, 1965; Mendelsohn and Griswold, 1964) and from anecdotal descriptions of creative.individuals at work (Ghiselin, 1952; Koestler, 1964) about the characteristic work habits, intellectual dispositions and coping styles of productive adults. Thus, it is possible even at present to take steps—although admittedly tentative ones—to identify those fundamental mental operations which are basic to any act of original thought.

The approach being explored by the Berkeley Creative Thinking Project is derived principally from these foregoing considerations. Basically the student is required to practice a number of skills, strategies and work habits recognized as fundamental to the effective operation of creative adults. Skill proficiency is gained in the course of working on complex intellectual tasks which require the creation of a product, whether it be an explanation of inexplicable phenomena, the planning of an effective course of action, or the development of an innovative set of ideas. To be sure, these skills and strategies, although appropriate in some form at any developmental level, are presented in a simplified manner so as to be readily understood by children yet at the same time without losing their broad inclusiveness and general utility. In a parallel fashion the practice problems used are simplified versions of tasks which in a more advanced form would challenge intellectually creative adults.

As the student progresses through a series of such problems over an extended period of time it is intended that the tasks increase in scope and difficulty, requiring the coordination of successively more complex strategies and skills. Thus, by presenting simulated models of the intellectual quest which progressively increase in complexity, the student's behavior hopefully approaches that of a creative adult through a series of successive approximations.

At present the Berkeley Group is developing instructional materials appropriate for students at the upper elementary level (fifth-grade and sixth-grade) with projected plans for extending these materials both up and down the grade levels. Within the upper elementary level where the bulk of the current research is being conducted, the effort is concentrated on developing several distinctive but interrelated series of programs, each covering a different aspect of productive thinking. Series One: GENERAL PROBLEM SOLVING (Covington, Crutchfield, and Davies 1966) has recently been completed and is available for regular classroom use.

Series One consists of 16 lessons each featuring a problem which permits extensive practice on a variety of crucial mental strategies basic to problem solving in its more general form, including formulating a problem in the most effective and least-biasing manner, transforming unfamiliar situations into more familiar analogical and metaphorical equivalents, and dividing a complex problem into a more manageable sub-parts. Each lesson is presented in a self-instructional booklet through which the student works by himself at his own pace. As a particular problem sequence unfolds, the reader is given repeated opportunities to practice various cognitive skills by asking questions, thinking of ideas, or plotting alternative courses of action. Feedback to the student's ideas, questions or proposals is given on subsequent pages of the booklet in the form of a range of possible responses which he might have thought of. These examples typically are ones which children regard as novel and ingenious. It is hoped that exposure to a number of such examples in a variety of problem situations will broaden the student's expectancies as to what constitute appropriate ideas, important questions to ask, or promising lines of investigation.

Another crucial pedagogical feature is the systematic attempt to shift the responsibility of decision-making from the programmed sequence to the student himself. The technique employed here involves the use of comprehensive monitoring in the early phases of the instructional program with a gradual reduction in guidance as the student becomes more proficient in applying the various skills and strategies. In this manner the student comes ultimately to rely on his own resources and initiative with only occasional redirection from the program.

The theme and content of these problems are of basically two types. One type focuses on situations which are neutral with respect to orthodox subject-matter, as when the student tries to construct a theory to explain some mysterious happening in a deserted and reputedly haunted house. It is hoped that such non-curricular themes will encourage the student to see the broader applications of the principles being taught than might otherwise be the case if the concepts were associated from the outset with a specific content area. In contrast the content of still other problems includes more traditional subject-matter concepts. This permits the student to practice applying the strategies in situations not unlike those which arise in the course of regular classroom work. One problem of this sort requires the student to come to understand the puzzling behavior of a group of aquanauts during the testing of a new piece of undersea rescue gear. Here the most elegant explanations depend jointly on an understanding of the aquanauts themselves—their perceptions, anxieties, and expectancies—and the application of various basic principles of mechanics, physics, and biology, such as the effects of air pressure on human body.

Psychological and Social Justifications for a Cognitive Curriculum

As for the psychological considerations, this approach permits the creation of the only kind of knowledge which will truly strengthen the self-generating mind—knowledge derived from personal experience as well as the sense of achievement which arises in the course of creating a satisfying personal product. Another point stems from the fact that the most notable characteristic of the truly productive innovator is an ability to coordinate his efforts and to plan and to sustain a long-term intellectual effort. The present approach in simulating the total act of productive thought—from initial recognition of a problem to the discovery of the most elegant solutions—requires that the student deal with all facets of this complex process on an interrelated, interlocking basis. Guided practice in realistic yet manageable situations is the only proper training-ground for strengthening both a sense of overall planfulness and an ability to coordinate a wide variety of intellectual skills.

Several additional remarks can be made from a social-cultural perspective. First, the cultural transmission of the values, beliefs and attitudes of the productive thinker implies, among other things, preparing children to act in adulthood with intelligent self-reliance and initiative. Yet our culture does not promote these aims with any degree of directness. For instance, we greatly prolong infancy and "schoolhood," forcing the child into a position of dependence on adults who far too often reward him for docility rather than for independence. In contrast, a central tenet of a cognitive curriculum is to provide the child with the kinds of experiences which cultivate pre-adult discipline and intellectual reliance.

Second, the rapid changes in knowledge, customs, and in society itself constitute a continuing challenge to the relevance and worth of one's education. No educative method can prevent these changes; it can only prepare the student to respond productively in the face of change. These considerations compel us to teach for principles and concepts of productive thought which have the broadest application in the face of unknown future contingencies rather than to teach merely for what is momentarily true or useful. The student cannot be expected to perpetuate his intellectual life if what he is taught in school becomes progressively outdated, unimportant, misleading, or false. As we have seen, a cognitive-curriculum approach stresses the teaching of mental skills and strategies of enduring relevance in a context which makes for maximum future transfer.

Illustrative Data

Now that we have explored the cognitive-curriculum model from a number of directions—its purpose, pedagogical rationale, and justifications—we come to the final and the most crucial question of all: what empirical evidence is there that instruction based on such an approach will actually promote the goal of achieving intellectually productive thinkers? Most of the data pertinent to this question come from research on the GENERAL PROBLEM SOLVING PROGRAM which to date has been administered on an experimental basis to several thousand school children throughout the United States.

As part of the larger research program, a number of criterion tests have been developed to assess the effectiveness of the Program (Olton, et al., 1967). One type of test is designed to reflect the degree to which the student is *willing* to engage in tasks which require productive thought and further to provide evidence on the appropriateness of his actions in situations where he alone must decide how to structure the task and what problem-solving steps should be taken—dispositions which, perhaps above all others, epitomize the essence of the productive thinker. The test is in a booklet format. At the beginning the student is presented with a welter of facts, information and data which contains a number of puzzling factual discrepancies and other curiosities. On several occasions throughout the remainder of the test sequence the student is given a choice of action. He can either deal directly with the puzzling data in any way he chooses or he can engage in a routine clerical task, which, although related to the problem requires a modicum of productive thought.

One such test deals with the concept of ecology—in this case, the various forces which affect the migratory behavior of birds. The student imagines himself a laboratory assistant whose regular job it is to record numerical data on the movement of robins spotted at various points in a region. After he masters this simple clerical routine, the student is interrupted by the chief scientist who shows him a report on the migration of a particular species with which he is unfamiliar. The report consists primarily of a map which plots the migration route. Imbedded in the map are several puzzling circumstances not commented on in the body of the text, such as the fact that the birds take a different route north in the spring from the one they take south in the fall and that the size of the flock dwindles precipitously over an uncharted area. On five subsequent pages in the test booklet the student is given a choice of either "raising any questions or adding any thoughts of your own to the report" or "going back to copying the information on the robins being sent in by observers." At two of these five choice points additional information is provided which is relevant to the interpretation of the puzzling events, such as the fact that the birds were flying over farm land when their numbers were so drastically reduced.

In recent study in the San Francisco Bay Area, sixty carefully matched upper elementary school children were drawn from within two intact classrooms and assigned to one of two treatment conditions. One group received the GENERAL PROBLEM SOLVING PROGRAM as a self-administering supplement to their regular school work over a seven week period. Concurrently, the remaining students in each of the two classes received self-instructional *control* materials featuring a curriculum-relevant topic—events in California history—but with no emphasis on productive thinking concepts. The migration problem was presented 90 school days after the regular training period had ended. At that time every precaution was taken to insure that the problem appeared to be part of a regular class assignment and unrelated to the earlier experimental program. To this end the problem was presented entirely by the teacher and the format and style of the booklet itself were deliberately modified so as to be distinctly different from the physical appearance of the previous materials.

As to the results, consider first that data reflecting the degree to which the student was willing to engage in productive thinking. A gross index of such a disposition was taken to be the number of times the student chose to deal in some way, however imperfectly, with the scientist's report, rather than to engage in the clerical routine. In summing over all five choice-points it was found that the instructed students chose to work on the report 50% more often than did the control students. Of course, however, choosing the clerical task does not necessarily indicate a willingness to deal with the more demanding aspects of the problem. For example, the student may have already expressed his ideas and has nothing new to add. Bearing on this point are the two choice-points where new and highly relevant information is introduced for the first time. If a student still chooses the clerical task in these situations then it can be reasonably assumed that he either is not motivated to act productively or that he lacks an appreciation of the importance of these facts. Again, in the case of these two choice-points the margin of superiority favoring the instructed students was of the same order of magnitude as that reported for all five choice points taken collectively.

Although the instructed group dealt more often with the more productive aspects of the problem, it is still possible that their responses were of marginal quality, as in simply paraphrasing various parts of the report. Actually, far from sacrificing quality of responses for quantity, the instructed students demonstrated a superior performance as reflected in the absolute incidence of satisfactory problem-solving responses. Several different scoring categories were constituted including among others, the number of puzzling circumstances identified and the number of different explanations for these oddities. In all cases, the instructed students generated 60%-100% more responses than did the control students.

These data pertain to the most central aspects of the self-directing intellect—a willingness to undertake intellectually demanding tasks, a sensitivity to problem situations and a facility for structuring complexity and reducing ambiguities. As such these findings are highly encouraging, not only because of the large and educationally significant training effect, but also because the effect was demonstrated some months after training.

These data taken in concert with a large volume of additional empirical indications gathered in the course of our research, suggest that the dispositions, attitudes and work habits which characterize the innovative thinker can be enhanced directly by methods and techniques which are presently available to educational planners.

The research reported in this paper is conducted by the Creative Thinking Project supported by a grant from the Carnegie Corporation of New York and under the joint direction of the author and Dr. Richard S. Crutchfield.

References

Covington, M. V., & Crutchfield, R. S. "Experiments in the use of programmed instruction for the facilitation of creative problem solving", PROGRAMMED INSTRUCTION, 4: 1965.

Covington, M. V., Crutchfield, R. S., & Davies, L. B. THE PRODUCTIVE THINKING PROGRAM. SERIES ONE: GENERAL PROBLEM SOLVING. Berkeley: Brazelton Printing Company, 1966. (This Program to be published by the Charles E. Merrill Company, 1300 Alum Creek Drive, Columbus, Ohio, 43216. Copies may be purchased on an interim basis from Educational Innovation, P. O. Box 9248, Berkeley, California, 94719.)

Crutchfield, R. S. "Independent thought in a conformist world", In S. M. Farber, & R. H. L. Wilson (Eds.), MAN AND CIVILIZATION: CONFLICT AND CREATIVITY. Part two of CONTROL OF MIND. New York: McGraw-Hill, pp. 208-228, 1963.

Duncker, K. "On problem solving", PSYCHOL. MONOGR., 58 (No. 5) (Whole No. 270): 1945.

Ghiselin, B. THE CREATIVE PROCESS: A SYMPOSIUM. New York: New American Library, 1952.

Kersh, B. Y. "The adequacy of 'meaning' as an explanation for superiority of learning by independent discovery", J. EDUC. PSYCHOL., 49: 282-292, 1958.

Kersh, B. Y. "The motivating effect of learning by direct discovery", J. EDUC. PSYCHOL., 53: 65-71, 1962.

Koestler, A. THE CREATIVE ACT. New York: The Macmillan Company, 1964.

Luchins, A. S. "Mechanization in problem solving: The effects of Einstellung", PSYCHOL. MONOGR., 54 (No. 248): 1942.

Olton, R. M., Wardrop, J. L., Covington, M. V., Goodwin, W. L., Crutchfield, R. S., Klausmeier, H. J., & Ronda, T. THE DEVELOPMENT OF PRODUCTIVE THINKING SKILLS IN FIFTH-GRADE CHILDREN, Technical Report No. 34, Wisconsin Research and Development Center for Cognitive Learning. The University of Wisconsin, Madison, Wisconsin, 39 pp.

MacKinnon, D. W. "Personality correlates of creativity", In Mary Jane Aschner, & C. E. Bish (Eds.), PRODUCTIVE THINKING IN EDUCATION. Washington, D. C. : National Education Association and The Carnegie Corporation of New York, pp. 139-171, 1965.

Mendelsohn, G. A., & Griswold, B. B. "Differential use of incidental stimuli in problem solving as a function of creativity". J. ABNORM. SOC. PSYCHOL., 1964, 68 (No. 4): 431-436, 1964.

Suchman, J. R. "Inquiry thinking in the elementary school", SCI. TEACHER, 27: 42-47, 1960.

Suchman, J. R. "Inquiry training: Building skills for autonomous discovery". MERRILL-PALMER QUART. BEHAV. DEVELOP., 7: 147-169, 1961.

as behavior control, 58-59
and cognition, 291, 309-10
and cognitive environment, 164-65
and cognitive skills, 390
and color recognition, 327-28
and concept attainment, 153-56
and conceptual ability, 292-294
and deafness, 291ff
deficiencies in, 312
and deprivation, 281
and discrimination learning, 151-53
and early learning, 148-49
effect on subjective attitudes, 365-67
and environment, 47
importance of, 146-47
inner, 294
and lower-class families, 258, 285
maternal influences on, 148
origins of, 147
and paleological cognition, 97-99
and sensorimotor development, 149-50
and symbolic behavior, 294, 321,
324-25
use in teaching, 370-72
Learning
age differences in, 234, 236
age as a factor in deafness, 321-24,
325-26
and aggression, 176-77
and anxiety interference, 173
and attention, 52, 59, 145-46, 457-62
and behavior modification, 417-22
conflict in, 378
conservation performance, 234ff, 248-51
developmental differences in, 66
discrimination, experiments in, 68-80, 267-71
durability in, 373-74
and exploratory drive, 434-42
incidental, 154
and insight, 376
and intelligence, 429
intentional, 454
use of language in, 370-72
and maturation, 124-26
and motivation, 165-67, 168-70
necessity a motive in, 375-76
and neurochemistry, 119ff
reinforcement in, 127, 167, 170-71, 390-41€
and relation to stimuli, 277-83
and resistance, 376-77
reversals in, 65-68, 71-72, 74, 80, 83
rules in, 377-78
and selective response, 279-80
and transfer theory, 374-75
and verbal input, 148-49
See also Cognitive learning;
Problem solving

Measurement
anxiety, 174
Griffiths Mental Development
Scale, 132
of kindergarten readiness, 462-66,
471, 478-79

of problem-solving abilities (CATB),
424ff
See also Tests
Memory
and deafness, 307-08, 327-30
and drug experiments, 120-22
and incidental learning, 454
in mentally retarded, 122-24
neurochemical theories of, 119ff
and reinforcement, 373-74
Mentally retarded
and acquisition difficulties, 123-24
anxiety in learning, 175-76
attention discrimination, 135-37
body image, 141-43
brain function in, 112-14
and brain injury, 114ff
and cognitive sequence, 126-28
and concept attainment, 154-56
congenital bases for, 160-62
and cultural deprivation, 275ff
diagnostic difficulties, 139-40
and discrimination ability, 63
and discrimination learning, 129-30,
153
and environmental factors, 163-67
and failure expectancy, 171-73
familial and organic distinctions,
159-60
and figure-ground perception, 133-35
and heredity, 157-59, 275-76
and hyperactivity, 284
and institutional environment, 275ff
and intersensory integration, 137-38
and language acquisition, 150-51
and laterality, 142-43
and maternal attitudes, 126
memory in, 122-24
and mental-age concept, 130-31
motivation in learning, 137, 165-67,
168-70
predicting in first year, 168-69
and prematurity, 162
and reinforcement in learning, 167,
403-04
and reinforcer heirarchies, 170-71
research needs in, 179-82
researches in, 111-12
stimulus-trace theory, 122
and visual perception, 132-33
Motor development. See Perceptual-Motor
development

Nonverbal learning. See Deafness;
Intellectual ability; Intelligence;
Language development

Perception
and attention, 135
and developmental behavior, 132
figure-ground, 133-37
influence on social judgment, 365-67
and language acquisition, 151-53
neurologically impaired, 115-16